Ubuntu

24.04

LTS

Server

Administration
and
Reference

to

George, Robert, and Mark

Ubuntu 24.04 LTS Server: Administration and Reference

Richard Petersen

Surfing Turtle Press

Alameda, CA

www.surfingturtlepress.com

Please send inquiries to: editor@surfingturtlepress.com

ISBN-13 978-1-949857-54-2

Preface

This book is designed as an Ubuntu 24.04 LTS Server administration and reference source, covering the Ubuntu servers and their support applications. Server tools are covered as well as the underlying configuration files and system implementations. The emphasis is on what administrators will need to know to perform key server support and management tasks. Coverage of the systemd service management system is integrated into the book. Topics covered include software management, systemd service management, systemd-networkd and Netplan network configuration, AppArmor security, OpenSSH, the Chrony time server, and Ubuntu cloud services. Key servers are examined, including Web, FTP, CUPS printing, NFS, and Samba Windows shares. Network support servers and applications covered include the Squid proxy server, the Domain Name System (BIND) server, DHCP, distributed network file systems, nftables firewalls, and cloud computing.

The book is organized into five parts: getting started, services, shared resources, network support, and shells.

Part 1 focuses on basic tasks such as installing the Ubuntu Live Server, configuring networking with Netplan, systemd-networkd, and NetworkManager, managing software from the Ubuntu Snap and APT repositories, and basic usage for the desktop and the command line interfaces.

Part 2 examines Internet servers as well as how services are managed by systemd using unit files. Configuration and implementation of the Postfix mail server, the vsftpd FTP server, the Apache Web server, as well as news and database servers are covered in detail.

Part 3 deals with servers that provide shared resources on a local network or the Internet. Services examined include the CUPS printing server, NFS Linux network file server, and Samba Windows file and printing server, clustering, and cloud computing services supported by Ubuntu.

Part 4 covers servers that provide network support, like the Squid proxy server, the Bind Domain Name System (DNS) server, DHCP servers, and the nftables firewall along with the configuration firewall tools FirewallD and UFW. IPtables is included for reference. Key networking operations are also examined like IPv6 auto-configuration, TPC/IP networking, and network monitoring tools.

Part 5 provides a review of shell commands, including those used for managing files, as well as shell scripts, variables, and configuration files. The Ubuntu Live Server only installs a command line interface, with no desktop. To manage your system and its files you will have to know the shell commands.

Overview

Contents

3. Usage Basics: Login, Interfaces, networking, and Help 69

Part 2: Services

Part 3: Shared Resources

11. Network File Systems and Distributed Network File Systems: NFS and clusters 341

Part 5: Shells

19. Shells 609

20. Working with files and directories 627

Part 1: Getting Started

Introduction
Installation
Usage Basics
Software Management

ubuntu

1. Introduction to Ubuntu Linux

Ubuntu releases

Ubuntu Editions

Ubuntu 24.04 Server Installation Options

Ubuntu 24.04

Ubuntu Software

Ubuntu Help and Documentation

Ubuntu Linux is currently one of the most popular end-user Linux distributions (**https://ubuntu.com**). Ubuntu Linux is managed by the Ubuntu foundation, which is sponsored by Canonical, Ltd (**https://canonical.com**), a commercial organization that supports and promotes open source projects. Ubuntu is based on Debian Linux, one of the oldest Linux distributions, which is dedicated to incorporating cutting-edge developments and features (**https://www.debian.org**). Mark Shuttleworth, a South African and Debian Linux developer, initiated the Ubuntu project. Debian Linux is primarily a Linux development project, trying out new features. Ubuntu provides a Debian-based Linux distribution that is stable, reliable, and easy to use.

Ubuntu is designed as a Linux operating system that can be used easily by everyone. The name Ubuntu means "humanity to others." As the Ubuntu project describes it: "Ubuntu is an African word meaning 'Humanity to others", or "I am what I am because of who we all are." The Ubuntu distribution brings the spirit of Ubuntu to the software world."

The official Ubuntu philosophy lists the following principles.

1. Every computer user should have the freedom to download, run, copy, distribute study, share, change, and improve their software for any purpose, without paying licensing fees.

2. Every computer user should be able to use their software in the language of their choice.

3. Every computer user should be given every opportunity to use software, even if they work under a disability.

The emphasis on language reflects Ubuntu's international scope. It is meant to be a global distribution that does not focus on any single market. Language support has been integrated into Linux in general by its internationalization projects, denoted by the term i18n.

Making software available to all users involves both full accessibility supports for users with disabilities as well as seamless integration of software access using online repositories, making massive amounts of software available to all users at the touch of a button. Ubuntu also makes full use of Linux's automatic device detection ability, greatly simplifying installation as well as access to removable devices and attached storage.

Ubuntu aims to provide a fully supported and reliable, open source and free, easy to use and modify, Linux operating system. Ubuntu makes the following promises about its distribution.

Ubuntu will always be free of charge, including enterprise releases and security updates.

Ubuntu comes with full commercial support from Canonical and hundreds of companies around the world.

Ubuntu includes the very best translations and accessibility infrastructure that the free software community has to offer.

Ubuntu DVDs contain only free software applications; we encourage you to use free and open source software, improve it and pass it on (Ubuntu repositories contain some proprietary software like vendor graphics drivers that is also free).

Ubuntu provides both long-term and short-term support releases. Long-term support releases (LTS), such as Ubuntu 24.04, are released every two years. Short-term releases, such as 23.10, are provided every six months between the LTS versions. They are designed to make available the latest applications and support for the newest hardware. Each has its own nickname, like Noble Numbat for the 24.04 release. The long-term support releases are supported for three years for desktops and five years for servers, whereas short-term support releases are supported for 18 months. In addition, Canonical sells subscriptions such as Ubuntu Pro, which provides full commercial support for companies that purchase it.

Installing Ubuntu is easy to do. A core set of applications are installed, and you can add to them as you wish. Following installation, additional software can be downloaded from online repositories. There are only a few install screens, which move quickly through default partitioning, user setup, and keyboard selection. Hardware components, such as graphics cards and network connections, are configured and detected automatically.

All Linux software for Ubuntu is currently available from online repositories. You can download applications for desktops, Internet servers, office suites, and programming packages, among others. Software packages are distributed primarily through the official Ubuntu repository.

Ubuntu Live Server

Those who want to run Ubuntu as a server in order to provide an Internet service such as a website would use the Ubuntu Server edition. The Ubuntu Live Server is a collection of Linux servers, like those for a Web or FTP site, as well as networking support like a DNS server. The Ubuntu Live Server will install the Ubuntu versions of the Linux servers, with a command line interface. Keeping just the command line interface provides significant efficiency gains for intensely used servers. The server edition also provides cloud support. Ubuntu maintains its own site for the server edition at:

`https://ubuntu.com/server/`

You can download the Server edition from:

`https://ubuntu.com/download/server/`

The **http://releases.ubuntu.com/noble/** site holds Ubuntu Live Server download configuration files for BitTorrent and metalink downloads from multiple mirrors, and zsync files for synchronizing downloads.

For more detailed information on configuration and management check the Ubuntu Server documentation for Ubuntu 24.04 at:

`https://ubuntu.com/server/docs`

For more specialized explanations, see the Ubuntu Community Discourse site for Servers.

`https://discourse.ubuntu.com/c/server/`

The Server edition provides only a simple command line interface. It does not install the desktop. It is designed primarily to run servers. You could just install the servers individually on a standard Ubuntu Desktop. You do not have to install the Server edition to install and run servers.

You now have the option during installation to install either the standard Ubuntu Server with a set of server software, or a minimal version with no added server software (designed for servers with no human interaction). You can install server software later.

Desktop on the Server installation

You could install the Ubuntu Live Server and then later install the Ubuntu desktop from the Ubuntu repository. You can install the complete Ubuntu desktop, one of the Ubuntu flavours, or just the minimal GNOME desktop interface. If you are running servers for a small or home network, the overhead involved with the desktop is not significant. Most likely your servers will be lightly used. At the same time, the additional support provided by the desktop server configuration tools would be helpful.

You can install the Ubuntu Desktop Minimal version that includes several administrative packages you may want to use, like the Network Manager, User management, and the Software Updater. Installing the Ubuntu Desktop Minimal version does not install software such as office, multimedia, and game applications. The minimal version only installs the Firefox browser and a few editors.

You install Ubuntu Desktop Minimal using the **ubuntu-desktop-minimal** meta-package and the **apt** software management tool (you could also use **tasksel**). Use **apt** the **ubuntu-desktop-minimal** meta-package, as shown here.

```
sudo apt install ubuntu-desktop-minimal
```

If, for some reason, you want the full desktop install the **ubuntu-desktop** package. The full Ubuntu desktop will install the complete set of desktop packages, including multimedia and graphics packages, which you may have no use for on your server.

```
sudo apt install ubuntu-desktop
```

Alternatively, you can install any of the Ubuntu Flavours, such as Ubuntu MATE, Kubuntu, or Xubuntu (Xfce). Flavours are alternative desktops supported by Ubuntu and available on the Ubuntu repositories, **https://ubuntu.com/download/flavours**. For Xubuntu (Xfce) install **xubuntu-desktop**. For the KDE desktop, including the KDM login screen, install the **kubuntu-desktop** package. For Ubuntu MATE install the **mate-desktop** package. Keep in mind that these are full packages with an extensive set of software applications.

```
sudo apt install mate-desktop
```

```
sudo apt install kubuntu-desktop
```

```
sudo apt install xubuntu-desktop
```

You could also run **tasksel** with the **sudo** command and then use the arrow keys to move to a desktop entry and press the spacebar. Then tab to the OK button and press ENTER. Desktop choices include Xfce (xubuntu-desktop), KDE Plasma (kubuntu-desktop), MATE (mate-desktop), Cinnamon, LXQt, and GNOME.

```
sudo tasksel
```

Server install options

To recap, your options are:

Install the Ubuntu Live Server only using the command line interface alone.

Install the Ubuntu Live Server first and then installing the Ubuntu Desktop Minimal (**ubuntu-desktop-minimal**). Will implement automatic X Window System startup for

GDM. You could also install any of the Ubuntu Flavours instead such as **mate-desktop**, **cinnamon-desktop**, **xubuntu-desktop**, and **kubuntu-desktop**.

Install the Ubuntu Desktop Minimal first, and then install server packages from the Ubuntu repository using the **apt** command or the Synaptic Package Manager. You will always have the X Window System running as additional overhead. Efficiency degradation would be minor for a small or home networks.

Choose the option that works best for you. Keep in mind that you do not need the Ubuntu Live Server to run servers. All the servers are also available on the Ubuntu repository and can be run from any desktop install.

Ubuntu Pro

Ubuntu sells an enterprise version of Ubuntu with full commercial support called Ubuntu Pro. Ubuntu Pro provides real time security updates, NIST cryptographic module validation, the Ubuntu Security Guide for DISA-STIG and CIS benchmark compliance, and common criteria evaluation assurance level (EAL). It also provides kernel livepatch and system management with Landscape. Ubuntu Pro is also available for personal use for free for up to 5 systems. It does require that you register with Ubuntu. To find out more about Ubuntu Pro see:

```
https://ubuntu.com/pro
```

Ubuntu Software

All Linux software for Ubuntu is currently available from online repositories. You can download applications for desktops, Internet servers, office suites, and programming packages, among others. Software packages are distributed primarily through the official Ubuntu repository. On a desktop, downloads and updates are handled automatically by your desktop software manager and updater. Many popular applications are included in separate sections of the repository. During installation, your system is configured to access Ubuntu repositories. On a desktop, you can update to the latest software from the Ubuntu repository using the software updater. On the Ubuntu server you would use the **apt update** and **apt upgrade** commands.

```
sudo apt update
sudo apt upgrade
```

A complete listings of software packages for the Ubuntu distribution, along with a search capability are located at:

```
https://packages.ubuntu.com
https://snapcraft.io/store
```

In addition, you could download from third-party sources software that is in the form of compressed archives or in DEB packages. DEB packages are archived using the Debian Package Manager and have the extension **.deb**. Compressed archives have an extension such as **.tar.gz**. You also can download the source version and compile it directly on your system. This has become a simple process, almost as simple as installing the compiled DEB versions.

There are two software management systems supported and used by Ubuntu 24.04, the older APT (Advanced Package Tool) software management system that uses DEB packages, and the newer Snap system that uses snap packages. Most servers are still available only as Apt packages.

Snap is the new package format that will replace the deb package management system on Ubuntu. The packages are called **snaps**. With Snap, the software files for an application are not installed in global directories. They are installed in one separate location, and any dependent software and libraries are included as part of the snap package.

All software packages in the Ubuntu repositories are accessible directly on the Ubuntu server with the **apt** commands, such as **apt install** and **apt list**. On the desktop you can access packages with the App Center and the Synaptic Package Manager, which provide easy software installation, removal, and searching. App Center is an implementation of the Snap Store and supports both APT and Snap packages, but gives priority to Snap packages.

Managing Systems with Landscape

Landscape is Ubuntu's administration and monitoring management service accessed through a hosted Web interface. You can register online with Ubuntu for the Landscape service. With Landscape you can administer, monitor, and maintain machines on your network, as well as install and update hosts software. You can find out more about Landscape at:

```
https://ubuntu.com/landscape
```

Machines can be organized into groups, letting you install packages on different groups. Your custom repository can be accessed directly with Landscape, using it to install software on your machines. You can also manage users and servers, adding and removing users, as well as starting and stopping servers.

Landscape also installs its own monitoring application on each machine, providing reports on usage, hardware status, and performance. You can also manage processes, detecting those that use the most resources.

In addition, Landscape supports cloud computing, letting you manage instances of a system on a cloud as you would computers on your network. Landscape can manage Ubuntu instances on the Amazon EC2 cloud and on the Ubuntu Cloud Infrastructure.

Ubuntu Help and Documentation

A great deal of help and documentation is available online for Ubuntu, ranging from detailed install procedures to beginner questions (see Table 1-1). The documentation for Ubuntu 24.04 is located at **https://help.ubuntu.com/**. A link on this site for the 24.04 server sends you to the Ubuntu 24.04 server documentation site at: **https://ubuntu.com/server/docs**. It provides tutorials and an extensive server reference. Also, check the Ubuntu tutorials site (**https://ubuntu.com/tutorials/**) for basic tutorials on different Ubuntu tasks, such as running the Live DVD/USB, setting up Samba, Install the Ubuntu desktop, and configuring the Apache Web server. The Ubuntu Discourse site provides community-based information on current Ubuntu features (**https://discourse.ubuntu.com/**).

Site	Description
https://ubuntu.com/server/docs/	Ubuntu Server documentation site with tutorial and reference
https://help.ubuntu.com/	Help pages and install documentation
https://packages.ubuntu.com	Ubuntu software package list and search
https://askubuntu.com	Ask Ubuntu Q&A site for users and developers (community based)
https://ubuntu.com/tutorials/	Tutorials for Ubuntu topics and tasks
https://discourse.ubuntu.com/	Ubuntu Discourse site with Ubuntu community development discussions as well as documentation
http://fridge.ubuntu.com	News and developments
http://planet.ubuntu.com	Member and developer blogs
https://ubuntu.com/blog	Latest Ubuntu news
http://www.tldp.org	Linux Documentation Project website
https://help.ubuntu.com/community	Community Documentation
https://lists.ubuntu.com	Ubuntu mailing lists

Table 1-1: Ubuntu help and documentation

In addition, there are blog and news sites as well as the standard Linux documentation. Ubuntu Community features Ubuntu documentation, support, blogs, and news. A Contribute section links to sites where you can contribute for development, artwork, documentation, and support. The Ask Ubuntu site is a question and answer site based on community support, which provides answers to many common questions (**https://askubuntu.com**). For mailing lists, check **https://lists.ubuntu.com**. There are lists for categories like Ubuntu announcements, community support for specific flavors, and development for areas like the desktop, servers, or mobile implementation.

help.ubuntu.com

Ubuntu-specific documentation is available at **https://help.ubuntu.com**. Here, on listed links, you can find specific documentation for different releases. Always check the release help page first for documentation, though it may be sparse and cover mainly changed areas. For 24.04, the Documentation section provides the Ubuntu Desktop Guide (Desktop) and the Ubuntu Server Documentation. The Ubuntu Server Documentation is available as a Web site and as a downloadble PDF. On the Web site, use the sidebar to select a tutorial for installation (Tutorials), and extensive set of server HowTo covering installation and configuration (How-To Guides), reference topics such as system requirements for installation and cloud images, and detailed explanations of server topics (Explanations).

```
https://documentation.ubuntu.com/server/
```

Explanations covers network configuration for netplan and DHCP (Networking) , virtualization, security for VPN connections (Security), encrypted connections for OpenSSL, Bind

9 DNSSEC, and JAVA (Cryptography), LVM management (Storage), and phase software updates (Software Management).

The Ubuntu Desktop Guide covers the GNOME interfaces and is the same guide installed with your desktop, accessible as Help (Applications overview).

```
https://help.ubuntu.com/stable/ubuntu-help/index.html
```

One of the more helpful pages is the Community Help page, **https://help.ubuntu.com/community**. Here you will find detailed documentation on the installation of all Ubuntu releases, using the desktop, installing software, and configuring devices. Always check the page for your Ubuntu release first. The page includes these main sections:

Installation: Link to Install page with sections on desktop, server, and alternate installations.

Hardware: Sections on managing hardware. Links to pages on drives and partitions, input devices, wireless configuration, printers, sound, and video.

Further Topics: Links to pages on system administration, security, and troubleshooting, servers, networking, and software development.

Ubuntu Flavours: Links to documentation on different Ubuntu versions such as Lubuntu and Kubuntu.

discourse.ubuntu.com

The Ubuntu Discourse site provides online support and discussion for users. Categories covers areas such as support, announcements, projects, and documentation. The Project Discussion category covers specific support areas like desktop, server, cloud, and the snap store. The "Support and Help" category provides an area where users can obtain answers to questions. You can use the search feature to find discussions on your topic of interest. You can also sort by latest and recent posts.

```
https://discourse.ubuntu.com
```

Linux documentation

The Linux Documentation Project (LDP) has developed a complete set of Linux manuals. The documentation is available at the LDP home site at **https://www.tldp.org**. The Linux documentation for your installed software will be available in your **/usr/share/doc** directory.

2. Installing the Ubuntu Server

Ubuntu Live Server

Upgrading

Installing Ubuntu from the Live Server Installer

Recovery and Rescue

Re-Installing the Boot Loader

Installing Ubuntu Linux has become a simple procedure with just a few screens with default entries for easy installation. A pre-selected collection of software is already installed. Most of your devices, like your monitor and network connection, are detected automatically. For Ubuntu 24.04 the server is installed using the Ubuntu Live Server USB/DVD. For Server specific installation details be sure to check the Ubuntu Live Server tutorial at:

```
https://ubuntu.com/tutorials/install-ubuntu-server
```

For detailed key installation topics such as information on partitioning and automatic installs, check the server guide at:

```
https://ubuntu.com/server/docs/install/general
```

The basic install procedures are covered in this chapter, though you should consult the Server Installation documentation for more detailed information.

Should you wish, you can even install the Ubuntu desktop and then use GNOME-based desktop tools like Synaptic Package Manager or the App Center to install the servers you want. You can also use desktop server configuration tools to manage your servers. These are not available on a direct Live Server install. The downside of installing from the desktop is that you incur the overhead of running the desktop interface, namely GNOME. Most commercial and professional enterprise servers are time-critical, managing a massive number of transactions. A desktop interface can seriously degrade performance. However, for a simple home or local server, which would have relatively few transactions, the desktop would incur little overhead. It would also make managing your server much easier.

Upgrading

You can upgrade directly from the Ubuntu 23.10 release. First, install the **update-manager-core** package, if not installed already.

Then run the **do-release-upgrade** command. This operation will perform any needed system configuration changes.

```
sudo do-release-upgrade
```

Ubuntu Server: Live Server Installer

The Ubuntu Live Server Installer is designed for hardware servers, systems that will run only servers and not perform any other tasks like desktop applications. The Ubuntu desktops are not installed. You will be presented with just a command line interface and command line tools like the **nano** editor to manage your server configuration. You will have to know how to edit server configuration files manually, typing in your entries. You can download the Live Server Installer from the Ubuntu website at:

```
https://www.ubuntu.com/download/server
```

The name of the Live Server Installer is:

```
ubuntu-24.04-live-server
```

It provides a simple and easy to use interface for installing a basic Ubuntu server. The Live Server Installer also supports more complex installations, such as LVM, RAID, VLANS, or re-using existing partitions. It is specifically geared to cloud installs, and installs cloud configured networking, though it can also be used as a standalone server. It installs **cloud-init** by default. A summary of the Live Server Installer is at:

`https://ubuntu.com/server/docs`

The Live Server Installer installs an Ubuntu server, with no additional server software. Once the server is installed, you can directly download and install any server from the Ubuntu repository using the **apt** command.

The Ubuntu Live Server has only a 64-bit version.

You can download the Live Server Installer directly, or by using the BitTorrent, Metalinks, or Zsync download methods. The Live Server Installer download files for these methods are located at:

`http://releases.ubuntu.com/noble/`

For BitTorrent, you can use a BitTorrent client such as transmission or ktorrent.

For information about using metalink with Ubuntu see:

`https://wiki.ubuntu.com/MetalinkIsoDownloads`

Installing Ubuntu from the Live Server Installer

The Live Server Installer CD uses a text-based install interface installer called Subiquity, with ENTER, TAB, SPACEBAR, and arrow keys used to make selections. The installation program used on Ubuntu is a screen-based program that takes you through all these processes, step-by-step, as one continuous procedure. You can use the keyboard to make selections. You can also use TAB, the arrow keys, SPACEBAR, and ENTER to make selections. When you finish with a screen, tab to the Done button at the bottom, and then press ENTER to move to the next screen. If you need to move back to the previous screen, tab to the Back button and press ENTER. You have little to do other than make selections and choose options.

Installation Overview

Installation is a straightforward process. The screen-based installation is easy to use.

For an overview, check the Ubuntu Live Server Installer tutorial at:

`https://ubuntu.com/tutorials/install-ubuntu-server`

Most systems today already meet hardware requirements and have automatic connections to the Internet (DHCP).

They also support booting from a DVD or USB, though this support may have to be explicitly configured in the system BIOS.

For a quick installation, you can start up the installation process, by inserting your Server USB/DVD and starting up your system. Installation is a simple matter of following the instructions in each window as you progress. Installation follows several easy steps:

1. **Language Selection**   A default is chosen for you, like English, so you can usually just press ENTER.

2. **Keyboard Layout**   You can choose to automatically detect the layout by pressing some keys, or choose one from a list, first by country and then by type. A default is chosen for you. You can usually press ENTER.

3. **Configure your network**. Network device configuration.

4. **Configure Proxy**   Enter your proxy address if you have one.

5. **Choose a mirror**   A default mirror is chosen, you can choose a different one if you want.

6. **Filesystem Setup**   Disks are scanned and the partition options presented. If you have a blank disk or one you want to overwrite entirely, you can use the "Use an entire disk" option to perform an automatic partitioning.

7. The base system is installed in the background as you continue with the next step.

8. **Profile Setup** Set up a username for your computer, as well as a password for that user.

9. **Asked to install OpenSSH server**   You are asked if you want to install an SSH server and whether you want ot import you SHH idendity.

10. **Snap software selection**   You can choose from a list of popular Snap packages to install.

11. **Finish the Installation**   After the install, you will be asked to Reboot your system. You can also view the install log at this time.

Starting the Ubuntu Live Server Installation

If your computer can boot from the USB/DVD, you can start the installation directly from the USB/DVD. After you turn on or restart your computer, the installation program will start up. Your system then detects your hardware, providing any configuration specifications that may be needed.

Keys	Action
TAB	Move to different entries and to the Done, Reset, and Back buttons
ENTER	Execute a selected button or menu entry
Arrow, up and down	Move to different entries and selections on a menu
Arrow, left and right	Move within an entry

Table 2-1: Installation Keys for Live Server Installer

As each screen appears during the installation, default entries will be already selected, usually by the auto-probing capability of the installation program. Selected entries will appear highlighted. If these entries are correct, you can simply press ENTER to accept them and go on to the next screen. Some screens will display a Done button. Use the Tab key to move to that button. Many screens will also have a Back button. The Tab key will cycle through to the Done and Back buttons. You can also use the arrow keys to move to different entries and between the Back and Done buttons. The install keys are listed in Table 2-1. For several screens, you can Tab to a Back key and press ENTER to display the previous screen.

Language and Keyboard

First, you select your Language (see Figure 2-1). Use the up/down arrow keys to move through the list. Press the ENTER key when you have reached your selection. The detected default will already be selected. If correct, just press ENTER.

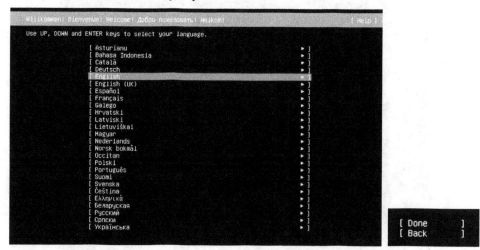

Figure 2-1: Language

If a new version of the Subiquity installer is available, you will be prompted to download it if you want (see Figure 2-2).

Figure 2-2: Subiquity installer update

You will then be asked to select a keyboard. The default keyboard will be selected already, such as U.S. English (see Figure 2-3). Should you want a different keyboard layout, click the plus button preceding the currently selected keyboard to display a list of different keyboard layouts (See figure 2-4). Use the arrow keys to find your selection and then press ENTER.

Figure 2-3: Keyboard configuration

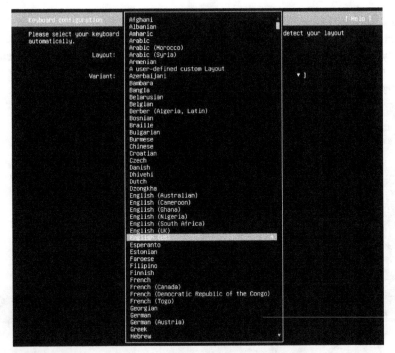

Figure 2-4: Keyboard configuration - keyboard layouts menu

If there is more than one keyboard layout for your region, a variant, there will be a plus sign before the Variant entry. Click the plus sign to display a menu of possible variants (see Figure 2-5). The USA keyboard will have several keyboard selections such as Macintosh, Dvorak, or International, as well as the standard.

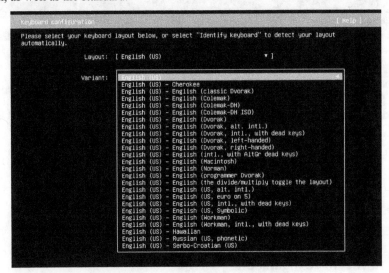

Figure 2-5: Keyboard configuration - keyboard variants menu

If your keyboard is not listed, you can choose the Identify Keyboard option to let you enter keys that can be used to detect your keyboard.

You can then choose between the full Ubuntu server and the Ubuntu minimized version, as well as choose to install third party drivers.

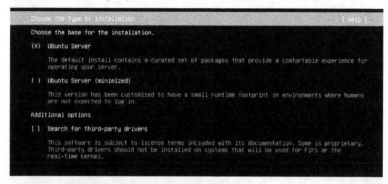

Figure 2-6: Choose the base for the installer

Network Connections

You then configure your network interfaces. They are automatically detected and listed. Normally you would have only one. If you have multiple hardware network connections, you are asked to choose one (usually the Ethernet connection, beginning with **en** for fixed or **wl** for wireless). If you are using a DCHP server to configure your network information, it will be detected (see Figure 2-7). The Ubuntu Live Server installer uses the device you select on this screen to generate the network configuration using netplan.

Figure 2-7: Network Configuration

Then you are asked if you use a proxy server (see Figure 2-8). Enter it if you use one, otherwise just leave the entry blank and press ENTER.

Figure 2-8: Proxy Server Configuration

You can then select another mirror if you wish, or just use the default (see Figure 2-9).

Figure 2-9: Mirror selection

Filesystem Setup

Then you are asked to designate the Linux partitions and hard disk configurations you want to use on your hard drives. For LVM partitions, an LVM Group has to be set up before you can configure any partitions. This means that the partition table is written to before you configure your partitions. This action cannot be reversed. This is true for both Guided LVM and manual LVM partitioning.

If you are setting up standard partitions manually, instead of LVM partitions, partitions will be changed or formatted at the end of the partitioning process. At the end of the partitioning procedure, you will be asked explicitly to write the partition changes to your disk. You can opt out of the installation at any time until that point, and your original partitions will remain untouched.

The partition options will change according to the number of hard disks on your system. If you have several hard disks, they will be listed. You can also select the disk on which to install Ubuntu.

Automatic Partitioning: "Use an Entire Disk"

Ubuntu provides automatic partitioning if you just want to use available drives and free space for your Linux system. You will have to have an entire blank disk free for use for your Ubuntu server.

On the "Guided storage configuration" screen the "Use the entire disk" and the "Set up this disk as an LVM group" are selected by default (see Figure 2-10). This option will format your entire disk and set up an LVM file system with a volume group and logical volumes. To use this option, just select the Done entry at the bottom of the screen and press ENTER.

Figure 2-10: Filesystem creation "Use An Entire Disk"

Figure 2-11: Filesystem Summary with LVM default

The "Storage configuration" screen displays the file systems in the "FILE SYSTEM Summary" section, with a logical volume set up for the root (/), an ext4 partition set up for the Ubuntu Linux **/boot** files, and a partition for the boot EFI file system (bios_grub) (see Figure 2-11). You cannot boot directly from an LVM file system, so you have to have a standard **/boot** and EFI/BIOS partitions to boot from.

If you do not want to use the LVM file system, you can deselect its entry on the "Guided storage configuration" screen. This will set up two partitions, one for the boot EFI/BIOS file system and a standard **ext4** partition for the entire file system (/) (see Figure 2-12).

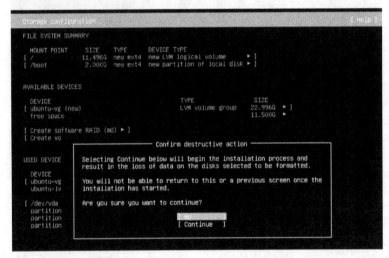

Figure 2-12: Filesystem Summary without LVM

The choices at the bottom of the Storage configuration" screen are Done, Reset, and Back (see Figure 2-9). For the "Use an Entire Disk" option, both Reset and Back return you to the first Filesystem Setup screen as shown in Figure 2-9.

Choosing Done displays the "Confirm destructive action" dialog with No and Continue options (see Figure 2-13). The No option is selected. To perform the partitioning, use the arrow key to move down to the Continue option and press Enter. The partitions are then created on the hard disk. Up until this moment no action has been taken. Once you choose Continue the partitions are then created. This action is irrevocable.

Figure 2-13: Creating partitions

Profile setup

On the Profile setup screen, you create a user to login with and specify your server's name (see Figure 2-14). Enter the user's full name (usually your own). Then enter the hostname you want to use for the server you are installing. Enter a user's login name and that user's password to create

the user to login with. The user you are creating will have administrative access, allowing you to
change your system configuration, add new users, and install new software.

Figure 2-14: Profile setup - user and hostname

Ubuntu Pro

On the "Upgrade to Ubuntu Pro" screen you can choose to enable the Ubuntu Pro service
(see Figure 2-15). Select the "About Ubuntu Pro" entry to display more information about Ubuntu
Pro. You have the option to enable Ubuntu Pro or to skip and sign up later. The "Skip for now"
option is selected by default. You could just press ENTER to continue.

Figure 2-15: Ubuntu Pro

SSH Configuration

On the SSH configuration screen you can choose to install the OpenSSH server (see
Figure 2-16). If you choose to install the SSH server, you can then also import an SSH identity
from either Github or Launchpad.

Figure 2-16: SSH Setup

Featured Server Snaps

The Featured Server Snaps screen then list popular server-related snaps that you can choose to install (see Figure 2-17). Use the SPACEBAR to select an entry.

Figure 2-17: Featured Server Snaps

Installing System and Installation Complete

The standard software for a basic Ubuntu server is installed. Remaining configuration and boot loader installation is performed for you. The "Installing System" screen shows a brief log of the install process. When complete, the "Installation Complete!" screen is displayed (see Figure 2-18). Buttons at the bottom of the screen let you choose to "View the full log" or to "Reboot ". When the installation is complete, security updates will be downloaded and installed. You will have the option to cancel the update. The Reboot button is selected by default. Press enter to reboot your system. You will be prompted to eject the install disk.

Figure 2-18: Finishing install

Manual Partitioning

To manually configure your hard drive, first, plan what partitions you want to set up and what their size should be. You can set up different partitions for any directory on your system. Many systems set up separate partitions for **/home**, **/var**, **/srv**, as well as / (root) and **/boot**. You no longer need a swap partition. A swap file is used instead.

/var directory holds data that constantly changes like printer spool files.

/srv directory holds server data, like Web server pages and FTP sites

/home directory holds user's folders and files along with any user data.

/ the root directory is the system directory. All other file systems and partitions attach to it.

/boot the boot directory holds the Linux kernel and the boot configuration. You will need a separate boot partition if you are using LVM partitions for your root partition. The boot directory cannot be on an LVM partition.

To perform a manual partition, use the SPACEBAR to select the "Custom storage layout" entry on the "Guided storage configuration" screen (see Figure 2-19). This will also deselect the "Use an entire disk" entry. The choose the Done entry at the bottom of the screen.

Figure 2-19: Choose Custom Storage Layout

The "Storage configuration" screen is then displayed showing your hard disks in the AVAILABLE DEVICES section. If you have only one hard disk, only that disk is listed.

Select the free space entry for the drive where you want to create your partitions. Press ENTER to display a menu where you can choose the "Add GPT Partition" entry (see Figure 2-20).

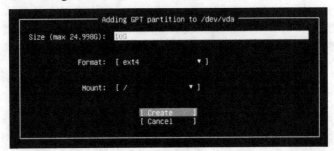

Figure 2-20: Add a partition

This opens the "Adding GPT partition to" dialog with entries for specifying the partition size, format, and mount point (see Figure 2-21). For the size, the maximum possible size is shown (the available free space). Specify the size of the partition in either M or G for megabytes and gigabytes. If you enter nothing, the maximum size is used.

```
┌──────────── Adding GPT partition to /dev/vda ────────────┐
│                                                          │
│  Size (max 24.998G):  10G                                │
│                                                          │
│           Format:  [ ext4              ▼ ]               │
│                                                          │
│            Mount:  [ /                 ▼ ]               │
│                                                          │
│                      [ Create     ]                      │
│                      [ Cancel     ]                      │
│                                                          │
└──────────────────────────────────────────────────────────┘
```

Figure 2-21: Creating a partition

Upon creating the first partition, the EFI/BIOS boot partition is also added, as shown on the "Storage configuration" screen (see Figure 2-22).

```
Storage configuration                                    [ Help ]

FILE SYSTEM SUMMARY

  MOUNT POINT    SIZE    TYPE    DEVICE TYPE
  /              24.000G new ext4  new partition of local disk ▶ ]

AVAILABLE DEVICES

  DEVICE                         TYPE        SIZE
[ /dev/vda                       local disk  25.000G  ▶ ]
  free space                                 1021.000M ▶

[ Create software RAID (md) ▶ ]
[ Create volume group (LVM) ▶ ]

USED DEVICES

  DEVICE                         TYPE        SIZE
[ /dev/vda                       local disk  25.000G  ▶ ]
  partition 1  new, BIOS grub spacer                 1.000M  ▶
  partition 2  new, to be formatted as ext4, mounted at /  24.000G  ▶
```

Figure 2-22: Root partition and EFI/BIOS boot file system

Default entries will be entered for the format and mount point (Mount). For the first partition this is the format **ext4** with a mount point for the root system, /. A third partition would also have the format **ext4**, but with the mount point **/home** (see Figure 2-23).

```
┌──────── Adding GPT partition to /dev/vda ────────┐
│                                                  │
│ Size (max 14.997G):  [4G                      ]  │
│                                                  │
│                                                  │
│        Format:  [ ext4          ▼ ]              │
│                                                  │
│        Mount:   [ /home         ▼ ]              │
│                                                  │
│                      [ Create    ]               │
│                      [ Cancel    ]               │
│                                                  │
└──────────────────────────────────────────────────┘
```

Figure 2-23: Additional partitions

For any partition you can choose a different format or mount point than the default. Press the ENTER key on the format or mount entries to see menus of possible options. The format option displays a menu with formats for **ext4**, **xfs**, **btrfs**, **swap**, and "leave unconfigured" (see figure 2-24). A standard Linux partition would use **ext4** and a swap partition would use **swap** should you want one. The **xfs** and **btrfs** formats are more advanced formats.

Pressing ENTER on the mount entry displays a menu with the commonly used mount points: / (root), **/boot**, **/home**, **/srv**, **/usr**, **/var**, **/var/lib**, and other (see Figure 2-25). You can also leave it unmounted.

```
┌──────── Adding GPT partition to /dev/vda ────────┐
│                                                  │
│ Size (max 14.997G):  [4G                      ]  │
│                                                  │
│        Format:  │ ext4              ◄ │          │
│                 │ xfs                 │          │
│                 │ btrfs               │          │
│        Mount:   │ ---                 │          │
│                 │ swap                │          │
│                 │ ---                 │          │
│                 │ Leave unformatted   │          │
│                                                  │
└──────────────────────────────────────────────────┘
```

Figure 2-24: Partition format menu

```
┌──────── Adding GPT partition to /dev/vda ────────┐
│                                                  │
│ Size (max 14.997G):  [4G                      ]  │
│                                                  │
│        Format:              ]                    │
│                 │ /                 │            │
│                 │ /boot             │            │
│        Mount:   │ /home           ◄ │            │
│                 │ /srv              │            │
│                 │ /usr              │            │
│                 │ /var              │            │
│                 │ /var/lib          │            │
│                 │ Other             │            │
│                 │ ---               │            │
│                 │ Leave unmounted   │            │
│                                                  │
└──────────────────────────────────────────────────┘
```

Figure 2-25: Partition Mount menu

Figure 2-26: File System Summary

You then return to the "Storage configuration" screen showing the File System Summary, which lists the partitions you have set up (see Figure 2-26). These are the partitions you will create. The boot EFI or BIOS partition is added automatically for you.

Partition entries will show the partition number, size, format type, and mount point. If there is still free space, you will still be able to add a partition using the remaining amount of free space shown, which you can choose to add another partition. You can edit any of the partition entries by moving to that entry in the USED DEVICES section and pressing ENTER to display a menu where you can choose the Edit entry to open that partition's "Editing partition" screen. You can then change the size, format, or mount point.

At the bottom of the screen you have buttons for Done, Reset, and Back (see Figure 2-20). The Back button returns you to the "Guided storage configuration" screen.

The Reset button removes all your partition settings and returns you to the initial "Storage configuration" screen, allowing you to start over. You will lose all the settings you just set up.

To actually create the partitions, select the Done entry at the bottom of the screen and press ENTER. This displays the "Confirm destructive action" dialog with No and Continue options (see Figure 2-12). The No option is selected. To perform the partitioning, use the arrow key to move down to the Continue option and press Enter. The partitions are then created on the hard disk. Once you choose Continue the partitions are then created. This action is irrevocable.

Manual Partitioning for LVM

You can also manually partition your drive using LVM. You must first set up a boot file system partition for both your Ubuntu Linux **/boot** directory and for the EFI/BIO file system. You cannot boot directly from an LVM file system. To do this add a standard (GPT) ext4 partition for the **/boot** directory (see Figure 2-27). The EFI file system partition is then automatically added. The boot file systems are then listed under the FILE "SYSTEM Summary" section (see Figure 2-28).

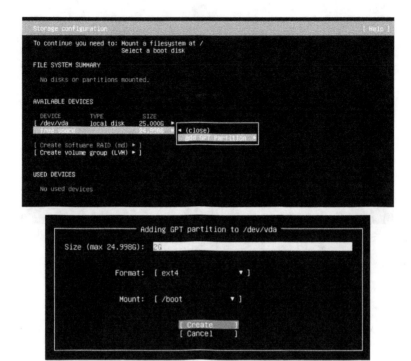

Figure 2-27: Create a /boot partition

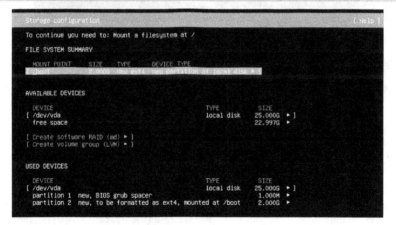

Figure 2-28: Boot file system partitions

You then have to specify the rest of the disk as unformatted. Open the "Add to GPT partition" dialog (see Figure 2-29). Then select the Unformatted option in the file system menu.

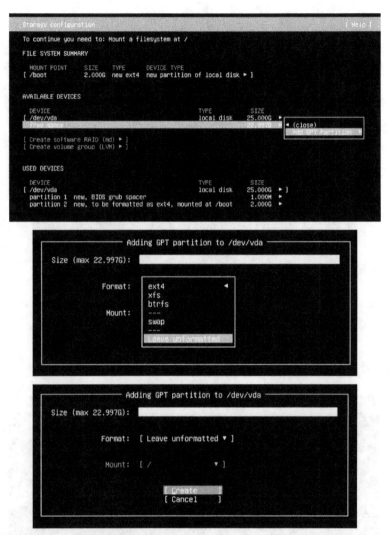

Figure 2-29: Specify unformatted disk

On the "Storage configuration" screen, there now will be an accessible entry for "Create volume group (LVM)" (see Figure 2-30). Select this entry and choose to create a volume group. On the "Create LVM volume group" dialog, you enter a name (the default is **vg0**) and select the device. You can also encrypt it.

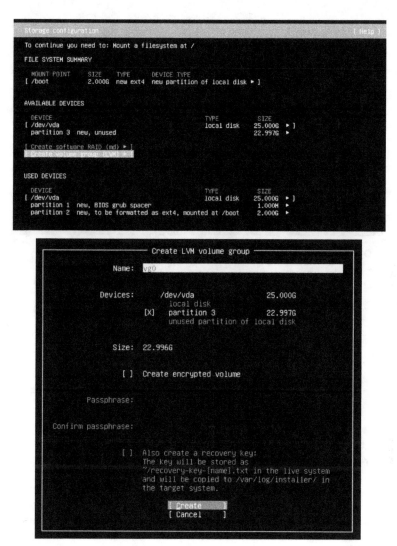

Figure 2-30: Create Volume Group

Upon returning to the "Storage configuration" screen, you will see an entry for the LVM volume group you created listed under the AVAILABLE DEVICES section. Choose the free space entry for that device to display a menu with the "Create Logical Volume" entry (see Figure 2-31). Choose this entry to open the "Adding logical volume to" dialog (see Figure 2-32). Enter the logical volume's name and size. The default name is **lv-0**. Select the format. The default is **ext4**. And then choose the mount point. The default for the first logical volume is the root, /. From the "Storage configuration" screen you can choose to add more logical volumes such as one for **/home**. The default name is incremented to the next number as in **lv-1**.

Figure 2-31: Logical Volume

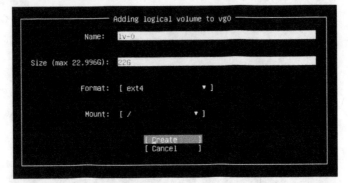

Figure 2-32: Creating a logical volumes

The "Storage configuration" screen will show all your LVM devices, listing your group volume and your logical volumes (see Figure 2-33). To actually create the partitions, select the Done button at the bottom of the screen and press ENTER. This displays the "Confirm destructive action" dialog with No and Continue options (see Figure 2-13). The No option is selected. To perform the partitioning, use the down arrow key to move down to the Continue option and press Enter. The partitions are then created on the hard disk.

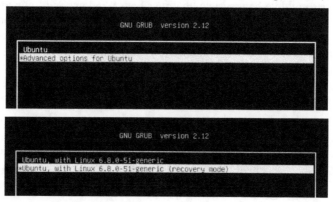

Figure 2-33: Storage Configuration for LVM

Recovery, rescue, and boot loader re-install

Ubuntu provides the means to start up systems that have failed for some reason. A system that may boot but fails to start up, can be started in a recovery mode, already set up for you as an entry on your boot loader menu.

Recovery

If for some reason your system is not able to start up, it may be due to conflicting configurations, libraries, or applications. On the GRUB menu, first, choose the "Advanced options for Ubuntu" to open the advanced options menu. Then select the recovery mode entry, the Ubuntu kernel entry with the (recovery mode) label attached to the end (see Figure 2-34).

Figure 2-34: Recovery kernel, GRUB

This will start up a dialog that asks you to select the root partition. Once selected, another dialog shows a menu where you can use the arrow and ENTER keys to select from several recovery options (see Figure 2-35). These include resume, fsck, network, and root. Short descriptions for each item are displayed on the menu.

```
Recovery Menu (filesystem state: read-only)

     resume           Resume normal boot
     clean            Try to make free space
     dpkg             Repair broken packages
     fsck             Check all file systems
     grub             Update grub bootloader
     network          Enable networking
     root             Drop to root shell prompt
     system-summary   System summary



                     <Ok>
```

Figure 2-35: Recovery menu

The root option will start up Ubuntu as the root user with a command line shell prompt. In this case, you can boot your Linux system in a recovery mode and then edit configuration files with a text editor such as Vi and nano, remove the suspect libraries, or reinstall damaged software with **apt** or **snap**.

If you forget your password, you can select the Recovery mode from the GRUB menu, then choose the "Drop to root shell prompt" entry. Then run the **passwd** command with the username. You will be prompted to re-enter the password for that user. You can then run the **poweroff** command to shut down the system. When you restart, the new password will work.

The resume entry will start up Ubuntu normally, but in the command line mode.

To rescue a broken system, choose the **root** entry. Your broken system will be mounted and made accessible with a command line interface. You can then use command line operations and editors to fix configuration files.

Re-Installing the Boot Loader

If you have a multiple-boot system, that runs both Windows and Linux on the same machine, you may run into a situation where you have to reinstall your GRUB boot loader. This problem occurs if your Windows system completely crashes beyond repair and you have to install a new version of Windows, if you added Windows to your machine after having installed Linux, or if you upgraded to a new version of Windows. A Windows installation will automatically overwrite your boot loader (alternatively, you could install your boot loader on your Linux partition instead of the primary boot record, MBR). You will no longer be able to access your Linux system.

You can manually reinstall your boot loader, using your Ubuntu Desktop USB/DVD. The procedure is more complicated, as you have to mount your Ubuntu system. On the Ubuntu Live DVD, you can use GParted to find out what partition your Ubuntu system uses. In a terminal window, create a directory on which to mount the system.

```
sudo mkdir myubuntu
```

Then mount it, making sure you have the correct file system type and partition name (usually **/dev/sda5** on dual boot systems).

```
sudo mount -t ext4 /dev/sda5  myubuntu
```

Then, use **grub-install** and the device name of your first partition to install the boot loader, with the **--root-directory** option to specify the directory where you mounted your Ubuntu file system. The **--root-directory** option requires a full path name, which for the Ubuntu Live DVD would be **/home/ubuntu** for the home directory. Using the **myubuntu** directory this example, the full pathname of the Ubuntu file system would be **/home/ubuntu/myubuntu**. You would then enter the following **grub-install** command.

```
sudo grub-install --root-directory=/home/ubuntu/myubuntu /dev/sda
```

This will re-install your current GRUB boot loader. You can then reboot, and the GRUB boot loader will start up.

ubuntu

3. Usage Basics: Login, Interfaces, networking, and Help

Ubuntu Server startup

Grub selection and editing

The Command Line Interface

Accessing Linux from the Command Line Interface

Help Resources accessible from the command line

Network Connections with systemd-networkd

Netplan

Network Manager and nmcli

Predictable Network Device Names

The Ubuntu Desktop

Terminal window

Ubuntu Desktop Help

Using Linux is an almost intuitive process, with easy-to-use interfaces, including graphical logins and desktops like GNOME and KDE. Even the standard Linux command line interface is user-friendly, with editable commands, history lists, and cursor-based tools. To start using Linux, you have to know how to access your Linux system and, once you are on the system, how to execute commands and run applications.

Linux is noted for providing easy access to extensive help documentation. It is easy to obtain information quickly about any Linux command and utility while logged in to the system. You can access an online manual that describes each command or obtain help that provides more detailed explanations of different Linux features. A complete set of manuals provided by the Linux Documentation Project is included on your system and is available to browse through or print. The Ubuntu desktop and its variants such as Kubuntu and Xubuntu, provide help systems with easy access to desktop, system, and application help files.

It is possible to first install the Ubuntu server, and then later install the Ubuntu desktop. This would provide you with all the configuration files for the Ubuntu server, as well as the desktop configuration tools available for those servers.

Ubuntu Server startup

If you installed with the Ubuntu Live Server Installer, no desktop is installed. When you start up, a command line interface is presented. The startup procedure uses tty1, the terminal one device, presenting a command line interface. Startup messages are displayed.

Ubuntu uses the systemd login manager, logind, to manage logins and sessions, replacing consolekit which is no longer supported. You can configure login manager options with the **/etc/systemd/logind.conf** file. You can set options such as the number of terminals (default is 6), the idle action, and hardware key operations, such as the power key. Check the **logind.conf** man page for details.

The startup procedure provides no interactive support by default. This is an issue if you have file system mount problems, where **fsck** is run to check or fix file systems. To enable interactive support, edit the GRUB boot entry as described in the next section, and add the splash option, then boot. The Plymouth start up splash screen is shown, and you are notified and prompted for any filesystem mount problems. To make the Plymouth splash screen the default, add the **splash** option to the **/etc/default/grub** file.

The login prompt then prompts you to enter your username. This is the username you set up during installation (see Figure 3-1).

Figure 3-1: Server login prompt

After you enter your username, you will be prompted to enter the password. Once logged in, you can then run commands. Basic server status information will be displayed such as the system load and the number of users logged in (see Figure 3-2).

To shut down the system enter the **poweroff** command with the **sudo** command. You will be prompted to enter your password.

```
sudo poweroff
```

To perform a reboot from the command line, you can use the **reboot** command.

```
sudo reboot
```

From the login prompt, you can reboot your system with the Ctrl-Alt-Del keys.

```
Ubuntu 24.04 LTS myserver tty1

myserver login: richard
Password:
Welcome to Ubuntu 24.04 LTS (GNU/Linux 6.8.0-51-generic x86_64)

 * Documentation:  https://help.ubuntu.com
 * Management:     https://landscape.canonical.com
 * Support:        https://ubuntu.com/pro

 System information as of Thu Jan 23 09:56:01 PM UTC 2025

  System load:  0.43             Processes:              146
  Usage of /:   40.5% of 11.21GB  Users logged in:        0
  Memory usage: 5%               IPv4 address for enp1s0: 192.168.122.15
  Swap usage:   0%

Expanded Security Maintenance for Applications is not enabled.

139 updates can be applied immediately.
To see these additional updates run: apt list --upgradable

Enable ESM Apps to receive additional future security updates.
See https://ubuntu.com/esm or run: sudo pro status


The programs included with the Ubuntu system are free software;
the exact distribution terms for each program are described in the
individual files in /usr/share/doc/*/copyright.

Ubuntu comes with ABSOLUTELY NO WARRANTY, to the extent permitted by
applicable law.

To run a command as administrator (user "root"), use "sudo <command>".
See "man sudo_root" for details.

richard@myserver:~$
```

Figure 3-2: Server login

GRUB Boot Loader

When your system starts, the GRUB boot loader will quickly select your default operating system and start up its login screen. If you have just installed Ubuntu, the default operating system will be Ubuntu.

If you have installed more than one operating system, the GRUB menu is displayed for several seconds at startup, before loading the default operating system automatically. To display the GRUB menu should you have only your Ubuntu system installed, press the SHIFT key at start up. Once displayed, press the ESC key to have GRUB wait until you have made a selection. Your GRUB menu is displayed as shown in Figure 3-3. The Advanced options entry allows you to start Ubuntu in recovery mode or choose a previously installed kernel to use.

The GRUB menu lists Ubuntu along with any other operating systems installed on your hard drive, such as Windows or other versions of Linux. Use the arrow keys to move to the entry you want and press ENTER.

For graphical installations, some displays may have difficulty running the graphical startup display. If you have this problem, you can edit your Linux GRUB entry and remove the **splash** term at the end of the **linux** line. Press the **e** key to edit a GRUB entry (see Figure 3-4).

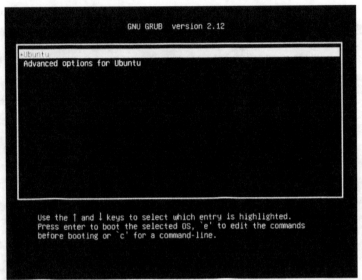

Figure 3-3: Ubuntu GRUB menu

Figure 3-4: Editing a GRUB menu item

To change a particular line, use the up and down arrow keys to move to the line. You can use the left and right arrow keys to move along the line. The Backspace key will delete characters and typing will insert characters. The editing changes are temporary. Permanent changes can only be made by directly editing the GRUB configuration **/etc/default/grub** file, and then running the following command:

```
sudo update-grub
```

If you have installed more than one operating system or wish to use the recovery kernel, you can select it using the GRUB menu.

If no other operating system is detected, by default, access to the GRUB menu is disabled. Disabling of the GRUB menu will also deny access to the recovery option. To enable the GRUB menu, you first have to edit the GRUB configuration file and comment out or modify the GRUB_HIDDEN_TIMEOUT option. By default, this option is set to 0, effectively disabling GRUB menu access.

```
GRUB_HIDDEN_TIMEOUT=0
```

If you want the GRUB menu displayed each time you start up, just comment out this line using a preceding # character.

```
# GRUB_HIDDEN_TIMEOUT=0
```

For the standard server installation and for systems with other operating systems installed, this entry will be commented out already (see Figure 3-5). Each time you start up, the GRUB menu will be displayed for a few seconds, allowing you to make selections.

If you only want the menu displayed when you choose to access it, change the numeric value to the number of seconds to wait. Pressing the ESC key in that time period will display the GRUB menu. On systems with other operating systems already installed, this option will be commented out. To enable the option, first, remove the preceding # comment character. The following example waits for 10 seconds.

```
GRUB_HIDDEN_TIMEOUT=10
```

The GRUB configuration file is **/etc/default/grub**. You can edit it from the command line interface with a text editor like **vi**, **emacs**, or **nano**. The **nano** editor provides a simple cursor-based interface for easy editing. Use **Ctrl-o** to write changes and **Ctrl-x** to exit.

```
sudo nano /etc/default/grub
```

Once you have made your changes, you must run the **update-grub** command to implement the configuration changes.

```
sudo update-grub
```

Figure 3-5: Editing the /etc/default/grub file with the nano editor

Help Resources accessible from the command line

There are several different resources you can access for help on your system. If you have installed a desktop, you can use the Ubuntu help center. The Ubuntu Live Server will not install the desktop. You will have access to command line help tools, like the man and info pages. The **/usr/share/doc** directory will hold any documentation installed for applications. A great deal of support documentation is already installed on your system, as well as accessible from online sources.

If you need to ask a question, you can obtain help support at **https://answers.launchpad.net** and **https://askubuntu.com**. Here you can submit your question, as well as check answered questions.

Application Documentation

On your system, the **/usr/share/doc** directory contains documentation files installed by each application. Within each directory, you can usually find HOW-TO, README, and INSTALL documents for that application. Some documentation will include detailed manuals. For many servers, like the Bind server, these include helpful examples or Web-based manuals. Often the documentation for applications like servers are included in a separate software package, usually with the suffix **-doc** in the name, like **bind9-doc** for the DNS BIND documentation. Such documentation may be located under their package name, instead of their application name, like **/usr/share/doc/bind9-doc** for the DNS server documentation.

The Man Pages

You can also access the Man pages, which are manuals for Linux commands available from the command line interface, using the **man** command. Enter **man** with the command for which you want information. The following example asks for information on the **ls** command.

```
$ man ls
```

Pressing the SPACEBAR key advances you to the next page. Pressing the **b** key moves you back a page. When you finish, press the **q** key to quit the Man utility and return to the command line. You activate a search by pressing either the slash (/) or question mark (**?**). The / searches forward, and the ? searches backward. When you press the /, a line opens at the bottom of your screen, and you then enter a word to search for. Press ENTER to activate the search. You can repeat the same search by pressing the **n** key. You do not have to reenter the pattern.

The Info Pages

Online documentation for GNU applications, such as the gcc compiler and the Emacs editor, also exist as info pages. You can access this documentation by entering the command **info**. This brings up a special screen listing different GNU applications. The **info** interface has its own set of commands. You can learn more about it by entering **info info** at the command prompt. Typing **m** opens a line at the bottom of the screen where you can enter the first few letters of the application. Pressing ENTER brings up the info file on that application.

The Command Line Interface

The Ubuntu Live Server USB/DVD, for efficiency reasons, will not install a desktop interface. Instead, you use the traditional UNIX command line interface, accessing your system from a login prompt and typing commands from your keyboard on a command line.

Accessing Linux from the Command Line Interface

For the command line interface, you are initially given a login prompt. The login prompt is preceded by the hostname you gave your system. In this example, the hostname is **myserver**. When you finish using Linux, you log out with the **logout** command. Linux then displays the same login prompt, waiting for you or another user to log in again. This is the equivalent of the login window provided by the GDM display manager. You can then log in to another account.

Once you log in as a user, you can enter and execute commands. To log in, enter your username and your password. If you make a mistake, you can erase characters with the **backspace** key. In the next example, the user enters the username **richard** and is then prompted to enter the password:

```
Ubuntu 24.04 LTS myserver tty1

myserver login: richard
Password:
```

When you type in your password, it does not appear on the screen. This is to protect your password from being seen by others. If you enter either the username or the password incorrectly, the system will respond with the error message "Login incorrect" and will ask for your username again, starting the login process over. You can then re-enter your username and password.

Once you enter your username and password, you are logged in to the system and the command line prompt is displayed, waiting for you to enter a command. The command line prompt is a dollar sign (**$**). On Ubuntu, your prompt is preceded by the hostname and the folder you are in. The home folder is indicated by a tilde (~).

```
richard@myserver:~$
richard@myserver:~$ cd Pictures
richard@myserver:~/Pictures$
```

To end your session, issue the **logout** or **exit** command. This returns you to the login prompt, and Linux waits for another user to log in.

```
richard@myserver:~$ logout
```

To shut down your system from the command line, you can use the **poweroff** command. If you are not an administrative user, you will have to also use the **sudo** command. The user you created for installation is an administrative user.

```
poweroff
```

To perform a reboot from the terminal window, you can use the **reboot** command.

```
reboot
```

If you want a time delay on the shutdown, you would use the **shutdown** command with **-h** and the time options with administrative access (**sudo** command). This command will log you out and shut down the system after 5 minutes.

```
richard@myserver:~$ sudo shutdown -h +5
```

Using the Command Line Interface

Linux commands make extensive use of options and arguments. Be careful to place your arguments and options in their correct order on the command line. The format for a Linux command is the command name followed by options, and then by arguments, as shown here.

```
$ command-name options arguments
```

An option is a one-letter code preceded by one or two dashes, which modifies the type of action the command takes. Options and arguments may or may not be optional, depending on the command. For example, the **ls** command can take an option, **-s**. The **ls** command displays a listing of files in your directory, and the **-s** option adds the size of each file in blocks. You enter the command and its option on the command line as follows.

```
$ ls -s
```

If you are uncertain what format and options a command uses, you can check the command syntax quickly by displaying its man page. Most commands have a man page. Enter the **man** command with the command name as an argument.

An argument is data the command may need to execute its task. In many cases, this is a filename. An argument is entered as a word on the command line that appears after any options. For example, to display the contents of a file, you can use the **more** or **less** commands with the file's name as its argument. The **less** or **more** command used with the filename **mydata** would be entered on the command line as follows.

```
$ less mydata
```

The command line is actually a buffer of text you can edit. Before you press ENTER to execute the command, you can edit the command on the command line. The editing capabilities provide a way to correct mistakes you may make when typing a command and its options. The BACKSPACE key lets you erase the character you just typed (the one to the left of the cursor) and the DEL key lets you erase one character to the right of the cursor. With this character-erasing capability, you can BACKSPACE over the entire line if you want, erasing what you entered. **Ctrl-u** erases the whole command line and lets you start over again at the prompt.

You can use the UP-ARROW key to redisplay your last-executed command. You can then re-execute that command, or you can edit it and execute the modified command. This is helpful when you have to repeat certain operations, such as editing the same file. This is also helpful when you have already executed a command you entered incorrectly.

Accessing USB drives from the Command line Interface on a Server.

When you attach a USB drive it is detected automatically, but not mounted. A message will be displayed indicating the device name for the drive. If you have one hard drive, which would be labeled device **sda**, then the USB device would be **sdb**. USB drives are normally formatted as **vfat** file systems. Your file system would be located on the first file system on the USB drive, which would be **sdb1** in this example. Use the **lsblk** command to find out the device name of the USB drive.

To access the USB drive you have to create a directory on which to mount it. Then use the mount command to mount the file system. You only create the directory once. Use the **mkdir** command to create the directory.

```
lsblk
mkdir myusb
```

To mount a USB drive to that directory, enter a mount command with the **vfat** type, mounting the **/dev/sdb1** device to the **myusb** directory. You have to have administrative access, so you need to use the **sudo** command.

```
sudo mount  -t vfat   /dev/sdb1  myusb
```

You can then access the USB drive by accessing the **myusb** directory.

```
$ cd myusb
$ ls
```

Write operations would still have to be run with administrative access.

```
sudo cp mydata  myusb
```

To write whole directories and their subdirectories, you need to add the **-R** option to **cp**.

```
sudo cp -R mydatadir  myusb
```

Once finished with the USB drive, be sure to first unmount it before removing it.

```
sudo umount /dev/sdb1
```

The USB drive's directory cannot be your working directory.

Setting the date and time

You can set the system date and time either manually or by referencing an Internet time server. You could also use your local hardware clock. To set the system time manually, you use the **date** command. The **date** command has several options for adjusting both displaying and setting the date and time. Check the date man page for a detailed list, **man date**. You can set the time with the **--set** option and a string specifying the date. You use human readable terms for the time string, such as Mon or Monday for the day and Jul or July for the month. Hour, minute, and second can be represented by numbers separated by colons. The following sets the date to July 9, 8:15 AM 2020.

```
sudo date --set=Thursday July 9 08:15 2024'
```

To just set the time you would enter something like:

```
sudo date --set='12:15:43'
```

To access the hardware clock, you use the **hwclock** command. The command itself will display the hardware clock time.

```
sudo hwclock
```

The **--hctosys** option will set the system clock using the hardware clock's time, and the **--systohc** option resets the hardware clock using the system time. Use the **--set** and **--date** options to set the hardware clock to a certain time.

```
sudo hwclock --systohc
```

Editing files with the command line interface: text editors

If you are using the command line interface only, you will often have to edit configuration files to configure your system and servers. You will have to use a command-line based editor to perform your editing tasks. Most command line editors provide a screen-based interface that makes displaying and editing a file fairly simple. Two standard command line editors are installed by default on your system, **vi** and **nano**. Several common command line text editors are listed in Table 3-1.

Editor	Description
vi	The Vi editor, difficult to use, considered the standard editor on Linux ad UNIX system, installed by default
nano	Easy to use screen-based editor, installed by default
emacs	Powerful and complex screen-based editor, though easier to use than Vi, Ubuntu repository
vim	Easier to use version of vi, Ubuntu repository
joe	Simple screen-based editor similar to Emacs, Universe repository
the	Screen based editor similar to Emacs, Universe repository
ne	Simple screen-based editor similar to nano, Universe repository

Table 3-1: Command line interface text editors

The commands you use to start the editors are also the editor names, in lower case, like **vi** for the Vi editor, **nano**, **joe**, and **emacs** for Emacs.

The **vi** editor is the standard editor used on most Linux and UNIX systems. It can be difficult to use by people accustomed to a desktop editor. The **nano** editor is easier to use, featuring a screen-based interface that you can navigate with arrow keys. If you do not already know **vi**, you may want to use **nano** instead.

The **nano** editor is a simple screen-based editor that lets you visually edit your file, using arrow and page keys to move around the file. You use control keys to perform actions. **Ctrl-x** will exit and prompt you to save the file, **Ctrl-o** will save it.

Start nano with the **nano** command. To edit a configuration file, you will need administrative access. You would start **nano** with the **sudo** command. Figure 3-6 shows the **nano** editor being used to edit the **/etc/default/keyboard** file. To edit a configuration file like **/etc/default/keyboard** you would enter the following.

```
sudo nano /etc/default/keyboard
```

Figure 3-6: Editing with nano

More powerful editors that you may find helpful are vim and emacs. You will have to first install them. The **vim** editor provides a slightly easier interface for **vi**. Emacs provides an interface similar to **nano**, but much more complex.

Other simple screen-based editors are **joe**, **ne**, **aee**, and **the**. All are available on the Universe repository. **joe** and **the** are similar to Emacs. **ne** and **aee** are more like **nano**.

Networking

Network devices now use a predictable naming method that differs from the older naming method. Names are generated based on the specific device referencing the network device type, its hardware connection and slot, and even its function. Some of the examples in later chapters in this book still use the older naming convention with the **eth** prefix for clarity. For some of the examples, it is easier to understand what is being referenced.

You configure your network connections using network managers. For the Ubuntu 24.04 server you have two network managers to choose from: systemd-networkd and NetworkManager. On the Ubuntu 24.04 server the systemd-networkd network manager is the default and is installed and activated at installation. The older NetworkManager network manager is still available for the server and can be downloaded and installed later. On the server, you can manage NetworkManager on the command line using **nmcli**. For the Ubuntu Desktop, NetworkManager is the default and can be managed by the Settings Network and Wi-Fi tabs.

Both network managers use Netplan to configure and manage network devices. Netplan is a network abstract configuration renderer, which generates network device configuration files using simple user-defined configuration files. The older **ifupdown** package along with its collection of network device management tools, such as **ifup** and **ifdown**, have been deprecated, but is still available and supported. Netplan provides a level of abstraction for network device configuration, making the process much more flexible. Netplan creates network device configuration files in the **/etc/netplan** directory, which users can edit. It then uses these files to generate the network device configuration files at startup.

Configuring a network with systemd-networkd

The systemd based network manager called **systemd-networkd** can currently be used for basic operations. You would use it as a small, fast, and simple alternative to a larger manager such as NetworkManager. systemd is described in detail in Chapter 5. The service, target, and socket files for systemd-networkd are located in the **/lib/systemd/system**: **systemd-networkd.service**, **systemd-networkd-wait-online.service**, and **systemd-networkd.socket.** Network resolvconf operations are handled with **systemd-resolved.service**. User configuration files for systemd-networkd are located in /etc/systemd/network.

In the **systemd-networkd.service** file several security features are enabled. A capability bounding set (CapabilityBoundingSet) lets you limit kernel capabilities to those specified. The man page for **capabilities** list the available capabilities. The CAP_NET capabilities limit the networkd service to network operations such as interface configuration, firewall administration, multicasting, sockets, broadcasting, and proxies. The CAP_SET capabilities allow for file and process GID and UIDs. The CAP_CHOWN, CAP_DAC_OVERRIDE, and CAP_FOWNER capabilities deal with bypassing permission checks for files. The CAP_SYS capabilities that provide system administrative capabilities are not included. In addition, the ProtectSystem option (**systemd.exec**) prevents the service from making any changes to the system (/**usr**, /**boot**, and /**etc** directories are read only for this service). The ProtectHome option makes the /**home**, /**root**, and /**run/user** directories inaccessible. WatchdogSec sets the watchdog timeout for the service. Check the **systemd.directives** man page for a list of all systemd directives.

systemd-networkd.service

```
[Unit]
Description=Network Service
Documentation=man:systemd-networkd.service(8)
ConditionCapability=CAP_NET_ADMIN
DefaultDependencies=no
# systemd-udevd.service can be dropped once tuntap is moved to netlink
After=systemd-udevd.service network-pre.target systemd-sysusers.service systemd-
sysctl.service
Before=network.target multi-user.target shutdown.target
Conflicts=shutdown.target
Wants=network.target

[Service]
AmbientCapabilities=CAP_NET_ADMIN CAP_NET_BIND_SERVICE CAP_NET_BROADCAST
CAP_NET_RAW
CapabilityBoundingSet=CAP_NET_ADMIN CAP_NET_BIND_SERVICE CAP_NET_BROADCAST
CAP_NET_RAW
ExecStart=!!/lib/systemd/systemd-networkd
LockPersonality=yes
MemoryDenyWriteExecute=yes
NoNewPrivileges=yes
ProtectControlGroups=yes
ProtectHome=yes
ProtectKernelModules=yes
ProtectKernelLogs=yes
ProtectSystem=strict
Restart=on-failure
RestartSec=0
RestrictAddressFamilies=AF_UNIX AF_NETLINK AF_INET AF_INET6 AF_PACKET AF_ALG
RestrictNamespaces=yes
RestrictRealtime=yes
RuntimeDirectory=systemd/netif
RuntimeDirectoryPreserve=yes
SystemCallArchitectures=native
SystemCallErrorNumber=EPERM
SystemCallFilter=@system-service
Type=notify
RestartKillSignal=SIGUSR2
User=systemd-network
WatchdogSec=3min

[Install]
WantedBy=multi-user.target
Also=systemd-networkd.socket
Alias=dbus-org.freedesktop.network1.service

# We want to enable systemd-networkd-wait-online.service whenever this service
# is enabled. systemd-networkd-wait-online.service has
# WantedBy=network-online.target, so enabling it only has an effect if
# network-online.target itself is enabled or pulled in by some other unit.
Also=systemd-networkd-wait-online.service
```

The **systemd-networkd.socket** file sets **systemd.socket** options for buffer size (ReceiveBuffer), network link (ListenNetlink), passing credentials (PassCredentials). As a condition for starting the service, the CAP_NET_ADMIN capability needs to be set in the capability bounding set (ConditionCapability).

systemd-networkd.socket

```
[Unit]
Description=Network Service Netlink Socket
Documentation=man:systemd-networkd.service(8) man:rtnetlink(7)
ConditionCapability=CAP_NET_ADMIN
DefaultDependencies=no
Before=sockets.target

[Socket]
ReceiveBuffer=128M
ListenNetlink=route 1361
PassCredentials=yes

[Install]
WantedBy=sockets.target
```

The **systemd-resolved.service** provides for the resolvconf operations (DNS server information). It has the same capabilities as **systemd-networkd.service**, except for the network capabilities.

systemd-resolved.service

```
[Unit]
Description=Network Name Resolution
Documentation=man:systemd-resolved.service(8)
Documentation=https://www.freedesktop.org/wiki/Software/systemd/resolved
Documentation=https://www.freedesktop.org/wiki/Software/systemd/writing-network-
configuration-managers
Documentation=https://www.freedesktop.org/wiki/Software/systemd/writing-resolver-
clients
DefaultDependencies=no
After=systemd-sysusers.service systemd-networkd.service
Before=network.target nss-lookup.target shutdown.target
Conflicts=shutdown.target
Wants=nss-lookup.target

[Service]
AmbientCapabilities=CAP_SETPCAP CAP_NET_RAW CAP_NET_BIND_SERVICE
CapabilityBoundingSet=CAP_SETPCAP CAP_NET_RAW CAP_NET_BIND_SERVICE
ExecStart=!!/lib/systemd/systemd-resolved
LockPersonality=yes
MemoryDenyWriteExecute=yes
NoNewPrivileges=yes
PrivateDevices=yes
PrivateTmp=yes
ProtectControlGroups=yes
ProtectHome=yes
ProtectKernelModules=yes
```

```
ProtectKernelTunables=yes
ProtectSystem=strict
Restart=always
RestartSec=0
RestrictAddressFamilies=AF_UNIX AF_NETLINK AF_INET AF_INET6
RestrictNamespaces=yes
RestrictRealtime=yes
RestrictSUIDSGID=yes
RuntimeDirectory=systemd/resolve
RuntimeDirectoryPreserve=yes
SystemCallArchitectures=native
SystemCallErrorNumber=EPERM
SystemCallFilter=@system-service
Type=notify
User=systemd-resolve
WatchdogSec=3min

[Install]
WantedBy=multi-user.target
Alias=dbus-org.freedesktop.resolve1.service
```

In addition, the **systemd-networkd-wait-online.service** delays activation of other services until **systemd-networkd** service comes online.

Netplan

On the Ubuntu Server, Netplan is used to configure and set up your network connections. The **/etc/netplan** directory holds network service and interface information for configuring your network device. The actual configuration file is generated when the system starts up and placed in the **/var/run/systemd/network** directory (or **/var/run/NetworkManager** if using NetworkManager). There is no fixed configuration file in the **/etc** directory. Instead a simple Netplan configuration file in the **/etc/netplan** directory is used to generate the network configuration file. The **/etc/netplan** files are written using YAML (YAML Ain't Markup Language) and have the extension **.yaml**. This method provides a level of abstraction that make configuration of different available network devices much more flexible. The default network service is **networkd**, which is used for the Ubuntu server. But you could use NetworkManager (network-manager) instead if you want. You can find out more about Netplan at:

```
https://netplan.io
```

Use the **networkctl status** command to check on the status of your network connections.

```
networkctl status
```

For information about a specific device add the device name to the **status** command.

```
networkctl status enp7s0
```

Ubuntu generates three different default Netplan configuration files, depending on the Ubuntu version installed: the Live server or the Desktop. The Live server installer, Subiquity, generates the Netplan configuration file, **50-cloud-init.yaml**. The Desktop generates a configuration file for NetworkManager, **01-network-manager-all.yaml**. NetworkManager is the default for the Ubuntu Desktop.

Detailed examples of Netplan configurations files can be found at:

```
/usr/share/doc/netplan/examples
```

These include examples for static, wireless, NetworkManager, dhcp, bridge, bonding, and vlans.

Live Server Installer Netplan Configuration File

The Live Server Installer, Subiquity, generates the Netplan default configuration file, **50-cloud-init.yaml**.

/etc/netplan/50-cloud-init.yaml

```
# This file is the network config written by subiquity.

network:
  ethernets:
    emp7s0:
      dhcp4: true
  version: 2
```

You can edit this file or add another one, replacing it. You would then have to know how networking on your system is configured. For many systems, especially those using DHCP, this is a simple configuration, but for others, such as a static connection, it can be complex. For a system using a standard DHCP connection, as shown in this chapter, you can simply copy the **dhcp.yaml** file from the **/usr/share/doc/netplan/examples** directory to the **/etc/netplan** directory.

```
cd /usr/share/doc/netplan/examples
sudo cp dhcp.yaml /etc/netplan
```

If you do not know it already, find out the name of your Ethernet device with **ip link** command. Then use a text editor like **nano** to edit the **dhcp.yaml** and replace the name of ethernet device, **enp3s0**, with the name of the one on your system. Be sure to use the **sudo** command to start the editor.

```
cd /etc/netplan
sudo nano dhcp.yaml
```

The final would look something like the following.

/etc/netplan/dhcp.yaml

```
network:
  version: 2
  renderer: networkd
  ethernets:
    enp7s0:
      dhcp4: true
```

If you reboot, the network configuration files will be read, and your device configured. To configure your device without rebooting, you can use the Netplan **generate** command to create the run time configuration file directly, and then use the **apply** command to have Netplan apply that configuration to your network connection.

```
sudo netplan generate
sudo netplan apply
```

You could then restart systemd-networkd.

```
sudo systemctl restart systemd-networkd
```

Should you want to use NetworkManager instead of systemd-networkd, there are a few added steps. Instead of the **dhcp.yaml** file you would copy the **network-manager.yaml** file from the **/usr/share/doc/netplan/examples** directory. There is no need to edit this file.

```
cd /usr/share/doc/netplan/examples
sudo cp network-manager.yaml /etc/netplan
```

Then, if Network Manager is not installed, install it.

```
sudo apt install network-manager
```

Then stop and disable systemd-networkd.

```
sudo systemctl stop systemd-networkd
sudo systemctl disable systemd-networkd
sudo systemctl disable systemd-networkd.target
```

Then enable and start the network-manager service.

```
sudo systemctl enable network-manager
sudo systemctl start network-manager
```

You can then use **nmcli** to manage your network connection.

Ubuntu Desktop Netplan Configuration File

The Ubuntu Desktop uses NetworkManager by default instead of systemd-networkd, which greatly simplifies it default Netplan configuration file. The file holds only the renderer information, as NetworkManager handles all the details. You would use the GNOME Settings Network and Wi-Fi tabs to configure your network.

/etc/netplan/01-network-manager-all.yaml

```
# Let NetworkManager manage all devices on this system
network:
  version: 2
  renderer: NetworkManager
```

Netplan wireless configuration for systemd-networkd

For systemd-networkd wireless devices you have to edit your Netplan configuration file to add your wireless device name, the wireless network you want to access, and the password for that network. Instead of editing the default file directly, you can copy the **02-dhcp.yaml** file with the 2 changed to 3 and give it a name such as **03-wireless.yaml**. Netplan will read any **yaml** file in the **/etc/netplan** folder. You can find an example of a wireless configuration file at **/usr/share/doc/netplan/examples**, but it is for the network that does not support dhcp and is more complicated.

```
cd /etc/netplan
sudo cp 2-dhcp.yaml 03-wireless.yaml
```

Then edit the file to add keys for Wi-Fi, access-points, the SSID, and the password.

```
sudo nano 3-wireless.yaml
```

An example of a wireless Netplan configuration is shown below. Instead of the **ethernets:** definition you use the **wifis:** definition. This is followed by a key consisting of the wireless device name, such as **wlp6s0:**. Below that key is the **dhcp4:** ID and the **access-points:** ID, used to configure the Wi-Fi device. Under the **access-points:** ID you add an ID consisting of the SSID of the wireless network you want to connect to (the wireless network's name). The SSID must be within quotes. Under this ID you add the **password:** ID and the password for accessing that wireless network. The password must be within quotes.

/etc/netplan/03-wireless.yaml

```
network:
  version: 2
  renderer: networkd
  wifis:
    wlp6s0:
        dhcp4: true
        access-points:
            "SSID":
                password: "password"
```

Netplan generates a wireless configuration file at startup in **/run/netplan**. A wireless file will have the name of the device added along with the name of wireless network (SSID), such as **netplan-wlp6s0-surfturtle**.

This file is then used the by **wpa_supplicant@service** to submit the SSID and password to **wpa_supplicant**, which then accesses the wireless network. The **wpa_supplicant@.service** file is shown here.

wpa_supplicant@.service

```
[Unit]
Description=WPA supplicant daemon (interface specific version)
Requires=sys-subsystem-net-devices-%i.device
After=sys-subsystem-net-devices-%i.device
Before=network.target
Wants=network.target

[Service]
Type=simple
ExecStart=/sbin/wpa_supplicant -c /etc/wpa_supplicant/wpa_supplicant-%I.conf -i%I
ExecReload=/bin/kill -HUP $MAINPID

[Install]
WantedBy-multi-user.target
```

If you reboot, the wireless netplan file will be read and your wireless device configured. To configure your device without rebooting, you can use the Netplan **generate** command to create the run time configuration file directly (**/var/run/systemd/network**), and then use the **apply** command to have Netplan apply that configuration to your network connection.

```
sudo netplan generate
sudo netplan apply
```

Then restart systemd-networkd.

```
sudo systemctl restart systemd-networkd
```

You can use the **networkctl** command to see if your wireless device has been properly configured and is connected. The **networkctl** command works only for systemd-networkd.

```
$ networkctl
IDX LINK          TYPE         OPERATIONAL SETUP
  1 lo            loopback     carrier     unmanaged
  2 enp7s0        ether        routable    configured
  3 wlp6s0        wlan         routable    configured

3 links listed.
```

Live Server Installer Netplan Configuration File

The Live Server Installer, Subiquity, generates the Netplan default configuration file, **50-cloud-init.yaml**.

/etc/netplan/50-cloud-init.yaml

```
network:
  ethernets:
    emp7s0:
      dhcp4: true
  version: 2
  wifi: {}
```

You can edit this file or add another one, replacing it. You would then have to know how networking on your system is configured. For many systems, especially those using DHCP, this is a simple configuration, but for others, such as a static connection, it can be complex. For a system using a standard DHCP connection, as shown in this chapter, you can simply copy the **dhcp.yaml** file from the **/usr/share/doc/netplan/examples** directory to the **/etc/netplan** directory.

```
cd /usr/share/doc/netplan/examples
sudo cp dhcp.yaml /etc/netplan
```

If you do not know it already, find out the name of your Ethernet device with **ip link** command. Then use a text editor like **nano** to edit the **dhcp.yaml** and replace the name of ethernet device, **enp3s0**, with the name of the one on your system. Be sure to use the **sudo** command to start the editor.

```
cd /etc/netplan
sudo nano dhcp.yaml
```

The final would look something like the following.

/etc/netplan/dhcp.yaml

```
network:
  version: 2
  renderer: networkd
  ethernets:
    enp7s0:
      dhcp4: true
```

If you reboot, the network configuration files will be read, and your device configured. To configure your device without rebooting, you can use the Netplan **generate** command to create the run time configuration file directly, and then use the **apply** command to have Netplan apply that configuration to your network connection.

```
sudo netplan generate
sudo netplan apply
```

You could then restart systemd-networkd.

```
sudo systemctl restart systemd-networkd
```

Should you want to use NetworkManager instead of systemd-networkd, there are a few added steps. Instead of the dhcp.yaml file you would copy the **network-manager.yaml** file from the **/usr/share/doc/netplan/examples** directory. There is no need to edit this file.

```
cd /usr/share/doc/netplan/examples
sudo cp network-manager.yaml /etc/netplan
```

Then, if Network Manager is not installed, install it.

```
sudo apt install network-manager
```

Then stop and disable systemd-networkd.

```
sudo systemctl stop systemd-networkd
sudo systemctl disable systemd-networkd
sudo systemctl disable systemd-networkd.target
```

Then enable and start the network-manager service.

```
sudo systemctl enable network-manager
sudo systemctl start network-manager
```

You can then use **nmcli** to manage your network connection.

Ubuntu Desktop Netplan Configuration File

The Ubuntu Desktop uses NetworkManager by default instead of systemd-networkd, which greatly simplifies it default Netplan configuration file. The file holds only the renderer information, as NetworkManager handles all the details. You would use the GNOME Settings Network and Wi-Fi tabs to configure your network.

/etc/netplan/01-network-manager-all.yaml

```
# Let NetworkManager manage all devices on this system
network:
  version: 2
  renderer: NetworkManager
```

Switching between systemd-networkd and network-manager

It is possible to use NetworkManager instead of systemd-networkd. First make sure you have installed NetworkManager. If not, then install it.

```
sudo apt install network-manager
```

You have to make sure you have stopped and disabled systemd-networkd. Be sure to also disable systemd-resolved and systemd-networkd-ail-online. These changes are made as the root user. Use **sudo**.

First stop systemd-networkd with the **systemctl** command.

```
sudo systemctl stop systemd-networkd
```

Then disable systemd-networkd.

```
sudo systemctl disable systemd-networkd
sudo systemctl disable systemd-networkd.target
```

Then enable NetworkManager. Use the service name for NetworkManager, network-manager. Also, enable NetworkManager-wait-online to use the DCHP supplied DNS servers.

```
sudo systemctl enable network-manager
```

You then have to create a Netplan NetworkManager configuration file like that shown previously for the Ubuntu Desktop. A simple way to do this is to copy the **network_manager.yaml** file from the netplan.io doc directory, **/usr/share/doc/netplan/examples**. You could rename to something like, **02-network-manager.yaml**, if you want.

```
cd /usr/share/doc/netplan/examples
sudo cp network_manager.yaml  /etc/netplan/02-network-manager.yaml
```

/etc/netplan/02-network-manager.yaml

```
network:
  version: 2
  renderer: NetworkManager
```

Then use the netplan command with the apply option to generate a new network configuration file.

```
sudo netplan generate
sudo netplan apply
```

The configuration files for NetworkManager are in the **/run/NetworkManager/system-connections** directory and have the NetworkManager name of the connection, such as **'Wired connection-1'.nmconnections**.

Then start networking by starting NetworkManager.

```
sudo systemctl start network-manager
```

You can use the status command for systemctl to see if your network device is active or inactive.

```
sudo systemctl status systemd-networkd
sudo systemctl status network-manager
```

You can check the status of your network device configuration and activation with the **networkctl** command.

```
networkctl
```

To change back to systemd-networkd, disable NetworkManager and enable systemd-networkd.

```
sudo systemctl stop network-manager
sudo systemctl disable network-manager

sudo systemctl enable systemd-networkd
sudo systemctl enable systemd-networkd.target
sudo systemctl start systemd-networkd
```

NetworkManager and nmcli

It is possible to still use NetworkManager instead of systemd-networkd. You will have to install the network-manager package. It is not installed by default.

```
sudo apt-get install network-manager
```

You then have to deactivate systemd-networkd and activate NetworkManager, as described in the previous section. You can then use **nmcli** command to manage your network connection. Keep in mind that the name of any network configuration created by Netplan will have the name **netplan-** prefixing the device name, as is the case for the default configuration. For a device named **enp7s0**, the device name of the default configuration will be **netplan-enp7s0**. If you are referencing the device directly (ifname), as with the connect and disconnect commands, you use just the device name, such as **enp7s0**.

The **nmcli** command is NetworkManager Command Line Interface command. Most network configuration tasks can be performed by **nmcli**. The **nmcli** command manages NetworkManager through a set of objects: general (**g**), networking (**n**), radio (**r**), connection (**c**), device (**d**), and agent (**a**). Each can be referenced using the full name or a unique prefix, such as **con** for connection or **dev** for device. The unique prefix can be as short as a single character, such as **g** for general, **c** for connections, or **d** for device. See Table 3-2 for a list of the objects and commonly used options. The **nmcli** man page provides a complete listing with examples.

The general object shows the current status of NetworkManager and what kind of devices are enabled. You can limit the information displayed using the **-t** (terse) and **-f** (field) options. The STATE field show the connection status, and the CONNECTIVITY field the connection.

```
$ nmcli general
STATE      CONNECTIVITY  WIFI-HW   WIFI     WWAN-HW   WWAN
connected  full          enabled   enabled  enabled   enabled

$ nmcli -t -f STATE general
connected
```

The **connection** object references the network connection and the **show** option displays that information. The following example displays your current connection.

Object	Description
`general`	NetworkManager status and enabled devices. Use the terse (**-t**) and field (**-f**) option to limit the information displayed.
`networking`	Manage networking, use `on` and `off` to turn networking on or off, and `connectivity` for the connection state.
`radio`	Turns on or off the wireless networking (on or off). Can turn on or off specific kinds of wireless: `wifi`, `wwan` (mobile broadband), and `wimax`. The `all` option turns on or off all wireless.
`connection`	Manage network connections.

	`show`	List connection profiles. With `--active` show only active connections.
	`up`	Activate a connection
	`down`	Deactivate a connection
	`add`	Add a new connection, specifying `type`, `ifname`, `con-name` (profile).
	`modify`	Edit an existing connection, use + and – to add new values to properties
	`edit`	Add a new connection or edit an existing one using the interactive editor
	`delete`	Delete a configured connection (profile)
	`reload`	Reload all connection profiles
	`load`	Reload or load a specific profile (use to load a new or modified connection profile)

device	Manage network interfaces (devices).

	`status`	Display device status
	`show`	Display device information
	`connect`	Connect the device
	`disconnect`	Disconnect the device
	`delete`	Delete a software device, such as a bridge.
	`wifi`	Display a list of available wifi access points
	`wifi rescan`	Rescan for and display access points
	`wifi connect`	Connect to a wifi network; specify `password`, `wep-key-type`, `ifname`, `bssid`, and `name` (profile name)
	`wimax`	List available WiMAX networks

agent	Run as a Network Manager secret agent or polkit agent.

	`secret`	As a secret agent, nmcli listens for secret requests.
	`polkit`	As a polkit agent it listens for all authorization requests.

Table 3-2: The nmcli objects

```
nmcli connection show
```

You can use **c** instead of **connection** and **s** instead of show. $ **nmcli c s**
```
NAME           UUID                                  TYPE          DEVICE
netplan-enp7s0     f7202f6d-fc66-4b81-8962-69b71202efc0  802-3-ethernet  enp7s0
AT&T LTE 1   65913b39-789a-488c-9559-28ea6341d9e1  gsm             --
```

As with the general object, you can limit the fields displayed using the **-f** option. The following only list the name and type fields.

```
$ nmcli -f name,type c s
NAME          TYPE
netplan-enp7s0        802-3-ethernet
AT&T LTE 1  gsm
```

Adding the **--active** option will only show active connections.

```
nmcli c s --active
```

To start and stop a connection (like **ifconfig** does), use the **up** and **down** options.

```
nmcli con up netplan-enp7s0.
```

Use the **device** object to manage your network devices. The **show** and **status** options provide information about your devices. To check the status of all your network devices, use the **device** object and **status** options.

```
nmcli device status
DEVICE  TYPE       STATE         CONNECTION
enp7s0  ethernet   connected     netplan-enp7s0
wlp6s0  wifi       disconnected  --
lo      loopback   unmanaged     --
```

You can abbreviate **device** and **status** to **d** and **s**.

```
nmcli d s
```

You also use the **device** object to connect and disconnect devices. Use the **connect** or **disconnect** options with the interface name (ifname) of the device, in this example, **enp7s0**. With the **delete** option you can remove a device.

```
nmcli device disconnect enp7s0
nmcli device connect enp7s0
```

To turn networking on or off you use the **networking** object and the **on** and **off** options. Use the **connectivity** option to check network connectivity. The networking object alone tells you if it is enabled or not.

```
$ nmcli networking
enabled

$ nmcli networking on

$ nmcli networking connectivity
full
```

Should you want to just turn on or off the Wifi connection, you would use the **radio** object. Use **wifi**, **wwan**, and **wimax** for a specific type of wifi connection and the **all** option for all of them. The radio object alone shows wifi status of all your wifi connection types.

```
$ nmcli radio
WIFI-HW   WIFI  WWAN-HW   WWAN
enabled   enabled  enabled   enabled

$ nmcli radio wifi on
```

```
$ nmcli radio all off
```

nmcli Wired Network Manager Configurations

You can use **nmcli** to add and edit NetworkManager network configurations. However, these configurations are not in any way integrated with Netplan. Such configurations could only be accessed with NetworkManager, whereas Netplan configurations can be used by either Network Manager or systemd-networkd. The NetworkManager configurations created and edited by **nmcli** are place in the **/etc/NetworkManager/system-connections** directory, not to the **/etc/netplan** directory. Netplan configurations take precedence unless you disable Netplan.

To add a new static configuration with **nmcli**, use the connection object with the **add** option. Specify the configuration's profile name with the **con-name** option, the interface name with the **ifname** option, the **type**, such as ethernet. For a static connection you would add the IP address (**ipv4** or **ipv6**), and the gateway address (**gw4** or **gw6**). For a DHCP connection simply do not list the IP address and gateway options. The profile name can be any name. The profile name is the configuration name, also known as the connection name. You could have several profile names for the same network device. For example, for your wireless device you could have several wireless connection profiles, depending on the different networks you want to connect to. Should you connect your Ethernet device to a different network, you would simply use a different connection profile that you have already set up, instead of manually reconfiguring the connection. If you do not specify a connection name, one is generated and assigned for you. The connection name can be the same as the device name as shown here, but keep in mind that the connection name refers to the profile and the device name refers to the actual device.

```
$ nmcli c s
NAME                UUID                                    TYPE            DEVICE
netplan-enp7s0      f7202f6d-fc66-4b81-8962-69b71202efc0    802-3-ethernet  enp7s0
```

For a DHCP connection, specify the profile name, connection type, and ifname. The following example creates an Ethernet connection with the profile name "my-wired."

```
nmcli con add con-name my-wired type ethernet ifname enp7s0
```

For a static connection add the IP (**ip4** or **ip6**) and gateway (**gw4** or **gw6**) options with their addresses.

```
nmcli con add con-name my-wired-static ifname enp7s0 type ethernet ip4
192.168.1.0/24 gw4 192.168.1.1
```

In most cases, the type is Ethernet (wired) or wifi (wireless). Check the **nmcli** man page for a list of other types, such as gsm, infiniband, vpn, vlan, wimax, and bridge.

You can also add a connection using the interactive editor. Use the **edit** instead of the **add** option, and specify the **con-name** (profile) and connection type.

```
nmcli con edit type ethernet con-name my-wired
```

To modify an existing connection, use the **modify** option. For an IP connection, the property that is changed is referenced as part of the IP settings, in this example, **ip4**. The IP properties include addresses, gateway, and method (ip4.addresses, ip4.gateway, and ip4.method).

```
nmcli con mod my-wired ip4.gateway 192.168.1.2
```

To add or remove a value for a property use the + and - signs as a prefix. To add a DNS server address you would use **+ip4.dns**. To remove one use **-ip4.dns**.

```
nmcli con mod my-wired +ip4.dns 192.168.1.5
```

You can also modify a connection using the interactive editor. Use the edit instead of the modify option with the connection name.

```
nmcli con edit my-wired
```

You are then placed in the interactive editor with an **nmcli>** prompt and the settings you can change are listed. The **help** command lists available commands. Use the **describe** command to show property descriptions.

Use **print** to show the current value of a property and **set** to change its value. To see all the properties for a setting, use the print command and the setting name. Once you have made changes, use the **save** command to effect the changes.

```
print ipv4
print ipv4.dns
print connection
set ipv4.address 192.168.0.1
```

The connection edit command can also reference a profile using the **id** option. The Name field in the connection profile information is the same as the ID. Also, each profile is given a unique system UUID, which can also be used to reference the profile.

Once you are finished editing the connection, enter the **quit** command to leave the editor.

nmcli Wireless NetworkManager Configurations

Wi-Fi network configuration should be done with Netplan. It is possible to use **nmcli** to connect to a Wi-Fi network configuration. Any configuration created with **nmcli** is placed in the **/etc/NetworkManager/system-connections** directory.

To see a list of all the available wifi networks in your area, you use the **wifi** option with the **device** object. You can further qualify it by interface (if you have more than one) by adding the **ifname** option, and by BSSID adding the **bssid** option.

```
nmcli device wifi
```

To connect to a new Wifi network, use the **wifi connect** option and the SSID. You can further specify a password, wep-key-type, key, ifname, bssid, name (profile name), and if it is private. If you do not provide a name (profile name), **nmcli** will generate one for you.

```
nmcli dev wifi connect surfturtle password mypass wep-key-type wpa ifname wlp6s0
name my-wireless1
```

To reconnect to a Wifi network for which you have previously set up a connection, use the **connection** object with the **up** command and the **id** option to specify the profile name.

```
nmcli connection up id my-wireless1
```

You can also add a new wireless connection using the **connection** object and the **wifi** type with the **ssid** option.

```
nmcli con add con-name my-wireless2 ifname wlp6s0 type wifi ssid ssidname
```

Then, to set the encryption type use the **modify** command to set the **sec.key-mgmt** property, and for the passphrase set the **wifi-sec.psk** property.

```
nmcli con mod my-wireless2 wifi-sec.key-mgmt wpa-psk
nmcli con modify my-wireless2 wifi-sec.psk mypassword
```

Predictable and unpredictable network device names

Network devices now use a predictable naming method that differs from the older naming method. Names are generated based on the specific device referencing the network device type, its hardware connection and slot, and even its function. The traditional network device names used the **eth** prefix with the number of the device for an Ethernet network device. The name **eth0** referred to the first Ethernet connection on your computer. This naming method was considered unpredictable as it did not accurately reference the actual Ethernet device. The old system relied on probing the network driver at boot, and if your system had several Ethernet connections, the names could end up being switched, depending on how the startup proceeded. With the current version of systemd udev, the naming uses a predictable method that specifies a particular device. The predictable method references the actual hardware connection on your system.

The name used to reference predictable network device names has a prefix for the type of device followed by several qualifiers such as the type of hardware, the slot used, and the function number. Instead of the older unpredictable name like **eth0**, the first Ethernet device is referenced by a name like **enp7s0**. The interface name **enp7s0** references an Ethernet (en) connection, at pci slot 7 (p7) with the hotplug slot index number 0 (s0). **wlp6s0** is a wireless (wl) connection, at pci slot 6 (p6) with the hotplug slot index number 0 (s0). **virvb0** is a virtual (vir) bridge (vb) network interface. Table 3-3 lists predictable naming prefixes.

Name	Description
en	Ethernet
sl	serial line IP (slip)
wl	wlan, wireless local area network
ww	wwan, wireless wide area network (mobile broadband)
p	pci geographical location (pci-e slot)
s	hotplug slot index number
o	onboard cards
f	function (used for cards with more than one port)
u	USB port
i	USB port interface

Table 3-3: Network Interface Device Naming

Unlike the older unpredictable name, the predictable name will most likely be different for each computer. Predictable network names, along with alternatives, are discussed at:

```
https://www.freedesktop.org/wiki/Software/systemd/PredictableNetworkInterfaceName
s/
```

The naming is carried out by the kernel and is describe in the comment section of the kernel source's **systemd/src/udev/udev-builtin-net_id.c** file.

Network device path names

The directory **/sys/devices** lists all your devices in subdirectories, including your network devices. The path to the devices progresses through subdirectories named for the busses connecting the device. To quickly find the full path name, you can us the **/sys/class** directory instead. For network devices use **/sys/class/net**. Then use the **ls -l** command to list the network devices with their links to the full pathname in the **/sys/devices** directory (the **../..** path references a **cd** change up two directories (**class/net**) to the **/sys** directory).

```
$ cd /sys/class/net
$ ls
enp7s0   lo   wlp6s0
$ ls -l
total 0
lrwxrwxrwx 1 root 0 Feb 19 12:27 enp7s0 ->
../../devices/pci0000:00/0000:00:1c.3/0000:07:00.0/net/enp7s0
lrwxrwxrwx 1 root 0 Feb 19 12:27 lo -> ../../devices/virtual/net/lo
lrwxrwxrwx 1 root 0 Feb 19 12:28 wlp6s0 ->
../../devices/pci0000:00/0000:00:1c.2/0000:06:00.0/net/wlp6s0
```

So the full path name in the **/sys/devices** directory for **enp7s0** is:

```
/sys/devices/pci0000:00/0000:00:1c.3/0000:07:00.0/net/enp7s0
```

You can find the pci bus slot used with the **lspci** command. This command lists all your pci connected devices. In this example, the pci bus slot used 7, which is why the pci part of the name enp7s0 is **p7**. The **s** part refers to a hotplug slot, in this example **s0**.

```
$ lspci
06:00.0 Network controller: Qualcomm Atheros QCA9565 / AR9565 Wireless Network
Adapter (rev 01)
07:00.0 Ethernet controller: Realtek Semiconductor Co., Ltd. RTL8101/2/6E PCI
Express Fast/Gigabit Ethernet controller (rev 07)
```

Devices have certain properties defined by udev, which manages all devices. Some operations, such as systemd link files, make use these properties. The ID_PATH, ID_NET_NAME_MAC, and INTERFACE properties can be used to identify a device to udev. To display these properties, you use the **udevadm** command to query the udev database. With the **info** and **-e** options, properties of all active devices are displayed. You can pipe (|) this output to a **grep** command to display only those properties for a given device. In the following example, the properties for the **enp7s0** device are listed. Preceding the properties for a given device is a line, beginning (^) with a "P" and ending with the device name. The **.*** matching characters match all other intervening characters on that line, **^P.*enp7s0**. The **-A** option displays the specified number of additional lines after that match, **-A 22**.

```
$ udevadm info -e | grep -A 22 ^P.*enp7s0
P: /devices/pci0000:00/0000:00:1c.3/0000:07:00.0/net/enp7s0
E: DEVPATH=/devices/pci0000:00/0000:00:1c.3/0000:07:00.0/net/enp7s0
E: ID_BUS=pci
E: ID_MM_CANDIDATE=1
E: ID_MODEL_FROM_DATABASE=RTL8101/2/6E PCI Express Fast/Gigabit Ethernet
controller
E: ID_MODEL_ID=0x8136
E: ID_NET_DRIVER=r8169
E: ID_NET_LINK_FILE=/lib/systemd/network/99-default.link
E: ID_NET_NAME_MAC=enx74e6e20ec729
E: ID_NET_NAME_PATH=enp7s0
E: ID_OUI_FROM_DATABASE=Dell Inc.
E: ID_PATH=pci-0000:07:00.0
E: ID_PATH_TAG=pci-0000_07_00_0
E: ID_PCI_CLASS_FROM_DATABASE=Network controller
E: ID_PCI_SUBCLASS_FROM_DATABASE=Ethernet controller
E: ID_VENDOR_FROM_DATABASE=Realtek Semiconductor Co., Ltd.
E: ID_VENDOR_ID=0x10ec
E: IFINDEX=2
E: INTERFACE=enp7s0
E: SUBSYSTEM=net
E: SYSTEMD_ALIAS=/sys/subsystem/net/devices/enp7s0
E: TAGS=:systemd:
E: USEC_INITIALIZED=1080179
```

For certain tasks, such as renaming, you many need to know the MAC address. You can find this with the **ip link** command, which you can abbreviate to **ip l**. The MAC address is before the brd string. In this example, the MAC address for **enp7s0** is **74:e6:e2:0e:c7:29**. The **ip link** command also provides the MTU (Maximum Transmission Unit) and the current state of the connection.

```
$ ip link
1: lo: <LOOPBACK,UP,LOWER_UP> mtu 65536 qdisc noqueue state UNKNOWN mode DEFAULT
group default qlen 1 link/loopback 00:00:00:00:00:00 brd 00:00:00:00:00:00
2: enp7s0: <BROADCAST,MULTICAST,UP,LOWER_UP> mtu 1500 qdisc fq_codel state UP
mode DEFAULT group default qlen 1000 link/ether 74:e6:e2:0e:c7:29 brd
ff:ff:ff:ff:ff:ff
3: wlp6s0: <BROADCAST,MULTICAST> mtu 1500 qdisc noop state DOWN mode DEFAULT
group default qlen 1000 link/ether 4c:bb:58:22:40:1d brd ff:ff:ff:ff:ff:ff
```

Renaming network device names for systemd-networkd with netplan

You can easily rename network devices using Netplan. Within the configuration definition for a network device, such as ethernets, you would add configuration IDs under the name of the device whose name you want to change). The **match:** IDs is added to select the device. As it its designed to select a wide range of devices, to choose just one, would require a unique property. You can use the hardware MAC address of the device as that property. The **ip link** command will list the MAC addresses of your network devices. Use the **macaddress:** ID under the **match:** ID to specify the MAC address of the network device. Then follow it with a **set-name:** ID where you specify the name you want the network device to have. The following example changes the network device name **enp7s0** to **eth0**.

/etc/netplan/dhcp.yaml

```
network:
  version: 2
  renderer: networkd
  ethernets:
    enp7s0:
      dhcp4: true
      match:
          macaddress: "74:e6:e2:0e:c7:29"
      set-name: eth0
```

You can use the **ip link** command to check on the name.

```
ip link
```

Due to timing issues, this may not work yet on reboot. In that case run the **netplan apply** command to change the name.

```
sudo netplan apply
```

Renaming network device names for systemd-networkd with systemd.link

The systemd-networkd manager provides an alternate way to change network device names (keep in mind that an udev rule also works for systemd-networkd). To change the name you would set up a systemd link file in the **/etc/systemd/network** directory. The **systemd.link** man page shows how to do this. A systemd link file consists of Match and Link sections. In the Match section you specify the network device, and in the Link section to specify the name you want to give it. The network device can be referenced by its predictable name (Path) or MAC address (MACAddress).

The default systemd link file is **/lib/systemd/network/99-default.link**. The file has only a Link section which lists policies to use in determining the name. The NamePolicy key lists the policies to be checked, starting with the kernel, then the udev database, udev firmware onboard information, udev hot-plug slot information, and the device path. In most cases, the slot policy is used. The MACAddressPolicy is set to persistent, for devices that have or need fixed MAC addresses.

99-default.link

```
[Link]
NamePolicy=kernel database onboard slot path
MACAddressPolicy=persistent
```

To rename a device, you would set up a systemd link file in the **/etc/systemd/network** directory. The **/etc/systemd** directory takes precedence over the **/lib/systemd** directory. A link file consists of a priority number, any name, and the **.link** extension. Lower numbers have a higher priority. In this example, the network device **enp7s0** has its named changed to **eth0**. The Match section uses the Path key to match on the device path, using the ID_PATH property for the device provided by udev.

You can query the udev database for information on your network device using the **udevadm info** command and match on the device. An added **grep** operation for ID_PATH= will display only the ID_PATH property.

```
$ udevadm info -e | grep -A 22 ^P.*enp7s0 | grep ID_PATH=
E: ID_PATH=pci-0000:07:00.0
```

For the Path key, use the udev ID_PATH value and a * glob matching character for the rest of the path. The Link section uses the Name key to specify the new name. The MacAddressPolicy should be set to persistent, indicating a fixed connection. Start the name of the link file with a number less than 99, so as to take precedence over the **99-default.link** file.

10-my-netname.link

```
[Match]
Path=pci-0000:07:00.0-*

[Link]
Name=eth0
MacAddressPolicy=persistent
```

Instead of the Path key, you could use the MACAddress key to match on the hardware address of the network device. The MAC address is udev ID_NET_NAME_MAC property without the prefix and with colon separation. The MAC address in this example is 74:e6:e2:0e:c7:29.   You can also use **ip link** to find the MAC address (the numbers before **brd**).

10-my-netname.link

```
[Match]
MACAddress=74:e6:e2:0e:c7:29

[Link]
Name=eth0
MacAddressPolicy=persistent
```

Alternatively, you could use the OriginalName key in the Match section instead of the Path. The original name is the udev INTERFACE property, which also the name of the device as displayed by **ifconfig**.

10-my-netname.link

```
[Match]
OriginalName=enp7s0*

[Link]
Name=eth0
MacAddressPolicy=persistent
```

Renaming network device names with udev rules

If you should change your hardware, like your motherboard with its Ethernet connection, or, if you use an Ethernet card and simply change the slot it is connected to, then the name will change. For firewall rules referencing a particular Ethernet connection, this could be a problem. You can, if you wish, change the name to one of your own choosing, even using the older unpredictable names. This way you would only have to update the name change, rather than all your rules and any other code that references the network device by name.

You can change device name by adding a user udev rule for network device names. Changes made with udev rules work for both NetworkManager and systemd-networkd. In the

/etc/udev/rules.d directory, create a file with the **.rules** extension and prefixed by a number less than 80, such as **70-my-net-names.rules**. The **.rules** files in **/etc/udev/rules.d** take precedence over those in the udev system directory, **/lib/udev/rules.d**.

In the udev rule, identify the subsystem as net (SUBSYSTEM=="net"), the action to take as add (ACTION=="add"), then the MAC address (ATTR[address}, the address attribute). Use **ip link** to obtain the mac address. The MAC address is also listed as the ID_NET_NAME_MAC entry in the **udevadm info** output (be sure to remove the prefix and add intervening colons). Use the NAME field to specify the new name for the device. Use the single = operator to make the name assignment.

/etc/udev/rules.d/70-my-net-names.rules

```
SUBSYSTEM=="net", ACTION=="add", ATTR{address}=="74:e6:e2:0e:c7:29", NAME="eth0"
```

To further specify the device you can add the kernel name (KERNEL) of the device. The kernel name is the INTERFACE entry.

```
SUBSYSTEM=="net", ACTION=="add", ATTR{address}=="74:e6:e2:0e:c7:29",
KERNEL=="enp7s0", NAME="eth0"
```

Installing the Ubuntu Desktop: ubuntu-desktop-minimal

For a server, you may want to install the Ubuntu desktop minimal version of the desktop. The Ubuntu desktop minimal installs all the basic administrative packages such as the Firefox Web browser, Network Manager, and the Update manager. You can install the Ubuntu desktop minimal on a server system using the **ubuntu-desktop-minimal** meta-package. Use **apt** with the **ubuntu-desktop-minimal** meta-package, as shown here.

```
sudo apt install ubuntu-desktop-minimal
```

Download and setup can take a while. You then log out and restart your system. The GDM will start up as shown in Figure 3-7.

Should you want to install the full set of software for the desktop you would install the **ubuntu-desktop** meta-package. The **ubuntu-desktop** meta-package will install the complete set of desktop packages, including multimedia and graphics packages you may have no use for on your server.

```
sudo apt install ubuntu-desktop
```

Instead of the Ubuntu desktop, you could install other desktops such as MATE or KDE Plasma. You can install a desktop directly with the **apt** command.

```
sudo apt install mate-desktop
```

Alternatively, you can use the **tasksel** software management tool. You can choose to install different basic desktops, including GNOME, Xfce, KDE Plasma, Cinnamon, and MATE. Run **tasksel** with the **sudo** command, then use the arrow keys to move to a desktop entry and press the spacebar. Then tab to the OK button and press ENTER.

```
sudo tasksel
```

Installing desktops with tasksel

An easy way to install a desktop is to use tasksel, which will display a list of desktop metapackages such as the Ubuntu, Kubuntu, and MATE desktops. To run tasksel, enter the **tasksel** command at the shell prompt. If you are using a desktop, open a terminal window and enter the **tasksel** command.

```
sudo tasksel
```

Should you want to quit tasksel without installing or removing any software, tab to the OK button and press ENTER. The tasksel application ends, and you return to the shell prompt.

The tasksel tool displays a keyboard-based dialog listing the package collections, as shown here. Those already installed have an asterisk next to their entries. Use the arrow keys to move to an entry and press the spacebar to select it. When you have made all your selections, use the Tab key to move to the OK button. Then press the ENTER key to install the selected software.

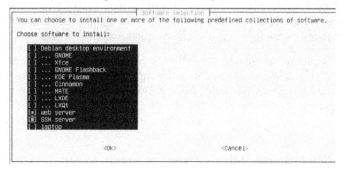

You can also use tasksel to uninstall packages. Installed packages will have an asterisk next to them. Move to the package you want to remove and press the spacebar. The asterisk will disappear, leaving you with empty brackets. Tab to the OK button and press ENTER. An installation window is displayed, and the deselected package collections are removed.

The tasksel dialog displays software collections for various desktops, the Web server (Apache2), the SSH server, and for a laptop. The desktops will install a complete desktop system, such as the Ubuntu desktop which includes the GDM. If you install a desktop, the X server and the desktop interface is started up automatically, just as if you installed from the Ubuntu desktop USB/DVD, instead of from the server USB/DVD. You will still be using the server kernel, though.

If you already know the name of the server or package collection you want to install, you can use **tasksel** command with the **install** option and the package name to install the package directly. You would not have to use the screen interface. The package names are usually the same as those listed on the screen interface, but in lower case with a dash connecting the words, as in web-server for Apache Web server. The option **--list-tasks** lists the server and meta package names with their associated descriptions used on the screen interface. The following command directly installs the Apache Web server.

```
sudo tasksel install web-server
```

You can use the **remove** option to remove a meta package. Check the tasksel Man page for a complete set of options. The following example removes the Web server.

```
sudo tasksel remove web-server
```

The Ubuntu Desktop

The Ubuntu 24.04 desktop uses the Ubuntu GNOME interface. Ubuntu uses the Ubuntu Yaru theme for its interface with the Ubuntu screen background, and menu icons as its default (see Figure 3-11). You can change themes using the GNOME Tweaks Appearance tab's. The Yaru theme places the window control buttons (close, maximize, and minimize buttons) on the right side of a window title bar, as shown here. There are three window buttons: an x for close, a dash (-) for minimize, and a square for maximize.

window buttons

The GNOME Display Manager: GDM

The graphical login interface displays a list of usernames. When you click a username, a login screen replaces the listing of users, displaying the selected user and a text box in which you then enter your password. Upon pressing ENTER, you log in and your desktop starts up.

Graphical logins are handled by the GNOME Display Manager (GDM). The GDM manages the login interface, in addition to authenticating a user password and username, and then starts up a selected desktop. From the GDM, you can shift to the command-line interface with CTRL+ALT+F2, and then shift back to the GDM with CTRL+ALT+F1. The keys F2 through F6 provide different command-line terminals, as in CTRL+ALT+F3 for the third command-line terminal.

When the GDM starts up, it shows a listing of users (see Figure 3-7). A System menu at the top right of the screen displays entries for sound adjustment, screen brightness (for laptops), the battery status (if a laptop), and a power button. Click the power button to display a Power Off menu with entries for Suspend, Restart, and Power Off. Clicking the Power Off entry displays the Power Off dialog with options to Power Off and Cancel. The System menu also shows Quick Settings buttons for networking (Wired, Wi-Fi, Bluetooth, and Airplane Mode), power mode, and buttons for several desktop settings such as night lighting, style, and keyboard.

At the top center of the screen is the date (day of the week) and time. Clicking on the time displays the calendar with the full date specified, and the notifications menu if allowed.

Next to the System menu button is an accessibility button, which displays a menu of switches that let you turn on accessibility tools and such features as the onscreen keyboard, enhanced contrast, and the screen magnifier.

To log in, click a username from the list of users. You are then prompted to enter the user's password (see Figure 3-8). A login screen replaces the user list, showing the username you selected and a Password text box in which you can enter the user's password. By default, the password you enter is hidden. Should you want to display the text of your password, you can click the eye button located to the right in the password text box. Click the eye button again to hide the password. Once you enter the password, press Enter. Your desktop starts up.

Figure 3-7: The GDM user listing

Figure 3-8: GDM login

If the name of a user you want to log in as is not listed, click the "Not listed?" entry at the end of the list, to open a text box, which prompts you first for a username, and then a password.

On the login screen, there is a session button (gear icon) located at the right bottom corner. You can click this button to display a menu listing other installed desktops or the same desktop using a different display server. When you installed the Ubuntu desktop, two display servers were installed, X11 and Wayland. On the session menu you can choose Ubuntu (the Wayland display server and the default) or "Ubuntu on X.org", which uses the older X.org display server.

The session menu will also show other installed desktops you could use instead of Ubuntu (GNOME). Though GNOME is the primary desktop for Ubuntu, it is possible to install and use other desktops, known as Ubuntu Flavors, such as Kubuntu (Plasma, KDE), Xubuntu (Xfce session), and Ubuntu MATE (MATE). These are available on the Ubuntu repository (see Figure 3-9).

Ubuntu uses the systemd login manager, logind. You can configure login manager options with the **/etc/systemd/logind.conf** file. You can set options such as the number of terminals, the idle action, and hardware key operations, such as the power key. Check the **logind.conf** man page for details.

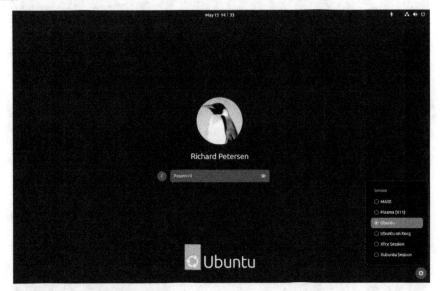

Figure 3-9: GDM Session menu

The System menu

Once logged in, the System menu button is displayed on the right side of the top bar of the desktop (see Figure 3-10). The button will display emblems for network, sound, and power. Clicking the button displays the System menu. At the top, it has buttons for the battery service indicator (battery image), taking a screenshot (camera image), opening Settings (gear image), activating the lock screen (lock image), and displaying the Power Off menu (power button image). The battery service indicator shows the current charge of the battery. Clicking on it opens the Setting Power tab showing the battery level. The Power Off menu lists Suspend, Restart, Power Off, Switch User (if you have more than one), and Logout entries.

Below these buttons are sliding bars for sound and brightness, which you can adjust the volume and brightness. If your display does not support brightness adjustments, only the sound slider is shown.

Below the sliders, a set of Quick Settings buttons lets you quickly activate or deactivate different services and devices. These will be different depending on your computer's capabilities. The network devices are listed first. Most will have either a Wired or Wi-Fi button or both, depending on the kind of network connections supported. If you have Bluetooth, a Bluetooth button is displayed. You can turn a device or service on or off by clicking its button. Activated buttons have a highlighted solid color, whereas deactivated ones are grayed out (dark for the dark style). In addition, the Wi-Fi button will also display your currently selected Wi-Fi connection, the Bluetooth button will show the number of selected Bluetooth devices, and the Power Mode button displays your current power mode (the default is Balanced for the desktop (full desktop install) and Power saver for the server (minimal desktop added to a server). An unselected Power Mode button, does not turn off the power mode, it just uses the default power mode. Clicking it will select a different power mode such as power saver. Clicking it again will deselect the power mode button, returning you to the default power mode.

Figure 3-10: System menu

If a device or service can be further configured, its button will have a menu button on its right side indicated by a right arrow, as is the case for Wired, Wi-Fi, Bluetooth, Power Mode, and Keyboard. Clicking on the menu button opens a small dialog where you can select settings. The Wired, Wi-Fi, Bluetooth, and Power Mode buttons will include a link in their menus to their appropriate Settings dialog, allowing you to perform a detailed configuration. The Wired dialog has a Wired Settings link to open the Settings Network tab, and the Power Mode dialog has a Power Settings link to open the Settings Power tab. The Wi-Fi button's dialog has an All Networks link that opens the Settings Wi-Fi tab.

Some button menus let you make simple setting selections, such as the Power Mode button's dialog that lets you choose Performance, Balanced, Power Saver power modes. The Bluetooth button's menu list your available Bluetooth devices. Wi-Fi shows your Wi-Fi connections.

Other buttons just turn a service on or off, such as the Night Light button that turns on night lighting for the display, the Dark Style that switches between the desktop dark and light styles, and Airplane Mode that turns airplane mode on and off. These have no menu buttons on button's right side.

You can also set the power profile from the System menu. You can choose from three profile modes: Performance, Balanced, and Power Saver. For the server, Power saver is the default, whereas for the desktop, Balanced is the default. Power Saver reduces performance to save power, especially for display operations. The Balanced mode balances power use and performance. Performance gives priority to CPU performance. Click on the Power Mode button on the System menu to turn the power mode on an off. On the Power Mode button, the current power mode is shown. Click on the Power Mode button's menu button (right arrow on the right side of the button) to display the Power Mode menu where you can choose the profile mode you want (see Figure 3-11). The current power mode has a check mark next to it. To access the Settings Power tab for more detailed power configuration, click the Power Settings link at the bottom of the menu.

Figure 3-11: System menu power profile modes

On systems that are not laptops, there will be no brightness slider or Battery entry on the System menu. If the system also has no wireless device, the Wi-Fi entry will also be missing.

Lock Screen

You can choose to lock your screen and suspend your system by clicking the Lock button on the top right of the System menu. The screen will go blank. Moving the mouse shows the time and date briefly (see Figure 3-12). To start up again, press any key and your Login screen appears with a password text box. Enter your password to start up your desktop session again. The password you enter is hidden. Should you want to display the text of your password, you can click the eye button located to the right in the password text box. Click the eye button again to hide the password.

Figure 3-12: Lock Screen

Logging Out and Switching Users

If you want to exit your desktop and return to the GDM login screen, or switch to a different user, you click the power button on the top right of the System menu to open the Power Off menu with entries for Suspend, Restart, Power Off, Log Out, and Switch User (see Figure 3-13). If you have only one user configured for your system, then the Switch User entry does not appear. Click the Switch User entry to log out and display the GDM with its list of users you can log into.

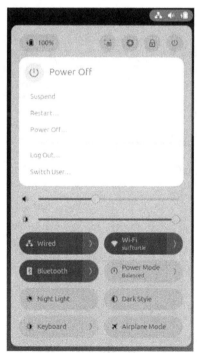

Figure 3-13: Power Off menu with Log Out entry

Click the Log Out entry to display a dialog that shows buttons for Cancel and Log Out (see Figure 3-14). Then click the Log Out button to log out of your account, returning to the login screen, where you can log in again as a different user or shut down the system. A countdown will commence in the dialog, showing how much time you have left before it performs the logout automatically.

Figure 3-14: Log Out dialog

The Switch User entry switches out from the current user and runs the GDM to display a list of users you can log in as. Click the name to open a password prompt and display a session button. You can then log in as that user. The sessions of users already logged will continue with the same open windows and applications that were running when the user switched off. You can switch back and forth between logged-in users, with all users retaining their session from where they left off. When you switch off from a user, that user's running programs will continue in the background.

Poweroff

From the login screen, you can poweroff (shut down) the system using the System menu on either the login screen or the desktop. Click the power button on the top right of the System menu to open the Power Off menu with entries for Suspend, Restart, Power Off, and Log Out. Click the Power Off" entry to display a Power Off dialog with options to Cancel or Power Off (see Figure 3-15). A countdown will commence in the dialog, showing how much time you have left before it performs the shutdown automatically. You can also just press the power button on your computer to display the Power Off dialog.

Figure 3-15: Power Off menu and Power Off dialog

Should your display freeze or become corrupted, one safe way to shut down and restart is to press a command line interface key (like CTRL-ALT-F2) to revert to the command line interface, and then press CTRL-ALT-DEL to restart. You can also log in on the command line interface (terminal) and then enter the **sudo poweroff** command.

On the desktop, you can also shut down your system from a terminal window, using the **poweroff** command with the **sudo** command. You will be prompted to enter your password.

```
sudo poweroff
```

To perform a reboot from a terminal window, you can use the **reboot** command.

```
sudo reboot
```

Ubuntu (GNOME)

Ubuntu 24.04 LTS uses the GNOME desktop. It provides easy-to-use overviews and menus, along with a flexible file manager and desktop. GNOME is based on the gnome-shell, which is a compositing window manager.

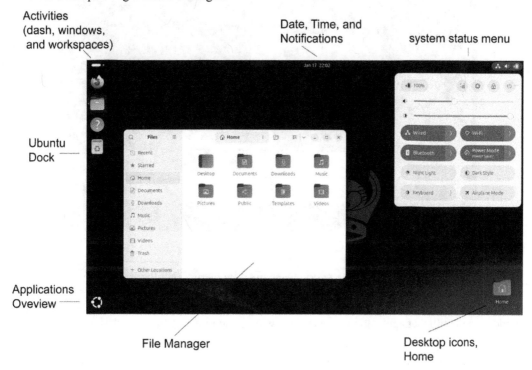

Figure 3-16: The Ubuntu desktop (minimal)

The Ubuntu desktop displays a top bar and a dock (dash) on the left side, through which you access your applications, windows, and settings (see Figure 3-16). Clicking the System menu button (network, sound, power indicators) at the right side of the top bar displays the System menu, from which you can access the desktop setting, lock the screen, and shut down (Power Off) the system. The dock is a bar on the left side with icons for your favorite applications along with icons for accessing applications. For the minimal Ubuntu desktop, there are icons for the Firefox web browser, Files (the GNOME file manager), Ubuntu help, the Trash folder, and the Applications overview. The last icon opens an Applications overview that you can use to start other applications. To open an application shown on the dock, click its icon or right-click on the icon and choose New Window from the pop-up menu. You can remove any of the dock icons except the Applications overview icon by right-clicking on the icon and choosing Unpin. Running applications will also be shown in the dock, which you can pin to the dock if you want by right-clicking and choosing "Pin to Dash." The Ubuntu dock is a GNOME extension implemented by Ubuntu and is a modified version of the GNOME Dock to Dash extension, which places a GNOME dash on the desktop.

You can access open windows and their running applications by using the Activities overview mode. Click the Activities button at the left side of the top bar (or press the Super (Windows) key) (see Figure 3-17). Large thumbnails of open windows are displayed on the windows overview (the desktop workspace area), along with workspaces, if you have more than one. You can use the Search box at the top to locate an application quickly. Part of your next desktop workspace is displayed on the right side. Clicking on that next workspace, moves you to it.

Figure 3-17: Activities overview

You can manually leave the overview at any time by pressing the ESC key, pressing the Super key (Windows key), or by clicking a window thumbnail. While in the Activities overview, the Ubuntu dock is still displayed on the left side of the screen. Clicking on an icon selects the window open with that application or opens a new one, and returns you to the desktop.

You can access windows from the windows overview, which is displayed when you start Activities. The windows overview displays thumbnails of all your open windows. When you pass your mouse over a window thumbnail, a close box appears, at the upper-right corner, with which you can close the window. You can also move the window on the desktop to another workspace.

To see just the windows open for a single application, such as several folders, click the application's icon on the dock to display the windows overview showing all the windows open for that application. Select the one you want.

To move a window on the desktop, click and drag its title bar. To maximize a window, double-click its title bar or drag it to the top bar. To return to normal, double-click the title bar again or drag it away from the top bar. To close a window, click its close box (upper right). To minimize a window, click its minimize button. To maximize a minimized window, click its icon in the dock.

The Ubuntu desktop also supports corresponding keyboard operations for desktop tasks, see Table 3-4.

Keypress	Action
SHIFT	Move a file or folder, default
CTRL	Copy a file or folder
CTRL-SHIFT	Create a link for a file or folder
F2	Rename selected file or folder
CTRL-ALT-Arrow (right, left, up, down)	Move to a different desktop
CTRL-w	Close current window
ALT-SPACEBAR	Open window menu for window operations
ALT-F2	Open Run command box
ALT-F1	Open Applications menu
CTRL-F	Find file

Table 3-4: Window and File Manager Keyboard shortcuts

Clicking the Applications icon on the dash or dock (bottom icon) opens the Applications overview listings all your installed applications (see Figure 3-18). Click an application icon to start that application. You can also right-click and choose the New Window entry on the pop-up menu. There is an application folder called Utilities on the applications overview. Utilities lists several tools, such as file roller, backup tool, log viewer, font manager, system monitor, terminal window, and, when installed, GNOME Tweaks.

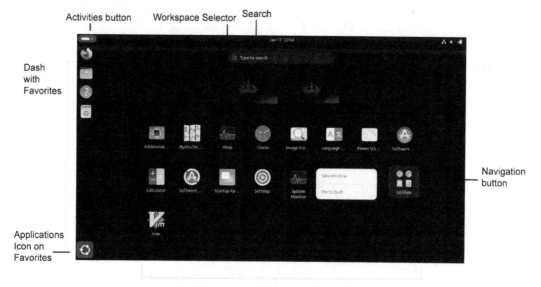

Applications Overview with workspace selector

Figure 3-18: Applications Overview

Files File Manager

You can access your home folder from the Files icon on the dash. A file manager window opens, showing your Home folder (see Figure 3-19). Your Home folder will already have default folders created for commonly used files. These include Documents, Downloads, Music, Pictures, and Videos. Your office applications will automatically save files to the Documents folder by default. Image and photo applications place image files in the Pictures folder. The Desktop folder will hold all files and folders saved to your desktop. When you download a file, it is placed in the Downloads folder.

The file manager window displays several components, including a header bar, which combines the title bar and toolbar, and a sidebar. When you open a new folder, the same window is used to display it, and you can use the forward and back arrows to move through previously opened folders. The header bar displays navigation folder buttons that show your current folder and its parent folders. You can click a parent folder to move to it. The GNOME file manager also supports tabs. You can open several folders in the same file manager window.

Figure 3-19: Files File manager

You can view a folder's contents as icons or as a detailed list, which you can choose by clicking the grid/list button between the search and view menu buttons on the right side of the toolbar (see Figure 3-20. This button toggles between grid (icon) and list views.

Figure 3-20: File manager grid/list button

There are three menus on the file manager header bar, the folder menu on the navigation button for the current folder, the view menu (down-arrow button) on the right side of the header bar, and tools menu (menu button), on the top right of the sidebar. The sidebar is located on the left side of file manager window (see Figure 3-21).

To the right of the location buttons, is the button for the current folder's folder menu (three vertical dots, ellipses), which you can click to display the folder menu). The menu shows common folder tasks such as creating a new folder (New Folder), open with a different file manager (Open With), and bookmarking the folder (Add to Bookmarks). The Reload button refreshes the display, updating any changes. The Edit Location entry changes the location buttons to an editable location textbox. The Copy Location entry copies the full pathname of the folder, which you can then paste to other documents (CTRL-v). The Properties entry displays the folder's Properties dialog, showing folder information and permissions. You can also open the folder in a terminal window, which is useful for running shell commands on the folder files and subfolders.

To the right of the grid/list button is a button for the View menu (down-arrow). The Views menu has entries for sorting your file manager icons. The sort entries allow you to sort your icons by name (A-Z and Z-A), size, type, and modification date. You can also reverse the order by name and modification date.

The file manager Tools menu (lines button) is located on the sidebar, to the right of the "Files" label. The Tools menu has entries for managing folders and files, as well as entries for configuring the file manager display. There are entries for showing hidden files, adjusting the icon size, and opening a new window or tab. The Keyboard Shortcuts entry displays the list of available shortcut keys, organized by function such as open operations, tabs, navigation, view operations, and edit tasks such as renaming, editing, and copying files.

Figure 3-21: File manager folder, view, and tools menus

Ubuntu Customization with GNOME Tweaks: Themes, Icons, Fonts, and Startup Applications

You can perform common desktop customizations using the GNOME Tweaks. Areas to customize include fonts, themes, startup applications, windows, and startup applications. You can access GNOME Tweaks from the Applications overview | Utilities. The GNOME Tweaks has tabs for Fonts, Appearance, Sound, Mouse & Touchpad, Keyboard, Windows, and Startup Applications (see Figure 3-22). GNOME Tweaks is not installed by default. It is available from the App Center as a Debian package.

The Appearance tab lets you set the theme for your icons, cursor, and legacy applications. Ubuntu uses the Yaru theme. Traditionally, GNOME uses the Adwaita Theme with its light and dark variants. As you add other desktops, such as MATE, the available themes increase. There would be many window themes and icons to choose from. On this tab, in the Background section, you can manage your background image, setting the default image for light and dark styles, and different adjustment options such as Zoom, Centered, Stretched, and Wallpaper.

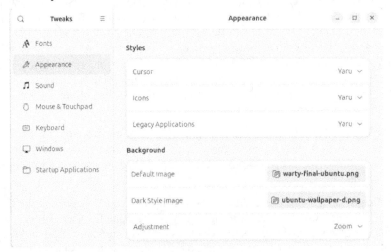

Figure 3-22: GNOME Tweaks - Appearance tab (themes)

Desktop fonts for interface (application or dialog text), documents, and monospace (terminal windows or code) can be changed in the Fonts tab (see Figure 3-23). You can adjust the size of the font or change the font style. Clicking the font name opens a "Pick a Font" dialog from which you can choose a different font. The quality of the text display can be further adjusted with Rendering and Antialiasing options. To simply increase or decrease the size of all fonts on your desktop interface, you can adjust the Scaling Factor.

Figure 3-23: GNOME Tweaks - Fonts tab

At times, there may be certain applications that you want started up when you log in, such as the Text Editor, the Firefox web browser, or the Videos movie player. On the Startup Applications tab, you can choose the applications to start up (see Figure 3-24). Click the plus (+) button to open an applications dialog from which you can choose an application. Click the Add button to add the application. Once added, you can later remove the application by clicking its Remove button.

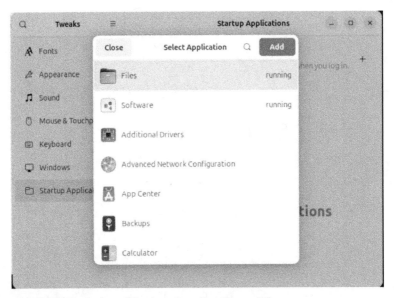

Figure 3-24: GNOME Tweaks - Startup Applications tab

Network Connections

Network connections on the desktop will be set up for you by NetworkManager, which will detect your network connections automatically, both wired and wireless. NetworkManager provides status information for your connection and allows you to switch easily from one configured connection to another, as needed. For initial configuration, it detects as much information as possible about the new connection.

NetworkManager is user specific. Wired connections will be started automatically. For wireless connections, when a user logs in, NetworkManager selects the connection preferred by that user. From a menu of detected wireless networks, the user can select a wireless connection to use.

NetworkManager displays active network connections in the System menu: the Wired button for the wired connection and the Wi-Fi button for a wireless connection. Each entry will indicate its status, as connected or disconnected. The buttons for these entries will vary according to their connection status: solid (colored) for an active connection and empty (faded) for a disconnected connection (see Figure 3-25). On wired systems that have no wireless devices, there is no Wi-Fi button in the System menu. Clicking all the network buttons, turns networking off, removing the network indicator from the Settings menu button.

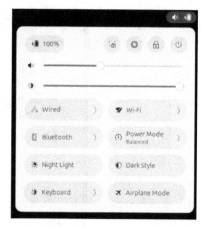

Figure 3-25: System menu with network Quick Settings buttons, on and off

NetworkManager Wired Connections

For computers connected to a wired network, such as an Ethernet connection, NetworkManager automatically detects and establishes the network connection. Most networks use DHCP to provide such network information as an IP address and DNS server. With this kind of connection, NetworkManager can connect automatically to your network whenever you start your system.

NetworkManager Wireless Connections

NetworkManager will scan for wireless connections, checking for Extended Service Set Identifiers (ESSIDs) . If an ESSID identifies a previously used connection, it is selected. If several are found, the recently used one is chosen. If only new connections are available, NetworkManager waits for the user to choose one.

Click the Wi-Fi button's menu link in the System menu to display the Wi-Fi menu showing a list of available Wi-Fi connections you can choose from (see Figure 3-26). Entries display the name of the wireless network and a wave graph showing the strength of its signal. To connect to a network click on an entry. If this is the first time you are trying to connect to that network, an Authentication dialog will prompt you to enter the password or encryption key (see Figure 3-27). The selected Wi-Fi connection will display a checkmark next to its name. Below the list of Wi-Fi connections is an All Networks link you can click to open the Settings Wi-Fi tab.

Figure 3-26: System Menu Wi-Fi button's menu showing Wi-Fi connections

Figure 3-27: Wi-Fi authentication

The Wi-Fi button on the System menu will also show the name of the connected Wi-Fi network. You can turn off wireless by clicking the Wi-Fi button (see Figure 3-28). When turned off, the button fades. To reactivate your wireless connection, click the Wi-Fi button again.

Figure 3-28: System menu with Wi-Fi button on and off

Configuring Network Connections with GNOME Settings

On the GNOME Settings dialog there is a Wi-Fi tab for wireless configuration and a Network tab for wired, VPN, and proxy configurations. Choose the All Networks link from the expanded Wi-Fi button (arrow on right side of the button) in the System menu, or click the Wi-Fi tab in the Settings dialog, to open the Wi-Fi tab (see Figure 3-29). On the Wi-Fi tab, an Airplane Mode switch and a list of visible wireless connections are listed (Visible Networks section). The currently active connection will have a "Connected" label next to its configuration button. At the top of the tab is a Wi-Fi switch for turning wireless on and off. Below the switch are links for dialogs for connections to hidden networks, turning on your computer's Wi-Fi hotspot capability, and listing previously accessed Wi-Fi Networks (Saved Networks). The "Saved Networks" link opens a "Save Wi-Fi Networks" dialog listing your previously accessed Wi-Fi networks, which you can choose to configure or delete (Trash button).

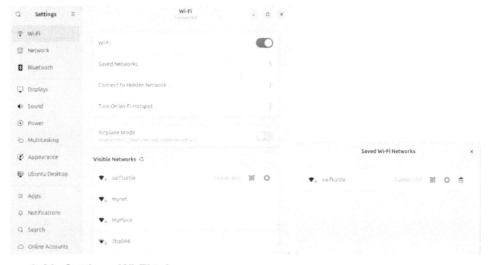

Figure 3-29: Settings Wi-Fi tab

Your current active connection will have a "Connected" label, scan button, and a configuration (gear) button to the right. The scan button displays a Share Network dialog displaying an image to scan to allow quickly sharing your network with yours or other people's devices such as phones and tablets (see Figure 3-30). The network name and password are also shown.

Figure 3-30: Settings Wi-Fi entry with scan button and Scan dialog

Click the configuration button to display a dialog with tabs for managing the connection. The Details tab provides information about the connection (see Figure 3-31). The Security, Identity, IPv4, and IPv6 tabs let you perform a detailed configuration of your connection, as described in Chapter 15. The settings are set to automatic by default. Should you make any changes, click the Apply button to have them take effect. The Details tab has options both for connecting automatically and for providing availability to other users. These are set by default. Should you not want to connect to the wireless network automatically, be sure to uncheck this option. To remove a network's connection information, click the Forget Connection button on the Details tab.

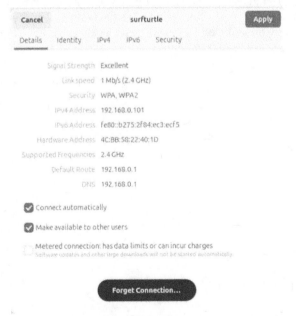

Figure 3-31: Settings Wi-Fi connection - Details tab

For a wired connection, click the Wired Settings entry on the Wired button's menu in the System menu or click the Network tab on GNOME Settings. This will display lists of Wired and VPN connections, as well as an entry for the Network Proxy. The Wired section shows your current wired connections with on and off switches for each. A plus button at the top right of the Wired section lets you add more wired connections. Next to a connection's switch a gear button is displayed (see Figure 3-32). Clicking the gear button opens a configuration dialog for that connection with tabs for Details, Identity, IPv4, IPv6, and Security (see Chapter 15).

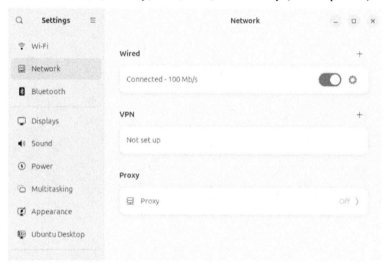

Figure 3-32: Settings Network tab with Wired connection

Clicking on the Network proxy gear button opens a Network Proxy tab with a Network Proxy switch for turning network proxy on and off. The Configuration entry shows a menu to the right with Manual and Automatic options (see Figure 3-33). For the Automatic option, you enter a URL address. The Manual option lets you enter address and port information for the proxy.

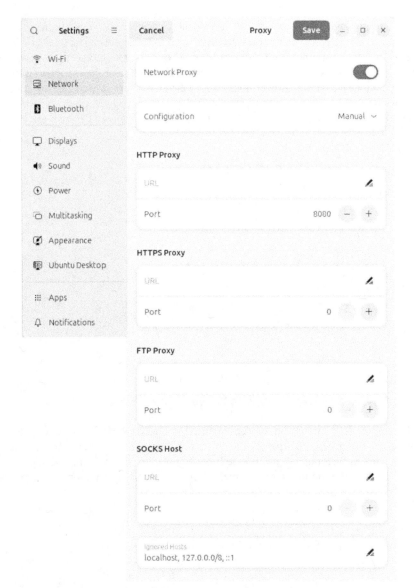

Figure 3-33: Settings Network tab with proxy settings

To add a vpn connection, click the plus (+) button at the top right of the VPN section to open the Add Vpn dialog listing the supported VPN protocols (see Chapter 15). Once a protocol is selected, an appropriate configuration dialog for your VPN network is displayed.

Shared Folders for your network (nautilus-share, Samba, and smbpasswd)

Your default configuration of Ubuntu does not let you share folders on a network. This is true even for those upgrading from a previous release. To enable the sharing of folders on Ubuntu 24.04, you have to install the **nautilus-share** and Samba server package (**samba**). Then, for a user to be allowed to share their folders, you use the **smbpasswd -a** command to give that user a Samba password and add that user to the **sambashare** group. Other local computers cannot access the shared folders on your Linux system until you install a sharing server, Samba for Windows systems and Linux/Unix systems. Be sure also to allow firewall access for Samba (see Chapter 15, Firewalls).

In previous releases the **nautilus-share** package was installed when you installed Ubuntu. It no longer is. You have to install the **nautilus-share** package yourself using the **sudo apt install** command in a terminal window.

```
sudo apt install nautilus-share
```

The **nautilus-share** package requires that the Samba server be installed. If Samba is not already installed, it will install it. You can also install the Samba server (**samba** package) directly with the Synaptic Package Manager or the **apt install** command. The Samba server is not installed with installation and you cannot install it from the App Center. Instead, you have to open a terminal window (Terminal application) and enter the **apt install** command on the command line as an administrator (**sudo**).

```
sudo apt install samba
```

Two servers are installed and run using the **smbd** and **nmbd** systemd service scripts. The **smbd** server is the Samba server, and the **nmbd** server is the network discovery server. Should the Samba server fail to start, you can start it manually in a terminal window with the commands:

```
sudo systemctl start nmbd
sudo systemctl start smbd
```

You can check the current status with the **status** option and restart with the **restart** option:

```
systemctl status nmbd
systemctl status smbd
```

When first installed, Samba imports the user accounts already configured on your Ubuntu system. Corresponding Windows users with the same username and password as an Ubuntu account on your Ubuntu system are connected automatically to the Ubuntu shared folders. Should the Windows user have a different password, that user is prompted on Windows to enter a username and password. This is an Ubuntu username and password. In the case of a Windows user with the same username but different password, the user would enter the same username with an Ubuntu user password, not the Windows password.

Each user attempting to access a Samba server will need a Samba server user name and a Samba password for that user. Such user-level security requires that this username and Samba password be stored in the Samba password database, which is maintained separately by the Samba server. To add a user Samba password, in a terminal window, enter the **smbpasswd** command with the **-a** option and the username you want to add. You are then prompted to enter a Samba password for that user.

```
richard@myserver:~$ sudo smbpasswd -a richard
[sudo] password for richard:
New SMB password:
Retype new SMB password:
Added user richard.
richard@myserver:~$
```

To enable sharing on a particular user account, including your own, you have to first give the user permission to share folders on a local network by adding the user to the **sambashare** group. The user that installed the **nautilus-share** packages is automatically added to the **sambashare** group. For other users, the **smbpasswd** operation not only creates a Samba password for the user, but should also add the user to the **sambashare** group. If it fails to add the user to the **sambashare** group, you can do so manually by opening a terminal window and use the **adduser** command to add a user to a group. The first argument is the user name and the second argument is the group name. To add the **george** user to the **sambashare** group you would enter.

```
sudo adduser george sambashare
```

You could also use **useradd** with the **-G** option, or **usermod** with the **-a** and **-G** options.

```
sudo useradd -G george sambashare
```

```
sudo usermod -a -G george sambashare
```

With these three elements in place (**nautilus-share**, **samba**, and setting up a Samba password for your user) you can now share your folders. You have to logout and login to your system for the changes to take effect.

The **nautilus-share** package adds a "Sharing Options" entry to the context menu for a folder. To share a folder on your Ubuntu system, right-click on it and select Sharing Options from the context menu. This opens a Folder Sharing dialog where you can allow sharing, and choose whether to permit modifying, adding, or deleting files in the folder (see Figure 3-34). You can also allow access to anyone who does not also have an account on your system (guest). Once you have made your selections, click the Create Share button. You can later change the sharing options if you want.

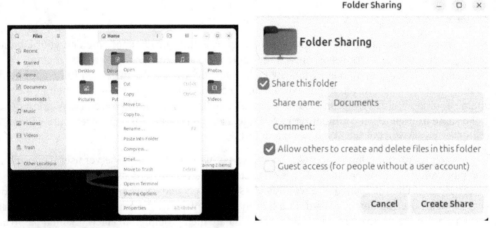

Figure 3-34: Folder Sharing Options

To allow access by other users, permissions on the folder will have to be changed. You will be prompted to allow the file manager to make these changes for you. Just click the "Add the permissions automatically" button (see Figure 3-36).

Figure 3-35: Folder Sharing permissions prompt

Note: If you are running a firewall, be sure to configure access for the NFS and Samba services, including browsing support. Otherwise, access to your shared folders by other computers may be blocked (see Chapter 15).

Once you click the Create Share button, the share is created and the button changes to a Modify Share button (see Figure 3-36). Folders that are shared display a sharing emblem next to their icon on a file manager window. To make changes, select the Sharing Options entry from the folder's context menu to open the Folder Sharing dialog. Make your selections, and then click the Modify Share button to make the changes.

Figure 3-36: Folder Sharing dialog

Once sharing is enabled, the Files file manager will display your system in the Networks entry of the Other Locations tab. You can click on it to display the shares on your system (see Figure 3-37).

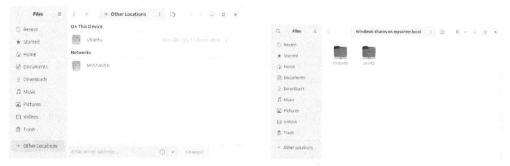

Figure 3-37: Other Locations with sharing enabled

If you are using a firewall, be sure that it is configured for access by Samba to allow multicast DNS discovery. For Gufw (Firewall Configuration), be sure that the rules are added for Samba. For FirewallD, on firewall-config (Firewall), be sure that the mdns, samba, and samba-client services are enabled (Zones | Services tab) (see Figure 3-38) .

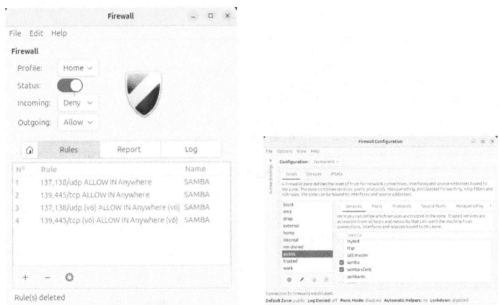

Figure 3-38: Samba Firewall Configuration, Gufw (UFW) and firewall-config (FirewallD)

Terminal Window

The Terminal window allows you to enter Linux commands on a command line. It is installed by default, and is accessible from the Applications overview as Terminal. Its package name is **gnome-terminal** and it is a GNOME 4.6 application for Ubuntu 24.04.

The terminal window provides you with a shell interface for using shell commands instead of your desktop. The command line is editable, allowing you to use the BACKSPACE key to erase characters on the line. Pressing a key will insert that character. You can use the left and right arrow keys to move anywhere on the line, and then press keys to insert characters, or use backspace to delete characters (see Figure 3-39). Folders, files, and executable files are color-coded: white for files (black if background is white), blue for folders, green for executable files, and aqua for links. Shared folders are displayed with a green background.

You can have several terminal windows open at the same time. On the Ubuntu dock, you can right-click on the terminal icon to list all your open terminal windows and use that list to move to a different one or to close a terminal. The Ubuntu dock menu's Quit entry will close all your open terminal windows.

Figure 3-39: Terminal Window

The terminal window menu lets you open a new terminal window and lock the current window to a read only status (see Figure 3-40). Use the Full Screen entry to expand the window and the scaling buttons at the top of the menu to increase or decrease the font size. The Preferences entry opens the terminal window Preferences dialog where you can configure your terminal windows. The Advanced sub-menu lets you reset and clear the window, erasing previously displayed commands. You can also change the size of the terminal window from a set of listed sizes.

Figure 3-40: Terminal Window menu

The terminal window will remember the previous commands you entered. Use the up and down arrows to have those commands displayed in turn on the command line. Press the ENTER key to re-execute the currently displayed command. You can even edit a previous command before running it, allowing you to execute a modified version of a previous command. This can be helpful if you need to re-execute a complex command with a different argument, or if you mistyped a complex command and want to correct it without having to re-type the entire command. The terminal window will display all your previous interactions and commands for that session. Use the scrollbar to see any previous commands you ran and their displayed results.

To quickly locate either a previous command or message in the terminal window you can use the search dialog (see Figure 3-41). Click on the search button (looking glass button) located on the right side of the terminal window's titlebar. This open a search dialog with options for case, words, regular expressions, and wrap around.

Figure 3-41: Terminal Window Search dialog

You can open as many terminal windows as you want, each working in its own shell. Instead of opening a separate window for each new shell, you can open several shells in the same window, using tabs. Use the keys SHIFT-CTRL-t or click the Tab button on the left side of the terminal window's titlebar (plus symbol) to open a new tab. A tab toolbar opens at the top of the terminal window with the folder name and a close button for each added tab. Each tab runs a separate shell, letting you enter different commands in each (see Figure 3-42). You can right-click on the tab's folder name to display a pop-up menu with options to move to the next or previous tab, close the tab, or detach the tab to a new terminal window. You can move to any tab by clicking on a tab's folder name, selecting its name from the Tabs menu, or pressing the **Ctrl-PageUp** and **Ctrl-PageDown** keys to move through the tabs sequentially. The Tabs menu is the down arrow on the right side of the terminal window and to the right of the tab names. It is displayed if multiple tabs are open.

The terminal window also supports desktop cut/copy and paste operations. You can copy a line from a Web page and then paste it to the terminal window by pressing SHIFT-CTRL-v. The command will appear and then you can press ENTER to execute the command. This is useful for command line operations displayed on an instructional Web page. Instead of typing in a complex command yourself, just select and copy from the Web page directly, and then paste to the Terminal window. You can also perform any edits on the command, if needed, before executing it. Also, should you want to copy a command on the terminal window, select the text with your mouse and then use SHIFT-CTRL-c keys to copy the command. You can select part of a line or multiple lines, as long as they are shown on the terminal window.

Figure 3-42: Terminal Window with tabs showing tabs menu

You can customize terminal windows using profiles. A default profile is set up already. To customize your terminal window, select Preferences from the terminal window menu. This opens a window for setting your default profile options with option categories on the sidebar for Global and Profiles. In the Profiles section there will be an "Unnamed" profile, the default. Click on the down menu button to the right to open a menu with the options to copy (clone) the profile or change the name. To add another profile, click on the plus button to the right of the "Profiles" heading to open a dialog to create a new profile. For profiles you create you have the added options to delete them and to set one as the default. A selected profile displays tabs for Text, Colors, Scrolling, Command, and Compatibility (see Figure 3-43). On the Text tab, you can select the default size of a terminal window in text rows and columns, as well as the font, spacing, and cursor shape.

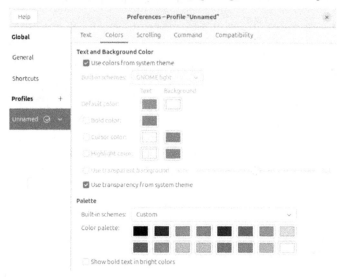

Figure 3-43: Terminal Window Profile configuration

Your terminal window will be set up to use a dark background with white text. To change this, you can edit the profile to change the background and text colors on the Colors tab. De-select the "Use colors from system theme" entry. This enables the "Built-in schemes" menu from which you can select a "Black on white" display. Other color combinations are also listed, such as "Black on light yellow" and "Green on black." The Custom option lets you choose your own text and background colors. The colors on your open terminal window will change according to your selection, allowing you to see how the color choices will look. For a transparent background, choose the "Use transparent background" entry and then set the amount of shading (none is completely transparent and full shows no transparency).

The Scrolling tab specifies the number of command lines your terminal history will keep, as well as other scroll options such as whether to display the scrollbar. These are the lines you can move back through and select to re-execute. You can de-select the Limit scrollback option to set this to unlimited to keep all the commands.

To later edit a particular profile, select Preferences from the terminal window menu to open the Preferences window, and then click on the one you want in the Profiles section.

Settings

You can configure desktop settings and perform most administrative tasks using the GNOME configuration tools (see Table 3-2) listed in the Settings application, accessible with the Settings button (gear image) located at the top right of the System menu (see Figure 3-44). Settings displays tabs on a left sidebar for different desktop and system configurations (see Figure 3-45). The tabs are segmented into five groups, beginning with those for networking, then the desktop, application related tabs, devices such as the keyboard and printers, and then several subheadings for accessibility, security, and system management and information, which have links to open several tabs. Should you use a link to open a tab, a left arrow is displayed at the upper left of the current tab's header bar. Click on it to return back to the tab with the link you used.

Figure 3-44: Ubuntu (GNOME) Settings

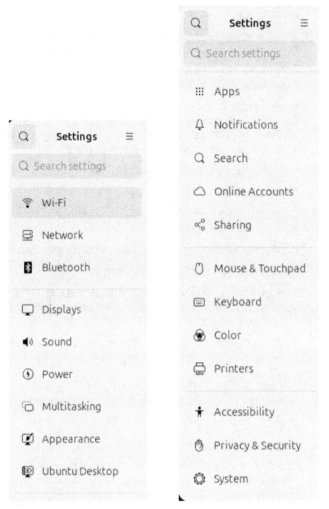

Figure 3-45: Settings Sidebar

Some tabs lists links that you can use to open other tabs or dialogs, such as the System, Privacy & Security, and Accessibility tabs. The links have a right arrow symbol at the end of the link entry. You can click on a link to open the tab or dialog. If the link is to a tab, when the tab opens, a left arrow button appears on the header bar to the left of the tab's name. You click on this button to return to the previous tab. Any tab you link to can, in turn, list links to yet other tabs and dialogs.

Setting	Description
Accessibility	Enables universal access features for the display, keyboard, and mouse. Displays tabs for Seeing, Hearing, Typing, Pointing and Clicking, and Zoom.
Appearance	Style (light, dark, and color accents) and backgrounds.
Apps	Opens a dialog where you can set permissions for applications such as file types and notifications. Also includes a tab for setting default applications such as your Web browser and image viewer, as well as setting default applications for removable media.
Bluetooth	Sets Bluetooth detection and configuration
Color	Sets the color profile for a device.
Displays	Changes your screen resolution, refresh rate, and screen orientation for your connected displays.
Keyboard	Configures input sources, alternate character keys, and shortcut keys.
Mouse & Touchpad	Sets mouse and touchpad configuration
Multitasking	Turn on hot corner, screen edge window resizing, dynamic or fixed workspaces, show workspaces on all displays, and application switching on workspaces and monitors.
Network	Turn wired networks on or off. Allows access to an available wired network. Also specifies proxy configuration, if needed.
Notifications	Turns on notifications for different applications
Online Accounts	Configures online accounts for use by e-mail and browser applications
Power	Sets the power saving options and lists battery levels.
Printers	Configure printers and access print queues
Privacy & Security	Turns on privacy and security features. Displays tabs for Connectivity, Screen Lock, Location, File History & Trash, Diagnostics, and Device Security.
Sharing	Turns on sharing for media.
Sound	Configures system levels, output and input sound devices, and sound effects.
Search	Specifies the resources and locations searched by the GNOME activities overview search box
System	Displays tabs for system information and management: Region & Language, Date & Time, Users, Remote Desktop, Secure Shell, and About. Also includes a link to Software Updates for updating your system.
Ubuntu Desktop	Set desktop icon, dock configuration, and enhanced tiling.
Wi-Fi	Configure and manage wireless networks.

Table 3-2: Settings

4. Managing Software

Ubuntu software distribution is implemented using the online Ubuntu software repositories, which contain an extensive collection of Ubuntu-compliant software. With the integration of repository access into your Linux system, you can think of that software as an easily installed extension of your current collection. You can add software to your system by accessing software repositories that support Debian packages (DEB) and the Advanced Package Tool (APT), or the newer Snap packages known as **snaps** and the Snap package manager. Software is packaged into DEB or Snap software package files. These files are, in turn, installed and managed by APT or Snap.

You can also download source code versions of applications, then compile, and install them on your system. Where this process once was complex, it has been streamlined significantly with the use of configure scripts. Most current source code, including GNU software, is distributed with a configure script, which automatically detects your system configuration and creates a binary file that is compatible with your system.

You can download Linux software from many online sources directly, but it is always advised that you use the Ubuntu prepared package versions if available. Most software for Linux systems have corresponding Ubuntu-compliant packages in the Ubuntu Universe and Multiverse sections. Several proprietary versions of popular software packages, such as Skype, are freely available as Snap packages.

Installing Software Packages: APT and Snap

Installing software is an administrative function performed by a user with administrative access. During the Ubuntu installation, only some of the many applications and utilities available for users on Linux were installed on your system. On Ubuntu, you can install or remove software from your system with the **apt** and **snap** commands, or, from the desktop, with the App Center and the Synaptic Package Manager. Alternatively, you could install software as separate DEB files, or by downloading and compiling its source code.

Ubuntu supports two packages management systems, Snap and DEB (Debian package format). For the older DEB formatted packages, the underlying software management tool is APT. Snap packages (**snaps**) have a different format from DEB, and cannot be managed by APT. Instead they are managed by the Snap package manager, which uses the **snapd** daemon to install, update, and run snap applications. Snap is a completely different package management system, though Snap packages can be installed alongside APT packages, and accessed seamlessly on Ubuntu.

APT (Advanced Package Tool) is the older tool for installing packages, and is still used for most applications. When you install a DEB package with Ubuntu Software or with the Synaptic Package Manager, APT will be invoked and will select and download the package automatically from the appropriate online APT managed repository. This will include the entire Ubuntu online repository, including the main, universe, multiverse, and restricted sections.

A DEB software package includes all the files needed for a software application. A Linux software application often consists of several files that must be installed in different directories. The application program itself is placed in a system folder such as **/usr/bin**, online manual files go in another folder, and library files go in yet another folder. When you select an application for installation, APT will install any additional dependent (required) packages. APT also will install all recommended packages by default. Many software applications have additional features that rely on recommended packages.

Snap is the new package format that will replace the DEB package management system on Ubuntu. The packages are called **snaps**. With the DEB format, as with other Linux package formats like RPM, the component software files for a software application are installed directly to global system folders such as **/lib**, **/etc**, and **/usr/bin**. In effect, such a package has access to your entire system during installation, posing security risks. In addition, a DEB software package usually has several dependent packages, which also have to be installed. These can be extensive. Under this system, shared libraries, used by different applications can be a problem for developers, as changes in software may have to wait for supporting changes in the shared libraries.

With Snap, the software files for an application are no longer installed in global folders. They are installed in one separate folder, and any dependent software and shared libraries are included as part of the snap package. In effect, there are no longer any dependencies, and libraries are no longer shared. This makes for more secure and faster updates, though a larger set of installed files. The installation process no longer needs access to your entire system. The entire application is isolated in one location. The problem of a failed update due to broken dependencies is no longer an issue. Applications that used to make use of the same shared library, will now have their own copies of that library. Developers that used to have to wait for changes to be made to a shared library, can now directly just change their own copy.

Keep in mind, that your Ubuntu Live Server will currently install APT supported software applications, even for those that have corresponding Snap packages.

Software Package Types

Ubuntu uses both Snap (snaps) and Debian-compliant software packages (DEB). Snap packages have the extension **.snap** and DEB packages have a **.deb** extension. Other packages, such as those in the form of source code that you need to compile, may come in a variety of compressed archives. These commonly have the extension **.tar.gz**, **.tgz**, or **.tar.bz2**. Packages with the **.rpm** extension are Red Hat Package software packages used on Red Hat, Fedora, SuSE and other Linux distributions that use RPM packages. They are not compatible directly with Ubuntu. You can use the **alien** utility to convert most RPM packages to DEB packages that you can then install on Ubuntu. Table 4-1 lists several common file extensions that you will find for the great variety of Linux software packages available. You can download any Ubuntu-compliant DEB package as well as the original source code package, as single files, directly from **https://packages.ubuntu.com/**.

Ubuntu Package Management Software

Software packages can be managed and installed using different package management software tools. The **snap** command supports only Snap packages (**snaps**), and all the other package managers support APT. On the desktop, the App Center package manager (snap-store) supports both Snap (snaps) and APT (DEB). The Software Updater application (desktop) supports both Snap and APT packages.

APT (Advanced Package Tool) performs the actual software management operations for all applications installed from an APT repository. The Synaptic Package Manager (desktop), **dpkg**, **apt**, and **apt-get** are all front-ends for APT. Ubuntu Software, though, is a front-end for Snap and the Snap Store, though it can also manage APT packages.

Extension	File
.deb	A Debian/Ubuntu Linux package
.gz	A **gzip**-compressed file (use **gunzip** to decompress)
.bz2	A **bzip2**-compressed file (use **bunzip2** to decompress; also use the **j** option with **tar**, as in **xvjf**)
.tar	A tar archive file (use **tar** with **xvf** to extract)
.tar.gz	A **gzip**-compressed **tar** archive file (use **gunzip** to decompress and **tar** to extract; use the **z** option with **tar**, as in **xvzf**, to both decompress and extract in one step)
.tar.bz2	A **bzip2**-compressed **tar** archive file (extract with **tar -xvzj**)
.tz	A **tar** archive file compressed with the **compress** command
.Z	A file compressed with the **compress** command (use the **decompress** command to decompress)
.bin	A self-extracting software file
.rpm	A software package created with the Red Hat Software Package Manager, used on Fedora, Red Hat, Centos, and SuSE distributions
.snap	A snap package, replacement for .deb

Table 4-1: Linux Software Package File Extensions

Snap is the alternative and eventual replacement for APT. Snap packages are downloaded and installed from the Snap Store using the **snapd** daemon. A snap package, in addition to an application, installs a copy of supporting libraries and configuration files, all located in a separate folder in the **/snap** folder, with user data located in a home folder's **snap** folder. They are not installed on the system globally as APT does. Snap packages and applications are run and updated by the **snapd** daemon. Each update to a snap package, has, in turn, a separate revision folder, each with a copy of supporting libraries and configuration files. Updates are easy to perform and require no system-wide updating of supporting libraries. You can easily switch from one revision to another. The App Center and the **snap** command are front-ends for Snap and the Snap Store. The App Center is a modified version of the **snap-store** application, which manages Snap packages. The App Center can also install and manage DEB packages from APT repositories, though priority is given to Snap packages.

Command Line tools

If you installed the Ubuntu Live Server, you will only have access to the following command line software management tools.

APT only package managers

apt is the primary command line tool for APT, and is used to install, update, and remove software. It is based on **apt-get** and does not have as many options. It uses the APT database, **/var/lib/apt** with repository information at **/var/cache/apt**

apt-get is the older command line tool for APT to install, update, and remove software. It has more options than **apt**. It uses the APT database, **/var/lib/apt** with repository information at **/var/cache/apt**

dpkg is the older command line tool used to install, update, remove, and query DEB software packages. It uses its own database, **/var/lib/dpkg**, Repository files are kept at **/var/cache/apt**, the same as APT.

aptitude Front end for tools like dpkg or apt-get, screen based, uses own database, **/var/lib/aptitude**.

Snap only package managers

snap is the command line command for managing snap packages (Snap). Packages are installed at **/snap**, with user data in the user home folder's **snap** folder.

Desktop tools

If you installed the Ubuntu Desktop USB/DVD or one of its variations like Kubuntu, you will have access to the following desktop interface tools, as well as using a terminal window to run the previously listed command line tools.

Snap and APT package managers

App Center is the primary desktop interface for locating and installing UBUNTU software. App Center is an implementation of the snap-store application. App Center can manage both snap packages (Snap) and DEB packages (APT). In App Center, snap packages are given priority.

Software updater is the Ubuntu graphical front end for updating installed software. It updates APT supported packages and, also, invokes the **snapd** daemon to update snap packages from the Snap Store.

GNOME Software is the is the GNOME Software manager that Ubuntu Software is based on. The basic install supports the APT repositories only (DEB packages). But you can install a Gnome Software plugin for snap packages, letting you use it to manage snap packages. You can also install a Flatpak plugin to manage Flatpak packages.

APT only package managers

Synaptic Package Manager is a Graphical front end for managing DEB packages on APT repositories. It does not support Snap.

GNOME Software: GNOME Graphical front end for managing packages, repository info at **/var/cache/apt**.

Discover Package Manager is the KDE software manager and is a graphical front end for APT.

Muon Package Manager is an older KDE software manager similar to the Synaptic Package Manager and is a graphical front end for APT.

Synaptic Package Manager: Graphical front end for managing packages, repository info at **/var/cache/apt**. Ubuntu no longer supports it.

Muon is the KDE software manager, a graphical front end for APT.

APT: Deb Package Management

Ubuntu provides Debian packages (DEB) and the Advanced Package Tool (APT) to manage them. The App Center manages both Snap and APT package systems, whereas the Synaptic Package Manager is a front-end for APT and only manages DEB packages. The command-line tools for managing DEB packages with APT are Aptitude, **apt** and **apt-get**.

Most server packages are still only available as APT (DEB) packages. You would use the **apt** and **apt-get** commands, as well as the Aptitude tool, to manage them. Snap provides very few server packages. Some are listed during the install process on the "Featured Server Snaps" screen.

Ubuntu APT Repositories

For Ubuntu, its APT-based software repository is organized into sections, depending on how the software is supported. Software supported directly is located in the main Ubuntu repository section. Other Linux software that is most likely compatible is placed in the Universe repository section. Many software applications, particularly multimedia applications, have potential licensing conflicts. Such applications are placed in the Multiverse repository section, which is not maintained directly by Ubuntu. Many of the popular multimedia drivers and applications, such as video and digital music support can be obtained from the Ubuntu Multiverse sections using the same simple APT commands you use for Ubuntu-supported software. Software from the Multiverse and Universe sections are supported by package managers like the App Center and the Synaptic Package Manager, and can be installed just as easily as Ubuntu main section software. Some drivers are entirely proprietary and supplied directly by vendors. This is the case with the NVIDIA vendor-provided drivers. These drivers are placed in a restricted section, noting that there is no open source support.

Four main components or sections make up the Ubuntu APT repository: main, restricted, universe, and multiverse. These components are described in detail at:

`https://help.ubuntu.com/community/Repositories/Ubuntu`

To see a listing of all packages in the Ubuntu APT repository see:

`https://packages.ubuntu.com`

To see available repositories and their sections, see the Ubuntu Software tab on Software & Updates, which is accessible from the Applications overview.

APT Repository Components

The following repository components are included in the Ubuntu APT repository:

main: Officially supported Ubuntu software (canonical), such as the GStreamer Good plug-in.

restricted: Software commonly used and required for many applications, but not open source or freely licensed. Because they are not open source, they are not guaranteed to work.

universe: All open source Linux software not directly supported by Ubuntu such as GStreamer Bad plug-ins.

multiverse: Linux software that does not meet licensing requirements and is not considered essential. It is not guaranteed to work. For example, the GStreamer ugly package is in this repository. Check **https://ubuntu.com/licensing**.

APT Repositories

In addition to the Ubuntu APT repository, Ubuntu maintains several other APT repositories used primarily for maintenance and support for existing packages. The updates repository holds updated packages for a release. The security updates repository contains critical security package updates every system will need.

Ubuntu repository: Collection of Ubuntu-compliant software packages for releases organized into main, universe, multiverse, and restricted sections.

Updates: Updates for packages in the main repository, including main, restricted, universe, and multiverse sections.

Backports: Software under development for the next Ubuntu release, but packaged for use in the current one. Not guaranteed or fully tested. Backports access is now enabled by default.

Security updates: Critical security fixes for Ubuntu repository software.

The Backports repository provides un-finalized or development versions for new and current software. They are not guaranteed to work, but may provide needed features.

Note: Though it is possible to add the Debian Linux distribution repository, it is not advisable. Packages are designed for specific distributions. Combining them can lead to irresolvable conflicts.

APT Ubuntu Repository Configuration file: ubuntu.sources and sources.list.d

Ubuntu APT repository configuration is managed by APT using configuration files in the **/etc/apt/sources.list.d** directory. The **/etc/apt/sources.list.d/ubuntu.sources** file holds repository entries. There are two different types of files that can be used to configure repositories, the one-line style format that has a **.list** extension, and the deb822 style format that has a **.sources** extension. Ubuntu now uses a **.sources** file with the deb822 style named **ubuntu.sources**, instead of the **sources.list** file with the One-Line style uses in previous release. The file name is **ubuntu.sources**, which is located in the **/etc/apt/sources.list.d** directory. The **/etc/apt/sources.list** file used in previous release is still present, but is just contains a message referring you to the **/etc/apt/sources.list.d/ubuntu.sources** file.

Both the deb822 style and the one-line style have the same elements in their formats: type, URI, suite, components, and options. The type is the type of repository, either **deb** or **deb-src**. The URI (universal resource identifier) provides the location of the repository, such as an FTP or Web URL. The suite name is a collection of packages in a release. In Ubuntu, it consist of the release name and a qualifier, such as **noble**, **noble-updates**, or **noble-security**. The primary collection normally, for Ubuntu, has no qualifier. It is just the release name, which for Ubuntu 24.04 is **noble**. Ubuntu 22.04 LTS, the previous LTS suite, used **jammy**, **jammy-updates**, and **jammy-security**. The components can be one or more terms that identify a section in that release's repository. There can be more than one term used to specify a component, like **restricted** to specify the restricted component in the Ubuntu APT repository. The Multiverse and Universe sections are referenced as **universe** and **multiverse**.

The URI is the address of the repository, such as **http://us.archive.ubuntu.com/ubuntu**. **jammy** is the name for Ubuntu 22.04, and **noble** is the name for 24.04.

The one-line format places all the information on a single line, with the following format:

```
format   URI   suite    components
```

The entry for the Jammy main, restricted, and universe sections is shown here.

```
deb http://us.archive.ubuntu.com/ubuntu/ jammy  main restricted universe
```

The one-line style requires multiple entries for different suites, such as jammy, jammy-security, and jammy-updates.

A deb822 **.sources** file has a very different format than the older one-line **.list** file. The deb822 style uses a series of stanzas separated by empty lines. Each stanza consists of a series of fields, each on its own line. Commonly used fields are Types, URIs, Suites, and Components. The name of the field is separated by a colon from its values. If the Types, URIs, and Component fields are the same for multiple suites, you would only need one stanza in which the suites are all listed in the Suites field.

The previous one-line style example written in a deb822 style would be:

```
Types: deb
URIs: http://us.archive.ubuntu.com/ubuntu/
Suites: jammy jammy-updates jammy-backports
Components: main restricted universe multiverse
```

In Ubuntu 24.04, **noble**, there is one stanza for the noble, noble-updates, and noble-backports suites.

```
Types: deb
URIs: http://us.archive.ubuntu.com/ubuntu/
Suites: noble noble-updates noble-backports
Components: main restricted universe multiverse
```

As the security suite uses a different URI, it needs a separate stanza.

```
Types: deb
URIs: http://security.ubuntu.com/ubuntu/
Suites: noble-security
Components: main restricted universe multiverse
```

To add source files to your repository configuration, the **deb-src** type is added to the Types field. This is what the Software & Updates Ubuntu Software tab's "Source code" option does.

```
Types: deb deb-src
URIs: http://us.archive.ubuntu.com/ubuntu/
Suites: noble noble-updates noble-backports
Components: main restricted universe multiverse
```

Following the Components field are any options. Ubuntu 24.04 uses the Signed-By option to specify that APT uses the Ubuntu keys in the **ubuntu-archive-keyring.gpg** file to perform verification. Keys for packages are located in the **/usr/share/keyrings** directory.

```
Signed-By: /usr/share/keyrings/ubuntu-archive-keyring.gpg
```

The fields used for Ubuntu 24.04 are Types, URIs, Suites, Components, and Signed-By. The Ubuntu 24.04 **ubuntu.sources** file is shown here.

/etc/apt/sources.list.d/ubuntu.sources

```
Types: deb
URIs: http://us.archive.ubuntu.com/ubuntu/
Suites: noble noble-updates noble-backports
Components: main restricted universe multiverse
Signed-By: /usr/share/keyrings/ubuntu-archive-keyring.gpg

Types: deb
URIs: http://security.ubuntu.com/ubuntu/
Suites: noble-security
Components: main restricted universe multiverse
Signed-By: /usr/share/keyrings/ubuntu-archive-keyring.gpg
```

Most entries can be managed using Software & Updates. Entries can also be managed by editing the **ubuntu.sources** file with Text Editor or with an editor such as **nano**.

```
sudo nano /etc/apt/sources.list.d/ubuntu.sources
```

You could remove an stanza by placing a comment symbol, the #, at the beginning of each line in the stanza. But it is easier to simply add the Enabled field and giving it a **no** value. To re-enable the stanza, change the **no** to **yes**.

```
Enabled: no
```

New APT repositories can be added using the Software & Updates's Other Software tab. You can simply add the repository entries directly. To do this, you do not have to edit the **/etc/apt/sources.list.d/ubuntu.sources** file. Editing such an important file always includes the risk of incorrectly changing the entries. Instead, new repository entries can be placed in a text file with a **.sources** extension with entries in the deb822 style in the **/etc/apt/sources.list.d** folder, which APT will read as if part of the **ubuntu.sources** file.

Managing APT Software Repositories on the Desktop with Software & Updates

On the desktop, you can manage your APT repositories with the Software & Updates dialog, allowing you to enable or disable repository sections, as well as add new entries. This dialog edits the **/etc/apt/sources.list.d/ubuntu.sources** file directly. You can access Software & Updates from the Applications overview. You can also access it on the Synaptic Package Manager from the Settings menu as the Repositories entry. The Software & Updates dialog displays seven tabs: Ubuntu Software, Other Software, Updates, Authentication, Additional Drivers, Developer Options, and Ubuntu Pro (see Figure 4-1).

Figure 4-1: Software & Updates - Ubuntu software repository sections

The Ubuntu Software tab lists all the Ubuntu APT repository section entries. These include the main repository, universe, restricted, and multiverse, as well as source code. Those that are enabled will be checked. Initially, all of them, except the source code, will be enabled. You can enable or disable a repository section by checking or un-checking its entry. You can select the repository server to use from the "Download from" drop-down menu.

On the Other Software tab, you can add repositories for third-party APT software (see Figure 4-2). To add a third-party repository manually, click the Add button. This opens a dialog where you are prompted to enter the complete APT entry, but in the older one-line style, starting with the deb type, followed by the URI, suite, and components. The line is place in a **.list** file in the **/etc/apt/sources.list.d** and will have a one-line style format. For a Personal Package Archives (PPA) APT repository, you would just enter the ppa: entry. Once entered, click the Add button.

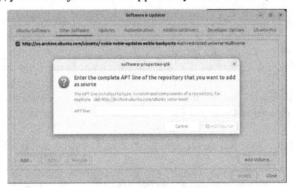

Figure 4-2: Software & Updates - Other Software configuration

The Authentication tab shows the repository software signature keys that are installed on your system (see Figure 4-3). Ubuntu requires a signature key for any package that it installs. Signature keys for all the Ubuntu repositories are installed and are listed on this tab.

Most other third party or customized APT repositories will provide a signature key file for you to download and import. You can add such keys manually from the Authentication tab. Click the "Import Key File" button to open a file browser where you can select the downloaded key file.

This procedure is the same as the **apt-key add** operation. Both add keys that APT then uses to verify DEB software packages downloaded from repositories before it installs them.

Figure 4-3: Software & Updates - Authentication, package signature keys

On the Developer Options tab, you can click the Pre-released software (noble-proposed) option to choose to receive development updates (see Figure 4-4). These are for testing and may introduce instability.

Figure 4-4: Software & Updates - Developer Options

After you have made changes, click the Close button. If you made any repository changes (Ubuntu Software and Other Software tabs) such as adding or disabling a repository, the Software & Updates tool will notify you that your software package information is out of date, displaying a Reload button. Click the Reload button to make the new repositories or components available on your package managers like the App Center and the Synaptic Package Manager. You also can reload your repository configuration by running the **sudo apt update** command or clicking the Reload button on the Synaptic Package Manager.

DEB Software Packages

A Debian package will automatically resolve dependencies, installing any other needed packages instead of simply reporting their absence. Packages are named with the software name, the version number, and the **.deb** extension. Check **https://www.debian.org/doc** for more information. The package filename format is as follows:

the package name

version number

distribution label and build number. Packages created specifically for Ubuntu have the ubuntu label here. Attached to it is the build number, the number of times the package was built for Ubuntu.

architecture The type of system on which the package runs, like i386 for Intel 32-bit x86 systems, or amd64 for both Intel and AMD 64-bit systems, x86_64.

package format. This is always **deb**

For example, the package name for 3dchess is 3dchess, with a version and build number 0.8.1-21, and an amd64 architecture for a 64-bit system.

```
3dchess_0.8.1-21ubuntu1_amd64.deb
```

The following package has an Ubuntu label, a package specifically created for Ubuntu that is not the same as the original Debian version (**dfsg**). In the following example, the version and build number is 2:4.15.5 The architecture is amd64 for a 64-bit system.

```
samba_2:4.15.5+dfsg-0ubuntu5_amd64.deb
```

Managing software with Aptitude

The Aptitude software tool provides a keyboard-based screen interface on command line interfaces for managing software. Because of its easy-to-use screen interface, Aptitude is an effective package management tool for Ubuntu server installs that do not have a desktop.

Check the Ubuntu Server Guide | Package Management | Aptitude for basic operations.

```
https://ubuntu.com/server/docs/package-management
```

A menu bar at the top lets you use your arrow keys to select menus and entries for package management, searching, and views (see Figure 4-5). You use the **Ctrl-t** keys to access the menu, and the arrow keys to move to different menus. To quit aptitude just press the **q** key if only one screen is open. Aptitude can have several screens open at the same time, though only one is shown at a time. The tabs for the screens are listed under the menubar. As you open a new screen, its label will be displayed below the menu. Pressing the **q** key will close the current screen, and, if there is only one screen open, will quit from Aptitude. To move from one tab screen to another, use the F6 and F7 keys. To see a listing of all the key commands, press the **?** key. Several commonly used key commands are listed in Table 4-2.

You start Aptitude by entering the **sudo aptitude** command on the command line. On desktops this open a terminal window.

```
sudo aptitude
```

Key	Description
Ctrl-t	Access menu, the Ctrl-t will toggle between the menu and the main screen. Menu entries will also show equivalent key operations.
Arrow and Page up/down	Move to a selection
ENTER	Expand a category or open a package description
q	Quit the current screen. If only one screen is open, quit Aptitude
+	Mark a package for installation
-	Mark a package for removal
g g	Install and removed marked packages, the first g displays a preview showing what packages will be installed and removed. Pressing g again performs the actual install and remove operations. Press **q** on the preview screen to leave the preview and not perform any install and remove operations.
/	Search for a package, the Find operation
u	Update the package list
U	Mark packages to be updated for updating, use **g g** to perform the actual update.
?	Display the list of key commands
F6 and F7	Move forward and backward between tabs (screens)

Table 4-2: Aptitude key commands

The screen will have two main views, the top one listing packages by category, and the bottom one displaying information about a selected package or category. On the top view, use the arrow keys to move to an entry, and then press the ENTER key to expand an entry. Categories will expand to a package listing, and packages will open a detailed description, along with a listing of dependent packages. Use the + key to mark a package for installation, and the - key to mark an installed package for removal. You can also use the Package menu's Install and Remove entries.

Figure 4-5: Aptitude package manager

Each package entry begins with a letter denoting the package state. Uninstalled packages will be labeled with a **p** indicating a purged package, one not on the system. Installed packages will have the letter **i**. Packages marked for installation or removal will have an additional letter indicating an action yet to be taken. When a package is marked for installation it will have both a **p** and **i** (see Figure 4-6), as shown for the **vsftpd** package entry. Table 4-3 lists the package codes for Aptitude.

Codes	Description
i	Installed package
c	Package not installed, but package configuration remains on system
p	Purged from system
v	Virtual package
B	Broken package
u	Unpacked files, but package not yet configured
C	Half-configured - Configuration failed and requires fix
H	Half-installed - Removal failed and requires fix

Table 4-3: Aptitude package codes

Figure 4-6: Aptitude: selecting packages

Once you have selected packages for installation (or removal), press the **g** key. A preview of the packages to be installed and removed will be listed (see Figure 4-7). Then press the **g** key again. You will have to press **g** twice to install. Aptitude will change to the shell interface, displaying the download, unpack, and setup messages as packages are being installed. You will then be prompted to press return (the ENTER key), to return to the Aptitude interface. To install you could also select the Actions | Install/remove packages menu entry twice.

If you know the package name, you can search for it to locate it more easily. To open a search window, press the / key (or from the menubar (**Ctrl-t**) use the right arrow key to move to the Search menu and select Find). Type in your search and press ENTER. The selected package will be listed and highlighted.

Figure 4-7: Aptitude: installing packages

In Figure 4-7, you will also see that two tabs (screens) are actually open, Packages and Preview. The Preview tab is currently displayed. You can use the F7 and F6 keys to move to the other tab (Packages) and back again. Use the **q** key to close a tab. With the Preview tab open, pressing **q** will quit and close the Preview screen.

Managing software with apt and apt-get

APT is designed to work with repositories, and will handle any dependencies for you. It uses **dpkg** to install and remove individual packages, but can also determine what dependent packages need to be installed, as well as query and download packages from repositories. Several popular tools for APT let you manage your software easily, like the App Center, the Synaptic Package Manager, GNOME Software, and Aptitude. The App Center, the Synaptic Package Manager, and GNOME Software, rely on a desktop interface like GNOME. If you are using the command line interface, you can use **apt** or **apt-get** to manage packages. Using the **apt** or **apt-get** commands on the command line you can install, update, and remove packages. Check the **apt** and **apt-get** man page for a detailed listing of **apt-get** commands (see Table 4-4). The **apt** command is a new version of **apt-get** with fewer options. For example, the **apt-get** command has the **check** option to check for broken dependencies. Older systems may want to continue using **apt-get**, especially if the command is used in customized system scripts. For basic operations, such as upgrading, installing, or removing packages, you would use **apt** instead.

```
apt-get command   package
apt command   package
```

Command	Description
update	Download and resynchronize the package listing of available and updated packages for APT supported repositories. APT repositories updated are those specified in **/etc/apt/sources.list.d/ubuntu.sources**
upgrade	Update packages, install new versions of installed packages if available.
install	Install a specific package, using its package name, not full package filename.
remove	Remove a software package from your system.
source	Download and extract a source code package
check	Check for broken dependencies (**apt-get** command)
clean	Removes the downloaded packages held in the repository cache on your system. Used to free up disk space (**apt-get** command)

Table 4-4: apt-get commands

The **apt** and **apt-get** commands usually take two arguments: the command to perform and the name of the package. Other APT package tools follow the same format. The command is a term such as **install** for installing packages or **remove** to uninstall a package. You only need to specify the software name, not the package's full filename. APT will determine that. To install the MPlayer package you would use:

```
sudo apt install mplayer
```

To make sure that **apt** or **apt-get** has current repository information, use the **update** command.

```
sudo apt update
```

To remove packages, you use the **remove** command.

```
sudo apt remove mplayer
```

The **remove** command alone will not remove any configuration files for that package on your system. To remove both the package and the configuration files, use the **--purge** option with the **remove** command. Should you have already removed the application and want to later remove the configuration files, also use the same **remove** operation with the **--purge** option.

```
sudo apt remove --purge mplayer
```

You can use the **-s** option to check the remove or install first, especially to check whether any dependency problems exist. For remove operations, you can use **-s** to find out first what dependent packages will also be removed.

```
sudo apt-get remove -s mplayer
```

The **apt-get** command can be helpful if your X Windows System server ever fails (your display driver). For example, if you installed a restricted vendor display driver, and then your desktop fails to start, you can start up in the recovery mode, start the root shell, and use **apt-get** to remove the restricted display driver. Your former X open source display drivers would be restored automatically. The following would remove the NVIDIA restricted display driver.

```
sudo apt-get remove nvidia*
```

A complete log of all install, remove, and update operations are kept in the **/var/log/dpkg.log** file. You can consult this file to find out exactly what files were installed or removed.

Configuration for APT is held in the **/etc/apt/sources.list.d** folder. Here the **ubuntu.sources** file lists the distribution repositories from where packages are installed. Source lists for additional third-party repositories are also kept in the **/etc/apt/sources.list.d** folder. GPG (GNU Privacy Guard) database files hold validation keys for those repositories. Specific options for **apt-get** can be found in an **/etc/apt/apt.conf** file or in various files located in the **/etc/apt/apt.conf.d** folder.

Command Line Search and Information: dpkg-query and apt-cache tools

The **dpkg-query** command lets you list detailed information about your packages. It operates on the command line (terminal window). Use **dpkg-query** with the **-l** option to list all your packages.

```
dpkg-query -l
```

The **dpkg** command can operate as a front end for **dpkg-query**, detecting its options to perform the appropriate task. The preceding command could also be run as:

```
dpkg -l
```

Listing a particular package requires and exact match on the package name unless you use pattern matching operators. The following command lists the **samba** package.

```
dpkg-query -l samba
```

A pattern matching operator, such as *, placed after a pattern will display any packages beginning with the specified pattern. The pattern with its operators needs to be placed in single quotation marks to prevent an attempt by the shell to use the pattern to match on filenames in your current directory. The following example finds all packages beginning with the pattern "samba". This would include packages with names such as **samba-client** and **samba-common**.

```
dpkg-query -l 'samba*'
```

You can further refine the results by using **grep** to perform an additional search. The following operation first outputs all packages beginning with **samba**, and from those results, the **grep** operations lists only those with the pattern "common" in their name, such as **samba-common**.

```
dpkg -l 'samba*' | grep 'common'
```

Use the **-L** option to list the files that a package has installed.

```
dpkg-query -L samba
```

To see the status information about a package, including its dependencies and configuration files, use the **-s** option. Fields will include Status, Section, Architecture, Version, Depends (dependent packages), Suggests, Conflicts (conflicting packages), and Conffiles (configuration files).

```
dpkg-query -s samba
```

The status information will also provide suggested dependencies. These are packages not installed, but likely to be used. For the samba package, the **chrony** time server package is suggested.

```
dpkg-query -s  samba | grep Suggests
```

Use the **-S** option to determine to which package a particular file belongs to.

```
dpkg-query -S filename
```

You can also obtain information with the **apt-cache** tool. Use the search command with **apt-cache** to perform a search.

```
apt-cache search samba
```

To find dependencies for a particular package, use the **depends** command.

```
apt-cache depends samba
```

To display the package information, use the **show** command.

```
apt-cache show samba
```

Note: If you have installed Aptitude software manager, you can use the aptitude command with the search and show options to find and display information about packages.

Managing non-repository packages with dpkg

You can use **dpkg** to install a software package you have already downloaded directly, instead of with an APT enabled software tools like **apt-get**, the App Center, or the Synaptic Package Manager. In this case, you are not installing from a repository. Instead, you have manually downloaded the package file from a Web or FTP site to a folder on your system. Such a situation would be rare, reserved for software not available on the Ubuntu repository or any APT enabled repository. Keep in mind that most software is already on your Ubuntu or APT enabled repositories. Check there first for the software package before performing a direct download and installing with **dpkg**. The **dpkg** configuration files are located in the **/etc/dpkg** folder. Configuration is held in the **dpkg.cfg** file. See the **dpkg** man page for a detailed listing of options.

One situation, for which you would use **dpkg**, is for packages you have built yourself, like packages you created when converting a package in another format to a Debian package (DEB). This is the case when converting an RPM package (Red Hat Package Manager) to a Debian package format.

For **dpkg**, you use the **-i** option to install a package and **-r** to remove it.

```
sudo dpkg -i package.deb
```

The major failing for **dpkg** is that it provides no dependency support. It will inform you of needed dependencies, but you will have to install them separately. **dpkg** installs only the specified package. It is useful for packages that have no dependencies.

You use the **-I** option to obtain package information directly from the DEB package file.

```
sudo dpkg -I package.deb
```

To remove a package, you use the **-r** option with the package software name. You do not need version or extension information like **.386** or **.deb**. With **dpkg** when removing a package with dependencies, you first have to remove all its dependencies manually. You will not be able to uninstall the package until you do this. Configuration files are not removed.

```
sudo dpkg -r packagename
```

If you install a package that requires dependencies, and then fail to install these dependencies, your install database will be marked as having broken packages. In this case, APT will not allow new packages to be installed until the broken packages are fixed. You can enter the **apt-get** command with the **-f** and install options to fix all broken packages at once.

```
sudo apt-get -f install
```

Source code files

Though you can install source code files directly, the best way to install one is to use **apt-get**. Use the **source** command with the package name. Packages will be downloaded and extracted.

```
sudo apt-get source alien
```

The **--download** option lets you just download the source package without extracting it. The **--compile** option will download, extract, compile, and package the source code into a Debian binary package, ready for installation.

No dependent packages will be downloaded. If you have a software package that requires any dependent packages to run, you will have to download and compile those also. To obtain needed dependent files, use the **build-dep** option. All your dependent files will be located and downloaded for you automatically.

```
sudo apt-get build-dep alien
```

Installing from source code requires that supporting development libraries and source code header files be installed. You can do this separately for each major development platform like

GNOME, KDE, or the kernel. Alternatively, you can run the APT meta-package **build-essential** for all the Ubuntu development packages. You will have to do this only once.

```
sudo apt-get install build-essential
```

Managing Snap: the snap command

You can simply use the **snap** command to install and manage Snap packages (see Table 4-8). To find a Snap package, use the **snap find** command with the search term (see Figure 4-8).

```
snap find skype
```

```
richard@richard-laptop:~$ snap find
No search term specified. Here are some interesting snaps:

Name              Version    Publisher            Notes    Summary
josm              r18969     mvo○                 -        Editor for OpenStreetMap
vault             1.16.2     canonical✓           -        Vault is a tool for securely accessing secrets.
artikulate        23.08.4    kde✓                 -        Artikulate Pronunciation Trainer
mumble            v1.5.517   snapcrafters○        -        Open Source, Low Latency, High Quality Voice Chat
kolourpaint       23.08.4    kde✓                 -        Paint Program
insomnia          9.1.1      getinsomnia          -        Insomnia
clion             2024.1.1   jetbrains✓           classic  A cross-platform IDE for C and C++
hey-mail          1.2.14     basecamp✓            -        Email at its best, by Basecamp
superproductivity 8.0.5      johannesjo           -        Super Productivity - The advanced ToDo List and Productivity Tool
terminal-parrot   1.1.1      kz6fittycent         -        A Dancing Parrot For Your Terminal
okular            23.08.5    kde✓                 -        Document Viewer
whalebird         6.1.0      h3poteto             -        Whalebird
warzone2100       4.4.2      warzone-2100-project -        Command the forces of The Project in a battle to rebuild the world.
tdhcad            24.04.02   timhirrel            -        Vector Graphics and Charting
minetest          5.8.0      snapcrafters○        -        Open source voxel game engine
helix             24.03      lauren-brock         classic  Helix is a modal text editor inspired by Vim and Kakoune

Provide a search term for more specific results.
richard@richard-laptop:~$ []
```

Figure 4-8: Listing of popular available Snaps: find

You can also search on a search term. The following example searches for FTP clients and servers, and for Web servers.

```
snap find ftp
snap find "web server"
```

Without the search term, a list of popular Snap packages is displayed.

```
snap find
```

Snaps are further organized into sections such as entertainment, games, and productivity. You can see the available sections with the **find --section** command.

```
snap find --section
```

To see available games you would enter the section name preceded by the = sign, as in **--section=games**.

```
snap find --section=games
```

To install a package, use the **snap** command with the **install** option. The following installs the skype Snap package.

```
sudo snap install skype
```

Command	Description
find *pattern*	Search for available snap packages. Without a search term, a list of popular packages is displayed.
find --section	List the available snap package categories (sections)
find --section=*section-name*	List the snap packages in a section
refresh	Manually update packages, installing new revisions of installed packages if available. Snaps are automatically updated every six hours by default.
install *snap-package*	Install a snap package
remove	Remove a snap package completely
revert [*revision-number*]	Revert to a previous installed revision of a snap. Without a revision number the previous installed revision is used.
disable *snap-package*	Disable a snap without uninstalling it. The installed snap remains on your system, but is unavailable to users. Will disable all snap applications installed by the package.
enable *snap-package*	Enable a disabled snap, making it available to users again. Will enable all snap applications installed by the package
list	List your installed snap packages
list --all	List all your snap packages along with the revisions for each package, which will also display the revision number of a revision
list --all *snap-package*	List all the revisions for a snap package, which will also display the revision number for each
connections	List interfaces with their plugs and slots
interface	List available interfaces with a description of each
install channel=*risk-level*	Install a snap package revision from a specified risk-level (**stable**, **candidate**, **beta**, and **edge**)
info *snap-package*	Display detailed information for an installed snap package, including all revisions
connect *plug slot*	Manually connect a snap application (plug) to a system resource (slot)
get	List configuration options for a package you can set if there are any
set	Change configuration options for a package if there are any
unset	Set configuration options to nothing for a package if there are any
run *snap-application*	Run a snap application

Table 4-5: snap commands

Once installed, the Snap applications installed by the package will appear on the Applications overview, just as any other application.

Use the **remove** command to remove a package completely from your system.

```
sudo snap remove skype
```

With Snap, you have the option of disabling a package, instead of removing it completely. The Snap package remains installed, but is unavailable to any users. Use the **disable** command to disable a package. You can enable a disabled package with the **enable** command. Keep in mind that if the package installed has several applications, all those applications are disabled by the **disable** command. The **enable** command will enable all of them.

```
sudo snap disable skype
sudo snap enable skype
```

Use the **refresh** command to update your Snap packages.

```
sudo Snap refresh skype
```

To see a list of Snap packages already installed, use the **list** command (see Figure 4-9). To include all installed versions of the different packages, add the **--all** option.

```
snap list
snap list --all
```

Figure 4-9: Listing of installed snaps: list

To display detailed information about a particular Snap package, you use the **info** command.

```
snap info skype
```

Snap applications are stored as revisions in the **/snap** folder under the package name. Each revision has its own folder, which includes the application executables, as well as all configuration and system support files. In effect, each revision of a Snap application has its own **/etc**, **/usr**, **/bin**, **/lib**, and **/var** folder. A link to the application program currently enabled is held in the **/snap/bin** folder. User data for a Snap application is held in a **snap** folder in your home folder. Systemd support for Snap is provided by the systemd **snapd.service** and **snapd.socket** files.

Should you want to create a Snap package, you can use **snapcraft**, which you can install with the App Center or the **snap install --classic** command.

Snap Channels: tracks and risk levels

Snap packages are managed by channels which organize a package into tracks and risk levels. Developers may also add a branch category for short-term versions of an applications. You will see track and risk-levels listed as possible channel selections in the App Center for a Snap package.

```
track/risk-level
```

The track indicates the revision of a package installed. By default this is **latest**. The risk level indicates the reliability of the software. There are four risk levels: **stable**, **candidate**, **beta**, and **edge**. The **stable** risk level is for reliable software considered ready for mass distribution. The **candidate** risk level is for a version of the application being readied for release but still being tested. The **beta** risk level is for beta versions of applications that may incorporate new features but is considered unstable. The **edge** risk level is for versions that are still under development with ongoing changes that may not always run.

Packages are installed with the latest risk level by default.

```
snap install
```

Should you want to use a different risk level, you can specify it with the appropriate risk level track: **--stable**, **--candidate**, **--beta**, and **--edge**. You can also use the **--channel** option.

```
snap install --candidate
snap install --channel=candidate
```

You can later change the risk level tracked using the **switch** command. This only changes the tracking. It does not install the version for that track. To do that you would have to run the **refresh** command.

```
snap switch --candidate
```

To both perform a switch to a different track and install the version of the applications from that track, you can run the **refresh** command directly.

```
snap refresh --channel=candidate
```

Snap Confinement

Most Snap packages are run using a strict confinement mode, running in isolation with only minimal access to system resources such as networks, system folders, and processes. Some Snap packages are allowed to run in the classic mode, if officially approved, letting them access system resources just as a traditional DEB package can. These packages can only be installed with the **--classic** option. For a package to obtain classic status, it must be carefully examined by Snapcraft for security and stability issues. There is also a **devmode** reserved for developers. To see the confinement mode for a package use the **snap info** command with the **--verbose** option. The **snap list** command, which lists all your Snap packages, will also display each package's confinement mode.

```
snap info --verbose inkscape
```

Access to system resources by a package is setup up by interfaces, which are determined by the developer and implemented when the package is installed. Interfaces usually allow access to resources such as devices. This often includes your home folder, network access, system files, and the display server (Wayland or X11). A Snap package can only access your system through these interfaces. Interfaces consist of plugs and slots. The plug is the package or process that needs the interface (the consumer), and the plug is the service that supports it (the provider). The **snap connections** command will list the interfaces for a package.

```
snap connections inkscape
```

The **snap connections** command with no package as an argument, will list all the packages (plugs) along with the interfaces and slots they use.

```
snap connections
```

A sample of the list is shown here.

Interface	Plug	Slot	Notes
appstream-metadata	snap-store:appstream-metadata	:appstream-metadata	-
audio-playback	chromium:audio-playback	:audio-playback	-
audio-record	chromium:audio-record	:audio-record	-
avahi-observe	firefox:avahi-observe	:avahi-observe	-
browser-support	chromium:browser-sandbox	:browser-support	-
browser-support	firefox:browser-sandbox	:browser-support	-
camera	chromium:camera	:camera	-
camera	firefox:camera	:camera	-
gsettings	chromium:gsettings	:gsettings	-
gsettings	firefox:gsettings	:gsettings	-
gsettings	inkscape:gsettings	:gsettings	-
gsettings	snap-store:gsettings	:gsettings	-
home	chromium:home	:home	-
home	firefox:home	:home	-
home	gwenview:home	:home	-
home	inkscape:home	:home	-
network	chromium:network	:network	-
network	firefox:network	:network	-
network	gwenview:network	:network	-
network	snap-store:network	:network	-
opengl	chromium:opengl	:opengl	-
opengl	firefox:opengl	:opengl	-
opengl	gwenview:opengl	:opengl	-
wayland	firefox:wayland	:wayland	-
wayland	inkscape:wayland	:wayland	-
wayland	snap-store:wayland	:wayland	-
x11	chromium:x11	:x11	-
x11	firefox:x11	:x11	-
x11	gwenview:x11	:x11	-
x11	inkscape:x11	:x11	-
x11	snap-store:x11	:x11	-

The **snap interface** command lists all your interfaces on your system with a description of each.

```
snap interface
```

A sample of the interface list is shown here.

```
Name                      Summary
appstream-metadata        allows access to AppStream metadata
audio-playback            allows audio playback via supporting services
audio-record              allows audio recording via supporting services
avahi-control             allows control over service discovery on a local network
via the mDNS/DNS-SD protocol suite
avahi-observe             allows discovery on a local network via the mDNS/DNS-SD
protocol suite
bluez                     allows operating as the bluez service
browser-support           allows access to various APIs needed by modern web
browsers
camera                    allows access to all cameras
content                   allows sharing code and data with other snaps
cups                      allows access to the CUPS socket for printing
cups-control              allows access to the CUPS control socket
desktop                   allows access to basic graphical desktop resources
desktop-launch            allows snaps to identify and launch desktop applications
in (or from) other snaps
desktop-legacy            allows privileged access to desktop legacy methods
fwupd                     allows operating as the fwupd service
gsettings                 allows access to any gsettings item of current user
hardware-observe          allows reading information about system hardware
home                      allows access to non-hidden files in the home directory
joystick                  allows access to joystick devices
login-session-observe     allows reading login and session information
mount-control             allows creating transient and persistent mounts
mount-observe             allows reading mount table and quota information
network                   allows access to the network
network-bind              allows operating as a network service
network-manager-observe   allows observing NetworkManager settings
network-status            allows access to network connectivity status
opengl                    allows access to OpenGL stack
optical-drive             allows access to optical drives
packagekit-control        allows control of the PackageKit service
personal-files            allows access to personal files or directories
pulseaudio                allows operating as or interacting with the pulseaudio
service
raw-usb                   allows raw access to all USB devices
removable-media           allows access to mounted removable storage
screen-inhibit-control    allows inhibiting the screen saver
shutdown                  allows shutting down or rebooting the system
snap-themes-control       allows use of snapd's theme installation API
snapd-control             allows communicating with snapd
system-files              allows access to system files or directories
system-packages-doc       allows access to documentation of system packages
u2f-devices               allows access to u2f devices
udisks2                   allows operating as or interacting with the UDisks2
service
unity7                    allows interacting with Unity 7 services
upower-observe            allows operating as or reading from the UPower service
wayland                   allows access to compositors supporting wayland protocol
x11                       allows interacting with or running as an X11 server
```

To see the slots and plugs used for an interface, use the **snap interface** command with the name of that interface. The following command lists all the plugs and slots for the network interface.

```
richard@richard-laptop:~$ snap interface network
name:    network
summary: allows access to the network
plugs:
  - chromium
  - digikam
  - gimp
  - firefox
  - gwenview
  - snap-store
slots:
  - snapd
```

You can use the **connect** and **disconnect** commands to manually connect or disconnect an interface for a package. They take as their arguments the plug and slot, with the plug preceded by the package name and a colon. As noted, interfaces for packages are normally set up for you and activated when a package is installed. The following connects the Gwenview image manager to your home folder.

```
sudo snap connect gwenview:home :home
```

Not all interfaces available to an application may be activated when you install it. You can also turn activated interfaces off, denying access for that package to the resource. On the

On the desktop, the Settings Apps tab, lets you easily manage the interfaces for an application by selecting the application in the Apps application's tab. The Permission section lists the permission supported by the application, with switches for each one to turn them on or off. For some permissions there will be a menu instead of a switch to allow you to choose an option. In Figure 4-10, the GIMP application is not allowed to read and write to removeable media, whereas it is allowed access to your network and home folder, as well as to print documents and to run in the background.

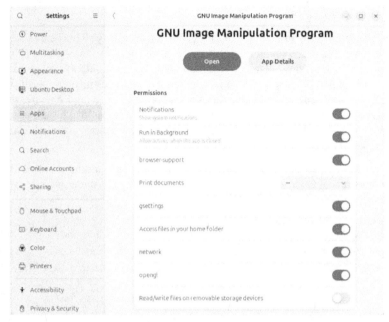

Figure 4-10: Snap application permissions - Settings

You can also check the connections (permissions) allowed using the connections command with the package name, showing the slots and plugs for that package. The following show the GIMP (**gimp**) interfaces. The plug for removable media has no slot, showing that it is disconnected. This permission is turned off.

```
richard@richard-laptop:~$ snap connections gimp
Interface                Plug                     Slot                            Notes
browser-support          gimp:browser-support     :browser-support                -
content[gnome-3-38-2004] gimp:gnome-3-38-2004     gnome-3-38-2004:gnome-3-38-2004 -
content[gtk-2-engines]   gimp:gtk-2-engines       gtk2-common-themes:gtk-2-engines -
content[gtk-3-themes]    gimp:gtk-3-themes        gtk-common-themes:gtk-3-themes  -
content[icon-themes]     gimp:icon-themes         gtk-common-themes:icon-themes   -
content[sound-themes]    gimp:sound-themes        gtk-common-themes:sound-themes  -
cups-control             gimp:cups-control        -                               -
dbus                     -                        gimp:dbus-gimp                  -
desktop                  gimp:desktop             :desktop                        -
desktop-legacy           gimp:desktop-legacy      :desktop-legacy                 -
gsettings                gimp:gsettings           :gsettings                      -
home                     gimp:home                :home                           -
network                  gimp:network             :network                        -
opengl                   gimp:opengl              :opengl                         -
removable-media          gimp:removable-media     -                               -
unity7                   gimp:unity7              :unity7                         -
wayland                  gimp:wayland             :wayland                        -
x11                      gimp:x11                 :x11                            -
```

If your application is not listed in the Settings Apps tab, you can manually set the permission using the **connect** and **disconnect** commands. Use the **snap connect** command to turn on a permission, and the **snap disconnect** command turn it off.

```
snap connect gimp:removable-media  :removable-media
```

Snap Revisions: revert

Snaps are installed as revisions. For any given application, you may have several revisions of an application installed. Each revision is able to run as the application. Priority is given to the current revision, the most recently installed. But you could easily decide to run a previous revision instead. This could happen if a new revision is installed that becomes unstable, or if the changes made to the software have deprecated capabilities you normally use. Major changes to an application are released as a version, which is also considered a revision. Though you could have several revisions for a given version, for most less complex applications you will usually have just the one revision per version.

Whereas a **list** command will display your installed snaps, adding the **--all** option will also display all the revisions of each snap. This operation will display the name, version, revision, tracking, publisher, and notes for each revision.

```
richard@richard-laptop:~$ snap list --all
Name            Version          Rev   Tracking        Publisher   Notes
chromium        81.0.4044.129    1135  latest/stable   canonical✓  disabled
chromium        81.0.4044.138    1143  latest/stable   canonical✓  -
digikam         6.4.0            6     latest/beta     sergiusens  -
dragon          19.04.2          27    latest/stable   kde✓        -
firefox         76.0.1-1         359   latest/stable   mozilla✓    -
gwenview        24.04.0          48    latest/stable   kde✓        -
sensors-unity   18.02            202   latest/stable   paroj       -
skype           8.59.0.77        123   latest/stable   skype✓      disabled,classic
skype           8.60.0.76        128   latest/stable   skype✓      classic
snap-store      3.36.0-80-g208fd61 454 latest/stable/… canonical✓  -
snap-store      3.36.0-74-ga164ec9 433 latest/stable/… canonical✓  disabled
snapd           2.44.3           7264  latest/stable   canonical✓  snapd
spectacle       19.04.3          25    latest/stable   kde✓        -
```

Instead of listing all the snaps, you could just list the revisions for a particular snap.

```
richard@richard-laptop:~$ snap list --all skype
Name   Version    Rev  Tracking      Publisher   Notes
skype  8.59.0.77  123  latest/stable  skype✓     disabled,classic
skype  8.60.0.76  128  latest/stable  skype✓     classic
```

The revision number is unique. You could have several revisions with the same version number, but the revision number is the unique identifier for that install. Previous revision can be run using their revision number.

Only one revision of an application can be enabled. This is the one that Snap will run. All other revision of that application are disabled, as shown in the Notes field of the **list --all** output.

You can enable a previous revision, disabling the current one, and thereby letting Snap run it. You do this with the **revert** command and the number of the revision you want to enable. The following example reverts GIMP (**gimp**) to revision 428.

```
sudo snap revert gimp 428
```

If you just want to enable the previous revision, you can leave out the number.

```
sudo snap revert gimp
```

If you decide, after reverting to a previous revision, that you want to return to using the latest revision, run the **revert** command with the revision number of the latest revision.

```
sudo snap revert skype 428
```

You could also just run the **refresh** command on that snap. The latest revision is automatically enabled.

```
sudo snap refresh gimp
```

Keep in mind, that if a new update of a snap is later released, the automatic **refresh** operation, will update the snap to that new revision.

Snap Package Configuration

Some Snap package, such as those for services, may have configuration options you can manage using the **snap get**, **snap set**, and **snap unset** commands. The **snap get** command list configuration options for a snap and their current setting. The **snap set** command can change an option, and the **snap unset** command removes a value. Some Snap packages, such as servers, have options that can be set when the application is started. Each revision will have a configuration that will be applied when that revision is run. Using the **revert** command you could change from using one revision of a server to another, each running separate configurations.

In addition, all snap applications have supporting environment variables. Environment variables will show folders that the snap can access, as well as application information such as the revision and version number. You can see the environment variable for an application by first starting that application's shell with the **run --shell** command.

```
sudo snap run --shell skype
```

Keep in mind that sometimes the package name may not be the same as the application name. A package could install several applications, as is the case with the nextcloud package. To access the Nextcloud web server you would use its application name, **nextcloud.apache**.

```
sudo snap run --shell nextcloud.apache
```

You can then use the shell **env** command to list your environment variables, filtering the output with **grep** and the SNAP pattern to show just the snap related ones.

```
env | grep SNAP
```

The environment variables for the current enabled revision is listed. The folder variables will show the folder of that revision. The SNAP_COMMON and SNAP_USER_DATA variables show the location of the folders that your application can write to.

To leave the shell enter the **exit** command.

Snap and systemd

Snap is managed by the **snapd** daemon, which runs several services. The service files for these are located in the **/lib/systemd/system** folder. Applications installed by a Snap package have access to the application configured by **systemd** using **.mount** files located in the **/etc/systemd/system** folder. The mount file will begin with the term **snap** and have the application name and its revision number. Each revision will have a separate mount file. The mount file for Skype revision 128 is **snap-skype-128.mount**.

/etc/systemd/system/snap-skype-128.mount

```
[Unit]
Description=Mount unit for skype, revision 128
Before=snapd.service

[Mount]
What=/var/lib/snapd/snaps/skype_128.snap
Where=/snap/skype/128
Type=squashfs
Options=nodev,ro,x-gdu.hide
LazyUnmount=yes

[Install]
WantedBy=multi-user.target
```

The file shows the revision number and the location of the revision.

```
Where=/snap/skype/128
```

Snap and Services

Services installed as Snap packages can be managed by **systemctl** commands such as **systemctl start** and **systemctl stop** to start and stop a service. In addition, some Snap packaged services will also provide configuration options you can manage using the snap **get**, **set**, and **unset** commands. There are few services currently available as Snap packages. For most services like the FTP and Web servers, you would still use APT.

Services installed as Snap packages have their systemd service files installed in the **/etc/systemd/system** folder, not in **/lib/systemd/system** as APT services are. All snap installed services are managed through the **snapd** server. The **snapd** server, in turn, has service files for **snapd** in the **/lib/system/system** folder. Furthermore, all the snap installed services have their service files begin with the term **snap**, as in **snap.nextcloud.apache.service** for the Nextcloud web server (part of the **nextcloud** Snap package). You can then use **systemctl** commands to manage the service.

```
systemctl status snap.nextcloud.apache
sudo system restart snap.nextcloud.apache
```

The format of the service file is much the same as other systemd service files, except that execution operation are run by the **snap run** command. The service also requires supporting snap systemd operations such as the **snap-nextcloud** mount and **snapd.apparmor.service**.

/etc/systemd/system/snap.nextcloud.apache.service

```
[Unit]
# Auto-generated, DO NOT EDIT
Description=Service for snap application nextcloud.apache
Requires=snap-nextcloud-20498.mount
Wants=network.target
After=snap-nextcloud-20498.mount network.target snapd.apparmor.service
X-Snappy=yes

[Service]
EnvironmentFile=-/etc/environment
ExecStart=/usr/bin/snap run nextcloud.apache
SyslogIdentifier=nextcloud.apache
Restart=always
WorkingDirectory=/var/snap/nextcloud/20498
ExecStop=/usr/bin/snap run --command=stop nextcloud.apache
TimeoutStopSec=30
Type=simple

[Install]
WantedBy=multi-user.target
```

Flatpak

Flatpak is an open source alternative to Snap. A Flatpak package installs its own set of supporting libraries that can be kept up to date without affecting those on your system, much like Snap does. In effect, Flatpak packages run inside their own environment, separate from your system. These include popular applications such as VLC, Spotify, Bookworm, Krita, Steam, and Blender. These applications are downloaded from the Flathub repository. Some applications, such as Bookworm, are only available as Flatpak packages.

You install the **flatpak** package with the **sudo apt install** command or from the Synaptic Package Manager.

```
sudo apt install flatpak
```

With the GNOME Software Flatpak plugin (**gnome-software-plugin-flatpak**), you can also manage Flatpak packages. You will have to install the plugin. You can install the plugin from the GNOME Software page on Software, or from a terminal window with a shell command. From a terminal window use the following.

```
sudo apt install gnome-software-plugin-flatpak
```

You will also have to add the **flathub** repository.

```
flatpak remote-add flathub https://dl.flathub.org/repo/flathub.flatpakrepo
```

Restart your system to load the repository.

Installing Software from Compressed Archives: .tar.gz

Linux software applications in the form of source code are available at different sites on the Internet. You can download any of this software and install it on your system. Recent releases are often available in the form of compressed archive files. Applications will always be downloadable as compressed archives if they do not have a DEB (Ubuntu) version.

Decompressing and Extracting Software

Before you unpack the archive, move it to the directory where you want it. When source code files are unpacked, they generate their own subdirectories from which you can compile and install the software. Once the package is installed, you can delete this directory, keeping the original source code package file (**.tar.gz**). For example, the file **antigrav_0.0.3.orig.tar** unpacks to a subdirectory called **antigrav_0.0.3.orig**. In certain cases, the software package that contains precompiled binaries is designed to unpack directly into the system subdirectory where it will be used.

Though you can decompress and extract software in separate operations, you will find that the more common approach is to perform both actions with a single command. The **tar** utility provides decompression options you can use to have **tar** first decompress a file for you, invoking the specified decompression utility. The **z** option automatically invokes **gunzip** to unpack a **.gz** file, and the **j** option unpacks a **.bz2** file. Use the **Z** option for **.Z** files. For example, to combine the decompressing and unpacking operation for a **tar.gz** file into one **tar** command, insert a **z** option to the option list, **xzvf**. The next example shows how you can combine decompression and extraction in one step.

```
tar xvzf antigrav_0.0.3.orig.tar.gz
```

For a **.bz2**-compressed archive, you use the **j** option instead of the **z** option.

```
tar xvjf antigrav_0.0.3.orig.tar.bz2
```

Files ending with **.bin** are self-extracting archives. Run the bin file as if it were a command. You may have to use **chmod** to make it executable. Then enter the file as a command on a command line, with **./** attached to the beginning of the filename.

```
sudo chmod 755 package
```

The extraction process creates a subdirectory consisting of the name and release of the software. In the preceding example, the extraction created a subdirectory called **antigrav_0.0.3.orig**. You can change to this subdirectory and examine its files, such as the **README** and **INSTALL** files.

```
cd antigrav_0.0.3.orig
```

Installation of your software may differ for each package. Instructions are usually provided along with an installation program. Be sure to consult the **README** and **INSTALL** files, if included.

Compiling Software

Some software may be in the form of source code that you need to compile before you can install it. This is particularly true of programs designed for cross-platform implementations. Programs designed to run on various Linux and UNIX systems may be distributed as source code that is downloaded and compiled in those different systems. Compiling such software has been greatly simplified in recent years by the use of configuration scripts that automatically detect a given system's hardware and software configuration and then allow you to compile the program accordingly. For example, the name of the C compiler on a system could be **gcc** or **cc**. Configuration scripts detect which is present and select it for use in the program compilation.

Note: Some software will run using scripting languages like Python, instead of programming language code like C++. These may require only a setup operation (a setup command), not compiling. Once installed, they will run directly using the scripting language interpreter, like Python.

A configure script works by generating a customized Makefile, designed for that particular system. A Makefile contains detailed commands to compile a program, including any preprocessing, links to required libraries, and the compilation of program components in their proper order. Many Makefiles for complex applications may have to access several software subdirectories, each with separate components to compile. The use of configure and Makefile scripts automates the compile process, reducing the procedure to a few simple steps.

First, change to the directory where the software's source code has been extracted, as shown in this example:

```
# cd /usr/local/src/antigrav_0.0.3.orig
```

Before you compile software, read the **README** or **INSTALL** files included with it. These give you detailed instructions on how to compile and install this particular program.

Most software can be compiled and installed in three simple steps. Their first step is the **./configure** command, which generates your customized Makefile. The second step is the **make** command, which uses a Makefile in your working directory (in this case, the Makefile you just generated with the **./configure** command) to compile your software. The final step also uses the **make** command, but this time with the **install** option. The Makefile generated by the **./configure** command also may contain instructions for installing the software on your system. Using the **install** option runs just those installation commands. To perform the installation, you have to be logged in as an administrative user, giving you the ability to add software files to system directories as needed. If the software uses configuration scripts, compiling and installing usually involves only the following three commands.

```
./configure
make
make install
```

In the preceding example, the **./configure** command performs configuration detection. The **make** command performs the actual compiling, using a Makefile script generated by the **./configure** operation. The **make install** command installs the program on your system, placing the executable program in a directory, such as **/usr/local/bin**, and any configuration files in **/etc**. Any shared libraries it created may go into **/usr/local/lib**.

Once you have compiled and installed your application, and you have checked that it is working properly, you can remove the source code directory that was created when you extracted the software. You can keep the archive file (**tar**) in case you need to extract the software again. Use **rm** with the **-rf** options so that all subdirectories will be deleted, and you do not have to confirm each deletion.

Tip: Be sure to remember to place the period and slash before the **configure** command. The ./ references a command in the current working directory, rather than another Linux command with the same name.

Certain software may have specific options set up for the ./**configure** operation. To find out what these are, you use the ./**configure** command with the **--help** option:

```
./configure --help
```

A useful common option is the **-prefix** option, which lets you specify the install directory:

```
./configure -prefix=/usr/bin
```

Note: If you are compiling an X, GNOME, or KDE-based program, be sure their development libraries have been installed.

Checking Software Package Digital Signatures

One effective use for digital signatures is to verify that a software package has not been tampered with. A software package could be intercepted in transmission and some of its system-level files changed or substituted. Software packages from your distribution, as well as those by reputable GNU and Linux projects, are digitally signed. The signature provides modification digest information with which to check the integrity of the package. The digital signature may be included with the package file or posted as a separate file. To import a key that APT can use to check a software package, you use the **apt-key** command. APT will automatically check for digital signatures. To check the digital signature of a software package file that is not part of the APT repository system, you use the **gpg** command with the **--verify** option. These would include packages like those made available as compressed archives, **.tar.gz**, whereas APT can check all DEB packages itself.

Importing Software Public keys with apt-key

First, however, you will need to make sure that you have the signer's public key. The digital signature was encrypted with the software distributor's private key. That distributor is the signer. Once you have that signer's public key, you can check any data you receive from them. In the case of third-party software repositories, you have to install their public key. Once the key is installed, you do not have to install it again.

Ubuntu includes and installs its public keys with its distribution. For any packages on the Ubuntu repositories, the needed public keys are already installed and checked by APT automatically. With other sites, you may need to download the public key from their site and install it. You may also have to add repository support to access their Ubuntu compatible software. Once downloaded, you can then use the **apt-key** command to install the public key for use by APT in software verification. Ubuntu uses the **apt-key** command to maintain public keys for software packages. Use the **apt-key** command with the **add** option to add the key. To actually access the software repository you would have to also install its APT configuration file in the **/etc/apt/sources.list.d** directory.

Checking Software Compressed Archives

Many software packages in the form of compressed archives, **.tar.gz** or **tar.bz2**, will provide signatures in separate files that end with the **.sig** extension. To check these, you use the **gpg** command with the **--verify** option. For example, the most recent Sendmail package is distributed in the form of a compressed archive, **.tar.gz**. Its digital signature is provided in a separate **.sig** file. First, you download and install the public key for Sendmail software obtained from the Sendmail website (the key may have the year as part of its name). Sendmail has combined all its keys into one armored text file, **PGPKEYS**.

```
gpg --import PGPKEYS
```

You can also use the **gpg** command with the **--search-key** and **--keyserver** options to import the key. Keys matching the search term will be displayed in a numbered list. You will be prompted to enter the number of the key you want. The 2020 Sendmail key from the results from the following example would be 1. This is the key used for 2020 released software.

```
gpg  --keyserver pool.sks-keyserver.net  --search-keys Sendmail
```

On a desktop, instead of using **gpg**, you could use Passwords and Keys application (Seahorse) to find and import the key (Passwords and Keys).

To check a software archive, a **tar.gz**, file, you need to also download its digital signature files. For the compressed archive (**.tar.gz**) you can use the **.sig** file ending in **.gz.sig**, and for the uncompressed archive use **.tar.sig**. Then, with the **gpg** command and the **--verify** option, use the digital signature in the **.sig** file to check the authenticity and integrity of the software compressed archive.

```
$ gpg --verify sendmail.8.15.2.tar.gz.sig sendmail.8.15.2.tar.gz
gpg: Signature made Wed 31 Oct 2020 08:23:07 PM PDT using RSA key ID 7093B841
gpg: Good signature from "Sendmail Signing Key/2020 <sendmail@Sendmail.ORG>"$
```

You can also specify just the signature file, and **gpg** will automatically search for and select a file of the same name, but without the **.sig** or **.asc** extension.

```
gpg --verify sendmail.8.15.2.tar.gz.sig
```

In the future, when you download any software from the Sendmail site that uses this key, you just have to perform the **--verify** operation. Bear in mind, though, that different software packages from the same site may use different keys. You will have to make sure that you have imported and signed the appropriate key for the software you are checking.

Tip: You can use the **--fingerprint** option to check a key's validity if you wish. If you are confident that the key is valid, you can then sign it with the **--sign-key** command.

Managing Software on the Ubuntu Desktop

If you have installed the Ubuntu desktop (either from the Server install or directly from a Desktop USB/DVD), you can use desktop-based software management tools for installing, updating, and removing software.

APT Software Management on the Desktop

The App Center software manager is a modified version of the snap-store application, and gives priority to Snap packages. It will, though, also display and manage a corresponding APT/DEB version of an application, should there be one. For example, there are both APT and Snap packages for the Inkscape. Should you install both the Snap and APT versions of Inkscape, you will then have two versions of Inkscape on your system. The Synaptic Package Manager only manages the APT versions of software applications.

Should you want to also use the GNOME Software manager instead of the App Center, you can install it as GNOME Software. This standard version of GNOME Software manages APT supported packages. The GNOME Software snap plugin lets it also manage Snap packages (**gnome-software-plugin-snap**). Should you also want to use Flatpak on GNOME Software, there is also a GNOME Software Flatpak plugin (**gnome-software-plugin-flatpak**).

The App Center

To perform simple installation and removal of software, you can use the App Center, which is the primary supported package manager for Ubuntu (see Figure 4-11). The App Center is modified to use the **snap-store** application, which manages Snap packages. The App Center is designed to be the centralized utility for managing your software. The App Center performs a variety of different software tasks, including installation, removal, updating of software.

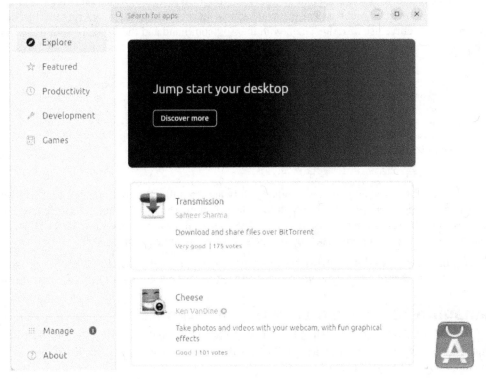

Figure 4-11: App Center

To use the App Center, click the App Center icon on the dock or on the Applications overview. A window opens with a search bar in the header bar and several tab headings in a sidebar. The tabs are Explore, Featured, Productivity, Development, and Games, and, at the bottom, Manage and About.

The Explore tab has sections for the desktop, featured Snap applications, games, developer applications, productivity. Some of these have links to corresponding App Center tabs, such as Feature, Productivity, and Development. All will also list a few popular applications, which you can click on to install directly. Midway through the tab, after games and before developers, there is a Categories section with links to different software categories, such as Art and Design, Music and Audio, Science, Social, and Photo and Video (see Figure 4-12). Click on a link to open a tab listing software in that category.

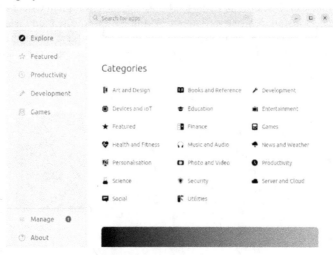

Figure 4-12: App Center Categories

Categories will allow you to further filter the selection a Sort menu, which lets you sort items by name, relevance, or size (Figure 4-13). The applications are listed as icons, which show the application's icon, name, full name, short description, and rating. Packages already installed have a checkmark displayed next to the application's name, just above the description.

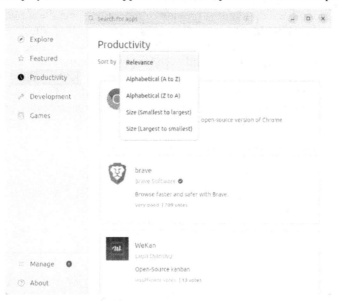

Figure 4-13: App Center category with Sort menu

To search for a package, in the search box on the header bar, enter part of the name or a term to describe the package (see Figure 4-14). Best results are listed in a menu, showing an icon and name for each applications. Applications are organized into a "Snap packages" section and a "Debian packages" section. Click on an entry to open its description page where you can perform possible actions such as install, remove, or launch. At the bottom of the menu is a "See all results for" link that will open a tab listing all the applications that match the search pattern. On that tab you can use menus to sort the packages, select either Snap or Debian packages, and choose packages from just a specific category.

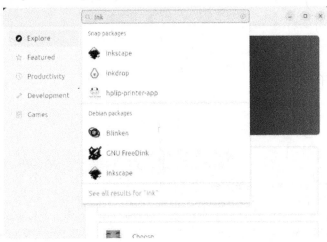

Figure 4-14: App Center, using the search box

The application's description page provides information about the application such as its rating size, version, and date published, as well as links to its related websites (see Figure 4-15). Snap applications show a Channel menu from which you can choose the Snap channel to install the application from such as stable, candidate, and edge (see Figure 4-16). The stable channel is selected by default. Uninstalled software displays an Install button to the right of the Channel menu. Further down the tab is a Gallery section showing a slideshow of images of the application. Below the Gallery is the Description section with a detailed description of the application.

Figure 4-15: App Center, software descriptor page

Figure 4-16: App Center, Snap package channels

Click the Install button to install the software. You are first asked to enter your password. As the software is installed, an Installing progress circle appears (see Figure 4-17). When complete, an Open button is displayed to the right, with an ellipses button below it. To later remove the application, if you wish, click on this button to display an Uninstall button, which you can click to uninstall the software (see Figure 4-18). Below the ellipses button are thumbs up and down button you can use to rate the application.

Figure 4-17: App Center, installing applications

Figure 4-18: App Center, removing applications

The Manage tab lists your installed applications (see Figure 4-19). Those that have to be updated are listed in the "Updates available" section. You can update individual applications (Update button), or click the "Update all" button to update all of them at once. To check for updates, click the "Check for updates" button. An ellipses menu to the right of the Update button display entries for Open and "Show details".

The "Installed and updated" section lists all your installed Snap applications, other than those that need updating. In the search box you can enter patterns to search for applications. You can also search by name (alphabetically), size, and the recency of the last update. A checkbox lets you display Snap system applications, such as the gtk themes or the snapd server.

The application entries show the name, version installed, when last updated, and the size. You can use an Open button to the right to open the application. The ellipses menu displays a menu with a "Show details" entry you can click to open the application's description page.

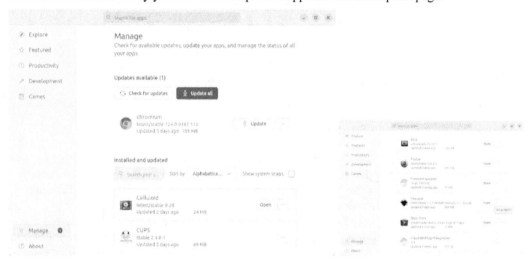

Figure 4-19: App Center, Manage tab

App Center for Snap packages

The App Center has a Snap backend that integrates Snap packages and allows you to install and remove them. The Synaptic Package Manager and the **apt** command do not support Snap packages. GNOME Software can support Snap packages, if you install its Snap plugin. The easiest way to find and install Snap packages is to use the App Center, which is modified to use the snap-store application (see Figure 4-20). A Channel button is shown on the App Center that lists various Snap tracks with their risk levels. the App Center supports packages both from the Snap Store (**snapcraft.io**) and APT repositories. Many packages, such as those part of the GNOME desktop like Text Editor, will the APT repositories. However, there could be corresponding Snap and Deb packages, as is the case with Inkscape. Should you install the Inkscape Snap package you are installing from the Snap Store (**snapcraft.io**), whereas if you install the Inkscape DEB package you are installing a separate application from the APT Universe repository.

Though installed with the ubuntu-desktop meta-package, the App Center is not installed with the ubuntu-desktop-minimal package. You would have to manually install it. The software name of the App Center is snap-store. You can install it with a **snap install** command.

```
sudo snap install snap-store
```

Figure 4-20: App Center - Snap Package

On the App Center, when you display the application page for a Snap package, a Channels menu is displayed on the left side below the application name. Clicking this menu lets you choose from the available versions for this Snap package on different channels, usually stable, beta, and edge (see Figure 4-21). Each version will list the URL, channel, and version. The URL is **snapcraft.io** for the Ubuntu Snap Store. The channel will list the track and risk level, usually **latest/stable** or **latest/beta**. The version shows the version of the software package. The **stable** and **candidate** risk levels usually have the same version, where the **beta** risk level will be different. Some applications will have tracks for special releases, such as the **esr/stable** channel for Firefox's Extended Support Release (**esr**).

Figure 4-21: App Center - Snap Tracks and Risk Levels

App Center for APT (Debian) packages

Though the App Center gives priority to Snap packages, you can also use it to also manage APT packages (see Figure 4-22). APT packages are referred to in the App Center as Debian packages. The categories with which you can browse the App Center, will only display Snap packages. To find and display APT packages, you have to perform a search. The menu of initial results will show a Snap and Debian section showing commonly installed packages. If the packages are only available as Debian packages only the Debian section is shown, and if the packages are only available as Snap packages, only the Snap section is shown. By clicking on the "See all results for" entry at the bottom of the menu, you open a results tab in which you can choose to see Snap or Debian packages. Use the "Filter by" menu to select "Snap packages" or "Debian packages".

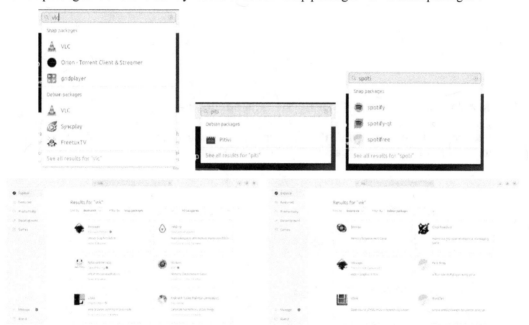

Figure 4-22: App Center, APT (DEB) package

The application page for an APT managed package will display an Install or Uninstall button (see Figure 4-23). It will list the package version, as well as a Gallery of images and a Description. There is no menu.

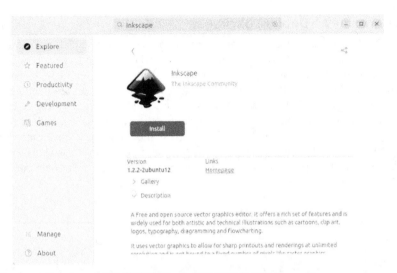

Figure 4-23: App Center, APT (DEB) package application page

If an application has both APT and Snap versions available, and you install both, you can run either of them from the Applications Overview (see Figure 4-24).

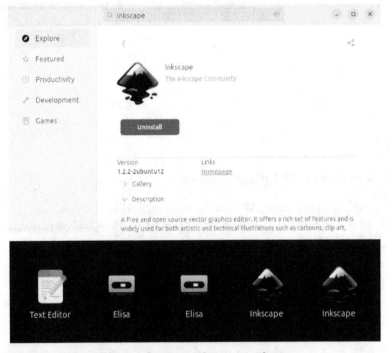

Figure 4-24: App Center, APT and Snap package versions

GNOME Software

You can install the original GNOME Software application using the App Center as a Debian package named Software, or with the Synaptic Package Manager, or the **sudo apt install** command. The name of the GNOME Software package is **gnome-software**.

```
sudo apt install gnome-software
```

Once installed, you can use it to manage Apt packages, and, if you have installed support for it, Flathub packages. The icon for it is labeled Software on the applications overview (see Figure 4-25). GNOME Software also has GNOME Other Categories section for GNOME addons, organized into three categories on the main page: codecs, fonts, and input sources (see Figure 4-26). Categories have a fully functional Show menu with a complete listing of sub-categories.

The GNOME Software Snap plugin is already installed and allows GNOME Software to manage Snap packages. Like the App Center (snap-store), for Snap packages it will display a menu on the right side of the titlebar of snap channels to install. On GNOME Software the menu item for a Snap package is labeled SNAP, whereas the menu item for a Debian package is labeled DEB. In addition, a menu item will indicate whether the package is from the Ubuntu managed repositories, or from another service such as Flathub. A menu item from the Flathub service is labeled FLATPAK.

Figure 4-25: GNOME Software

Figure 4-26: GNOME Software Addons for codecs

For Flatpak packages, GNOME Software will list the **dl.flathub.org** site as the source on the application description page. Should there also be an APT version of an application available, a Flathub menu is displayed on the right side of the titlebar showing the Flatpak application and the DEB (Ubuntu) application (see Figure 4-27). Choose the one you want to install. Should GNOME

Software be configured to support Snap, APT, and Flatpak, applications available on all of them, such as VLC, will list separate entries for each.

Figure 4-27: GNOME Software Flatpak

Synaptic Package Manager: APT only

The Synaptic Package Manager has been replaced by the App Center as the primary package manager. It is not installed by default. Synaptic is no longer supported by Ubuntu, though support is still provided by the Ubuntu community. Packages are listed by name and include supporting packages like libraries and system critical packages. Once installed, you can access the Synaptic Package Manager on the Applications overview. You can install the Synaptic Package Manager from the App Center as a Debian package, or by using the **sudo apt install** command in a terminal window.

```
sudo apt install synaptic
```

The Synaptic Package Manager is a front-end for the APT system and can only access APT repositories. It cannot manage Snap packages. Some packages are available both as Snap and APT packages. Should you install such a Snap package using the App Center and then, again, using the Synaptic Package Manager, you would have two installations of the same software application, one managed by APT and the other by Snap.

Many APT software packages will not be available from the App Center. But you can install them using the Synaptic Package Manager or the **apt** command. Many servers, such as the Vsftpd FTP server and Apache Web server, and desktops, such as Kubuntu and Xfce, are not listed by the App Center, as well as many applications in Universe and Multiverse. You will have to use the Synaptic Packages Manager or the **apt** command to install them.

The Synaptic Package Manager displays three panes: a side pane for listing software categories and buttons, a top pane for listing software packages, and a bottom pane for displaying a selected package's description. When a package is selected, the description pane also displays a Get Screenshot button. Clicking this button will download and display an image of the application if there is one. Click the Get Changelog button to display a window listing the application changes.

Buttons at the lower left of the Synaptic Package Manager window provide options for organizing and refining the list of packages shown (see Figure 4-28). Five options are available: Sections, Status, Origin, Custom Filters, Search results, and Architecture. The dialog pane above the buttons changes depending on which option you choose. Clicking the Sections button will list section categories for your software such as Graphics, Communications, and Development. The Status button will list options for installed and not installed software. The Origin button shows entries for different repositories and their sections, as well as those locally installed (manual or disc based installations). Custom filters lets you choose a filter to use for listing packages. You can create your own filter and use it to display selected packages. Search results will list your current and previous searches, letting you move from one to the other.

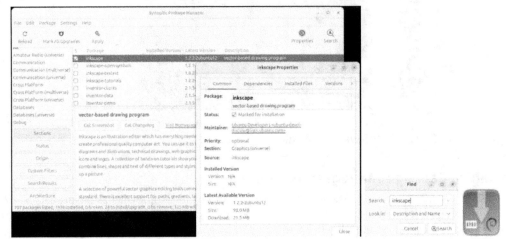

Figure 4-28: Synaptic Package Manager

The Sections option is selected by default (see Figure 4-29). You can choose to list all packages, or refine your listing using categories provided in the pane. The All entry in this pane will list all available packages. Packages are organized into categories such as Cross Platform, Communications, and Editors. Each category is subdivided by multiverse, universe, and restricted software.

Figure 4-29: Synaptic Package Manager: Sections

To perform a search, you use the Search tool. Click the Search button on the toolbar to open a Search dialog with a text box where you can enter search terms. A pop-up menu lets you specify what features of a package to search such as the "Description and Name" feature. You can search other package features like the Name, the maintainer name (Maintainer), the package version (Version), packages it may depend on (Dependencies), or associated packages (Provided Packages). A list of searches will be displayed in Search Results. You can move back and forth between search results by clicking on the search entries in this listing.

Status entries further refine installed software as manual or as upgradeable (see Figure 4-30). Local software consists of packages you download and install manually.

Figure 4-30: Synaptic Package Manager: Status

With the Origin options, Ubuntu-compliant repositories may further refine access according to multiverse, universe, and restricted software. A main section selects Ubuntu-supported software. The Architecture options let you select software compatible with a specified architecture, such as 64-bit or 32-bit.

Properties

To find out information about a package, select the package and click the Properties button. This opens a window with Common, Dependencies, Installed Files, Versions, and Description tabs (see Figure 4-28). The Common tab provides section, versions, and maintainer information. The Installed Files tab show you exactly what files are installed, which is useful for finding the exact location, and names for configuration files, as well as commands. The Description tab displays detailed information about the software. The Dependencies tab shows all dependent software packages needed by this software, usually libraries.

Installing packages

Before installing software, you should press the Reload button to load the most recent package lists from the active repositories

To install a package, single click on its empty checkbox or right-click on its name to display a pop-up menu and select the "Mark for installation" entry. Should any dependent packages exist, a dialog opens listing those packages. Click the Mark button in the dialog to mark those packages for installation. The package entry's checkbox will then be marked in the Synaptic Package Manager window.

Once you have selected the packages you want to install, click the Apply button on the toolbar to begin the installation process. A Summary dialog opens showing all the packages to be installed. You have the option to download the package files only. The number of packages to be installed is listed, along with the size of the download and the amount of disk space used. Click the Apply button on the Summary dialog to download and install the packages. A download window will then appear showing the progress of your package installations. You can choose to show the progress of individual packages, which opens a terminal window listing each package as it is downloaded and installed.

Once downloaded, the dialog name changes to Installing Software. You can choose to have the dialog close automatically when finished. Sometimes installation requires user input to configure the software. You will be prompted to enter the information if necessary.

When you right-click a package name, you also see options for Mark Suggested for Installation or Mark Recommended for Installation. These will mark applications that can enhance your selected software, though they are not essential. If there are no suggested or recommended packages for that application, then these entries will be grayed out.

Certain software, like desktops or office suites that require a significant number of packages, can be selected all at once using metapackages. A metapackage has configuration files that select, download, and configure the range of packages needed for such complex software. For example, the **kubuntu-desktop** meta package will install the entire Kubuntu desktop (Sections | Meta Packages (universe)).

Removing packages

To remove a package, first, locate it. Then right-click it and select the "Mark package for removal" entry. This will leave configuration files untouched. Alternatively, you can mark a package for complete removal, which will also remove any configuration files, "Mark for Complete Removal." Dependent packages will not be removed.

Once you have marked packages for removal, click the Apply button. A summary dialog displays the packages that will be removed. Click Apply to remove them.

The Synaptic Package Manager may not remove dependent packages, especially shared libraries that might be used by other applications. This means that your system could have installed packages that are never being used.

Search filters

You can further refine your search for packages by creating search filters. Select the Settings | Filters menu entry to open the Filters window. The Filters window shows two panes, a filter list on the left, and three tabs on the right: Status, Section, and Properties. To create a new filter, click the New button located just below the filter listing. Click the New Filter 1 entry in the filter list on the left pane. On the Status tab, you can refine your search criteria according to a package's status. You can search only uninstalled packages, include installed packages, include or exclude packages marked for removal, or search for those that are new in the repository. Initially, all criteria are selected. Uncheck those you do not want included in your search. The Section tab lets you include or exclude different repository sections like games, documentation, or administration. If you are looking for a game, you could choose to include just the game section, excluding everything else. On the Properties tab, you can specify patterns to search on package information such as package names, using Boolean operators to refine your search criteria. Package search criteria are entered using the two pop-up menus and the text box at the bottom of the tab, along with AND or OR Boolean operators.

Note: For KDE you can use the Discover Software Center and the Muon package manager to install and update packages.

GNOME Software for separate DEB packages

You can also use the GNOME Software (not the App Center) to perform an installation of a single DEB software package. Usually, these packages are downloaded directly from a website and have few or no dependent packages. When you right-click on a deb package, you should see the entry "Open With Software Install." Choose this entry to open GNOME Software, listing the package name, description, details (version number, size, and source), and an Install button.

Updating Ubuntu

New updates are continually being prepared for particular software packages as well as system components. These are posted as updates you can download from software repositories and install on your system. These include new versions of applications, servers, and the kernel. Such updates may range from single software packages to whole components. When updates become available, a message appears on your desktop.

Updating packages (Upgrading) with apt

The **apt** tool also lets you update your entire system at once. The terms **update** and **upgrade** are used differently from other software tools. In **apt**, the **update** command just updates your package listing, checking for packages that may need to install newer versions, but not installing those versions. Technically, it updates the package list that APT uses to determine what packages need to be updated. The term **upgrade** is used to denote the actual update of a software package. A new version is downloaded and installed. What is referred to as updating by **apt**, other package managers refer to as obtaining the list of software packages to be updated (the reload operation). In **apt**, upgrading is what other package managers refer to as performing updates.

Note: The terms **update** and **upgrade** can be confusing when used with **apt**. The update operation updates the Apt package list only, whereas an upgrade actually downloads and installs updated packages.

Upgrading is a simple matter of using the **upgrade** command. With no package specified, using **apt** with the **upgrade** command will update your entire system. Add the **-u** option to list packages as they are updated. First, make sure your repository information (package list) is up to date with the **update** command, then issue the **upgrade** command.

```
sudo apt update
sudo apt -u upgrade
```

Updating Snaps

Snap packages (snaps) are updated automatically by the **snapd** daemon, four times a day (every six hours). You can manually update your snaps with the **snap refresh** command. You can to this for an individual package or for all snaps.

```
sudo snap refresh
sudo snap refresh skype
```

See the Snapcraft update documentation for more details.

```
https://snapcraft.io/docs/keeping-snaps-up-to-date
```

With the **--time** option you can check the time of the last update and when the next one will take place.

```
snap refresh --time
```

To see the list of packages updated with the last refresh, use the **snap changes** command.

```
snap changes
```

The listing will show the number of the package change ID (ID), its status (Status), the time of its revision (Spawn), when it was available (Ready), and a short description of the update including the name of the application affected (Summary).

```
richard@richard-laptop:~$ snap changes
ID   Status  Spawn              Ready              Summary
33   Done    today at 11:37 PDT today at 11:38 PDT Auto-refresh snap "skype"
```

To see the changes performed for a particular software package update use the **snap change** command with the change ID of the update.

```
richard@richard-laptop:~$ snap change 33
Status   Spawn               Ready               Summary
Done     today at 11:37 PDT  today at 11:37 PDT  Ensure prerequisites for "skype"
are available
Done     today at 11:37 PDT  today at 11:37 PDT  Download snap "skype" (128) from
channel "latest/stable"
Done     today at 11:37 PDT  today at 11:37 PDT  Fetch and check assertions for
snap "skype" (128)
Done     today at 11:37 PDT  today at 11:37 PDT  Mount snap "skype" (128)
Done     today at 11:37 PDT  today at 11:37 PDT  Run pre-refresh hook of "skype"
snap if present
Done     today at 11:37 PDT  today at 11:37 PDT  Stop snap "skype" services
Done     today at 11:37 PDT  today at 11:37 PDT  Remove aliases for snap "skype"
Done     today at 11:37 PDT  today at 11:37 PDT  Make current revision for snap
"skype" unavailable
Done     today at 11:37 PDT  today at 11:37 PDT  Copy snap "skype" data
Done     today at 11:37 PDT  today at 11:37 PDT  Setup snap "skype" (128) security
profiles
Done     today at 11:37 PDT  today at 11:37 PDT  Make snap "skype" (128) available
to the system
Done     today at 11:37 PDT  today at 11:37 PDT  Automatically connect eligible
plugs and slots of snap "skype"
Done     today at 11:37 PDT  today at 11:38 PDT  Set automatic aliases for snap
"skype"
Done     today at 11:37 PDT  today at 11:38 PDT  Setup snap "skype" aliases
Done     today at 11:37 PDT  today at 11:38 PDT  Run post-refresh hook of "skype"
snap if present
Done     today at 11:37 PDT  today at 11:38 PDT  Start snap "skype" (128) services
Done     today at 11:37 PDT  today at 11:38 PDT  Clean up "skype" (128) install
Done     today at 11:37 PDT  today at 11:38 PDT  Run configure hook of "skype"
snap if present
Done     today at 11:37 PDT  today at 11:38 PDT  Run health check of "skype" snap
```

You can configure snap updates by adjusting the time, suspending updates, and setting a limit on how many package revisions you want to keep. Use the **snap set system** command with various options to configure snap updates. The **refresh.timer** option lets you specify times for updates and how many you want performed. The time is specified by the Snap timer string format (**https://snapcraft.io/docs/timer-string-format**). Use the dash to indicate a range. The following first entry updates only on Monday and Friday. The second entry updates Tuesday through Thursday.

```
sudo snap set system refresh.timer=mon,fri
sudo snap set system refresh.timer=tue-thu
```

Use the **refresh.hold** option to delay updates to a specified time. The **time-metered** option pauses updates, and the **refresh.retrain** option sets the number of stored revisions. The default is 3, and the maximum allowed is 20.

```
sudo snap set system refresh.retrain=4
```

Updating Ubuntu on the Desktop

On the Ubuntu desktop, you can update APT software easily with Software Updater. With Software & Updates you can configure updates. The Firmware updater lets you update the firmware for your devices.

Updating Ubuntu APT software with Software Updater

Updating your APT software on your Ubuntu system is a simple procedure, using Software Updater, which provides a graphical update interface for APT. The Software Updater icon appears on the Dock when updates are available. The Software Updater then displays a simple dialog that shows the amount to be downloaded with "Remind Me Later" and "Install Now" buttons (see Figure 4-31). The Settings button opens the Software & Update dialog to the Updates dialog where you can configure updates (see Figure 4-36). You can also manually update by starting the Software Updater from the Applications overview.

Software Updater will also invoke the **snapd** daemon to update your Snap packages. It does not update them directly. The Software Updater interface only explicitly manages APT packages.

Figure 4-31: Software Updater with selected packages

To see actual packages to be updated, click the "Details of updates" arrow. Packages are organized into application categories such as Ubuntu base for the Ubuntu desktop and Linux OS packages, Firefox for Firefox updates, and LibreOffice for office updates. You can expand these to individual packages. The checkboxes for each entry lets you de-select any particular packages you do not want to update (see Figure 4-32). All the APT-compatible repositories that are configured on your system will be checked for updates.

Figure 4-32: Details of updates

To see a detailed description of a particular update, select the update and then click the "Technical description" arrow (see Figure 4-33). The Technical description section displays information about the software, and the Changes and Versions sections lists the changes to be made by the update.

Click the Install Now button to start updating. The packages will be downloaded from their appropriate repository. Once downloaded, the packages are updated.

Figure 4-33: Details of updates, Technical description

When downloading and installing, a dialog appears showing the download and install progress (see Figure 4-34). You can choose to show progress for individual files. A window will open up that lists each file and its progress. Once downloaded, the updates are installed. Click the Details arrow to see install messages for particular software packages.

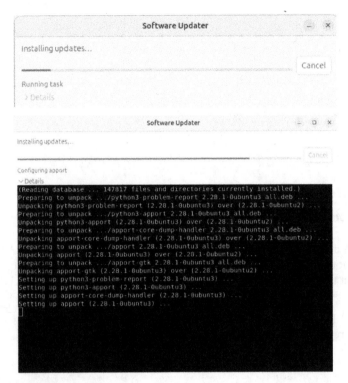

Figure 4-34: Downloading updates

When the update completes, Software updater will display a message saying that your system is up-to-date. If a critical package was installed such as a new kernel, you will be prompted to restart your system. You can restart now or later (see Figure 4-35).

Figure 4-35: Downloaded updates

You can configure Software Updater using the dconf editor. The Software Updater keys are located at apps | update-manager. There are keys to auto-close the install window, check for distribution upgrades, show details and versions, and set the window dimensions.

Configuring Updates with Software & Updates

The Updates tab in Software & Updates lets you configure how updates are managed (see Figure 4-36). Snap packages are updated automatically, which is a feature of the Snap system. You do not configure their updates. For packages that are not installed by Snap, which includes many of the Ubuntu main, universe, and multiverse packages, you can configure updates. Keep in mind that the options listed on this tab have no effect on Snap updates.

Figure 4-36: Software & Updates Update configuration

From the menu labeled "For other packages, subscribe to:" you can choose All updates, security and recommended updates, and security updates only (noble-security). The "All updates" entry is already selected. Your system is already configured to check for updates automatically on a daily basis. For packages not installed by Snap, you can opt not to check for updates by choosing never from the "Automatically check for updates" menu. You also have options for how security updates are handled. You can download and install any security updates automatically, without confirmation. You can download them and install them later. Or you can just be notified of available security updates, and then choose to install them when you want. For all other updates you can adjust when you want to be notified of updates (immediately, weekly, or every two weeks). On this tab, you also can choose what Ubuntu releases to be notified of: the long term support (LTS) releases only, all releases, or none.

The UbuntuPro tab lets you extend Ubuntu security updates for your Main and Universe repository packages to 2034, and it lets you use the Canonical Livepatch service, which allows you to install security updates that do not require a restart immediately (see Figure 4-37). You will need a Canonical account to use it. When turned on, you can click on the Livepatch menu on the top bar to see the current status and access the Livepatch settings directly.

Figure 4-37: Software & Updates - Ubuntu Pro (Livepatch)

Firmware Updater

With the Firmware Updater utility you can update the firmware for your devices directly (see Figure 4-38). A sidebar lists tabs for your hardware firmware. The UEFI entry is your motherboard. You may have others for hard disks and wireless devices. Each tab shows the current version and information about the firmware. The All Versions button shows your current version, with detailed information about the update. A Reinstall button lets you reinstall the update. If there was no update, just the current version information is provided. If previous updates were installed, there will be an "Older Versions" link at the bottom you can click to list the previous updates. They will have a Downgrade button you can click should you need to reinstall a previous version for some reason.

The **ubuntu-desktop-minimal** meta package does not install firmware updater. It is a Snap package you can install with the following command for the **firmware-updater** package.

```
sudo snap install firmware-updater
```

Figure 4-38: Firmware Updater

Part 2: Services

Managing Services
Mail Servers
FTP Servers
Web Servers
News and Database Servers

ubuntu

5. Managing Services

systemd

systemd unit files: /lib/systemd/system

special targets (runlevels)

managing services

Network Time Protocol, Chrony

AppArmor security

OpenSSH

A single Linux system can provide several different kinds of services, ranging from security to administration, and including more obvious Internet services like Web and FTP sites, e-mail, and printing. Security tools, such as the Secure Shell (SSH) run as services, along with administrative network tools, such as Dynamic Host Control Protocol (DHCP) and the BIND Domain Name Server. The network connection interface is itself, a service that you can restart at will. Each service operates as a continually running daemon looking for requests for its particular services. In the case of a web service, the requests come from remote users. You can turn services on or off by starting or shutting down their daemons. System startup is managed by the **systemd** service. The original System V init system for starting individual services has been phased out.

systemd

Linux systems traditionally used the Unix System V init daemon to manage services by setting up runlevels at which they could be started or shutdown. Linux has since replaced the System V init daemon with the **systemd** init daemon. Whereas the System V init daemon would start certain services when the entire system started up or shut down using shell scripts run in sequence, **systemd** uses sockets for all system tasks and services. **systemd** sets up sockets for daemons and coordinates between them as they start up. This allows **systemd** to start daemons at the same time (in parallel). Should one daemon require support from another, **systemd** coordinates the data from their sockets (buffering), so that one daemon receives the information from another daemon that it needs to continue. This parallel startup compatibility allows for very fast boot times.

In effect, you can think of **systemd** as a combination of System V init scripts and the inetd daemon (xinetd), using socket activation applied to all system startup tasks and to network servers. The socket activation design was originally inspired by the inetd service that used sockets (AT_INET) to start internet daemons when requested. The socket activation design was used by in Apple's OS X system to apply to all sockets (AF_UNIX). This allowed all start up processes to start at the same time in parallel, making for fast boot times. Such sockets are set up and managed by **systemd**. When D-BUS needs to write to journald (logging), it writes to the systemd-journald socket managed by **systemd**. It does not have to communicate directly with journald. This means that services no longer have to be started and shutdown in a particular sequence as they were under System V. They can all start and stop at the same time. Also, as **systemd** controls the socket, if a service fails, its socket remains in place. The service can be restarted using the same socket with no loss of information. **systemd** manages all types of sockets including UNIX (system), INET (network), NETLINK (devices), FIFO (pipes), and POSIX (messages). See the following for more details.

```
https://docs.fedoraproject.org/en-US/quick-docs/understanding-and-administering-
systemd/index.html
https://www.freedesktop.org/wiki/Software/systemd/
```

systemd sets up sockets for all system tasks and services. Configuration for systemd tasks is defined in unit files in **/lib/systemd** directory. System unit files are held in the **/lib/systemd/system** directory and user application unit files are in the **/lib/systemd/user** directory. In this respect, **systemd** files replace the entries that used to be in the Sys V init's **/etc/inittab** file. **systemd** also has its own versions of **shutdown**, **reboot**, **halt**, **init**, and **telinit**, each with their own man page.

systemd is entirely compatible with both System V scripts in the **/etc/init.d** directory and the **/etc/fstab** file. The SystemV scripts and **/etc/fstab** are treated as additional configuration files for **systemd** to work with. If System V scripts are present in the **/etc/init.d** directory, it will use them to generate a corresponding unit configuration file, if there are no corresponding **systemd** unit configuration files already. **systemd** configuration always takes precedence. **systemd** will also, if needed, use the start and stop priority files in the System V init **/etc/init.d** directories to determine dependencies. Entries in **/etc/fstab** are used to generate corresponding **systemd** unit files that are then used to manage file systems. **systemd** also supports snapshots that allow restoring services to a previous state.

The systemd configuration (**.service**) files are located in the **/lib/systemd/system** and **/lib/systemd/user** directories, and are considered system files that you should not modify. It is possible to copy them to the **/etc/systemd/system** or **/etc/systemd/user** directories and make changes to the copies. Files in the **/etc/systemd/system** and **/etc/systemd/user** directories take precedence. The configuration file for the logind daemon, **logind.conf**, is located in the **/etc/systemd** directory.

Ubuntu also uses systemd services for time (**timedated**), location (**localed**), login (**logind**), and hostname (**hostnamed**) (**systemd-services** package). They can be managed with corresponding systemd control applications: **timedatectl**, **localectl**, and **hostnamectl**.

systemd basic configuration files

You can configure **systemd** for system, login manager, users, and journal service using the configuration files located in the **/etc/systemd** directory. When run for a system service, systemd uses the **system.conf** file, otherwise it uses the **user.conf** file. You can set options such as the log level (LogLevel) and resource size limits. See the man page for **systemd.conf** (**system.conf** and **user.conf**), **logind.conf**, and **journald.conf** for details on the options available.

units

systemd organizes tasks into units, each with a unit configuration file. There are several types of units (see Table 5-1). A unit file will have an extension to its name that specifies the type of unit it is. Service types have the extension **.service**, and mount types have the extension **.mount**. The service type performs much the same function as System V init scripts. Services can be stopped, started, and restarted. The **systemctl** command will list all units.

Units can also be used for socket, device, and mount tasks. The socket type implements the kind of connection used for inetd and xinetd, allowing you to start a service on demand. The device type references devices as detected by udev. The mount type manages a file system's mount point, and automount activates that mount point should it be automounted. An automount unit file has a corresponding mount unit file, which it uses to mount a file system. Similarly, a socket type usually has a corresponding service type file used to perform a task for that socket.

Within each unit are directives that control a service, socket, device, or mount point. Some directives are unique to the type of unit. These are listed in the man page for that service, such as **systemd.service** for the service unit, or **systemd.mount** for a mount unit (see Table 5-1).

```
man systemd.service
```

Options common to units are listed in the **systemd.exec** and **systemd.unit** pages. The **systemd.unit** page lists directives common to all units such as Wants, Conflicts, Before, SourcePath, and Also. The **systemd.exec** pages list options for the execution of a program for a unit, such as the starting of a server daemon. These include options such as User, Group, WorkingDirectory, Nice, Umask, and Environment. The **systemd.exec** page covers options for service, socket, mount, and swap units. The **systemd.directives** man page provides a listing of all systemd unit options and the man page for each option.

Unit Type	Unit Man page	Description
`service`	systemd.service	Services such as servers, which can be started and stopped.
`socket`	systemd.socket	Socket for services (allows for inetd like services, AF_INET).
`device`	systemd.device	Devices.
`mount`	systemd.mount	File system mount points.
`automount`	systemd.automount	Automount point for a file system. Use with mount units.
`target`	systemd.target	Group units.
`path`	systemd.path	Manage directories.
`snapshot`	systemd.snapshot	Created by systemd using the **systemctl snapshot** command to save runtime states of systemd. Use **systemctl isolate** to restore a state.
`swap`	systemd.swap	Swap unit file generated by systemd for the swap file system.
`timer`	systemd.timer	Time-based activation of a unit. Corresponds to a service file. Time formats are specified on the **systemd.time** man page.
	systemd.unit	Man page with configuration options common to all units.
	systemd.exec	Man page for execution environment options for service, socket, mount, and swap units.
	systemd.special	Man page for systemd special targets such as **multi-user.target** and **printer.target**.
	systemd.time	Time and date formats for **systemd.**
	systemd.directives	Listing of all systemd options and the man page they are described on.

Table 5-1: systemd unit types and man pages

The target unit is used to group units. For example, targets are used to emulate runlevels. A multi-user target groups units (services) together that, in System V, would run on runlevel 3. In effect, targets group those services that run on a certain runlevel for a certain task. The printer target activates the CUPS service, and the graphical target emulates runlevel 5. A target can also be used to reference other targets. A default target designates the default runlevel. Some unit files are automatically generated by **systemd**. For example, operations specified in the **/etc/fstab** are performed by mount units, which are automatically generated from the **fstab** entries.

Units can be dependent on one another, where one unit may require the activation of other units. This dependency is specified using directories with the **.wants** extension. For example, the **poweroff.target** is dependent on the **plymouth-poweroff** service. The directory **poweroff.target.wants** has a symbolic link to this service. Should you want a service dependent on your graphical desktop, you can add symbolic links to it in the **graphical.target.wants** directory.

It is important to distinguish between the wants directories in the **/etc/systemd/system** and **/etc/systemd/user** directories and those in the **/lib/systemd/system** and **/etc/systemd/user** directories. Those in the **/lib/systemd** directory are set up by your system and should be left alone. To manage your own dependencies, you can set up corresponding wants directories in the **/etc/systemd/system** and **/etc/systemd/user** directories. The **/etc/systemd** directory always takes priority. For example, in the **/etc/systemd/system/multi-user.target.wants** directory you can place links to services that you want started up for the multi-user.target (runlevel 3). Your system automatically installs links for services you enable, such as **ufw.service** and **vsftpd.service**. These are all links to the actual service files in the **/lib/systemd/system** directory. The **multi-user.target.wants** directory holds a link to **ufw.service**, starting up the firewall. The **printer.target.wants** directory has a link to the cups service.

Disabling a service removes its link from its wants directory in **/etc/systemd/system**. For example, disabling the vsftpd service removes its link from the **/etc/systemd/system/multi-user.target.wants** directory. The original service file, in this case, **vsftpd.service**, remains in the **/lib/systemd/system** directory. If you enable the service again, a link for it is added to the **/etc/systemd/system/multi-user.target.wants** directory.

The **/etc/systemd/system** directory also hold links to services. The **/etc/systemd/system/syslog.service** file is a link to **/lib/systemd/system/rsyslog.service.** The **/etc/systemd/system/dbus-org.freedesktop.Avahi.service** link references **/lib/systemd/system/avahi-daemon.service.**

To manage **systemd** you can use **systemctl**. The older service management tool, **service**, has been modified to use **systemctl** to perform actions on services such as starting and stopping.

unit file syntax

A unit file is organized into sections designated by keywords enclosed in brackets. All units have a unit section, **[Unit]**, and an install section, **[Install]**. The options for these sections are described in the **systemd.unit** Man page. Comments can be written by beginning a line with the # or ; characters. See Table 5-2 for a listing of commonly used Unit and Install section options.

The Unit section of a unit file holds generic information about a unit. The Description option provides information about the task the unit manages, such as the Vsftpd server as shown here.

```
Description=vsftpd FTP server
```

The Documentation option lists URIs for the application's documentation.

```
Documentation=man:dhcpd(8)
```

Note: The syntax for unit file is based on .desktop files, which in turn are inspired by Windows ini files. The .desktop type of file conforms to the XDB Desktop Entry Specification.

Types of dependencies can be specified using the Before, After, Requires, Wants, and Conflicts options in the unit section. After and Before configure the ordering of a unit. In the following After option in the **vsftpd.service** file, the vsftpd service is started after networking.

```
After=network.target
```

Unit options	Description
[Unit]	
Description	Description of the unit.
Documentation	URIs referencing documentation.
Requires	Units required by the service. This is a strict requirement. If the required units fail, so will the unit.
PartOf	Dependent units started and stopped by the service. This is not a strict requirement. If the dependent units fail, the unit will still start up.
Wants	Units wanted by the service. This is not a strict requirement. If the required units fail, the unit will still start up. Same functionality as the wants directories.
Conflicts	Negative unit dependency. Starting the unit stops the listed units in the Conflicts option.
Before	Unit ordering. Unit starts before the units listed.
After	Unit ordering. Unit waits until the units listed start.
OnFailure	Units to be run if the unit fails.
SourcePath	File the configuration was generated from, such as the mount unit files generated from **/etc/fstab**.
[Install]	
WantedBy	Sets up the unit's symbolic link in listed unit's **.wants** subdirectory. When the listed unit is activated, so is the unit. This is not a strict requirement.
RequiredBY	Sets up the unit's symbolic link in listed unit's **.requires** subdirectory. When the listed unit is activated, so is the unit. This is a strong requirement.
Alias	Additional names the unit is installed under. The aliases are implemented as symbolic links to the unit file.
Also	Additional units to install with this unit.

Table 5-2: systemd Unit and Install section options (common to all units, systemd.unit)

The Requires option sets up a dependency between units. This is a strong dependency. If one fails, so does the other. In the following Requires option from the **graphical.target** unit file, the graphical target can only be started if the multi-user and rescue targets are activated.

```
After=multi-user.target rescue.service rescue.target
```

The Wants option sets up a weaker dependency, requiring activation, but not triggering failure should it occur. This is the case with the graphical target and the display manager service.

```
Wants=display-manager.service
```

Several condition options are available such as ConditionACPower which, if true, checks to see if a system is using AC power. In the following example, ConditionPathExists checks for the existence of a file with runtime options for the DHCP server in the **/etc/default** directory.

```
ConditionPathExists=/etc/default/isc-dhcp-server
```

Some unit files are automatically generated by systemd, allowing you to use older configuration methods. For example, the unit file used to manage the mounting of your file systems is generated from the configuration information in the **/etc/fstab** file. The SourcePath option specifies the configuration file used to generate the unit file. The SourcePath option for the **boot.mount** unit file is shown here.

```
SourcePath=/etc/fstab
```

The Install section provides installation information for the unit. The WantedBy and RequiredBy options specify units that this unit wants or requires. For service units managing servers like Vsftpd and the DCHP servers, the install section has a WantedBy option for the **multi-user.target**. This has the effect of running the server at runlevels 2, 3, 4, and 5. When the multi-user target becomes activated so does that unit.

```
WantedBy=multi-user.target
```

The WantedBy option is implemented by setting up a link to the unit in a **.wants** subdirectory for the wanted by unit. For the **multi-user.target** unit, a subdirectory called **multi-user.target.wants** has symbolic links to all the units that want it, such as **vsftpd.service** for the vsfptd FTP service. These wants symbolic links are set up in the **/etc/systemd/system** directory, which can be changed as you enable and disable a service. Disabling a service removes the link. RequiredBy is a much stronger dependency.

The Alias option lists other unit names that could reference this unit. In the **ssh.service** file you will find an Alias option for **sshd.service**.

```
Alias=sshd.service
```

The Also option lists other units that should be activated when this unit is started. The CUPS service has an Also option to start the CUPS socket and path.

```
Also=cups.socket cups.path
```

Different types of units have their own options. Service, socket, target, and path units all have options appropriate for their tasks.

special targets

A target file groups units for services, mounts, sockets, and devices. **systemd** has a set of special target files designed for specific purposes (see Table 5-3). Some are used for on-demand services such as bluetooth and printer. When a Bluetooth device is connected, the bluetooth target becomes active. When you connect a printer, the printer target is activated which, in turn, activates the CUPS print server. The sound target is activated when the system starts and runs all sound-related units. See the **special.target** Man page for more details.

There are several special target files that are designed to fulfill the function of runlevels in System V (see Table 5-4). These include the rescue, multi-user, and graphical targets. On boot, **systemd** activates the default target, which is a link to a special target, such as **multi-user.target** and **graphical.target**.

You can override the default target with a **systemd.unit** kernel command line option for GRUB. On the GRUB startup menu, you could edit the kernel boot line and add the following option to boot to the command line instead of the desktop.

```
systemd.unit=multi-user.target
```

The following will start up the graphical target.

```
systemd.unit=graphical.target
```

Should you need to boot as a rescue system (base system and rescue shell), you would specify the rescue target.

```
systemd.unit=rescue.target
```

Special units	Description
`basic.target`	Units to be run at early boot.
`bluetooth.target`	Starts when a Bluetooth device becomes active.
`printer.target`	Starts printer service when a printer is attached.
`sound.target`	Starts when sound device is detected, usually at boot.
`display-manager.service`	Link to a display service such as GDM or KDM.
`ctrl-alt-del.target`	Activated when the user presses Ctrl-Alt-Del keys, this is a link to the **reboot.target** which reboots the system.
`system-update.target`	Implements an offline system update. After downloading, the updates are performed when your system reboots, at which time it detects the presence of the target.

Table 5-3: special units

Special RunlevelTargets	Description
`default.target`	References a special target to be activated on boot.
`rescue.target`	Starts up base system and rescue shell.
`emergency.target`	Starts base system, with option to start full system.
`multi-user.target`	Starts up command line interface, multi-user and non-graphical (similar to runlevel 3).
`graphical.target`	Start graphical interface (desktop) (similar to runlevel 5).

Table 5-4: special runlevel targets (boot)

You could also simply add a 3 as in previous releases, as runlevel links also reference the special targets in **systemd**. The 3 would reference the runlevel 3 target, which links to the multi-user target. A copy of the **multi-user.target** file follows. The multi-user target requires the basic target which loads the basic system (Requires). It conflicts with the rescue target (Conflicts), and it is run after the basic target. It can be isolated allowing you to switch special targets (AllowIsolate).

multi-user.target

```
[Unit]
Description=Multi-User System
Documentation=man:systemd.special(7)
Requires=basic.target
Conflicts=rescue.service rescue.target
After=basic.target rescue.service rescue.target
AllowIsolate=yes
```

The **graphical.target** depends on the **multi-user.target**. A copy of the **graphical.target** unit file follows. It requires that the **multi-user.target** be activated (Requires). Anything run for the multi-user target, including servers, is also run for the graphical target, the desktop. The desktop target is run after the **multi-user.target** (After). It is not run for the **rescue.target** (Conflicts). It also wants the display-manager service to run (GDM or KDM) (Wants). You can isolate it to switch to another target (AllowIsolate).

graphical.target

```
[Unit]
Description=Graphical Interface
Documentation=man:systemd.special(7)
Requires=multi-user.target
Wants=display-manager.service
Conflicts=rescue.service rescue.target
After=multi-user.target rescue.service rescue.target display-manager.service
AllowIsolate=yes
```

Modifying unit files: /etc/systemd/system

systemd uses unit files to manage devices, mounts, and services. These are located in the **/lib/systemd/system** and **/lib/systemd/user** directories and are considered system files that you should not modify. You can modify a unit file either by specifying features that override those in the original, or by creating a separate copy that you can edit, which takes precedence over the original. In each case it is best to create the modifications using the **systemctl** command with the **edit** option.

To simply override or add entries to the unit file, you can create an associated drop in directory that contains configuration files with entries. Such a directory has the same name as the unit file with a **.d** extension. It contains configuration files with the extension **.conf**. To create a drop in directory and its configuration file, you simple edit the unit file with the **systemctl edit** command.

```
sudo systemctl edit vsftpd.service
```

This opens your default line editor and lets you add in the new entries. When you save, if the drop in directory does not exist, it is created. This creates an **override.conf** file in the **/etc/systemd/system/vsftpd.service.d** directory.

Should you want to make more extensive changes, you can create a copy of the original unit file in the **/etc/systemd/system** or **/etc/systemd/user** directories. Unit files in this directory take precedence over those in the **/lib/systemd/system** and **/lib/systemd/user** directories. You can then modify the unit file version in **/etc/systemd/system**. You would create this copy using the **systemctl edit --full** command.

```
sudo systemctl edit --full vsftpd.service
```

This opens your default line editor to display the copy of the unit file, now in your **/etc/systemd/system** directory, and lets you modify or add entries.

Alternatively, you could copy a unit file to the **/etc/systemd/system** directory directly, and then edit it with a text editor. Use the **sudo cp** command to copy the file. The following command copies the Samba service unit file.

```
sudo cp /lib/systemd/system/smbd.service   /etc/systemd/system/smbd.service
```

Execution Environment Options

The unit files of type service, sockets, mount, and swap share the same options for the execution environment of the unit (see Table 5-5). These are found in the unit section for that type such as **[Service]** for service units or **[Socket]** for socket unit. With these options, you can set features such as the working directory (WorkingDirectory), the file mode creation mask (UMask), and the system logging level (SysLogLevel). Nice sets the default scheduling priority level. User specifies the user id for the processes the unit runs.

```
User=mysql
```

Exec options	Description
WorkingDirectory	Sets the working directory for an application.
RootDirectory	Root directory for an application.
User, Group	Application's user and group ids.
Nice	Sets priority for an application.
CPUSchedulingPriority	CPU Scheduling priority for the applications.
UMask	File mode creation mask, default is 022.
Environment	Set environment variables for an application.
StandardOutput	Direct standard output a connection such as log, console, or null.
SysLogLevel	System logging level such as warn, alert, info, or debug.
DeviceAllow, DeviceDeny	Control applications access to a device.
ControlGroup	Assign application to a control group.

Table 5-5: systemd exec options (Service, Socket, Mount, Swap) (systemd.exec)

service unit files

A service unit file is used to run applications and commands such as the Samba (**smbd**) and Web (**apache2**) servers. They have a **[Service]** section with options specified in the **systemd.service** Man page. See Table 5-6 for a listing of several common service options. A service unit file has the extension **.service** and the prefix is the name of the server program, such as **isc-dhcp-server.service** for the DHCP server and **vsftpd.service** for the Very Secure FTP server. Table 5-7 lists several popular servers.

A copy of the Vsftpd service unit file, **vsftpd.service**, follows. The Vsftpd FTP service is started after the network has started. The server program to run is specified, **/usr/sbin/vsftpd** (ExecStart). The service is installed by the **multi-user.target** (WantedBy) when the system starts up.

vsftpd.service

```
[Unit]
Description=vsftpd FTP server
After=network.target
[Service]
Type=simple
ExecStart=/usr/sbin/vsftpd /etc/vsftpd.conf
ExecReload=/bin/kill -HUP $MAINPID
ExecStartPre=-/bin/mkdir -p /var/run/vsftpd/empty
[Install]
WantedBy=multi-user.target
```

Service options	Description
ExecStart	Commands to execute when service starts, such as running an application or server.
Type	Startup type such as simple (the default), forking, dbus, notify, or idle.
ExecStartPre, ExecStartPost	Commands executed before and after the ExecStart command.
TimeStartSec	Time to wait before starting the ExecStart command.
Restart	Restart when the ExecStart command end.
PermissionsStartOnly	Boolean value, If true the permission based options are applied, such as User.
RootDirectoryStartOnly	Boolean value, if true, the RootDirectory option applies only to the ExecStart option.

Table 5-6: systemd service options [Service] (systemd.service)

The **named.service** file is even simpler, incorporating runtime options into the program command. It is run after the network service and is started by the **multi-user.target**. It also has an alias, which lets you manage the service either as **named** or as **bind9**.

named.service

```
[Unit]
Description=BIND Domain Name Server
Documentation=man:named(8)
After=network.target
Wants=nss-lookup.target
Before=nss-lookup.target
[Service]
Type=forking
EnvironmentFile=/etc/default/named
ExecStart=/usr/sbin/named -f $OPTIONS
ExecReload=/usr/sbin/rndc reload
ExecStop=/usr/sbin/rndc stop
Restart=on-failure
[Install]
WantedBy=multi-user.target
Alias=bind9.service
```

Service unit files	Description
apache2	Apache Web server.
bind9	Bind 9 DNS server.
cups	The CUPS printer daemon.
isc-dhcp-server	Dynamic Host Configuration Protocol daemon.
mysql	MySQL database server.
network	Operations to start up or shut down your network connections.
nis	The NIS server.
nfs-server	Network Filesystem.
postfix	Postfix mail server.
sendmail	The Sendmail MTA daemon.
smbd	Samba for Windows hosts.
squid3	Squid proxy-cache server.
ssh	Secure Shell daemon.
systemd-journald	System logging daemon.
vsftpd	Very Secure FTP server.
ufw	Controls the UFW firewall.

Table 5-7: Collection of Service unit files

On Demand and Standalone Services (socket)

The On Demand activation of services, formerly implemented by inetd, is the default in systemd. Should you want a standalone service, you can specify that it is wanted by a special target so that it will be started up at boot time, instead of when it is first activated. In the Install section of a service unit file, a WantedBy option specifying the multi-user target will start the service at boot, making it a standalone service. In the following, the service is wanted by the **multi-user.target**. To put it another way, the service starts at runlevels 2, 3, 4, and 5. Note that the graphical target (5) is dependent on (Requires) the multi-user target (2, 3, and 4), so by specifying the multi-user target, the service is also started with the graphical target.

```
[Install]
WantedBy=multi-user.target
```

The Bluetooth service only wants the **bluetooth.target** which is only activated if a Bluetooth device is present. It is not started at boot.

```
[Install]
WantedBy=bluetooth.target
```

Use the basic target, should you want the service started at all runlevels.

```
[Install]
WantedBy=basic.target
```

To emulate an on-demand server service, as inetd used to do, you would use a **.socket** file to compliment a **.service** file. This is the case with CUPS, which has a cups service file and corresponding cups socket file (CUPS is not installed by default on the Server edition). The WantedBy option for **sockets.target** ties the socket to the special target **sockets.target**, which makes the unit socket-activated.

The Socket section lists options for the socket, usually what socket to listen on (ListenStream). The **systemd.socket** Man page lists socket options. Table 5-8 lists common options.

Socket options	Description
ListenStream	Address to listen on for a stream. The address can be a port number, path name for a socket device, or an IPv4 or IPv6 address with a port number.
Accept	If true, service instance is set up for each connection; if false, only one service instance is set up for all connections.
MaxConnections	Maximum number of connections for a service.
Service	Service unit to run when the socket is active. Default is a service name that is the same as the socket name.

Table 5-8: systemd socket file options [Socket] (systemd.socket)

cups.socket

```
[Unit]
Description=CUPS Scheduler
PartOf=cups.service

[Socket]
ListenStream= /run/cups/cups.sock
RemoveOnStop=on

[Install]
WantedBy=sockets.target
```

cups.service

```
[Unit]
Description=CUPS Scheduler
Documentation=man:cupsd(8)
After=network.target nss-user-lookup.target nslcd.service
Requires=cups.socket

[Service]
ExecStart=/usr/sbin/cupsd -l
Type=notify
Restart=on-failure

[Install]
Also=cups.socket cups.path
WantedBy=printer.target multi-user.target
```

Path units

      systemd uses path units to monitor a path. Sometimes a service unit has a corresponding path unit to monitor directories, as is the case with **cups.path** and **cups.service**. Options for the Path section are listed in Table 5-9 and on the **systemd.path** Man page. The **cups.path** unit file is shown here. The PathExists option checks if the printer spool files exist.

cups.path

```
[Unit]
Description=CUPS Scheduler
PartOf=cups.service

[Path]
PathExists=/var/cache/cups/org.cups.cupsd

[Install]
WantedBy=multi-user.target
```

path options	Description
PathExists	Activates if a file exists.
PathExistsGlob	Activates if there exists a file matching a pattern, such as any file in a specified directory.
PathModified	Activates if a file has been modified.

Table 5-9: path option (systemd.path)

Template unit files

There is a special type of unit file called a template file, which allows for the generation of several unit files at runtime using one template file. Templates are used for services that generate instances of a service such as a getty terminal, an OpenVPN connection, and an rsync connection. A template filename ends with an **@** sign. If a corresponding unit file is not found for a service, **systemd** will check to see if there is a template file that can be applied to it. **systemd** matches the service name with the template name. It then generates an instance unit file for that particular service.

For example, a terminal uses the getty service (get TTY). As you do not know how many terminals you may use, they are generated automatically using the **getty@.service** unit file.

In the configuration file, the **%I** specifier is used to substitute for the service name. Given the service name **getty@tty3**, the **%I** specifier substitutes for **tty3**.

```
ExecStart=-/sbin/agetty -o '-p -- \\u' --noclear %I $TERM
```

The **getty@.service** template file is shown here.

getty@.service

```
[Unit]
Description=Getty on %I
Documentation=man:agetty(8) man:systemd-getty-generator(8)
Documentation=http://0pointer.de/blog/projects/serial-console.html
After=systemd-user-sessions.service plymouth-quit-wait.service getty-pre.target
After=rc-local.service

# If additional gettys are spawned during boot then we should make
# sure that this is synchronized before getty.target, even though
# getty.target didn't actually pull it in.
Before=getty.target
IgnoreOnIsolate=yes

# IgnoreOnIsolate causes issues with sulogin, if someone isolates
# rescue.target or starts rescue.service from multi-user.target or
# graphical.target.
Conflicts=rescue.service
Before-rescue.service

# On systems without virtual consoles, don't start any getty. Note
# that serial gettys are covered by serial-getty@.service, not this
# unit.
ConditionPathExists=/dev/tty0
```

```
[Service]
# the VT is cleared by TTYVTDisallocate
# The '-o' option value tells agetty to replace 'login' arguments with an
# option to preserve environment (-p), followed by '--' for safety, and then
# the entered username.
ExecStart=-/sbin/agetty -o '-p -- \\u' --noclear $TERM
Type=idle
Restart=always
RestartSec=0
UtmpIdentifier=%I
StandardInput=tty
StandardOutput=tty
TTYPath=/dev/%I
TTYReset=yes
TTYVHangup=yes
TTYVTDisallocate=yes
IgnoreSIGPIPE=no
SendSIGHUP=yes
ImportCredential=agetty.*
ImportCredential=login.*

# Unset locale for the console getty since the console has problems
# displaying some internationalized messages.
Environment=LANG= LANGUAGE= LC_CTYPE= LC_NUMERIC= LC_TIME= LC_COLLATE=
LC_MONETARY= LC_MESSAGES= LC_PAPER= LC_NAME= LC_ADDRESS= LC_TELEPHONE=
LC_MEASUREMENT= LC_IDENTIFICATION=

[Install]
WantedBy=getty.target
DefaultInstance=tty1
```

Runlevels and Special Targets

Under the old System V, a Linux system could run in different levels, called **runlevels**, depending on the capabilities you wanted to give it. Under System V, Linux had several runlevels, numbered from 0 to 6. When you power up your system, you enter the default runlevel. Runlevels 0, 1, and 6 are special runlevels that perform specific functions. Runlevel 0 was the power-down state. Runlevel 6 was the reboot state (it shuts down the system and reboots). Runlevel 1 was the single-user state, which allowed access only to the administrative user and does not run any network services.

systemd uses special targets instead of runlevels to create the same effect as runlevels, grouping services to run for specified targets. Runlevels are no longer implemented. There are two major special targets: **multi-user** and **graphical**. The **multi-user** target is similar to runlevel 3, providing you with a command line login. The **graphical** target is similar to runlevel 5, providing you with a graphical login and interface.

You set the default target (runlevel) by linking a target's **systemd** service file to the **systemd default.target** file. This operation replaces the way inittab was used to specify a default runlevel in previous releases. The following makes the graphical interface the default (runlevel 5).

```
ln -s /lib/systemd/system/graphical.target  /etc/systemd/system/default.target
```

systemd does provide compatibility support for runlevels. Runlevel compatibility is implemented using symbolic links in **/lib/system/systemd** directory to **systemd** targets. The **runlevel0.target** link references the systemd **poweroff.target**. Runlevel 2, 3, and 4 targets all link to the same **multi-user.target** (command line interface). The **runlevel6.target** links to the **reboot.target**, and **runlevel5.target** links to **graphical.target** (desktop interface). The runlevels and their targets are listed in Table 5-10.

System Runlevel links	systemd targets
runlevel0	poweroff.target
runlevel1	rescue.target
runlevel2	multi-user.target
runlevel3	multi-user.target
runlevel4	multi-user.target
runlevel5	graphical.target
runlevel6	reboot.target

Table 5-10: System Runlevels (States)

You can still use the **runlevel** command to see what state you are currently running in. It lists the previous state followed by the current one. If you have not changed states, the previous state will be listed as N, indicating no previous state. This is the case for the state you boot up in. In the next example, the system is running in state 3, with no previous state change.

```
# runlevel
N 3
```

Changing runlevels can be helpful if you have problems at a particular runlevel. For example, if your video card is not installed properly, then any attempt to start up in runlevel 5 (**graphical.target**) will likely fail, as this level immediately starts your graphical interface. Instead, you could use the command line interface, runlevel 3 (**multi-user.target**), to fix your video card installation.

No matter what runlevel you start in, you can change from one runlevel to another with the **telinit** command. If your default runlevel is 3, you power up in runlevel 3, but you can change to, say, runlevel 5 with **telinit 5**. The command **telinit 0** shuts down your system. In the next example, the **telinit** command changes to runlevel 1, the administrative state.

```
telinit 1
```

Before **systemd** was implemented, you could also use **init** to change runlevels. With **systemd**, both **telinit** and **init** are now **systemd** emulation versions of the original Unix commands. The **telinit** command is always used to change runlevels. If you use **init** with a runlevel number, it now merely invokes **telinit** to make the change.

Alternatively, you can use the **systemctl** command directly to change runlevels (targets). The **systemctl** command with the **isolate** option and the name of the target file changes to that target (runlevel). This is what the **telinit** command actually does. The following command changes to the **multi-user** target.

```
sudo systemctl isolate multi-user.target
```

You could also use the runlevel link instead.

```
sudo systemctl isolate runlevel3.target
```

systemd and automatically mounting file systems: /etc/fstab

The **systemd** unit files with the extension **.mount** can be used to mount file systems automatically. Normally systemd will read the **/etc/fstab** file for mount information. If a mount unit file exists in the **/etc/systemd** directory, it takes precedence, but **/etc/fstab** takes precedence over any unit mount files in the **/lib/systemd** directory. The **/etc/fstab** file is used for mount configuration information. Most of the options for a mount unit file correspond to those of the **/etc/fstab** file, specifying the device path name, the mount point, file system type, and mount options (see Table 5-11). The entries in the **/etc/fstab** file are converted to mount unit files at boot, which are then used by systemd to perform the actual mount operations. These mount unit files are created by the systemd-fstab-generator and can be found in the **/run/systemd/generator** directory.

The following fstab file entries have corresponding mount files created in the **/run/systemd/generator** directory: **boot.mount** for the boot file system (**boot-efi.mount** for an EUFI boot system), **home.mount** for the home file system, and **-.mount** for the root file system. For the swap file system, a swap file is generated.

mount options	Description
What	Path of the device.
Where	Directory of the mount point.
Type	File system type.
Options	Mount options.
DirectoryMode	Permissions for created file system mount directories.
TimeoutSec	Time to wait for a mount operation to finish.
automount options	**Description**
Where	Mount point for the file system. If it does not exist, it will be created.
DirectoryMode	Permissions for any directories created.

Table 5-11: systemd mount and automount file options [Mount] [Automount]

```
UUID=1059a-4a86-4072-982e-000717229b9f / ext4    errors=remount-ro   0 1
UUID-=5537-AF41 /boot/efi    vfat    umask=0077   0 1
UUID=147b-4a86-4072-982e-000717229b6g /home ext4    default   0 1
/swapfile  none    swap    sw   0 0
```

For this example, the **-.mount** file used for the root file system will have the following mount options. The root directory is represented in the mount filename as a dash, **-**, instead of a slash, **/**. The mount options are listed in a **[Mount]** section.

```
[Mount]
What=/dev/disk/by-uuid/1059a-4a86-4072-982e-000717229b9f
Where=/
Type=ext4
Options=errors=remount-ro
```

The **home.mount** file references partition for the home file system and mounts it to the **/home** directory.

```
[Mount]
What=/dev/disk/by-uuid/147b-4a86-4072-982e-000717229b6g
Where=/home
Type=ext4
```

The **boot.mount** file mounts the ext4 file system that holds the kernel in the **/boot** directory.

```
[Mount]
What=/dev/disk/by-uuid/e759aa59-4a86-4072-982e-000717229b4a
Where=/boot
Type=ext4
```

On EFI boot systems, the **boot-efi.mount** file mounts the vfat EFI file system that holds the boot information.

```
[Mount]
What=/dev/disk/by-uuid/5537-AF41
Where=/boot/efi
Type=vfat
```

All the unit files will designate the **/etc/fstab** file as the SourcePath, the file from which the configuration was generated.

```
SourcePath=/etc/fstab
```

All are mounted before any local file systems.

```
Before=local-fs.target
```

Local and remote file systems are distinguished by Wants options in their unit files for **local-fs.target** or **remote-fs.target**.

A mount unit file has to be named for the mount point it references. The path name slashes are replaced by dashes in the unit name. For example, the **proc-fs-nfsd.mount** file references the mount point **/proc/fs/nfsd**. The root path name, /, becomes a dash, -.

For file systems to be automatically mounted when accessed you can use the automount unit type. An automount unit must have a corresponding mount unit of the same name.

The **systemd-fsck@service** file provides a file system check with **fsck**, using the disk name as an argument.

```
RequiresOverridable=system-fsck@dev-disk-by\x2duuid-5537\x2dAF41.service
After=system-fsck@dev-disk-by\x2duuid-5537\x2dAF41.service
```

systemd slice and scope units

The slice and scope units are designed to group units to easily control their processes and resources. The scope units are generated by systemd to manage a process and its subprocesses. An example of a scope unit is a user session scope that groups the processes for a user session together. A slice is used to manage resources for processes, such as the machine slice for virtual machines, the system slice for system services, and the user slice for user sessions.

System V: /etc/init.d

For Ubuntu 24.04, compatible System V management scripts are located in the **/etc/init.d** directory. These are accessed by links in rc.d directories The rc.d directories correspond to the different runlevels, such as **rc3.d** for runlevel 3, and **rc5.d** for runlevel 5.

For a very few system tasks, such as the **lpd** service, that are not implemented as systemd services and have no unit files, **systemd** will read their System V scripts in the **/etc/init.d** directory and generate a corresponding unit configuration file for it. Such unit files are generated by **systemd-sysv-generator** and located in the **/var/run/systemd/generator.late** directory.

An **rc-local.service** unit file in the **/lib/systemd/system** directory will run a **/etc/rc.local** file, if present. This is to maintain compatibility with older System V configuration.

Shutdown and Poweroff

You can use the **shutdown** and **poweroff** commands to power down the system. The **shutdown** command provides more options. Keep in mind that the **shutdown** command used is the **systemd** version, which will use **systemctl** to actually shut down the system.

You can also shut down your system immediately using the **poweroff** command with the **sudo** command. You may be prompted to enter your password.

```
sudo poweroff
```

To perform a reboot, you can use the **reboot** command.

```
sudo reboot
```

The **shutdown** command has a time argument that gives users on the system a warning before you power down. You can specify an exact time to shut down, or a period of minutes from the current time. The exact time is specified by *hh:mm* for the hour and minutes. The period of time is indicated by a + and the number of minutes.

The **shutdown** command takes several options with which you can specify how you want your system shut down. The **-h** option, which stands for halt, simply shuts down the system, whereas the **-r** option shuts down the system and then reboots it. In the next example, the system is shut down after ten minutes.

```
shutdown -h +10
```

To shut down the system immediately, you can use **+0** or the word **now**. The shutdown options are listed in Table 5-12. The following example shuts down the system immediately and then reboots.

```
shutdown -r now
```

Command	Description
shutdown **[-rkhncft]** *time* [*warning*]	Shuts the system down after the specified time period, issuing warnings to users; you can specify a warning message of your own after the time argument; if neither **-h** nor **-r** is specified to shut down the system, the system sets to the administrative mode, runlevel state 1.
Argument	
Time	Has two possible formats: it can be an absolute time in the format *hh:mm,* with *hh* as the hour (one or two digits) and *mm* as the minute (in two digits); it can also be in the format *+m,* with *m* as the number of minutes to wait; the word **now** is an alias for +0.
Option	
-t *sec*	Tells **init** to wait *sec* seconds between sending processes the warning and the kill signals, before changing to another runlevel.
-k	Doesn't actually shut down; only sends the warning messages to everybody.
-r	Reboots after shutdown, runlevel state 6.
-h	Halts after shutdown, runlevel state 0.
-n	Doesn't call **init** to do the shutdown; you do it yourself.
-f	Skips file system checking (fsck) on reboot.
-c	Cancels an already running shutdown; no time argument.

Table 5-12: System Shutdown Options

With the **shutdown** command, you can include a warning message to be sent to all users currently logged in, giving them time to finish what they are doing before you shut them down.

```
shutdown -h +5 "System needs a rest"
```

If you do not specify either the **-h** or the **-r** options, the **shutdown** command shuts down the multi-user mode and shifts you to an administrative single-user mode. In effect, your system state changes from 3 (multi-user state) to 1 (administrative single-user state). Only the root user is active, allowing the root user to perform any necessary system administrative operations with which other users might interfere.

The shutdown process works through systemd using the **systemctl** command. The **poweroff**, **halt**, and **reboot** commands invoke systemd service files activated through corresponding target files. The **systemctl** command, in turn, uses the **/lib/systemd/system-shutdown** program to perform the actual shut down operation. In the **/lib/systemd/system** directory, the **systemd-poweroff.halt** file shows the **systemctl poweroff** command. The man page for the shutdown service is **systemd-halt-service**. Always use the **poweroff**, **reboot**, and **halt** commands to shut down, not the **systemctl** command. The corresponding systemd target and service files for these commands ensure that the shutdown process proceeds safely.

systemd-poweroff.service

```
#  This file is part of systemd.
#
#  systemd is free software; you can redistribute it and/or modify it
#  under the terms of the GNU Lesser General Public License as published by
#  the Free Software Foundation; either version 2.1 of the License, or
#  (at your option) any later version.

[Unit]
Description=System Power Off

Documentation=man:systemd-poweroff.service(8)
DefaultDependencies=no
Requires=shutdown.target umount.target final.target
After=shutdown.target umount.target final.target

SuccessAction=poweroff-force
```

Note: The halt command merely halts the system, it does not turn it off.

Managing Services

You can select certain services to run. Most services are servers like a Web server or FTP server. Other services provide security, such as SSH or Kerberos. You can decide which services to use with the **systemctl** command.

Enabling services: starting a service automatically at boot

Services such as the Apache Web server, Samba server, and the FTP server are handled by the **systemd** daemon. You can manage services using the **systemctl** command. The older **service** command is simply a front end to the **systemctl** command.

To have a service start up at boot, you need to first enable it using the **systemctl** tool as an administrative user. Use the **enable** command to enable the service. The following command enables the **vsftpd** server and the Samba server (**smbd**). The **systemctl** command uses the service's service configuration file located in the **/lib/systemd/system** or the **/etc/systemd/system** directory.

```
sudo systemctl enable vsftpd.service
sudo systemctl enable smbd
```

Managing services manually: systemctl

Use the **start**, **stop**, and **restart** commands with **systemctl** to manually start, stop, and restart a service. The **enable** command only starts up a service automatically. You could choose to start it manually using the **start** command. You can stop and restart a service any time using the **stop** and **restart** commands. The **condrestart** command only starts the server if it is already stopped. Use the **status** command to check the current status of service.

```
sudo systemctl start vsftpd
sudo systemctl restart vsftpd
sudo systemctl condrestart vsftpd
sudo systemctl stop vsftpd
sudo systemctl status vsftpd
```

The service Command

The older **service** command is now simply a front end for the **systemctl** command which performs the actual operation using **systemd**. The **service** command cannot enable or disable services. It only performs management operations such as start, stop, restart, and status. With the **service** command, you enter the service name with the **stop** argument to stop it, the **start** argument to start it, and the **restart** argument to restart it. You will have to use the **sudo** command. The following will start the **vsftpd** FTP service.

```
sudo service vsftpd start
```

The **systemd** version of the **service** command actually invokes the **systemctl** command to run the service's systemd **.service** unit file in **/lib/systemd/system**. If a service is not enabled, **systemd** will enable it. You can perform the same operations as the **service** command, using the **systemctl** command. The following is the equivalent of the previous command.

```
sudo systemctl start vsftpd
```

Cockpit

The Cockpit management console (provided by Red Hat) provides a Web interface for managing both system administration and internet servers on your system, as well as servers on your network (**https://cockpit-project.org**). The Web interface works best on a desktop system. You can use it to manage your system resources, including services, storage, and networking. The package name is **cockpit**.

```
sudo apt install cockpit
```

Figure 5-1: Cockpit

You can access Cockpit using a Web browser and accessing port 9090 on your local system (**localhost:9090**). The cockpit page initially prompts you for your username and password. The top menu on the left side shows a listing of the systems on your network. Your current system is already chosen. Links on the left side show administration categories such as System, services, networking, and storage. Click on the Services link to list your services, showing whether they are enabled or disabled, including the network services such as Samba, the Apache Web server, and the vsftpd FTP server (see Figure 5-1). The "Limited access" button at the top with a lock icon prevents you from making changes. To manage the services as an administrator, click on this button to open an "Switch to administrative access" dialog that prompts you for your password. Click the Authenticate button. Then click on the Services tab to list enabled and disabled services. Clicking on a service opens a page where you can manage the service. The current status is shown. Clicking on an vertical alliteration button to the right of the service name displays a menu for actions you may want to take, such as stopping or restarting a service. To disable a service click its enable/disable button to the right of the service name. If disabled, its status on the services list will show disabled.

Cockpit dynamically updates with **systemctl**. Should you make changes in a terminal window using **systemctl**, the changes are immediately shown on Cockpit.

The default port for Cockpit is the same as that used by Prometheus (Chapter 18), port 9090. Should you install and run Prometheus, it will block access on port 9090 for Cockpit. In this case, you can change the port that Cockpit uses. Create a **listen.conf** file in a cockpit configuration directory (**cockpit.conf.d**) in the **/etc/systemd/system** directory. Use the Socket and ListenStream directives to change the port. To access immediately reload the systemd configuration files (**daemon-reload**) and restart the Cockpit socket, otherwise restart the system. First create the **cockpit.conf.d** directory in the **/etc/systemd/system** directory if it does not already exist. Then, in the **cockpit.conf.d** directory create the **listen.conf** file and enter the Socket and ListenStream directives, assigning a new port.

```
cd /etc/systemd/system
sudo mkdir cockpit.conf.d
cd cockpit.conf.d
sudo nano listen.conf
```

A sample **listen.conf** file is shown here, setting the port to 9095 instead of 9090.

/etc/systemd/system/cockpit.conf.d/listen.conf

```
[Socket]
ListenStream=
ListenStream=9095
```

To access immediately reload the systemd configuration files (**daemon-reload**) and restart the Cockpit socket, otherwise restart the system.

```
sudo systemctl daemon-reload
sudo systemctl restart cockpit.socket
```

/etc/default

The **/etc/default** directory holds scripts for setting runtime options when a service starts up. For example, the **/etc/default/apache2** script sets cache cleaning options. The **/etc/default/ufw** scripts sets firewall default policies. You can edit these scripts and change the values assigned to options, changing the behavior of a service.

Network Time Protocol: Chrony

For servers to run correctly, they need to always have the correct time. Internet time servers worldwide provide the time in the form of the Universal Time Coordinated (UTC). Local time is then calculated using the local system's local time zone. The time is obtained from Internet time servers from an Internet connection. You have the option of using a local hardware clock instead, though this may be much less accurate.

Normally, the time on a host machine is kept in a Time of Year chip (TOY) that maintains the time when the machine is off. Its time is used when the machine is rebooted. A host using the

Network Time Protocol then adjusts the time, using the time obtained from an Internet time server. If there is a discrepancy of more than 1000 seconds (about 15 minutes), the system administrator is required to manually set the time. Time servers in the public network are organized in stratum levels, the highest being 1. Time servers from a lower stratum obtain the time from those in the next higher level.

The time is synchronized for your host by the **systemd-timesyncd** daemon. You can manage and set the time on your host with the **timedatectl** command. However, if you want to set up a time server on your local network, you can use Chrony.

For servers on your local network, you may want to set up your own time server, ensuring that all your servers are using a synchronized time. If all your servers are running on a single host system that is directly connected to the Internet and accessing an Internet time server, you will not need to set up a separate time server.

The Chrony time server replaces the older NTP time server. You can find documentation for Chrony at:

```
https://chrony.tuxfamily.org
```

There is a package on the Ubuntu repository for the Chrony server. You can install it with the **apt** command, as well as the App Center or the Synaptic Package Manager on the desktop.

```
sudo apt install chrony
```

There are man pages for the **chronyd**, **chrony.conf**, and **chronyc**. The command line interface for the **chronyd** server is **chronyc**.

```
chronyc
```

The Chrony server

The Chrony server name is **chronyd** and is managed by the **/lib/systemd/system/chrony.service** script. Use the **start**, **stop**, and **restart** options with the **systemctl** command to manage the server.

```
sudo systemctl start chronyd
```

Your host systems can then be configured to use Chrony and access your Chrony time server.

The chrony.conf configuration file

The Chrony server configuration file is **/etc/chrony/chrony.conf**. This file lists the Internet time servers that your own time server used to determine the time. Check the **chrony.conf** Man page for a complete listing of the Chrony server configuration directives.

In the **chrony.conf** file, the server directive specifies the Internet time server's Internet address that your Chrony server uses to access the time. There is a default entry for the pool of Ubuntu time servers, but you can add server entries for other time servers. You would use the **server** directive for a specific time server.

```
pool ntp.ubuntu.com
```

The default **/etc/chrony/chrony.conf** file is shown here.

```
# Welcome to the chrony configuration file. See chrony.conf(5) for more
# information about usuable directives.

# This will use (up to):
# - 4 sources from ntp.ubuntu.com which some are ipv6 enabled
# - 2 sources from 2.ubuntu.pool.ntp.org which is ipv6 enabled as well
# - 1 source from [01].ubuntu.pool.ntp.org each (ipv4 only atm)
# This means by default, up to 6 dual-stack and up to 2 additional IPv4-only
# sources will be used.
# At the same time it retains some protection against one of the entries being
# down (compare to just using one of the lines). See (LP: #1754358) for the discussion.
# About using servers from the NTP Pool Project in general see (LP: #104525).
# Approved by Ubuntu Technical Board on 2011-02-08.
# See http://www.pool.ntp.org/join.html for more information.
pool ntp.ubuntu.com          iburst maxsources 4
pool 0.ubuntu.pool.ntp.org iburst maxsources 1
pool 1.ubuntu.pool.ntp.org iburst maxsources 1
pool 2.ubuntu.pool.ntp.org iburst maxsources 2

# Use time sources from DHCP.
sourcedir /run/chrony-dhcp

# Use NTP sources found in /etc/chrony/sources.d.
sourcedir /etc/chrony/sources.d

# This directive specify the location of the file containing ID/key pairs for
# NTP authentication.
keyfile /etc/chrony/chrony.keys

# This directive specify the file into which chronyd will store the rate
# information.
driftfile /var/lib/chrony/chrony.drift

# Save NTS keys and cookies.
ntsdumpdir /var/lib/chrony

# Uncomment the following line to turn logging on.
#log tracking measurements statistics

# Save NTS keys and cookies.
ntsdumpdir /var/lib/chrony

# Log files location.
logdir /var/log/chrony

# Stop bad estimates upsetting machine clock.
maxupdateskew 100.0

# This directive enables kernel synchronisation (every 11 minutes) of the
# real-time clock. Note that it cannot be used along with the 'rtcfile' directive.
rtcsync

# Step the system clock instead of slewing it if the adjustment is larger than
# one second, but only in the first three clock updates.
makestep 1 3
# Get TAI-UTC offset and leap seconds from the system tz database.
# This directive must be commented out when using time sources serving
# leap-smeared time.
leapsectz right/UTC
```

The **allow** directive permits access by hosts on a local network to your time server, and the **deny** directive denies access. Those hosts can then use your time server. The **deny** directive denies access to specified hosts.

You can use the **cmdallow** command to allow client hosts to see your time server monitoring information. A host can then run the **cronyc** command line interface to run monitoring commands. The **cmddeny** will deny access.

You can also run the time server in broadcast mode where the time is broadcast to your network clients. Use the **broadcast** directive and your network's broadcast address.

```
broadcast 192.168.123.255
```

cronyc

The **cronyc** command line interface lets you monitor your **chronyd** server, generating status reports, as well as letting you change the **chronyd** configuration as it is running. You start the cronyc interface with the **cronyc** command. This places you in an interactive shell with the **chrony>** prompt where you can enter **cronyc** commands. To leave the shell enter the **quit** command.

For security purposes, only monitoring commands can be used by normal users or from users on other hosts. The activity command will check for how many NTP sources are online, and **sourcestats** will list performance information for NTP sources.

```
$ chronyc
chronyc>
```

Should you want to enter configuration commands you have to start **chronyc** as the root user. Use the **sudo** command. Keep in mind that the changes are not permanent. The **chrony.conf** file is not affected.

```
sudo chronyc
```

To set the time manually you would enter the **chronyc** shell as the root user, and use the **settime** command to specify the time. You may first have to run the **manual** command to enable the **settime** command.

```
$ sudo chronyc
chronyc> manual on
chronyc> settime Apr 7, 2024 18:24:09
chronyc> quit
```

AppArmor security

Ubuntu installs AppArmor as its default security system. AppArmor (Application Armor) is designed as an alternative to SELinux (Security-Enhanced Linux, **http://selinuxproject.org/page/Main_Page**). It is much less complicated but makes use of the same kernel support provided for SELinux. AppArmor is a simple method for implementing mandatory access controls (MAC) for specified Linux applications. It is used primarily for servers like Samba, the CUPS print servers, and the time server. In this respect, it is much more limited in scope than SELinux, which tries to cover every object. Instead of labeling each object, which

SELinux does, AppArmor identifies an object by its path name. The object does not have to be touched. Originally developed by Immunix and later supported for a time by Novell (OpenSUSE), AppArmor is available under the GNU Public License. You can find out more about AppArmor at **https://gitlab.com/apparmor/apparmor/-/wikis/Documentation**.

AppArmor works by setting up a profile for supported applications. Essentially, this is a security policy similar to SELinux policies. A profile defines what an application can access and use on the system. Ubuntu will install the **apparmor** package. Also available are the **apparmor-profiles**, **apparmor-utils**, and **apparmor-doc** packages.

AppArmor is implemented with systemd, using the **/lib/systemd/system/apparmor.service** script. You can use the **systemctl** command to start, stop, and restart AppArmor.

```
sudo systemctl start apparmor
```

AppArmor utilities

The **apparmor-utils** packages install several AppArmor tools, including **aa-enforce**, which enables AppArmor and **aa-complain**, which instructs AppArmor to just issue warning messages (see Table 5-13). The **aa-unconfined** tool will list applications that have no AppArmor profiles. The **aa-audit** tool will turn on AppArmor message logging for an application (uses enforce mode).

Utility	Description
apparmor_status	Status information about AppArmor policies.
aa-audit *applications*	Enable logging for AppArmor messages for specified applications.
aa-complain	Set AppArmor to complain mode.
aa-enforce	Set AppArmor to enforce mode.
aa-autodep *application*	Generate a basic profile for new applications.
aa-logprof	Analyzes AppArmor complain messages for a profile and suggests profile modifications.
aa-genprof *application*	Generate profile for an application.
aa-unconfined	Lists applications not controlled by AppArmor (no profiles).

Table 5-13: AppArmor Utilities

The **apparmor_status** tool will display current profile information. The **--complaining** options lists only those in complain mode, and **--enforced** for those in enforcing mode.

```
sudo apparmor_status
```

The **aa-logprof** tool will analyze AppArmor logs to determine if any changes are needed in any of the application profiles. Suggested changes will be presented, and the user can allow (**A**) or deny them (**D**). In complain mode, allow is the default, and in enforce mode, deny is the default. You can also make your own changes with the new (**N**) option. Should you want the change applied to all files and directories in a suggested path, you can select the glob option (**G**), essentially replacing the last directory or file in a path with the * global file matching symbol.The **aa-logprof** tool will analyze AppArmor logs to determine if any changes are needed in any of the application profiles. Suggested changes will be presented, and the user can allow (**A**) or deny them (**D**). In complain mode, allow is the default, and in enforce mode, deny is the default. You can also make your own changes with the new (**N**) option. Should you want the change applied to all files and directories in a suggested path, you can select the glob option (**G**), essentially replacing the last directory or file in a path with the * global file matching symbol.

The **aa-autodep** tool will generate a basic AppArmor profile for a new or unconfined application. If you want a more effective profile, you can use **aa-genprof** to analyze the application's use and generate profile controls accordingly.

The **aa-genprof** tool will update or generate a detailed profile for a specified application. **aa-genprof** will first set the profile to complain mode. You then start up the application and use it, generating complain mode log messages on that use. Then, **vgenprof** prompts you to either scan the complain messages to further refine the profile (**S**), or to finish (**F**). When scanned, different violations are detected, and the user is prompted to allow or deny recommended controls. You can then repeat the scan operation until you feel the profile is acceptable. Select finish (**F**) to finalize the profile and quit.

AppArmor configuration

AppArmor configuration is located in the **/etc/apparmor** directory. Configurations for different profiles are located in the **/etc/apparmor.d** directory. Loaded profile configuration files have the name of their path, using periods instead of slashes to separate directory names. The profile file for the **smbd** (Samba) application is **usr.sbin.smbd**. For CUPS (**cupsd**) it is **usr.sbin.cupsd**. Additional profiles like the Samba and Apache profiles are installed with the **apparmor-profiles** package (not installed by default).

```
sudo apt-get install apparmor-profiles
```

Configuration rules for AppArmor profiles consist of a path and permissions allowable on that path. A detailed explanation of AppArmor rules and permissions can be found in the **apparmor.d** Man page, including a profile example. A path ending in a * matching symbol will select all the files in that directory. The ** symbol selects all files and subdirectories. All file matching operations are supported (* [] ?). Permissions include **r** (read), **w** (write), **x** (execute), and **l** (link). The **u** permission allows unconstrained access. The following entry allows all the files and subdirectories in the **/var/log/samba/cores/smbd** directory to be written to.

```
/var/log/samba/cores/smbd/** rw,
```

The **/etc/apparmor.d/abstractions** directory has files with profile rules that are common to different profiles. Rules from these files are read into actual profiles using the **include** directive. There are abstractions for applications like audio, samba, and video. Some abstractions will include yet other more general abstractions, like those for the X server (**X**) or GNOME (**gnome**). For example, the profile for the Samba **smbd** server, **usr.sbin.smbd**, will have an include directive for the **samba** abstraction. This abstraction holds rules common to both the **smbd** and **nmbd** servers, both used by the Samba service. The <> used in an **include** directive indicates the **/etc/apparmor.d** directory. A list of abstraction files can be found in the **apparmor.d** Man page. The **include** directive begins with a # character.

```
#include <abstractions/samba>
```

In some cases, a profile may need access to some files in a directory that it normally should not have access to. In this case, it may need to use a sub-profile to allow access. In effect, the application changes profiles, taking on permissions it does not have in the original profile.

The **armor-profiles** package will activate several commonly used profiles, setting up profile files for them in the **/etc/apparmor.d** directory, like those for samba (**usr.sbin.nmbd** and **usr.sbin.smbd**), the Dovecot mail pop and imap server (**usr.sbin.dovecot**), and Avahi (**usr.sbin.avahi-daemon**).

The package also will provide profile default files for numerous applications in the **/usr/share/doc/apparmor-profiles/extras** directory, such as the vsftpd FTP server (**usr.sbin.vsftpd**), the ClamAV virus scanner (**usr.bin.freshclam**), and the Squid proxy server (**usr.sbin.squid**). Some service applications are located in the **/usr/lib** directory, and will have a **usr.lib** prefix such as those for the Postfix server, which uses several profiles, beginning with **usr.lib.postfix**. To use these extra profiles, copy them to the **/etc/apparmor.d** directory. The following example copies the profile for the vsftpd FTP server.

```
sudo cp /usr/share/doc/apparmor-profiles/extras/usr.sbin.vsftpd  /etc/apparmor.d
```

Remote Administration

For remote administration, you can use OpenSSH and Puppet. OpenSSH lets you remotely control and transfer files securely over your network. Puppet lets you manage the remote configuration of services.

Puppet

Puppet allows you to configure remote systems automatically, even though they may be running different Linux distributions with varying configuration files. Instead of configuring each system on a network manually, you can use Puppet to configure them automatically. Puppet abstracts administration tasks as resources in a resource abstraction layer (RAL). You then specify basic values or operations for a particular resource using a Puppet configuration language. Administration types include services, files, users, and groups. For example, you could use puppet to perform an update for a service (server) on systems using different package managers such as apt or Synaptic.

Puppet configuration can become very complex. Once set up, it fully automates configuration changes across all your networked systems. For detailed documentation and guides see the following.

```
https://puppet.com/docs/
```

Puppet configuration is located in the **/etc/puppet** directory. Puppet operations on services are specified in modules programmed in the **init.pp** file located in a **manifests** directory. In the Ubuntu example for Apache (Ubuntu Server Guide, Puppet), the apache2 module is created in the **init.pp** file:

```
/etc/puppet/modules/apache2/manifests/init.pp
```

On Ubuntu, clients use the puppet client (**puppet** package) and the server uses the puppetmaster daemon (**puppet-master** package). On puppet clients, use the **sytemctl** command to manually start and stop the **puppet** service. For the server, enable the **puppetmaster** service.

On the firewall add access for the Puppet port, 8140.

For the client, the puppet runtime configuration is set in the **/etc/default/puppet** file. Here you set the daemon to start by setting the **START** variable to yes

If your network is running a DNS server, you can set up a CNAME puppet entry for the puppet server. The puppet clients can then use the CNAME to locate the puppet server.

```
puppet   IN   CNAME   turtle.mytrek.com
```

You could also add a host entry for the puppet server in each client's **/etc/host** file.

On the server, the puppetmaster configuration in **/etc/default/puppetmaster** file lets you set port entries and the log service. Default entries are commented out. Remove the comment character, #, to enable.

When you first set up a client server puppet connection, the client and server have to sign the client's SSL certificate. First, run puppet on the client. On the server run the **puppet cert --list** command to see the clients certificate request. Then use **puppet cert --sign** to sign the certificate.

The Secure Shell: OpenSSH

Although a firewall can protect a network from attempts to break into it from the outside, the problem of securing legitimate communications to the network from outside sources still exists. A particular problem is one of users who want to connect to your network remotely. Such connections could be monitored, and information such as passwords and user IDs used when the user logs in to your network could be copied and used later to break in. One solution is to use SSH for remote logins and other kinds of remote connections such as FTP transfers. SSH encrypts any communications between the remote user and a system on your network.

The SSH protocol has become an official Internet Engineering Task Force (IETF) standard. A free and open source version is developed and maintained by the OpenSSH project, supported by the OpenBSD project. OpenSSH is the version supplied with most Linux distributions, including Ubuntu. You can find out more about OpenSSH at **https://www.openssh.com/**, where you can download the most recent version, though Ubuntu will provide current versions from its repository. Traditionally there were two versions of SSH, the older SSH1 and its replacement SSH2. In the current release of OpenSSH, SSH1 is disabled by default. The OpenSSH server only supports SSH2. Should you need SSH1 tools for accessing an old SSH1 only server, you can install the **openssh-client-ssh1** package.

SSH secures connections by both authenticating users and encrypting their transmissions. The authentication process is handled with public key encryption. Once authenticated, transmissions are encrypted by a cipher agreed upon by the SSH server and client for use in a particular session. SSH supports multiple ciphers. Authentication is applied to both hosts and users. SSH first authenticates a particular host, verifying that it is a valid SSH host that can be securely communicated with. Then the user is authenticated, verifying that the user is who they say they are.

Encryption

The public key encryption used in SSH authentication makes use of two keys: a public key and a private key. The public key is used to encrypt data, while the private key decrypts it. Each host or user has its own public and private keys. The public key is distributed to other hosts, who can then use it to encrypt authenticated data that only the host's private key can decrypt. For example, when a host sends data to a user on another system, the host encrypts the authentication data with a public key, which it previously received from that user. The data can be decrypted only by the user's corresponding private key. The public key can safely be sent in the open from one host to another, allowing it to be installed safely on different hosts. You can think of the process as taking place between a client and a server. When the client sends data to the server, it first encrypts the data using the server's public key. The server can then decrypt the data using its own private key.

It is recommended that SSH transmissions be authenticated with public-private keys controlled by passphrases. Unlike PGP, SSH uses public-key encryption for the authentication process only. Once authenticated, participants agree on a common cipher to use to encrypt transmissions. Authentication will verify the identity of the participants. Each user who intends to use SSH to access a remote account first needs to create the public and private keys along with a passphrase to use for the authentication process. A user then sends their public key to the remote account they want to access and installs the public key on that account. When the user attempts to access the remote account, that account can then use the user's public key to authenticate that the user is who they claim to be. The process assumes that the remote account has set up its own SSH private and public key. For the user to access the remote account, they will have to know the remote account's SSH passphrase. SSH is often used in situations where a user has two or more accounts located on different systems and wants to be able to securely access them from each other. In that case, the user already has access to each account and can install SSH on each, giving each its own private and public keys along with their passphrases.

Authentication

For authentication in SSH, a user creates both public and private keys. For this, you use the **ssh-keygen** command. The user's public key then has to be distributed to those users that the original user wants access to. Often this is an account a user has on another host. A passphrase further protects access. The original user will need to know the other user's passphrase to access it.

When a remote user tries to log in to an account, that account is checked to see if it has the remote user's public key. That public key is then used to encrypt a challenge (usually a random number) that can be decrypted only by the remote user's private key. When the remote user receives the encrypted challenge, that user decrypts the challenge with its private key. The remote user will first encrypt a session identifier using its private key, signing it. The encrypted session identifier is then decrypted by the account using the remote user's public key. The session identifier has been previously set up by SSH for that session.

SSH authentication is first carried out with the host, and then with users. Each host has its own host keys, public and private keys used for authentication. Once the host is authenticated, the user is queried. Each user has their own public and private keys. Users on an SSH server who want to receive connections from remote users will have to keep a list of those remote user's public keys. Similarly, an SSH host will maintain a list of public keys for other SSH hosts.

SSH Packages, Tools, and Server

SSH is implemented on Linux systems with OpenSSH. The full set of OpenSSH packages includes the OpenSSH meta-package (ssh), the OpenSSH server (openssh-server), and the

OpenSSH client (openssh-clients). These packages also require OpenSSL (openssl), which installs the cryptographic libraries that SSH uses.

The SSH tools are listed in Table 5-14. They include several client programs such as **scp**, **ssh**, as well as the **ssh** server. The **ssh** server (**sshd**) provides secure connections to anyone from the outside using the **ssh** client to connect. Several configuration utilities are also included, such as **ssh-add**, which adds valid hosts to the authentication agent, and **ssh-keygen**, which generates the keys used for encryption.

Application	Description
ssh	SSH client.
sshd	SSH server (daemon).
sftp	SSH FTP client, Secure File Transfer Program. Version 2 only. Use ? to list sftp commands(SFTP protocol).
sftp-server	SSH FTP server. Version 2 only (SFTP protocol).
scp	SSH copy command client.
ssh-keygen	Utility for generating keys. **-h** for help.
ssh-keyscan	Tool to automatically gather public host keys to generate ssh_known_hosts files.
ssh-add	Adds RSD and DSA identities to the authentication agent.
ssh-agent	SSH authentication agent that holds private keys for public key authentication (RSA, DSA).
ssh-askpass	X Window System utility for querying passwords, invoked by **ssh-add** (openssh-askpass).
ssh-askpass-gnome	GNOME utility for querying passwords, invoked by **ssh-add**.
ssh-signer	Signs host-based authentication packets. Version 2 only. Must be suid root (performed by installation).
slogin	Remote login (version 1).

Table 5-14: SSH Tools

You can start, stop, and restart the server manually with the **systemctl** commands.

```
sudo systemctl restart sshd
```

You have to configure your firewall to allow access to the **ssh** service. The service is set up to operate using the TCP protocol on port 22, tcp/22. If you are managing your IPTables or nftables firewall directly, you would add the following IPtables and nftables rules. This accepts input on port 22 for TCP/IP protocol packages.

iptables rule:

```
iptables -A INPUT -p tcp --dport 22 -j ACCEPT
```

nftables rule:

```
nft add rule ip filter INPUT tcp dport 22 counter accept
```

SSH Setup

Using SSH involves creating your own public and private keys and then distributing your public key to other users you want to access. These can be different users or simply user accounts of your own that you have on remote systems. Often people remotely log in from a local client to an account on a remote server, perhaps from a home computer to a company computer. Your home computer would be your client account, and the account on your company computer would be your server account. On your client account, you need to generate your public and private keys and then place a copy of your public key in the server account. Once the account on your server has a copy of your client user's public key, you can access the server account from your client account. You will be also prompted for the server account's passphrase. You will have to know this to access that account. Figure 5-1 illustrates the SSH setup that allows a user **george** to access the account **cecelia**.

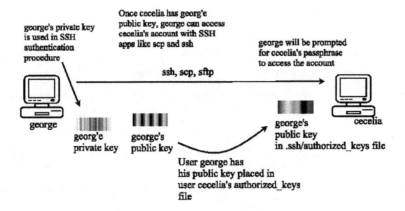

Figure 5-2: SSH setup and access

To allow you to use SSH to access other accounts follow these steps.

You must create public and private keys on your account along with a passphrase. You will need to use this passphrase to access your account from another account.

You must distribute your public key to other accounts you want to access, placing them in the **.ssh/authorized_keys** file.

Other accounts also have to set up public and private keys along with a passphrase.

You must know the other account's passphrase to access it.

Creating SSH Keys with ssh-keygen

You create your public and private keys using the **ssh-keygen** command. You need to specify the kind of encryption you want to use. You can use either DSA or RSA encryption. Specify the type using the **-t** option and the encryption name in lowercase (**rsa**, **dsa**, **ecdsa**, and **ed25519**). In the following example, the user creates a key with the RSA encryption.

```
ssh-keygen -t rsa
```

The **ssh-keygen** command prompts you for a passphrase, which it will use as a kind of password to protect your private key. The passphrase should be several words long. You are also prompted to enter a filename for the keys. If you do not enter one, SSH will use its defaults. The public key will be given the extension **.pub**. The **ssh-keygen** command generates the public key and places it in your public key file, such as **.ssh/id_dsa.pub** or **.ssh/id_rsa.pub**, depending on the type of key you specified. It places the private key in the corresponding private key file, such as **.ssh/id_dsa** or **.ssh/id_rsa**.

If you need to change your passphrase, you can do so with the **ssh-keygen** command and the **-p** option. Each user will have their own SSH configuration directory, called **.ssh**, located in their own home directory. The public and private keys, as well as SSH configuration files, are placed here. If you build from the source code, the **make install** operation will automatically run **ssh-keygen**. Table 5-15 lists the SSH configuration files.

File	Description
$HOME/.ssh/known_hosts	Records host keys for all hosts the user has logged in to (that are not in **/etc/ssh/ssh_known_hosts**).
$HOME/.ssh/random_seed	Seeds the random number generator.
$HOME/.ssh/id_rsa	Contains the RSA authentication identity of the user.
$HOME/.ssh/id_dsa	Contains the DSA authentication identity of the user.
$HOME/.ssh/id_rsa.pub	Contains the RSA public key for authentication. The contents of this file should be added to **$HOME/.ssh/authorized_keys** on all machines where you want to log in using RSA authentication.
$HOME/.ssh/id_dsa.pub	Contains the DSA public key for authentication.
$HOME/.ssh/config	The per-user configuration file.
$HOME/.ssh/authorized_keys	Lists the RSA or DSA keys that can be used for logging in as this user.
/etc/ssh/ssh_known_hosts	Contains the system-wide list of known host keys.
/etc/ssh/ssh_config	Contains the system-wide configuration file. This file provides defaults for those values not specified in the user's configuration file.
/etc/ssh/sshd_config	Contains the SSH server configuration file.
/etc/ssh/sshrc	Contains the system default. Commands in this file are executed by ssh when the user logs in just before the user's shell (or command) is started.
$HOME/.ssh/rc	Contains commands executed by ssh when the user logs in just before the user's shell (or command) is started.

Table 5-15: SSH Configuration Files

Authorized Keys

A public key is used to authenticate a user and its host. You use the public key on a remote system to allow that user access. The public key is placed in the remote user account's **.ssh/authorized_keys** file. The public key is held in the **.ssh/id_dsa.pub** file. If a user wants to log in remotely from a local account to an account on a remote system, they would first place their public key in the **.ssh/authorized_keys** file in the account on the remote system they want to access. If the user **larisa** on **turtle.mytrek.com** wants to access the **aleina** account on **rabbit.mytrek.com**, **larisa**'s public key from **/home/larisa/.ssh/id_dsa.pub** first must be placed in **aleina**'s **authorized_keys** file, **/home/aleina/.ssh/authorized_keys**. User **larisa** can send the key or have it copied over. A simple **cat** operation can append a key to the authorized key file. In the next example, the user adds the public key for **aleina** in the **larisa.pub** file to the authorized key file. The **larisa.pub** file is a copy of the **/home/larisa/.ssh/id_dsa.pub** file that the user received earlier.

```
cat larisa.pub >> .ssh/authorized_keys
```

Note: You can also use seahorse to create and manage SSH keys.

Note: The .ssh/identity filename is used in SSH version 1; it may be installed by default on older distribution versions. SSH version 2 uses a different filename, .ssh/id_dsa or .ssh/id_rsa, depending on whether RSA or DSA authentication is used.

Loading Keys

If you regularly make connections to a variety of remote hosts, you can use the **ssh-agent** command to place private keys in memory where they can be accessed quickly to decrypt received transmissions. The **ssh-agent** command is intended for use at the beginning of a login session. For GNOME, you can use the **openssh-askpass-gnome** utility, invoked by **ssh-add**, which allows you to enter a password when you log in to GNOME. GNOME will automatically supply that password whenever you use an SSH client.

Although the **ssh-agent** command enables you to use private keys in memory, you also must specifically load your private keys into memory using the **ssh-add** command. **ssh-add** with no arguments loads your private key from your private key file, such as. **.ssh/id_rsa**. You are prompted for your passphrase for this private key. To remove the key from memory, use **ssh-add** with the **-d** option. If you have several private keys, you can load them all into memory. **ssh-add** with the **-l** option lists those currently loaded.

SSH Clients

SSH was originally designed to replace remote access operations, such as **rlogin**, **rcp**, and Telnet, which perform no encryption and introduce security risks. You can also use SSH to encode X server sessions as well as FTP transmissions (**sftp**). Corresponding SSH clients replace these applications. With **slogin** or **ssh**, you can log in from a remote host to execute commands and run applications, much as you can with **rlogin** and **rsh**. With **scp**, you can copy files between the remote host and a network host, just as with **rcp**. With **sftp**, you can transfer FTP files secured by encryption.

ssh

With **ssh**, you can remotely log in from a local client to a remote system on your network operating as the SSH server. The term local client here refers to one outside the network, such as your home computer, and the term remote refers to a host system on the network to which you are connecting. In effect, you connect from your local system to the remote network host. It is designed to replace **rlogin**, which performs remote logins, and **rsh**, which executes remote commands. With

ssh, you can log in from a local site to a remote host on your network and then send commands to be executed on that host. The **ssh** command is also capable of supporting X Window System connections. This feature is automatically enabled if you make an ssh connection from an X Window System environment, such as GNOME. A connection is set up for you between the local X server and the remote X server. The remote host sets up a dummy X server and sends any X Window System data through it to your local system to be processed by your own local X server.

The ssh login operation function is much like the **rlogin** command. You enter the **ssh** command with the address of the remote host, followed by a **-l** option and the login name (username) of the remote account you are logging in to. The following example logs in to the **aleina** user account on the **rabbit.mytrek.com** host.

```
ssh rabbit.mytrek.com -l aleina
```

You can also use the username in an address format with **ssh**, as in:

```
ssh aleina@rabbit.mytrek.com
```

The following listing shows how the user **george** accesses the **cecelia** account on **turtle.mytrek.com**.

```
[george@turtle george]$ ssh turtle.mytrek.com -l cecelia
cecelia@turtle.mytrek.com's password:
[cecelia@turtle cecelia]$
```

A variety of options is available to enable you to configure your connection. Most have corresponding configuration options that can be set in the configuration file. For example, with the **-c** option, you can designate which encryption method you want to use, for instance, **idea**, **des**, **blowfish**, or **arcfour**. With the **-i** option, you can select a particular private key to use. The **-c** option enables you to have transmissions compressed at specified levels (see the **ssh** Man page for a complete list of options).

scp

You use **scp** to copy files from one host to another on a network. Designed to replace **rcp**, **scp** uses **ssh** to transfer data and employs the same authentication and encryption methods. If authentication requires it, **scp** requests a password or passphrase. The **scp** program operates much like **rcp**. Directories and files on remote hosts are specified using the username and the host address before the filename or directory. The username specifies the remote user account that **scp** is accessing, and the host is the remote system where that account is located. You separate the user from the host address with an **@**, and you separate the host address from the file or directory name with a colon. The following example copies the file **party** from a user's current directory to the user **aleina**'s **birthday** directory, located on the **rabbit.mytrek.com** host.

```
scp party aleina@rabbit.mytrek.com:/birthday/party
```

Of particular interest is the **-r** option (recursive) option, which enables you to copy whole directories. See the **scp** Man page for a complete list of options. In the next example, the user copies the entire **reports** directory to the user **justin**'s **projects** directory.

```
scp -r reports justin@rabbit.mytrek.com:/projects
```

In the next example, the user **george** copies the **mydoc1** file from the user **cecelia**'s home directory.

```
[george@turtle george]$ scp cecelia@turtle.mytrek.com:mydoc1  .
cecelia@turtle.mytrek.com's password:
mydoc1    0% |                                    |   0 --:--
ETA
mydoc1  100% |****************************|  17 00:00
[george@turtle george]$
```

sftp and sftp-server

With **sftp**, you can transfer FTP files secured by encryption. The **sftp** program uses the same commands as **ftp**. This client operates much like **ftp**, with many of the same commands.

```
sftp download.ubuntu.com
```

To use the **sftp** to connect to an FTP server, that server needs to be operating the **sftp-server** application. The SSH server invokes **sftp-server** to provide encrypted FTP transmissions to those using the **sftp** client. The sftp server and client use the SSH File Transfer Protocol (SFTP) to perform FTP operations securely.

Port Forwarding (Tunneling)

If for some reason, you can connect to a secure host only by going through an insecure host, SSH provides a feature called port forwarding. With port forwarding, you can secure the insecure segment of your connection. This involves simply specifying the port at which the insecure host is to connect to the secure one. This sets up a direct connection between the local host and the remote host, through the intermediary insecure host. Encrypted data is passed through directly. This process is referred to as tunneling, creating a secure tunnel of encrypted data through connected servers.

You can set up port forwarding to a port on the remote system or to one on your local system. To forward a port on the remote system to a port on your local system, use **ssh** with the **-R** option, followed by an argument holding the local port, the remote host address, and the remote port to be forwarded, each separated by a colon. This works by allocating a socket to listen to the port on the remote side. Whenever a connection is made to this port, the connection is forwarded over the secure channel, and a connection is made to a remote port from the local machine. In the following example, port 22 on the local system is connected to port 23 on the **rabbit.mytrek.com** remote system.

```
ssh -R 22:rabbit.mytrek.com:23
```

To forward a port on your local system to a port on a remote system, use the **-L** option, followed by an argument holding the local port, the remote host address, and the remote port to be forwarded, each two arguments separated by a colon. A socket is allocated to listen to the port on the local side. Whenever a connection is made to this port, the connection is forwarded over the secure channel and a connection is made to the remote port on the remote machine. In the following example, port 22 on the local system is connected to port 23 on the **rabbit.mytrek.com** remote system.

```
ssh -L 22:rabbit.mytrek.com:23
```

You can use the LocalForward and RemoteForward options in your **.ssh/ssh_config** file to set up port forwarding for particular hosts or to specify a default for all hosts you connect to.

SSH Configuration

The SSH configuration file for each user is in their **.ssh/ssh_config** file. The **/etc/ssh/ssh_config** file is used to set site-wide defaults, with possible additional configuration files in the **/etc/ssh/ssh_config.d** directory that are read by the **/etc/ssh/ssh_config** file. In the configuration file, you can set various options, as listed in the **ssh_config** Man document. The configuration file is designed to specify options for different remote hosts to which you might connect. It is organized into segments, where each segment begins with the keyword **HOST**, followed by the IP address of the host. The following lines hold the options you have set for that host. A segment ends at the next **HOST** entry. Of particular interest are the **User** and **Ciphers** options. Use the **User** option to specify the names of users on the remote system who are allowed access. With the **Ciphers** option, you can select which encryption method to use for a particular host (the **Cipher** option is an SSH1 option, which is no longer supported):

```
Host turtle.mytrek.com
    User larisa
    Compression no
    Ciphers aes128-ctr
```

Most standard options, including ciphers, are already listed as commented entries. Remove the # to activate.

```
#   Ciphers aes128-ctr,aes192-ctr,aes256-ctr,aes128-cbc,3des-cbc
```

To specify global options that apply to any host you connect to, create a **HOST** entry with the asterisk as its host, **HOST ***. This entry must be placed at the end of the configuration file because an option is changed only the first time it is set. Any subsequent entries for an option are ignored. Because a host matches on both its own entry and the global one, its specific entry should come before the global entry. The asterisk (*****) and the question mark (**?**) are both wildcard matching operators that enable you to specify a group of hosts with the same suffix or prefix.

```
  Host *
    PasswordAuthentication yes
    ConnectTimeout 0
    Ciphers aes128-ctr
```

You use the **/etc/ssh/sshd_config** file to configure an SSH server, with possible additional configuration files in the **/etc/ssh/sshd_config.d** directory that are read by the **/etc/ssh/sshd_config** file. Here you will find server options like the port to use, password requirement, and PAM usage. Once configured, you can check the validation of your configuration file with the **sshd** command and the **-T** option.

```
sudo sshd -T
```

Watchdog

Watchdog is designed for unattended dedicated servers. It checks on a timer to see if a system has hanged. If so, then watchdog automatically reboots the system. Most hardware servers have a watchdog timer built into the motherboard. Debian (Ubuntu) Linux also has software watchdog support for the kernel, though it is not as effective as a hardware timer. To implement watchdog, install and run the watchdog daemon (watchdog software package). The systemd service files for watchdog are **watchdog.service** and **wd_keepalive.service**, which loads the watchdog kernel module and runs the watchdog daemon. Watchdog runtime options are located in the

/etc/default/watchdog file (see the watchdog man page). Set **watchdog_options** to use an option, such as **watchdog_options="-v"**.

The watchdog configuration file is **/etc/watchdog.conf**. Check the man page for **watchdog.conf** for a list of possible options. Most options are commented. The default interval time and log directory are also listed. Watchdog can also ping a network or address on an interface to see if it is still accessible (**ping** and **interface**). The maximum load for a system can be checked (the **max-load** options). You can set up and specify test and repair scripts and binaries for watchdog to use (**test-binary** and **repair-binary** options). The **/usr/share/doc/watchdog/examples** directory has samples of such scripts. The user test and repair scripts should be placed in **/etc/watchdog.d**. The **wd_keepalive** daemon is a simplified version of watchdog that only performs a reset.

ubuntu

6. Mail Servers

Mail Transport Agents

Postfix

Postfix Configuration

Postfix Greylisting Policy Server

Controlling User and Host Access

POP and IMAP Servers

Dovecot

Other POP and IMAP Servers

Spam: SpamAssassin

Mail servers provide Internet users with electronic mail services. They have their own TCP/IP protocols such as the Simple Mail Transfer Protocol (SMTP), the Post Office Protocol (POP), and the Internet Mail Access Protocol (IMAP). Messages are sent across the Internet through mail servers that service local domains. A domain can be seen as a subnet of the larger Internet, with its own server to handle mail messages sent from or received for users on that subnet. When a user emails a message, it is first sent from his or her host system to the mail server. The mail server then sends the message to another mail server on the Internet, the one servicing the subnet on which the recipient user is located. The receiving mail server then sends the message to the recipient's host system.

At each stage, a different type of operation takes place using different agents (programs). A mail user agent (MUA) is a mail client program, such as Evolution, Thunderbird, Kmail, or mailx. With an MUA, a user composes a mail message and sends it. Then a mail transfer agent (MTA) transports the messages over the Internet. MTAs are mail servers that use SMTP to send messages across the Internet from one mail server to another, transporting them among subnets. On Ubuntu, the commonly used MTAs are Postfix and Exim. These are mail server daemons that constantly check for incoming messages from other mail servers and send outgoing messages to appropriate servers (see Table 6-1). Incoming messages received by a mail server are distributed to a user using mail delivery agents (MDAs). Ubuntu supports the procmail and dovecot MDAs, taking messages received by the mail server and delivering them to user accounts. Dovecot refers to its delivery function as an LDA (Local Delivery Agent) which is the same as MDA.

For those systems not supported by a mail server directly, a mail retrieval agent (MRA), like fetchmail, will manually retrieve mail from a remote mail server and direct the mail to the system's mail clients (MUAs).

Mail Transport Agents

On Ubuntu, you can install and configure the Exim, Postfix, or Sendmail mail servers. You can also set up your Linux system to run a POP server. POP servers hold users' mail until they log in to access their messages, instead of having mail sent to their hosts directly. The two recommended MTAs are Exim and Postfix, both in the main Ubuntu repository. Sendmail is also available from the Universe repository.

Exim is a fast and flexible MTA similar to Sendmail. Developed at the University of Cambridge, it has a different implementation than Sendmail. You can find out more about Exim at **https://wiki.debian.org/PkgExim4** and at **http://www.exim.org**. Exim is a Debian Linux project. Ubuntu, as a version a Debian Linux, implements Exim reliably.

Courier (Universe repository) is a fast, small, and secure MTA that maintains some compatibility with Sendmail. The Courier software package also includes POP, IMAP, and webmail servers along with mailing list services. It supports extensive authentication methods including shadow passwords, PAM, and LDAP.

Qmail (Multiverse repository) is also a fast and secure MTA, but it has little compatibility with Sendmail. It has its own configuration and maintenance files. Like Postfix, it has a modular design, using a different program for each mail task. It also focuses on security, speed, and easy configuration.

Agent	Description
Postfix	Fast, easy-to-configure, and secure mail transfer agent compatible with Sendmail and designed to replace it (Ubuntu repository) **www.postfix.org**
Exim	MTA based on smail3 (Ubuntu repository) **www.exim.org**
Sendmail	Sendmail mail transfer agent, supported by the Sendmail consortium (Universe repository)
Courier	Courier MTA (Universe repository) **www.courier-mta.org**
Qmail	Fast, flexible, and secure MTA with its own implementation and competitive with Postfix (Multiverse repository) **https://cr.yp.to/qmail.html**

Table 6-1: Mail Transfer Agents

Postfix

Postfix is a fast, secure, and flexible MTA designed to replace Sendmail while maintaining as much compatibility as possible. Written by Wietse Venema and originally released as the IBM Secure Mailer, it is now available under the GNU license (**www.postfix.org**). Postfix was created with security in mind, treating all incoming mail as potential security risks. Postfix uses many of the same Sendmail directories and files and makes use of Sendmail wrappers, letting Sendmail clients interact seamlessly with Postfix servers. Postfix is also easier to configure than Sendmail.

Check the Ubuntu Server Guide | Services | Mail - Postfix for basic configuration.

`https://ubuntu.com/server/docs/mail-postfix`

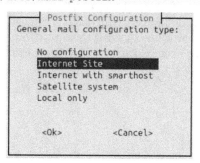

Figure 6-1: Postfix standard configuration selection

Postfix is available on the main Ubuntu repository. When you install Postfix, two configuration screens will appear to prompt you for the kind of installation you want. The first screen asks you select a standard configuration, with Internet site already selected as the default (see Figure 6-1). You can choose from Internet site, Internet with smarthost, Satellite system, Local, or No configuration. If you install using the desktop (Synaptic Package Manager or Ubuntu Software), the screen will look different, but the prompts will be the same.

Instead of one large program, Postfix is implemented as a collection of smaller programs, each designed to perform a specific mail-related task. A Postfix primary daemon runs continuously and manages the use of the other Postfix daemons, running them only as needed. A **bounce** daemon handles undeliverable mail, a **trivial-rewrite** daemon redirects messages, and the **showq** daemon provides information on the print queues.

The options are as follows:

Internet site: The default configuration. Mail server interacts directly with the Internet. Mail sent directly with SMTP.

Internet site with smarthost: Mail server for a local network that uses an ISP mail server to interact with the Internet. Mail is received and sent to and from the ISP mail server with mail server access tools like fetchmail. Mail can be received, but not sent, directly from the Internet.

Local only: System only mail server (no network access) for users on the mail server's system (localhost).

No configuration: No configuration to standard configuration files (requires detailed configuration on your part).

Satellite system: Outgoing forwarding mail server for sent mail only (no received mail).

The following configuration screen will prompt you for your system mail name, displaying your computer hostname as the default.

Several other support packages are also available on the Ubuntu repository for Postfix. These include the Postfix documentation with examples (**postfix-doc**), LDAP (**postfix-ldap**), PGSQL (**postfix-pgsql**) and MySQL (**postfix-mysql**), as well as Postfix greylisting support (**postgrey**).

Postfix is managed by **systemd** using the **postfix.service** and **postfix@.service** unit files in the **/lib/systemd/system** directory. Postfix is started as a standalone daemon for the multi-user and graphical targets (Before). The **/lib/systemd/system/postfix@.service** file is used to start, stop, and reload the server (ExecStart, ExecReload, and ExecStop). This template unit file is used to generate different instances of the server.

postfix.service

```
[Unit]
Description=Postfix Mail Transport Agent
Documentation=man:postfix(1)
Conflicts=sendmail.service exim4.service
ConditionPathExists=/etc/postfix/main.cf

[Service]
Type=oneshot
RemainAfterExit=yes
ExecStart=/bin/true
ExecReload=/bin/true

[Install]
WantedBy=multi-user.target
```

postfix@.service

```
[Unit]
Description=Postfix Mail Transport Agent (instance %i)
Documentation=man:postfix(1)
PartOf=postfix.service
Before=postfix.service
ReloadPropagatedFrom=postfix.service
After=network-online.target nss-lookup.target
Wants=network-online.target

[Service]
Type=forking
GuessMainPID=no
ExecStartPre=/usr/lib/postfix/configure-instance.sh %i
ExecStart=/usr/sbin/postmulti -i %i -p start
ExecStop=/usr/sbin/postmulti -i %i -p stop
ExecReload=/usr/sbin/postmulti -i %i -p reload

[Install]
WantedBy=multi-user.target
```

Postfix Commands

Several Postfix commands allow you to manage your server tasks. The **sendmail** command sends messages. You use **mailq** to display the status of your mail queues. The **newaliases** command takes mail aliases listed in the aliases files and stores them in a database file that can be used by Postfix.

The **postmap** command is used to maintain various database files used by Postfix, such as the alias file for mail aliases and the access file that restricts messages received by the server. You can also implement these database files as SQL databases like MySQL, allowing for easier management. The **mysql_table** Man page provides detailed information on how to configure SQL database support (check **pgsql_table** for Postgresql database support). You could also use LDAP instead of SQL (**ldap_table**).

In addition, Postfix provides lower-level tools, all beginning with the term **post**, such as the **postalias** command, which maintains the alias database, and **postcat**, which displays print queue files.

Quick configuration with dpkg-reconfigure

Instead of manually editing the **main.cf** file directly, you can perform an automatic configuration using the **dpkg-reconfigure** command. With the postfix option, **dpkg-reconfigure** will run a series of screens prompting you to enter basic Postfix configuration options. As when you first installed Postfix, you are prompted to enter the configuration type and the system mail name. Additional screens let you enter more detailed options, like the administrator account and the domains supported.

Before you use the **dpkg-reconfigure** command, be sure to back up your **main.cf** file, with a command like the following. The **dpkg-reconfigure** operation will replace the **main.cf** file entirely.

```
sudo cp /etc/postfix/main.cf  mainback.cf
```

You can then start up the **dpkg-reconfigure** operation in a terminal window or from the command line with the following command.

```
sudo dpkg-reconfigure postfix
```

The **dpkg-reconfigure** operation uses a screen-based keyboard interface. Use the TAB key to move to the button labels at the bottom of the screen. Use the ENTER key to select a button. Some screens will display menus, from which you can select an entry using the arrow keys and then, using the TAB key move to the OK button to choose it. You can use the ESC key to move back to the previous screen. The screens are as follows.

Welcome screen with configuration descriptions (see Figure 6-2).

Select the Postfix configuration such as Internet Site, Satellite system, and Local only (see Figure 6-1). Usually you would select Internet.

Enter the system domain name (the hostname of your current system will already be entered), see Figure 6-3.

Enter the user that will be the Postfix administrator.

Enter the domains that this mail server supports (the final destination (your current host and domain are entered for you. You should change this to the network domain that this mail server is meant to serve), see Figure 6-4.

You are then asked if you want to force synchronous updates. "No" will be selected by default. Normally you do not need synchronous updates. The ext4 file system used on all Ubuntu systems supports journaling, which easily recovers from any crashes.

You are then asked to specify the networks for which the server will relay mail. IP address entries will already be displayed for your local host (IPv4 and IPv6 versions). To use the postfix default, leave this entry blank.

If you have already installed procmail, you are then asked if you want procmail for local delivery

You can then specify a limit to your mailbox files, 0 is no limit (the default). A size limit can prevent large email attachments.

You then have the option to change the character used for the local address. The default is the plus sign (+) and is already entered. Normally you would use this sign.

You are then given the option to choose which IP protocol to use. The default is the one already in use on your system and will be selected already. You can choose to use IPV4, IPV6, or both (all).

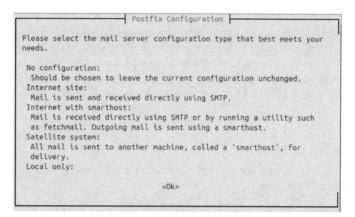

Figure 6-2: Postfix dpkg-reconfigure, first screen (press TAB and ENTER)

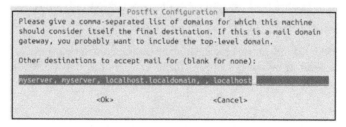

Figure 6-3: Postfix dpkg-reconfigure, domain name

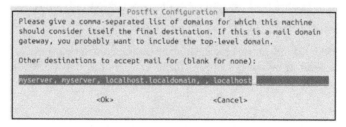

Figure 6-4: Postfix dpkg-reconfigure, domains

Postfix Configuration: /etc/postfix/main.cf

Postfix configuration is handled by setting parameters in its configuration file, **main.cf**. In addition, the **master.cf** file holds parameters for running Postfix services and the **dynamicmaps.cf** file for additional runtime capabilities.

A default **/etc/postfix/main.cf** file is installed with Postfix, with most of the essential configuration values already set. Parameter names tend to be user-friendly. For example, directory locations are specified by parameters ending in the term **directory**, such as **queue_directory** for the location of Postfix queues and **daemon_directory** for the location of the Postfix daemons. Defaults are already implemented for most parameters. For example, defaults are set for particular resource controls, such as message size, time limits, and the number of allowed messages per queue. You can edit the **main.cf** file to change the parameter values to meet your own needs. After making any changes, you need only to reload the configuration using the **postfix reload** command.

```
postfix reload
```

The Ubuntu main.cf file

Ubuntu installs a customized version of **main.cf**, using only a few options, several of which are Debian specific.

Instead of editing the **main.cf** file directly with an editor, you can use the **postconf** command with the **-e** option and a quoted option assignment. The following **postconf** command will set the **biff** option to no in the **main.cf** file. You will need administrative access, so you have to use the **sudo** command. The **postconf** command provides numerous options you can use to manage the **main.cf** file, such as **-v** to enable verbose logging and **-#** to comment out an option. See the **postconf** man page for a complete listing..

```
sudo postconf -e  'biff = no'
```

The **myorigin** parameter specifies the origin address for e-mail sent by the server. On Debian/Ubuntu, this is commented out. On Ubuntu, the **myorigin** value is set to the **myhostname** value, which you entered in the second configuration screen during the Postfix installation. This is the hostname for your mail server. Alternatively, the commented entry is set to the file that holds the hostname, the same value as **myhostname**. If enabled, the entry line would read the origin address from a designated file, like **/etc/mailname**.

```
#myorigin = /etc/mailname
```

One of the first lines in the **main.cf** file will set the banner. On the Ubuntu version, the term Ubuntu is displayed with the hostname and software name (**mail_name** is set to Postfix).

```
smtpd_banner = $myhostname ESMTP $mail_name (Ubuntu)
```

Several of the Ubuntu entries are designed to make your server more efficient. For efficiency purposes, the **biff** option is set to no, turning off the biff notification operation for the mail server.

```
biff = no
```

The **append_dot_mydomain** option adds the domain name to the email address. This operation is now handled by mail clients (MUA) like Thunderbird and Evolution. Ubuntu turns it off.

```
# appending .domain is the MUA's job.
append_dot_mydomain = no
```

Ubuntu will include a commented entry to the **delay_warning_time** option. This option will notify the sender of undelivered mail after a specified time period. The time period default is four hours.

```
# Uncomment the next line to generate "delayed mail" warnings
#delay_warning_time = 4h
```

The **readme_directory** option specifies the location of the Postfix documentation. On Ubuntu, Postfix documentation is held in the **postfix-doc** package which is installed separately. If the package is not installed, the option will be set to no. If installed, the location is set to **/etc/share/doc/postfix**.

```
readme_directory = /usr/share/doc/postfix
```

The **html_directory** entry holds the location of documentation in the Web page format.

```
html_directory = /usr/share/doc/postfix/html
```

Several TLS options are specified to provide Secure Socket Layer (SSL) security. See the following section on SMTP Authentication.

Network options are then set, including **myhostname**, **mydestination**, and **mynetworks**. These were set up during configuration. **myhostname** is the server URL, **mydestination** is a list of domains supported by the server, and **mynetworks** is the list of supported networks. The **alias_maps** directive specifies the file that holds aliases associated with users, like that for postprimary. The **alias database** specifies the file that holds aliases for destination addresses. Usually, these are the same file, **/etc/aliases**. The **relay_host** directive is used if you are using another mail server to send and receive mail. This is empty if your mail server sends and receives mail directly.

```
myhostname = myserver
alias_maps = hash:/etc/aliases
alias_database = hash:/etc/aliases
mydestination = $myhostname, myserver, localhost.localdomain, , localhost
relayhost =
mynetworks = 127.0.0.0/8 [::ffff:127.0.0.0]/104 [::1]/128
```

To easily control spam, relay restrictions are put in place with **smtpd_relay_restrictions** for relay operation. With Postfix 2.10, relay restrictions are specified with their own options, instead of using recipient restrictions. Relay operations are allowed from local networks (**permit_mynetworks**), from authenticated sources (Simple Authentication and Security Layer, SASL) (**permit_sasl_authenticated**), and rejects unauthorized destinations (**defer_unauth_destination**).

```
smptd_relay_restrictions = permit_mynetworks permit_sasl_authenticated
defer_unauth_destination
```

Several mailbox configuration entries are listed. The **mailbox_size** directive is used to restrict the size of user's mailbox files, the files that hold their messages. It is set to 0 by default, meaning an unlimited size. The **recipient_delimiter** character is usually set to +.

```
mailbox_size_limit = 0
recipient_delimiter = +s
```

Certain basic network options are set. The **inet_interfaces** directive specifies the network device that supports the mail server. Usually, this is set to **all**. The **inet_protocols** directive specifies the network protocols used (IPv4 and IPv6).

```
inet_interfaces = all
inet_protocols = all
```

The Ubuntu server default **main.cf** file is shown here with the **procmail** option.

```
# See /usr/share/postfix/main.cf.dist for a commented, more complete version

# Debian specific:  Specifying a file name will cause the first
# line of that file to be used as the name.  The Debian default
# is /etc/mailname.
#myorigin = /etc/mailname

smtpd_banner = $myhostname ESMTP $mail_name (Ubuntu)
biff = no

# appending .domain is the MUA's job.
append_dot_mydomain = no

# Uncomment the next line to generate "delayed mail" warnings
#delay_warning_time = 4h

readme_directory = /usr/share/doc/postfix

# See http://www.postfix.org/COMPATIBILITY_README.html -- default to 2
# on fresh installs.
compatibility_level = 3.6

# TLS parameters
smtpd_tls_cert_file = /etc/ssl/certs/ssl-cert-snakeoil.pem
smtpd_tls_key_file = /etc/ssl/private/ssl-cert-snakeoil.key
smtpd_security_level = may

smtp_tls_CApath=/etc/ssl/certs
smtp_security_level = may
smtp_tls_session_cache_database = btree:${data_directory}/smtp_scache

smptd_relay_restrictions = permit_mynetworks permit_sasl_authenticated
defer_unauth_destination
myhostname = myserver
alias_maps = hash:/etc/aliases
alias_database = hash:/etc/aliases
mydestination = $myhostname, myserver, localhost.localdomain, , localhost
relayhost =
mynetworks = 127.0.0.0/8 [::ffff:127.0.0.0]/104 [::1]/128
mailbox_size_limit = 0
recipient_delimiter = +
inet_interfaces = all
inet_protocols = all
html_directory = /usr/share/doc/postfix/html
mailbox_command = procmail -a "$EXTENSION"
```

SMTP Authentication

Several TLS options in the **main.cf** file provide Secure Socket Layer (SSL) security for the SMTP server (outgoing mail) and for the SMTPD server (incoming mail). Encryption uses Transport Layer Security (TLS). These options have the prefix **smtpd_tls**. The **smtpd_tls_cert_file** and **smtpd_tls_key_file** options specify the files for the TLS certificate and key in the **/etc/ssl** directory. The **smtpd_use_tls** option is set to yes to enable the use of TLS encryption. The **tls_session_cache_database** option designate a secure cache to hold passwords for the extent of a session. The **smtpd_tls_CApath** option is the directory that holds your Certificate Authority files.

```
# TLS parameters
smtpd_tls_cert_file = /etc/ssl/certs/ssl-cert-snakeoil.pem
smtpd_tls_key_file = /etc/ssl/private/ssl-cert-snakeoil.key
smtpd_security_level = may

smtp_tls_CApath=/etc/ssl/certs
smtp_security_level = may
smtp_tls_session_cache_database = btree:${data_directory}/smtp_scache
```

For an actual mail server, you should obtain a certificate and key for that server, and set the **smtpd_tls_cert_file** and **smtpd_tls_key_file** options to the new certificate and key files. To specify your own certificate authority, use the **smtp_tls_CApath** option.

```
https://ubuntu.com/server/docs/security-certificates
```

In addition you could add logging options. The **smtp_tls_note_starttls_offer** option logs the host name of an SMTP server that does not have TLS enabled and is using STARTTLS for encryption. For incoming mail you could set the loglevel for TLS activity and received header option to generate message headers with protocol, cypher, and client information.

```
smtp_tls_note_startls_offer = yes
smtpd_tsl_loglevel = 1
smtpd_tls_received_header = yes
```

Mail User Agent Options and Authentication: Dovecot

When you install a Mail User Agent like dovecot or procmail, several options will be added to the **main.cf** file, denoting the MUA installed and specifying security options to use. The **mailbox_command** directive specifies the mail delivery agent to use for delivering mail to user's mailboxes (be sure one is installed, **dovecot** or **procmail**). If you install procmail, it will be listed.

```
mailbox_command = procmail -a "$EXTENSION"
```

If you have installed dovecot, you will have to manually configure the Postfix **main.cf** file.

Configure the **home mailbox** to use the Maildir format.

```
home_mailmox = Maildir/
```

The **mailbox command** is then set to use the dovecot local delivery agent.

```
mailbox_command = /usr/lib/dovecot/dovecot-lda -f "$SENDER" -a "$RECIPIENT"
```

Dovecot uses SASL (Simple Authentication Security Layer) for all its messages and Postfix has to be configured to support it. Dovecot SASL specifies authentication methods and protocols to be used. On Ubuntu, Postfix can support Dovecot SASL. You configure this support with several SASL and SASL TLS options, as well as the configuration of the Dovecot **service auth** directive.

The **smtpd_sasl_auth_enable** option will enable SASL security. The **smtpd_sasl_type** option specifies the MUA used, such as dovecot. **smtpd_sasl_security_options** will list nonanonymous to deny anonymous authentication and noplaintext to deny passwords in plain text. **smtpd_sasl_local_domain** is set to the server hostname.

The **smtpd_relay_restrictions** option sets several conditions for accepting mail, such as **permit_mynetworks** and **reject_unauth_destination**. The **smtpd_sender_restrictions** place restrictions on outgoing mail, like **reject_unknown_sender_domain**.

In additions, the MUA also has **smtpd_tls** options such as **smtpd_sasl_tls_security_options**, and **smtpd_tls_mandatory_ciphers**.

```
smtpd_sasl_auth_enable = yes
smtpd_sasl_type = dovecot
smtpd_sasl_path = private/auth
smtpd_sasl_security_options = noanonymous,noplaintext
smtpd_sasl_local_domain = $myhostname
smtpd_relay_restrictions =
permit_sasl_authenticated,permit_mynetworks,reject_unauth_destination
smtpd_sender_restrictions = reject_unknown_sender_domain
broken_sasl_auth_clients = yes

smtpd_sasl_tls_security_options = noanonymous
smtpd_tls_mandatory_protocols = SSLv3, TLSv1
smtpd_tls_mandatory_ciphers = medium
tls_random_source = dev:/dev/urandom
```

For Dovecot, to enable Postfix for DovecotSASL, you will have to edit the **/etc/dovecot/conf.d/10-master.conf** file and remove the comment characters in the **smtp-auth** section following the "Postfix smtp-auth" comment. You then set the user to the value of **default_internal_user**, which is defined as **dovecot** at the beginning of the file.

```
#Postfix smtp-auth
unix_listerner /var/spool/postfix/private/auth  {
   mode = 066

#Auth process is run as this user
  user = $default_internal_user
}
```

To enable support for Outlook clients, change to **auth_mechanisms** entry in **/etc/dovecot/conf.d/10-auth.conf** to **plain login**. Windows requires the **login** mechanism.

```
auth_mechanisms = plain login
```

Postfix directives for main.cf

Postfix provides an extensive set of configuration directives letting you set up more complex configurations. The **/usr/share/postfix** directory has sample **main.cf** files listing available directives, many with detailed comments (install **postfix-doc**). You can find the complete version of **main.cf** with detailed comments at:

```
/usr/share/postfix/main.cf.dist
```

Network Parameters

You will most likely need to set several network parameters. To ease this process, Postfix defines parameters that hold key network information, such as **myhostname**, which holds the hostname of your system, and **mydomain**, which holds the domain name of your network. For example, **myhostname** would be set to the host **turtle.mytrek.com**, whereas **mydomain** would be just **mytrek.com**. Parameters like **myhostname** and **mydomain** are themselves used as values assigned to other parameters. On Ubuntu, **myhostname** will be set to the system mail name you entered in the second configuration screen during the Postfix installation. In the next example, **myhostname** and **mydomain** are set to the host the mail server is running on and its network domain.

```
myhostname=turtle.mytrek.com
mydomain=mytrek.com
```

The **myorigin** parameter specifies the origin address for e-mail sent by the server. On Debian/Ubuntu, this is commented out. It is set to the file that holds the hostname, the same value as **myhostname**. You could assign the value of **myhostname** to it directly as shown here and described in the **main.cf.dist** sample version.

```
myorigin=$myhostname
```

On Ubuntu/Debian, the line would read the origin address from a designated file, like **/etc/mailname**.

```
#myorigin=/etc/mailname
```

If you are using a single system directly attached to the Internet, you may want to keep this configuration, labeling mail as being sent by your host. However, if your system is operating as a gateway for a network, your mail server is sending out mail from different hosts on that network. You may wish to change the origin address to the domain name so that mail is perceived as sent from the domain.

```
myorigin=$mydomain
```

The **inet_protocols** option specifies the IP protocol to use. This can be IPV4, IPV6, or all for both.

```
inet_protocols = all
```

Local Networks

The **mydestination** parameter holds the list of domains that your mail server will receive mail for. By default, these include **localhost** and your system's hostname.

```
mydestination = $myhostname, localhost.$mydomain, localhost
```

If you want the mail server to receive mail for an entire local network, you need to also specify its domain name. That way, the server can receive mail addressed just to the domain, instead of your specific host.

```
mydestination = $myhostname, localhost.$mydomain, localhost, $mydomain
```

Also, if your host goes by other hostnames and there are DNS records identifying your host by those names, you need to specify those names as well. For example, your host could also be a web server to which mail could be directed. A host **turtle.mytrek.com** may also be identified as the website **mytrek.com**. Both names would have to be listed in the **mydestination** parameter.

```
mydestination = $myhostname, localhost.$mydomain, localhost, $mydomain,
www.$mydomain
```

If your system is a gateway for one or more local networks, you can specify them with the **mynetworks** parameter. This allows your mail server to relay mail addressed to those networks. Networks are specified using their IP addresses. The **relay_domains** parameter lets you specify domain addresses of networks for which you can relay messages. By default, this is set to **mydestination**:

```
mynetworks=192.168.0.0
relay_domains=$mydestination
```

Hosts within the local network connected to the Internet by a gateway need to know the identity of the relay host (the mail server). You set this with the **relayhost** parameter. Also, **myorigin** should be set to just **mydomain**. If there is a DNS server identifying the gateway as the mail server, you can just set **relayhost** to the value of **mydomain**. If not, then **relayhost** should be set to the specific hostname of the gateway/mail server. If your local network is not running a DNS server, be sure to set **disable_dns_lookups** to yes.

```
relayhost=$mydomain
```

Direct Connections

If your system is directly connected to the Internet and you use an ISP (Internet service provider) for receiving mail, you can configure Postfix as a null client to only send mail. Set the **relay_host** parameter to just your own domain name. Also, in the **master.cf** file, comment out the SMTP server and local delivery agent entries.

```
relayhost = $mydomain
```

Masquerading

If your mail server is operating on a gateway for a local network and you want to hide the hosts in that network, you can opt to masquerade the local hosts, letting it appear that all mail is coming from the domain in general, instead of a particular host. To set this option, you use the **masquerade_domains** parameter. In the following example, all mail sent by a local host such as **rabbit.mytrek.com** will be addressed as coming from **mytrek.com**. Thus a message sent by the user **chris@rabbit.mytrek.com** is sent out as coming from **chris@mytrek.com**:

```
masquerade_domains = $mydomain
```

Received mail is not masqueraded by default. This allows Postfix to still deliver received mail to particular hosts. If you want received mail to also be masqueraded, you have to add the **envelope_recipients** parameter to the list of values assigned to the **masquerade_class** parameter. In that case, Postfix will no longer be able to deliver received mail.

Virtual Domains and Virtual Accounts

If your network has implemented virtual domains, you will need to set up a virtual domain table and specify that table with the **virtual_maps** option. Setting up a table is a simple matter of listing virtual names and their real addresses in a text file such as **/etc/postfix/virtual**. Then use the **postmap** command to create a Postfix table.

```
postmap /etc/postfix/virtual
```

In the **main.cf** file, specify the table with the **virtual_maps** parameter. Postfix will then use this table to look up virtual domains.

```
virtual_maps = hash:/etc/postfix/virtual
```

Note: See the Postfix FAQ at **http://www.postfix.org/** for detailed information on how to set up Postfix for a gateway, a local workstation, or a host directly connected to the Internet (null server).

Instead of using mail accounts for actual users on a system, you can set up virtual accounts. Virtual accounts can be managed either in standard Postfix text files, in SQL databases, or as LDAP entries. SQL databases are preferred for managing a large number of virtual accounts. For SQL support, you first create tables in a MySQL database for domains (the virtual domains), users (user accounts), and forwarding (aliases). Corresponding virtual domain configuration files will list information like the database, tables, and host to use, such as a **mysql_virt.cf** for SQL database access and **mysql_users.cf** for accessing the user table.

Postfix Greylisting Policy Server

Postfix also supports greylisting with the Postfix Greylisting Policy Server. Greylisting blocks spammers based on their mailing methods rather than content, relying on the idea that spammers will not attempt retries if rejected. Messages from new previously unknown sources are rejected, where upon a valid MTA will retry, whereas a spammer will not. To support the Greylisting Policy Server, Postfix is configured to delegate Policy access to a server. In the **/etc/postfix** directory you can use the **postgrey_whitelist** files to exclude email addresses from greylisting.

The Greylisting Policy Server is run as a standalone server, using its own startup script. The postgrey Man page provides detailed information about the server's options.

Controlling User and Host Access

With an access file, you can control access by certain users, hosts, and domains. The access file works much like the one used for Sendmail. Entries are made in a text file beginning with the user, host, or domain name or address, followed by an action to take. A user, host, or domain can be accepted, rejected with no message, or rejected with a message. Once entries are made, they can be installed in a Postfix database file with the **postmap** command.

```
postmap /etc/postfix/access
```

You can then use the access file in various Postfix operations to control clients, recipients, and senders.

Access can also be controlled by use of the Mail Abuse Prevention System (MAPS), which provides the RBL+ service, a collection of mail address DNS-based databases (**mail-abuse.com**). These databases, like the Realtime Blackhole List (RBL), list mail addresses that are known be used by mail abusers. A domain or host is matched against a list maintained by the service, which can be accessed on a local server or directly from an online site. Various Postfix operations let you use MAPS databases to control access by clients, recipients, or senders.

Header and Body Checks

With the **header_checks** parameter, you can specify a Postfix table where you can list criteria for rejecting messages. Check the **/etc/postfix/header_checks** file for details. The criteria are patterns that can match message headers. You can have matching messages rejected, rejected with a reply, simply deleted, or logged with a warning. You have the option of taking several actions, including REJECT, DISCARD, WARN, HOLD, and IGNORE.

```
header_checks = regexp:/etc/postfix/header_checks
```

The database, in this case, **/etc/postfix/header_checks**, will have lines, each with a regular expression and a corresponding action. The regular expression can either be a standard regular expression as denoted by **regexp** in the **header_checks** parameter, or conform to a Perl Compatible Regular Expression, **prece**.

The **body_checks** parameter lets you check the body of text messages, line by line, using regular expressions and actions like those used for **header_checks** in a **/etc/postfix/body_checks** file.

Controlling Client, Senders, and Recipients

Combined with Dovecot, Postfix defines sender and recipient controls in the **/etc/postfix/main.cf** file a shown here.

```
smtpd_recipient_restrictions = reject_unknown_sender_domain,
    reject_unknown_recipient_domain, reject_unauth_pipelining, permit_mynetworks,
    permit_sasl_authenticated, reject_unauth_destination
smtpd_sender_restrictions = reject_unknown_sender_domain
```

You could also configure Postfix with added or different client, sender, and recipient options. With the **smtpd_client_restrictions** parameter, you can restrict access to the mail server by certain clients. Restrictions you can apply include **reject_unknown_client_hostname**, which will reject any clients with unresolved addresses; **permit_mynetworks**, which allows access by any clients defined by **mynetworks**; and **check_client_access**, which will check an access database to see if a client should be accepted or rejected. The **reject_rbl_client** and **reject_rhsbl_client** parameters will reject clients from specified domains.

```
smtpd_client_restrictions = permit_mynetworks, \
            reject_unknown_client, check_client_access, reject_maps_rbl
```

The **reject_rbl_client** restriction rejects domain addresses according to a specified MAPS service. The site can be an online site or a local one set up to provide the service. The **reject_rhsbl_client** restriction rejects host addresses.

```
smtpd_client_restrictions = reject_rbl_client relays.mail-abuse.org
```

To implement restrictions from an access file, you can use the **hash** directive and the name of the file.

```
smtpd_client_restrictions = hash:/etc/postfix/access
```

The corresponding **smtpd_sender_restrictions** parameter works much the same way as its client counterpart but controls access from specific senders. It has many of the same restrictions but adds **reject_non_fqdn_sender**, which will reject any mail header without a fully qualified domain name, and **reject_sender_login_mismatch**, which will require sender verification. The **reject_rhsbl_sender** restriction rejects domain addresses according to a specified MAPS service.

The **smtpd_recipient_restrictions** parameter will restrict the recipients the server will accept mail for. Restrictions include **permit_auth_destination**, which allows authorized messages, and **reject_unauth_destination**, which rejects unauthorized messages. The **check_recipient_access** restriction checks local networks for a recipient address. The **reject_unknown_recipient_domain** restriction rejects recipient addresses with no DNS entry. The **reject_rhsbl_recipient** restriction rejects domain addresses according to a specified MAPS service.

You can further refine restrictions with parameters such as **smtpd_helo_restrictions**, which requires a HELO command from a client. Restriction parameters include **reject_invalid_hostname**, which checks for faulty syntax, **reject_unknown_hostname**, for hosts with no DNS entry, and **reject_non_fqdn_hostname** for hosts whose names are not fully qualified. The **strict_rfc821_envelopes** parameter will implement strict envelope protocol compliance.

Note: Sendmail operates as a server to both receive and send mail messages (**sendmail** package). Sendmail listens for any mail messages received from other hosts and addressed to users on the network hosts it serves and, at the same time, handles messages users are sending out to remote users, determining what hosts to send them to.

POP and IMAP Server: Dovecot

The protocols Internet Mail Access Protocol (IMAP) and Post Office Protocol (POP) allow a remote server to hold mail for users who can fetch their mail from it when they are ready. Unlike procmail, which delivers mail messages directly to a user account on a Linux system, the IMAP and POP protocols hold mail until a user accesses an account on the IMAP or POP server. The servers then transfer any received messages to the user's local mailbox. Such servers are often used by ISPs to provide Internet mail services for users. Instead of being sent directly to a user's machine, the mail resides in the IMAP or POP server until it is retrieved. Ubuntu installs Dovecot as its recommended IMAP and POP servers. It will be installed as part of the **dovecot-postfix** package, and used by Postfix as the delivery agent.

You can access the POP server from different hosts. When you do, all the messages are transferred to that host. They are not kept on the POP server (though you can set an option to keep them). The POP server forwards your messages to the requesting host. When you access your messages from a certain computer, they will be transferred to that computer and erased from the POP server. If you access your POP server again from a different computer, those previous messages will be gone.

The Internet Mail Access Protocol (IMAP) allows a remote server to hold mail for users who can log in to access their mail. Unlike the POP servers, IMAP servers retain user mail messages. Users can even save their mail on the IMAP mail server. This has the advantage of keeping a user's mail in one centralized location accessible anywhere on the network. Users can log in to the mail server from any host on the network and read, send, and save their mail.

Unlike POP, IMAP allows users to set up multiple folders on their mail server in which they can organize their mail. IMAP also supports the use of shared folders to which several users can access mail on a given topic.

Dovecot

Dovecot is a combination IMAP and POP server (**dovecot-pop3d** and **dovecot-imapd** packages), as well as an LDA (Local Delivery Agent). Using its own indexing methods, Dovecot is able to handle a great deal of e-mail traffic. It features support for SSL, along with several authentication methods. Password database support includes shadow passwords, LDAP, PAM, and MySQL. Dovecot is available in POP, IMAP, common packages, on the Ubuntu main repository. Dovecot can function as a local delivery agent for the major mail servers, including Postfix, Exim, and Sendmail. For detailed configuration information check **https://wiki.dovecot.org/**. For information about the Dovecot LDA check **https://wiki.dovecot.org/LDA**.

The dovecot configuration files are located in the **/etc/dovecot** directory. The main configuration file is **/etc/dovecot/dovecot.conf**, which includes configuration files located in the **conf.d** subdirectory such as **10-logging.conf**, **10-ssl.conf**, **10-auth.conf**, and **10-mail.conf**. Options specific to **imap** and **pop3** are placed in their own files (**20-pop3.conf** and **20-imap.conf**). Corresponding copies are placed in the **/usr/share/dovecot/conf.d** directory.

These are some basic settings to configure:

protocols   This can be set to **imap** and **pop3**, as well as **imaps** and **pop3s** for SSL encrypted connections. Protocols are listed in the **/usr/share/dovecot/protocols.d** directory. They are read by the **dovecot.conf** file.

listen   This can be set to IPv4 or IPv4 addresses on which to listen for connections. The * character indicates all IPv4 network interfaces, and **::** all IPv6 interfaces.

Authentication processes are listed in the **10-auth.conf** file in the **/etc/dovecot/conf.d** directory.

auth_mechanism in **10-auth.conf** file is plain by default. The digest-MD5 and cran-MD5 methods are supported, but they are not needed if you are using SSL.

mail_location   The default mail storage method and location (**/etc/dovecot/conf.d/10-mail.conf** file).

service auth in **10-master.conf**   Configuration for DovecotSASL support for services such as Postfix.

On Ubuntu, the standard dovecot configuration options are set up in the **.conf** files. These files are read in at the end of the **dovecot.conf** file as part of the dovecot configuration. It will set the **protocols**, **ssl**, and **mail_location** options, as well as set options for the IMAP, POP3, and LDA.

```
!include conf.d/*.conf
```

Dovecot supports either mailbox or maildir (IMAP) storage formats. The mailbox format uses single large mailbox files to hold several mail messages. This will be the user's **mbox** file at **/var/mail**. Updates can be time consuming. The maildir format uses a separate file for each message, making updates much more efficient. You can configure Dovecot to use a maildir format by setting the **mail_location** option to use a **maildir** setting, specifying the directory to use. The **%u** symbol can be used to represent the username, **%h** for the home directory. Messages will be stored in a user's **maildir** directory instead of an **mbox** file. Be sure to create the **maildir** directory and give it read, write, and execute access The default **maildir** entry in the /etc/dovecot/conf.d/10-**mail.conf** file uses the **mail** subdirectory in the user's home directory, but for inboxes uses the **/var/mail** directory with a subdirectory for the user .

```
mail_location=mbox:~/mail:INBOX=/var/mail/%u
```

Alternatively, you could place mail in separate files instead of an mbox file in the user's home directory.

```
mail_location=maildir:~/Maildir
```

If you have installed Postfix, then dovecot configures the user mail directory with the **home_mailbox** option in the **/etc/postfix/main.cf** file. This sets the mail box directory to the **Maildir** directory in the user's home directory.

```
home_mailbox = Maildir/
```

Other POP and IMAP Servers

Many distributions also include the Cyrus IMAP server, which you can install and use instead of Dovecot. In addition, several other IMAP and POP servers are available for use on Linux:

The **Cyrus IMAP** server (**https://www.cyrusimap.org/**) features security controls and authentication, using a private mailbox structure that is easily scalable (Universe repository). It is designed to be run on dedicated mail servers. The name of the Cyrus IMAP server daemon is **imapd**.

The **Courier-IMAP** server (**http://courier-mta.org**) is a small, fast IMAP server that provides extensive authentication support including LDAP and PAM (Universe repository).

Spam: SpamAssassin

With SpamAssassin, you can filter sent and received e-mail for spam. The filter examines both headers and content, drawing on rules designed to detect common spam messages. When they are detected, it then tags the message as spam, so that a mail client can then discard it. SpamAssassin will also report spam messages to spam detection databases. The version of SpamAssassin distributed for Linux is the open source version developed by the Apache project, located at **https://spamassassin.apache.org/**. There you can find detailed documentation, FAQs, mailing lists, and even a listing of the tests that SpamAssassin performs.

Note: For dovecot IMAP server you can use **dovecot-antispam** plugin to implement spam detection.

SpamAssassin rule files are located at **/usr/share/spamassassin**. The files contain rules for running tests such as detecting the fake hello in the header. Configuration files for SpamAssassin are located at **/etc/spamassassin**. The **local.cf** file lists system-wide SpamAssassin options such as how to rewrite headers. The **init.pre** file holds spam system configurations. Server options such as enabling SpamAssassin, are listed in the **/etc/default spamassassin** file.

Users can set their own SpamAssassin option in their **.spamassassin/user_prefs** file. Common options include **required_scorei**, which sets a threshold for classifying a message as SPAM, numerous whitelist and blacklist options that accept and reject messages from certain users and domains, and tagging options that either rewrite or just add SPAM labels. Check the **Mail::SpamAssassin::Conf** man page for details.

Mail Filtering: Amavisd-new

On Ubuntu, you can set up mail filtering using Amavisd-new, which invokes the ClamAV virus protection utility and SpamAssassin to filter mail. You can also use external filters such as opendkim for Sendmail and python-policy-spf for Postfix. Check **https://www.ijs.si/software/amavisd/** for more details.

amavisd-new calls filtering tools as needed. First, a message is filtered using an external filter such as opendkim or python-policy-spf (Postfix will use both), then **amavisd-new** has the message scanned by ClamAV for viruses, followed by an analysis by SpamAssassin to see if it is spam. Only then does **amavisd-new** allow the message to be placed in the inbox.

To implement mail filtering, be sure you have installed amavisd-new, spamassassin, and clamav, along with the external filters.

```
sudo apt-get install amavisd-new spamassassin clamav-daemon
sudo apt-get install opendkim postfix-policyd-spf-python
```

Ubuntu also recommends that you install supporting applications such as pyzor, razor, and the extraction utilities if you have not already done so (arg, capextract, cpio, lha, nomarch, pax, rar, unrar, unzip, zip).

Add the clamav user to the amavis group to allow amavis to use clamav to scan files.

```
sudo adduser calmav amavis
sudo adduser amavis clamav
```

Enable spamassassin by editing the spamassassin configuration file, **/etc/default/spamassassin**, and setting the ENABLED entry to 1.

```
ENABLED=1
```

Then start spamassassin.

```
sudo service spamassasin start
```

You can then configure Amavisd-new using files in the **/etc/amavis/conf.d** directory. To activate virus detection and spamassassin, edit the **/etc/amavis/conf.d/15_content_filter_mode** file and uncomment the lines for virus detection and spamassassin as indicated by the comments.

Ubuntu also recommends that you disable the bounce response for spam emails by settings the **final_spam_destiny** option in the **20_debian_defaults** file to D_DISCARD instead of D_BOUNCE. You can also adjust the level of spam detection

```
$final_spam_destiny  =  D_DISCARD;
```

Should your mail server DNS address be different from the DNS MX record, you have to specify the mail server's domain name in the **50_user** file. If your server supports different domains, you would list them in the **local_domain_acl** directive.

Amavisd-new also supports whitelists for domains and subdomains with valid Domain Keys (DKIM whitelists). These are configured in the **40-policy_banks** file.

Mailing Lists: Mailman

Mailman provides a Web interface for managing email mailing lists used for email discussions and newsletters. It supports Postfix, Sendmail, Exim, and Qmail mail servers. To use mailman you configure the Apache Web server to run a mailman virtual Web server. A default Apache configuration file for a mailman Web host is located at **/etc/mailman/apache.conf**. You can copy this file to the Apache **sites-available** directory as **mailman.conf.** ,

```
sudo cp /etc/mailman/apache.conf /etc/apache2/sites-available/mailman.conf
```

Enable the mailman virtual host with the **a2ensite** command and then restart Apache.

```
sudo a2ensite mailman.conf
sudo service apache2 restart
```

For Postfix, you have to specify the mailing list domain, in the **/etc/postfix/main.cf** file. You can use the **postconf –e** command to add the mailman configuration entries.

```
sudo postconf -e 'relay_domains = lists.example.com'
sudo postconf -e 'transport_maps = hash:/etc/postfix/transport'
sudo postconf -e 'mailman_destination_recipient_limit = 1'
```

In the **/etc/postfix/transport** file specify the domain for the mailman lists.

```
lists.example.com      mailman:
```

Then rebuild the transport map.

```
sudo postmap -v /etc/postfix/transport
```

You can then start the mailman server.

```
sudo service mailman start
```

Use the **newlist** command to create a default mailing list.

```
sudo newlist mailman
```

The mailman Web server is managed using CGI scripts in the **/usr/lib/chi-bin/mailman** directory. Administrators can access mailman at (*hostname* is the name of your machine):

```
http://hostname/cgi-bin/mailman/admin
```

Users can access the mailing list at:

```
http://hostname/cgi-bin/mailman/listinfo
```

ubuntu

7. FTP

FTP Servers

Anonymous FTP: vsftpd

The FTP User Account: anonymous

The Very Secure FTP Server

vsftpd Virtual Hosts

rsync and FTP

The File Transfer Protocol (FTP) is designed to transfer large files across a network from one system to another. Like most Internet operations, FTP works on a client/server model. FTP client programs can enable users to transfer files to and from a remote system running an FTP server program. Any Linux system can operate as an FTP server. It runs the server software, an FTP daemon with the appropriate configuration. Transfers are made between user accounts on client and server systems. A user on the remote system has to log in to an account on a server and can then transfer files to and from that account's directories only. A special kind of user account named FTP, allows any user to log in to it with the username "anonymous." This account has its own set of directories and files that are considered public, available to anyone on the network who wants to download them. The numerous FTP sites on the Internet are FTP servers supporting FTP user accounts with anonymous login. Any Linux system can be configured to support anonymous FTP access, turning them into FTP sites.

FTP Servers

FTP server software consists of an FTP daemon and configuration files. The daemon is a program that continuously checks for FTP requests from remote users. When a request is received, it manages a login, sets up the connection to the requested user account, and executes any FTP commands the remote user sends. For anonymous FTP access, the FTP daemon allows the remote user to log in to the FTP account using **anonymous** as the username. The user then has access to the directories and files set up for the FTP account. As a further security measure, the daemon changes the root directory for that session to be the FTP home directory. This hides the rest of the system from the remote user. Normally, any user on a system can move around to any directories open to them. A user logging in with anonymous FTP can see only the FTP home directory and its subdirectories. The remainder of the system is hidden from that user. This effect is achieved by the **chroot** operation (discussed later) that changes the system root directory for that user to that of the FTP directory. By default, the FTP server also requires a user to be using a valid shell. It checks for a list of valid shells in the **/etc/shells** file. Most daemons have options for turning off this feature.

FTP Servers	Site
Very Secure FTP Server (vsftpd)	**vsftpd.beasts.org**
ProFTPD	**proftpd.org**
PureFTP	**https://www.pureftpd.org/**

Table 7-1: FTP Servers

Available Servers

Several FTP servers are available for use on Linux systems (see Table 7-1). Three of the more common servers include **vsftpd**, **pureftpd**, and **proftpd**. The Very Secure FTP Server provides a simple and very secure FTP server (**vsftpd** package). The Pure FTPD servers is a lightweight, fast, and secure FTP server, based upon Troll-FTPd (**pure-ftpd** package), **https://www.pureftpd.org**. ProFTPD is a popular FTP daemon based on an Apache web server design (**proftpd-basic** package). It features simplified configuration and support for virtual FTP hosts, **http://proftpd.org**.

You can only have one FTP server installed. Should you decide to install another, the currently installed one will be removed.

FTP Users

Normal users with accounts on an FTP server can gain full FTP access simply by logging into their accounts. Such users can access and transfer files directly from their own accounts or any directories they may have access to. You can also create users, known as guest users that have restricted access to the FTP publicly accessible directories. This involves setting standard user restrictions, with the FTP public directory as their home directory. Users can also log in as anonymous users, allowing anyone on the network or Internet to access files on an FTP server.

Anonymous FTP: vsftpd

An anonymous FTP site is basically a special kind of user on your system with publicly accessible directories and files in its home directory. Anyone can log in to this account and access its files. Because anyone can log in to an anonymous FTP account, you must be careful to restrict a remote FTP user to only the files on that anonymous FTP directory. Normally, a user's files are interconnected to the entire file structure of your system. Normal users have write access that lets them create or delete files and directories. The anonymous FTP files and directories can be configured in such a way that the rest of the file system is hidden from them and remote users are given only read access.

For a workable FTP site, you need an FTP user account, an FTP home directory, as well as controlled access to certain configuration and support files. These are set up for you when you installed your FTP server. The FTP home directory also contains a publicly accessible directory with files that are available to remote users. It is usually named **pub**, for public.

The FTP User Account: anonymous

To provide anonymous FTP access by other users, you will need a separate FTP user account named "FTP." This account is created automatically when the FTP server is installed. Restrictions are then placed on the FTP account to keep any remote FTP users from accessing any other part of your system. The entry for this account in your **/etc/passwd** file is set up to prevent normal user access to it. The following is the entry you find in your **/etc/passwd** file on Ubuntu that sets up an FTP login as an anonymous user.

```
ftp:x:121:129:ftp daemon,,,:/srv/ftp:/usr/sbin/nologin
```

The **x** in the password field blocks the account. This will prevent other users from accessing it, and in that way taking control of its files, and then possibly accessing other parts of your system. The next field is the user ID, 121. The comment field follows, in this case, "ftp daemon". The following field is the login directory, which for the FTP server is **/srv/ftp**. When FTP users log in, they are placed in this directory. The **/srv** directory is commonly used for servers.

Should you want to change your FTP server to use a different directory, you would simply change the FTP user's home directory to be that new directory. You can use the **usermod** command with the **-d** option to make the change. First be sure to create the new directory. In the following example, the FTP directory is changed to **/srv/myftp**.

```
sudo mkdir /srv/myftp
sudo usermod -d /srv/myftp  ftp
```

The FTP home directory is owned by the root user, not by the FTP user. The FTP user has no administrative control over the FTP home directory. Use the **ls -d** command to check on the ownership of the FTP directory.

```
ls -ld /srv/ftp
```

If you set up a different FTP directory, be sure to change a directory's ownership. You use the **chown** command, as shown in this example for a **myftp** directory:

```
sudo chown root.nogroup /srv/myftp
```

The permission for the FTP directory is set to 755; read, write and execute permission for the root user, but only read and execute permission for everyone else. If you create your own FTP directory, be sure to change the permissions on that directory to 755. Use the **chmod** command.

```
sudo chmod 755 /srv/myftp
```

An important part of protecting your system is preventing remote users from using any commands or programs, not in the restricted directories. For example, you would not let a user use your **ls** command to list filenames because **ls** is located in your **/bin** directory. At the same time, you want to let the FTP user list filenames using an **ls** command. FTP daemons such as **vsftpd** and ProFTPD solve this problem by creating secure access to needed system commands and files while restricting remote users to only the FTP site's directories.

An alternative solution is to make copies of selected system directories, files, and commands the remote users need, and placing them in a **bin** directory within the **ftp** directory. Remote users are then restricted to that local **bin** directory, instead of the system's **bin** directory. Whenever a remote user runs the **ls** command, that user is running the copy in **ftp/bin**, not the one in **/bin**. To set this up on your FTP server, you would make a new **bin** directory in the **ftp** directory, and then make a copy of the **ls** command and place it in **ftp/bin**. Then do this for any commands you want to make available to FTP users. Also, create an **ftp/etc** directory to hold a copy of your **passwd** and **group** files. This is to prevents access to the original files in the **/etc** directory by FTP users. You should edit the **ftp/etc/passwd** to remove all entries for regular users on your system. All other entries should have their passwords set to **x** to block access. Do essentially the same for the **group** file, removing all user groups and set all passwords to **x**. You will also have to create an **ftp/lib** directory where you would place copies of the libraries you need to run the commands in the local **ftp/bin** directory.

Anonymous FTP Files

The downloadable files you are making available to remote FTP users are located in a directory named **pub**. FTP users log in to the FTP home directory (**/srv/ftp**). They can then change to the **pub** directory and access the downloadable files (**/srv/ftp/pub**). The **pub** directory can, of course, have subdirectories. Some of the subdirectories can be used as upload directories, where FTP users can upload files.

Each subdirectory in the **pub** directory to hold FTP files, you should have a **README** file and an **INDEX** file as a courtesy to FTP users. The **README** file provides a brief description of the kind of files held in this directory. The **INDEX** file displays a listing of the files and a description of each.

The Very Secure FTP Server

The Very Secure FTP Server (**vsftpd**) runs fast, is easy to configure, and provides excellent security. It avoids the overhead of other large FTP server software while, at the same time, providing a high level of security. Though a small application, it can handle a large workload, managing high traffic levels on an FTP site. It may be best suited for sites where many anonymous and guest users are downloading the same files. The **vsftpd** FTP server is available on the Ubuntu main repository and with critical updates provided.

Very Secure FTP Server was designed with a special focus on security. The server is divided into privileged and unprivileged processes. The unprivileged process receives FTP requests, which it then interprets and passes onto the privileged process. The privileged process securely filters the requests. The privileged process does not run with full root permission. It only uses those system-level functions that are needed to perform its tasks. The Very Secure FTP Server also uses separate versions of directory commands like **ls**, instead of the system's versions.

Check the Ubuntu Server Guide | Services | Service - FTP for basic configuration.

```
https://ubuntu.com/server/docs/service-ftp
```

See Table 7-2 for a list of vsftpd configuration and support files.

File	Description
/etc/ftpusers	Users always denied access
vsftpd.user_list	Specified users denied access (allowed access if `userlist_deny` is NO)
vsftpd.chroot_list	Local users allowed access (denied access if `chroot_local_user` is on)
/etc/vsftpd.conf	vsftpd configuration file
/etc/pam.d/vsftpd	PAM vsftpd script
/lib/systemd/system/vsftpd.service	Service file for vsftpd server, standalone
/srv/ftp	FTP directory

Table 7-2: Configuration and support files for vsftpd

The Very Secure FTP server package is **vsftpd**. Use **apt**, **aptitude**, or the Synaptic Package Manager to install it. The package also installs anonymous FTP support.

```
sudo apt install vsftpd
```

The Very Secure FTP Server is managed by **systemd** using the **vsftpd.service** unit file, shown here. It is a simple file that is run after the network starts (After) and is started by the **multi-user.target** (runlevels 2, 3, 4, and 5) (WantedBy). It is run by the **/usr/sbin/vsftpd** command with reads the **/etc/vsftpd.conf** file for configuration.

vsftpd.service

```
[Unit]
Description=vsftpd FTP server
After=network.target

[Service]
Type=simple
ExecStart=/usr/sbin/vsftpd /etc/vsftpd.conf
ExecReload=/bin/kill -HUP $MAINPID
ExecStartPre=-/bin/mkdir -p /var/run/vsftpd/empty

[Install]
WantedBy=multi-user.target
```

Running vsftpd

The Very Secure FTP Server's daemon is named **vsftpd**. It is designed to be run as a stand-alone server, which can be started and stopped using the **/lib/systemd/system/vsftpd.service** server script. To start, stop, and restart **vsftpd**, you can use the **systemctl** command. If you previously enabled another FTP server such as ProFTPD, be sure to disable it first. Whenever you make changes to your configuration, be sure to restart the FTP server to make the changes take effect.

```
sudo systemctl restart vsftpd
```

The anonymous FTP directory will be **ftp** user's home directory, **/srv/ftp**. Here will be located the file and directories for an anonymous FTP server.

Firewall access

To allow firewall access to the FTP port, usually port 21, you should enable access using a firewall configuration tool like **ufw**.

For the **ufw** default firewall, you would use the following command. The **ufw** firewall maintains its IPtables files in **/etc/ufw**. You can also use the Gufw tool (desktop) to add access for the FTP port, port 21.

```
sudo ufw allow tcp/21
```

If you are managing your firewall directly, you could add the following nftables or IPtables rules. This accepts input on port 21 for TCP/IP protocol packages.

nftables

```
nft add rule ip filter INPUT tcp dport 21 counter accept
```

iptables

```
iptables -A INPUT -p tcp --dport 21 -j ACCEPT
```

Configuring vsftpd

The **vsftpd** server is configured using one configuration file, **/etc/vsftpd.conf**. The configuration options are kept simple and precise. Entries in the **vsftpd.conf** file consist of directives composed of an option that is assigned a value. The assignment operation uses a = operator and there are spaces around it. The value for options can be on and off flags assigned a **YES** or **NO** value, numeric values, or a string (see Table 7-3). The default **vsftpd.conf** file, installed in the **/etc** directory, lists many of the commonly used options available with detailed comments for each. Those that are not active are commented out with a preceding # character. The names for the options are meant to be self-explanatory. You would use the **anon_upload_enable** to let anonymous users upload files, and the **anon_mkdir_write_enable** to let anonymous users create directories. To see a list of all the options, check the Man page for **vsftpd.conf**. The page has detailed documentation for each option.

The vsftpd server runs as the **nobody** user for unsecured tasks. The **nobody** user is used by various services. You can change this to a user dedicated to FTP server, something like **ftpsecure**. Set the username in the **nopriv_user** option.

```
nopriv_user=ftpsecure
```

Enabling Standalone Access

For **vsftpd** to run as a standalone server, the **listen** or **listen_ipv6** options have to be set to **YES**. With is option set, **vsftpd** continually listens on its assigned port for requests. Use the **listen_port** option to specify which port to use. By default, the **listen_ipv6** option is set to yes and the listen option (IPv4) is set to no. Keep in mind that the **listen_ipv6** option accepts connections from both IPv6 and IPv4 sockets, whereas the **listen-ipv4** option would only accept IPv4 connections.

```
listen=NO
```

```
listen_ipv6=YES
```

Enabling Login Access

Use the **anonymous_enable** option, with the **YES** value assigned to it, to enable anonymous FTP. Setting it to **NO** disables anonymous FTP. This is the default entry in the **vsftpd.conf** file, as shown below.

To allow local users on your system to use the FTP server the **local_enable** option is set to **YES**. This is the default, as shown here.

```
# Allow anonymous FTP? (Disabled by default).
anonymous_enable=NO
#
# Uncomment this to allow local users to log in.
local_enable=YES
```

Should you want to let anonymous users log in without providing a password, you can set **no_anon_password** to YES.

Local User Permissions

With permission options you can control how local users manage files on the FTP server. Use the **write_enable** option to let local users to create, rename, and delete files and directories, With this option active users can upload, rename, and delete their files, as well as to the same for subdirectories. The **user_config_dir option** lets you configure specific users.

```
write_enable=YES
```

Option	Description
listen	Set standalone mode
listen_port	Specify port for standalone mode
anonymous_enable	Enable anonymous user access
local_enable	Enable access by local users
write_enable	Enable write access by local users (modify and create files)
no_anon_password	Specify whether anonymous users must submit a password
anon_upload_enable	Enable uploading by anonymous users
anon_mkdir_write_enable	Allow anonymous users to create directories
aonon_world_readable_only	Make uploaded files read-only to all users
idle_session_timeout	Set time limit in seconds for idle sessions
data_connection_timeouts	Set time limit in seconds for failed connections
dirmessage_enable	Display directory messages
ftpd_banner	Display FTP login message
xferlog_enable	Enable logging of transmission transactions
xferlog_file	Specify log file
deny_email_enable	Enable denying anonymous users, whose e-mail addresses are specified in **vsftpd.banned**
userlist_enable	Deny access to users specified in the **vsftp.user_list** file
userlist_file	Deny or allow users access depending on setting of userlist_deny
userlist_deny	When set to **YES**, **userlist_file** deny list users access.
chroot_list_enable	Restrict users to their home directories
chroot_list_file	Allow users access to home directories. Unless chroot_local_user is set to **YES**, this file contains a list of users not allowed access to their home directories
chroot_local_user	Allow access by all users to their home directories
pam_service_name	Specify PAM script
ls_recurse_enable	Enable recursive listing
user_config_dir	Directory for user specific configuration

Table 7-3: Configuration Options for vsftpd.conf

You can also set the default permissions for uploaded files with the **local_umask** option. The permission value works inversely, The 022 value is the permission 755. The 022 value is the recommended default set in **vsftpd.conf**. This turns off the write permission for other users (Others and Groups) and gives the owner read, write, and execute permission, whereas all other users have only read and execute permission, a 755 permission setting.

```
local_umask=022
```

Because ASCII uploads entail certain security risks, they are turned off by default. However, if you are uploading large text files, you may want to enable them in special cases. Use **ascii_upload_enable** to allow ASCII uploads.

Anonymous User Permissions

You can set options to let anonymous users manage files. To allow anonymous users to upload a file you set the **anon_upload_enable** option. To let them rename or delete their files, you use the **anon_other_write_enable** option. To directories, set the **anon_mkdir_write_enable** option.

```
anon_upload_enable=YES
anon_other_write_enable=YES
anon_mkdir_write_enable=YES
```

To prevent other users from removing or changing a file, you can set the permission of the file to read-only with the **anon_world_readable_only** option. Only the user who uploaded the file can change or remove it.

All files uploaded by anonymous users are normally owned by the anonymous FTP user. It is possible for files to be owned by another user, as a security measure. This would hide the actual owner from any anonymous users. Use the **chown_uploads** option to enable this feature, and specify the new user with **chown_username** option. As a further security precaution, you should never specify an administrative user like **root**.

```
chown_uploads=YES
chown_username=myftp
```

The upload directory permissions must have write permission for other users (777) so the they can access the directory and add files.

```
sudo chmod 777 /srv/ftp/upload
```

You can use **anon_umask** option to set default read/write permissions for all uploaded files. The permission number works inversely. The default is 077, which gives read/write/execute permission to the owner only (700). If you want to give all users read access, you would set the umask to 022. In this case, the 2 turns off write permission but sets read and execute permission (755). The value 000 allows both read, write, and execute for all users, the equivalent of 777.

Messages

You can display a message at FTP login and when users enter certain directories. Enabling the **dirmessage_enable** option, allows the display of a directory message held in that directory's **.message** file. It is displayed whenever that that directory is accessed. You use the **ftpd_banner** option to enable and specify your FTP login message.

```
dirmessage_enable=YES
ftpd_banner=Welcome to blah FTP service.
```

Logging

You use the **xferlog** options to enable logging, specify the log format, and designate a log file.

```
xferlog_enable=YES
```

The **xferlog_file** option specifies the log file. The default on Ubuntu is **/var/log/vsftpd.log**.

```
xferlog_file=/var/log/vsftpd.log
```

Log entries can be saved in the standard ftpd xferlog format.

```
xferlog_std_format=YES
```

Connection Time Limits

To reduce the workload on an FTP server, you can detect and cutoff dropped connections, as well as put time limits on idle users. The **idle_session_timeout** option sets a time limit for idle users, and **data_connection_timeouts** will end failed data connections. The options are already enabled, with defaults in seconds, as shown here.

```
idle_session_timeout=600
data_connection_timeout=120
```

vsftpd Access Controls

There are options that lets you control access to a FTP site, such as the **anonymous_enable** option, which allows anonymous users access, and **local_enable** option that lets local users log in to their accounts. Files set up to control access will have a **vsftpd.** prefix, like **vsftpd.banned_emails** for email addresses of banned anonymous users.

Restricting Access

The **deny_email_enable** option lets you deny access by anonymous users, and the **banned_email_file** option designates the file (usually **vstfpd.banned_emails**) that holds the e-mail addresses of those users. The **/etc/ftpusers** file lists those users that can never be accessed. These are usually system users like **root**, **mail**, and **nobody**.

User Access

To control access by users, you would enable the The **userlist_enable** and the **userlist_deny** options. These will allow access by all users, except those listed in the file specified by the **userlist_file** option (usually **vsftpd.user_list**). This approach allows everyone access, except of few listed users. If, instead, you wanted to deny access to everyone, except a specific list of users, you would set the **userlist_deny** option to **NO** (its default is **YES**). This changes the **vsftpd.user_list** file (**userlist_file** option) to be a list of those users allowed access, instead of those denied access. As such, only the users listed in the **vsftpd.user_list** file are granted access to the FTP site.

User Restrictions

You can limit local users to accessing just their home directories, denying them access they would normally have to the entire system. The **chroot_list_enable** option turns on this feature, and the **chroot_list_file** option specifies the file (usually **vsftpd.chroot_list**) that lists those users allowed access.

```
chroot_list_enable=YES
chroot_list_file=/etc/vsftpd.chroot_list
```

Should you want to allow access by all local users, you can set the **chroot_local_user** option to YES.

```
chroot_local_users=YES
```

When this option is set, the file specified by the **chroot_list_file** option will be taken to mean the list of users not allowed access. In the following example, access by local users is denied to those listed in **vsftpd.chroot_list**, but allowed for all other local users.

```
chroot_local_users=YES
chroot_list_file=/etc/vsftpd.chroot_list
```

On Ubuntu, the **secure_chroot_dir** option is used to specify a non-user secure non-writeable directory used when FTP does not require file system access.

```
secure_chroot_dir=/var/run/vsftpd/empty
```

User Authentication and SSL Encryption

The PAM service is used by the **vsftpd** server to authenticate local users that remotely access their accounts through an FTP client. In the **vsftpd.conf** file, the PAM script used for the server is specified with the **pam_service_name** option.

```
pam_service_name=vsftpd
```

A PAM file named **vsftpd**, located in the **etc/pam.d** directory, lists entries used to control access to the **vsftpd** server. PAM is currently set up to authenticate users with valid accounts. The default **/etc/pam.d/vsftpd** file is shown here:

```
# Standard behavior for ftpd(8)
auth required  pam_listfile.so  item=user sense=deny  file=/etc/ftpusers  onerr=succeed
# Note: vsftpd handles anonymous logins on its own. Do not enable pam_ftp.so.
# Standard pam includes
@include common-account
@include common-session
@include common-auth
auth    required   pam_shells.so
```

The **rsa_cert_file** option specifies the location of the RSA certificate file, and the **rsa_private_key_file** option specifies the SSL encryption key to use for SSL connections.

```
rsa_cert_file=/etc/ssl/certs/ssl-cert-snakeoil.pem
rsa_private_key_file=/etc/ssl/private/ssl-cert-snakeoil.key
ssl_enable=NO
```

Command Access

The vsftpd server limits the commands you can run. Most options for the **ls** command that lists files are not permitted, though, the asterisk file-matching function is allowed. To allow listing of files in subdirectories (the **-R** option), you have to set the **ls_recurse_enable** option to **YES**.

vsftpd Virtual Hosts

It is possible to configure the vsftpd server for virtual hosts. In virtual hosting a single FTP server functions as if it has two or more IP addresses. You can access the same server with multiple IP addresses. Each host will have its own FTP user directory and files. You will have to manually create FTP users and directories for each virtual host, as well as vsftpd configuration files for each virtual host in the **/etc/** directory. You can set up virtual hosts for running vsftpd either as a standalone server or on demand, using a systemd template.

Virtual Hosts on a standalone server

On Ubuntu, **vsftpd** is configured to run as a standalone service. Adding virtual hosts is a simple matter of creating a separate vsftpd configuration file for each virtual host. Then run an instance of **vsftpd** for each using a different configuration file. The configuration files are placed in the **/etc** directory and can have the prefix **vsftpd-**, for example **/etc/vsftpd-mysite1.conf**. In the configuration file, use the **listen_address** option to specify which IP address that virtual host will use.

```
listen_address=192.168.0.5
```

When you run vsftpd, specify the configuration file to use.

```
sudo service vsftpd /etc/vsftpd-mysite1.conf
```

See the **/usr/share/doc/vsftpd/examples/INTERNET_SITE_NOINETD** directory for more information.

You will, of course, have to set up a user and a directory for each virtual host. For example, for the first virtual host, you could use **mysite1** and use the directory **/srv/mysite1**. Be sure to set root ownership and the appropriate permissions.

```
sudo useradd -d /srv/mysite1
sudo chown root.root /srv/mysite1
sudo chmod a+rx /srv/mysite1
sudo unmask 022
sudo mkdir /srv/mysite1/pub
```

vsftpd Virtual Hosts with systemd

As currently installed, vsftpd does not support virtual hosts using systemd directly. But you can create the appropriate template service file and corresponding target file to have systemd run vsftpd virtual hosts. The **vsftpd@.service** systemd template file reads the configuration files listed in the **/etc/vsftpd** directory. The **vsfptd@.service** file is shown here.

vsftpd@.service

```
 [Unit]
Description=Vsftpd ftp daemon
After=network.target
PartOf=vsftpd.target

[Service]
Type=forking
ExecStart=/usr/sbin/vsftpd /etc/vsftpd/%i.conf

[Install]
WantedBy=vsftpd.target
```

The following example uses two IP addresses for an FTP server. Create an FTP user for each host. Create directories for each host (you can use the one already set up for one of the users). For example, for the first virtual host, you could use **FTP-host1**. Be sure to set root ownership and the appropriate permissions.

```
useradd -d /var/ftp-host1
chown root.root /var/ftp-host1
chmod a+rx /var/ftp-host1
umask 022
mkdir /var/ftp-host1/pub
```

Within the **/etc/vsftpd** directory, create separate configuration files for each virtual host. Within each, specify the FTP user you created for each, using the **ftp_username** entry.

```
ftp_username = FTP-host1
```

The **vsftpd@.service** file needs a corresponding target file, **vsftpd.target**, which provides group configuration of all the vsftpd servers you start with the **vsftpd@.service** file. The **vsftpd.target** file starts the servers after the **network.target** file (network service files) and it is wanted by **multi-user.target**.

vsftpd.target

```
[Unit]
Description=FTP daemon
After=network.target

[Install]
WantedBy=multi-user.target
```

vsftpd Virtual Users

For a virtual user, you would use PAM to authenticate an authorized user. You do not have to set up separate FTP accounts for a virtual user, just use PAM to allow access by that user. You will have to create a PAM login database file and a PAM file in the **/etc/pam.d** directory that that can access the database (for sample files and documentation check **/usr/share/doc/vsftpd/examples/VIRTUAL_USERS**). Then create a virtual FTP user and corresponding directories for the virtual user. In the **vsftpd.conf** file, you disable anonymous FTP.

```
anonymous_enable=NO
local_enable=YES
```

Then enable guest access:

```
guest_enable=YES
guest_username=virtual
```

For more refined user control, you can set up a user configuration directory with files for different permissions for each user. Set the **user_config_dir** option in the **/etc/vsftpd.conf** file to the directory that will hold user configuration files. For example:

```
user_config_dir=/etc/vsftpd_user_conf
```

Be sure to create that directory.

```
sudo mkdir /etc/vsftpd_user_conf
```

In separate files named with a username, enter the vsftpd permissions and options you want for that user. See **/usr/share/doc/vsftpd/examples/VIRTUAL_USERS_2** for more information.

Using FTP with rsync

FTP servers can support rsync operations using **rsync** as a server. This feature lets you sync your local files with corresponding versions on an FTP server. In effect, you can use **rsync** to update local files and directories, changing only those that have been modified. You could update multiple files in a directory or a single file such as a large ISO image.

Accessing FTP Sites with rsync

To sync directories and files on an FTP server running an rsync server, you enter the **rsync** command, the hostname, two double colons, and then either the path of the directory you want to access or one of the FTP server's modules. In the following example, the user updates a local **myreport** directory from the one on the **mystuff.com** FTP site.

```
sudo rsync ftp.mytrek.com::/home/ftp/pub/myreport  /home/mystuff
```

The rsync modules will show the directories on that site that are supported by rsync. The modules are defined by the site's **/etc/rsyncd.conf** configuration file. An rsync module references a directory and its subdirectories. To see what rsync modules are available, use the FTP site with a double colon only as an option to the **rsync** command.

```
sudo rsync ftp.mystuff.com::
```

The previous example shows that the **ftp.mystuff.com** site has an FTP module. If you want to display a list for all the files and directories referenced by an rsync module, you use the **rsync** command with the **-r** option.

```
rsync -r ftp.mystuff.com::ftp
```

Configuring an rsync Server

To work with your FTP site, you have to configure rsync to run as a server. The rsync configuration file is **/etc/default/rsync**. Set the **RSYNC_ENABLE** entry to **true**.

```
RSYNC_ENABLE=true
```

You can then manage the server with the **systemctl** command.

```
sudo systemctl start rsync
```

Should you make configuration changes, you will have to restart the **rsync** server with the **systemctl** command to have the changes take effect.

```
sudo systemctl restart rsync
```

When run as a server, **rsync** reads the **/etc/rsyncd.conf** file, loading configuration options such as the location for the FTP site files. There is no default configuration file set up for you in the **/etc** directory. You will have to create one. You could copy a default version from the **/usr/share/doc/rsync/examples** directory.

```
sudo cp /usr/share/doc/rsync/examples/rsyncd.conf   /etc
```

The configuration file is organized into sections called modules. Each section references a tree (a directory and its subdirectories) with options that are applied to the tree. A module name is enclosed in brackets, for example, **[ftp]** for an FTP module. For the FTP module, the **path** option specifies the location of your FTP site directories and files. The user and group IDs can be specified with the **uid** and **gid** options. The default is **nobody**. If you copied the example, you have to change the **path** option to **/srv/ftp/**, the location for the vsftpd server files on Ubuntu. A sample FTP module heading with the **vsftpd** path setting for Ubuntu is shown here.

```
[ftp]
      comment = public archive
      path = /srv/ftp/
```

The sample version of **rsyncd.conf** will have an ftp module set up for you with default values assigned. Many less common options will be commented out with a # character.

By default, rsync allows anonymous access to all users. Should you want to restrict access by users, you can use the **auth users** option to list authorized users. To restrict access by host, you can use the **hosts allow** and **hosts deny** access controls. To restrict access by areas on the FTP site by rsync, you can set up a secret file, usually **/etc/rsyncd.secrets**. This file would consist of a colon-separated list of usernames and passwords.

```
aleina:mypass3
larisa:yourp5
```

Below is an example of the corresponding module for the controlled area.

```
[specialftp]
      comment = special projects
      path = /var/projects/special
      command = restricted access
      auth users = aleina,larisa
      secrets file = /etc/rsyncd.secrets
```

If a local user is on the FTP server and wants to know what modules are available, the user can run **rsync** with the **localhost** option followed by just the double colon.

```
$ rsync localhost::
ftp             public archive
specialftp      special projects
```

Should a remote user want to know what modules are available, the user would enter by your hostname and double colon only.

```
rsync ftp.mytrek.com::
```

rsync Mirroring

A site may let you use rsync for mirroring. Using rsync you would need to copy only the files that have been modified. You would not have to maintain a completely separate copy of the site.

Below, the mytrek FTP site is mirrored to the **/srv/ftp/mirror/mytrek** directory on a local system. The **-a** option is used to include several common rsync options, such as **-r** (recursive) option which include all subdirectories, the **-t** option that preserves file times and dates, the **-l** option to recreate symbolic links, and the **-p** option which preserve all permissions. The **--delete** option is will delete files that have been removed on the sending side. It removes any obsolete files on the mirror site.

```
rsync -a --delete ftp.mytrek.com::ftp /srv/ftp/mirror/mytrek
```

ProFTPD

ProFTPD is based on the same design as the Apache web server, implementing a similar simplified configuration structure and supporting such flexible features as virtual hosting. ProFTPD is an open source project made available under a GPL license. At **http://proftpd.org** you can find detailed documentation including FAQs, user manuals, and sample configurations. Check the site for new releases and updates. ProFTPD is available on the Universe repository as **proftpd-basic** and **proftpd-doc**, with additional authentication modules for mysql, ldap, odbc, sqlite, and pgsql.

You cannot have both vsftpd and ProFTPD installed at the same time. If you install ProFTPD, then vsftpd will be removed.

When you install ProFTPD configuration files are located in the **/etc/proftpd** directory. The primary configuration file is **/etc/proftpd/proftpd.conf**. Virtual servers are configured in the **virtual.conf** file. Modules have their own configuration files such as **sql.conf** and **ldap.conf**. You can choose what modules to load in the **modules.conf** file.

ubuntu

8. Web Servers

Apache Web Server

Ubuntu Apache Installation

Apache Configuration

Apache Configuration Directives

Virtual Hosting on Apache

NGINX Web Server

The primary web server for Ubuntu is Apache, which has become the standard web server for most Linux distributions. It is a powerful, stable, and fairly easy-to-configure server. Ubuntu provides a default configuration for the Apache, making it usable as soon as it is installed. The NGINX server is also available. NGINX is a small fast server capable of handling very high Web traffic and is often used in support for an Apache server. See Table 8-1 for a list of Web servers and associated sites.

Apache Web Server

The Apache web server is a full-featured, free HTTP (Web) server, developed and maintained by the Apache Server Project. The aim of the project is to provide a reliable, efficient, and easily extensible Web server, with free open source code made available under its own Apache Software License. The server software includes the server daemon, configuration files, management tools, and documentation. The Apache Server Project is one of the several projects currently supported by the Apache Software Foundation (formerly known as the Apache Group). This nonprofit organization provides financial, legal, and organizational support for various Apache Open Source software projects. The website for the Apache Software Foundation is **https://apache.org**. Table 8-1 lists some Apache-related websites.

Apache was originally based on the NCSA web server developed at the National Center for Supercomputing Applications, University of Illinois, Urbana-Champaign. Apache has since emerged as a server in its own right, and become one of the most popular Web servers in use. Although originally developed for Linux and UNIX systems, Apache has become a cross-platform application with Windows versions. Apache provides online support and documentation for its web server at **https://httpd.apache.org**. An HTML-based manual also is provided with the server installation. Also, check the Ubuntu Server Guide | Services | Web Servers - Apache for basic configuration.

```
https://ubuntu.com/server/docs/web-servers-apache
```

Website	Description
https://apache.org	Apache Software Foundation
https://httpd.apache.org	Apache HTTP Server Project
https://www.php.net/	PHP Hypertext Preprocessor, embedded web page programming language
https://nginx.org	NGINX Web server

Table 8-1: Web Servers and Related Websites

LAMP

During installation, you can install the Apache Web server as part of the LAMP collection of packages. LAMP stands for Linux Apache MySQL and PHP. It consists of the Web server (Apache) with database support (MySQL) and programming capability (PHP). For programming, PHP is selected by default, though you could use Python or Perl instead. Together they provide a commercially capable website, supporting multiple users and complex data with application support. For a basic informational website, you only need the Apache Web server.

The LAMP packages include the following from the Ubuntu main repository.

apache2   The Apache Web server and all supporting packages

mysql-server   The MySQL database server

php5-mysql and **libapache2-mod-php5**   The PHP support for MySQL and Apache

Ubuntu Apache Installation

Ubuntu will provide you with the option of installing the Apache web server during the Ubuntu Server installation (LAMP package). Alternatively, you can install the Apache web server later as the **apache2** package (use apptitude, the Synaptic Package Manager, or **apt**). All the necessary directories and configuration files are automatically generated for you. Then, whenever you run Linux, your system is already a fully functional website. Every time you start your system, the web server will also start up, running continuously. On Ubuntu, the directory reserved for your website data files is **/var/www**. Place your web pages in this directory. Your system is already configured to operate as a web server. All you need to do is perform any needed network server configuration, and then designate the files and directories open to remote users. Once your website is connected to a network, remote users can access it.

The web server normally sets up your website in the **/var/www** directory. A simple **index.html** test page is installed for you in the **html** subdirectory to check if your Web server is working. Your configuration files are located in a different directory, **/etc/apache2**. Table 8-2 lists the various Apache web server directories and configuration files.

The Apache manual is installed from the **apacha2-doc** package, and is placed in the **/usr/share/doc/apache2-doc/manual** directory in html format. You can access it with any browser as:

```
http://localhost/manual/index.html
```

Apache also installs several management applications, such as **apache2ctl** for starting and stopping the server, **a2ensite** for activating a website, and **a2enmod** for enabling particular modules. The **apache2.service** unit file is designed to safely run **apache2ctl** and should also be used to start and stop the server manually. Table 8-3 lists the applications.

The Apache server is managed by **systemd** using the **apache2.service** unit file in the **/lib/systemd/system** directory. The server is started after the network and file system mounts (After). The **/usr/sbin/apachectl** program is used to start, stop, and restart the server (ExecStart, ExecStop, ExecReload).

Directories and Files	Description
.htaccess	Directory-based configuration files; an **.htaccess** file holds directives to control access to files within the directory in which it is located
/var/www	Directory for Apache website HTML files, the location of the default server HTML files. Virtual sites will be located here
/etc/apache2	Directory for Apache web server configuration files
/lib/systemd/system/apache2.service	Apache Web server systemd service file for start up and shut down
/etc/default/apache2	Apache Web start up configuration
/usr/sbin	Location of the Apache web server program file and utilities
/usr/share/doc/apache2-doc	Apache web server manual, **apache2-doc** package
/var/log/apache2	Location of Apache log files
/usr/lib/apache2	Directory holding Apache modules
/usr/lib/cgi-bin	Directory holding Web CGI scripts
/var/cache/apache2	Directory holding Apache cache

Table 8-2: Apache Web Server Files and Directories

Application	Description
apache2ctl	Control start, stop, and restart the apache server
a2enmod	Enable an Apache module
a2dismod	Disable an Apache module
a2enconf	Enable an Apache configuration file in **conf-available**
a2disconf	Disable an Apache configuration file in **conf-available**
a2ensite	Enable a website, loading its configuration file
a2dissite	Disable an Apache website
/lib/systemd/system/apache2.service	Systemd service file designed for Ubuntu to start, stop, and restart server, invokes **apache2ctl**.

Table 8-3: Apache management tools

apache2.service

```
[Unit]
Description=The Apache HTTP Server
After=network.target remote-fs.target nss-lookup.target
Documentation=https://httpd.apache.org/docs/2.4/

[Service]
Type=forking
Environment=APACHE_STARTED_BY_SYSTEMD=true
ExecStart=/usr/sbin/apachectl start
ExecStop=/usr/sbin/apachectl graceful-stop
ExecReload=/usr/sbin/apachectl graceful
killMode=mixed
PrivateTmp=true
Restart=on-abort

[Install]
WantedBy=multi-user.target
```

Apache Multiprocessing Modules: MPM

Apache uses an architecture with multiprocessing modules (MPMs), which are designed to customize Apache to different operating systems, as well as handle certain multiprocessing operations. For the main MPM, a Linux system uses the prefork, worker, or event MPM, whereas Windows uses the mpm_winnt MPM. The prefork is a standard MPM module designed to be compatible with older UNIX and Linux systems, particularly those that do not support threading. Currently, Ubuntu uses the worker modules. You can configure the workload parameters for both in their module configuration files in the **mods-available** directory: the **mpm_prefork.conf**, **mpm_worker.conf**, and **mpm_event.conf** files.

Starting and Stopping the Web Server

On Ubuntu, Apache is installed as a standalone server. Your system will use a systemd service script to automatically start up the web server daemon, invoking it whenever you start your system. A systemd unit script for the web server called **apache2.service** is in the **/lib/systemd/system** directory. This script uses the **apache2ctl** tool to manage the Apache server, allowing you to start, stop, and restart the server from the command line. The **apache2.service** file can take different arguments: **start** to start the server, **stop** to stop it, and **restart** to shut down and restart the server.

To check your web server, start your web browser on the host that is running the Web server, and use localhost as the domain name. Your Web server will be providing access on port 80. You would enter **http://localhost/**. You can also just enter your hostname. If you already have an Internet domain name address already supported by DNS servers, you could use that instead. This should display the home page you placed in your web root directory. A test page **index.html** file is set up for you that will display the words, It Works. Your website will be located in the **/var/www/html** directory. Here is where you would place the Web pages for your website.

As you configure your website, you will need to reload your configuration settings and restart the Web server, so that the new settings will take effect. You can do this by running the

apache2.service file first with the **reload** option, and then with the **restart** option. Use the **systemctl** command to invoke the **apache2** script.

```
sudo systemctl reload apache2
sudo systemctl restart apache2
```

You also can use the **apache2.service** file to start and stop the Web server using the **start** and **stop** options. With the **status** option, you can check if your Web server is running.

```
sudo systemctl start apache2
```

The **apache-htcacheclean.service** systemd unit file can be used to run the **htcacheclean** daemon, which will periodically check and clean the disk cache used by the Web server. Use the **apache-htcacheclean** command to start and stop the htcacheclean server.

```
sudo systemctl start apache-htcacheclean
sudo systemctl stop apache-htcacheclean
```

Once you have your server running, you can check its performance with the **ab** benchmarking tool, also provided by Apache. **ab** shows you how many requests at a time your server can handle. It takes as its argument the website URL. Options include **-v**, which enables you to control the level of detail displayed, **-n**, which specifies the number of requests to handle (default is 1). and **-t**, which specifies a time limit.

```
ab -v -n localhost/index.htm.
```

Apache Configuration

Configuration directives are run from the **apache2.conf** configuration file. A documented version of the **apache2.conf** configuration file is installed automatically in **/etc/apache2/apache2.conf**. It contains detailed descriptions and default entries for global Apache directives. Though the **apache2.conf** file runs the entire configuration, it does so by including the contents of other configuration files. In effect, Apache configuration is distributed among other configuration files tailored for specific tasks. Configuration files for Apache are listed in Table 8-4.

The **apache2.conf** file is configured to include and run all the directives in the **/etc/apache2/ports.conf**, **/etc/apache2/envvars**, all the configuration files linked to in the **/etc/apache2/conf-enabled** and **/etc/apache2/mods-enabled** directories, and all the configuration files linked to in the **/etc/apache2/sites-enabled** directory. The **/etc/apache2/ports.conf** file holds the port directives determining what port Apache will use (normally 80). The **/etc/apache2/envvars** file holds variable definitions such as APACHE_LOG_DIR, which are used by Apache tools, site configuration files, and scripts like **apache2ctl**. Currently, these include user and group definitions for running Apache.

Any of the directives in the main configuration files can be overridden on a per-directory basis using an **.htaccess** file located within a directory. Although originally designed for access directives, the **.htaccess** file can also hold any resource directives, enabling you to tailor how web pages are displayed in a particular directory. You can configure access to **.htaccess** files in the **apache2.conf** file. In addition, default start-up settings for **htcacheclean** are set up in the **/etc/default/apache2** file for managing the Web server cache.

File or Directory	Description
apache2.conf	Apache web server configuration file, will run all other configuration files
conf-available	Directory holding specialized and local configuration files
conf-enabled	Active configuration files, links to their configuration files in conf-available Read by apache2.conf
ports.conf	Directives for defining the port the Web server will use
envvars	Variable definitions used by apache2.conf and other scripts, defines user, groups, and pid for Apache
mods-available	Configuration files for particular modules, including their directives Also includes modules.
mods-enabled	Active modules, links to their configuration files in mods-available Read by apache2.conf
sites-available	Configuration files for particular sites, including Directory directives
sites-enabled	Active sites, links to their configuration files in sites-available. Read by apache2.conf

Table 8-4: Apache configuration files in the /etc/apache2 directory.

Module configuration files

Many directives that once resided in the Apache core are now placed in respective modules and MPMs. With this modular design, several directives have been dropped, such as ServerType. Available modules and their configuration files are located in the **/etc/apache2/mods-available** directory. The enabled modules are listed in the **/etc/apache2/mods-enabled** directory as links to their corresponding modules in the **mods-available** directory. A module is disabled by removing its link. Use the **a2enmod** command to enable a module, and the **a2dismod** command to disable a module. These commands work by adding or removing links for available modules in the **/etc/apache2/mods-enabled** directory.

Modules will have both a **.conf** and **.load** configuration file. For example, the SSL module has both an **ssl.conf** and **ssl.load** file. The **.conf** file holds directives for configuring the module, and the **.load** file holds the LoadModule directive for performing the actual load operation, specifying the location and name of the module. Their corresponding links in the **mods-enabled** directory also have **.conf** and **.load** extensions.

Configuration files in conf-available

Additional configuration files, not associated with a particular module, are located in the **/etc/apache2/conf-available** directory. Sometimes these are links to configuration files set up by other applications. The configuration files have the extension **.conf**, such as **security.conf**. The configuration files are not active unless enabled. The enabled configuration files are listed in the **/etc/apache2/conf-enabled** directory as links to their corresponding modules in the **conf-available** directory. The links also have the same **.conf** extension. A configuration file is disabled by removing its link. Use the **a2enconf** command to enable a module, and the **a2disconf** command to disable a module. These commands work by adding or removing links for available modules in the /etc/apache2/conf-enabled directory.

Site configuration files

All sites on the Web server are configured as virtual hosts, with a special site called default for the main Web server. Normally you would create your site as a virtual host, reserving the default for administration. Virtual hosts can then be enabled or disabled, letting you turn access to a site on and off. You use the **a2dissite** and **a2ensite** commands to enable or disable sites.

The configuration files for sites you have set up on your server are listed in the /etc/apache2/sites-available directory. Configuration files will contain Directory directives specifying the location of the site and controls and features you have set up for it. The **000-default.conf** file holds configuration directives for the default Web server, such as the directory directives locating the default site at /var/www/html. All site configuration files have the extension **.conf**. To make a site accessible, a link to its configuration file must be created in the /etc/apache2/sites-enabled directory. Use the **ensite** command to create such a link. There will already be a link for the **default** site (**000-default.conf**). The links also have a **.conf** extension.

Apache Configuration Directives

Apache configuration takes the form of directives entered into the Apache configuration files (**/etc/apache2**). With these directives, you can enter basic configuration information, such as your server name, or perform more complex operations, such as implementing virtual hosts. The design is flexible enough to enable you to define configuration features for particular directories and different virtual hosts. Apache has a variety of different directives performing operations as diverse as controlling directory access, assigning file icon formats, and creating log files. Most directives set values such as **DirectoryRoot**, which holds the root directory for the server's web pages, or **Port**, which holds the port on the system that the server listens on for requests. The syntax for a simple directive is shown here:

```
directive option ...
```

Certain directives create blocks able to hold directives that apply to specific server components (also referred to as block directives). For example, the **Directory** directive is used to define a block within which you place directives that apply only to a particular directory. Block directives are entered in pairs: a beginning directive and a terminating directive. The terminating directive defines the end of the block and consists of the same name beginning with a slash. Block directives take an argument that specifies the particular object to which the directives apply. For the **Directory** block directive, you must specify a directory name to which it will apply. The **<Directory** *directory*> block directive creates a block whose directives within it apply to the specified directory. The block is terminated by a **</Directory>** directive. The **<VirtualHost** *hostaddress*> block directive is used to configure a specific virtual web server, and must include the IP or domain name address used for that server. **</VirtualHost>** is its terminating directive. Any directives you place within this block are applied to that virtual web server. The **<Limit** *method*> directive specifies the kind of access method you want to limit such as GET or POST. The access control directives located within the block list the controls you are placing on those methods. The syntax for a block directive is as follows:

```
<block-directive option ... >
 directive option ...
 directive option ...
</block-directive>
```

Global directives are placed in one of the main configuration files. Directives for particular sites are located in that site's configuration file in **/etc/apache2/sites-available** directory. Directory directives in those files can be used to configure a particular directory. However, Apache also makes use of directory-based configuration files. Any website directory may have its own **.htaccess** file that holds directives to configure only that directory. If your site has many directories, or if any directories have special configuration needs, you can place their configuration directives in their **.htaccess** files, instead of filling the main configuration file with specific **Directory** directives for each one. You also can control what directives in an **.htaccess** file take precedence over those in the main configuration files. If your site allows user or client-controlled directories, you may want to monitor or disable the use of **.htaccess** files in them. It is possible for directives in an **.htaccess** file to override those in the standard configuration files unless disabled with AllowOverride directives.

You can find a listing of Apache web configuration directives both at the Apache website, **http://httpd.apache.org/docs/2.4/mod/quickreference.html** and, if you have installed the **apache2-doc** package, on your own system as **http://localhost/manual/en/mod/quickreference.html**.

Access controls: require

With the access control directive **require** you can control access to your website by remote users and hosts (see Table 8-5). With Apache 2.4, the **require** directive replaces the **allow**, **order**, **deny**, and **satisfy** directives used in Apache 2.2. It is implemented by the **mod_authz_host** module. Access can be granted or denied. The **all** term refers to all hosts. The **require** directive can be used globally to control access to the entire site or placed within **Directory** directives to control access to individual directives. In the following example, all users are allowed access.

```
require all granted
```

The **require** directive performs authentication on users. Authentication can refer to all users (**all**), specific users (**user**), groups (**group**), the domain name of a host the users are on (**host**), IP address (**ip**) of a host, authorized users (**valid-user**), an expression (**expr**), HTTP method (**method**), or environment variable (**env**). In most cases, it is used to determine access by all users (**all**), or those from specified hosts (**host** or **ip**), or those users with password set up by the **htpasswd** command in the Apache user password file (**valid-user**).

Directory blocks

A Directory block begins with a **<Directory** *pathname***>** directive, where *pathname* is the directory to be configured. The ending directive uses the same <> symbols, but with a slash preceding the word "Directory": **</Directory>**. Directives placed within this block apply only to the specified directory. The following example denies access to only the **mypics** directory by requests from www.myvids.com.

```
<Directory /var/www/mypics>
    Require all granted
    Require host www.myvids.com denied
</Directory>
```

With the **Options** directive, you can enable certain features in a directory, such as the use of symbolic links, automatic indexing, execution of CGI scripts, and content negotiation. The default is the **All** option, which turns on all features except content negotiation (**Multiviews**). The following example enables automatic indexing (**Indexes**), symbolic links (**FollowSymLinks**), and content negotiation (**Multiviews**). A simple **index.html** file has been placed in the **/var/www** directory to disable automatic indexing (Indexes) for that top level directory (DocumentRoot). The Indexes option can be a security risk.

```
Options Indexes FollowSymLinks Multiviews
```

Configurations made by directives in main configuration files or in upper-level directories are inherited by lower-level directories. Directives for a particular directory held in **.htaccess** files and Directory blocks can be allowed to override those configurations. This capability can be controlled by the **AllowOverride** directive. With the **all** argument, **.htaccess** files can override any previous configurations. The **None** argument disallows overrides, effectively disabling the **.htaccess** file. You can further control the override of specific groups of directives. **AuthConfig** enables use of authorization directives, **FileInfo** is for type directives, **Indexes** is for indexing directives, **Limit** is for access control directives, and **Options** is for the options directive.

```
AllowOverride all
```

Authentication

Your web server can also control access on a per-user or per-group basis to particular directories on your website. You can require various levels of authentication. Access can be limited to particular users and require passwords, or expanded to allow members of a group access. You can dispense with passwords altogether or set up an anonymous type of access, as used with FTP.

To apply authentication directives to a certain directory, you place those directives within either a **Directory** block or the directory's **.htaccess** file. Use the **require** directive to determine what users can access the directory. You can list particular users or groups. The **AuthName** directive provides the authentication realm to the user, the name used to identify the particular set of resources accessed by this authentication process. The **AuthType** directive specifies the type of authentication, such as basic or digest. A **require** directive requires also **AuthType**, **AuthName**, and directives specifying the locations of group and user authentication files. In the following example, only the users **george**, **robert**, and **mark** are allowed access to the **newpics** directory:

```
<Directory /var/www/newpics
    AuthType Basic
    AuthName Newpics
    AuthUserFile "/web/users"
    AuthGroupFile "/web/groups"
    <Limit GET POST>
        require user george robert mark
    </Limit>
</Directory>
```

To set up anonymous access for a directory, place the **Anonymous** directive with the user anonymous as its argument in the directory's Directory block or **.htaccess** file. You can also use the **Anonymous** directive to provide access to particular users without requiring passwords from them.

Apache maintains its own user and group authentication files, specifying what users and groups are allowed access to which directories. These files are normally simple flat files, such as your system's password and group files. They can become large, however, possibly slowing down authentication lookups. As an alternative, many sites have used database management files in place of these flat files. Database methods are then used to access the files, providing a faster response time. Apache has directives for specifying the authentication files, depending on the type of file you are using. The **AuthUserfile** and **AuthGroupFile** directives are used to specify the locations of authentication files that have a standard flat file format. The **AuthDBUserFile** and **AuthDBGroupFile** directives are used for DB database files, and the **AuthDBMGUserFile** and **AuthDBMGGroupFile** are used for DBMG database files.

The programs **htdigest**, **htpasswd**, and **htdbm** are tools provided with the Apache software package for creating and maintaining user authentication files, which are user password files listing users who have access to specific directories or resources on your website. The **htdigest** and **htpasswd** programs manage a simple flat file of user authentication records, whereas **htdbm** uses a more complex database management format. If your user list is extensive, you may want to use a database file for fast lookups. **htdigest** takes as its arguments the authentication file, the realm, and the username, creating or updating the user entry. **htpasswd** can also employ encryption on the password. **htdbm** has an extensive set of options to add, delete, and update user entries. A variety of different database formats is used to set up such files. Three common ones are Berkeley DB2, NDBM, and GNU GBDM. **htdbm** looks for the system libraries for these formats in that order. Be careful to be consistent in using the same format for your authentication files. The following example creates the user **dylan** and password in the **/web/users** authentication file. You will be prompted to enter the password. The **-c** option create the **/web/users** file if it does not exist.

```
sudo htpasswd.-c /web/users  dylan
```

Directory-level Configuration

One of the most flexible aspects of Apache is its ability to configure individual directories. With the **Directory** directive, you can define a block of directives that apply only to a particular directory (see Table 8-5).

Such a directive can be placed in a site configuration file. Global default directives are located in the **apache2.conf** configuration file. You can also use an **.htaccess** file within a particular directory to hold configuration directives. Those directives are then applied only to that directory. The name **.htaccess** is set with the **AccessFileName** directive. You can change this if you want.

```
AccessFileName .htaccess
```

A Directory block begins with a **<Directory** *pathname***>** directive, where *pathname* is the directory to be configured. The ending directive uses the same **<>** symbols, but with a slash preceding the word "Directory": **</Directory>**. Directives placed within this block apply only to the specified directory.

With the **Options** directive, you can enable certain features in a directory, such as the use of symbolic links, automatic indexing, execution of CGI scripts, and content negotiation. The default is the **All** option, which turns on all features except content negotiation (**Multiviews**). The following example enables automatic indexing (**Indexes**), symbolic links (**FollowSymLinks**), and content negotiation (**Multiviews**).

```
Options Indexes FollowSymLinks Multiviews
```

Directive	Description
require *user-authentication*	Authenticates users that can access a given directory or site. Authentication can refer to all users (**all**), userids (**user**), groups (**group**), domain name (**host**), IP address (**ip**), and even an expression, HTTP method, or environment variable.
require host *hosts*	Determines hosts (domain names) that can access a given directory.
require ip *addresses*	Determines hosts (IP addresses) that can access a given directory.
require all granted	Grant access to all hosts
require all denied	Deny access to all hosts
<Files *filename***>** ... **</Files>**	Provides for access control by filename. Similar to the **<Directory>** directive and **<Location>** directive. **<Files>** sections are processed in the order they appear in the configuration file, after the **<Directory>** sections and **.htaccess** files are read, but before **<Location>** sections. **<Files>** can be nested inside **<Directory>** sections to restrict the portion of the file system to which they apply.
<FilesMatch *regex***>** ... **</FilesMatch>**	Provides for access control by filename like the **<Files>** directive, but uses a regular expression.
<Limit *method method* ... **>** ... **</Limit>**	**<Limit>** and **</Limit>** specify a group of access control directives that apply only to the specified access methods, any valid HTTP method. Access control directives appearing outside a **<Limit>** directive apply to all access methods. Method names are GET, POST, PUT, DELETE, CONNECT, and OPTIONS.
<LimitExcept *method method* ... **>** ... **</LimitExcept>**	**<LimitExcept>** and **</LimitExcept>** specify a group of access control directives, which then apply to any HTTP access method *not* listed in the arguments.
<Location *URL***>** ... **</Location>**	The **<Location>** directive provides for access control by URL. Similar to the **<Directory>** directive.
<LocationMatch *regex***>** ... **</LocationMatch>**	Provides access control by URL, in an identical manner to **<Location>**, using a regular expression as an argument.
LimitRequestBody *number*	Limits the size of an HTTP request message body.

Table 8-5: Access Control Directives

Configurations made by directives in main configuration files or in upper-level directories are inherited by lower-level directories. Directives for a particular directory held in **.htaccess** files and Directory blocks can be allowed to override those configurations. This capability can be controlled by the **AllowOverride** directive. With the **all** argument, **.htaccess** files can override any previous configurations. The **none** argument disallows overrides, effectively disabling the **.htaccess** file. You can further control the override of specific groups of directives. **AuthConfig** enables use of authorization directives, **FileInfo** is for type directives, **Indexes** is for indexing directives, **Limit** is for access control directives, and **Options** is for the options directive.

```
AllowOverride all
```

When given a URL for a directory instead of an HTML file, and when no default web page is in the directory, Apache creates a page on the fly and displays it. This is usually only a listing of the different files in the directory. In effect, Apache indexes the items in the directory for you. You can set several options for generating and displaying such an index using **IndexOptions**. With **FancyIndexing**, web page items are displayed with icons and column headers that can be used to sort the listing. With **VersionSort**, items are sorted alphabetically and numerically. **NameWidth** sets column width, with the * value setting the width as needed. **Charset** sets the character set, usually UTF-8. For a complete list of options see **http://httpd.apache.org/docs/2.2/mod/mod_autoindex.html#indexoptions**

```
IndexOptions FancyIndexing VersionSort NameWidth=* HTMLTable Charset=UTF-8
```

Global Configuration: apache2.conf, ports.conf, and envvars

The Apache configuration places global settings in the **apache2.conf** file, as well as the **ports.conf** and **envvars** files. Configurations for particular modules are located in the **modules-conf** directory. The global settings control the basic operation and performance of the web server. Here is where you set configuration locations, process ID files, timing, ports, environmental variable definitions, and default directory controls. Apache uses several global variables, which are set in the **envvars** file.

The **ServerRoot** directive specifies where your web server configuration files and modules are kept. This server root directory is then used as a prefix to other directory entries.

```
ServerRoot "/etc/apache2"
```

The lock directory is specified by the Mutex directive using the APACHE_LOCK_DIR variable set in the **/etc/apache2/envvars** file.

```
Mutex file:${APACHE_LOCK_DIR} default
```

The location of runtime files is specified with the APACHE_RUN_DIR, also in the **/etc/apache2/envvars** file.

```
DefaultRuntimeDir ${APACHE_RUN_DIR}
```

The server's process ID (PID) file is set by **PidFile**. On Ubuntu, the Process ID file is defined by APACHE_PID_FILE variable in the **/etc/apache2/envvars** file.

```
PidFile ${APACHE_PID_FILE}
```

Connection and request timing is handled by **Timeout, KeepAlive, MaxKeepAliveRequest**, and **KeepAliveTimeout** directives. **Timeout** is the time in seconds that the web server times out a send or receive request. **KeepAlive** allows persistent connections, several requests from a client on the same connection. This is turned off by default.

MaxKeepAliveRequests sets the maximum number of requests on a persistent connection. **KeepAliveTimeout** is the time that a given connection to a client is kept open to receive more requests from that client.

Additional directives set user and group, local directory configuration files, and logs. The User and Group directives set the User and Group that run the Apache server. The APACHE_RUN_USERS and the APACHE_RUN_GROUP variables are set in the **/etc/apache2/envvars** file. The name of the user and group is **www-data**.

```
User ${APACHE_RUN_USERS}
Group ${APACHE_RUN_GROUP}
```

The **Listen** directive will bind the server to a specific port or IP address. By default, this is port 80. The Listen directive is defined in the **/etc/apache2/ports.conf** file.

```
Listen 80
```

Directory security defaults in apache2.conf

One of the most flexible aspects of Apache is its ability to configure individual directories. With the **Directory** directive, you can define a block of directives that apply only to a particular directory. Such a directive can be placed in the **apache2.conf** configuration file.

Several default Directory blocks are defined in the **apache2.conf** file to control access to your website. All of them prevent the use of **.htaccess** files in their directories by setting the AllowOverride directive to none.

```
AllowOverride None
```

For the website's root directory, /, symbolic links are allowed. The **/usr/share** directory allows access to everyone.

```
<Directory />
    Options FollowSymLinks
    AllowOverride None
    Require all denied
</Directory>

<Directory /usr/share>
    AllowOverride None
    Require all granted
</Directory>
```

Then the directory block is defined for the website directory, **/var/www/**. This is the location for all the website files. The "Require all granted" directive will allow anyone to access the files. Keep in mind that the website's document directory is defined by the DocumentRoot directive as **/var/www/html** in the site's **sites-available** configuration file.

```
<Directory "/var/www">
    Options Indexes FollowSymLinks
    AllowOverride None
    Require all granted
</Directory>
```

An additional commented directive is listed for the **srv** directory, should you want to enable it.

```
#<Directory "/srv ">
#    Options Indexes FollowSymLinks
#    AllowOverride None
#    Require all granted
#</Directory>
```

The Options directive specifies options to display default indexes, allows symbolic links, and supports MultiViews. The Indexes option will list files, should there be no default page for the directory (DirectoryIndex). MultiViews supports content negotiation, like using a particular language or a preferred image type.

```
Options Indexes FollowSymLinks MultiViews
```

You can also use an **.htaccess** file within a particular directory to hold configuration directives. Those directives are then applied only to that directory. The name ".htaccess" is set with the **AccessFileName** directive. You can change this if you want.

```
AccessFileName .htaccess
```

To deny access to the **.htaccess** files by Web clients, a FilesMatch block is defined with the access control directives "Require all denied", which denies access to all users. The FilesMatch directive references any file beginning with **.ht** (the period is quoted with a backslash). The FilesMatch directive allows the use of regular expressions, in this case, the ^ expression. The **</FilesMatch>** entry ends the **<Files>** block.

```
<FilesMatch ~ "^\.ht">
    Require all denied
</Files>
```

logs

For efficiency, the **HostnameLookups** operation is turned off. **HostnameLookups**, if turned on, would log all Web clients, generating a DNS server search for each client that accesses the Web server.

```
HostnameLookups Off
```

ErrorLog specifies the location of the log file (APACHE_LOG_DIR is set in the **/etc/apache2/envvars** file).

```
ErrorLog ${APACHE_LOG_DIR}/error.log
```

LogLevel sets the level at which messages should be logged. The warn level is usually used, though you can choose others like notice, info, debug, as well as more serious ones like crit, alert, and emerg.

```
LogLevel warn
```

The **LogFormat** directive defines some nicknames to be used with the **CustomLog** directive, like host_combined, common, and referrer. These are the formats in which messages are saved in the log file. The formats use substitution symbols like **%h** for the host, **%t** for the time, and **%u** for the user. The following defines a common format that displays the host, remote logname, user, time, the first line of the request in quotes, status, and size. The substitution characters are listed at **http://httpd.apache.org/docs/2.4/mod/mod_log_config.html**.

```
LogFormat "%h %l %u %t \"%r\" %>s %0" common
```

The **CustomLog** directive defines a default log for virtual hosts that do not define one. It is now defined in the **/etc/apache2/conf-available/other-vhosts-access-log.conf** file, which is read by the **apache2.conf** file. The format used is the **vhost_combined** format.

```
CustomLog ${APACHE_LOG_DIR}/other_vhosts_access.log   vhost_combined
```

Included files in apache2.conf

The **apache2.conf** file will include all module, port, and site configuration files with the **Include** and **IncludeOptional** directives. Specialized configurations will be located in the **conf-available** directory.

```
# Include module configuration:
IncludeOptional mods-enabled/*.load
IncludeOptional mods-enabled/*.conf
# Include list of ports to listen on
Include ports.conf

# Include generic snippets of statements
IncludeOptional conf-enabled/*.conf
# Include the virtual host configurations:
IncludeOptional sites-enabled/*.conf
```

MPM Configuration: mods-available

Configuration settings for MPM prefork, worker, and event modules let you tailor your Apache web server to your workload demands. Default entries will already be set for a standard web server operating under a light load. You can modify these settings for different demands. These setting are located in the **mods-available** directory in the **mpm_prefork.conf**, **mpm_worker.conf**, and **mpm_event.conf** files. A link in the **mods-enabled** directory shows the one enabled, usually the **mpm_prefork** module. Use **a2enmod** to enable the module you want.

Three MPM modules commonly available to UNIX and Linux systems are prefork, worker, and event. The prefork module supports one thread per process, which maintains compatibility with older systems and modules. The worker module supports multiple threads for each process, placing a much lower load on system resources. The event module serves more requests simultaneously. They share several of the same directives, such as **StartServer** and **MaxRequestPerChild**. Ubuntu currently uses the worker module.

Apache runs a single parent process with as many child processes as are needed to handle requests. Configuration for MPM modules focuses on the number of processes that should be available. The prefork module will list server numbers as a process is started for each server; the worker module will control threads since it uses threads for each process. The **StartServer** directive lists the number of server processes to start for both modules. This will normally be larger for the prefork than for the worker module.

In the prefork module (**mpm_prefork.conf**) you need to set minimum and maximum settings for spare servers. **MaxRequestWorkers** sets the maximum number of servers that can be started, and **ServerLimit** sets the number of servers allowed. The **MaxRequestsPerChild** sets the maximum number of requests allowed for a server.

```
StartServers           5
MinSpareServers        5
MaxSpareServers        10
MaxRequesWorkers       150
MaxRequestsPerChild    0
```

The directives serve as a kind of throttle on the web server access, controlling processes to keep available, and limiting the resources that can be used. In the prefork configuration, the **StartServer** is set to 5, and the spare minimum to 5, with the maximum spare as 20. This means that initially 5 server processes will be started up and will wait for requests, along with 5 spare processes. When server processes are no longer being used, they will be terminated until the number of these spare processes is less than 10. The maximum number of server processes that can be started is 150.

In the worker MPM (**mpm_worker.conf**), only 2 server processes are initially started (**StartServer**). Spare threads are set at 25 and 75. The maximum number of threads is set at 150, with the threads per child at 25. **MaxRequestWorkers** sets the maximum number of client threads, and **ThreadsPerChild** sets the number of threads for each server. **MaxConnectionsPerChild** limits the maximum number of requests for a server.

```
StartServers           2
MinSpareThreads        25
MaxSpareThreads        75
ThreadLimit            64
ThreadsPerChild        25
MaxRequestWorkers      150
MaxConnectionsPerChild    0
```

The event MPM is based on the worker MPM and has the same configuration. It is designed to pass off processing to supporting threads, freeing up the main threads to handle new requests.

Error Messages: conf-available/localized-error-pages.conf

Configured in the **conf-available/localized-error-pages.conf** file, and included in the **apache2.conf** file with other **conf-available** files are directives for internationalized error messages. The **LanguagePriority** directive lets you rank the languages to use. The mod_alias, mod_include, and mod_negotiation modules have to be loaded. The Alias and Directory directives specify the error directory as **/usr/share/apache2/error**. Here you will find **.var** files for different error messages, like HTTP_BAD_GATEWAY.html.var. These **.var** files contain configuration for displaying the messages in the languages specified by LanguagePriority directive. Some of the key internationalization error directives are shown here.

```
Alias /error/ "/usr/share/apache2/error'
LanguagePriority en cs de es fr it nl sv pg-br ro
ErrorDocument 502 /error/HTTP_BAD_GATEWAY.html.var
```

Security: conf-available/security.conf

Configured in the **conf-available/security.conf** file, and included in the **apache2.conf** file with other **conf-available** files are directives for site security. Most entries are commented out. **ServerTokens** determines the content of the site's response header. On Ubuntu, it is set to OS to return the operating system type. **ServerSignature** is set to On, which adds server version and hostname information for server-generated pages. **TraceEnable** is set to Off to disable trace requests.

cgi-bin: conf-available/serve-cgi-bin.conf

Configured in the **conf-available/serve-cgi-bin** file, and included in the **apache2.conf** file with other **conf-available** files are directives for site **cgi-bin** directory access. The **cgi-bin** directory holds the website's executable scripts like the CGI (Common Gateway Interface) and SSI (Server Side Includes) scripts.

First, a check is made to see if the CGI module has been loaded, either the traditional single server CGI bin module (**mod_cgi.c**) or the multi-tasking CGI bin daemon module (**mod_cgid.c**). If either is present the ENABLE_USR_LIB_CGI_BIN variable is defined. If defined, then a series of Apache CGI related directives are run.

An alias is set up for the **cgi-bin** directory, which is actually located at **/usr/lib/cgi-bin**.

```
Alias /cgi-bin/ /usr/lib/cgi-bin/
```

Controls are then placed on the **/usr/lib/cgi-bin** directory. All users are allowed access. Options designate that CGI programs can be executed and symbolic links are allowed if the owner's match. Multiviews are not allowed. The ExeCGI option allows the execution of CGI scripts. The + and - signs are used to indicate whether an option is turned on or off. If you use a + and - sign for one option, you have to use them for all.

```
<Directory "/usr/lib/cgi-bin">
   AllowOverride None
   Options +ExecCGI -MultiViews +SymLinksIfOwnerMatch
   Require all granted
</Directory>
```

Documentation: conf-available/apache2-doc.conf

If you installed the **apache2-doc** package, documentation is set up for you at **/usr/share/doc/apache2-doc**. The configuration file for the Apache documentation is at **/etc/apache2/conf-available/apache2-doc.conf**. The manual directory is aliased (**/usr/share/doc/apache2-doc/manual**) and controls are set up to allow access from all users.

```
Alias /manual/ /usr/share/doc/apache2-doc/manual/

<Directory "/usr/share/doc/apache2-doc/manual/">
    Options Indexes FollowSymLinks
    AllowOverride None
    Require all granted
    AddDefaultCharset off
</Directory>
```

Site-Level Configuration Directives

Site specific information is kept in the site's configuration files in **/etc/apache2/sites-available** directory. The **000-default.conf** site configuration file will hold directives for the main server. A **default-ssl.conf** file holds configuration for a main server with SSL support. The site configuration files hold site-specific information like Directory directives for their Web pages and server information like the administrator address. Authentication controls can be placed on particular directives. You can use the default configuration file as a partial model.

The site configuration files begin with few directives. Most global, module, and default directives are already enabled by the **apache2.conf** file, the added configuration files (**conf-available** directory), and the module configuration files (**modules-conf** directory). The actual site configuration file initially has only a few directives. You can add ones that you want to apply to that site.

A site configuration begins with a **VirtualHost** directive. The directive can name a particular IP address of a site or ***:80** for the main server (you can use a fully qualified domain name instead of the IP address, but this is not recommended). The directive block ends with a **</VirtualHost>** directive at the end of the file. Your site-specific directives like Directory directives are placed within the block. Keep in mind that all the site level configurations that are enabled will be read directly as if they were part of one large **apache2.conf** file.

```
<VirtualHost *:80>

</VirtualHost>
```

The following is an example of the **ServerAdmin** directive used to set the address where users can send mail for administrative issues. The default entry is **webmaster@localhost**. You can replace this with the address you want to use to receive system administration mail.

```
ServerAdmin webmaster@localhost
```

The **DocumentRoot** directive specifies where the Web server's HTML files are located. On Ubuntu this is the **/var/www/html** directory.

```
DocumentRoot /var/www/html
```

The **ServerName** directive (not used for the default host) determines the name of the virtual host.

```
ServerName www.example.com
```

Virtual Hosting on Apache

All sites are treated as virtual hosts configured by their site configuration files in **/etc/apashe2/sites-available** directory. In effect, the server can act as several servers, each hosted website appearing separate to outside users.

Apache supports both IP address-based and name-based virtual hosting. IP address-based virtual hosts use valid registered IP addresses, whereas name-based virtual hosts use fully qualified domain addresses. These domain addresses are provided by the host header from the requesting browser. The server can then determine the correct virtual host to use on the basis of the domain name alone. See **http://httpd.apache.org/docs/2.4/vhosts/** for more information.

You can enable or disable a virtual site with the **a2dissite** and **a2ensite** commands. Enabled sites are listed as symbolic links in the **/etc/apache2/sites-enabled** directory.

Virtual Host for main server: 000-default.conf

The main server must also have a virtual host configuration. This is set up by Ubuntu as the default configuration in the **sites-available** directory, **/etc/apache2/sites-available/000-default**. For the main server, the **VirtualHost** directive uses an * as its name with its port, 80. The directive block begins with **<VirtualHost *:80>** and ends with **</VirtualHost>**. The DocumentRoot is set to **/var/www/**, the location of the Web server's HTML files and subdirectories.

```
<VirtualHost *:80>
 ServerAdmin webmaster@localhost
 DocumentRoot /var/www/html
...
</VirtualHost>
```

For logging, the **ErrorLog** location is specified and the **LogLevel** is set at warn. The log display format used is combined (APACHE_LOG_DIR is defined in **/etc/apache2/envvars**).

```
 LogLevel info ssl:warn
 ErrorLog ${APACHE_LOG_DIR}/error.log
 CustomLog ${APACHE_LOG_DIR}/access.log combined
```

Should you have an alias for your main host, you can specify that using an added Virtual host directive that also uses the ***:80** name, but with the alias as the **ServerName**. The following example sets up the default for the main Web server host as well as an alias, **www.turtle.com** and **www.turtle.org**.

```
<VirtualHost *:80>
 ServerName www.turtle.com
 ServerAdmin webmaster@mail.turtle.com
 DocumentRoot /var/www/html
</VirtualHost>

<VirtualHost 192.168.1.5>
 ServerName www.turtle.org
 ServerAdmin webmaster@mail.turtle.com
 DocumentRoot /var/www/html
</VirtualHost>
```

You may want to modify the **/etc/apache2/sites-available/000-default.conf** configuration file to reflect the server name and mail address you want to use for your site.

A copy of the **/etc/apache2/sites-available/000-default.conf** file is shown here.

```
<VirtualHost *:80>

 ServerAdmin webmaster@localhost
 DocumentRoot /var/www/html

 # Possible values include: trace8, ..., trace1, debug, info, notice, warn,
 # error, crit, alert, emerg.
 #LogLevel info ssl:warn

 ErrorLog ${APACHE_LOG_DIR}/error.log
 CustomLog ${APACHE_LOG_DIR}/access.log combined

</VirtualHost>
```

Site and Global Configuration

It may be the case that certain directives that are configured globally, you may want to configure just for particular sites. This would entail turning off their global configuration, and enabling them on a site by site basis. As an example, access to the cgi-bin directory is currently global, with its **conf-available/serve-cgi-bin.conf** file enabled by a link to it in the **conf-enabled** directory. If you only want a few sites to have access to the **cgi-bin** directory, instead of all of them (global), you would disable the global link. Then, in the **sites-available** files for those sites you want to give access to the cgi-bin directory, you would insert an **include** statement for the **serve-cgi-bin.conf** file.

Use the **a2disconf** command to disable the global use of the configuration file. This removes its link in the **/etc/apache2/conf-enabled** directory.

```
a2disconf serve-cgi-bin.conf
```

Add the following **include** statement to the site files for the sites you want to have access to the **cgi-bin** directory.

```
include conf-available/serve-cgi-bin.conf
```

Virtual Host for main server: default-ssl.conf

The **default-ssl.conf** file has the same entries as the default site file but adds directives for SSL. The directives are explained with detailed comments. Several directives are commented out, which you can enable as you need them, like those for the certificate authority, revocation lists, client authentication, SSL options, and access control. The virtual host is set to use port 443, **<Virtualhost_default_:443>**.

In the SSL Engine Switch section, SSL is enabled.

```
SSLEngine on
```

A self-signed SLL certificate is specified

```
SSLCertificateFile    /etc/ssl/certs/ssl-cert-snakeoil.pem
SSLCertificateKeyFile /etc/ssl/private/ssl-cert-snakeoil.key
```

SSL options are applied to the website files and the cgi-bin.

```
<FilesMatch "\.(cgi|shtml|phtml|php)$">
        SSLOptions +StdEnvVars
</FilesMatch>
<Directory /usr/lib/cgi-bin>
        SSLOptions +StdEnvVars
</Directory>
```

For an SSL enabled Web server to work you will need an SSL certificate and key specific to your website to implement SSL encryption. See the followings section in the Ubuntu Server Guide for details.

```
https://ubuntu.com/server/docs/security-certificates
```

In the **/etc/apache2/ports.conf** file, Apache is configured to listen on port 443 should the **ssl_module** be active.

```
<IfModule ssl_module>
     Listen 443
</IfMOdule>
```

Creating Virtual Hosts

The easiest way to create a new Virtual host is to copy the default file, giving it the name of the new website. Then edit the file to add the ServerName directive with the domain name of the website. Be sure to change the ServerAdmin, DocumentRoot, ErrorLog, and CustomLog directives. You also could remove the document directives. The following example implements a name-based virtual host, **www.mypics.com**. A subdirectory for the website has to be created in the **/var/www** directory, in this case, **/var/www/mypics/**, with the DocumentRoot at **/var/www/mypics/**. The Directory directive now references the **/var/www/mypics/** directory. The **/usr/share/doc** Directory directives are not needed. If you wanted to allow the use of **.htaccess** files on this site you would change the AllowOverride directive to **all**. You also have to add a subdirectory in the Apache log directory for the logs such as **/var/log/apache2/mypics**, (APACHE_LOG_DIR). Basic steps would include the following:

Create a configuration file in **/etc/apache2/sites-available**

Create a directory for the website documents at **/var/www/**

Create a subdirectory for the website log files at **/var/log/apache2/**

If your virtual host is referenced by other domain names, you can specify them with the **ServerAlias** directive, listing the domain names within the selected **VirtualHost** block.

```
ServerAlias www.greatpics.org
```

A sample configuration file, called here **mypics**, would be placed in the **sites-available** directory. The file is shown here with ServerName and ServerAlias directives included.

```
<VirtualHost *:80>
 ServerName www.mypics.com
 ServerAdmin webmaster@mail.mypics.com
 ServerAlias www.greatpics.org
 DocumentRoot /var/www/mypics/


  <Directory /var/www/mypics/>
    Options Indexes FollowSymLinks MultiViews
    AllowOverride None
    Require all granted
  </Directory>

 ErrorLog ${APACHE_LOG_DIR}/mypics/error_log
 LogLevel warn
 CustomLog ${APACHE_LOG_DIR}/mypics/access.log combined

</VirtualHost>
```

Once configured, you would then activate the site with the **a2ensite** command.

```
sudo a2ensite mypics
```

Name-based Virtual Hosts

The Apache default configuration described in the previous section uses name-based virtual hosting. With name-based virtual hosting, you can support any number of virtual hosts using no additional IP addresses. With only a single IP address for your machine, you can still support an unlimited number of virtual hosts. Such a capability is made possible by the HTTP/1.1 protocol, which lets a server identify the name by which it is being accessed. This method requires the client, the remote user, to use a browser that supports the HTTP/1.1 protocol, as current browsers do. A browser using such a protocol can send a host header specifying the particular host to use on a machine.

If you are using a particular IP address for your website, you would use that address instead of the port number in the VirtualHost directive. To implement name-based virtual hosting for a particular IP address, you use a **VirtualHost** directive and a **NameVirtualHost** directive to specify the IP address you want to use for the virtual hosts. If your system has only one IP address, you need to use that address. Within the **VirtualHost** directives, you use the **ServerName** directive to specify the domain name you want to use for that host. Using **ServerName** to specify the domain name is important to avoid a DNS lookup. A DNS lookup failure disables the virtual host. The **VirtualHost** directives each take as their argument the same IP address specified in the **NameVirtualHost** directive. You use Apache directives within the **VirtualHost** blocks to configure each host separately. Name-based virtual hosting uses the domain name address specified in a host header to determine the virtual host to use. If no such information exists, the first host is used as the default.

Here, **www.mypics.com** and **www.myproj.org** are implemented as name-based virtual hosts instead of IP-based hosts. Though on Ubuntu these would be placed in separate **sites-available** files, they are shown here together to make for a clearer example, with directives for the main server added (turtle.mytrek.com).

```
ServerName turtle.mytrek.com
NameVirtualHost 192.168.1.5

<VirtualHost 192.168.1.5>
 ServerName www.mypics.com
 ServerAdmin webmaster@mail.mypics.com
 DocumentRoot /var/www/mypics/html
 ErrorLog /var/www/mypics/logs/error_log
 ...
</VirtualHost>

<VirtualHost 192.168.1.5>
 ServerName www.myproj.org
 ServerAdmin webmaster@mail.myproj.org
 DocumentRoot /var/www/myproj/html
 ErrorLog /var/www/myproj/logs/error_log
 ....
</VirtualHost>
```

If your system has only one IP address, implementing virtual hosts prevents access to your main server with that address. You could no longer use your main server as a Web server directly. You could use it only indirectly to manage your virtual host. You could configure a virtual host to manage your main server's Web pages. You would then use your main server to support a set of virtual hosts that would function as websites, rather than the main server operating as one site directly. This is the approach implemented by Ubuntu for the Apache Web server.

If your machine has two or more IP addresses, you can use one for the main server and the other for your virtual hosts. You can even mix IP-based virtual hosts and name-based virtual hosts on your server. You can also use separate IP addresses to support different sets of virtual hosts.

Dynamic Virtual Hosting

If you have implemented many virtual hosts on your server that have the same configuration, you can use a technique called dynamic virtual hosting to have these virtual hosts generated dynamically. The code for implementing your virtual hosts becomes much smaller, and as a result, your server accesses them faster. Adding yet more virtual hosts becomes a simple matter of creating appropriate directories and adding entries for them in the DNS server.

To make dynamic virtual hosting work, the server uses commands in the **mod_vhost_alias** module (supported in Apache version 1.3.6 and up) to rewrite both the server name and the document root to those of the appropriate virtual server (for older Apache versions before 1.3.6, you use the mod_rewrite module). Dynamic virtual hosting can be either name-based or IP-based. In either case, you have to set the **UseCanonicalName** directive in such a way as to allow the server to use the virtual hostname instead of the server's own name. For name-based hosting, simply turn off **UseCanonicalName**. This allows your server to obtain the hostname from the host header of the user request. For IP-based hosting, you set the **UseCanonicalName** directive to DNS. This allows the server to look up the host in the DNS server.

```
UseCanonicalName Off
UseCanonicalName DNS
```

You then have to enable the server to locate the different document root directories and CGI bin directories for your various virtual hosts. You use the **VirtualDocumentRoot** directive to specify the template for virtual host directories. For example, if you place the different host directories in the **/var/www/hosts** directory, you can then set the **VirtualDocumentRoot** directive accordingly.

```
VirtualDocumentRoot /var/www/hosts/%0/html
```

The **%0** will be replaced with the virtual host's name when that virtual host is accessed. It is important that you create the dynamic virtual host's directory using that host's name. For example, for a dynamic virtual host called **www.mygolf.org**, you first create a directory named **/var/www/hosts/www.mygolf.org**, and then create subdirectories for the document root and CGI programs, as in **/var/www/hosts/www.mygolf.org/html**. For the CGI directory, use the **VirtualScriptAlias** directive to specify the CGI subdirectory you use.

```
VirtualScriptAlias /var/www/hosts/%0/cgi-bin
```

A simple example of name-based dynamic virtual hosting directives follows.

```
UseCanonicalName Off
VirtualDocumentRoot /var/www/hosts/%0/html
VirtualScriptAlias /var/www/hosts/%0/cgi-bin
```

A request for **www.mygolf.com/html/mypage** evaluates to:

```
/var/www/hosts/www.mygolf.com/html/mypage
```

A simple example of dynamic virtual hosting is shown here.

```
UseCanonicalName Off
NameVirtualHost 192.168.1.5
<VirtualHost 192.168.1.5>
 ServerName www.mygolf.com
 ServerAdmin webmaster@mail.mygolf.com
 VirtualDocumentRoot /var/www/hosts/%0/html
 VirtualScriptAlias /var/www/hosts/%0/cgi-bin
 ...
</VirtualHost>
```

To implement IP-based dynamic virtual hosting instead, set the **UseCanonicalName** to DNS instead of Off.

```
UseCanonicalName DNS
VirtualDocumentRoot /var/www/hosts/%0/html
VirtualScriptAlias /var/www/hosts/%0/cgi-bin
```

Interpolated Strings

The **mod_vhost_alias** module supports various interpolated strings, each beginning with a **%** symbol and followed by a number. The **%0** symbol references the entire web address. **%1** references only the first segment, **%2** references the second, **%-1** references the last part, and **%2+** references from the second part on. For example, to use only the second part of a web address for the directory name, use the following directives:

```
VirtualDocumentRoot /var/www/hosts/%2/html
VirtualScriptAlias /var/www/hosts/%2/cgi-bin
```

In this case, a request made for **www.mygolf.com/html/mypage** uses only the second part of the web address. This would be "mygolf" in **www.mygolf.com**, and would evaluate to

```
/var/www/hosts/mygolf/html/mypage
```

If you used **%2+** instead, as in **/var/www/hosts/%2/html**, the request for **www.mygolf.com/html/mypage** would evaluate to

```
/var/www/hosts/mygolf.com/html/mypage
```

The same method works for IP addresses, where **%1** references the first IP address segment, **%2** references the second, and so on.

Logs for Dynamic Virtual Hosts

One drawback of dynamic virtual hosting is that you can set up only one log for all your hosts. However, you can create your own shell program to simply cut out the entries for the different hosts in that log.

```
LogFormat "%V %h %l %u %t \"%r\" %s %b" vcommon
CustomLog logs/access_log vcommon
```

Note: Apache also supports IP address–based virtual hosting. Your server must have a different IP address for each virtual host. Your machine can have separate physical network connections for each. You can have Apache run a separate daemon for each virtual host, separately listening for each IP address, or you can have a single daemon running that listens for requests for all the virtual hosts.

Apache Instances

Apache also supports the implementation of additional Web server instances on the same Ubuntu system. An instance is, in effect, a separate Web server with its own copy of the **/etc/apache2** directory. Maintaining such an instance can pose problems for updates. Ubuntu updates are made only to the default **/etc/apache2** directory, not to the corresponding directories for any instances. You would have to manage any updates manually. See the **README.multiple-instances** file in the **/usr/share/doc/apache2** directory for details on how to create and maintain an Apache instance.

A new Apache instance will have the prefix **apache2-** and the name you give it. Use the **setup-instance** script in the **/usr/share/doc/apache2/examples** directory to create the instance. The **setup-instance** script takes as an argument the name you decided to give the instance. It then creates a copy of the **/etc/apache2** directory, using the instance name and the **apache2-** prefix. The following command creates an instance called **apache2-myapache1** and copies the **/etc/apache2** directory to **/etc/apache2-myapache1**.

```
cd /usr/share/doc/apache2/examples
sudo sh setup-instance myapache1
```

The **apache2@.service** systemd file in the **/lib/systemd/system** directory is used run the service. You attach the instance name to the **apache2@** prefix, for example **apache2@myapache1**. The **setup-instance** command will also enable and start the instance. Use the **systemctl** command to manage the new instance, just as you would the original **apache2**.

```
sudo systemctl enable apache2@myapache1
sudo systemctl start apache2@myapache1
sudo systemctl status apache2@myapache1
```

The **apache2@.service** file is the same as the **apache2.service** file listed as the beginning of this chapter, except that it has a different ENVIRONMENT variable that specifies the location of that Apache instance's configuration directory. The **%i** parameter substitutes the instance's name.

```
Environment=APACHE_CONFDIR=/etc/apache2-%i APACHE_STARTED_BY_SYSTEMD=true
```

For an Apache instance, the corresponding appropriate values are detected for Apache global variables (the $SUFFIX variable in the **envvars** file). For the **apache2-myapche1** example, the value of the APACHE_PID_FILE variable would be **/var/run/apache2-myapche1**, instead of just **/var/run/apache2**.

NGINX Web Server

The NGINX Web server is fast becoming a key support server for the Apache Web server, providing a reverse proxy to allow Apache to better handle high load demands. NGINX has an event-based asynchronous design that lets it handle requests at the same time using very little memory, instead of discretely threading requests as Apache does. This approach makes for a fast Web server, though one that is not easily customized. Apache's easy modular design still makes it easier to deploy. Often NGINX is used as a front end processor for an Apache server, handling a large number of request, and then sending them on to the Apache server. You can find out more about NGINX at **http://nginx.org**, with documentation at **http://nginx.org/en/docs/**.

You can install NGINX with the **nginx** and **nginx-doc** packages, part of the Ubuntu Main repository. Configuration is located in the **/etc/nginx** directory. Documentation and examples can be found in the **/usr/share/doc/nginx-doc** directory (**nginx-doc** package). NGINX has a similar configuration directory structure as Apache, with main configuration files in the **/etc/nginx** directory, and site configuration files in the **sites-available** directory, with links to a **sites-enabled** directory. Initially, a **default** site is set up.

The configuration files are simple, with an **/etc/nginx/nginx.conf** file as the main configuration file for the NGINX server, and several supporting configuration files, as well as an additional **conf.d** configuration directory. The format for commands uses a block structure, encased in braces. In the **nginx.conf** file, an http block sets the global settings for the Web server, with include directives for configuration files and the sites-enabled server files. A **default** file in the **sites-available** directory shows the configuration **default** website. You can set up a Web server with very few directives and blocks. It is advised that you create a new file for the website configuration, to better tailor it to your needs. There is a **server** block for each port a server listens on, and location blocks to access website files. The **server** block in the **/etc/nginx/sites-available/default** file installed for Ubuntu is shown here.

```
server {
        listen 80 default_server;
        listen [::]:80 default_server;

        root /var/www/html;

        # Add index.php to the list if you are using PHP
        index index.html index.htm index.nginx-debian.html;

        server_name _;

        location / {
                # First attempt to serve request as file, then
                # as directory, then fall back to displaying a 404.
                try_files $uri $uri/ =404;
        }
```

The **http** block in the **/etc/nginx/nginx.conf** file is shown here. The block includes basic, SSL, log file location, and **gzip** directives. Website configuration files are read in from the **/etc/nginx/sites-enabled** directory, which contains links to files in the **sites-available** directory.

```
http {

        # Basic Settings
        sendfile on;
        tcp_nopush on;
        types_hash_max_size 2048;
        include /etc/nginx/mime.types;
        default_type application/octet-stream;

        # SSL Settings
        ssl_protocols TLSv1 TLSv1.1 TLSv1.2 TLSv1.3; # Dropping SSLv3, ref: PO
        ssl_prefer_server_ciphers on;

        # Logging Settings
        access_log /var/log/nginx/access.log;

        # Gzip Settings
        gzip on;

        # Virtual Host Configs
        include /etc/nginx/conf.d/*.conf;
        include /etc/nginx/sites-enabled/*;
}
```

9. News and Database Services

News Servers

Database Servers: MySQL and PostgreSQL

Relational Database Structure

MySQL

PostgreSQL

Newsgroup servers are used for setting up newsgroups for local networks or for supporting the Internet's Usenet News service. Database servers manage large collections of data on local networks as well as for Internet services.

News Servers

News servers provide Internet users with Usenet news services. They have their own TCP/IP protocol, the Network News Transfer Protocol (NNTP). On most Linux systems, the InterNetNews (INN) news server is used to provide news services (**https://www.isc.org/**). INN news servers access Usenet newsfeeds, providing news clients on your network with the full range of newsgroups and articles. Newsgroup articles are transferred using NNTP, and servers that support this protocol are known as NNTP servers. INN was written by Rich Salz and is currently maintained and supported by the Internet Software Consortium (ISC). You can download current versions from its website at **https://www.isc.org/othersoftware/#INN**. The documentation directory for INN in **/usr/share/doc** contains extensive samples. The primary program for INN is the **innd** daemon. There are two versions of INN, a smaller INN used for local networks, and a much more complex INN2 used for large networks. Ubuntu uses INN. Both are available for Ubuntu (**inn** and **inn2** packages).

INN also includes several support programs to provide maintenance and crash recovery and to perform statistical analysis on server performance and usage. The **cleanfeed** program implements spam protection, and **innreport** generates INN reports based on logs. INN also features a strong filter system for screening unwanted articles.

Leafnode is an NNTP news server designed for small networks that may have slow connections to the Internet. You can install the Leafnode software package (**leafnode**) using **apt** or the Synaptic Package Manager. Documentation is available at **https://www.leafnode.org/**. Along with the Leafnode NNTP server, the software package includes several utilities such as Fetchnews, Texpire, and NewsQ that send, delete, and display news articles. **slrnpull** is a simple single-user version of Leafnode that can be used only with the **slrn** newsreader.

Database Servers: MySQL and PostgreSQL

Two fully functional database servers are included with most Linux distributions, MySQL and PostgreSQL. MySQL is the most popular of the two, though PostgreSQL is noted for providing more features. You can learn more about these products through the sites listed in Table 9-1. Check the Ubuntu Server Guide | Services | Databases for basic configuration.

```
https://ubuntu.com/server/docs/databases-introduction
```

Relational Database Structure

MySQL and PostgreSQL both use a relational database structure. In a relational database, data is placed in tables, with identifier fields used to relate the data to entries in other tables. Each row in the table is a record, each with a unique identifier, like a record number. The connections between records in different tables are implemented by special tables that associate the unique identifiers from records in one table with those of another.

Database	Resource	Packages
MySQL	https://www.mysql.com/	**mysql-server** **mysql-client**
PostgreSQL	https://www.postgresql.org/	**postgresql**

Table 9-1: Database Resources

A simple, single-table database has no need for a unique identifier. A simple address book listing names and addresses is an example of a single-table database. However, most databases access complex information of different types, related in various ways. Instead of having large records with repeated information, you divide the data among different tables, each holding the unique instance of the data. This way, data is not repeated. You have only one table that holds a single record for a person's name, rather than repeating that person's name each time the data references him or her. The relational organization then takes on the task of relating one piece of data to another. This way, you can store a great deal of information using relatively small database files.

Though there are many ways to implement a relational database, a simple rule of thumb is to organize data into tables where you have a unique instance of each item of data. Each record is given a unique identifier, usually a number. To associate the records in one table with another, you create tables that associate their identifiers.

The Structured Query Language (SQL) is used by most relational database management systems (RDBMSs), including both MySQL and PostgreSQL. The following command will create the database:

```
CREATE DATABASE myphotos
```

Before performing any operations on a database, you first access it with the USE command.

```
USE myphotos
```

The tables are created using the CREATE TABLE command. The fields for each table are listed within parentheses following the table name. For each field, you need to specify a name, data type, and other options, such as whether it can have a null value or not.

```
CREATE TABLE names (
    personid INT(5) UNSIGNED NOT NULL,
    name VARCHAR(20) NOT NULL,
    street VARCHAR(30) NOT NULL,
    phone CHAR(8)
    );
```

MySQL

MySQL is structured on a client/server model with a server daemon (**mysqld**) filling requests from client programs. MySQL is designed for speed, reliability, and ease of use. It is meant to be a fast database management system for large databases and, at the same time, a reliable one, suitable for intensive use. To create databases, you use the standard SQL language. User access can be controlled by assigning privileges.

On Ubuntu, you can install MySQL server and client packages, along with numerous MySQL configuration packages for certain services like Postfix, Exim, and Apache. The packages to install are **mysql-client**, **mysql-common**, and **mysql-server**. Documentation is held in the **mysql-doc** package and installed at **/usr/share/doc/mysql-doc**. Check the Ubuntu Server Guide | Services | Databases - Mysql for basic configuration and management.

```
https://ubuntu.com/server/docs/databases-mysql
```

MySQL is managed by **systemd** using the **/lib/systemd/system/mysql.service** unit file. To customize the service file, you can create a version of it in the **/etc/systemd/system** directory, which includes the original version. You would create a version in **/etc/systemd/system** that includes the system version in **/lib/systemd/system**. Then you add a Service section with added options, as shown here.

/etc/systemd/system/mysql.service

```
.include /lib/systemd/system/mysqld.service
 [Service]
  LimitNOFILE=10000
```

Alternatively you can create a **.conf** in the **/etc/systemd/system/mysql.service.d** directory.

The **/lib/systemd/system/mysql.service** file is shown here.

mysql.service

```
# MySQL systemd service file

[Unit]
Description=MySQL Community Server
After=network.target

[Install]
WantedBy=multi-user.target

[Service]
Type=notify
User=mysql
Group=mysql
PermissionsStartOnly=true
ExecStartPre=/usr/share/mysql/mysql-systemd-start pre
ExecStart=/usr/sbin/mysqld
TimeoutSec=infinity
Restart=on-failure
RuntimeDirectory=mysqld
RuntimeDirectoryMode=755
LimitNOFILE=10000

# Set enviroment variable MYSQLD_PARENT_PID. This is required for restart.
Environment=MYSQLD_PARENT_PID=1
```

MySQL Configuration

MySQL supports three different configuration files, one for global settings, another for server-specific settings, and an optional one for user-customized settings.

The **/etc/mysql/my.cnf** configuration file is used for global settings applied to both clients and servers. It is a link to the **/etc/alternatives/my.cnf** file, which, in turn, is a link to the **/etc/mysql/mysql.cnf** file, which includes configuration files from the **/etc/mysql/conf.d** and the **/etc/mysql/mysql.conf.d** directories. The **conf.d** directory holds the **mysql.cnf** file, which provides user configuration, and the **mysql.conf.d** directory holds the **mysqld.cnf** file.

The **/etc/mysql/mysql.conf.d/mysqld.cnf** file provides the MySQL server settings, and the **/etc/mysql/mysql.conf.d/mysql.cnf** file holds MySQL client options.

The **.my.cnf** file allows users to customize their access to MySQL. It is located in a user's home directory. Note that this is a dot file.

Global Configuration:/etc/mysql/mysql.conf.d/mysqld.cnf

MySQL specifies options according to different groups, usually the names of server tools. The options are arranged in group segments. The group name is placed within brackets, and options applied to it follow. A selection of MySQL directives in the **mysqld** section of the **/etc/mysql/mysql.conf.d/mysqld.cnf** file is shown here. The section is organized into basic settings, fine tuning, and logging and replication parts.

```
#
# The MySQL database server configuration file.
#
# One can use all long options that the program supports.
# Run program with --help to get a list of available options and with
# --print-defaults to see which it would actually understand and use.
#
# For explanations see
# http://dev.mysql.com/doc/mysql/en/server-system-variables.html


# Here is entries for some specific programs
# The following values assume you have at least 32M ram

[mysqld]
#
# * Basic Settings
#
user            = mysql
# pid-file      = /var/run/mysqld/mysqld.pid
# socket        = /var/run/mysqld/mysqld.sock
# port          = 3306
# datadir       = /var/lib/mysql


# If MySQL is running as a replication secondary, this should be
# changed. Ref https://dev.mysql.com/doc/refman/8.0/en/server-system-
variables.html#sysvar_tmpdir
# tmpdir               = /tmp
#
# Instead of skip-networking the default is now to listen only on
# localhost which is more compatible and is not less secure.
bind-address          = 127.0.0.1
```

```
mysqlx-bind-address    = 127.0.0.1
#
# * Fine Tuning
#
key_buffer_size        = 16M
# max_allowed_packet   = 64M
# thread_stack         = 256K

# thread_cache_size        = -1

# This replaces the startup script and checks MyISAM tables if needed
# the first time they are touched
myisam-recover-options   = BACKUP

# max_connections          = 151

# table_open_cache         = 4000


#
# * Logging and Replication
#
# Both location gets rotated by the cronjob.
#
# Log all queries
# Be aware that this log type is a performance killer.
# general_log_file       = /var/log/mysql/query.log
# general_log            = 1
#
# Error log - should be very few entries.
#
log_error = /var/log/mysql/error.log
#
# Here you can see queries with especially long duration
# slow_query_log             = 1
# slow_query_log_file = /var/log/mysql/mysql-slow.log
# long_query_time = 2
# log-queries-not-using-indexes
#
# The following can be used as easy to replay backup logs or for replication.
# note: if you are setting up a replication secondary, see README.Debian about
#       other settings you may need to change.
# server-id    = 1
# log_bin      = /var/log/mysql/mysql-bin.log
# binlog_expire_logs_seconds = 2592000
max_binlog_size    = 100M
# binlog_do_db       = include_database_name
# binlog_ignore_db   = include_database_name
```

Options are set up according to groups that control different behaviors of the MySQL server: **mysqld** for the daemon. The **datadir** directory, **/var/lib/mysql**, is where your database files will be placed. Server tools and daemons are located in the **basedir** directory, **/usr**, and the user that MySQL will run as, has the name **mysql**, as specified in the **user** option.

To see what options are currently set for both client and server, you run **mysqld** directly with the **--help** option.

```
/usr/libexec/mysqld --help
```

MySQL networking

The network services for which MySQL databases are used, such as the Apache Web server, require that hosts on your network be allowed to access a MySQL database. In effect, the MySQL database can operate as a network database server. To allow other hosts on your network to access your MySQL database, you have to set the MySQL server to accept access from a network source. You do this with the **bind-address** option in the **mysqld** section of the **/etc/mysql/my.cnf configuration** file. Initially, this is set to the localhost, 127.0.0.1, allowing access only for your local machine.

```
bind-address = 127.0.0.1
```

If the address is allocated dynamically by a DHCP server, comment out the bind-address entry with a # sign. If the bind-address option is not set, the default is to allow any access. This is also a quick way to enable network access to MySQL databases used by a network server like the Apache Web server.

```
# bind-address = 127.0.0.1
```

To allow access from a specific local network, you can change the bind-address entry to the IP address of your machine on that network. Should your local network access on your machine use an additional dedicated network device, you can use the IP address of that network device.

```
bind-address = 192.168.0.52
```

If you want to allow MySQL to use several network interfaces, including **localhost**, you would set the bind-address to 0.0.0.0. This allows MySQL to use all your network interfaces.

```
bind-address = 0.0.0.0
```

To deny any kind of network access, including localhost, you can use the skip-networking option.

```
skip-networking
```

Also, make sure that your firewall has enabled access on the port that the MySQL server is using. The default port for MySQL is 3306.

For the **ufw** default firewall, you would use the following command. The ufw firewall maintains its IPtables files in **/etc/ufw**. You can also use the Gufw tool (desktop) to add access for port 3306. Keep in mind that the ufw firewall IPtables rules are automatically converted to nftables rules.

```
sudo ufw allow 3306/tcp
```

If you are managing your firewall directly, you could manage access by adding the following nftables or IPtables rules. This accepts input on port 3306 for TCP/IP protocol packages.

nftables

```
nft add rule ip filter INPUT tcp dport 3306 counter accept
```

iptables

```
iptables -A INPUT -p tcp --dport 3306 -j ACCEPT
```

User Configuration: .my.cnf

Users who access the database server will have their own configuration file in their home directory: **.my.cnf**. Here the user can specify connection options, such as the password used to access the database and the connection timeouts.

```
[client]
password=mypassword

[mysql]
no-auto-rehash
set-variable = connect_timeout=2
[mysql-hotcopy]
interactive-timeout
```

MySQL Tools

MySQL provides a variety of tools (as shown in Table 9-2), including server, client, and administrative tools. Backups can be handled with the **mysqldump** command. The **mysqlshow** command will display a database, just as issuing the SQL command **SELECT *.*** does, and **mysqlimport** can import text files, just like LOAD INFILE.

Command	Description
`mysqld`	MySQL server
`mysql`	MySQL client
`mysqladmin`	Creates and administers databases
`mysqldump`	Database backup
`mysqlimport`	Imports text files
`mysqlshow`	Displays databases

Table 9-2: MySQL Commands

To manage your MySQL database, you use **mysql** as the **root** user. The **mysql** client starts up the MySQL monitor. As the root user, you can enter administrative commands to create databases and database tables, add or remove entries, and carry out standard client tasks such as displaying data. Open a terminal window. Then enter the **mysql** command with the **-u root** and the **-p** option. You will be prompted for a MySQL password. When you installed MySQL server, you were prompted to enter a password. This is the password you need to use to access the MySQL monitor shell.

```
mysql -u root -p
mysql>
```

The **mysql** command will start a MySQL monitor shell with a **mysql>** prompt. Be sure to end your commands with a semicolon, otherwise, the monitor shell will provide an indented arrow prompt waiting for added arguments. In the monitor shell, the semicolon, not the ENTER key, ends commands. Once you enter the semi-colon, you then press the ENTER key to execute the command.

You can use the **status** command to check the status of your server and **show databases** to list current databases.

```
mysql> status;
mysql> show databases;
```

Note: You can use **mysqltuner** to analyze your Mysql database and suggest optimization recommendations (**mysqltuner** package).

PostgreSQL

PostgreSQL is based on the POSTGRESQL database management system, though it uses SQL as its query language. POSTGRESQL is a next-generation research prototype developed at the University of California, Berkeley. You can learn more about it from the PostgreSQL website at **https://www.postgresql.org/**. PostgreSQL is an open source project, developed under the GPL license. You can install PostgreSQL using the **postgresql** package.

PostgreSQL is often used to provide database support for Internet servers with heavy demands, such as web servers. With a few simple commands, you can create relational database tables. Use the **createuser** command to create a PostgreSQL user with which you can log in to the server. You can then create a database with the **createdb** command and construct relational tables using the **create table** directive. With an **insert** command, you can add records and then view them with the **select** command.

Part 3: Shared Resources

Print Services: CUPS

Network File System (NFS) and Distributed File System (GFS)

Samba (Windows)

Cloud Computing

ubuntu

10. Print Services

Printer Services: CUPS

Printer Devices and Configuration

Installing Printers

CUPS Configuration files

CUPS Command Line Print Clients

CUPS Command Line Administrative Tools

Print services configure and make available printers on your local system, as well as on your network. Printers are managed as network resources by print servers. As a network resource, several hosts on a network could access the same printer. Printing sites and resources are listed in Table 10-1.

CUPS

The Common Unix Printing System (CUPS) provides printing services, developed by Apple as an open source project, and is freely available under the GNU Public License. CUPS is the primary print server for most Linux distributions, including Ubuntu. The CUPS site at **https://www.cups.org/** provides detailed documentation on installing and managing printers. CUPS uses the Internet Printing Protocol (IPP), which provides a printing standard for the Internet (**https://pwg.org/ipp/**). The IPP protocol provides support for networking, PostScript, and web interfaces. The older line printer (LPD) printing systems only supported line printers. CUPS functions as network server, using a configuration format similar to the Apache web server. The networking supports lets users access printers remotely. GNOME provides integrated support for CUPS, allowing GNOME-based applications to directly access CUPS printers.

Resource	Description
https://www.cups.org/	Common Unix Printing System
https://pwg.org/ipp/	Internet Printing Protocol
http://lprng.sourceforge.net/	LPRng print server (Universe repository)

Table 10-1: Print Resources

Once you have installed your printers and configured your print server, you can print and manage your print queue using print clients. A variety of print configuration tools is available for the CUPS server such as Settings Printers, system-config-printer, the CUPS configuration tool, and various line printing tools such as **lpq** and **lpc**, described in detail later in this chapter. Check the Ubuntu Server Guide | Services | Service - CUPS for basic configuration.

```
https://ubuntu.com/server/docs/service-cups
```

CUPS is managed by systemd using an on demand socket implementation with **cups.service**, **cups.socket**, **cups.path**, and **cups-browsed** files. In addition, a special **printer.target** unit detects when a printer is connected to your system. The **cups.service** file runs the CUPS server, **/usr/sbin/cupsd** (ExecStart). It is run when the **printer.target** is activated, which happens when a user connects a printer (WantedBy). The **cups.socket** unit file has CUPS listen for request at the CUPS socket, **/var/run/cups/cups.sock** (ListenStream). In effect, CUPS runs like the old inetd daemons, activated only when requested. The **cups.path** unit sets up CUPS print directories at **/var/cache/cups** (PathExists) when the system starts up (WantedBy=multi-user.target). The **cups-browsed.service** file supports access remote printers on your network.

cups.service

```
[Unit]
Description=CUPS Scheduler
Documentation=man:cupsd(8)
After=network.target nss-user-lookup.target nslcd.service
Requires=cups.socket

[Service]
ExecStart=/usr/sbin/cupsd -l
Type=notify
Restart=on-failure

[Install]
Also=cups.socket cups.path
WantedBy=printer.target multi-user.target
```

cups.socket

```
[Unit]
Description=CUPS Scheduler
PartOf=cups.service

[Socket]
ListenStream=/run/cups/cups.sock
RemoveOnStop=on

[Install]
WantedBy=sockets.target
```

cups.path

```
[Unit]
Description=CUPS Scheduler
PartOf=cups.service

[Path]
PathExists=/var/cache/cups/org.cups.cupsd

[Install]
WantedBy=multi-user.target
```

cups-browsed.service

```
[Unit]
Description=Make remote CUPS printers available locally
Requires=cups.service
After=cups.service avahi-daemon.service network-online.target
Wants=avahi-daemon.service network-online.target

[Service]
ExecStart=/usr/sbin/cups-browsed
User=cups-browsed
AmbientCapabilities=CAP_NET_BIND_SERVICE
```

```
[Install]
WantedBy=multi-user.target
```

Note: Line Printer, Next Generation (LPRng) was the traditional print server for Linux and UNIX systems, but it has since been dropped from many Linux distributions. You can find out more about LPRng at **http://lprng.sourceforge.net/**.

Driverless Printing

Most newer printer models support driverless printing. Instead of installing a driver, the printer supports a driverless driver. You can print to any of these printers without first downloading and installing a driver for them. The printers are automatically detected through DNS Service Discovery (DNS-SD). The CUPS Web configuration interface, system-config-printer, GNOME printers, and lpadmin already support driverless printing.

CUPS uses the **driverless** utility to detect available driverless printers and to generate PPD configuration files for them. The drivers may not be as complete in features as their official drivers, but will print. Currently printers compatible with IPP Anywhere and Apple Raster supported printers can make use of driverless drivers, usually newer printers. Settings Printer, system-config-printer, and the CUP Web interface all use the driverless tool to detect and configure driverless printers. See the man page for **driverless** for more information.

Conflicts may occur with the cups-browsed daemon, which was an earlier effort to implement a version of driverless printing, and is still useful for printers that do not support driverless printing. You may have to set option in the **/etc/cups/cups-browsed.conf** file to support driverless printing. You need to set the OnlyUnsupportedByCUPS and CreateIPPPrinterQueues options.

Printer Devices and Configuration

To use a printer, you have to install the configuration for it on your Linux system. Configuring a printer is a simple procedure where you choose options. Upon configuration, Linux creates the device name for a printer. USB-connected printers are removable devices and can be recognized no matter what USB port they are connected to. Older printers, such as parallel printers, have to be connected to a particular port and are assigned a specific device name. For parallel printers the device names are **lp0**, **lp1**, and **lp2**. The numbers used in these names correspond to a parallel port on your system. The **lp0** name is the LPT1 parallel port, and **lp1** is the LPT2 parallel port. Serial printers will use serial ports, using the device names such as **ttyS0**, **ttyS1**, and **ttyS2**.

Printer URI (Universal Resource Identifier)

Printers can be local or remote. Both are referenced using Universal Resource Identifiers (URI). URIs support both network protocols used to communicate with remote printers, and device connections used to reference local printers.

Remote printers are referenced by the protocol used to communicate with it, like **ipp** for the Internet Printing Protocol used for UNIX network printers, **smb** for the Samba protocol used for

Windows network printers, and **lpd** for the older LPRng Unix servers. Their URIs are similar to a Web URL, indicating the network address of the system the printer is connected to.

```
ipp://mytsuff.com/printers/queue1
smb://guest@lizard/myhp
```

For attached local printers, especially older ones, the URI will use the device connection and the device name. The **usb:** prefix is used for USB printers, **parallel:** for older printers connected to a parallel port, **serial:** for printers connected to a serial port, and **scsi:** for SCSI connected printers.

In the CUPS **/etc/cups/printers.conf** file the DeviceURI entry will reference the URI for a printer. For USB printers, the URI uses **usb:**.

```
DeviceURI usb://Canon/S330
```

Spool Directories

When your system prints a file, it makes use of special directories called spool directories. A print job is a file to be printed. When you send a file to a printer, a copy of it is made and placed in a spool directory set up for that printer. The location of the spool directory is obtained from the printer's entry in its configuration file. On Linux, the spool directory is located at **/var/spool/cups** under a directory with the name of the printer. For example, the spool directory for the **myepson** printer would be located at **/var/spool/cups/myepson**. The spool directory contains several files for managing print jobs. Some files use the name of the printer as their extension. For example, the **myepson** printer has the files **control.myepson**, which provides printer queue control, and **active.myepson** for the active print job, as well as **log.myepson,** which is the log file.

CUPS start and restart

You can start, stop, and restart CUPS using the **systemctl** command and the **cups** script. When you make changes or install printers, be sure to restart CUPS to have your changes take effect. You can use the following command.

```
sudo systemctl restart cups
```

The CUPS server is configured to start up when your system boots. The **/etc/default/cups** file holds startup options for the cups server, such as the LOAD_LP_MODULE option to load the parallel printer driver module.

Installing Printers

Several tools are available for installing CUPS printers. On the desktop, the easiest method is to use the Settings Printers tab. You could also still use the older **system-config-printer** tool. You can also use the CUPS Web browser-based configuration tools, included with the CUPS software (will work with **elinks** or **lynx** command line browser). Or you can just edit the CUPS printer configuration files directly.

Remote Printers

Most newer printers support driverless printing. Available remote printers are detected automatically, and driverless configurations are generated by CUPS. To manually search for a remote printer remote printer that is attached to a Windows system or another Linux system running CUPS, you specify its location, using special URL protocols. For another CUPS printer on a remote host, the protocol used is **ipp**, for Internet Printing Protocol, whereas for a Windows printer, it would be **smb**. Older Unix or Linux systems using LPRng would use the **lpd** protocol. Be sure your firewall is configured to allow access to remote printers.

Shared Windows printers on any of the computers connected to your local network are automatically accessible once configured. Be sure the Samba server is installed to let you access shared Windows printers.

Should you want to share a printer on your Ubuntu computer with users on other computers, you need to install the Samba server (Samba package) and have the Server Message Block services enabled using the **smbd** and **nmbd** daemons. You would then configure the printer as a shared device. You can use the **systemctl** command to restart, stop, and start the services.

```
sudo systemctl restart smbd
sudo systemctl restart nmbd
```

Also, be sure that the **smbclient** package is installed. Ubuntu does not install it by default.

```
sudo apt install smbclient
```

Configuring remote printers manually

In the **printers.conf** file, for a remote printer, instead of listing the device, the DeviceURI entry, will have an Internet address, along with its protocol. For example, a remote printer on a CUPS server (**ipp**) would be indicated as shown here (a Windows printer would use the **smb** protocol):

```
DeviceURI ipp://mytsuff.com/printers/queue1
```

When you install the Windows printer on CUPS, you specify its location using the URL protocol **smb**. The username of the user allowed to log in to the printer is entered before the hostname and separated from the hostname by an @ sign. On most configurations, this is the **guest** user. The location entry for a Windows printer called **myhp** attached to a Windows host named **lizard** is shown next. It's Samba share reference would be **//lizard/myhp**.

```
DeviceURI smb://guest@lizard/myhp
```

To enable CUPS on Samba, you also have to set the printing option in the **/etc/samba/smb.conf** file to **cups**, as shown here.

```
printing = cups
printcap name = cups
```

Configuring Printers on the Ubuntu desktop

On the Ubuntu desktop you can use the Ubuntu Settings Printers tab, the Print Settings application, and the CUPS Web browser configuration tool to configure your printers.

Settings Printers tab

The Printers tool is accessible from the Settings Printers tab. It lists installed printers, letting you configure them and access their job queues (see Figure 10-1). If no printers are detected, an Add button is displayed on the tab, which you can use to detect your printer. Once you have added a printer, the Add Printer button is displayed in the Printers tab's header, which you can use to detect additional printers. The Printers tab will list entries for detected and configured printers. A printer entry displays the printer name, model, status, a jobs button with the number of jobs, and a configuration button (gear icon). Click the jobs button to open a dialog listing active jobs for this printer (see Figure 10-2). For each job entry there are buttons to the right to pause or remove the job.

Figure 10-1: Settings Printers tab

Figure 10-2: Settings Printers - Jobs

To configure a printer, click the ellipsis button to display a menu with entries for the printer's options, details, default, and removal (see Figure 10-3). Choosing the "Use Printer by Default", makes it your default printer. The "Remove Printer" entry removes the printer configuration from your system. The "Printer Details" entry opens a dialog with printer's details, such as the name, location, address, and driver. There are buttons for selecting a driver from a search, database, or a PPD file. Clicking on the "Printing Options" entry open the printer's options dialog (see Figure 10-3). You can configure printer features, such as page setup, image quality, and color. The Advanced tab lets you set specialized options, such as contrast, ink type, and saturation.

Figure 10-3: Settings Printers - Details and Options

On the Settings Printers tab, you can click the Add button to open the Add Printer dialog, which lists printers attached to your system (see Figure 10-4). They are detected automatically. If you know the address of a printer on your network, you can enter it in the search box at the bottom to have it detected and displayed.

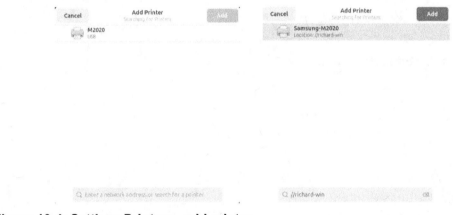

Figure 10-4: Settings Printers - add printer

For remote printers, click the Add button to open the Add Printer dialog listing Printers attached to your system. Remote printers will be automatically detected and listed. To manually add a remote printer and you know the address of the printer on your network, you can enter it in the search box at the bottom to have it detected and displayed.

Print Settings (system-config-printer)

You can also use the older **system-config-printer** tool to edit a printer configuration or to add a remote printer. You can install **system-config-printer** from the App Center as a Debian package named "Print Settings". You can open the Print Settings application from the Applications overview as Printers. A printer configuration window is displayed, showing icons for installed printers. As you add printers, icons for them are displayed in the Printer configuration window (see Figure 10-5).

Figure 10-5: Print Settings (system-config-printer0

      To see the printer settings, such as printer and job options, access controls, and policies, double-click the printer icon or right-click and select Properties. The Printer Properties window opens with six tabs: Settings, Policies, Access Control, Printer Options, Job Options, and Ink/Toner Levels (see Figure 10-6).

Figure 10-6: Printer Properties window

      The Printer configuration window Printer menu lets you rename the printer, enable or disable it, and make it a shared printer. Select the printer icon and then click the Printer menu. The Delete entry will remove a printer configuration. Use the Set As Default entry to make the printer a system-wide or personal default printer. There are also entries for accessing the printer properties and viewing the print queue.

      The Printer icon menu is accessed by right-clicking the printer icon. If the printer is already a default, there is no Set As Default entry. The Properties entry opens the printer properties window for that printer.

      The View Print Queue entry opens the Document Print Status window, which lists the jobs for that printer. You can change the queue position as well as stop or delete jobs. From the toolbar, you can choose to display printed jobs and reprint them. You will be notified if a job should fail.

To check the server settings, select Settings from the Server menu. This opens a new window showing the CUPS printer server settings. The Common UNIX Printing System (CUPS) is the server that provides printing services (**www.cups.org**).

To select a particular CUPS server, select the Connect entry in the Server menu. This opens a Connect to CUPS Server window with a drop-down menu listing all current CUPS servers from which to choose.

Again, when you edit any printer's configuration settings, you will be prompted for authorization. Whenever you try to change a printer setting, such as its driver or URI, you are prompted to enter the administrative password for device authorization.

To make a printer the default, either right-click the printer icon and select Set As Default or single-click the printer icon and then, from the Printer configuration window's Printer menu, select the Set As Default entry. A Set Default Printer dialog opens with options for setting the system-wide default or setting the personal default. The system-wide default printer is the default for your entire network served by your CUPS server, not just your local system. The system-wide default printer will have a green check mark emblem on its printer icon in the Printer configuration window (see Figure 10-7).

Figure 10-7: Default Printer

Should you wish to use a different printer as your default, you can designate it as your personal default. To make a printer your personal default, select the entry Set as My Personal Default Printer in the Set Default Printer dialog. A personal emblem, a heart, will appear on the printer's icon in the Printer configuration window.

If you have more than one printer on your system, you can make one the default by clicking the Make Default Printer button in the printer's properties Settings pane.

The Class entry lets you create a printer class. You can access the New menu from the Server menu or from the Add button. This feature lets you select a group of printers to print a job, instead of selecting just one. That way, if one printer is busy or down, another printer can be automatically selected to perform the job. Installed printers can be assigned to different classes.

To edit an installed printer, double-click its icon in the Printer configuration window or right-click and select the Properties entry. This opens a Printer Properties window for that printer. A sidebar lists the configuration tabs. Click one to display that tab. There are configuration entries for Settings, Policies, Access Control, Printer Options, Job Options, and Ink/Toner Levels.

To install a new printer, choose the Server | New | Printer menu entry or click the Add button on the toolbar (see Figure 10-8). A New Printer window opens and displays a series of dialog boxes from which you select the connection, model, drivers, and printer name with location. The location is specified using special URI protocols. For another CUPS printer on a remote host, the protocol used is **ipp**, for Internet Printing Protocol, whereas for a Windows printer, it is **smb**. Older UNIX and Linux systems using LPRng use the **lpd** protocol.

Figure 10-8: New Printer

You can also use Print Settings (system-config-printer) to set up a remote printer on Linux, UNIX, or Windows networks. When you add a new printer or edit one, the New Printer dialog will list possible remote connection types under the Network entry. When you select a remote connection entry, a pane will be displayed to the right where you can enter configuration information.

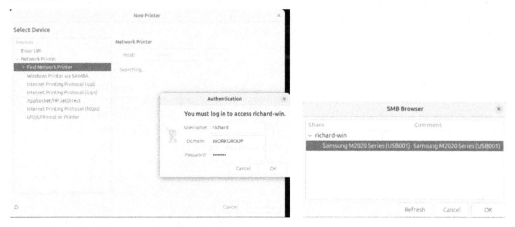

Figure 10-9: Finding a network printer

To find a connected printer on your network automatically, click the Find Network Printer entry. This is a simple easy way to find a printer for a small network. Enter the hostname of the system the remote printer is connected to, then click the Find button. The host is searched and the detected printers are displayed as entries under the Network Printer heading (see Figure 10-9). You may be asked to login as a qualified user. You can then click the Find button to open a dialog listing shared printers on the host. Choose the one you want. For more refined access you can use the "Windows Printer via Samba" operation. The selected printer will appear under the Network Printer heading in the sidebar (see Figure 10-10).

Figure 10-10: Selecting a network printer

The location is specified using special URI protocols. For another CUPS printer on a remote host, the protocol used is **ipp**, for Internet Printing Protocol, whereas for a Windows printer, it is **smb**. Older UNIX and Linux systems using LPRng use the **lpd** protocol.

To configure a specific type of printer, choose from the available entries. For a remote Linux or UNIX printer, select either Internet Printing Protocol (ipp), which is used for newer systems, or LPD/LPR Host or Printer, which is used for older systems. Both panes display entries for the Host name and the queue. For the Host name, enter the hostname of the system that controls the printer. For an Apple or HP jet direct printer on your network, select the AppSocket/HP jetDirect entry.

A "Windows printer via Samba" printer is one located on a Windows network, and provides more refined access than the Find Network Printer operation. You need to specify the Windows server (hostname or IP address), the name of the share, the name of the printer's workgroup, and the username and password. The format of the printer SMB URL is shown on the SMP Printer pane. The share is the hostname and printer name in the **smb** URI format *//workgroup/hostname/printername*. The workgroup is the windows network workgroup that the printer belongs to. On small networks, there is usually only one. The hostname is the computer where the printer is located. The username and password can be for the printer resource itself, or for access by a particular user. The pane will display a box at the top where you can enter the share host and printer name as an **smb** URI. Click the Browse button to open a dialog that will list shared printers on the host. Choose the one you want.

If the Browse operation accessed by the Browse button does not work, you may have to enter the exact name of the printer, including special characters such as spaces and parenthesis. These special characters are referenced with a preceding percent sign, **%**, followed by the ASCII hexadecimal value for the character. A space is referenced as **%20**, an open parenthesis as **%28**, and a close parenthesis as **%29**. In these examples, the Windows name of the Samsung M2020 printer is:

```
Samsung M2020 Series (USB001)
```

This would be:

```
Samsung%20M2020%20Series%20%28USB001%29
```

Be sure to also include your host name. If you have multiple workgroups on your network, include the workgroup name also. The full entry for the previous example, with the host 'richard-win" would be:

```
richard-win/Samsung%20M2020%20Series%20%28USB001%29
```

With the workgroup name "workgroup" it would be:

```
workgroup/richard-win/Samsung%20M2020%20Series%20%28USB001%29
```

You also can enter in any needed Samba authentication, if required, such as a username and password. Check "Authentication required" to allow you to enter the Samba Username and Password. The Connections section to the lower right will list "Windows Printer via Samba" as the connection. With the current version of Samba, if you do not enter it now, it will prompt you for a user name and password when you try to use the printer. This may not work. To be sure of access you should enter the user and password on this dialog now.

You then continue with install screens for the printer model, driver, and name. Once installed, you can then access the printer properties just as you would any printer (see Figure 10-11).

Figure 10-11: Remote Windows printer Settings

The configured remote printer is then listed in the system-config-printer window, along with other printers (see Figure 10-12). When you choose to print from an application, the remote printer will be listed along with your local printers.

Figure 10-12: Remote Windows Printers

CUPS Web Browser-based configuration tool

The CUPS configuration Web interface is a web-based tool that can also manage printers and print jobs. A Web page is displayed with tabs for managing jobs and printers and performing administrative tasks. You can access the CUPS configuration tool using the **localhost** address and specifying port **631**. Enter the following URL into your Web browser:

```
http://localhost:631
```

Entering the **localhost:631** URL in your Web browser opens the Home screen for the CUPS Web interface. There are tabs for various sections, as well as links for specialized tasks like adding printers or obtaining help (see Figure 10-13). Tabs include Administration, Classes, Help, Jobs, and Printers. You can manage and add printers on the Administration tab. The Printers tab will list installed printers with buttons for accessing their print queues, printer options, and job options, among others. The Jobs tab lists your print jobs and lets you manage them.

If you installed the ubuntu-desktop-minimal desktop on an Ubuntu server, you have to add the **lpadmin** group to your user name. Use the **usermod** command with the **-a** and **-G** options. In this example the user name is richard. You then have to restart the Cups server with **systemctl**.

```
sudo usermod -a -G lpadmin richard
sudo systemctl restart cups
```

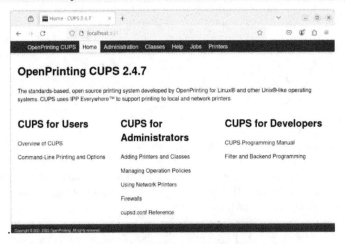

Figure 10-13: CUPS Web-based Configuration Tool: Home tab

When you try to make any changes for the first time during the session, you will first be asked to enter a username with administrative access (your username) and password (your user password), just as you would for the **sudo** command.

The Administration tab displays segments for Printers, Classes, Jobs, and the Server (see Figure 10-14). The server section is where you allow printer sharing. Buttons allow you to view logs and change settings.

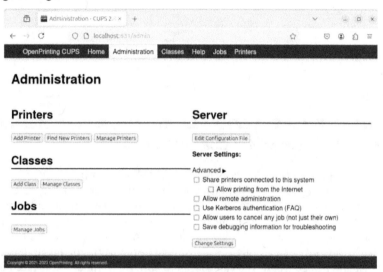

Figure 10-14: CUPS Web-based Configuration Tool: Administration tab

With the CUPS configuration tool, local printers are automatically detected and configured. You can install a printer manually on CUPS through a series of Web pages, each of which requests different information. To install a printer, click the Add Printer button either on the Home page or the Administration page. You must first specify the protocol. On the next screen, you enter a URI to use for the printer. For a local printer, this is the protocol and the hostname. A page is displayed where you enter the printer name and location (see Figure 10-15). A Sharing checkbox lets you choose to share the printer. The location is the host to which the printer is connected. The procedure is similar to **system-config-printer**. Subsequent pages will prompt you to enter the make and model of the printer, which you select from available listings. You can also load a PPD driver file instead if you have one. Click the Add Printer button when read. On the following page, you then set default options for your printer, like paper size and type, color, print quality, and resolution.

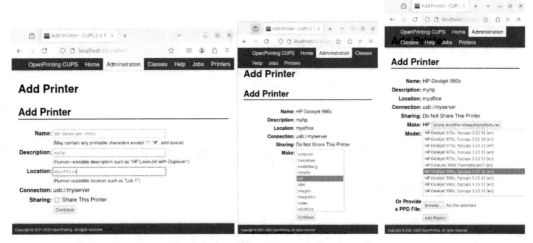

Figure 10-15: Adding a new printer: CUP Web Interface

To manage a printer, click the Printers tab or the Manage Printers button in the Administration page. The Printers page will list your installed printers (see Figure 10-16). Clicking a printer link opens a page for managing your jobs and performing administrative tasks (see Figure 10-17). From the Maintenance drop down menu you can perform printer and job tasks like pausing the printer, printing a test page, and canceling all jobs. The Administration menu lets you modify the printer, delete it, and set default options. Choosing the Administration menu's Set Default Options entry displays a page where you can configure how your printer prints (see Figure 10-18). Links at the top of the page display pages for setting certain options like general options, output control, banners, and extra features such as printer direction, ink type, color density, and drop size. The general options are listed first, where you can set basic features like the resolution and paper size.

Printers

Search in Printers: [_____] [Search] [Clear]

Showing 2 of 2 printers.

Queue Name	Description	Location	Make and Model	Status
HP-Deskjet-980c	myhp	myoffice	HP Deskjet 980c, hpcups 3.23.12	Idle
M2020-Series	M2020-Series		HP Designjet T920 PostScript	Paused - "Unplugged or turned off"

Figure 10-16: CUPS Web-based Configuration Tool: Printers tab

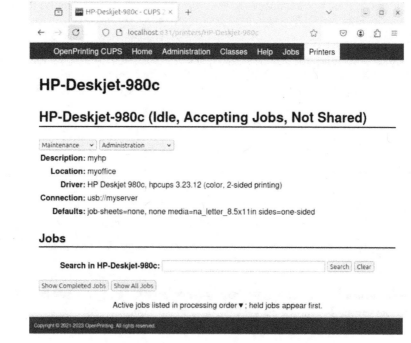

Figure 10-17: CUPS Web-based Configuration Tool: Managing Printers

Figure 10-18: CUPS Web-based Configuration Tool: Printer Options

Note: You can perform all administrative tasks from the command line using the **lpadmin** command. See the CUPS documentation for more details.

To use the CUPS configuration tool to install a remote printer, specify the remote printer network protocol on the initial Add Printer page. You can choose from Windows, Internet Printing Protocol (other UNIX or Linux systems), Apple and HP JetDirect connected printers, and the older LPD line printers (see Figure 10-19). If a network printer is connected currently, it may be listed in the Discovered Network Printers list.

Figure 10-19: CUPS Web-based Configuration Tool: Network Printers

CUPS Printer Classes

CUPS lets you select a group of printers to print a job, instead of selecting just one. If one printer is busy or down, another printer can be selected automatically to print the job. Such groupings of printers are called classes. Once you have installed your printers, you can group them into different classes. For example, you may want to group all inkjet printers into one class and laser printers in another, or you may want to group printers connected to one specific printer server in their own class.

On the Ubuntu desktop, you can use system-config-printer to set up classes for printers. The Class entry in the Server | New menu lets you create a printer class. You can access the New menu from the Server menu or from the Add button. This feature lets you select a group of printers to print a job, instead of selecting just one. That way, if one printer is busy or down, another printer can be selected automatically to perform the job. Installed printers can be assigned to different classes. When you click the Class entry in the New menu, a New Class window opens. Here you can enter the name for the class, any comments, and the location (your hostname is entered by default). The next screen lists available printers on the right side (Other printers) and the printers you assigned to the class on the left side (Printers in this class). Use the arrow button to add or remove printers to the class. Click Apply when finished. Tabs for a selected class are much the same as for a printer, with a Members tab instead of a Printer Options tab. In the Members tab, you can change which printers belong to the class. You can also select a printer or set of printers and choose "Create class" from the Printer menu, automatically adding them to the new class.

You can also create classes on the CUPS Web Configuration tool. Select the Administration tab, and click the Add Class button. On the Add Class page, you enter the name of the class, its location and then select the printers to add to the class from the Members list. The class will then show up on the Classes tab, showing its members and status.

CUPS Configuration files

The configuration files for the CUPS server are located in the **/etc/cups** directory (see Table 10-2). The **classes.conf** and **printers.conf** files can be managed by desktop applications such as GNOME Printer and the CUPS Web Configuration tool. Others, such as **cupsd.conf**, you have to edit with a text editor.

Filename	Description
classes.conf	Contains configurations for different local printer classes
client.conf	Lists specific options for specified clients
cupsd.conf	Configures the CUPS server, **cupsd**
printers.conf	Contains printer configurations for available local printers
cups-files.conf	File and directories used by CUPS
cups-browsed.conf	Access to remote and local printers
subscriptions.conf	Subscription controls for printer and print job information

Table 10-2: CUPS Configuration Files

cupsd.conf

The configuration file for the CUPS server is **/etc/cups/cupsd.conf**. To configure the CUPS server, use a text editor to edit the configuration entries in this file. When the CUPS software package was installed, it installed a detailed commented version of the **cupsd.conf** file. Most options are listed, though many are commented out, with a # symbol at the beginning of their entries. The CUPS server is configured using directives, similar in syntax to that used by the configuration for the Apache web server. Just as with Apache, directives can be organized into blocks.

For a detailed explanation of **cupsd.conf** directives check the CUPS documentation for **cupsd.conf**. You can also reference this documentation from the Online Help page | References link on the CUPS browser-based administration tool, **http://localhost:631**.

```
https://www.cups.org/documentation.html
```

The **cupsd.conf** file begins with log settings.

```
LogLevel warn
```

On Ubuntu, CUPS logging is disabled.

```
MaxLogSize 0
```

The Listen directives set the machine and socket on which to receive connections. These are set by default to the local machine, localhost port 631. If you are using a dedicated network interface for connecting to a local network, you would add the network card's IP address, allowing access from machines on your network.

```
# Only listen for connections from the local machine.
Listen localhost:631
Listen /run/cups/cups.sock
```

Browsing directives allow your local printers to be detected on your network, enabling them to be shared. For shared printing, the Browsing directive is set to on (it is set to Off by default). The BrowseLocalProtocols directive lists the network protocols to use for advertising the printers on a local network. The default is set to **dnssd**.

```
# Show shared printers on the local network.
Browsing On
BrowseLocalProtocols dnssd
```

A BrowseOrder of **allow,deny** will deny all browse transmissions, then first check the BrowseAllow directives for exceptions. A reverse order (**deny,allow**) does the opposite, accepting all browse transmissions, and first checks for those denied by BrowseDeny directives. The default **cupsd.conf** file has a BrowseOrder **allow,deny** directive followed by a BrowseAllow directive, which is set to **all**. To limit this to a particular network, use the IP address of the network instead of **all**. The BrowseAddress directive will make your local printers available as shared printers on the specified network. It is set to **@LOCAL** to allow access on your local network. You can add other BrowseAddress directives to allow access by other networks.

```
BrowseOrder allow,deny
BrowseAllow all
BrowseAddress @LOCAL
```

CUPS supports both Basic and Digest forms of authentication, specified in the **AuthType** directive. Basic authentication requires a user and password. For example, to use the web interface, you are prompted to enter the root user and the root user password. Digest authentication makes use of user and password information kept in the CUPS **/etc/cups/passwd.md5** file, using MD5 versions of a user and password for authentication. In addition, CUPS also supports a BasicDigest and Negotiate authentication. BasicDigest will use the CUPS md5 password file for basic authentication. Negotiate will use Kerberos authentication. The default authentication type is set, using the DefaultAuthType directive, set to Basic.

```
# Default authentication type, when authentication is required...
DefaultAuthType Basic
```

The Web interface setting is set to yes.

```
WebInterface Yes
```

Location Directives

Certain directives allow you to place access controls on specific locations. These can be printers or resources, such as the administrative tool or the spool directories. Location controls are implemented with the **Location** directive. There are several Location directives that control access. The first controls access to the server root directory, /. The Order allow, deny entry activates restrictions on access by remote systems. If there are no following Allow or Deny entries then the default is to deny all. There is an implied Allow localhost with the "Order allow, deny" directive, always giving access to the local machine. In effect, access here is denied to all systems, allowing access only by the local system.

```
# Restrict access to the server...
<Location />
  Order allow,deny
</Location>
```

Another **Location** directive is used to restrict administrative access, the **/admin** resource. The **Order allow,deny** directive denies access to all systems, except for the local machine. The **AuthType default** directive refers to the default set by DefaultAuthType. The **Require user** directive references the **SystemGroup** directive, **@SYSTEM** (defined in the **cups-files.conf** file). Only users from that group are allowed access.

```
# Restrict access to the admin pages...
<Location /admin>
  AuthType Default
  Require user @SYSTEM
  Order allow,deny
</Location>
```

Allow from and **Deny from** directives can permit or deny access from specific hosts and networks. If you wanted to just allow access to a particular machine, you would use an **Allow from** directive with the machine's IP address. CUPS also uses **@LOCAL** to indicate your local network, and **IF(***name***)** for a particular network interface (*name* is the device name of the interface) used to access a network. Should you want to allow administrative access by all other systems on your local network, you can add the **Allow from @LOCAL**. If you add an **Allow** directive, you also have to explicitly add the **Allow localhost** to ensure access by your local machine.

```
# Restrict access to the admin pages...
<Location /admin>
  Allow from localhost
  Allow from @LOCAL
  Order allow,deny
</Location>
```

The following entry would allow access from a particular machine.

```
  Allow From 192.168.0.5
```

The next location directive restricts access to the CUPS configuration files, **/admin/conf**.

```
# Restrict access to configuration files...
<Location /admin/conf>
  AuthType Default
  Require user @SYSTEM
  Order allow,deny
</Location>
```

The next location directive sets the same restrictions for the log files **/admin/log**.

```
# Restrict access to log files...
<Location /admin/log>
  AuthType Default
  Require user @SYSTEM
  Order allow,deny
</Location>
```

Default Operation Policy: Limit Directives

A default operation policy is then defined for access to basic administration, printer, print job, and owner operations. The default operation policy section begins with the **<Policy default>** directive. Limit directives are used to implement the directives for each kind of operation. Job operations covers tasks like sending a document, restarting a job, suspending a job, and restarting a job. Administrative tasks include modifying a printer configuration, deleting a printer, managing printer classes, and setting the default printer. Printer operations govern tasks like pausing a printer, enabling or disabling a printer, and shutting down a printer. The owner operations consist of just canceling a job and authenticating access to a job.

See the CUPS documentation on managing operations policies for more details.

```
https://www.cups.org/doc/policies.html
```

On all the default **Limit** directives, access is allowed only by the local machine (localhost), **Order allow,deny**.

The default policy section begins with a <Policy> directive followed by access controls for user and job information. The default for **JobPrivateAccess** limits access to owner, system, and access control lists. **JobPrivateValues** specifies values made private, such as the job name, originating host, and originating user. **SubscriptionPrivateAccess** and **SubscriptionPrivateValues** specify access for subscription attributes such notifications of printer events like job completed or job stopped.

```
<Policy default>
    JobPrivateAccess default
    JobPrivateValues default
    SubscriptionPrivateAccess default
    SubscriptionPrivateValues default
```

Limit directives are then set up to create and print jobs.

```
<Limit Create-Job Print-Job Print-URI Validate-Job>
    Order deny,allow
</Limit>
```

Both the administrative and printer **Limit** directives are set to the **AuthType default** and limited to access by administrative users, **Require user @SYSTEM**. The administrative directive is shown here.

```
# All administration operations require an administrator to authenticate...
<Limit CUPS-Add-Modify-Printer CUPS-Delete-Printer CUPS-Add-Modify-Class CUPS-
Delete-Class CUPS-Set-Default CUPS-Get-Devices>
    AuthType Default
    Require user @SYSTEM
    Order deny,allow
</Limit>
```

Both the job related and owner Limit directives require either owner or administrative authentication, **Require user @OWNER @SYSTEM**.

```
# Only the owner or an administrator can cancel or authenticate a job...
<Limit Cancel-Job CUPS-Authenticate-Job>
  Require user @OWNER @SYSTEM
  Order deny,allow
</Limit>

<Limit CUPS-Authenticate-Job>
  Require user @OWNER @SYSTEM
  Order deny,allow
</Limit>
```

For all other tasks, **<Limit All>**, access is restricted to the local machine (localhost).

```
<Limit All>
 Order deny,allow
</Limit>
```

The default policy section closed with a </Policy> directive.

```
</Policy>
```

An authenticated set of policy directives follows the default policy, with similar entries and an added **AuthType** entry in the Limit directive to create and print jobs, **<Policy authenticated>**. The **AuthClass** directive can be used within a **Limit** directive to specify the printer class allowed access. The **System** class includes the root, sys, and system users.

```
<Limit Create-Job Print-Job Print-URI Validate-Job>
  AuthType Default
  Order deny,allow
</Limit>
```

In addition there is also a policy section for kerberized policies, **<Policy kerberos>**.

cupsctl

You can use the **cupsctl** command to modify your **cupsd.conf** file, rather than editing the file directly. Check the **cupsctl** Man page for details. The **cupsctl** command with no options will display current settings.

```
cupsctl
```

The changes you can make with this command are limited to turning off remote administration or disabling shared printing. The major options you can set are:

remote-admin   Enable or disable remote administration

remote-any   Enable or disable remote printing

user-cancel-any   Enable or disable users to cancel the print jobs of others

share-printers   Enable or disable sharing of local printers with other systems

printers.conf

Configured information for a printer will be stored in the **/etc/cups/printers.conf** file. You can examine this file directly, even making changes. Here is an example of a printer configuration entry. The **DeviceURI** entry specifies the device used, in this case, a USB printer. It is currently idle, with no jobs.

```
# Printer configuration file for CUPS
# Written by cupsd
<Printer mycannon>
Info Cannon s330
Location richard-server
MakeModel Canon S330
DeviceURI usb://Canon/S330
State Idle
StateTime 1166554036
Accepting Yes
Shared Yes
ColorManaged Yes
JobSheets none
QuotaPeriod 0
PageLimit 0
KLimit 0
OpPolicy default
ErrorPolicy retry-job
</Printer>
```

subscriptions.conf

Configured information for printer and job information is located in the **/etc/cups/subscriptions.conf** file. Those receiving the information are specified by the **SubscriptionPrivateAccess** and **SubscriptionPrivateValues** directives in the policy section of the **cupd.conf** file. The **Events** directive specifies notifications of events to be sent, events such as job-completed, printer-stopped, and server-started. The **Owner** directive lists the users for this subscription. **LeaseDuration** is the time the subscription remains valid (0 value is the life of the print job or forever). **Interval** is the time between notifications. **Recipient** is the recipient URI for the notification. In the following example it is dbus:// (your desktop). The **subscriptions.conf** file is managed by **cupsd** directly and is not to be edited. A sample **subscriptions.conf** file is shown here.

```
# Subscription configuration file for CUPS v2.4.7
NextSubscriptionId 10
<Subscription 8>
Events printer-state-changed printer-restarted printer-shutdown printer-stopped
printer-added printer-deleted job-state-changed job-created job-completed job-
stopped
Owner richard
Recipient dbus://
LeaseDuration 86400
Interval 60
ExpirationTime 1639584373
NextEventId 1
</Subscription>
```

cups-files.conf

The files and directories that CUPS uses to manage print jobs can be configured in the **/etc/cups/cups-files.conf** file. The LogFileGroup directive indicates the group name for the log files, and the ErrorLog directive specifies the CUPS error log file.

```
LogFileGroup  adm
ErrorLog  /var/log/cups/error_log
```

The SystemGroup directive defines the users referenced by **@SYSTEM** in **cupsd.conf**.

```
SystemGroup lpadmin root
```

cups-browsed.conf

The **cups-browsed.conf** file configures the **cups-browsed** daemon, used for browsing remote and local printers. With driverless printing this is now managed by CUPS directly. The **cups-browsed** daemon is used for those printers not yet covered by CUPS driverless printing.

The BrowseRemoteProtocols defines the protocols to use.

```
BrowseRemoteProtocols  dnssd cups
```

The BrowseAllow directive can be used to restrict browsing to specified servers or networks.

```
BrowseAllow 192.168.1.0/24
```

The CreateIPPPrinterQueues directive allows the detection of non-CUPS IPP printers.

CUPS Command Line Print Commands

On the desktop, you can use the print clients such as the Setting Printers tab, system-config-printers and the CUPS Printer Configuration tool to manage your print jobs. For the shell command line, you can use several command line print commands instead. These include the **lpr**, **lpc**, **lpq**, and **lprm** commands. These commands let you print documents, display the print queue, and delete print jobs. For network connections, CUPS provides the **-E** encryption option, which allows you to encrypt print jobs. The command line print commands are listed in Table 10-3.

lpr

The **lpr** command stands for line print and submits a print job to the print queue. Its argument is the name of the file to be printed. With the **-P** option you can select a particular printer. Otherwise the default printer is used. In the following example, the file **myletter** is printed, and then prints the file **report** to the printer with the name **myprinter**.

```
$ lpr myletter
```

In this example, the file **myreport** is printed on the **myprinter** printer.

```
$ lpr -P myprinter myreport
```

Printer Management	Description
`lpr` *options file-list*	Prints a file, copies the file to the printer's spool directory, and places it on the print queue to be printed in turn. `-P` *printer* prints the file on the specified printer
`lpq` *options*	Displays the print jobs in the print queue. `-P` *printer* prints the queue for the specified printer `-l` prints a detailed listing
`lpstat` *options*	Displays printer status
`lprm` *options printjob-id* `or` *printer*	Removes a print job from the print queue. You identify a particular print job by its number as listed by `lpq`. `-P` *printer* removes all print jobs for the specified printer
`lpc`	Manages your printers. At the `lpc>` prompt, you can enter commands to check the status of your printers and take other actions

Table 10-3: CUPS Print Clients

lpc

With the **lpc** command you can enable or disable a printer, reorder print queues, and reload configuration files. When you enter the command **lpc** on the command line, an **lpc>** prompt is displayed. You can then enter **lpc** commands to manage your printers and reorder print jobs. The **status** command with the name of the printer displays a printer's status, displaying information such as the readiness of the printer and the number of print jobs in its queue. To stop or start printing use the **stop** and **start** commands. The **lpc** command shows the printers configured for your CUPS print server.

```
$ lpc
lpc> status myprinter
myprinter:
 printer is on device 'usb' speed -1
 queuing is enabled
 printing is enabled
 1 entry in spool area
```

lpq and lpstat

Use the **lpq** command to list the print jobs in the print queue. To see the jobs for a particular printer use the **-P** option with the printer name. To list the jobs for a specific user, enter the username. Use the **-l** option to display detailed information for each job. To display information for a specific job, use that job's ID number. The **lpstat** command lets you check the status of a printer.

```
$ lpq
myprinter is ready and printing
Rank    Owner   Jobs  File(s)         Total Size
active  chris   1     report          1024
```

lprm

You can remove a print job from the printer queue with the **lprm** command, deleting the job before it could be printed. **lprm** uses many of the same options as **lpq**. To remove a job, use **lprm** with the job number. You can use **lpq** to list the job number. Use the **-P** option with a printer name to remove all jobs for that printer. If no options are specified for **lprm** then the current print job printing is removed. The next command removes the first print job in the print queue.

```
lprm 1
```

CUPS Command Line Administrative Tools

CUPS command-line administrative tools includes such commands as **lpadmin**, **lpoptions**, **lpinfo**, **cupsenable**, **cupsdisable**, **cupsaccept**, and **cupsreject** (**cups-client** package). You can use the **cupsenable** and **cupsdisable** commands to start and stop print queues, and use the **cupsaccept** and **cupsreject** commands start and stop print jobs. With the **lpinfo** command you can display printer information. The **lpoptions** allows you to set print options. With the **lpadmin** command you can perform administrative tasks such as adding printers and changing configurations. CUPS administrative tools are listed in Table 10-4.

Note: The command line clients have the same name, and much the same syntax, as the older LPR and LPRng command line clients used in Unix and older Linux systems.

Administration Tool	Description
lpadmin	CUPS printer configuration
lpoptions	Sets printing options
cupsenable	Activates a printer
cupsdisable	Stops a printer
cupsaccept	Allows a printer to accept new jobs
cupsreject	Prevents a printer from accepting print jobs
lpinfo	Lists CUPS devices available

Table 10-4: CUPS Administrative Tools

lpadmin

The **lpadmin** command lets you choose the default printer and to configure options for a printer. Use the **-d** option to select a printer as the default. In the next example, **myprinter** is chosen as the default printer.

```
lpadmin -d myprinter
```

To set options for a printer, first use the **-p** option to select a printer. The next example sets printer description information (**-D** option) for the **myprinter** printer.

```
lpadmin -p myprinter  -D  Epson550
```

Some of the options allow you to set per-user quotas for print jobs. The **job-k-limit** option limits the size of a job allowed per user, **job-page-limit** determines the page limit for a job, and **job-quota-period** restrict the number of jobs using a specified time period. The next command sets a page limit of 100 for each user.

```
lpadmin -p myprinter  -o job-page-limit=100
```

You can control access by users with the **-u** option and an **allow** or **deny** list. Use an allow list for users permitted access. The allow list has an **allow:** label followed by a list of users. To deny access use a **deny:** list. In the following command, access is granted to **cora** but denied to **orrin** and **harlow**.

```
lpadmin -p myprinter -u allow:cora  deny:orrin,harlow
```

To simply deny or allow access to all users or none, use the terms **all** or **none** to permit or deny access to all or no users. You can create exceptions by having both an allow and deny list where one uses the **all** or **none** list. The next command allows access to all users except **dylan**.

```
lpadmin -p myprinter  -u allow:all   deny:dylan
```

lpoptions

With the **lpoptions** command, you can set print formatting options and defaults, such as the color or page format. Use the **-l** option to see a list of possible option for a printer. The **-p** option selects a printer, and the **-d** option sets the default printer. The following command lists the current options for the myprinter printer.

```
lpoptions -p myprinter -l
```

To assign a value to an option, you would use the **-o** option with the option name and value, **-o** *option=value.* You can use the **-r** option to remove a printer option. In the next example, the **sides** option is assigned the value **two-sided** to enable printing on both sides of a paper.

```
lpoptions -p myprinter -o sides=two-sided
```

You could later use the **-r** option to remove that option.

```
lpoptions -p myprinter -r sides
```

To see a list of available options, check the standard printing options in the CUPS Software Manual at **https://www.cups.org/**.

cupsenable and cupsdisable

The **cupsenable** command starts a printer, and the **cupsdisable** command stops it. With the **-c** option, you can cancel all jobs on the printer's queue, and the **-r** option broadcasts a message explaining the shutdown. This command disables the printer named **myepson.**

```
cupsdisable myepson
```

cupsaccept and cupsreject

With the **cupsaccept** and **cupsreject** commands you can control access to a printer's printer queue. You can use the **cupsreject** command to stop a printer accepting jobs. The

cupsaccept command allows print jobs. The following command prevents the **myepson** printer from accepting print jobs.

```
cupsreject myepson
```

lpinfo

The **lpinfo** command displays information about the CUPS devices and drivers that are available on your system. The **-v** options show information about devices and the **-m** option for drivers.

```
lpinfo -m
```

ubuntu

11. Network File Systems and Distributed Network File Systems: NFS and clusters

Network File Systems: NFS and /etc/exports

NFS Configuration: /etc/exports

Controlling and Accessing to NFS Servers

Mounting NFS File Systems: NFS Clients

Name Service Switch: nsswitch.conf

Distributed Network File Systems (clusters)

Red Hat Global File System (GFS and GFS 2)

The Network File System (NFS) lets you to connect to and access file systems on remote hosts. Distributed Network File Systems build on the basic concept of NFS as well as RAID techniques to create a file system implemented on multiple hosts across a large network, in effect, distributing the same file system among different hosts. The implementation used on Ubuntu is the Red Hat's Global File System (GFS).

Note: The Network Information Service (NIS), which maintains configuration files for all systems on a network, is very old server software and may soon be deprecated. It is not considered secure and has already been deprecated on Red Hat Linux and other Linux versions using the Red Hat Package management system (RPM). Instead of NIS, many networks now use LDAP to manage user information and authentication. NIS support is still available on Ubuntu with the **nis** package.

Network File Systems: NFS and /etc/exports

With NFS you can mount a file system located on a remote computer and access it as if it were local a file system on your system. In this way, different hosts on a network could access the same file system. The NFS website is **http://nfs.sourceforge.net**. Check the Ubuntu Server Guide | Services | Service - NFS for basic configuration and management.

```
https://ubuntu.com/server/docs/service-nfs
```

To set up the NFS service for your system, install the **nfs-kernel-server**, **nfs-common**, and **rpcbind** packages (selecting just the **nfs-kernel-server** will select the others automatically).

```
sudo apt install nfs-kernel-server
```

NFS Daemons

NFS uses Remote Procedure Calls (RPC) to provide remote access to file systems on a TCP/IP network. A host system makes some of its file systems available to other hosts on the network by exporting those file systems. The export operations are configured with entries in the **/etc/exports** file. The exports are implemented by several daemons such as **rpc.mountd**, **rpc.nfsd**, and **rpc.gssd**, which support access by remote hosts. You can control the NFS server with entries in the **/etc/hosts.allow** and **/etc/hosts.deny** files. The NFS server daemons provided in the **nfs-kernel-server** package are listed here. You can configure options in the **/etc/default/nfs-kernel-server** file.

rpc.nfsd   Receives NFS requests from remote systems and translates them into requests for the local system.

rpc.mountd   Performs requested mount and unmount operations.

Additional NFS support daemons are provided by the **nfs-common** package. You can configure options in the **/etc/default/nfs-common** file.

rpc.svcgssd   Performs security for rpc operations (rpcsec_gss protocol).

rpc.gssd   Client support for the rpcsec_gss protocol for gss-api security in NFSv4.

rpc.idmapd   Maps user and group IDs to names.

rpc.statd   Provides locking services when a remote host reboots.

rpc.blkmapd   Provides device discovery and mapping.

The **rpcbind** server converts remote procedure calls program number to appropriate port numbers.

The NFS daemons are managed by **systemd** using several service unit files located in **/lib/systemd/system**. The NFS daemons and their **systemd** unit files are listed in Table 11-1.

The **nfs-server.service** file is shown here. Runtime configuration information is read from **/etc/default/nfs-kernel-server** (EnvironmentFile).

nfs-server.service

```
[Unit]
Description=NFS server and services
DefaultDependencies=no
Requires=network.target proc-fs-nfsd.mount
Requires=nfs-mountd.service
Wants=rpcbind.socket network-online.target
Wants=rpc.statd.service nfs-idmapd.service
Wants=rpc-statd.nofify.service
wants=nfsdcld.service


After=network-online.target local-fs.target
After=proc-fs-nfsd.mount rpcbind.target nfs-mountd.service
After=nfs-idmapd.service rpc-statd.service
After=nfsdcld.service
Before=rpc-statd-notify.service

# GSS services dependencies and ordering
Wants=auth-rpcgss-module.service rpc-svcgssd.service
After=rpc-gssd.service gssproxy.service rpc-svcgssd.service


[Service]

Type=oneshot
RemainAfterExit=yes
ExecStartPre=/usr/sbin/exportfs -r
ExecStart=/usr/sbin/rpc.nfsd
ExecStop=/usr/sbin/rpc.nfsd 0
ExecStopPost=/usr/sbin/exportfs -au
ExecStopPost=/usr/sbin/exportfs -f

ExecReload=/usr/sbin/exportfs -r

[Install]
WantedBy=multi-user.target
```

Use the **systemctl** command to start, stop, and restart the NFS server manually.

```
sudo systemctl start nfs-kernel-server
```

The corresponding **systemd** unit files for the **nfsd**, **mountd**, **idmapd**, **statd**, and **svcgssd** daemons, will run these daemons (**nfs-** and **rpc-** prefixes).

To see if NFS is actually running, you can use the **rpcinfo** command with the **-p** option. You should see entries for **mountd** and **nfs**. If not, NFS is not running.

The **rpc.statd**, **rpc.idmapd**, and **rpc.gssd** daemons can be accessed using the **systemctl** command.

```
sudo systemctl restart statd
sudo systemctl restart idmapd
sudo systemctl restart gssd
```

Options for the **nfs-kernel-server** are now located in the **/etc/nfs.conf** file. To see what options are specified use the **nfsconf** command with the **--dump** option. Results are listed according to sections. Each server has a section. In the current Ubuntu install, there are only two options active.

```
nfsconf --dump
[general]
pipefs-directory = /run/rpc_pipefs

[mound]
  manage-fids - y
```

The **/etc/nfs.conf** file arranges options into different sections for the different NFS servers, such as gssd, nfsd, and statd. Most options are commented out. To activate an option remove the preceding comment character, #. A safer way to activate an option is to use the **nfsconf** command with the **--set** option.

```
nfsconf --file /etc/nfsconf --set statd debug 1
nfsconf --file /etc/nfsconf --set nfsd gracetime 80
```

See the man page for **nfs.conf** and **nfsconf** for more details.

```
man nfs.conf
man nfsconf
```

Options were previously specified in the configuration files located in the **/etc/default** folder (**nfs-kernel-server** and **nfs-common**). Though these are still present, they are ignored. Should you modify these files, the conversion script **/usr/share/nfs-common/nfsconvert.py** will generate a compatible configuration file as **/etc/nfs/conf.d/local.conf**. This may not work. If not, you will have to set options directly in the **/etc/nfs.conf** file.

The following is a listing of the **/etc/nfs.conf** file. Section are encased in brackets.

/etc/nfs.conf

```
#
# This is a general configuration for the
# NFS daemons and tools
#
[general]
pipefs-directory=/run/rpc_pipefs
#
[infsrahead]
```

```
# nfs=15000
# nfs4=15000
#
[exports]
# rootdir=/export
#
[exportfs]
# debug=0
#
[gssd]
# verbosity=0
# rpc-verbosity=0
# use-memcache=0
# use-machine-creds=1
# use-gss-proxy=0
# avoid-dns=1
# limit-to-legacy-enctypes=0
# context-timeout=0
# rpc-timeout=5
# keytab-file=/etc/krb5.keytab
# cred-cache-directory=
# preferred-realm=
# set-home=1
# upcall-timeout=30
# cancel-timed-out-upcalls=0
#
[lockd]
# port=0
# udp-port=0
#
[exported]
# debug="all|auth|call|general|parse"
# manage-gds=n
# state-directory-path=/var/lib/nfs
# threads=1
# cache-use-lpaddr=n
# ttl=1800
#
[mountd]
# debug="all|auth|call|general|parse"
manage-gids=y
# descriptors=0
# port=0
# threads=1
# reverse-lookup=n
# state-directory-path=/var/lib/nfs
# ha-callout=
# cache-use-lpaddr=n
# ttl=1800
#
[nfsdcld]
# debug=0
# storagedir=/var/lib/nfs/nfsdcld
```

```
#
[nfsdcltrack]
# debug=0
# storagedir=/var/lib/nfs/nfsdcltrack
#
[nfsd]
# debug=0
# threads=8
# host=
# port=0
# grace-time=90
# lease-time=90
# udp=n
# tcp=y
# vers2=n
# vers3=y
# vers4=y
# vers4.0=y
# vers4.1=y
# vers4.2=y
# rdma=n
# rdma-port=20049
#
[statd]
# debug=0
# port=0
# outgoing-port=0
# name=
# state-directory-path=/var/lib/nfs/statd
# ha-callout=
# no-notify=0
#
[sm-notify]
# debug=0
# force=0
# retry-time=900
# outgoing-port=
# outgoing-addr=
# lift-grace=y
#
[svcgssd]
# principal=
```

NFS Configuration: /etc/exports

Exported file systems are listed in the **/etc/exports** file. An entry consists of the pathname of the folder where the file system is located on the host system, followed by the list of hosts that can access it and any control access options. The options for each host are placed within parentheses in a comma-separated list. The options may be different for certain hosts. Some may have read-only access and others read and write access. If you want to specify options that can be applied to all hosts, you use an asterisk (*****) in place of a host name, followed by the options lists. A list of options is provided in Table 11-1. The syntax of an export entry in the **/etc/exports** file follows.

```
folder-pathname    host-designation(options)
```

General Option	Description
secure	Requires that requests originate on secure ports, those less than 1024 This is on by default
insecure	Turns off the **secure** option
ro	Allows only read-only access. This is the default
rw	Allows read/write access
sync	Performs all writes when requested. This is the default
async	Performs all writes when the server is ready
no_wdelay	Performs writes immediately, not checking to see if they are related
wdelay	Checks to see if writes are related, and if so, waits to perform them together. Can degrade performance. This is the default.
hide	Automatically hides an exported directory that is the subdirectory of another exported directory
subtree_check	Checks parent directories in a file system to validate an exported subdirectory. This is the default.
no_subtree_check	Does not check parent directories in a file system to validate an exported subdirectory
insecure_locks	Does not require authentication of locking requests. Used for older NFS versions
User ID Mapping	**Description**
all_squash	Maps all UIDs and GIDs to the anonymous user. Useful for NFS-exported public FTP directories, news spool directories, and so forth
no_all_squash	The opposite option to **all_squash**. This is the default setting.
root_squash	Maps requests from remote root user to the anonymous UID/GID. This is the default.
no_root_squash	Turns off root squashing. Allows the root user to access as the remote root
anonuid	Sets explicitly the UID and GID of the anonymous account used for **all_squash** and **root_squash** options. The defaults are nobody and nogroup

Table 11-1: The /etc/exports Options

NFS Host Entries

The same folder can have several host entries, each with different access options.

```
folder-pathname    host(options) host(options)  host(options)
```

There are various ways to designate a host. For those hosts located within your domain, you just have to specify the hostname. Hosts in other domains require a fully qualified domain name. Instead of a hostname, you can use the host's IP address. To reference multiple hosts at once, such as those in a certain domain, you can use the asterisk, *****, followed by the domain name. For example, ***.mytrek.com** references all the hosts in the **mytrek.com** domain. Should you want to use IP addresses instead of domain names, you would use the IP network addresses. The network address uses a netmask to reference a range of IP addresses. Alternatively, you could use an NIS netgroup name for a designated group of hosts. NIS netgroup names are preceded by an **@** sign.

```
folder       host(options)
folder       *(options)
folder       *.domain(options)
folder       192.168.1.0/255.255.255.0(options)
folder       @netgroup(options)
```

NFS Options

Several NFS options in **/etc/exports** let you control access to exported folders. The **ro** option provides read-only access, and the **rw** option specifies read/write access, allowing changes. Write tasks can be performed at once (the **sync** option), or when the server decides (the **async** option). For better efficiency, by default, related write requests are written at the same time (**wdelay**). This can cause a delay which can degrade performance. Should you wish, you can use the **no_wdelay** to have writes executed immediately instead. If a folder you have exported, is actually a subfolder of another exported folder, then that subfolder is not accessible unless it is mounted. This feature is implemented with the **hide** option, the default. The subfolder is, in a sense, hidden until it is explicitly mounted. The **no_hide** option will override this feature, allow a folder to be accessed if its parent is mounted, even though the folder is exported and has not been mounted.

The **subtree_check** option checks the validity of the parent folders of an exported folder. Though this check works with read-only file systems, problems can occur with read/write file systems, where filenames and folder may be changed at any time. The **no_subtree_check** option lets you override this check.

NFS User-Level Access

Several NFS options and features apply to user-level access. As a matter of security, the NFS server treats an NFS client's root user as an anonymous user, a procedure known as squashing the user. This squashing will not allow the client to appear as the NFS server's root user. The **no_root_squash** option lets you override this squashing, allowing a particular client's root user to have root-level control over the NFS server.

Squashing can also be applied to all users. The **all_squash** option treats all NFS users as anonymous users, restricting them to the anonymous group. This will prevent a client user from attempting to appear as a user on the NFS server.

A user can only mount and access folders on the NFS server if that user has a corresponding account on the NFS server with the same user ID. If the user IDs are different, they are considered to be two different users.

NFSv4

NFS version 4 is the latest version of the NFS protocol with enhanced features, such as better security, speed, and reliability. Only a few of the commands are different. When you mount an NFSv4 file system, you have to use the **nfs4** file type, not **nfs**.

```
mount -t nfs4  rabbit.mytrek.com:/  /home/dylan/projects
```

You can also use the **fsid=0** option to reference the root export location. The following entry would let you mount a file system to the **/home/richlp** folder without having to specify it in the mount operation.

```
/home/richlp          *(fsid=0,ro,sync)
```

NFSv4 also supports the RPCSEC_GSS (Remote Procedure Call Security, Generic Security Services) security mechanism which provides for private/public keys, encryption, and authentication with support for Kerberos. Kerberos comes in two flavors: **krb5i** which validates the integrity of the data, and **krb5p** which encrypts all requests but involves a performance cost. Samples for using the GSS and Kerberos security are listed as comments in the **/etc/exports** file. Instead of specifying a remote location, the rpcsec_gss protocol (**gss**) is used with **krb5i** security, **gss/krb5i**. The directory mounted in the sample is the **/srv/nfs4/homes** directory.

```
# /srv/nfs4/homes  gss/krb5i(rw,sync,no_subtree_check)
```

NFS File and Directory Security with NFS4 Access Lists

NFS4 allows you to set up access control lists (ACL) for folders and files. Use the NFS4 ACL tools to manage these lists (**nfs4-acl-tools** package). The NFS4 file system ACL tools include **nfs4_getfacl**, **nfs4_setfacl**, and **nfs4_editfacl**. Check the Man page for each for detailed options and examples. **nfs4_getfacl** will list the access controls for a specified file or directory. **nfs4_setfacl** will create access controls for a directory or file, and **nfs4_editfacl** will let you change them. **nfs4_editfacl** simply invokes **nfs_setfacl** with the **-e** option. When editing access controls, you are placed in an editor where you can make your changes. For setting access controls, you can read from a file, the standard input, or list the control entries on the command line.

The format for ACL entries is described on the **nfs4_acl** Man page. The first element in an ACL entry is the entry type such as an accept or deny entry (**A** or **D**). The entry type is followed by an ACL flag to denote group or inheritance capability. After the flag is the principal to which the ACL is applied. This is usually the URL of a user that is to be permitted or denied access. You could also specify groups, but you would have to include the **g** group flag. There are special URLs (OWNER@, GROUP@, and EVERYONE@) that correspond to the owner, group, and other access used for standard permissions. After the principal there follows the list of access options, such as **r** for read or **w** for write. The read, write, and execute permissions are **r,w,x**. The following example provides full access to the owner but gives only read and execute access to the user **mark@mypics.com**. Group write and execute access is denied.

```
A::OWNER@:rwadtTnNcCy
A::mark@mypics.com:rxtncy
D:g:GROUP@:waxtc
```

ACL permissions can be further refined by attributes. There are attribute reads (**t,n**) and attribute writes (**T,N**), as well as ACL read (**c**) and write (**C**) access. The **y** option enables NFS read and write synchronization. The **d** option lets you to delete files and directories, and the **D** option allows deleting of subdirectories. With the **a** option you can append data and create subdirectories. The **rtncy** options are the read options and **wadDTNC** are the write options, whereas **x** is the execute option. The **y** option is required for synchronized access. The **C** option allows a user to change the access controls. The lowercase **c** lets users display the access controls.

NFS /etc/exports Example

The following example of the **/etc/exports** file shows samples of file system exports. In the first entry, all hosts have read-only access to the file system mounted at the **/srv/pub** folder. The **/srv** folder is normally used for the folders maintained by different servers. The **all_squash** option treats users as anonymous. The next entry provides read and write access to the **lizard.mytrek.com** host for the file system mounted at the **/home/mypics** folder. The following entry lets the **rabbit.mytrek.com** host to have read-only access to the NFS server's DVD-ROM. With the last entry users have secure access to the **/home/richlp** folder.

/etc/exports

```
/srv/pub           *(ro,insecure,all_squash,sync)
/home/mypics       lizard.mytrek.com(rw,sync)
/media/dvdrom      rabbit.mytrek.com(ro,sync)
/home/richlp       *(secure,sync)
```

The default **/etc/options** file shows examples for using NFSv2, NFSv3, and NFSv4 formats.

/etc/exports

```
# /etc/exports: the access control list for filesystems which may be exported
#               to NFS clients.  See exports(5).
#
# Example for NFSv2 and NFSv3:
# /srv/homes     hostname1(rw,sync,no_subtree_check)   hostname2(ro,sync,no_subtree_check)
#
# Example for NFSv4:
# /srv/nfs4       gss/krb5i(rw,sync,fsid=0,crossmnt,no_subtree_check)
# /srv/nfs4/homes gss/krb5i(rw,sync,no_subtree_check)
#
```

Applying Changes

Whenever the NFS server is started, the file systems listed in the **/etc/exports** file are exported. The export process involves reading the entries in the **/etc/exports** file and creating corresponding entries in the **/var/lib/nfs/xtab** file. NFS reads the **/var/lib/nfs/xtab** file uses it to perform the actual exports. In this sense, the **xtab** file holds the list of active exports.

Should you add entries to the **/etc/exports** file, and then want to export them without rebooting your system, you would use the **exportfs** command with the **-a** option. The added entries are exported. Adding the **-v** option displays messages showing the tasks NFS is performing.

```
exportfs -a -v
```

Should you edit the **/etc/exports** file, making changes to the entries, you can use the **-r** option to re-export those entries. The **-r** option will re-sync the **/var/lib/nfs/xtab** file with the **/etc/exports** entries, removing any missing exports in the **/etc/exports** file and re-exporting those with different options. In effect, you are applying any changes you made to the **/etc/exports** file.

```
exportfs -r -v
```

If you both add entries and also change current ones, you can combine the added and re-export options (**-r** and **-a**) to export the added entries and re-export edited ones, as well as removing deleted entries.

```
exportfs -r -a -v
```

Manually Exporting File Systems

Instead of using entries in the **/etc/exports** file, you can use the **exportfs** command on a shell command line to export file systems. The exported filesystems are added to the **/var/lib/nfs/xtab** file. When using the **exportfs** command, use the **-o** option to specify permissions. After the options, enter the host and file system to export. Be sure to separate the host and file system names with a colon. For example, to export the **/home/myprojects** directory to **golf.mytrek.com** with the permissions **ro** and **insecure**, you use the following:

```
exportfs -o rw,insecure golf.mytrek.com:/home/myprojects
```

You can also use **exportfs** with the **-u** option to un-export an exported filesystem. This operation removes the exported filesystem's entry from the **/var/lib/nfs/xtab** file. The next example performs an un-export operation on the **/home/foodstuff** folder.

```
exportfs -u lizard.mytrek.com:/home/foodstuff
```

Controlling Accessing to NFS Servers

You can control access on your local network to the NFS server using the **hosts.allow** and **hosts.deny** files. You can also use firewall rules to control access from external hosts, those outside your local network.

/etc/hosts.allow and /etc/hosts.deny

The **/etc/hosts.allow** and **/etc/hosts.deny** files are used to restrict access to services provided by your server to hosts on your network or on the Internet (if accessible). For example, you can use the **hosts.allow** file to permit access by certain hosts to your FTP server. Entries in the **hosts.deny** file explicitly denies access to certain hosts. For NFS, you can provide the same kind of security by controlling access to specific NFS daemons.

rpcbind Service

The rpcbind service informs hosts where the NFS services are located on your system. The name used to reference rpcbind is **rpcbind**. The rpcbind configuration file is **/etc/default/rpcbind**. Here you can set options for the rpcbind service.

By denying access to it, a remote host cannot locate NFS. To secure NFS, you would deny access to all hosts and then make exceptions for those you want to allow. In the **hosts.deny** file, the following entry will deny access to all hosts. The rpcbind service is referenced with the name **rpcbind**. ALL is a special term referencing all hosts.

```
rpcbind:ALL
```

For those hosts you want to allow access to NFS, you would place their names in the **hosts.allow** file. Each entry would have the term rpcbind followed by a colon, and then a list of IP addresses of allowed hosts, separated by commas. The addresses can be single addresses or a range of addresses specified with a netmask. The next example permits access only by the hosts in the local network, 192.168.0.0 (indicated using a range), and to the single host 10.0.0.43.

```
rpcbind: 192.168.0.0/255.255.255.0, 10.0.0.43
```

Keep in mind, though, that **rpcbind** is also used by other services such as NIS. Should you close all access to the rpcbind in **hosts.deny**, you will have to allow access to NIS services, such as ypbind and ypderser, in **hosts.allow**. Also, should you want to allow access to remote commands such as **ruptime** and **rusers**, you will have to add entries for them.

You should also add the same controls for the other NFS services, such as **mountd** and **statd**, as shown here for the **hosts.deny** file.

```
mountd:ALL
statd:ALL
```

Corresponding entries for them in the **hosts.allow** file, allows access to certain hosts.

```
mountd:  192.168.0.0/255.255.255.0, 10.0.0.43
statd:   192.168.0.0/255.255.255.0, 10.0.0.43
```

Netfilter Rules

With Netfilter, you can control access to NFS services from hosts outside your local network, usually Internet access. The **rpcbind** service uses port 111, and **nfsd** uses 2049. Should you want to deny access to NFS from networks outside your local network, you can set up Netfilter rules to deny that access. In the next examples, access is denied to ports 111 and 2049 for transmissions on the eth1 network device. Internet packets attempting access on port 111 or 2049 are rejected. In these examples, the eth1 device connects to outside networks.

iptables rules:

```
iptables -A INPUT -p tcp -i eth1 --dport 111 -j DENY
iptables -A INPUT -p tcp -i eth1 --dport 2049 -j DENY
```

nftables rules:

```
nft add rule ip filter INPUT iifname "eth1" tcp dport 111 counter jump DENY
nft add rule ip filter INPUT iifname "eth1" tcp dport 2049 counter jump DENY
```

For NFS to work on your local network, you will have to allow packet fragments with the **-f** option. With **eth0** as the device used for the local network, the next example enables packet fragments locally.

iptables rules:

```
iptables -A INPUT -p tcp -i eth0 -f -j ACCEPT
```

nftables rules:

```
nft add rule ip filter INPUT iifname "eth0" ip frag-off & 0x1fff != 0 ip protocol
tcp counter accept
```

Mounting NFS File Systems: NFS Clients

Hosts can mount and access folders that NFS has made available. The hosts, of course, have to be functioning as NFS clients. NFS client capability is built in to the Linux kernel. Any Linux host can mount a remote NFS folder with a mount operation.

Mounting NFS Automatically: /etc/fstab

NFS folders can be mounted by an entry in the **/etc/fstab** file, as well as by a **mount** command. In effect, an entry for the NFS mount operation in the **/etc/fstab** file will mount the NFS file systems automatically at startup. The mount type for an NFS entry in the **/etc/fstab** file is **nfs**. To reference an NFS file system in a mount operation, you need to provide both the folder name and the hostname of the remote host where it is located. The folder and hostname are separated by a colon. For example, **rabbit.trek.com:/home/project** references a file system mounted at **/home/project** on the **rabbit.trek.com** host. The mount operation also requires the pathname of the folder where it is to be mounted on your system. The format for an NFS entry in the **/etc/fstab** file is shown below. The file type for NFS versions 1 through 3 is **nfs**, whereas for NFS version 4 it is **nfs4**.

```
host:remote-directory    local-directory      nfs    options   0   0
```

An NFS mount operation, can also include NFS mount options, such as the size of datagrams for reading and writing (**rsize** and **wsize**), and the wait time for responses from remote host (**timeo**). There are also options to let you perform a hard or soft mount (**hard** and **soft**). If a file system is to be hard mounted, should the remote host fail to respond, your system will repeatedly try to make contact. A hard mount is the default. If a file system is to be soft-mounted, then, if the remote host fails to respond, repeated attempts will stop after a specified time limit and an error message displayed. To avoid using system resources for continually failing hard-mount attempts, it may be preferable to use soft mount instead, which will stop such attempts. You can find a list of NFS mount options in the **mount** Man page (see Table 11-2).

In the following NFS mount example, the remote system is **rabbit.mytrek.com**, and the file system to be mounted is **/home/projects**. It will be mounted on the local system as the **/home/dylan/projects** folder, which must already exist on the local system. The filesystem type is **nfs** for NFS, and the **timeo** option sets up a wait time of 20 tenths of a second (two seconds) for a response. The **soft** options indicates that this is a soft mount.

```
rabbit.mytrek.com:/home/projects /home/dylan/myprojects  nfs   soft,intr,timeo=20
```

Mounting NFS Manually: mount

With the **mount** command and the **-t nfs** option you can mount an NFS file system manually. Use **-t nfs4** option for an NFSv4 file system. The next command mounts the previous example manually.

```
mount -t nfs -o soft,intr,timeo=20  rabbit.mytrek.com:/home/projects  /home/dylan/myprojects
```

Use the **umount** command to unmount an NFS folder. The mountpoint can be either a local folder or one on a remote host as shown the in the next example.

```
umount  /home/dylan/projects
umount  rabbit.mytrek.com:/home/projectsMounting
```

Option	Description
`rsize=n`	The number of bytes NFS uses when reading files from an NFS server. The default is 1,024 bytes. A size of 8,192 can greatly improve performance.
`wsize=n`	The number of bytes NFS uses when writing files to an NFS server. The default is 1,024 bytes. A size of 8,192 can greatly improve performance.
`timeo=n`	The value in tenths of a second before sending the first retransmission after a timeout. The default value is seven-tenths of a second.
`retry=n`	The number of minutes to retry an NFS mount operation before giving up. The default is 10,000 minutes (one week).
`retrans=n`	The number of retransmissions or minor timeouts for an NFS mount operation before a major timeout (default is 3). At that time, the connection is canceled or a "server not responding" message is displayed.
`soft`	Mount system using soft mount.
`hard`	Mount system using hard mount. This is the default.
`intr`	Allows NFS to interrupt the file operation and return to the calling program. The default is not to allow file operations to be interrupted.
`bg`	If the first mount attempt times out, continues trying the mount in the background. The default is to fail without backgrounding.
`tcp`	Mounts the NFS file system using the TCP protocol, instead of the default UDP protocol.

Table 11-2: NFS Mount Options

NFS on Demand: autofs

NFS file systems can be mounted automatically with the automount service, autofs (**autofs** package). With the autofs service active, a file system is mounted when it is accessed. For example, a directory change command (**cd**) to a folder configured to autofs mounting, will mount that remote folder.

The autofs configuration uses a primary file to reference map files, which designate the file systems to be automatically mounted. The autofs primary file is **/etc/auto.primary** file. In the primary file you will find a list of the full pathnames of folders to be mounted and their corresponding map files. A map file holds a key (the folder's name), mount options, and the file systems that can be mounted (its host and pathname). The configuration file for autofs is **/etc/autofs.conf**. Here you can define options such as the primary map file and the default timeout.

```
primary_map_name = /etc/auto.primary
```

The **/misc** folder is already configured as the pathname for automatically mounted file systems. You can then add file systems in the **/etc/auto.primary** file, including their corresponding map files. In the **/etc/auto.primary** file, you will find an entry for the **/misc** directory, showing **auto.misc** as its map file.

```
/misc     /etc/auto.misc
```

A map file entry in the primary file can also have options for mounting the folder, such as the **timeout** option, which set up a waiting period of inactivity before performing an automatic unmount.

A map file holds the key, mount options, and the full pathname and host of the file system to be mounted. The key is the folder name of the folder on the local system where the file system is mounted. For example, to mount the **/home/projects** folder on the **rabbit.mytrek.com** host to the **/auto/projects** folder, use the following entry. The **/etc/auto.misc** file holds samples of map file entries.

```
projects   soft,intr,timeo=20   rabbit.mytrek.com:/home/projects
```

To mount to a folder other than **/misc**, you place an entry for it in the primary file. The next entry mounts to the **/myprojects** folder using the **auto.myprojects** map file.

```
/myprojects    auto.myprojects    --timeout 60
```

The **/etc/auto.myprojects** map file would then have entries for NFS files system mounts, as shown here.

```
dylan     soft,intr,rw   rabbit.mytrek.com:/home/projects
newgame   soft,intr,ro   lizard.mytrek.com:/home/supergame
```

/etc/nsswitch.conf: Name Service Switch

Different functions in the standard C Library must be configured to operate on your Linux system. Previously, database-like services, such as password support and name services like NIS or DNS, directly accessed these functions, using a fixed search order. This configuration is carried out by a scheme called the Name Service Switch (NSS), which is based on the method of the same name used by Sun Microsystems Solaris 2 OS. The database sources and their lookup order are listed in the **/etc/nsswitch.conf** file.

The **/etc/nsswitch.conf** file holds entries for the different configuration files that can be controlled by NSS. The system configuration files that NSS supports are listed in Table 11-3. An entry consists of two fields: the service and the configuration specification. The service consists of the configuration file followed by a colon. The second field is the configuration specification for that file, which holds instructions on how the lookup procedure will work. The configuration specification can contain service specifications and action items. Service specifications are the services to search. Currently, valid service specifications are nis, nis-plus, files, db, dns, systemd, and compat (see Table 11-4). Not all are valid for each configuration file. For example, the dns service is valid only for the **hosts** file, whereas nis is valid for all files. The following example will first check the local **/etc/password** file and then systemd.

```
passwd:  files systemd
```

For more refined access to passwd, group, and shadow sources, you can use the + and - symbols in file entries to determine if the entry can be accessed by the nsswitch service. The **compat** service provides a compatible mode that will check for such entries. With no such entries, the nis service will be used for all entries. The **compat** service can only be applied to the passwd, group, and shadow databases. This provides the equivalent of the files and nis services.

File	Description
ethers	Ethernet numbers
group	Groups of users
hosts	Hostnames and numbers
netgroup	Network-wide list of hosts and users, used for access rules; C libraries before glibc 2.1 only support netgroups over NIS
network	Network names and numbers
passwd	User passwords
protocols	Network protocols
publickey	Public and secret keys for SecureRPC used by NFS and NIS+
rpc	Remote procedure call names and numbers
services	Network services
shadow	Shadow user passwords

Table 11-3: NSS-Supported databases

Service	Description
files	Checks corresponding **/etc** file for the configuration (for example, **/etc/hosts** for hosts); this service is valid for all files
db	Checks corresponding **/var/db** databases for the configuration; valid for all files except **netgroup**
compat	Provides **nis** and **files** services, with compatibility support for + and - entries. Valid only for **passwd**, **group**, and **shadow** files
dns	Checks the DNS service; valid only for **hosts** file
nis	Checks the NIS service; valid for all files
nisplus	NIS version 3
hesiod	Uses Hesiod for lookup

Table 11-4: NSS Configuration Services

If your passwd, group, and shadow files already have + and - entries, and you need to have the file entries take precedence over the nis service, you can specify the files database before the compat entry.

```
passwd:  files compat
```

An action item specifies the action to take for a specific service. An action item is placed within brackets after a service. A configuration specification can list several services, each with its own action item. In the following example, the entry for the **hosts** file has a configuration specification that says to check the **/etc/hosts** files and **mdns4_minimal** service and, if not found, to check the DNS server and the **mdns4** service (multicast DNS name resolution).

```
hosts: files mdns4_minimal [NOTFOUND=return] dns mdns4
```

An action item consists of a status and an action. The status holds a possible result of a service lookup, and the action is the action to take if the status is true. Currently, the possible status values are SUCCESS, NOTFOUND, UNAVAIL, and TRYAGAIN (service temporarily unavailable). The possible actions are return and continue. return stops the lookup process for the configuration file, whereas continue continues on to the next listed service. In the preceding example, if the record is not found in NIS, the lookup process ends.

Shown here is a copy of the **/etc/nsswitch.conf** file, which lists commonly used entries. Comments and commented-out entries begin with a # sign:

/etc/nsswitch.conf

```
# /etc/nsswitch.conf
#
# Example configuration of GNU Name Service Switch functionality.
# If you have the `glibc-doc-reference' and `info' packages installed, try:
# `info libc "Name Service Switch"' for information about this file.

passwd:         files  systemd
group:          files  systemd
shadow:         files  systemd
gshadow:        files  systemd

hosts:          files mdns4_minimal [NOTFOUND=return] dns
networks:       files

protocols:      db files
services:       db files
ethers:         db files
rpc:            db files

netgroup:       nis
```

Distributed Network File Systems

For very large distributed systems like Linux clusters, Linux also supports distributed network file systems, such as the Oracle Cluster File System for Linux (OCFS2), Lustre, the Gluster Storage Platform (GlusterFS), and the Red Hat Global File System (GFS and GFS 2). These systems build on the basic concept of NFS as well as RAID techniques to create a file system implemented on multiple hosts across a large network, in effect, distributing the same file system among different hosts at a low level (see Table 11-5). You can think of it as a kind of RAID array implemented across network hosts instead of just a single system. Instead of each host relying on its own file systems on its own hard drive, they all share the same distributed file system that uses hard drives collected on different distributed servers. This provides far more efficient use of storage available to the hosts, as well as providing for more centralized management of file system use.

GFS can be run either directly connected to a SAN (storage area network) or using GNBD (Global Network Block Device) storage connected over a LAN. The best performance is obtained from a SAN connection, whereas a GNBD format can be implemented easily using the storage on

LAN (Ethernet) connected systems. As with RAID devices, mirroring, failover, and redundancy can help protect and recover data.

High Availability clusters are groups of systems that use clustering to support servers, insuring that they do not go down. If one or more systems fail, the others continue with the same level of support. On Ubuntu, Hight Availability clusters relies on the Kronosnet network protocol (also known as **knet**), which is used by Corosync to manage High Availability clusters.

Website	Name
https://ubuntu.com/server/docs/ubuntu-ha-introduction	Ubuntu Server Guide - High Availability Clusters
https://fedoraproject.org/wiki/Features/Cluster	Fedora Cluster status and links
https://corosync.github.io/corosync/	Corosync Cluster Engine
https://wiki.clusterlabs.org/wiki/Pacemaker	Pacemaker cluster services and PCS documentation
https://oss.oracle.com/projects/ocfs2/	OCFS2, Oracle Cluster File System for Linux
https://access.redhat.com/documentation/en-us/red_hat_enterprise_linux/7/html/high_availability_add-on_overview/index	Red Hat High Availability Addon
https://www.gluster.org	Gluster Storage Platform
http://wiki.lustre.org	Lustre cluster file system
https://kronosnet.org/	Kronosnet (knet) High Availability clustering protocol

Table 11-5: Distributed File Systems

For more information on clusters as implemented on Ubuntu, check the Ubuntu Server Guide | Ubuntu High Availability:

```
https://ubuntu.com/server/docs/ubuntu-ha-introduction
```

Ubuntu also make available the HAProxy load balancer and reverse proxy for high availability systems. Install the **haproxy** package. A reverse proxy provides resources on your system or local network to your servers, instead of each server having to manage resources directly.

Note: OrangeFS is the current implementation of the Parallel Virtual File System (PVFS), which implements a distributed network file system using a management server that manages the files system on different I/O servers, **http://www.orangefs.org**. You can install it with the **orangefs** packages.

The OCFS2 cluster file system is provided by Oracle as open source software. You can install it with the **ocfs2-tools** and **ocfs2-tools-dev** packages. You can find out more about OCFS2 at **https://oss.oracle.com/projects/ocfs2/**.

Corosync Cluster Engine

The Corosync Cluster Engine is a "user space kernel" for clustering services. It provides the basis of communication, membership, and other services used in clustering environments. This is an open source Linux project. Corosync uses the Kronosnet protocol to manage High Availability clusters. Ubuntu provides Ubuntu compliant binaries in the **corosync** and **corosynclib** packages. Corosync packages include **corosync**. Corosync is managed by systemd using the **corosync.service** unit file, which starts the Corosync service for the multi-user.target using the **corosync** script located at **/usr/share/corosync**. You can use the **systemctl** command to start and stop corosync. Derived from the OpenAIS project, Corosync provides the underlying cluster infrastructure. You can find out more about Corosync at:

```
https://corosync.github.io/corosync/
```

Corosync is a plug-in cluster engine with a modular design. Modules, known as service engines, are plugged in to the Corosync engine to make use of Corosync cluster services. Corosync components include the Totem communications protocol, which is based on the OpenAIS virtual synchrony communications model, a live component replacement (LCR) plugin system, an object database for the service engines and their configuration, a logging system, and a inter-process communications (IPC) manager. Service engine modules include configuration for LDAP and corosync/openeais file format, the cluster manager (**pacemaker**) operates as part of corosync, both fence and fence agents.

Corosync manages the validity of a cluster through a quorum system the detects if more than half of the cluster nodes are active and can communicate with each other. The quorum process is managed with the Corosync quorum daemon (**corosync-qdevice** and **corosync-qnetd** packages).

Corosync is configured by the **/etc/corosync.conf** configuration file. Currently, there are four directives, forming blocks, within which options can be specified. They are the same as those used for OpenAIS. The four directives are totem for the Totem protocol, logging, amf for the AMF service, and event for the event service. See the **corosync.conf** man page for a complete description of directives and options.

Corosync uses its own protocol called Totem to perform multicast communications. Totem configuration is specified in the **totem** directive of the **corosync.conf** file as shown here.

```
totem {
    version: 2
    secauth: off
    threads: 0
    interface {
        ringnumber: 0
        bindnetaddr: 192.168.1.1
        mcastaddr: 226.94.1.1
        mcastport: 5405
    }
}
```

Pacemaker

To manage your clusters you use a cluster manager. The recommended one for Ubuntu is the Pacemaker Cluster Resource Manager (**pacemaker** and **pcs** packages). The older **cman** cluster manager has been deprecated. The pacemaker package installs the pacemaker service. The **pcs** package installs the pacemaker configuration service. Pacemaker can work with Redhat's GFS2, Oracle's OCFS2, and with Cluster LVM (CLVM2). On Ubuntu you would normally use GFS2. Pacemaker is managed by **systemd** using the **pacemaker.service** unit file.

Once installed, you can use the Pacemaker Configuration Service (**pcs**) to manage your clusters. The **pcs** daemon is managed by **systemd** using the **pcsd.service** unit file. You can use **pcs** commands to setup and manage your clusters. Check the Pacemaker website for detailed documentation on Pacemaker and Corosync for PCS.

```
https://wiki.clusterlabs.org/wiki/Pacemaker
```

Red Hat Global File System (GFS)

The Red Hat Global File System (GFS2) is the preferred distributed file system for Ubuntu. GFS separates the physical implementation from the logical format. A GFS appears as a set of logical volumes on one seamless logical device that can be mounted easily to any directory on your Linux file system. The logical volumes are created and managed by the Cluster Logical Volume Manager (CLVM), which is a cluster-enabled LVM. Physically, the file system is constructed from different storage resources, known as cluster nodes, distributed across your network. The administrator manages these nodes, providing needed mirroring or storage expansion. Should a node fail, GFS can fence a system off until it has recovered the node. Setting up a GFS requires planning. You have to determine ahead of time different settings like the number and names of your Global File Systems, the nodes that will be able to mount the file systems, fencing methods, and the partitions and disks to use.

The Red Hat Global File System (GFS2), the Gluster Storage Platform (GlusterFS), and the Oracle Cluster File System for Linux (OCFS2) are available from the Ubuntu repository. GlusterFS is open source and freely available, though support can be purchased commercially. On Ubuntu it is installed with the **glusterfs-server**, **glusterfs-common**, and **glusterfs-client** packages. See the GlusterFS site for more details, **https://www.gluster.org**. Configuration is located at **/etc/glusterfs**. Detailed examples are located in the **/usr/share/doc/glusterfs-server** directory.

Red Hat provides the Global File System (GFS) as an open source freely available distributed network file system. The original GFS version has been replaced with the new version of GFS, GFS 2, which uses a similar set of configuration and management tools, as well as native kernel support. Instead of a variety of seemingly unrelated packages, native kernel support for GFS 2 provides much of the kernel-level operations. GFS 2 now works through the Corosync Cluster Engine. You would use Corosync cluster commands for your cluster. GFS2 tools have been placed in the **gfs2-utils**, package, and the Distributed Lock Manager (DLM) commands in the **dlm** package.

Many former cluster packages and applications have been deprecated with Ubuntu, including cman, rgmanager, openais, heartbeat, luci, and system-config-cluster. Though lower level GFS commands are available in the **gfs2-utils** package, you are expected to use Corosync and Pacemaker commands to manage your clusters.

To run a cluster, you need both a cluster manager and locking mechanism. Pacemaker with the Distributed Lock Manager (**dlm**) implements cluster management and locking. Pacemaker manages connections between cluster devices and services, using **dlm** to provide locking. The **dlm** locking mechanism operates as a daemon with supporting libraries.

To set up a GFS 2 file system, you first need to create cluster devices using the physical volumes and organizing them into logical volumes. You use the CLVM (Clustering Logical Volume Manager) to set up logical volumes from physical partitions (in the past you used a volume manager called pool to do this). You can then install GFS file systems on these logical volumes directly. CLVM operates like LVM, using the same commands. It works over a distributed network and requires that the **clvmd** server be running (**clvm** package).

Several GFS commands manage the file system, such as **mkfs.gfs2** to make a GFS file system, **fsck.gfs2** to check and repair, and **gfs2_grow** to expand a file system. Check their respective Man pages for detailed descriptions. The GFS commands for managing GFS file systems are listed in Table 11-6.

Command	Description
dlm_tool	Distributed Lock Manager, implemented as a kernel module.
fsck.gfs2	The GFS 2 file system checker
gfs2_grow	Grows a GFS 2 file system
gfs2_jadd	Adds a journal to a GFS 2 file system
mkfs.gfs2	Makes a GFS 2 file system
gfs2_convert	Convert GFS 1 filesystem to GFS 2
gfs2_edit	Edit a GFS 2 file system
getfacl	Gets the ACL permissions for a file or directory
setfacl	Sets access control (ACL) for a file or directory

Table 11-6: GFS2 Tools

To mount a GFS file system, you use the **mount** command specifying **gfs2** as the mount type, as in

```
mount -t gfs2 /dev/vg0/mgfs /mygfs
```

This will invoke the **mkfs.gfs2** tool to perform the mount operation. Several GFS-specific mount options are also available, specified with the **-o** option, such as **lockproto** to specify a different lock protocol and **acl** to enable ACL support.

To check the status of a file system, you can use **fsck.gfs2**. This tool operates much like fsck, checking for corrupt systems and attempting repairs. You must first unmount the file system before you can use **fsck.gfs2** on it.

Should you add available space to the device on which a GFS file system resides, you can use **gfs2_grow** to expand the file system to that available space. It can be run on just one node to expand the entire cluster. If you want journaling, you first have to add journal files with the **gfs2_jadd** tool. **gfs2_grow** can only be run on a mounted GFS file system.

Journal files for GFS are installed in space outside of the GFS file system but on the same device. After creating a GFS file system, you can run **gfs2_jadd** to add the journal files for it. If you are expanding a current GFS file system, you need to run **gfs2_jadd** first. Like **gfs2_grow**, **gfs2_jadd** can only be run on mounted file systems. With the **setfacl** command you can set permissions for files and directories.To create new file systems on the cluster devices, you use the

mkfs.gfs2 command and mount them with the **-t gfs2** option. The following command creates a GFS file system on the **/dev/gv0/mgfs** and then mounts it to the **/mygfs** directory. For **mkfs.gfs2**, the **-t** option indicates the lock table used and the **-p** option specifies the lock protocol. The **-j** option specifies the number of journals, and the **-p** option specifies the lock protocol to use.

```
mkfs.gfs2 -t mycluster:mygfs -p lock_dlm -j 2 /dev/vg0/mgfs
mount -t gfs /dev/vg0/mgfs /gfs1
```

To have the **gfs** service script mount the GFS file system for you, you need to place an entry for it in the **/etc/fstab** file. If you do not want the file system automatically mounted, add the **noauto** option.

```
/dev/vg0/mgfs   /mygfs   gfs2   noauto,defaults   0   0
```

GFS also supports access controls. You can restrict access by users or groups to certain files or directories, specifying read or write permissions. With the **setfacl** command, you can set permissions for files and directories. You use the **-m** option to modify an ACL permission and **-x** to delete it. The **getfacl** obtains the current permissions for file or directory. The following sets read access by the user **dylan** to **myfile**.

```
setfacl -m u:dylan:r myfile
```

ubuntu

12. Samba

The Linux Samba server lets your Windows clients on a Microsoft Windows network to access shared files and printers on your Linux system, and also allows Linux systems to access shared files and printers on Windows systems. It allows you to connect to Windows systems over a Windows network. In effect, Samba allows a Linux system to operate as if it were a Windows server, using the same protocols as used in a Windows network.

UNIX and Linux systems use the TCP/IP protocol for networking, whereas Microsoft Windows networking uses the Server Message Block (SMB) protocol. The SMB protocol makes use of a network interface called Network Basic Input Output System (NetBIOS) that allows Windows systems to share resources, such as printers and folders. SMB was originally designed for small networks. For large networks, Microsoft developed the Common Internet File System (CIFS), which still uses SMB and NetBIOS for Windows networking.

The Samba server and client was created by Andrew Tridgell in an effort to connect a Linux system to a Windows PC. They allow UNIX and Linux systems to connect to a Windows network seamlessly. UNIX/Linux systems can share resources on Windows systems, and Windows systems can share resources on Unix/Linux systems. In a sense, Samba is a professional-level, open source, and free version of CIFS. With Samba you can mount shared Windows folders directly to your Linux system, using the Linux **cifs** file system.

Package name	Description
samba	The Samba server
samba-common	Samba Ubuntu configuration files and support tools
smbclient	Samba clients for accessing Windows shares
kdenetwork-filesharing	Samba sharing configuration on KDE
nautilus-share	Quick sharing configuration using the GNOME Nautilus file manager

Table 12-1: Samba packages on Ubuntu

You can obtain extensive documentation from the Samba Web and FTP sites at **https://www.samba.org/**. Examples are provided on your system in the **/usr/share/doc/samba/examples** directory.

On Ubuntu, Samba software is organized into several packages (see Table 12-1). By selecting the **samba** server package, necessary supporting packages such as **smbclient** and **samba-common** will be automatically selected. Configuration tools have to be selected manually. Samba software packages can be obtained from the Ubuntu repositories using **apt** or the Synaptic Package Manager. Check the Ubuntu Server | Doc | How-to Guides | Samba for basic configuration and management.

```
https://ubuntu.com/server/docs/samba-as-a-file-server
```

Samba Applications

The Samba server provides four services: file and printer services, authentication and authorization, name resolution, and service announcements. Two server daemons (**smbd** and **nmbd**) and several utility programs are installed by the Samba software package (see Table 12-2). The SMB daemon, **smbd**, provides the file and printer services, along with the authentication and authorization for those services. This allows users on the network to share folders and printers.

Access to these services is controlled by user passwords. When users try to access a shared folder, they are prompted for the password. A different password is provided for each user, and Samba maintains a separate Samba password file.

Application	Description
nautilus-share	Basic file sharing configuration built into the GNOME Nautilus file manager.
smbd	Samba server daemon that provides file and printer services to SMB clients.
nmbd	Samba daemon that provides NetBIOS name resolution and service browser support.
winbind	Uses authentication services provided by Windows domain.
mount.cifs	Mounts Samba share directories on Linux clients (used by the `mount` command with the **-t cifs** option).
smbpasswd	Changes SMB-encrypted passwords on Samba servers
pdbedit	Edit the Samba users database file. This is a Secure Accounts Manager (SAM) database.
tdbbackup	Backup the Samba .tdb database files.
smbcontrol	Send the Samba servers administrative messages, like shutdown or close-share.
smbstatus	Displays the current status of the SMB network connections.
testparm	Tests the Samba configuration file, **smb.conf.**
nmblookup	Maps the NetBIOS name of a Windows PC to its IP address.
/etc/default/samba	Samba startup options.

Table 12-2: Samba Server Applications

The **nmbd** server provides Name resolution and service announcements. Name resolution resolves IP addresses with NetBIOS names. Service announcements makes known the available services on a network, enabling browsing.

Basic Samba configuration support is already implemented by **nautilus-share**, letting you use your file manager to browse Samba shares. For a more complex configuration, you can edit the **/etc/samba/smb.conf** file directly. Configuration files are kept in the **/etc/samba** directory.

You can also install the **winbind** package which runs the **winbind** daemon. This daemon allows Samba servers to use authentication services provided by a Windows domain. With **winbind**, a Samba server can make use of a Windows domain authentication service to authenticate users, instead of using its own set of users.

The Samba package also includes support tools such as **smbstatus**, which displays the current status of the SMB server and who is using it, and **pdbedit**, which is used to edit the SMB password database. Additional packages provide support tools, like **smbclient** which lets a Linux system access Samba services (command line only). The **mount.cifs** and **umount.cifs** commands let Linux systems mount and unmount Samba shared folders. They are invoked by the **mount** command with the **-t cifs** option. You use **testparm** to test your Samba configuration. **smbtar** is a shell script that backs up SMB/CIFS-shared resources directly to an archive. The **nmblookup** command will map the NetBIOS name of a Windows PC to its IP address. With the **smbcontrol** command you can send administrative messages to the Samba servers (smbd, nmbd, and winbindd) such as to close shares, reload the configuration, or shutdown the server.

Starting up and accessing Samba

Once installed, Samba is normally configured to start up automatically. You can edit the **/etc/samba/smb.conf** file directly to make changes. If you make changes, you must restart the Samba server for them to take effect. To restart Samba with your new configuration, use the **systemctl** command. The **start**, **stop**, and **restart** options will start, stop, and restart the server. Run the following command from the command line or a terminal window to restart Samba.

```
sudo systemctl restart smbd
sudo systemctl restart nmbd
```

The Samba server consists of two daemons: **smbd** and **nmbd**. After installing the Samba package, you may have to enable and then start the Samba server. Use the **sudo** command for administrative access followed by a **systemctl** command for the **smbd** server with the **enable** command to enable the server. Do the same for the **nmbd** server. Then use **systemctl** command with the **start** command to start them. Once enabled, the server should start automatically whenever your system starts up.

```
sudo systemctl enable nmbd
sudo systemctl enable smbd
sudo systemctl start nmbd
sudo systemctl start smbd
```

Samba is managed by **systemd** using the **smbd.service** and **nmbd.service** unit files in **/lib/systemd/system** directory. The **smbd.service** file is shown here. Samba is started after networking (After). It is dependent on the **multi-user.target** (WantedBy). The service is started using the **smbd** script in the **/usr/sbin** directory (ExecStart).

smbd.service

```
[Unit]
Description=Samba SMB Daemon
Documentation=man:smbd(8) man:samba(7) man:smb.conf(5)
Wants=network-online.target
After=network.target network-online.target nmbd.service winbind.service

[Service]
Type=notify
PIDFile=/var/run/samba/smbd.pid
LimitNOFILE=16384
EnvironmentFile=-/etc/default/samba
ExecStartPre=/usr/share/samba/update-apparmor-samba-profile
ExecStart=/usr/sbin/smbd --foreground --no-process-group $SMBDOPTIONS
ExecReload=/bin/kill -HUP $MAINPID
LimitCORE=infinity
ExecCondition=/usr/share/samba/is-configured smb
```

```
[Install]
WantedBy=multi-user.target
# Upstream name:
Alias=smb.service
```

The NMB daemon is started after networking (After). It starts the **nmbd** server using the **/usr/sbin/nmbd** script.

nmbd.service

```
[Unit]
Description=Samba NMB Daemon
Documentation=man:nmbd(8) man:samba(7) man:smb.conf(5)
After=network-online.target
Wants= network.target network-online.target

[Service]
Type=notify
PIDFile=/var/run/samba/nmbd.pid
EnvironmentFile=-/etc/default/samba
ExecStart=/usr/sbin/nmbd --foreground --no-process-group $NMBDOPTIONS
ExecReload=/bin/kill -HUP $MAINPID
LimitCORE=infinity
ExecCondition=/usr/share/samba/is-configured smb

[Install]
WantedBy=multi-user.target
# Upstream name:
Alias=nmb.service
```

Firewall access

The UFW firewall used on Ubuntu prevents browsing Samba and Windows shares from your Linux desktop. To work around this restriction, you need to make sure your firewall treats Samba as a trusted service. To allow firewall access to the Samba ports you should enable access using a firewall configuration tool like ufw. The Samba ports are 125/TCP, 137/UDP, and 138/UDP. In addition, Samba uses the Microsoft Service Discovery service which uses port 445/TCP.

On the command line interface, using the UFW default firewall, you would use the following **ufw** commands. The UFW firewall maintains its IPtables files in **/etc/ufw**.

```
ufw allow 135/tcp
ufw allow 137:138/udp
ufw allow 445/tcp
```

If you are working from a desktop interface, you can use the Gufw tool to set the Samba ports for the UFW firewall. You will have to add the ports as simple rules (see Chapter 17). If you are using a firewall, be sure that it is configured for access by Samba to allow multicast DNS discovery. For Gufw (Preferences | Firewall Configuration), be sure that the rules are added for Samba. For FirewallD, on firewall-config (Administration | Firewall), be sure that the mdns, samba, and samba-client services are enabled (Zones | Services tab) (see Figure 12-1).

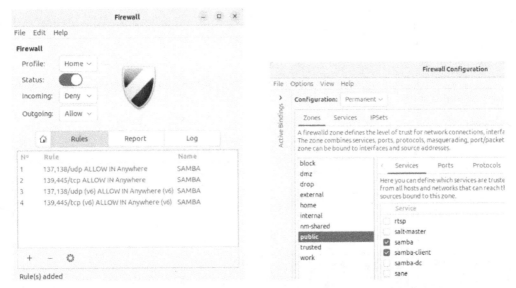

Figure 12-1: Samba Firewall Configuration, Gufw (UFW) and firewall-config (FirewallD)

If you are managing your IPtables or nftables firewall directly, you could manage access by adding the following IPtables or nftables rules. This accepts input on ports 137, 138, and 139 for TCP/IP protocol packages.

iptables rules:

```
iptables -A INPUT -p tcp --dport 139 -j ACCEPT
iptables -A INPUT -p udp --dport 137:138 -j ACCEPT
iptables -A INPUT -p tcp --dport 445 -j ACCEPT
iptables -A INPUT -p udp --dport 5353 -j ACCEPT
```

nftables rules:

```
nft add rule ip filter INPUT tcp dport 139 counter accept
nft add rule ip filter INPUT udp dport 137-138 counter accept
nft add rule ip filter INPUT tcp dport 445 counter accept
nft add rule ip filter INPUT udp dport 5353 counter accept
```

User-Level Security

Security for Samba is based on usernames and passwords, known as user level security. Users on a remote client log in to the Samba server with Samba passwords. The need for Samba passwords came about to accommodate Windows password encryption and login requirements, which are different from that used for Linux. To manage such passwords, Samba has to maintain a separate Windows-compatible password database. It cannot use the Linux password database. For logins, Windows also uses additional information such as user log in location.

For a user to login to a Samba share from a Windows system, the user has to already have a corresponding user account on that Samba server. That user account must also have a Samba password. In effect, the account has two password, the Linux user account password for accessing the account on Linux, and a Samba password used to access Samba shares from remote systems. In this way, a Linux user also becomes a Samba user.

Often, the Samba user account is not the same name as that of the Window account attempting to log in. To deal with this situation, a Windows username can be associated with a corresponding Samba user name. The name may or may not be the same. The mapping of windows users to Samba (Linux) users is stored in the **/etc/samba/smbusers** file. The following maps the Windows user **rpetersen** to the Samba (Linux) user **richard**.

```
richard = rpetersen
```

When a Windows user in Windows tries to access a Samba share, the user will be prompted to login. With the previous example, the Windows user would then enter **rpetersen** as the username and the Samba password that was set up for **richard**.

On Ubuntu, user-level security is managed by a password **tdb** (trivial data base) back-end database. A **tdb** database file stores Samba passwords with Windows extended information. By default, the **tdbsam** back-end database is used. The **tdbsam** database is designed for small networks. For systems using LDAP to manage users, you can use the LDAP-enabled back-end, **ldbsam**, which is designed for larger networks.

For standalone Samba servers, user level security and the tdbsam database is the default. So they are not specified in the **smb.conf** configuration file. You can explicitly configure them with the **security** and **passdb backend** options.

```
security = user
passdb backend = tdbsam
```

You can use the **username map** option to designate the file used to associate Windows and Linux users. A Windows user can use a Windows username to login as the associated user. The username map file is usually **/etc/samba/smbusers**.

```
username map = /etc/samba/smbusers
```

For an LDAP Samba database, **ldbsam**, you use LDAP Samba tools to manage users (the **smbldap-tools** package). These tools have the prefix smbldap. The tools include those for adding, modifying, and deleting users and groups (**smbldap-useradd**, **smbldap-userdelete**, and **smbldap-groupmod**). The **sbmldap-passwd** command manages Samba passwords with LDAP. The **smbldap-userinfo** command displays user information. LDAP Samba tools are configured in the **/etc/smbldap-tools/smbldap.conf** file.

The Samba server has a password Pluggable Authentication Module (PAM) module, **pam_smbpass.so**, which provides PAM authentication for Samba passwords. This will allow Windows hosts to work on a PAM-controlled network. The module is configured in your PAM **samba** file. The following entries in the PAM **samba** file require PAM authentication and passwords for the Samba server.

```
auth required pam_smbpass.so nodelay
password required pam_smbpass.so nodelay
```

For PAM to work with Samba, enable PAM in the **smb.conf** file.

```
obey pam restrictions = yes
```

Note: The **smbpasswd** file previously used is still available, but it is included only for backward compatibility.

Samba Passwords: smbpasswd

Each user attempting to access a Samba server will need a Samba server user name and password. Such user-level security requires that this username and Samba password be stored in the Samba password database, which is maintained separately by the Samba server. To add or change a user Samba password, use the **smbpasswd** command with the username.

```
$ sudo smbpasswd dylan
New SMB Password: new-password
Repeat New SMB Password: new-password
```

Any user can use the **smbpasswd** command to change their password, as shown here. If you have no Samba password, just press ENTER.

```
$ sudo smbpasswd
Old SMB password: old-password
New SMB Password: new-password
Repeat New SMB Password: new-password
```

If you want to give a user access without having to use a password, you would use **smbpasswd** with the **-n** option. In addition, the **smb.conf** file will need to have the **null passwords** option set to yes.

If you are using the older smb passwords file (not the tdbasm database), you should configure Samba to use encrypted passwords. Set the **encrypt passwords** option to **yes** and specify the SMB password file. You can also use the **mksmbpasswd** script to create a smbpasswd file from the users in your **/etc/passwd** file. Pipe the contents of the passwd file to **mksmbpasswd** and then use redirection (>) to create the file.

Managing Samba Users: smbpasswd and pdbedit

You can use the **smbpasswd** command or the **pdbedit** tool to manage Samba user passwords. For the **smbpasswd** command, the **-a** option will add a user and the **-x** option will remove one. Use the **-e** and **-d** options to enable or disable users.

```
sudo smbpasswd -a aleina
```

The **smbpasswd** command can save Samba passwords to either the older smbpasswd file or the newer tdbsam backend database file. Ubuntu currently uses the tdbasm backend database. The **pdbedit** command was designed to work with this database. Normally you would use the **pdbedit** command, instead of **smbpasswd** to manage your Samba users. To add a user with **pdbedit** you would use the **-a** option and to remove a user you use the **-x** option. You can also change passwords and set the user's home directory, as well as import or export the user entries to or from other back-end databases.

```
sudo pdbedit -a dylan
```

Unlike **smbpasswd**, with the **pdbedit** command you can display more information about users. The **-L** option displays users from the back-end database. Add the **-v** option for detailed information. For a particular user, add the username, as shown here.

```
sudo pdbedit -Lv richard
```

You can even display domain policies (the **-P** option) such as minimum password lengths or retries.

```
sudo pdbedit -P
```

If you want to import and export database entries, use the **-i** and **-e** options. The following will import entries from the old **smbpasswd** file to the new **tdbsam** back-end database.

```
sudo pdbedit -i smbpasswd -e tdbsam
```

Note: If your system is using an LDAP-enabled Samba database, use the **smbldap** tools to manage users and groups.

The Samba smb.conf Configuration File

Samba configuration is held in the **smb.conf** file located in the **/etc/samba** directory. It holds the configuration for the various shared resources, as well as global options that apply to all resources.

You use the **testparm** command in a terminal window to check the syntax of any changes you have made to the **/etc/samba/smb.conf** file.

```
testparm
```

The **/etc/samba/smb.conf** file is organized into two basic parts: one for global options and the other for shared services. Shared services, also known as shares, can either be file space services (used by clients as an extension of their native file systems) or printable services (used by clients to access print services on the host running the server). The file space service is a directory to which clients are given access. Clients can use the space in it as an extension of their local file system. A printable service provides access by clients to print services, such as printers managed by the Samba server.

The **/etc/samba/smb.conf** file contains default settings used for Ubuntu. You can edit the file to customize the configuration. Comment lines are preceded with a # sign. Entries that are disabled are preceded by a semicolon, **;**. To enable such an entry, remove its initial semi-colon character. For a complete listing of the Samba configuration parameters, check the Man page for **smb.conf**.

The **smb.conf** file is organized into two main groups with the labels (comments) Global Settings and Share Definitions. The Global Settings section has several subsections: Browsing/Identification, Networking, Debugging/Accounting, Authentication, Domains, Printing, and Misc. The global options are set first, followed by each shared resource's configuration.

Samba is configured according to resources such as shared folders and printers. Each resource in the **smb.conf** file is defined in its own section. A section is the basic element of the **smb.conf** file. A section holds its service name, enclosed in brackets, followed by options applied to the resource. For example, a section for a shared folder holds options that reference the folder and define the access rights for users. Global options are placed in a special section named **global**. There are also special sections, called **printers** and **homes**, which provide default options for user folders and for all shared printers. After these special sections, you can enter services for specific folders and printers on your server.

The format of a section always begins with a section label, the name of the shared resource encased in brackets. Other than the special sections, the section label can be any name you choose. Following the section label, on separate lines, different parameters (options) for this service are entered. Most of the parameters define the access rights for the service. For example, you may want a shared folder to be browseable, but read-only, and use a certain printer. Parameters are entered in the format *parameters name = value.* You can place comments in a section by placing a semicolon at the beginning of the comment line.

A simple example of a section configuration follows. The section label is encased in brackets and followed by two parameter entries. The **path** parameter references the shared folder. The **writeable** parameter specifies whether the user has write access to this folder.

```
[mysection]
path = /home/chris
writeable = true
```

A printer service has the same format but requires certain other parameters. The path parameter specifies the location of the printer spool folder. The **read-only** and **printable** parameters are set to **true**, indicating the service is read-only and printable. The **public** parameter lets anyone access the service.

```
[myprinter]
path = /var/spool/samba
read only = true
printable = true
public = true
```

The **writeable** option is an alias for the inverse of the **read only** option. The **writeable = yes** entry is the same as **read only = no** entry. The **read only = no**, **writeable = yes**, and **write ok = yes** options all provide write access to the user.

Variable Substitutions

For string values assigned to parameters, you can incorporate substitution operators. This provides greater flexibility in designating values that may be context-dependent, like usernames.

For example, suppose a service needs to use a separate directory for each user who logs in. The path for such directories could be specified using the **%u** variable that substitutes in the name of the current user. The string **path = /tmp/%u** would become **path = /tmp/justin** for the **justin** user and **/tmp/dylan** for the **dylan** user. Table 12-3 lists several of the more common substitution variables.

Global Settings

The Global Settings section provides configuration for the Samba server, as well as specifying defaults that may be used in the home and folder sections. In this section, you will find entries for the workgroup name, password configuration, browsing, and log files. The Global section begins with the **[global]** label.

Browsing/Identification

The Workgroup entry specifies the workgroup name you want to give to your network. The default Workgroup entry in the **smb.conf** file is shown here:

Variable	Description
%S	Name of the current service.
%P	Root directory of the current service.
%u	Username of the current service.
%H	Home directory of the user.
%h	Internet hostname on which Samba is running.
%m	NetBIOS name of the client machine.
%L	NetBIOS name of the server.
%M	Internet name of the client machine.
%I	IP address of the client machine.

Table 12-3: Samba Substitution Variables

```
[global]

# Change this to the workgroup/NT-domain name your Samba server will part of
 workgroup = WORKGROUP
```

The workgroup name has to be the same for each Windows client that the Samba server supports. On many Windows networks, this is defaulted to WORKGROUP. This is also the default name specified in the **smb.conf** file. If you want to use another name, you have to change the **workgroup** entry in the **smb.conf** file. The **workgroup** entry in the **smb.conf** file and the workgroup name on each Windows client has to be the same. In this example the workgroup name is **mygroup**.

```
workgroup = mygroup
```

The server string entry holds the descriptive name you want displayed for the server on the client systems. On Windows systems, this is the name displayed on the Samba server icon. The default is Samba Server, but you can change this to any name you want.

```
# server string is the equivalent of the NT Description field
   server string = %h server (Samba, Ubuntu)
```

Note: You can also configure Samba to be a Primary Domain Controller (PDC) for Windows NT networks. As a PDC, Samba sets up the Windows domain that other systems will use, instead of participating in an already established workgroup.

Networking

This subsection has interface directives for assigning a network interface device to a particular network to use for your server. The entries are commented out by default. The commented default entry is shown here for localhost on the first Ethernet device. Be sure to replace eth0 with the actual name of your network device (predictable name), such as enp7s0. You can use **ifconfig** to find the name.

```
;    interfaces = 127.0.0.0/8 eth0
```

If the system your Samba server runs on is not protected by a firewall, or the firewall is running on the same system, you should also enable the following.

```
;   bind interfaces only = yes
```

Debugging/Accounting

This section has directives for setting up logging for the Samba server. The log file directive is configured with the **%m** substitution symbol so that a separate log file is set up for each machine that connects to the server.

```
log file = /var/log/samba/log.%m
```

The maximum size of a log file is set to 1000 lines.

```
max log size = 1000
```

To have Samba log to the Samba log file, set logging to file. Add syslog01 to log also through syslog.

```
# We want Samba to only log to /var/log/samba/log.{smbd,nmbd}.
# Append syslog@1 if you want important messages to be sent to syslog too.
logging = file
```

The panic action directive notifies the administrator in case of a crash.

```
panic action = /usr/share/samba/panic-action %d
```

Authentication

The server role for the Samba server can be standalone, a member server, or a domain controller (classic primary, classic backup, or active directory). Usually the server is a standalone server. The server role determines the security. For a standalone server the security is user, which requires a password logon. Keep in mind, that with Ubuntu 24.04 the Classic Primary Domain Controller and the Classic Backup Domain Controller have both been deprecated. For a domain controller, it is recommended that you use the Active Directory Controller instead.

```
server role = standalone server
```

Windows clients use encrypted passwords for the login process. Passwords are encrypted by default and managed by the password database.

You can use the security option to specify the security: **user** (user password), **domain** (Windows domain), or **ads** (Kerberos) security. The **auto** setting is the default, which derives the security from the server role. If the server role is **standalone server**, then the security is **user** and is not specified in the **smb.conf** file. In the **smb.conf** file, as the **server role** is set to **standalone server**, the security is set to the user-level (**user**) and the password database file uses **tdbsam**.

Support for Pluggable Authentication Modules (PAM) security is then turned on.

```
obey pam restrictions = yes
```

When Samba passwords are changed, they need to be synced with UNIX passwords. The **unix password sync** directive turns on syncing, and the **passwd program** and **passwd chat** directives use the **passwd** command and specified prompts to change the password.

```
unix password sync = yes
```

```
passwd program = /usr/bin/passwd %u
passwd chat = *Enter\snew\s*\spassword:* %n\n *Retype\snew\s*\spassword:* %n\n
*password\supdated\ssuccessfully* .
```

PAM is also used for password changes by Samba clients.

```
pam password change = yes
```

As a security measure, you can restrict access to SMB services to certain specified local networks. On the host's network, type the network addresses of the local networks for which you want to permit access. To deny access to everyone in a network except a few particular hosts, you can use the EXCEPT option after the network address with the IP addresses of those hosts. The localhost (127) is always automatically included. The next example allows access to two local networks.

```
hosts allow = 192.168.1. 192.168.2.
```

The map to guest directive is set to bad user. This will allow any unknown users to login as guests. Samba users that fail to login though will not be allowed access, even as guests.

```
map to guest = bad user
```

Domains

The Domains subsection configures your Samba server as a Microsoft Public Domain Controller (PDC). All of these directives are commented out by default. See the section later in this chapter on Public Domain Controller on how to set up your Samba server as a PDC on a Microsoft network. In previous releases Ubuntu has supported both the older Classic Domain Controller and the newer Active Directory Controller. With Ubuntu 24.04, the Classic Domain Controller has been deprecated. It is recommended that the Active Directory Controller be used instead. Window clients primarily support the Active Directory Controller.

Misc

The Misc subsection has entries used to customize your server. Most are commented out, except for the **usershare** directive that allows users to create public shares. An **include** directive lets you set up configuration files for particular machines in the **/home/samba/etc** directory, that are then read when the machine connects.

```
;    include = /home/samba/etc/smb.conf.%m
```

There are also entries for those using the Winbind server, specifying the user and group id ranges, and the shell to use.

```
# Some defaults for winbind (make sure you're not using the ranges
# for something else.)
;    idmap config * :              backend = tdb
;    idmap config * :              range   = 3000-7999
;    idmap config YOURDOMAINHERE : backend = tdb
;    idmap config YOURDOMAINHERE : range   = 100000-999999
;    template shell = /bin/bash
```

The **usershare** directives allow non-root users to share folders. A commented entry for user max shares can be used to limit the number of shares a user can set up.

```
;         usershare max shares = 100
```

The **user allow guests** directive permits users to create public shares, allowing guests to access the shares.

```
# Allow users who've been granted usershare privileges to create
# public shares, not just authenticated ones
usershare allow guests = yes
```

You can use a guest user login to make resources available to anyone without requiring a password. A guest user login would handle any users who log in without a specific account. Samba is usually set up to use the **nobody** user as the guest user. Alternatively, you can set up and designate a specific user to use as the guest user. You can designate the guest user with the **guest ok** and **guest account** entries in the **smb.conf** file. Be sure to add the guest user to the password file.

```
guest ok = yes
guest account = nobody
```

In addition, this section provides several performance tweaks, such as setting socket options for Linux systems.

Share Definitions

The Share Definitions part will hold sections for the definition of commonly used shares, as well as any shares you have set up yourself, like shared folders or printers. There are three special sections: homes, netlogon, and profiles that are used for special purposes. Users can be referenced in the share definitions either by their user names or by groups. A group is indicated the a preceding @ character. Certain groups reference administrative users such as **@lpadmin**, **@syslog**, and **@adm**.

Homes Section

The Homes section applies to the home folders of users on the system. It sets the default controls for accessing a user home folder by remote users. Setting the **browseable** option to **no** prevents a remote user from listing the files in a file browser. Read access to files by remote users is determined by the **read only** option. The **create mask** and **directory mask** options set default permissions for new files and folders created in the home folder by remote users. Normally these permissions are set to 0700, which allows owner read/write/execute permission. The **valid users** option uses the **%S** macro to map to the current service. You can add the **writeable** directive to allow write access.

```
writeable = yes
```

The home entries are commented out in the **smb.conf** configuration file, disabling access to user home directories by default. To enable access to home directories, remove the semi-colon comment in front of each entry in the **smb.conf** file.

If you are setting up a PDC and chose to save user profiles in the user home directories, then the homes section and its entries have to be un-commented.

```
[homes]
 comment = Home Directories
 browseable = no
 read only = yes
 create mask = 0700
 directory mask = 0700
 valid users = %S
```

The printers and print$ Sections

The printers section specifies the default controls for accessing printers. These are used for printers for which no specific sections exist. Setting **browseable** to **no** simply hides the Printers section from the client, not the printers. The **path** option lists the location of the spool folder that Samba will use for printer files. The **printable** option must be set to yes to allow any printing. Otherwise, printing is disabled. To allow guest users to print, set the **guest ok** option to **yes**. The Printers section is shown here.

```
[printers]
 comment = All Printers
 browseable = no
 path = /var/tmp
 printable = yes
 guest ok = no
 read only = yes
 create mask = 0700
```

The **print$** section, shown next, specifies where a Windows client can find a print driver on your Samba server. The printer drivers are located in the **/var/lib/samba/printers** directory and are read-only. The browseable, read-only, and guest directives are commented out. They can be enabled to allow browsing of the drivers. The **write list** directive would allow you to remotely administer the Windows print drivers. **lpadmin** is the name of your administrator group.

```
# Windows clients look for this share name as a source of downloadable
# printer drivers
[print$]
  comment = Printer Drivers
  path = /var/lib/samba/printers
  browseable = yes
  read only = yes
  guest ok = no
;  write list = root, @lpadmin
```

Shares

The sections for shared resources, such as folders on your system, are placed after the Homes and Printers sections. A section for a shared folder, begins with a label for that share. It is followed by options for its pathname and permissions, each on a separate line. The **path** = *option* entry holds the full pathname for the folder. In the **comment** = *option* entry you can describe the share. Permission options let you make the folder writeable, public, or read-only. The **valid users** option lets you control access to shares by certain user. For any options not entered, the defaults in the Global, Homes, and Printers sections are used.

The following example, the **myprojects** share defines the **/myprojects** folder as a shared resource that is open to any user with guest access.

```
[myprojects]
    comment = Project Ideas
    path = /myprojects
    read only = no
    guest ok = yes
```

Use the **valid users** option to limit access to certain users. To then shut off access to all other users, the **guest ok** option is set to **no**.

```
[mynewmusic]
 comment =  New Music
 path = /home/specialprojects
 valid users = mark, richard
 guest ok = no
 read only = no
```

In the following example, the Documents folder is accessible and writeable to the george and richard users.

```
[Documents]
path = /home/richard/Documents
writeable = yes
browseable = yes
valid users = george, richard
```

If you want to allow public access to a folder, set the **guest ok** entry to **yes**, with no valid users entry.

```
[newdocs]
comment =  New Documents
path = /home/newdocs
guest ok = yes
read only = no
```

The users listed in a **valid users** option gives each user control of the files they create. You can further manage control of their files by using the **create mask** option to specify file permissions. In this example, the permissions are set to 765, which provides read/write/execute access to owners, read/write access to members of the group, and only read/execute access to all others (the default is 744, read-only for group and other permission).

```
[myshare]
 comment = Writer's projects
 path = /usr/local/drafts
 valid users = Justin, chris, dylan
 guest ok = no
 read only = no
 create mask = 0765
```

You can further refine control with the **read list** and **write list** options. The **read list** option provides read only access to the listed users, whereas the **write list** option provides both read and write access.

```
[myshare]
 comment = Writer's projects
 path = /usr/local/drafts
 read list = Justin, chris
 write list dylan
 guest ok = no
 read only = no
 create mask = 0765
```

Printer shares

Access to specific printers is defined in the Printers section of the **smb.conf** file. For a printer, you need to include the Printer and Printable entries, as well as specify the type of Printing server used. With the Printer entry, you name the printer, and by setting the Printable entry to yes, you allow it to print. You can control access to specific users with the **valid users** entry and by setting the Public entry to no. For public access, set the **public** entry to yes. For the CUPS server, set the printing option to **cups**.

The following example sets up a printer accessible to guest users, which allows the printer to be used by any user on the network. The **read only** option is set to **no** to allow users write-access to the printer's spool directory, located in **/var/spool/samba**. The printer should already be installed. The printer in this example was installed as **myhp**. You use the CUPS administrative tool to set up printers for the CUPS server. The Printing option can be inherited from the Printers share.

```
[myhp]
        path = /var/spool/samba
        read only = no
        guest ok = yes
        printable = yes
        printer = myhp
        oplocks = no
        share modes = no
        printing = cups
```

Should you want, you can also restrict printer use to certain users, denying it to public access, just as you can for shares. The next example, the printer is accessible only by the users **larisa** and **aleina**. You could add other users if you want.

```
[larisalaser]
        path = /var/spool/samba
        read only = no
        valid users = larisa aleina
        guest ok = no
        printable = yes
        printing = cups
        printer = larisalaser
        oplocks = no
        share modes = no
```

Testing the Samba Configuration

If you have modified the **smb.conf** file, you should test it to check for errors. Use the **testparm** command to see if the entries are correct. **testparm** checks the syntax and validity of Samba entries. By default, **testparm** checks the **/etc/samba/smb.conf** configuration file. If you want to use different configuration file, you can enter it as an argument to **testparm**.

Samba Public Domain Controller: Samba PDC

Samba can also operate as a Public Domain Controller (PDC). The domain controller will be registered and advertised on the network as the domain controller. The PDC provides a much more centralized way to control access to Samba shares. It provides the netlogon service and a NETLOGON share. The PDC will set up machine trust accounts for each Windows and Samba client. Though you can do this manually, Samba will do it for you automatically. Keep in mind that Samba cannot emulate a Microsoft Active PDC, but can emulate a Windows NT4 PDC.

In previous releases Ubuntu has supported both the older Classic Domain Controller and the newer Active Directory Domain Controller. With Ubuntu 24.04, the Classic Domain Controller has been deprecated. Only the Active Directory Domain Controller is supported.

For basic configuration check the Ubuntu Server Guide | Services | Samba - Domain Controller.

```
https://ubuntu.com/server/docs/samba-domain-controller
```

Microsoft Domain Security

As noted in the Samba documentation, the primary benefit of Microsoft domain security is single-sign-on (SSO). In effect, logging into your user account also logs you into access to your entire network's shared resources. Instead of having to be separately authenticated any time you try to access a shared network resource, you are already authenticated. Authentication is managed using Security IDs (SID) that consists of a network ID (NID) and a relative ID (RID). The RID references your personal account. A separate RID is assigned to every account, even those for groups or system services. The SID is used to set up access control lists (ACL) for the different shared resources on your network, allowing a resource to automatically identify you.

Samba Classic Domain Controller configuration

To configure a classic domain controller, edit the **Domains** section in the **smb.conf** file. Here you will find entries for configuring your Samba PDC options. You will need to add the **domain logons** and **domain primary** entries.

The essential PDC options are shown here.

```
workgroup = myworkgroup
domain logons = yes
domain primary = yes
security = user
```

If the netbios name is different from the hostname on which the server is run, you can add a **netbios name** option to specify it.

```
netbios name = myserver
```

Like most Samba configurations, the PDC requires a Samba back-end. The **tdbsam** is already configured for you. The security level should be **user**. This is normally the default and is already set. The **smb.conf** entry is shown here.

```
passdb backend = tdbsam
```

The PDC must also be designated the domain primary. This is set to auto by default. For a PDC, set it to yes, and for a BDC (backup domain controller) set it to no.

```
domain primary = yes
```

The PDC has browser functionality, with which it locates systems and shares on your network. These features are not present in the Ubuntu **smb.conf** file, but you can add them if needed. The **local primary** option is used only if you already have another PDC that you want to operate as the local primary. You could have several domain controllers operating on your network. Your Microsoft network holds an election to choose which should be the primary. The **os level** sets the precedence for this PDC. It should be higher than 32 to gain preference over other domain controllers on your network, ensuring this PDC's election as the primary master controller. The **preferred primary** option starts the browser election on startup.

```
;        local primary = no
os level = 33
preferred primary = yes
```

Domain Logon configuration

Samba domain controller uses the domain logons service whereby a user can log on to the network. The domain logon service is called the netlogon service by Microsoft. The samba share it uses is also called netlogon. To configure the domain logon service, you set the **domain logons** option to yes, or set the **server role** option to " classic primary domain controller" or to " classic backup domain controller." Keep in mind that both the Classic Primary Domain Controller and the Classic Backup Domain Controller have been deprecated with Ubuntu 22.04.

```
domain logons = yes
```

The logon path references the profile used for a user. The **%N** will be the server name, and the **%U** references the username. Profiles can be set up either in a separate profiles share or in the user home directories. The following would reference user profiles in the profiles share. You would also have to define the profiles share by un-commenting the profiles share entries in the **smb.conf** file.

```
logon path = \\%N\profiles\%U
```

If the profile is stored in the user's home directory instead of the Profiles share, you would uncomment the following entry instead. You will also have to allow access to user home directories, un-commenting the homes share entries.

```
logon path = \\%N\%U\profile
```

The **logon drive** and **logon home** specify the location of the user's home directory. The logon drive is set as the H: drive. The **%N** evaluates to the server name and **%U** to the user.

```
logon drive = H:
logon home = \\%N\%U
```

The login script can be one set by the system or by users.

```
logon script = logon.cmd
```

You can then enable user add operations for adding users, groups, and machines to the PDC. The add machine entry allows Samba to automatically add trusted machine accounts for Windows systems when they first join the PDC controlled network.

```
add user script = /usr/sbin/adduser --create-home %u
add machine script = /usr/sbin/useradd -g machines -c "%u machine account" -d
/var/lib/samba -s /bin/false %u
add group script = /usr/sbin/addgroup --force-badname %g
```

You then need to set up a netlogon share in the **smb.conf** file. This share holds the **netlogon** scripts, in this case, the **/var/lib/samba/netlogon** directory, which should not be writable, but should be accessible by all users (Guest OK). In the share definitions section of the **smb.conf** file, you will find the **[netlogon]** section commented. Remove the semi-colon comments from the entry, as shown here.

```
# Un-comment the following and create the netlogon directory for Domain Logon
# (you need to configure Samba to act as a domain controller too.)
[netlogon]
comment = Network Logon Service
path = /home/samba/netlogon
guest ok = yes
read only = yes
```

If you choose to use a profiles share to store user profiles in, then you should enable the **profiles** share. Un-comment the following to define a **profiles** share. The entries are located just after the **netlogon** shares.

```
[profiles]
comment = Users profiles
path = /home/samba/profiles
guest ok = no
browseable = no
create mask = 0600
directory mask = 0700
```

The **profile** share is where user netlogon profiles are stored. If instead, you are using the user's home directories to store their profiles, you will not need to define and use a **profiles** share. If you choose to store user profiles in the user home directories, you would uncomment the **homes** share entries instead.

Samba Active Directory Domain Controller

With Samba version 4 you can run Samba as an Active Directory Domain Controller, instead of as a classic domain controller. You will also have to run a DNS server and Kerberos authentication server. You will have to select and configure a server to operate as the domain controller. It must have a static IP address. To allow the Active Directory software to be more easily updated, it is advised that the domain controller should not also function as a file server. See the Samba documentation for detailed instructions on how to set up a server as an Active Directory Domain Controller.

```
https://wiki.samba.org/index.php/Setting_up_Samba_as_an_Active_Directory_Domain_C
ontroller
```

Be sure to remove any previous installation of Samba, including **winbindd**. Do a restart to ensure that all Samba processes have ended, or manually detect and stop them. Also, if you previously installed Samba, remove any Samba configuration files, including Samba databases. On Ubuntu, the Samba configuration files are located at **/etc/samba**. If you previously installed Kerberos, remove the Kerberos configuration file **/etc/krb5.conf**.

Take care in choosing a hostname for the server running the Active Directory Domain Controller. See the Samba documentation on selecting an appropriate hostname.

```
https://wiki.samba.org/index.php/Active_Directory_Naming_FAQ
```

In order to coordinate with the DNS server, disable any support for automatically updating the **/etc/resolvconf** file. This means disabling the **resolved** daemon. In the **/etc/hosts** file, be sure that the domain controller server name is correctly resolved to the static IP address you are using for it.

You then use the **samba-tool** command to provision the Active Directory, configuring it by setting up databases, an administration account, DNS entries, and configuration files. You use the **samba-tool** command to administer and manage your Active Directory.

The **samba-tool** command has an interactive and non-interactive mode. The interactive mode prompts for options such as the domain name you are using for the Active Directory Domain Controller, and the static IP address you are using for it. Use the **--interactive** option to use the interactive mode. You may want to include several options with the **samba-tool** command. The **--rfc2307** option will provide NIS support, which is difficult to add later should you need it. If your server has several network interfaces, you should specify the one to use, as in eth0 in this example.

```
-option="interfaces=lo eth0" --option="bind interfaces only=yes"
```

To see a listing of the **samba-tool** options for provisioning use the following command.

```
samba-tool domain provision --help
```

The command to perform an interactive provisioning follows. Be sure to add any other options you may need.

```
samba-tool domain provision --use-rfc2307 --interactive
```

In the non-interactive mode you would have to list all the options and their values with the **samba-tool** command.

Once the provisioning is finished, be sure the **/etc/resolv.conf** file has entries to search your Active Directory server's domain and that there is an entry specifying your DNS nameserver's IP address. Also, to configure Kerberos for the Active Directory, copy the version of the **krb5.conf** file generated by the provisioning in the **/var/lib/samba/private** directory to the **/etc** directory. In the **/etc/samba/smb.conf** file the **server role** option must be set to "active directory domain controller."

```
server role = active directory domain controller
```

The service name for the Samba Active Directory Domain Controller is **samba-ac-dc**. You can manage it with the **systemctl** command.

```
sudo systemctl enable samba-ac-dc
sudo systemctl start samba-ac-dc
```

Accessing Samba Services with Clients

Any client systems connected to the SMB network can access the shared services provided by the Samba server. You can use the **smblclient** command to access a shared folder and then run commands to manage the files there. If you want to mount a shared folder to a local folder on your system, providing direct access, you can use the the **mount** command with the **-t cifs** option. Be sure that firewall access for Samba is enabled.

Accessing Windows Samba Shares from the Ubuntu desktop

On the desktop, you can use a file manager like the Ubuntu desktop's Files file manager to access your Samba shares. With Samba version 4.13.3 (Ubuntu 24.04), the older SMBv1 (Secure Message Block) protocol has been fully deprecated. Linux and Windows have transitioned from the older SMBv1 protocol to the more secure SMBv3 protocol. As a result, network browsing by a Linux file manager such as Files on the Ubuntu desktop does not currently work. You can access Windows shares directly using the Connect to Server entry on the Ubuntu desktop Files file manager's Other Locations window. Enter in the **smb://** protocol and the name of the shared folder or that of the remote Windows system you want to access. After being prompted to enter your Samba password, the particular shared folder or the shared folders on that host will be displayed.

Accessing Samba Shares from Windows

You can browse Samba Shares from a Windows network window. On a Windows window, click the Network entry in the sidebar to open a list or icons for available systems on your network (see Figure 12-1). Click on system to display the shares available from that system. The first time you access the share, you may be prompted to enter your Samba password. The folder shares for that system are then displayed (see Figure 12-2).

Figure 12-1: Samba shares on Windows

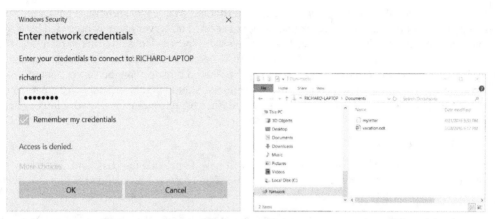

Figure 12-2: Accessing a Samba share on Windows

If you are having difficulty accessing a Samba share, you can use an alternative method using Windows network location shortcuts. You can add a new network location for it, that will be accessible from a shortcut you can set up for it on your Windows file manager "This PC" folder. To set up the shortcut, open the Windows file manager to any folder and right-click on the "This PC" entry in the sidebar to display a menu. Click on the "Add a network location" entry to open the "Add Network Location Wizard" and click Next. Click on the "Choose a custom network location" entry and click Next. In the text box labeled "Internet or network address:" enter the host name of your Linux system that holds the shares you want to access, beginning with the two backward slashes and followed by a backward slash (you may have to also enter the name of one of the shared folders on that system).

```
\\richard-laptop\
```

You can then click the Browse button to open a dialog showing a tree of all the shared folders on that host. You can choose a share, or any of a share's subfolders. Their file pathname is automatically added to the address textbox. Alternatively, you could enter the folder path name in the text box directly with the subfolders separated by single backward slashes. If you are sharing your Linux home folders, then the shared folder is the name of the user's Home folder, the user name. Samples are shown here.

```
\\richard-laptop\richard
```

```
\\richard-laptop\richard\Pictures
```

```
\\richard-laptop\mydocs
```

Once the locations for your shared folders are set up in Windows, you can access them again quickly from their shortcuts in the "This PC" folder.

smbclient

You can use **smbclient** to access SMB-shared services and folders on the Samba server or on a Windows system. It works much like FTP but has different protocols, the SMB protocols. **smbclient** has many of the same commands as FTP, for example, **mget** to transfer a file or **del** to delete a file. **smbclient** also provides options to query and connect to a remote system. For a complete list of options and commands, check the **smbclient** Man page. **smbclient** has as its argument a server name and the service you want to access. The server name is preceded by a double slash, and the service is preceded by a single slash. The service is any shared resource, such as a folder or a printer. The server name is its NetBIOS name, which may or may not be the same as its IP name. For example, to specify the **myreports** shared directory on the server named **turtle.mytrek.com**, use **//turtle.mytrek.com/myreports**. Should you have to specify a pathname, keep in mind that, though Windows uses backward slashes for its path names, Unix/Linux systems use forward slashes.

```
//server-name/service
```

If the service is password protected, you will have to provide the password. Enter the password as an argument following the service name. If no password is provided, and it is required for the service, you will be prompted to enter it.

The **smbclient** command provides several options for accessing shares. The **-I** option references a system by its IP address. To specify a login name you use **-U**. Should a password be needed, attach **%** with the password. The **-L** option displays a list of the services provided on a server, such as shared folders or printers. The following command will list the shares available on the host **turtle.mytrek.com**:

```
smbclient -L turtle.mytrek.com
```

In order to access a particular folder on a remote system, you enter the folder name and any options you want. Be sure to use backslashes for Windows path names. Upon connecting to the server, an SMB prompt is displayed. You can then enter **smbclient** commands such as **get** and **put** to transfer files. Use the **quit** and **exit** commands to quit and end the connection. The **recurse** command lets you to turn on recursion to copy whole subfolders at a time. With the UNIX file-matching operators, you can reference multiple files. The file-matching operators are *****, **[]**, and **?**. The default mask is *****, which matches everything. The following example uses **mget** to copy all files with a **.c** suffix, as in **myprog.c**:

```
smb> mget *.c
```

In the following example, **smbclient** accesses the folder **myreports** on the **turtle.mytrek.com** system, using the **dylan** login name and the **-I** option, the IP address of the server.

```
smbclient //turtle.mytrek.com/myreports -I 192.168.0.1 -U dylan
```

Normally you just use the server name to reference the server, as shown here. You do not need to specify the IP address.

```
smbclient //turtle.mytrek.com/myreports -U dylan
```

Should you want to access a user's home folder on the Samba server, you would use the **homes** service. In the next example, the user accesses the home folder of the **aleina** account on the Samba server. As the password is not provided, the user will be prompted for it.

```
smbclient //turtle.mytrek.com/homes -U aleina
```

smbclient also lets you access Windows shared resources. Enter the computer name of the Windows client and the shared folder on that client you want access to. In the next example, the user accesses the **windata** folder on the Windows client named **mycomp**. If the folder allows access to anyone, you just press ENTER at the password prompt.

```
smbclient //mycomp/windata
```

mount.cifs: mount -t cifs

You can mount a shared folder onto your local system by using the **mount** command and the **-t cifs** option. The **cifs** option will run the **mount.cifs** command, which, in turn, invokes the **smbclient** command to perform the mount. The **mount.cifs** command requires the names of the Samba server, shared folder, and the local folder where the shared folder is to be mounted. The following example mounts the **mybooks** folder to the **/mnt/mybks** folder on the local system.

```
mount -t cifs //turtle.mytrek.com/mybooks /mnt/mybks -U dylan
```

If you want to unmount a folder, you run the **umount** command with the **-t cifs** option and the folder name. The **umount** command will invoke the **umount.cifs** command which performs the unmount.

```
umount -t cifs  /mnt/mybks
```

Should you want to mount the home folder of a user, specify the **homes** service and the user's login name. The following example mounts the home folder of the user **aleina** to the **/home/harlow/aleinastuff** folder on the local system.

```
mount -t cifs //turtle.mytrek.com/homes /home/harlow/aleinastuff -U aleina
```

It is also possible to mount shared folders on Windows clients. Use two forward slashes to precede the name of the Windows computer and the Windows folder. If the folder name contains spaces, enclose it in single quotes. In the following example, the user mounts the **mydocs** folder on **mywin** as the **/mywindocs** folder. For a folder with access to anyone, just press ENTER at the password prompt without entering a password.

```
$ mount -t cifs //mywin/mydocs /mywindocs
Password:
$ ls /mydocs
mynewdoc.doc myreport.txt
```

When you are finished with that shared folder, you can use the **umount** command and the **-t cifs** option to unmount it as you would a Linux folder.

```
umount -t cifs /mywindocs
```

Should you want to control user access to the folder, you can specify a username and password as options when you mount it, as shown here.

```
mount -t cifs -o username=harlow passwd=mypass //mywin/mydocs /mywindocs
```

If you want the folder mounted automatically whenever you start up the system, you can create an entry for the mount operation in the **/etc/fstab** file. Use the **cifs** file type in the entry:

```
//mywin/mydocs   /mywindocs   cifs   defaults   0  0
```

ubuntu

13. Cloud Computing

Cloud Computing

Amazon EC2 Cloud for Ubuntu

Ubuntu Cloud (OpenStack)

Ubuntu features fully integrated support for cloud computing. It provides private and public cloud support. Ubuntu provides a managed service for private OpenStack cloud systems. It also supports Ubuntu systems on public clouds such as those provided by Amazon (Amazon Web Services), Google, Microsoft (Azure), and IBM (Softlayer).

You will need to use a Web browser to set up access and manage your cloud. Use either a command line browser like elinks or lynx, or, if you have installed the Ubuntu desktop, you can use the Firefox or Web browsers.

Ubuntu Cloud

The Ubuntu Cloud refers to the full range of cloud software and services that Ubuntu offers. These include both Public cloud (instances of Ubuntu on public clouds such as the Amazon AWS), and Ubuntu OpenStack (OpenStack supported clouds that you can set up yourself).

```
https://ubuntu.com/public-cloud
https://ubuntu.com/openstack
```

The Ubuntu OpenStack refers to a cloud you can build yourself or have managed by Ubuntu, using the OpenStack applications and servers provided by Ubuntu. An OpenStack cloud can be private, public, or a hybrid of both. They can be managed using Juju charms (apps).

In addition, the Ubuntu Advantage service (Cloud management) provides professional support for Ubuntu OpenStack. You can then use Landscape to manage your Ubuntu clouds. For more information see:

```
https://www.ubuntu.com/support
```

Service Orchestration

To implement cloud application services, Canonical provides JuJu, Metal as a Service (MAAS), and LXD. JuJu is a service orchestration toolset and MAAS provides hardware provisioning. With JuJu you can manage installation, configuration, and availability of your cloud services, and with MAAS set up hardware resources for them. Juju (formerly Ensemble) is a service orchestration system, which provides the tools to configure, upgrade, and deploy cloud services. It allows you to monitor use and scale deployment of services.

JuJu orchestrates application components such as dependencies on other software and various configuration settings, by combining them into an entity referred to as a charm. Using charms, JuJu can quickly manage a cloud service. A charm is basically a script, a set of instructions, for deploying a cloud service. Several are already available. With a JuJu charm, you can easily deploy a cloud service, specifying the number of nodes to use and choosing the cloud service such as AmazonEC2 or OpenStack. Using a charm you can scale back the number of nodes, or shut down the service quickly. You can find out more about JuJu at:

```
https://juju.is/docs
```

Containers

Ubuntu offers three container services for which it provides consulting support: LXD, Kubernetes, and Docker. Containers are the software that support virtual machines.

```
https://www.ubuntu.com/containers
```

LXD is a container hypervisor that maintains efficient access to devices. Kubernets is a container orchestration system. Ubuntu provides its own Canonical version. Whereas LXD implements a complete virtual machine with a full operating system, Docker implements just a particular service. Both are fully supported by Ubuntu. Keep in mind that Docker is a commercial service.

Ubuntu provides Docker, a technology that allows any application to be deployed as a container that will run on any type of server (bare-metal, virtual machine, public, and Open Stack), **https://www.docker.com**.

As an alternative to Docker, Ubuntu has developed LXD, a container hypervisor for deploying and managing containers. It is effectively a virtual machine, but without the overhead of an actual virtual machine. LXD is based on the Linux LXC container hypervisor. On any Ubuntu system, you can install the LXD hypervisor, which runs as a server, and then, on the hypervisor install an Ubuntu container image. You use **lxc** commands to manage a container such as launching or stopping a container. You can find out more about LXD at

```
https://linuxcontainers.org/
```

OpenStack

OpenStack is the private/public cloud software currently supported by Ubuntu, replacing Eucalyptus. You can find out more about OpenStack at:

```
https://www.openstack.org
```

Detailed documentation, including the end user guide, is available at:

```
https://docs.openstack.org
```

The Ubuntu OpenStack is the Ubuntu version of OpenStack. Ubuntu offers managed, supported, and manual versions. The managed and supported versions are commercial products, whereas the manual version is free. They are managed using Juju charms (apps).

```
https://www.ubuntu.com/openstack
```

You can use the OpenStack dashboard (horizon) to manage your cloud. It provides a Web interface for administering the OpenStack Nova cloud controller.

OpenStack comprises several services, including compute (Nova), storage (Cinder), imaging (Glance), networking (Neutron), orchestration (Heat), and database support (Trove). The computer packages on Ubuntu begin with the term nova. OpenStack supports several kinds of hypervisors, as well as database backends such as MySQL. It also supports LDAP user databases.

Ubuntu Cloud Images for private systems

Ubuntu cloud images that you can download directly for use on a private system are located at:

```
http://cloud-images.ubuntu.com
```

The Cloud Images page requires that you have access to a Web browser.

Click on the folder with the release name you want, such as noble for Ubuntu 24.04. This opens the page for the daily build folder. Click on the current folder for the latest link.

Ubuntu Cloud Image IDs for public systems

The official cloud image IDs for Ubuntu images available on public cloud systems are listed using the Ubuntu Cloud Locater site at:

```
https://cloud-images.ubuntu.com/locator/daily/
```

You can sort the various cloud images by Cloud (Amazon, Google, Oracle, and Microsoft), by Name (the Ubuntu release such as noble), Zone (location such as us-west or eu-east), Arch (architecture), and release (version release date). The cloud images are listed to the right under ID. Each image ID is a link to an associated Cloud service, which you can use to select an image to that service.

Public Cloud: Amazon EC2 Cloud

The Ubuntu public cloud Web page provides links to public clouds supported by Ubuntu including Amazon (Amazon Web Services), Google, Microsoft (Azure), and IBM (Softlayer). These are commercial services that you have to sign up and pay for. Once you have access, you can then access a cloud image for an Ubuntu server and set up applications to run on that cloud. See the Ubuntu public cloud page for an overview.

```
https://ubuntu.com/public-cloud
```

Ubuntu has long had support for Amazon Web services. Once you have access to the Amazon EC2 (Elastic Compute) cloud you can then run an Amazon Machine Image (AMI) for an Ubuntu server.

The EC2StartGUide shows how to set up access (link is on the Ubuntu public cloud page).

```
https://help.ubuntu.com/community/EC2StartersGuide
```

You can find out more about Amazon EC2 cloud at:

```
https://aws.amazon.com/ec2/
```

Check the Amazon EC2 documentation for more details, including the User Guide at:

```
https://docs.aws.amazon.com/ec2/index.html
```

To find out what Ubuntu cloud images are available, you can use the Ubuntu Cloud Locator site, discussed earlier.

Cloud tools

You can install a tool to allow you to start and stop instances. The recommended tools are the Amazon EC2 tools in the **ec2-api-tools** package. The Eucalyptus tool is an open source tool supported by Ubuntu.

Amazon EC2 tools

You can use the Amazon EC2 tools (Multiverse repository) to manage an Amazon cloud instance. The examples in this chapter use these tools.

First, install the Amazon EC2 API package.

```
ec2-api-tools
```

There are an extensive number of EC2 tools provided by this package. A listing and explanation of these tools are located at:

```
http://awsdocs.s3.amazonaws.com/EC2/ec2-clt.pdf
```

Locate the Commands (CLI Tools) chapter on this document. These explanations also apply to their Eucalyptus counterparts (**euca** prefix).

Setting up access

On the Amazon cloud, you can access a public Amazon Machine Image (AMI) for an Ubuntu 24.04 server system provided by Ubuntu. You will have to create an Amazon EC2 account, set up security, and then set up your cloud. Check the Ubuntu EC2 starter guide on how to set up access.

```
https://help.ubuntu.com/community/EC2StartersGuide
```

Create an account

To set up an Amazon EC2 account, you first have to have a basic Amazon account. Set one up if you do not already have one. Then sign in and set up an Amazon EC2 account at (click the Sign Up button):

```
https://aws.amazon.com/ec2
```

Set up Security:

To ensure access to the Amazon EC2 cloud, you have to make sure your security certificates and keys are installed and made available to the EC2 API tools that will manage your access to the AMI. You will create a certificate and private key on your AWS account. Click on the Account tab and choose Security Credentials. Click the **X.509 Certificates** tab. On this tab, click the "Create a new Certificate" link. This opens a dialog with buttons to download both a private key and certificate. Take note where you are downloading the certificate and private key. The private key file begins with the prefix **pk-** and the certificate file begins with **cert-**.

If you have set up an account already, but your Ubuntu system does not have access, you will have to generate a new certificate in order to download a private key. Sign in and click the Account tab, choosing the Security Credentials link. Click on the "X.509 Certificates" tab, and then click on the "Create a new Certificate" link. A dialog opens with buttons to download the Private key and the X.509 certificate.

Note your account ID which is listed at the bottom of the Security Credentials page.

You then set up three shell variables and export them to make them global. These are set up in your **.bashrc** file in your home directory. The variables hold the locations of your private key, Amazon certificate, and the JAVA OpenJDK.

EC2_PRIVATE_KEY	The location and name of your Amazon EC2 private key file
EC2_CERT	The location and name of your Amazon EC2 certificate file
JAVA_HOME	The location of the JAVA OpenJDK software

The EC2StartGUide provides an example format.

```
https://help.ubuntu.com/community/EC2StartersGuide
```

Here is the example.

```
export EC2_PRIVATE_KEY=$HOME/<where your private key is>/pk-XXXXXXXXXXXXXXXXX.pem
export EC2_CERT=$HOME/<where your certificate is>/cert-XXXXXXXXXXXXXXXXXXXX.pem
export JAVA_HOME=/usr/lib/jvm/java-11-openjdk-amd64/
```

The name of the certificate and key files can be very complex. On the command line interface, a simple way to copy the filenames is to list them with the **ls** command and save the names in a file that you can then copy and paste from in nano.

```
ls *.pem > mykeyname
nano mykeyname
```

To access the Ubuntu Server public AMI, you also have to generate an SSH key. Use the **ec2-add-keypair** command to create an SSH key. Be sure to save the output to a file, named in this example **myec2key.pem**. You can also set up the SSH keys using the AWS console.

```
ec2-add-keypair myec2key > myec2key.pem
```

Set the file permissions to 600.

```
chmod 600 myec2key.pem
```

Authorize access through the SHH port, port 22, using the **ec2-authorize** command.

```
ec2-authorize default -p 22
```

You can assign the SSH key you made to the EC2_KEYPAIR variable, and then use that variable to reference the key in your ec2 commands.

```
export EC2_KEYPAIR=<your keypair name> # name only, not the file name
```

In addition, you can specify the EC2 region site for your cloud instances. These are listed on the EC2StartersGuide Web page. For example, **us-east-1** indicates the Eastern US, and **eu-west-1** indicates Europe. The region site URL is assigned to the EC2_URL variable.

```
export EC2_URL=https://ec2.<your ec2 region>.amazonaws.com
```

You can then edit the **.bashrc** file, adding the EC2 variables at the end and copying and pasting the key filenames.

```
nano .bashrc
```

On a desktop interface, you can edit the **.bashrc** file and copy and paste using **gedit** (tools menu | Show Hidden Files).

A sample of the lines you would add is listed on the EC2StartersGuide Web page and is shown here, with example key and certificate names. In this example, the keys are in the user's HOME directory (**$HOME**), though you may want to place them in a more secure directory. On a desktop interface, you could copy and paste directly from the Web page to the **.bashrc** file, being edited with gedit.

```
export EC2_KEYPAIR=myec2key # name only, not the file name
export EC2_URL=https://ec2.us-west-1.amazonaws.comexport
EC2_PRIVATE_KEY=$HOME/pk-ABCDE2MA6RCNEC7LCXEDULV7H6JBZZZZ.pem
```

```
export EC2_CERT=$HOME/cert-ABCDE2MA6RCNEC7LCXEDULV7H6JBZZZZ.pem
export JAVA_HOME=/usr/lib/jvm/java-11-openjdk-amd64/
```

Accessing the AMI with the ec2 commands

The EC2 Starter Guide describes the use of the Amazon EC2 tools (**ec2-api-tools**), but the examples also apply to the Eucalyptus EC2 tools (**euca2ools**). Just replace the **ec2** prefix for these tools with the **euca** prefix, as in **euca-describe-images** instead of **ec2-describe-images**.

You will first have to find the AMI ID for the Ubuntu Server AMI. You have to reference the Ubuntu AMI ID to access that image. The official AMI IDs for Ubuntu are listed on the Ubuntu Cloud Images Locator site at:

```
https://cloud-images.ubuntu.com/locator/daily/
```

For the Cloud column choose Amazon AWS and for the Name column choose noble. Then you can choose the AMI ID you want in the ID column. The IDs are links that when you click, opens the Amazon Web Services page and selects the image you choose.

The "ec2 command" column lists the actual ec2 command you have to enter to start the instance. It shows the **ec2-run-instance** command with the AMI ID and the cloud region.

To list all available Ubuntu images, you can use the **ec2-describe-images** command with the **-a** option, and use **grep** to filter the results with the ubuntu pattern. These will include images posted by third parties, not just the official Ubuntu images.

```
ec2-describe-images -a | grep ubuntu
```

To list the current official Noble Ubuntu AMI images, use the **ec2-describe-images** command and pipe the results through a series of **grep** operations beginning with a **099720109477/ubuntu-images/ubuntu-noble** pattern. Be sure to specify the official Canonical user Amazon ID, 099720109477. Add a grep operation to show just the AMI images. This will display the original release Ubuntu images.

```
ec2-describe-images -a | grep 099720109477/ubuntu/images/ubuntu-noble
```

Add a grep operation for an **instance-store**, or **ebs** for an Elastic Block Store volume.

The images are periodically rebuilt and have the name **images-testing** instead of just **images**. The latest (daily build) images have the name **daily**. You can add the image type and the date to narrow your search.

To access an Amazon Machine Image (AMI), you first run the instance using the **ec2-run-instances** command. You will have to specify the AMI image, the SSH keys you created (use the EC2_KEYPAIR variable), and the type (small or micro). For a 64-bit AMI, specify the size. For 64-bit systems, you can add the **-t c1.large** option.

The reservation and instance information are displayed.

Run the **ec2-describe-instances** command to find out your instance ID and the external host the instance is running on.

There are two lines; the second is lengthy and will wrap around. The first entry in the INSTANCE line is the instance ID, and begins with **i-** prefix. The AMI image follows, and then the external hostname on which the instance is being run.

Once the AMI is running, you log in using the **ssh** command, your private key, and the external host listed in the **ec2-describe-instances** output preceded with **ubuntu@**.

When finished, you can log out to return to your shell.

When you are finished, be sure to shut down your AMI instance with the **ec2-terminate-instances** command. Otherwise, your AMI will continue to run and you will be charged for its use. For this command, you use the instance ID listed in the **ec2-describe-instances** output.

```
ec2-terminate-instances <instance_id>
```

Use the **ec2-describe-instances** command to check the status of your AMI, as well as to make sure it is shut down.

Amazon AWS Management Console

If you have access to a desktop Web browser on your system, you can also use the AWS management console to manage and access your Amazon EC2 cloud. Click the EC2 tab to manage your AWS EC2 service. Tasks are listed in the Navigation panel organized by Instances, Images, EBS, and Networking & Security. You can create private keys (SSH) for access and launch instances of AMI images.

```
https://aws.amazon.com/console/
```

The easiest way to access Ubuntu Images is to use the Ubuntu Cloud Images site to first find the image you want, and then click on the Launch button, which is a link to open the AWS management console to configure an instance of that image. You are taken through the steps of creating and starting an instance, as well as creating a private key (SSH) to access the instance. Once the instance is created, you can manage it by clicking on the Instance link in the Navigation bar. You can terminate an instance, click its check box and then choose Terminate from the Instance Actions menu.

Information on creating an AMI

You can create your own AMI with the Amazon AMI tools. Install the **ec2-ami-tools** package.

```
ec2-ami-tools
```

To create an AMI, you use the **ec2-bundle-image** tool. You then use the **ec2-upload-bundle** tool to upload it to the Amazon EC2 cloud. The **/etc/ec2/amitools** directory will hold the EC2 certificate.

A listing and explanation of the EC2 AMI tools are located at:

```
http://awsdocs.s3.amazonaws.com/EC2/ec2-clt.pdf
```

Cloud-Init

The **cloud-init** package provides scripts for the configuration and customization of cloud instances. It applies to AMI images. It includes support for installing an SSH key during instance initialization, login credentials (EC2 SSH keys), repository access, and to set your hostname. The **/etc/cloud** directory holds the **cloud.cfg** configuration file specifying scripts to run, and a

templates subdirectory for your hostname and Ubuntu repository configuration. See
https://help.ubuntu.com/community/CloudInit for more details.

   If your server does not operate from a cloud and has no need of a cloud configuration, it is
possible to disable cloud-init completely, instead of just disabling the its networking configuration.
Keep in mind that this removes all cloud configuration tasks performed by cloud-config. Not just
the networking part.

```
sudo systemctl disable cloud-config
sudo systemctl disable cloud-init
```

Part 4: Network Support

Proxy Servers
Domain Name System
Network Autoconfiguration and DHCP
Firewalls
Administering TCP/IP Networks

14. Proxy Servers: Squid

A proxy server operates as an intermediary between a local network and services available on a larger one, such as the Internet. Requests from local clients for web services can be handled by the proxy server, speeding transactions as well as controlling access. Proxy servers maintain current copies of commonly accessed web pages, speeding web access times by eliminating the need to access the original site constantly. They also perform security functions, protecting servers from unauthorized access.

Protocol	Description and Port
HTTP	Web pages, port 3128
FTP	FTP transfers through websites, port 3128
ICP	Internet Caching Protocol, port 3130
HTCP	Hypertext Caching Protocol, port 4827
CARP	Cache Array Routing Protocol
SNMP	Simple Network Management Protocol, port 3401
SSL	Secure Socket Layer

Table 14-1: Protocols Supported by Squid

Squid is a free, open source, proxy-caching server for web clients, designed to speed Internet access and provide security controls for web servers. It implements a proxy-caching service for web clients that caches web pages as users make requests. Copies of web pages accessed by users are kept in the Squid cache, and as requests are made, Squid checks to see if it has a current copy. If Squid does have a current copy, it returns the copy from its cache instead of querying the original site. If it does not have a current copy, it will retrieve one from the original site. Replacement algorithms periodically replace old objects in the cache. In this way, web browsers can then use the local Squid cache as a proxy HTTP server. Squid currently handles web pages supporting the HTTP, FTP, HTTPS protocols (Squid cannot be used with FTP clients), each with an associated default port (see Table 14-1). It also supports ICP (Internet Cache Protocol), HTCP (Hypertext Caching Protocol) for web caching, and SNMP (Simple Network Management Protocol) for providing status information.

You can find out more about Squid at **http://squid-cache.org**. For detailed information, check the Squid FAQ and the user manual located at their website. The FAQ is also installed in your **/usr/share/doc** under the **squid** directory.

As a proxy, Squid does more than just cache web objects. It operates as an intermediary between the web browsers (clients) and the servers they access. Instead of connections being made directly to the server, a client connects to the proxy server. The proxy then relays requests to the web server. This is useful for situations where a web server is placed behind a firewall server, protecting it from outside access. The proxy is accessible on the firewall, which can then transfer requests and responses back and forth between the client and the web server. The design is often used to allow web servers to operate on protected local networks and still be accessible on the Internet. You can also use a Squid proxy to provide web access to the Internet by local hosts. Instead of using a gateway providing complete access to the Internet, local hosts can use a proxy to allow them just web access. You can also combine the two, allowing gateway access, but using the proxy server to provide more control for web access. In addition, the caching capabilities of Squid can provide local hosts with faster web access.

Technically, you could use a proxy server to simply manage traffic between a web server and the clients who want to communicate with it, without doing caching at all. Squid combines both capabilities as a proxy-caching server.

Squid also provides security capabilities that let you exercise control over hosts accessing your web server. You can deny access by certain hosts and allow access by others. Squid also supports the use of encrypted protocols such as TLS. Encrypted communications are tunneled (passed through without reading) through the Squid server directly to the web server.

Squid is supported and distributed under a GNU Public License by the National Laboratory for Applied Network Research (NLANR) at the University of California, San Diego. The work is based on the Harvest Project to create a web indexing system that includes a high-performance cache daemon called **cached**. You can obtain current source code versions and online documentation from the Squid home page at **http://squid-cache.org**. The Squid software package (squid) consists of the Squid server and support scripts for services like LDAP and HTTP. You can also install the cache manager script called **cachemgr.cgi**, the **squid-cgi** package. The **cachemgr.cgi** script lets you view statistics for the Squid server as it runs. Squid version 4 is available on the main Ubuntu repository as the **squid** package.

```
sudo apt-get install squid
```

Check the Ubuntu Server Guide | Services | Proxy Servers - Squid for basic configuration.

```
https://ubuntu.com/server/docs/proxy-servers-squid
```

Also, check the Ubuntu Community Documentation on Squid at:

```
https://help.ubuntu.com/community/Squid
```

The Squid server is managed by systemd using the **squid.service** file in the **/lib/systemd/system** directory, shown here. It is started for the multi-user.target (WantedBy). The **/usr/sbin/squid** application is used to start, stop, and restart the server (ExecStart, ExecReload, ExecStop). The runtime directory is set to **squid** and its group is **proxy**.

squid.service

```
[Unit]
Description=Squid Web Proxy Server
Documentation=man:squid(8)
After=network.target network-online.target nss-lookup.target

[Service]
Type=notify
PIDFile=/var/run/squid.pid
Group=proxy
RuntimeDirectory=squid
RuntimeDirectoryMode=0775
ExecStartPre=/usr/sbin/squid --foreground -z
ExecStart=/usr/sbin/squid -sYC
ExecReload=/bin/kill -HUP $MAINPID
KillMode=mixed
NotifyAccess=all
```

```
[Install]
WantedBy=multi-user.target
```

You can use the **systemctl** command to manually stop, start, and restart the server, as well as enable for disable it.

```
sudo systemctl enable squid
sudo systemctl start squid
```

Configuring Client Browsers

Squid supports both standard proxy caches and transparent caches. With a standard proxy cache, users will need to configure their browsers to specifically access the Squid server. A transparent cache, on the other hand, requires no browser configuration by users. The cache is transparent, allowing access as if it were a normal website. Transparent caches are implemented by your firewall, using net filtering to intercept requests and direct them to the proxy cache.

With a standard proxy cache, users need to specify their proxy server in their web browser configuration. For this, they will need the IP address of the host running the Squid proxy server as well as the port it is using. Proxies usually make use of port 3128. To configure the use of a proxy server running on the private network, you enter the following. The proxy server is running on **turtle.mytrek.com** (192.168.0.1) and using port 3128.

```
192.168.0.1 3128
```

On Firefox, the user on the local network goes to the Network Settings dialog (Options | General | Network | Settings link).

On the Ubuntu desktop use the Settings Network tab. Click on the Network Proxy gear button to open a dialog where you can specify Automatic, Manual, and Disabled options. With the Manual option you can enter the proxy server address and port numbers.

On Linux and UNIX systems, local hosts can set the **http_proxy** and **ftp_proxy** shell variables to configure access by Linux-supported web browsers such as Lynx. You can place these definitions in your **.profile** or **/etc/profile** file to have them automatically defined whenever you log in.

```
http_proxy=192.168.0.1:3128
ftp_proxy=192.168.0.1:3128
export http_proxy ftp_proxy
```

Alternatively, you can use the proxy's URL.

```
http_proxy=http://turtle.mytrek.com:3128
```

For the Elinks browser, you can specify a proxy in its configuration file, **/etc/elinks.conf**. Set both FTP and web proxy host options, as in:

```
protocol.http.proxy.host   turtle.mytrek.com:3128
protocol.ftp.proxy.host    turtle.mytrek.com:3128
```

Before a client on a local host can use the proxy server, access permission has to be given to it in the server's **squid.conf** file, described in the later section "Security." Access can easily be provided to an entire network. For the sample network used here, you would have to place the following entries in the **squid.conf** file. These are explained in detail in the following sections.

```
acl mylan src 192.168.0.0/255.255.255.0
http_access allow mylan
```

Tip: Web clients that need to access your Squid server as a standard proxy cache will need to know the server's address and the port for Squid's HTTP services, by default 3128.

The squid.conf File

The Squid configuration file is **squid.conf**, located in the **/etc/squid** directory. In the **/etc/squid/squid.conf** file, you set general options such as ports used, security options controlling access to the server, and cache options for configuring caching operations. The default version of **squid.conf** provided with Squid software includes detailed explanations of all standard entries, along with commented default entries. Entries consist of tags that specify different attributes. For example, **maximum_object_size** sets a size limit on objects transferred.

```
maximum_object_size 4 MB
```

Note: Ubuntu installs Squid version 4.1, which provides many changes to previous options. The commented TAG entries will list deprecated options and, in some cases, recommend alternatives.

The **squid.conf** file is a large file that you may want to backup before editing. It is arranged in several commented sections such as:

```
OPTIONS FOR AUTHENTICATION
ACCESS CONTROLS
NETWORK OPTIONS
TLS OPTIONS
SSL OPTIONS
MEMORY CACHE OPTIONS
DISK CACHE OPTIONS
LOGFILE OPTIONS
HTTPS OPTIONS
TIMEOUTS
ADMINISTRATIVE PARAMETERS
DNS OPTIONS
```

As a proxy, Squid will use certain ports for specific services, such as port 3128 for HTTP services like web browsers. Default port numbers are already set for Squid. Should you need to use other ports, you can set them in the **/etc/squid/squid.conf** file. The following entry shows how you set the web browser port,

```
http_port 3128
```

Should you want to give your proxy server a name other that your system's hostname, you can specify one with the **visible_hostname** option (ADMINISTRATIIVE PARAMETERS section).

```
visible_hostname myproxy
```

Note: Squid uses the Simple Network Management Protocol (SNMP) to provide status information and statistics to SNMP agents managing your network. You can

406 *Part 4: Network Support*

control SNMP with the **snmp access** and **port** configurations in the **squid.conf** file.

Proxy Security

Squid can use its role as an intermediary between web clients and a web server to implement access controls, determining who can access the web server and how. Squid does this by checking access control lists (ACLs) of hosts and domains that have had controls placed on them. When it finds a web client from one of those hosts attempting to connect to the web server, it executes the control. Squid supports a number of controls with which it can deny or allow access to the web server by the remote host's web client (see Table 14-2). In effect, Squid sets up a firewall just for the web server. See the **/etc/squid/squid.conf** file's **TAG: acl** comments for a complete listing of **acl** options.

The first step in configuring Squid security is to create ACLs. These are lists of hosts and domains for which you want to set up controls. You define ACLs using the **acl** command, creating a label for the systems on which you are setting controls. You then use commands such as **http_access** to define these controls. You can define a system, or a group of systems, by use of several **acl** options, such as the source IP address, the domain name, or even the time and date. For example, the **src** option is used to define a system or group of systems with a certain source address. To define a **mylan acl** entry for systems in a local network with the addresses 192.168.0.0 through 192.168.0.255, use the following ACL definition.

```
acl mylan src 192.168.0.0/255.255.255.0
```

Once it is defined, you can use an ACL definition in a Squid option to specify a control you want to place on those systems. For example, to allow access by the mylan group of local systems to the web through the proxy, use an **http_access** option with the **allow** action specifying **mylan** as the **acl** definition to use, as shown here.

```
http_access allow mylan
```

The default **squid.conf** file provides entries for a recommended minimum configuration, beginning with entries for controlling access to your local net and server ports. Local net entries are listed for different local addresses (see Chapter 18).

```
acl localnet src 192.168.0.0.0/16  # RFC1918 local private network (LAN)
```

Access is supported on the HTTPS port (443), and server ports such as 80 for the Web server and 21 for the FTP server. These are designated as safe.

```
acl Safe_ports port 443      # https
acl Safe_ports port 80       # http
acl Safe_ports port 21       # ftp
```

Default **http_access** entries deny access to outside users, and allow access by hosts on the local network and the local host (Squid server host). Access is also denied on ports not deemed safe or without secure SSL ports. The **http_access** entries already defined in the **squid.conf** file are shown here.

```
http_access deny !Safe_ports
http_access deny CONNECT !SSL_ports
http_access allow localhost manager
http_access deny manager
http_access allow localhost
http_access deny all
```

Options	Description
src *ip-address/netmask*	Client's IP address
src *addr1-addr2/netmask*	Range of addresses
dst *ip-address/netmask*	Destination IP address
localip *ip-address/netmask*	Local socket IP address
srcdomain *domain*	Reverse lookup, client IP
dstdomain *domain*	Destination server from URL; for **dstdomain** and **dstdom_regex**, a reverse lookup is tried if an IP-based URL is used
srcdom_regex [-i] *expression*	Regular expression matching client name
dstdom_regex [-i] *expression*	Regular expression matching destination
time *[day-abbrevs] [h1:m1-h2:m2]*	Time as specified by day, hour, and minutes. Day abbreviations: S = Sunday, M = Monday, T = Tuesday, W = Wednesday, H = Thursday, F = Friday, A = Saturday
url_regex [-i] *expression*	Regular expression matching on whole URL
urlpath_regex [-i] *expression*	Regular expression matching on URL path
port *ports*	A specific port or range of ports
proto *protocol*	A specific protocol, such as HTTP or FTP
method *method*	Specific methods, such as GET and POST
browser [-i] *regexp*	Pattern match on user-agent header
ident *username*	String match on **ident** output
src_as *number*	Used for routing of requests to specific caches
dst_as *number*	Used for routing of requests to specific caches
proxy_auth *username*	List of valid usernames
snmp_community *string*	A community string to limit access to your SNMP agent

Table 14-2: Squid ACL Options

By defining ACLs and using them in Squid options, you can tailor your website with the kind of security you want. You should add your own ACLs after the comment label located near the middle of the file after the **http_access** entries for safe ports, and before the **http_access** entries for the localnet and local host.

```
#
# INSERT YOUR OWN RULE(S) HERE TO ALLOW ACCESS FROM YOUR CLIENTS
#
```

The following example allows access to the web through the proxy by only the **mylan** group of local systems, denying access to all others. Two **acl** entries are set up: one for the local system and one for all others; **http_access** options first allow access to the local system and then deny access to all others.

```
acl mylan src 192.168.0.0/255.255.255.0
acl all src 0.0.0.0/0.0.0.0
http_access allow mylan
http_access deny all
```

Basic default entries that you will find in your **squid.conf** file, along with an entry for the **mylan** sample network, are shown here.

```
acl manager proto cache_object
acl localhost src 127.0.0.1/32 ::1
acl to_localhost dst 127.0.0.1/0.0.0.0/32  ::1
acl mylan src 192.168.0.0/255.255.255.0
acl SSL_ports port 443
```

The order of the **http_access** options is important. Squid starts from the first and works its way down, stopping at the first **http_access** option with an ACL entry that matches. In the preceding example, local systems that match the first **http_access** command are allowed, whereas others fall through to the second **http_access** command and are denied.

For hosts and networks using the proxy, you can also control what sites they can access. For a destination address, you create an **acl** entry with the **dst** qualifier. The **dst** qualifier takes as its argument the site address. Then you can create an **http_access** option to control access to that address. The following example denies access by anyone using the proxy to access the destination site **rabbit.mytrek.com**. If you have a local network accessing the web through the proxy, you can use such commands to restrict access to certain sites.

```
acl myrabbit dst rabbit.mytrek.com
http_access deny myrabbit
```

Proxy Caches

Squid primarily uses the Internet Cache Protocol (ICP) to communicate with other web caches. It also provides support for the more experimental Hypertext Cache Protocol (HTCP) and the Cache Array Routing Protocol (CARP).

Using the ICP protocols, your Squid cache can connect to other Squid caches or other cache servers, such as the Microsoft proxy server. This way, if your network's Squid cache does not have a copy of a requested Web page, it can contact another cache to see if it is there instead of accessing the original site. You can configure Squid to connect to other Squid caches by connecting it to a cache hierarchy. Squid supports a hierarchy of caches denoted by the terms *child, sibling,* and *parent.* Sibling and child caches are accessible on the same level and are automatically queried whenever a request cannot be located in your own Squid's cache. If these queries fail, a parent cache is queried, which then searches its own child and sibling caches or its own parent cache, if needed, and so on.

Use **cache_peer** to set up parent, sibling, and child connections to other caches. This option has five fields. The first two consist of the hostname or IP address of the queried cache and the cache type (parent, child, or sibling). The third and fourth are the HTTP and the ICP ports of that cache, usually 3128 and 3130. The last is used for **cache_peer** options such as **proxy-only** to not save fetched objects locally, **no-query** for those caches that do not support ICP, and **weight**, which assigns priority to a parent cache. The following example sets up a connection to a parent cache.

```
cache_peer parent.foo.net parent 3128 3130
```

Squid provides several options for configuring cache memory. The **cache_mem** option sets the memory allocated primarily for objects currently in use (objects in transit). If available, space can also be used for frequently accessed objects (hot objects) and failed requests (negative-cache objects). The default is 8MB. The following example sets it to 256MB.

```
cache_mem 256 MB
```

You can use the cache manager (**cachemgr.cgi**) to manage the cache and view statistics on the cache manager as it runs. To run the cache manager, use your browser to execute the **cachemgr.cgi** script (this script should be placed in your web server's **cgi-bin** directory).

Logs

Squid keeps several logs detailing access, cache performance, and error messages. The log files are located in the **/var/log/squid** directory. Check the **/etc/squid/squid.conf** file's **TAG: logformat** comments for a detailed explanation of log format codes. There is also a bug with the **logformat squid** option. You cannot use the term **squid**. Use another name which you then define with an **access daemon** option. See the Ubuntu 24.04 release notes for details. The Squid logs are listed here.

access.log holds requests sent to your proxy.

cache.log holds Squid server messages such as errors and startup messages.

store.log holds information about the Squid cache such as objects added or removed.

ubuntu

15. Domain Name System

DNS Address Translations

Local Area Network Addressing

BIND

Domain Name System Configuration

named.conf

The options Statement

The named configuration files

Resource Records for Zone Files

Zone Files

Subdomains and Secondaries

IP Virtual Domains

Cache File

Dynamic Update: DHCP and Journal Files

DNS Security: Access Control Lists, TSIG, and DNSSEC

Split DNS: Views

The Domain Name System (DNS) is an Internet service that locates and translates domain names into their corresponding Internet Protocol (IP) addresses. All computers connected to the Internet are addressed using an IP address. Since an average user on a network might have to access many different hosts, keeping track of the IP addresses needed quickly became a problem. It was much easier to label hosts with names and use the names to access them. Names were associated with IP addresses. When a user used a name to access a host, the corresponding IP address was looked up first and then used to provide access.

With the changeover from IPv4 to IPv6 addressing, DNS servers will have some configuration differences. Both are covered here, though some topics will use IPv4 addressing for better clarity, as they are easier to represent.

DNS Address Translations

The process of translating IP addresses into associated names is fairly straightforward. Small networks can be set up easily, with just the basic configuration. The task becomes much more complex when you deal with larger networks and with the Internet. The sheer size of the task can make DNS configuration a complex operation.

Fully Qualified Domain Names

IP addresses were associated with corresponding names, called fully qualified domain names. A fully qualified domain name is composed of three or more segments. The first segment is the name that identifies the host, and the remaining segments are for the network in which the host is located. The network segments of a fully qualified domain name are usually referred to simply as the domain name, while the host part is referred to as the hostname (though this is also used to refer to the complete fully qualified domain name). In effect, subnets are referred to as domains. The fully qualified domain name **https://www.linux.org** could have an IPv4 address 198.182.196.56, where 198.182.196 is the network address and 56 is the host ID. Computers can be accessed only with an IP address, so a fully qualified domain name must first be translated into its corresponding IP address to be of any use. The parts of the IP address that make up the domain name and the hosts can vary.

IPv4 Addresses

The IP address may be implemented in either the newer IPv6 (Internet Protocol Version 6) format, or the older and more common IPv4 (Internet Protocol Version 4) format. Since the IPv4 addressing is much easier to read, that format will be used in these examples. In the older IPv4 format, the IP address consists of a number composed of four segments, separated by periods. Depending on the type of network, several of the first segments are used for the network address and one or more of the last segments are used for the host address. In a standard class C network used in smaller networks, the first three segments are the computer's network address and the last segment is the computer's host ID (as used in these examples). For example, in the address 192.168.0.2, 192.168.0 is the network address and 2 is the computer's host ID within that network. Together, they make up an IP address by which the computer can be addressed from anywhere on the Internet.

IPv6 Addressing

IPv6 addressing uses a very different approach designed to provide more flexibility and support for very large address spaces. There are three different types of IPv6 addresses: unicast, multicast, and anycast, of which unicast is the most commonly used. A unicast address is directed to a particular interface. There are several kinds of unicast addresses, depending on how the address is used. For example, you can have a global unicast address for access through the Internet or a unique-level unicast address for private networks.

Though consisting of 128 bits in eight segments (16 bits, 2 bytes, per segment), an IPv6 address is made up of several fields that conform roughly to the segments and capabilities of an IPv4 address: networking information, subnet information, and the interface identifier (host ID). The network information includes a format prefix indicating the type of network connection. In addition, a subnet identifier can be used to specify a local subnet. The network information takes up the first several segments. The remainder is used for the interface ID. The interface ID is a 64-bit (four-segment) Extended Unique Identifier (EUI-64) generated from a network device's Media Access Control (MAC) address. IP addresses are written in hexadecimal numbers, making them difficult to use. Each segment is separated from the next by a colon, and a set of consecutive segments with zero values can be left empty.

Manual Translations: /etc/hosts

Any computer on the Internet can maintain a file that manually associates IP addresses with domain names. On Linux and UNIX systems, this file is called the **/etc/hosts** file. Here, you can enter the IP addresses and domain names of computers you commonly access. Using this method, however, requires each computer to have a complete listing of all other computers on the Internet, and that listing must be updated constantly. Early on, this became clearly impractical for the Internet, though it is still feasible for small, isolated networks, as well as simple home networks.

DNS Servers

The Domain Name System has been implemented to deal with the task of translating the domain name of any computer on the Internet to its IP address. The task is carried out by interconnecting servers that manage the Domain Name System (also referred to as DNS servers or name servers). These DNS servers keep lists of fully qualified domain names and their IP addresses, matching one up with the other. This service is referred to as the Domain Name System. The Internet is composed of many connected subnets called domains, each with its own Domain Name System (DNS) servers that keep track of all the fully qualified domain names and IP addresses for all the computers on its network. DNS servers are hierarchically linked to root servers, which, in turn, connect to other root servers and the DNS servers on their subnets throughout the Internet. The section of a network for which a given DNS server is responsible is called a zone. Although a zone may correspond to a domain, many zones may, in fact, be within a domain, each with its own name server. This is true for large domains where too many systems exist for one name server to manage.

DNS Operation

When a user enters a fully qualified domain name to access a remote host, a resolver program queries the local network's DNS server requesting the corresponding IP address for that remote host. With the IP address, the user can then access the remote host. In Figure 15-1, the user at **rabbit.mytrek.com** wants to connect to the remote host **lizard.mytrek.com**. The host **rabbit.mytrek.com** first sends a request to the network's DNS server, in this case, **turtle.mytrek.com**, to look up the name **lizard.mytrek.com** and find its IP address. The DNS server at **turtle.mytrek.com** then returns the IP address for **lizard.mytrek.com**, 192.168.0.3, to the requesting host, **rabbit.mytrek.com**. With the IP address, the user at **rabbit.mytrek.com** can then connect to **lizard.mytrek.com**.

Figure 15-1: DNS server operation

DNS Clients: Resolvers

The names of the DNS servers that service a host's network are kept in the host's **/etc/resolv.conf** file. When setting up an Internet connection, the DNS servers, also referred to as name servers, provided by your Internet service provider (ISP) were placed in this file. These name servers resolve any fully qualified domain names that you use when you access different Internet sites. For example, when you enter a website name in your browser, the name is looked up by the name servers and the name's associated IP address is then used to access the site. In this file, the term **nameserver** references the IP address of a DNS server.

/etc/resolv.conf

```
search mytrek.com  mytrain.com
nameserver  192.168.0.1
nameserver  192.168.0.3
```

Local Area Network Addressing

If you are setting up a DNS server for a local area network (LAN) that is not connected to the Internet, you should use a special set of IP numbers reserved for such local networks (also known as private networks or intranets). This is especially true if you are implementing IP masquerading, where only a gateway machine has an Internet address, and the others make use of that one address to connect to the Internet. The IPv4 and IPv6 protocols use different addressing formats for local addresses. Many local and home networks still use the IPv4 format, and this is the format used in the following local addressing example.

IPv4 provides a range of private addresses for the three classes supported by IPv4. The class C IPv4 network numbers use the special network number 192.168. Numbers are also reserved for class A and class B non-Internet local networks. Table 15-1 lists these addresses. The possible addresses available span from 0 to 255 in the host segment of the address. For example, class B network addresses range from 172.16.0.0 to 172.16.255.255, giving you a total of 65,534 possible hosts. The class C network ranges from 192.168.0.0 to 192.168.255.255, giving you 254 possible subnetworks, each with 254 possible hosts. The number 127.0.0.0 is reserved for a system's loopback interface, which allows it to communicate with itself, as it enables users on the same system to send messages to each other.

Address	Networks
10.0.0.0	Class A network
172.16.0.0–172.31.255.255	Class B network
192.168.0.0	Class C network
127.0.0.0	Loopback network (for system self-communication)

Table 15-1: Non-Internet Private Network IP Addresses

IPv4 Private Networks

These numbers were originally designed for class-based addressing. However, they can just as easily be used for Classless Interdomain Routing (CIDR) addressing, where you can create subnetworks with a smaller number of hosts. For example, the 254 hosts addressed in a class C network could be split into two subnetworks, each with 125 hosts.

IPv6 Private Networks

IPv6 supports private networks with unique-local addresses that provide the same functionality of IPv4 private addresses. The unique-local addresses have no public routing information. They cannot access the Internet. They are restricted to the site they are used on. The unique-local addresses use only three fields: a format prefix, subnet identifier, and interface identifier. A site-level address has the format prefix **fc00**. If you have no subnets, it will be set to 0. This will give you a network prefix of **fc00:0:0:0**. You can drop the set of empty zeros to give you **fc00::**. The interface ID field will hold the interface identification information, similar to the host ID information in IPv4.

```
fc00::            IPv6 unique-local prefix
```

The loopback device will have the special address of **::1**, also known as localhost.

```
::1        IPv6 loopback network
```

Rather than using a special set of reserved addresses as IPv4 does, with IPv6 you only use the unique-local prefix, **fc00**, and the special loopback address, **::1**.

Tip: Once your network is set up, you can use ping6 or ping to see if it is working. The ping6 tool is designed for IPv6 addresses, whereas ping is used for IPv4.

Local Network Address Example Using IPv4

If you are setting up a LAN, such as a small business or home network, you are free to use a class C IPv4 network (254 hosts or less), that have the special network number 192.168, as used in these examples. These are numbers for your local machines. You can set up a private network, such as an intranet, using network cards, such as Ethernet cards and Ethernet hubs, and then configure your machines with IP addresses starting from 192.168.0.1. The host segment can range from 1 to 254, where 255 is used for the broadcast address. If you have three machines on your home network, you can give them the addresses 192.168.0.1, 192.168.0.2, and 192.168.0.3. You can then set up domain name system services for your network by running a DNS server on one of the machines. This machine becomes your network's DNS server. You can then give your machines fully qualified domain names and configure your DNS server to translate the names to their corresponding IP addresses. As shown in Figure 15-1, for example, you could give the machine 192.168.0.1 the name **turtle.mytrek.com** and the machine 192.168.0.2 the name **rabbit.mytrek.com**. You can also implement Internet services on your network such as FTP, Web, and mail services by setting up servers for them on your machines. Then you can configure your DNS server to let users access those services using fully qualified domain names. For example, for the **mytrek.com** network, the Web server could be accessed using the name **www.mytrek.com**. Instead of a Domain Name System, you could have the **/etc/hosts** files on each machine contain the entire list of IP addresses and domain names for all the machines in your network. But in this case, for any changes, you would have to update each machine's **/etc/hosts** file.

BIND

The DNS server software currently in use on Linux systems is Berkeley Internet Name Domain (BIND). BIND was originally developed at the University of California, Berkeley, and is currently maintained and supported by the Internet Software Consortium (ISC). You can obtain BIND information and current software releases from its website at **https://www.isc.org/**. Web page documentation and manuals are included with the software package. At that site, you can also access the BIND Administration Manual for detailed configuration information. The BIND documentation directory, **bind9-doc**, in **/usr/share/doc** contains the Administrative Reference Manual in the **arm** subdirectory. It is also available at:

```
https://downloads.isc.org/isc/bind9/9.16.4/doc/arm/html/
```

The DNS server packages on Ubuntu are:

```
bind9
bind9-doc
```

You can find out more about Bind9 at:

```
https://www.isc.org/bind/
```

The version of Bind9 used on Ubuntu 24.04 is 16.4. New features include the DNSSEC Key Manager, DNSTAP (logging), DNS Cookies (security), and Dynamic Database Interface (records). You can find out more about this release at:

```
https://downloads.isc.org/isc/bind9/9.16.4/doc/arm/html/notes.html
```

Check the Ubuntu Server documentation How-To guide (Networking | Domain Name Service) for basic configuration. The Guide takes you through the implementation of a simple DNS server, addressing topics such as zone files, secondary servers, DNS tools, and logging. You can also check the BIND9 Server Howto.

```
https://documentation.ubuntu.com/server/how-to/networking/install-dns/
```

```
https://help.ubuntu.com/community/BIND9ServerHowto
```

BIND Servers and Tools

The BIND DNS server software consists of a name server daemon, several sample configuration files, and resolver libraries. As of 1998, a new version of BIND, beginning with the series number 8.*x,* implemented a new configuration file using a new syntax. Version 9.0 adds new security features and support for IPv6. Older versions, which begin with the number 4.*x,* use a different configuration file with an older syntax. Most distributions, including Ubuntu, currently install the 9.*x* version of BIND.

The name of the BIND name server daemon is **named**. To operate your machine as a name server, simply run the **named** daemon with the appropriate configuration. The **named** daemon listens for resolution requests and provides the correct IP address for the requested hostname. On Ubuntu, **named** runs as a stand-alone daemon, starting up when the system boots and constantly running. You can start, stop, and restart the daemon manually using the **systemctl** command and the **named** service script.

```
sudo systemctl restart named
```

You can also use the older name for the service script, **bind9**. This is now an alias for **named**.

```
sudo systemctl restart bind9
```

You can also use the Remote Name Daemon Controller utility, **rndc**, provided with BIND (**bind9utils** package) to start, stop, restart, and check the status of the server as you test its configuration. **rndc** with the **stop** command stops **named** and, with the start command, starts it again, reading your **named.conf** file. **rndc** with the **help** command provides a list of all **rndc** commands. Configuration is set in the **/etc/rndc.conf** file. Once your name server is running, you can test it using the **dig** or **nslookup** utility, which queries a name server, providing information about hosts and domains. If you start **dig** with no arguments, it enters an interactive mode where you can issue different **dig** commands to refine your queries.

To check the syntax of your DNS server configuration and zone files, BIND provides the **named-checkconfig**, **named-checkzone**, and **named-rrchecker** tools: **named-checkconfig** will check the syntax of DNS configuration file, **named.conf**, **named-checkzone** will check a zone file's syntax, and **named-rrchecker** will check the syntax of a resource record. Other syntax checking tools are also available, such as **nslint**, which operates like the programming tool **lint,** and

arpaname which translates an IP address to its corresponding IN-ADDR.ARPA address used for reverse resolutions. Table 15-2 lists several DNS administrative tools.

Tool	Description
`dig` *domain*	Domain Information Groper, tool to obtain information on a DNS server. Preferred over `nslookup`
`host` *hostname*	Simple lookup of hosts
`nslookup` *domain*	Tool to query DNS servers for information about domains and hosts
`named-checkconf`	BIND tool to check the syntax of your DNS configuration file, **/etc/named.conf**
`named-checkzone`	BIND tool to check the syntax of your DNS zone files
`named-rrchecker`	BIND tool to check the syntax of your DNS resource records
`nslint`	Tool to check the syntax of your DNS configuration and zone files
`arpaname`	Tool to translate IP address to an IN-ADDR.ARPA address used for reverse resolutions
`rndc` *command*	Remote Name Daemon Controller, an administrative tool for managing a DNS server (version 9.*x*)
`ndc`	Name Daemon Controller (version 8.*x*)
`bind9`	Start, stop, and restart the **named** server with the **bind9**.**service** file

Table 15-2: BIND Diagnostic and Administrative Tools

The **named** daemon is managed by **systemd** using the **named.service** unit file. It is started for the **multi-user.target** (WantedBy). Runtime configuration is read from **/etc/default/bind9**. Though the **/usr/sbin/named** command starts the server (ExecStart), the **rndc** command is used to restart or stop the server (ExecReload and ExecStop). The **named.service** file has as an alias **bind9.service**, which was the name used in previous releases.

named.service

```
[Unit]
Description=BIND Domain Name Server
Documentation=man:named(8)
After=network.target
Wants=nss-lookup.target
Before=nss-lookup.target

[Service]

Type=forking
EnvironmentFile=/etc/default/named
ExecStart=/usr/sbin/named -f $OPTIONS
ExecReload=/usr/sbin/rndc reload
ExecStop=/usr/sbin/rndc stop
Restart=on-failure
```

```
[Install]
WantedBy=multi-user.target
Alias=bind9.service
```

Domain Name System Configuration

You configure a DNS server using a configuration file, several zone files, and a cache file. The part of a network for which the name server is responsible is called a zone. A zone is not the same as a domain because in a large domain you could have several zones, each with its own name server. You could also have one name server servicing several zones. In this case, each zone has its own zone file.

DNS Zones

The zone files hold resource records that provide hostname and IP address associations for computers on the network for which the DNS server is responsible. Zone files exist for the server's network and the local host. Zone entries are defined in the **named.conf** file. Here, you place zone entries for your primary, secondary, and forward DNS servers. The most commonly used zone types are described here:

Primary zone   This is the primary zone file for the network supported by the DNS server. It holds the mappings from domain names to IP addresses for all the hosts on that network.

Secondary zone   These are references to other DNS servers for your network. Your network can have a primary DNS server and several secondary DNS servers to help carry the workload. A secondary DNS server automatically copies its configuration files, including all zone files, from the primary DNS server. Any changes to the primary configuration files trigger an automatic download of these files to the secondary servers. In effect, you only have to manage the configuration files for the primary DNS server, since they are automatically copied to the secondary servers.

Forward zone   The forward zone lists name servers outside your network that should be searched if your network's name server fails to resolve an address.

IN-ADDR.ARPA zone   DNS can also provide reverse resolutions, where an IP address is used to determine the associated domain name address. Such lookups are provided by **IN-ADDR.ARPA** zone files. Each primary zone file usually has a corresponding **IN-ADDR.ARPA** zone file to provide reverse resolution for that zone. For each primary zone entry, a corresponding reverse mapping zone entry named **IN-ADDR.ARPA** also exists, as well as one for the localhost. This entry performs reverse mapping from an IP address to its domain name. The name of the zone entry uses the domain IP address, which is the IP address with segments listed starting from the host, instead of the network. So for the IP address 192.168.0.4, where 4 is the host address, the corresponding domain IP address is 4.0.168.192, listing the segments in reverse order. The reverse mapping for the localhost is 1.0.0.127.

IP6.ARPA zone   This is the IPv6 equivalent of the **IN-ADDR.ARPA** zone, providing reverse resolution for that zone. The IP6.ARPA zone uses bit labels that provide a bit-level format that is easier to write, requiring no reverse calculation on the part of the DNS administrator.

IP6.INT zone   This is the older form of the IPv6 IP6.ARPA zone, which is the equivalent of the IPv4 **IN-ADDR.ARPA** zone, providing reverse resolution for a zone. IP6.INT uses a nibble format to specify a reverse zone. In this format, a hexadecimal IPv6 address is segmented into each of its 32 hexadecimal numbers and listed in reverse order, each segment separated by a period.

Hint zone   A hint zone specifies the root name servers and is denoted by a period (.). A DNS server is normally connected to a larger network, such as the Internet, which has its own DNS servers. DNS servers are connected this way hierarchically, with each server having its root servers to which it can send resolution queries. The root servers are designated in the hint zone.

In accordance with RFC 9499 which specifies DNS terminology, the term master has been replaced by primary, and slave by secondary. This can be confusing because the examples and default files in the bind package still use the master/slave terminology. This chapter will use the approved terms primary and secondary.

DNS Servers Types

There are several kinds of DNS servers, each designed to perform a different type of task under the Domain Name System. The basic kind of DNS server is the primary server. Each network must have at least one primary server that is responsible for resolving names on the network. Large networks may need several DNS servers. Some of these can be secondary servers that can be updated directly from a primary server. Others may be alternative primary servers that hosts in a network can use. Both are commonly referred to as secondary servers. For DNS requests a DNS server cannot resolve, the request can be forwarded to specific DNS servers outside the network, such as on the Internet. DNS servers in a network can be set up to perform this task, and are referred to as forwarder servers. To help bear the workload, local DNS servers can be set up within a network that operate as caching servers. Such a server merely collects DNS lookups from previous requests it sent to the main DNS server. Any repeated requests can then be answered by the caching server.

A server that can answer DNS queries for a given zone with authority is known as an authoritative server. An authoritative server holds the DNS configuration records for hosts in a zone that will associate each host's DNS name with an IP address. For example, a primary server is an authoritative server. So are secondary and stealth servers. A caching server is not authoritative. It only holds whatever associations it picked up from other servers and cannot guarantee that the associations are valid. A listing of the different types of servers follows.

Primary server   This is the primary DNS server for a zone.

Secondary server   A DNS server that receives zone information from the primary server.

Forwarder server   A server that forwards unresolved DNS requests to outside DNS servers. Can be used to keep other servers on a local network hidden from the Internet.

Caching only server   Caches DNS information it receives from DNS servers and uses it to resolve local requests.

Stealth server   A DNS server for a zone not listed as a name server by the primary DNS server.

Location of Bind Server Files: /etc/bind/

Both the configuration and zone files used by BIND are placed in the **/etc/bind** directory. Zone files begin with the prefix **db**, as in **db.127** for the localhost zone file.

```
/etc/bind/named.conf          BIND configuration file
/etc/bind/db.*                BIND zone files
```

BIND Configuration Files

The configuration files for the **named** daemon are located in **/etc/bind/** directory and have a **.conf** extension, such as **named.conf**. Configuration statements use a flexible syntax similar to C programs. The format enables easy configuration of selected zones, enabling features such as access control lists and categorized logging. A configuration file consists of BIND configuration statements with attached blocks within which specific options are listed. A configuration statement is followed by arguments and a block that is delimited with braces. Within the block are lines of option and feature entries. Each entry is terminated with a semicolon. Comments can use the C, C++, or Shell/Perl syntax: enclosing /* */, preceding //, or preceding #. The following example shows a zone statement followed by the zone name and a block of options that begin with an opening brace ({). Each option entry ends with a semicolon. The entire block ends with a closing brace, also followed by a semicolon. The format for a statement is shown here, along with the different kinds of comments allowed. Tables 15-4, 15-5, and 15-6 list several commonly used statements and options.

```
// comments
/* comments */
# comments

statements {
 options and features; //comments
};
```

The following example shows a simple caching server entry.

```
// a caching only nameserver config
//
zone "." {
      type hint;
      file "named.ca";
      };
```

Once you have created your configuration file, you should check its syntax with the **named-checkconfig** tool. Enter the command on a shell command line. If you do not specify a configuration file, it will default to **/etc/bind/named.conf**.

```
named-checkconfig
```

The zone Statement

The zone statement is used to specify the domains that the name server will service. To create a zone statement, enter the keyword zone, followed by the name of the domain placed within double quotes. Do not place a period at the end of the domain name. In the following example, a period is within the domain name, but not at the end, "**mytrek.com**"; this differs from the zone file, which requires a period at the end of a complete domain name.

After the zone name, you can specify the class **in**, which stands for Internet. You can also leave it out, in which case it is assumed (there are only a few other esoteric classes that are rarely used). Within the zone block, you can place several options (see Table 15-3). Two essential options are type and file. The type option is used to specify the zone's type. The file option is used to specify the name of the zone file to be used for this zone. You can choose from several types of zones: **primary**, **secondary**, **stub**, **forward**, and **hint**. A **primary** zone specifies that the zone holds primary information and is authorized to act on it. A primary server was called a primary server in the older BIND 4 configuration. A **secondary** zone indicates that the zone needs to update its data periodically from a specified primary name server. Use this entry if your name server is operating as a secondary server for another primary (primary) DNS server. A **stub** zone copies only other name server entries, instead of the entire zone. A **forward** zone directs all queries to name servers specified in a forwarders statement. A **hint** zone specifies the set of root name servers used by all Internet DNS servers. You can also specify several options that can override any global options set with the options statement. Table 15-3 lists the BIND zone types. The following example shows a simple **zone** statement for the **mytrek.com** domain. Its class is Internet (**in**), and its type is **primary**. The name of its zone file is usually the same as the zone name, in this case, "**mytrek.com**."

```
zone "mytrek.com" in {
      type primary;
      file "mytrek.com";
      };
```

Type	Description
primary	Primary DNS zone
secondary	Secondary DNS server; controlled by a primary DNS server
hint	Set of root DNS Internet servers
forward	Forwards any queries in it to other servers
stub	Like a secondary zone, but holds only names of DNS servers

Table 15-3: DNS BIND Zone Types

Configuration Statements

Other statements, such as **acl**, **server**, **options**, and **logging**, enable you to configure different features for your name server (see Table 15-4). The **server** statement defines the characteristics to be associated with a remote name server, such as the transfer method and key ID for transaction security. The **control** statement defines special control channels. The **key** statement defines a key ID to be used in a server statement that associates an authentication method with a particular name server (see "DNSSEC" later in this chapter). The **logging** statement is used to configure logging options for the name server, such as the maximum size of the log file and a severity level for messages. Table 15-5 lists the BIND statements.

Statement	Description
/* comment */	BIND comment in C syntax.
// comment	BIND comment in C++ syntax.
# comment	BIND comment in Unix shell and Perl syntax.
acl	Defines a named IP address matching list.
include	Includes a file, interpreting it as part of the **named.conf** file.
key	Specifies key information for use in authentication and authorization.
logging	Specifies what the server logs and where the log messages are sent.
options	Global server configuration options and defaults for other statements.
controls	Declares control channels to be used by the ndc utility.
server	Sets certain configuration options for the specified server basis.
sortlists	Gives preference to specified networks according to a queries source.
trust-anchors	When used with **static key**, it defines DNSSEC keys preconfigured into the server and implicitly trusted (same as the deprecated **trusted-keys**). When used with **initial key**, it defines DNSSEC keys to be maintained (same as the deprecated **managed-keys**).
zone	Defines a zone.
view	Defines a view.

Table 15-4: BIND Configuration Statements

Option	Description
type	Specifies a zone type.
file	Specifies the zone file for the zone.
directory	Specifies a directory for zone files.
forwarders	Lists hosts for DNS servers where requests are to be forwarded.
primarys	Lists hosts for DNS primary servers for a secondary server.
notify	Allows primary servers to notify their secondary servers when the primary zone data changes and updates are needed.
allow-transfer	Specifies which hosts are allowed to receive zone transfers.
allow-query	Specifies hosts that are allowed to make queries.
allow-recursion	Specifies hosts that are allowed to perform recursive queries on the server.

Table 15-5: Zone Options

The **sortlists** statement lets you specify preferences to be used when a query returns multiple responses. For example, you could give preference to your localhost network or to a private local network such a 192.168.0.0.

The options Statement

The options statement defines global options and can be used only once in the configuration file. An extensive number of options cover such components as forwarding, name checking, directory path names, access control, and zone transfers, among others (see Table 15-6). A complete listing can be found in the BIND documentation. The options statement is listed in the **/etc/bind/named.conf.options** file. It is included in the **named.conf** file with an **include** statement.

```
include  "/etc/bind/named.conf.options"
```

Option	Description
sortlist	Gives preference to specified networks according to a queries source.
directory	Specifies a directory for zone files.
forwarders	Lists hosts for DNS servers where requests are to be forwarded.
allow-transfer	Specifies which hosts are allowed to receive zone transfers.
allow-query	Specifies hosts that are allowed to make queries.
allow-recursion	Specifies hosts that are allowed to perform recursive queries on the server.
notify	Allows primary servers to notify their secondary servers when the primary zone data changes and updates are needed.
blackhole	Option to eliminate denial response by allow-query.

Table 15-6: Bind Options for the options Statement

The directory Option

An important option found in most configuration files is the directory option, which holds the location of links for the name server's zone and cache files on your system. The following example is taken from the **/etc/bind/named.conf.options** file, with sample entries added for forward servers. The example uses IPv4 addresses.

```
options {
        directory "/var/cache/bind";
        forwarders { 192.168.0.34;
                192.168.0.47;
                };
        };
```

The forwarders Option

Another commonly used global option is the forwarders option. With the forwarders option, you can list several DNS servers to which queries can be forwarded if they cannot be resolved by the local DNS server. This is helpful for local networks that may need to use a DNS server connected to the Internet. The forwarders option can also be placed in forward zone entries.

The notify Option

With the notify option turned on, the primary zone DNS servers send messages to any secondary DNS servers whenever their configuration has changed. The secondary servers can then perform zone transfers in which they download the changed configuration files. Secondary servers always use the DNS configuration files copied from their primary DNS servers. The notify option takes one argument, yes or no, where yes is the default. With the no argument, you can have the primary server not send out any messages to the secondary servers, in effect preventing any zone transfers.

The named configuration files

BIND configuration uses three named configuration files for your zones and server options. These files are located in the **/etc/bind** directory.

named.conf The primary BIND configuration file. This file will read in the **named.conf.local**, the **named.conf.options**, and the **named.conf.default-zones** files. The DNS server actually only looks for the **named.conf** file.

named.conf.options This file includes global options for your DNS server.

named.conf.local Here you add your own zone configuration entries.

named.conf.default-zones This file lists the entries for the localhost and broadcast zones, used by a DNS server to access its own host.

The named.conf configuration file

The **named.conf** configuration file consist of three **include** statements for reading in the contents of the **named.conf.local**, the **named.conf.options**, and the **named.conf.default-zones** files. You should make any changes to these files, not to the **named.conf** file, though you can add changes to the **named.conf** file if you want. First the **named.conf.options** file is read to set global options, then the **named.conf.local** file which holds your DNS server zone statements, and then the **named.conf.default-zones** file which holds the standard zone definitions for root level access, the localhost, and broadcast. The **named.conf** file installed by the BIND server package to the **/etc/bind** directory is shown here. The file begins with comments using //.

/etc/bind/named.conf

```
// This is the primary configuration file for the BIND DNS server named.
//
// Please read /usr/share/doc/bind9/README.Debian.gz for information on the
// structure of BIND configuration files in Debian, *BEFORE* you customize
// this configuration file.
//
// If you are just adding zones, please do that in /etc/bind/named.conf.local

include "/etc/bind/named.conf.options";
include "/etc/bind/named.conf.local";
include "/etc/bind/named.conf.default-zones";
```

The named.conf.options configuration file

The **named.conf.options** file contains an options statement with global options listed. The **directory** option sets the directory for the zone and cache files to **/var/cache/bind**. In this directory, you will find links to your zone files and reverse mapping files, along with the cache file, **named.ca**. The original files will be located in **/etc/bind**. The **forwarders** option can be used for your ISP DNS servers. The **dnssec-validation** option enables the DNSSEC validation of signed zone. The **auto** option uses the DNSSEC default key in the **bind.key** file for the DNS root zone.

/etc/bind/named.conf.options

```
options {
    directory "/var/cache/bind";

// If there is a firewall between you and nameservers you want
// to talk to, you may need to fix the firewall to allow multiple
// ports to talk.  See http://www.kb.cert.org/vuls/id/800113

// If your ISP provided one or more IP addresses for stable
// nameservers, you probably want to use them as forwarders.
// Uncomment the following block, and insert the addresses
// replacing the all-0's placeholder.

    // forwarders {
    //      0.0.0.0;
    // };


//========================================================================
// If BIND logs error messages about the root key being expired,
// you will need to update your keys.  See https://www.isc.org/bind-keys
//========================================================================

    dnssec-validation auto;

    listen-on-v6 { any; };
    };
```

The named.conf.local configuration file

In the **named.conf.local** file you add the zone statements for your particular DNS server. Initially, this file will be empty, except for a few comments.

A sample **named.conf.local** file follows.

```
//
// A simple BIND configuration
//

zone "mytrek.com" {
                type primary;
                file "/etc/bind/db.mytrek.com";
                };
zone "1.168.192.IN-ADDR.ARPA" {
                        type primary;
                        file "/etc/bind/db.192.168.0";
                        };
```

The first zone statement defines a zone for the **mytrek.com** domain. Its type is primary, and its zone file is named "**mytrek.com**." The next zone is used for reverse IP mapping of the previous zone. Its name is made up of a reverse listing of the **mytrek.com** domain's IP address with the term **IN-ADDR.ARPA** appended. The domain address for **mytrek.com** is 192.168.0, so the reverse is 1.168.192. The **IN-ADDR.ARPA** domain is a special domain that supports gateway location and Internet address-to-host mapping.

The **named.conf.local** file is also where you would include the local address zone definitions for private non-Internet local addresses (those beginning with **192**, **10**, and **172.16** through **172.31**) (see Chapter 18). If you are not using them, you should include the dummy definitions for them located in the **zones.rfc1918** file.

```
include "/etc/bind/zones.rfc1918";
```

The named.conf.default-zones configuration file

The **named.conf** configuration file will read in any default zones from the **named.conf.default-zones** file, using the **include** directive. The zone statements in the **named.conf.default-zones** file will configure the localhost, broadcast, and root level zones.

The example file still uses the master and slave terms for primary and secondary. It has been edited here to use the official terminology.

You should not have to modify the **named.conf.default-zones** file. The **named.conf.default-zones** file installed by the BIND server package to the **/etc/bind** directory is shown here.

The "." zone is set up for accessing the root DNS servers file using the **/usr/share/dns/root.hints** file.

The localhost zone statement configures the localhost network addresses. The **127** statement defines a reverse mapping zone for the loopback interface (localhost), the method used by the system to address itself and enable communication between local users on the system. The zone file for the local host is **db.local**, and its reverse lookup file is **db.127**.

Two reverse lookup zones are then set up for the broadcast zone, 0 and 255, in the **db.0** and **db.255** zone files.

/etc/bind/named.conf.default-zones

```
// prime the server with knowledge of the root servers
zone "." {
    type hint;
    file "/usr/share/dns/root.hints";
};
// be authoritative for the localhost forward and reverse zones, and for
// broadcast zones as per RFC 1912

zone "localhost" {
    type primary;
    file "/etc/bind/db.local";
};

zone "127.in-addr.arpa" {
    type primary;
    file "/etc/bind/db.127";
};

zone "0.in-addr.arpa" {
    type primary;
    file "/etc/bind/db.0";
};

zone "255.in-addr.arpa" {
    type primary;
    file "/etc/bind/db.255";
};
```

An IPv6 named.conf.local Example

The IPv6 version for the preceding **named.conf.local** file appears much the same, except that the IN-ADDR.ARPA domain is replaced by the IP6.ARPA domain in the reverse zone entries. IP6.ARPA uses bit labels providing bit-level specification for the address. This is simply the full hexadecimal address, including zeros, without intervening colons. You need to use IP6.ARPA format of the IPv6 address for both the **mytrek.com** domain and the localhost domain.

named.conf.local

```
//
// A simple BIND 9 configuration
//

zone "mytrek.com" {
                type primary;
                file "/etc/bind/db.mytrek.com";
                };

zone "\[xFC00000000000000/64].IP6.ARPA" {
                        type primary;
                        file "/etc/bind/db.fc0";
                        };
```

Resource Records for Zone Files

Your name server holds domain name information about the hosts on your network in resource records placed in zone and reverse mapping files. Resource records are used to associate IP addresses with fully qualified domain names. You need a record for every computer in the zone that the name server services. A record takes up one line, though you can use parentheses to use several lines for a record, as is usually the case with SOA records. A resource record uses the Standard Resource Record Format as shown here.

```
name [<ttl>] [<class>] <type> <rdata> [<comment>]
```

Here, name is the name for this record. It can be a domain name or a hostname (fully qualified domain name). If you specify only the hostname, the default domain is appended. If no name entry exists, the last specific name is used. If the @ symbol is used, the name server's domain name is used. ttl (time to live) is an optional entry that specifies how long the record is to be cached (the **$TTL** directive sets the default). class is the class of the record. The class used in most resource record entries is IN, for Internet. By default, it is the same as that specified for the domain in the **named.conf** file. type is the type of the record. rdata is the resource record data. The following is an example of a resource record entry. The name is **rabbit.mytrek.com**, the class is Internet (IN), the type is a host address record (A), and the rdata is the IP address 192.168.0.2.

```
rabbit.mytrek.com.     IN   A   192.168.0.2
```

You can use the **named-rrchecker** tool to check the syntax of just the resource record class. type, and rdata. It checks a single record sent to it from the standard input. You can use the **echo** command with a pipe operation to send the record. It returns nothing if successful.

```
echo " IN A 192.168.0.2"  | named-rrchecker
echo " IN   NS      turtle.mytrek.com." | named-rrchecker
```

Resource Record Types

Different types of resource records exist for different kinds of hosts and name server operations (see Table 15-7 for a listing of resource record types). A, NS, MX, PTR, and CNAME are the types commonly used. A is used for host address records that match domain names with IP addresses. NS is used to reference a name server. MX specifies the host address of the mail server that services this zone. The name server has mail messages sent to that host. The PTR type is used for records that point to other resource records and is used for reverse mapping. CNAME is used to identify an alias for a host on your system.

All zone files begin with a Time To Live directive, which specifies the time that a client should keep the provided DNS information before refreshing the information again from the DNS server. Realistically this should be at least a day, though if changes in the server are scheduled sooner, you can temporarily shorten the time, later restoring it. Each record, in fact, has a Time To Live value that can be explicitly indicated with the TTL field. This is the second field in a resource record. If no TTL field is specified in the record, then the default, as defined by the $TLL directive, can be used. The $TTL directive is placed at the beginning of each zone file. By default, it will list the time in seconds, usually 86400, 24 hours.

```
$TTL 86400
```

Type	Description
A	An IPv4 host address, maps hostname to IPv4 address
AAAA	An IPv6 host address
A6	An IPv6 host address supporting chained addresses
NS	Authoritative name server for this zone
CNAME	Canonical name, used to define an alias for a hostname
SOA	Start of Authority, starts DNS entries in zone file, specifies name server for domain, and other features such as server contact and serial number
WKS	Well-known service description
PTR	Pointer record, for performing reverse domain name lookups, maps IP address to hostname
RP	Text string that contains contact information about a host
HINFO	Host information
MINFO	Mailbox or mail list information
MX	Mail exchanger, informs remote site of your zone's mail server
TXT	Text strings, usually information about a host
KEY	Domain private key
SIG	Resource record signature
NXT	Next resource record

Table 15-7: Domain Name System Resource Record TypesTime To Live Directive and Field: $TTL

You can also specify the time in days (d), hours (h), or minutes (m), as in

```
$TTL 2d3h
```

When used as a field, the TTL will be a time specified as the second field. In the following example, the turtle resource record can be cached for three days. This will override the default time in the TTL time directive:

```
turtle     3d     IN     A     192.168.0.1
```

Start of Authority: SOA

A zone or reverse mapping file always begins with a special resource record called the Start of Authority (SOA) record. This record specifies that all the following records are authoritative for this domain. It also holds information about the name server's domain, which is to be given to other name servers. An SOA record has the same format as other resource records, though its data segment is arranged differently. The format for an SOA record follows.

```
name {ttl} class SOA Origin Person-in-charge (
                            Serial number
                            Refresh
                            Retry
                            Expire
                            Minimum )
```

Each zone has its own SOA record. The SOA begins with the zone name specified in the **named.conf** zone entry. This is usually a domain name. An **@** symbol is usually used for the name, and acts like a macro expanding to the domain name. The class is usually the Internet class, IN. SOA is the type. Origin is the machine that is the origin of the records, usually the machine running your name server. The person-in-charge is the e-mail address for the person managing the name server (use dots, not **@**, for the e-mail address, as this symbol is used for the domain name). Several configuration entries are placed in a block delimited with braces. The first is the Serial number. You change the serial number when you add or change records so that it is updated by other servers. The serial number can be any number, as long as it is incremented each time a change is made to any record in the zone. A common practice is to use the year-month-day-number for the serial number, where number is the number of changes in that day. For example, 2020120403 would be the year 2020, December 4, for the third change. Be sure to update it when making changes.

Refresh specifies the time interval for refreshing SOA information. Retry is the frequency for trying to contact an authoritative server. Expire is the length of time a secondary name server keeps information about a zone without updating it. Minimum is the length of time records in a zone live. The times are specified in the number of seconds.

The following example shows an SOA record. The machine running the name server is **turtle.mytrek.com,** and the e-mail address of the person responsible for the server is **hostprimary.turtle.mytrek.com**. Notice the periods at the ends of these names. For names with no periods, the domain name is appended. **turtle** would be the same as **turtle.mytrek.com**. When entering full hostnames, be sure to add the period so that the domain is not appended.

```
@ IN SOA turtle.mytrek.com. hostprimary.turtle.mytrek.com. (
                                2020022700 ; Serial
                                28800 ; Refresh
                                14400 ; Retry
                                3600000 ; Expire
                                86400 ) ; Minimum
```

Name Server: NS

The name server record specifies the name of the name server for this zone. These have a resource record type of NS. If you have more than one name server, list them in NS records. These records usually follow the SOA record. As they usually apply to the same domain as the SOA record, their name field is often left blank to inherit the server's domain name specified by the **@** symbol in the previous SOA record.

```
        IN   NS      turtle.mytrek.com.
```

You can, if you wish, enter the domain name explicitly as shown here.

```
mytrek.com.  IN   NS      turtle.mytrek.com.
```

Address Record: A, AAAA, and A6

Resource records of type A are address records that associate a fully qualified domain name with an IP address. Often, only their hostname is specified. Any domain names without a terminating period automatically have the domain appended to them. Given the domain **mytrek.com**, the **turtle** name in the following example is expanded to **turtle.mytrek.com**.

```
rabbit.mytrek.com. IN    A    192.168.0.2
turtle             IN    A    192.168.0.1
```

BIND supports IPv6 addresses. IPv6 IP addresses have a very different format from that of the IPv4 addresses commonly used. Instead of the numerals arranged in four segments, IPv6 uses hexadecimal numbers arranged in seven segments. In the following example, **turtle.mytrek.com** is associated with a unique-local IPv6 address: **fc00::**. There are only three fields in a unique-local address: format prefix, subnet identifier, and interface identifier. The empty segments of the subnet identifier can be represented by an empty colon pair (::). The interface identifier follows, **8:800:200C:417A**.

```
turtle.mytrek.com. IN    AAAA    FC00::8:800:200C:417A
```

IPv6 also supports the use of IPv4 addresses as an interface identifier, instead of the MAC-derived identifier. The network information part of the IPv6 address would use IPv6 notation, and the remaining interface (host) identifier would use the full IPv4 address. These are known as mixed addresses. In the next example, **lizard.mytrek.com** is given a mixed address using IPv6 network information and IPv4 interface information. The IPv6 network information is for an IPv6 unique-local address.

```
lizard.mytrek.com. IN    AAAA    fc00::192.168.0.3
```

The AAAA record is used in most networks for an IPv6 record. An AAAA record operates much like a standard A address record, requiring a full IPv6 address. An A6 record is an experimental version of the IPv6 record. It can be more flexible, in that it does not require a full address. Instead, you chain A6 records together, specifying just part of the address in each. For example, you could specify just an interface identifier for a host, letting the network information be provided by another IPv6 record (you can implement an A6 record with a full address, just like an AAAA record). In the next example, the first A6 record lists only the address for the interface identifier for the host **divit**. Following the address is the domain name, **mytrek.com**, whose address is to be used to complete **divit**'s address, providing network information. The next A6 record provides the network address information for **mytrek.com**.

```
divit.mygolf.com. IN    A6    0:0:0:0:1234:5678:3466:af1f  mytrek.com.
mytrek.com.       IN    A6    3ffe:8050:201:1860::
```

Mail Exchanger: MX

The Mail Exchanger record, MX, specifies the mail server that is used for this zone or for a particular host. The mail exchanger is the server to which mail for the host is sent. In the following example, the mail server is specified as **turtle.mytrek.com**. Any mail sent to the address for any machines in that zone will be sent to the mail server, which in turn will send it to the specific machines. For example, mail sent to a user on **rabbit.mytrek.com** will first be sent to **turtle.mytrek.com**, which will then send it on to **rabbit.mytrek.com**. In the following example, the host 192.168.0.1 (**turtle.mytrek.com**) is defined as the mail server for the **mytrek.com** domain.

```
mytrek.com. IN    MX   10   turtle.mytrek.com.
```

You could also inherit the domain name from the SOA record, leaving the domain name entry blank.

```
         IN    MX   turtle.mytrek.com.
```

You could use the IP address instead, but in larger networks, the domain name may be needed to search for and resolve the IP address of a particular machine, which could change.

```
mytrek.com. IN    MX   10   192.168.0.1
```

An MX record recognizes an additional field that specifies the ranking for a mail exchanger. If your zone has several mail servers, you can assign them different rankings in their MX records. The smaller number has a higher ranking. This way, if mail cannot reach the first mail server, it can be routed to an alternate server to reach the host. In the following example, mail for hosts on the **mytrek.com** domain is first routed to the mail server at 192.168.0.1 (**turtle.mytrek.com**), and if that fails, it is routed to the mail server at 192.168.0.2 (**rabbit.mytrek.com**).

```
mytrek.com. IN MX 10 turtle.mytrek.com.
            IN MX 20 rabbit.mytrek.com.
```

You can also specify a mail server for a particular host. In the following example, the mail server for **lizard.mytrek.com** is specified as **rabbit.mytrek.com**.

```
lizard.mytrek.com. IN    A      192.168.0.3
                   IN    MX  10 rabbit.mytrek.com.
```

Aliases: CNAME

Resource records of type CNAME are used to specify alias names for a host in the zone. Aliases are often used for machines running several different types of servers, such as both Web and FTP servers. They are also used to locate a host when it changes its name. In this case, the old name becomes an alias for the new name. In the following example, **ftp.mytrek.com** is an alias for a machine actually called **turtle.mytrek.com**:

```
ftp.mytrek.com. IN CNAME turtle.mytrek.com.
```

The term CNAME stands for canonical name. The canonical name is the actual name of the host. In the preceding example, the canonical name is **turtle.mytrek.com**. The alias, also known as the CNAME, is **ftp.mytrek.com**. In a CNAME entry, the alias points to the canonical name. Aliases cannot be used for NS (name server) or MX (mail server) entries. For those records, you need to use the original domain name or IP address.

A more stable way to implement aliases is to create another address record for a host or domain. You can have as many hostnames for the same IP address as you want, provided they are certified. For example, to make **www.mytrek.com** an alias for **turtle.mytrek.com**, you only have to add another address record for it, giving it the same IP address as **turtle.mytrek.com**.

```
turtle.mytrek.com. IN A 192.168.0.1
www.mytrek.com. IN A 192.168.0.1
```

Pointer Record: PTR

A PTR record is used to perform reverse mapping from an IP address to a host. PTR records are used in reverse mapping files. The name entry holds a reversed IP address, and the data entry holds the name of the host. The following example maps the IP address 192.168.0.1 to **turtle.mytrek.com**.

```
1.1.168.192 IN PTR turtle.mytrek.com.
```

In a PTR record, you can specify just that last number segment of the address (the host address) and let DNS fill in the domain part of the address. In the next example, 1 has the domain address, 1.168.192, automatically added to give 1.1.168.192.

```
1 IN PTR turtle.mytrek.com.
```

Host Information: HINFO, RP, MINFO, and TXT

The HINFO, RP, MINFO, and TXT records are used to provide information about the host. The RP record enables you to specify the person responsible for a certain host. The HINFO record provides basic hardware and operating system identification. The TXT record is used to enter any text you want. MINFO provides a host's mail and mailbox information. These are used sparingly, as they may give too much information out about the server.

Zone Files

A DNS server uses several zone files covering different components of the DNS. Each zone uses two zone files: the principal zone file and a reverse mapping zone file. The zone file contains the resource records for hosts in the zone. A reverse mapping file contains records that provide reverse mapping of your domain name entries, enabling you to map from IP addresses to domain names. The name of the file used for the zone file can technically be any name, but on the Ubuntu server zone files, they use the prefix **db**, as in **db.local** for the localhost zone. The name of the file is specified in the zone statement's file entry in the **named.conf** and **named.conf.local** files. If your server supports several zones, you may want to use a name that denotes the specific zone. The domain name is used as the name of the zone file. For example, the zone **mytrek.com** would have a zone file with the same name and the prefix **db**, as in **db.mytrek.com**. The zone file used in the following example is called **db.mytrek.com**. The reverse mapping file can also be any name, though it is usually the reverse IP address domain specified in its corresponding zone file. For example, in the case of **mytrek.com.zone** zone file, the reverse mapping file would be called **db.192.168.0**, the IP address of the **mytrek.com** domain defined in the **db.mytrek.com** zone file. This file would contain reverse mapping of all the host addresses in the domain, allowing their hostname addresses to be mapped to their corresponding IP addresses. In addition, BIND sets up a cache file and a reverse mapping file for the localhost. The localhost reverse mapping file, **db.local**, holds reverse IP resource records for the local loopback interface, localhost.

Once you have created your zone files, you should check their syntax with the **named-checkzone** tool. This tool requires that you specify both a zone and a zone file. In the following example, in the **/etc/bind** directory, the zone **mytrek.com** in the zone file **db.mytrek.com** is checked.

```
named-checkzone  mytrek.com db.mytrek.com
```

Zone Files for Internet Zones

A zone file holds resource records that follow a certain format. The file begins with general directives to define default domains or to include other resource record files. These are followed by a single SOA record, name server and domain resource records, and then resource records for the different hosts. Comments begin with a semicolon and can be placed throughout the file. The @ symbol operates like a special macro, representing the domain name of the zone to which the records apply. The @ symbol is used in the first field of a resource or SOA record as the zone's domain name. Multiple names can be specified using the * matching character. The first field in a resource record is the name of the domain to which it applies. If the name is left blank, the previous explicit name entry in another resource record is used automatically. This way, you can list several entries that apply to the same host without having to repeat the hostname. Any host or domain name used throughout this file that is not terminated with a period has the zone's domain appended to it. For example, if the zone's domain is **mytrek.com** and a resource record has only the name **rabbit** with no trailing period, the zone's domain is automatically appended to it, giving you **rabbit.mytrek.com.**. Be sure to include the trailing period whenever you enter the complete fully qualified domain name, for example, **turtle.mytrek.com.**.

Directives

You can use several directives to set global attributes. $ORIGIN sets a default domain name to append to address names that do not end in a period. $INCLUDE includes a file. $GENERATE can generate records whose domain or IP addresses differ only by an iterated number. The $ORIGIN directive is often used to specify the root domain to use in address records. Be sure to include the trailing period. The following example sets the domain origin to **mytrek.com** and will be automatically appended to the **lizard** hostname that follows.

```
$ORIGIN   mytrek.com.
lizard   IN   A   192.168.0.2
```

SOA Record

A zone file begins with an SOA record specifying the machine the name server it is running on, among other specifications. The @ symbol is used for the name of the SOA record, denoting the zone's domain name. After the SOA, the name server resource records (NS) are listed. Just below the name server records are resource records for the domain itself. Resource records for host addresses (A), aliases (CNAME), and mail exchangers (MX) follow. The following example shows a sample zone file, which begins with an SOA record and is followed by an NS record, resource records for the domain, and then resource records for individual hosts.

db.turtle.mytrek.com

```
; Authoritative data for turle.mytrek.com
;
$TTL 86400
@ IN SOA turtle.mytrek.com. hostprimary.turtle.mytrek.com.(
                          2020022700; Serial number
                              10800 ; Refresh 3 hours
                               3600 ; Retry 1 hour
                            3600000 ; Expire 1000 hours
                              86400 ) ; Minimum 24 hours

            IN      NS         turtle.mytrek.com.
            IN      A          192.168.0.1
            IN      MX    10   turtle.mytrek.com.
            IN      MX    15   rabbit.mytrek.com.

turtle      IN      A          192.168.0.1
            IN      HINFO      PC-686 LINUX
ftp         IN      CNAME      turtle.mytrek.com.
www         IN      A          192.168.0.1

rabbit      IN      A          192.168.0.2

lizard      IN      A          192.168.0.3
            IN      HINFO      MAC MACOS
```

The first two lines are comments about the server for which this zone file is used. As comments, the lines begin with a semicolon. The class for each of the resource records in this file is IN, indicating these are Internet records. The SOA record begins with an @ symbol that stands for the zone's domain. In this example, it is **mytrek.com**. Any host or domain name used throughout this file that is not terminated with a period has this domain appended to it. For example, in the following resource record, **turtle** has no period, so it automatically expands to **turtle.mytrek.com**. The same happens for **rabbit** and **lizard**. These are read as **rabbit.mytrek.com** and **lizard.mytrek.com**. Also, in the SOA, notice that the e-mail address for hostprimary uses a period instead of an @ symbol. The @ symbol is a special symbol in zone files and cannot be used for any other purpose.

Nameserver Record

The next resource record specifies the name server for this zone. Here, it is **mytrek.com.**. Notice the name for this resource record is blank. If the name is blank, a resource record inherits the name from the previous record. In this case, the NS record inherits the value of @ in the SOA record, its previous record. This is the zone's domain, and the NS record specifies **turtle.mytrek.com** as the name server for this zone.

```
            IN   NS    turtle.mytrek.com.
```

Here the domain name is inherited. The entry can be read as the following. Notice the trailing period at the end of the domain name.

```
mytrek.com. IN   NS    turtle.mytrek.com.
```

Address Record

The following address records set up an address for the domain itself. This is often the same as the name server, in this case, 192.168.0.1 (the IP address of **turtle.mytrek.com**). This enables users to reference the domain itself, rather than a particular host in it. A mail exchanger record follows that routes mail for the domain to the name server. Users can send mail to the **mytrek.com** domain and it will be routed to **turtle.mytrek.com**.

```
            IN    A     192.168.0.1
```

Here the domain name is inherited. The entry can be read as the following.

```
mytrek.com. IN   A    192.168.0.1
```

Mail Exchanger Record

The next records are mail exchanger (MX) records listing **turtle.mytrek.com** and **fast.mytrek.com** as holding the mail servers for this zone. You can have more than one mail exchanger record for a host. More than one host may exist through which mail can be routed. These can be listed in mail exchanger records for which you can set priority rankings (a smaller number ranks higher). In this example, if **turtle.mytrek.com** cannot be reached, its mail is routed through **rabbit.mytrek.com**, which has been set up also to handle mail for the **mytrek.com** domain.

```
            IN    MX    100    turtle.mytrek.com.
            IN    MX    150    rabbit.mytrek.com.
```

Again the domain name is inherited. The entries can be read as the following.

```
mytrek.com.   IN    MX  100    turtle.mytrek.com.
mytrek.com.   IN    MX  150    rabbit.mytrek.com.
```

Address Record with Hostname

The following resource record is an address record (A) that associates an IP address with the fully qualified domain name **turtle.mytrek.com**. The resource record name holds only **turtle** with no trailing period, so it is automatically expanded to **turtle.mytrek.com**. This record provides the IP address to which **turtle.mytrek.com** can be mapped.

```
turtle   IN    A     192.168.0.1
```

Inherited Names

Several resource records immediately follow that have blank names. These inherit their names from the preceding full record, in this case, **turtle.mytrek.com**. In effect, these records also apply to that host. Using blank names is an easy way to list additional resource records for the same host (notice that an apparent indent occurs). The first record is an information record, providing the hardware and operating system for the machine.

```
            IN    HINFO    PC-686 LINUX
```

Alias Records

If you are using the same machine to run several different servers, such as Web and FTP servers, you may want to assign aliases to these servers to make accessing them easier for users. Instead of using the actual domain name, such as **turtle.mytrek.com**, to access the Web server running on it, users may find that using the following is easier: for the Web server, **www.mytrek.com**, and for the FTP server, **ftp.mytrek.com**. You can implement such a feature using alias records. In the example zone file, one CNAME alias records exist for the **turtle.mytrek.com** machine: FTP. The next record implements an alias for **www**, using another address record for the same machine. None of the name entries ends in a period, so they are appended automatically with the domain name **mytrek.com**. **www.mytrek.com** and **ftp.mytrek.com** are aliases for **turtle.mytrek.com**. Users entering those URLs automatically access the respective servers on the **turtle.mytrek.com** machine.

Loopback Record

Address and mail exchanger records are then listed for the two other machines in this zone: **rabbit.mytrek.com** and **lizard.mytrek.com**. You could add HINFO, TXT, MINFO, or alias records for these entries.

IPv6 Zone File Example

This is the same zone file using IPv6 addresses. The addresses are unique-local (FC00), instead of global (3), providing private network addressing. The AAAA IPv6 address records are used.

Note: On Ubuntu, if your network does not use zones for private address space, you can redirect those addresses to an empty configuration file, **db.empty**. Load the RFC 1912 configuration file, **zones.rfc1918**, into the **named.conf.local** file using an **include** statement.

```
; Authoritative data for turle.mytrek.com, IPv6 version
;
$TTL 1d
@ IN SOA turtle.mytrek.com. hostprimary.turtle.mytrek.com.(
                          2020022700 ; Serial number
                             10800 ; Refresh 3 hours
                              3600 ; Retry 1 hour
                           3600000 ; Expire 1000 hours
                             86400 ) ; Minimum 24 hours

            IN      NS      turtle.mytrek.com.
            IN      AAAA    FC00::8:800:200C:417A
            IN      MX   10 turtle.mytrek.com.
            IN      MX   15 rabbit.mytrek.com.

turtle      IN      AAAA    FC00::8:800:200C:417A
            IN      HINFO   PC-686 LINUX
ftp         IN      CNAME   turtle.mytrek.com.
www         IN      AAAA    FC00::8:800:200C:417A

rabbit      IN      AAAA    FC00::FEDC:BA98:7654:3210

lizard      IN      AAAA     FC00::E0:18F7:3466:7D
            IN      HINFO   MAC MACOS
```

Localhost zone file: named.local

The **db.local** zone file implements mapping for the local loopback interface known as localhost. This file includes support for both for IPv4 and for IPv6 addressing. The IPv4 address for localhost is **127.0.0.1**, and the IPv6 address is **::1**. These are special addresses that function as the local address for your machine. It allows a machine to address itself. The IPv4 address has the type A and the address 127.0.0.1, whereas the IPv6 address has the type AAAA and the address ::1.

```
A        127.0.0.1
AAAA     ::1
```

The **db.local** zone file is shown here.

db.local

```
$TTL 604000
@        IN SOA @ localhost.  root.localhost. (
                               2        ; Serial
                               604800 ; Refresh
                               86400   ; Retry
                               2419200; Expire
;                              604800) ; Negative Cache TTL
@        IN     NS     localhost.
@        IN     A      127.0.0.1
@        IN     AAAA   ::1
```

Reverse Mapping File

Reverse name lookups are enabled using a reverse mapping file. Reverse mapping files map fully qualified domain names to IP addresses. This reverse lookup capability is unnecessary, but it is convenient to have. With reverse mapping, when users access remote hosts, their domain name addresses can be used to identify their own host, instead of only the IP address. The name of the file can be anything you want. On Ubuntu, it is usually the first part of the zone's domain address (the network part of a zone's IP address). For example, the reverse mapping file for a zone with the IP address of 192.168.0 is **db.192**. It's full pathname would be something like **/etc/bind/db.192**. For the localhost which has address 127.0.0.1, the reverse zone file is **db.127**. Two reverse lookup zones are setup for the broadcast zone, 0 and 255, in the **db.0** and **db.255** files.

IPv4 IN-ADDR.ARPA Reverse Mapping Format

In IPv4, the zone entry for a reverse mapping in the **named** configuration files use a special domain name consisting of the IP address in reverse, with an **in-addr.arpa** extension. This reverse IP address becomes the zone domain referenced by the @ symbol in the reverse mapping file. For example, the reverse mapping zone name for a domain with the IP address of **192.168.43** would be **43.168.192.in-addr.arpa**. In the following example, the reverse domain name for the domain address **192.168.0** is **168.192.in-addr.arpa**:

```
zone "168.192.in-addr.arpa" in {
        type primary;
        file "db.192";
        };
```

You can use the **arpaname** tool to see what the IN-ADDR.ARPA address should be for any IP address.

```
$ arpaname 192.168.0.1
1.0.169.192.IN-ADDR.ARPA
```

A reverse mapping file begins with an SOA record, which is the same as that used in a forward mapping file. Resource records for each machine defined in the forward mapping file then follow. These resource records are PTR records that point to hosts in the zone. These must be actual hosts, not aliases defined with CNAME records. Records for reverse mapping begin with a reversed IP address. Each segment in the IP address is sequentially reversed. Each segment begins with the host ID, followed by reversed network numbers.

If you list only the host ID with no trailing period, the zone domain is automatically attached. In the case of a reverse mapping file, the zone domain as specified in the zone statement is the domain IP address backward. The 1 expands to 1.1.168.192. In the following example, **turtle** and **lizard** inherit the domain IP address, whereas **rabbit** has its address explicitly entered.

```
; reverse mapping of domain names 1.168.192.IN-ADDR.ARPA
;
$TTL 86400
@ IN SOA turtle.mytrek.com. hostprimary.turtle.mytrek.com. (
                    2020022700 ; Serial (yymmddxx format)
                         10800 ; Refresh 3hHours
                          3600 ; Retry 1 hour
                       3600000 ; Expire 1000 hours
                         86400 ) ; Minimum 24 hours


@             IN    NS     turtle.mytrek.com.
1             IN    PTR    turtle.mytrek.com.
2.1.168.192   IN    PTR    rabbit.mytrek.com.
3             IN    PTR    lizard.mytrek.com.
```

IPv6 IP6.ARPA Reverse Mapping Format

In IPv6, reverse mapping can be handled either with the current IP6.ARPA domain format, or with the older IP6.INT format. With IP6.ARPA, the address is represented by a bit-level representation that places the hexadecimal address within brackets. The first bracket is preceded by a backslash. The address must be preceded by an **x** indicating that it is a hexadecimal address. Following the address is a number indicating the number of bits referenced. In a 128-bit address, usually the first 64 bits reference the network address and the last 64 bits are for the interface address. The following example shows the network and interface addresses for lizard.

```
FC00:0000:0000:0000:00E0:18F7:3466:007D   lizard IPv6 address
\[xFC00000000000000/64]                   lizard network address
\[x00E018F73466007D/64]                   lizard interface address
```

The zone entry for a reverse mapping in a **named** configuration file with an **IP6.ARPA** extension would use the bit-level representation for the network address.

```
zone "\[xfc00000000000000/64].IP6.ARPA" in {
        type primary;
        file "fec.ip6.arpa";
        };
```

A reverse mapping file then uses the same bit-level format for the interface addresses.

```
$TTL 1d
@ IN SOA turtle.mytrek.com. hostprimary.turtle.mytrek.com.(
                    2020022700 ; Serial (yymmddxx format)
                       10800 ; Refresh 3hHours
                        3600 ; Retry 1 hour
                     3600000 ; Expire 1000 hours
                       86400 ) ; Minimum 24 hours


@                               IN    NS      turtle.mytrek.com.
\[x00080800200C417A/64]         IN    PTR     turtle.mytrek.com.
\[xFEDCBA9876543210/64]         IN    PTR     rabbit.mytrek.com.
\[x00E018F73466007D/64]         IN    PTR     lizard.mytrek.com.
```

Localhost Reverse Mapping

A localhost reverse mapping file implements reverse mapping for the local loopback interface known as localhost, whose network address is 127.0.0.1. The localhost reverse mapping filename uses the network part of the IP address, 127.0.0, and is named **db.127**. The address 127.0.0.1 is a special address that functions as the local address for your machine. In the zone statement for this file in the **named.conf.default-zones** file, the name of the zone is **127.in-addr.arpa**. The zone entry is shown here.

```
zone "127.in-addr.arpa" {
        type primary;
        file " /etc/bind/db.127";
        };
```

The name of the file used for the localhost reverse mapping file is **db.127**, though it can be any name. The zone file supports both IPv4 and IPv6 addresses.

```
;
; BIND reverse data file for local loopback interface
;
$TTL    604800
@      IN      SOA     localhost. root.localhost. (
                             1          ; Serial
                        604800          ; Refresh
                         86400          ; Retry
                       2419200          ; Expire
                        604800 )        ; Negative Cache TTL
;
@      IN      NS      localhost.
1.0.0  IN      PTR     localhost.
```

The NS record specifies the name server localhost should use. This file has a PTR record that maps the IP address to the localhost. The 1.0.0 used as the name expands to append the zone domain, in this case, giving you 1.0.0.127, a reverse IP address. The contents of the **db.127** file are shown here. Notice the trailing periods for localhost.

Subdomains and Secondary Servers

Adding a subdomain to a DNS server is a simple matter of creating an additional primary entry in the **named** configuration file, and then placing name server and authority entries for that subdomain in your primary DNS server's zone file. The subdomain, in turn, has its own zone file with its SOA record and entries listing hosts, which are part of its subdomain, including any of its own mail and news servers.

Subdomain Zones

The name for the subdomain could be a different name altogether or a name with the same suffix as the primary domain. In the following example, the subdomain is called **beach.mytrek.com**. It could just as easily be called **mybeach.com**. The name server to that domain is on the host **crab.beach.mytrek.com**, in this example. Its IP address is 192.168.0.33, and its zone file is **db.beach.mytrek.com**. The **beach.mytrek.com** zone file holds DNS entries for all the hosts being serviced by this name server. The following example shows zone entries.

```
zone "beach.mytrek.com" {
        type primary;
        file "db.beach.mytrek.com";
        };

zone "1.168.192.IN-ADDR.ARPA" {
        type primary;
        file "192.168.0";
        };
```

Subdomain Records

On the primary DNS server, in the example **turtle.mytrek.com**, you would place entries in the primary zone file to identify the subdomain server's host and designate it as a name server. Such entries are also known as glue records. In this example, you would place the following entries in the **mytrek.com** zone file on **turtle.mytrek.com**.

```
beach.mytrek.com.     IN    NS    beach.mytrek.com.
beach.mytrek.com.     IN    A     192.168.0.33.
```

URL references to hosts serviced by **beach.mytrek.com** can now be reached from any host serviced by **mytrek.com**, which does not need to maintain any information about the **beach.mytrek.com** hosts. It simply refers such URL references to the **beach.mytrek.com** name server.

Secondary Servers

A secondary DNS server is tied directly to a primary DNS server and periodically receives DNS information from it. You use a primary DNS server to configure its secondary DNS servers automatically. Any changes you make to the primary server are automatically transferred to its secondary servers. This transfer of information is called a zone transfer. Zone transfers are initiated automatically whenever the secondary zone's refresh time is reached or the secondary server receives a notify message from the primary. The refresh time is the second argument in the zone's SOA entry. A notify message is sent automatically by the primary whenever changes are made to the primary zone's configuration files and the **named** daemon is restarted. In effect, secondary zones are configured automatically by the primary zone, receiving the primary zone's zone files and making them their own.

Secondary Zones

To set up a secondary server on **rabbit.mytrek.com**, zone entries, as shown in the following example, are set up in the **named** configuration file for the secondary DNS server. The secondary server is operating in the same domain as the primary, and so it has the same zone name, **mytrek.com**. Its SOA file is named **secondary.mytrek.com**. The term "secondary" in the filename is merely a convention that helps identify it as a secondary server configuration file. The primarys statement lists its primary DNS server, in this case, 192.168.0.1. Whenever the secondary needs to make a zone transfer, it transfers data from that primary DNS server. The entry for the reverse mapping file for this secondary server lists its reverse mapping file as **secondary.192.168.0**.

```
zone "mytrek.com" {
        type secondary;
        file "secondary.mytrek.com";
        primarys { 192.168.0.1;
        };

zone "1.168.192.IN-ADDR.ARPA" {
        type secondary;
        file "secondary.192.168.0";
        primarys { 192.168.0.1;
        };
```

Secondary Records

On the primary DNS server, the primary SOA zone file has entries in it to identify the host that holds the secondary DNS server and to designate it as a DNS server. In this example, you would place the following in the **mytrek.com** zone file.

```
        IN        NS        192.168.0.2
```

You would also place an entry for this name server in the **mytrek.com** reverse mapping file.

```
        IN        NS        192.168.0.2
```

Controlling Transfers

The primary DNS server can control which secondary servers can transfer zone information from it using the **allow-transfer** statement. Place the statement with the list of IP addresses for the secondary servers to which you want to allow access. Also, the primary DNS server should be sure that its notify option is not disabled. The notify option is disabled by a "notify no" statement in the options or zone **named** configuration entries. Simply remove the "no" argument to enable notify.

Incremental Zone Transfers

BIND supports incremental zone transfers (IXFR). Previously, all the zone data would be replaced in an update, rather than changes such as the addition of a few resource records simply being edited in. With incremental zone transfers, a database of changes is maintained by the primary zone. Then only the changes are transferred to the secondary zone, which uses this information to update its own zone files. To implement incremental zone transfers, you have to turn on the **maintain-ixfr-base** option in the options section.

```
maintain-ixfr-base yes;
```

You can then use the **ixfr-base** option in a zone section to specify a particular database file to hold changes.

```
ixfr-base "db.mytrek.com.ixfr";
```

IP Virtual Domains

IP-based virtual hosting allows more than one IP address to be used for a single machine. If a machine has two registered IP addresses, either one can be used to address the machine. If you want to treat the extra IP address as another host in your domain, you have to create an address record for it in your domain's zone file. The domain name for the host would be the same as your domain name. If you want to use a different domain name for the extra IP, you have to set up a virtual domain for it. This entails creating a new zone statement for it with its own zone file. For example, if the extra IP address is 192.168.0.42 and you want to give it the domain name **sail.com**, you must create a new zone statement for it in a **named** configuration file with a new zone file. The zone statement would look something like this. The zone file is called **sail.com**.

```
zone "sail.com" in {
        type primary;
        file "sail.com";
        };
```

In the **db.sail.com** file, the name server name is **turtle.mytrek.com** and the e-mail address is **hostprimary@turtle.mytrek.com**. In the name server (NS) record, the name server is **turtle.mytrek.com.**

```
; Authoritative data for sail.com
;
$TTL 1d
@ IN SOA turtle.mytrek.com. hostprimary.turtle.mytrek.com. (
                        93071200 ; Serial (yymmddxx)
                           10800 ; Refresh 3 hours
                            3600 ; Retry 1 hour
                         3600000 ; Expire 1000 hours
                           86400 ) ; Minimum 24 hours

        IN      NS         turtle.mytrek.com.
        IN      MX     10  turtle.mytrek.com.
        IN      A          192.168.0.42 ;address of the sail.com domain

jib     IN      A          192.168.0.42
www     IN      A          jib.sail.com.
ftp     IN      CNAME      jib.sail.com.
```

This is the same machine using the original address that the name server is running as. **turtle.mytrek.com** is also the host that handles mail addressed to **sail.com** (MX). An address record then associates the extra IP address 192.168.0.42 with the **sail.com** domain name. A virtual host on this domain is then defined as **jib.sail.com**. The **www** and **ftp** aliases are created for that host, creating **www.sail.com** and **ftp.sail.com** virtual hosts.

In your reverse mapping file (**/var/named/1.168.192**), add PTR records for any virtual domains.

```
42.1.168.192      IN      PTR     sail.com.
42.1.168.192      IN      PTR     jib.sail.com.
```

You also have to configure your network connection to listen for both IP addresses on your machine.

Cache File

The cache file is used to connect the DNS server to root servers on the Internet. The file can be any name. On Bind 9, the cache file is implemented using the **/usr/share/dns/root.hints** file. The cache file is usually a standard file installed by your BIND software, which lists resource records for designated root servers for the Internet. The following example shows sample entries taken from the **root.hints** file.

```
; formerly NS.INTERNIC.NET
;
. 3600000 IN NS A.ROOT-SERVERS.NET.
A.ROOT-SERVERS.NET.   3600000   A   198.41.0.4
;
; formerly NS1.ISI.EDU
;
. 3600000 NS B.ROOT-SERVERS.NET.
B.ROOT-SERVERS.NET.   3600000   A   199.9.14.201
```

If you are creating an isolated intranet, you need to create your own root DNS server until you connect to the Internet. In effect, you are creating a fake root server. This can be another server on your system pretending to be the root or the same name server.

Dynamic Update: DHCP and Journal Files

There are situations wherein you will need to have zones updated dynamically. Instead of manually editing a zone file to make changes in a zone, an outside process updates the zone, making changes and saving the file automatically. Dynamic updates are carried out both by primary zones updating secondary zones, and by DHCP servers providing IP addresses they generated for hosts to the DNS server.

A journal file is maintained recording all the changes made to a zone, having a **.jnl** extension. Should a system crash occur, this file is read to implement the most current changes. Should you manually want to update a dynamically updated zone, you will need to erase its journal file first. Otherwise, your changes would be overwritten by the journal file entries.

You allow a zone to be automatically updated by specifying the **allow-update** option. This option indicates the host that can perform the update.

```
allow-update {turtle.mytrek.com;};
```

Alternatively, for primary zones, you can create a more refined set of access rules using the **update-policy** statement. With the **update-policy** statement, you can list several grant and deny rules for different hosts and types of hosts.

TSIG Signatures and Updates

With BIND 9, TSIG signature names can be used instead of hostnames or IP addresses for both **allow-update** and **update-policy** statements (see the following sections on TSIG). Use of TSIG signatures implements an authentication of a host performing a dynamic update, providing a much greater level of security. For example, to allow a DHCP server to update a zone file, you would place an **allow-update** entry in the zone statement listed in a **named** configuration file.

The TSIG key is defined in a key statement, naming the key previously created by the **dnssec-keygen** command. The algorithm is HMAC-MD5, and the secret is the encryption key listed in the **.private** file generated by **dnssec-keygen**.

```
key mydhcpserver {
algorithm HMAC-MD5;
secret "ONQAfbBLnvWU9H8hRqq/WA==";
};
```

The key name can then be used in an **allow-update** or **allow-policy** statement to specify a TSIG key.

```
allow-update { key mydhcpserver; };
```

Manual Updates: nsupdate

You can use the update procedure to perform any kind of update you want. You can perform updates manually or automatically using a script. For DHCP updates, the DHCP server is designed to perform dynamic updates of the DNS server. You will need to configure the DHCP server appropriately, specifying the TSIG key to use and the zones to update.

You can manually perform an update using the **nsupdate** command, specifying the file holding the key with the **-k** option.

```
nsupdate -k myserver.private
```

At the prompt, you can use **nsupdate** commands to implement changes. You match on a record using its full or partial entry. To update a record, you would first delete the old one and then add the changed version, as shown here:

```
update delete  rabbit.mytrek.com.  A  192.168.0.2
update add  rabbit.mytrek.com.  A  192.168.0.44
```

DNS Security: Access Control Lists, TSIG, and DNSSEC

DNS security currently allows you to control specific access by hosts to the DNS server, as well as providing encrypted communications between servers and authentication of DNS servers. With access control lists, you can determine who will have access to your DNS server. The DNS Security Extensions (DNSSEC), included with BIND 9 provide private/public key–encrypted authentication and transmissions. TSIGs (transaction signatures) use shared private keys to provide authentication of servers to secure actions such as dynamic updates between a DNS server and a DHCP server.

Once you have configured DNSSEC you can enable the DNSSEC validation of signed zone by placing the **dnssec-validation** option in the **/etc/bind/named.conf.options** file. You will also have to have defined **trust-anchors** keys (formerly **trusted-keys** and **managed-keys**). DNSSEC itself is enabled by default (the **dns-enable** option is deprecated).

```
dnssec-validation yes;
```

Access Control Lists

To control access by other hosts, you use access control lists, implemented with the **acl** statement. Using allow and deny options with access control host lists enables you to deny or allow access by specified hosts to the name server. With allow-query, you can restrict queries to specified hosts or networks. Normally, this will result in a response saying that access is denied. You can further eliminate this response by using the blackhole option in the options statement.

You define an ACL with the **acl** statement followed by the label you want to give the list and then the list of addresses. Addresses can be IP addresses, network addresses, or a range of addresses based on CNDR notation. You can also use an ACL as defined earlier. The following example defines an ACL called **mynet**.

```
acl mynet { 192.168.0.1; 192.168.0.2; };
```

If you are specifying a range, such as a network, you also add exceptions to the list by preceding such addresses with an exclamation point (!). In the following example, the **myexceptions** ACL lists all those hosts in the 192.168.0.0 network, except for 192.168.0.3.

```
acl myexceptions {192.168.0.0; !192.168.0.3; };
```

Four default ACLs are already defined for you. You can use them wherever an option uses a list of addresses as an argument. These are any for all hosts, none for no hosts, localhost for all local IP addresses, and localnet for all hosts on local networks served by the DNS server.

In the next example, an ACL of **mynet** is created. Then in the **mytrek.com** zone, only these hosts are allowed to query the server. As the server has no secondary DNS servers, zone transfers are disabled entirely. The blackhole option denies access from the myrejects list, without sending any rejection notice.

```
acl mynet { 192.168.0.0; };
acl myrejects { 10.0.0.44; 10.0.0.93; };

zone "mytrek.com" {
        type primary;
        file "mytrek.com";
        allow-query { mynet; };
        allow-recursion { mynet; };
        allow-transfer { none; };
        blackhole {myrejects};
        };
```

Once a list is defined, you can use it with the allow-query, allow-transfer, allow-recursion, and blackhole options in a zone statement to control access to a zone. allow-query specifies hosts that can query the DNS server. allow-transfer is used for primary/secondary zones, designating whether update transfers are allowed. allow-recursion specifies those hosts that can perform recursive queries on the server. The blackhole option will deny contact from any hosts in its list, without sending a denial response.

Secret Keys

Different security measures will use encryption keys generated with the **dnssec-keygen** command. You can use **dnssec-keygen** to create different types of keys, including zone (ZONE), host (HOST), and user (USER) keys. You specify the type of key with the **-n** option. A zone key will require the name ZONE and the name of the zone's domain name. A zone key is used in DNSSEC operations. The following example creates a zone key for the **mytrek.com** zone.

```
dnssec-keygen -n ZONE mytrek.com.
```

To create a host key, you would use the HOST type. HOST keys are often used in TSIG operations.

```
dnssec-keygen -n HOST turtle.mytrek.com.
```

The **dnssec-keygen** command will create public and private keys, each in corresponding files with the suffixes **.private** and **.key**. The **.key** file is a KEY resource record holding the public key. For DNSSEC, the private key is used to generate signatures for the zone, and the public key is used to verify the signatures. For TSIG, a shared private key generated by the HMAC-MD5 algorithm is used instead of a public/private key pair.

DNSSEC

DNSSEC provides encrypted authentication to DNS. With DNSSEC, you can create a signed zone that is securely identified with an encrypted signature. This form of security is used primarily to secure the connections between primary and secondary DNS servers, so that a primary server transfers update records only to authorized secondary servers, and does so with a secure encrypted communication. Two servers that establish such a secure connection do so using a pair of public and private keys. In effect, you have a parent zone that can securely authenticate child zones, using encrypted transmissions. This involves creating zone keys for each child, and having those keys used by the parent zone to authenticate the child zones.

Zone Keys

You generate a zone key using the **dnssec-keygen** command and specifying the zone type, ZONE, with the **-n** option. For the key name, you use the zone's domain name. The following example creates a zone key for the **mytrek.com** zone.

```
dnssec-keygen -n ZONE mytrek.com.
```

You can further designate an encryption algorithm (**-a**) and a key size (**-b**). Use the **-h** option to obtain a listing of the **dnssec-keygen** options. Since you are setting up a public/private key pair, you should choose either the RSA or DSA algorithm. The bit range will vary according to the algorithm. RSA ranges from 512 to 4096, and DSA ranges from 512 to 1024. The following example creates a zone key using a 768-bit key and the DSA encryption algorithm:

```
dnssec-keygen -a DSA -b 768 -n ZONE mytrek.com.
```

The **dnssec-keygen** command will create public and private keys, each in corresponding files with the suffixes **.private** and **.key**. The private key is used to generate signatures for the zone, and the public key is used to verify the signatures. The **.key** file is a KEY resource record holding the public key. This is used to decrypt signatures generated by the corresponding private key. You add the public key to a DNS **named** configuration file using the $INCLUDE statement to include the **.key** file.

DNSSEC Resource Records

In the zone file, you then use three DNSSEC DNS resource records to implement secure communications for a given zone: KEY, SIG, and NXT. In these records, you use the signed keys for the zones you have already generated. The KEY record holds public keys associated with zones, hosts, or users. The SIG record stores digital signatures and expiration dates for a set of resource records. The NXT record is used to determine that a resource record for a domain does not exist. In addition, several utilities let you manage DNS encryption. With the **dnskeygen** utility, you generated the public and private keys used for encryption. **dnssigner** signs a zone using the zone's private key, setting up authentication.

```
mytrek.com. KEY 0x4101 3 3 (
AvqyXgKk/uguxkJF/hbRpYzxZFG3x8EfNX38917GX6w7rlLy
BJ14TqvrDvXr84XsShg+OFcUJafNr84U4ER2dg6NrlRAmZA1
jFfVOUpWDWcHBR2jJnvgV9zJB2ULMGJheDHeyztM1KGd2oGk
Aensm74NlfUqKzy/3KZ9KnQmEpj/EEBr48vAsgAT9kMjN+V3
NgAwfoqgS0dwj5OiRJoIR4+cdRt+s32OUKsclAODFZTdtxRn
vXF3qYV0S8oewMbEwh3trXi1c7nDMQC3RmoY8RVGt5U6LMAQ
KITDyHU3VmRJ36vn77QqSzbeUPz8zEnbpik8kHPykJZFkcyj
jZoHT1xkJ1tk )
```

To secure a DNS zone with DNSSEC, you first use **dnskeygen** to create public and private keys for the DNS zone. Then use **dnssigner** to create an authentication key. In the DNS zone file, you enter a KEY resource record in which you include the public key. The public key will appear as a lengthy string of random characters. For the KEY record, you enter the domain name followed by the KEY and then the public key.

For authentication, you can sign particular resource records for a given domain or host. Enter the domain or host followed by the term SIG and then the resource record's signature.

```
mytrek.com. SIG KEY 3 86400 19990321010705 19990218010705 4932 com. (
Am3tWJzEDzfU1xwg7hzkiJ0+8UQaPtlJhUpQx1snKpDUqZxm
igMZEVk= )
```

The NXT record lets you negatively answer queries.

```
mytrek.com. NXT ftp.mytrek.com. A NS SOA MX SIG KEY NXT
```

Signing Keys

To set up secure communications between a parent (primary) DNS server and a child (secondary) DNS server, the public key then needs to be sent to the parent zone. There, the key can be signed by the parent. As you may have more than zone key, you create a keyset using the **dnssec-makekeyset** command. This generates a file with the extension **.keyset** that is then sent to the parent. The parent zone then uses the **dnssec-signkey** command to sign a child's keyset. This generates a file with the prefix **signedkey-**. This is sent back to the child and now contains both the child's keyset and the parent's signatures. Once the child has the **signedkey-** files, the **dnssec-signedzone** command can be used to sign the zone. The **dnssec-signedzone** command will generate a file with the extension **.signed**. This file is then included in a **named** configuration file with the INCLUDE operation. The **trust-anchors** statement with **static key** term needs to list the public key for the parent zone (replaces the **trusted-keys** statement).

TSIG Keys

TSIG (transaction signatures) also provide secure DNS communications, but they share the private key instead of a private/public key pair. They are usually used for communications between two local DNS servers, and to provide authentication for dynamic updates such as those between a DNS server and a DHCP server.

Generating TSIG keys

To create a TSIG key for your DNS server, you use the **dnssec-keygen** command as described earlier. Instead of using the same keys you use for DNSSEC, you create a new set to use for transaction signatures. For TSIG, a shared private key is used instead of a public/private key pair. For a TSIG key, you would use an HMAC-MD5 algorithm that generates the same key in the both the **.key** and **.private** files. Use the **-a** option to specify the HMAC-MD5 algorithm to use and the **-b** option for the bit size. (HMAC-MD5 ranges from 1 to 512.) Use the **-n** option to specify the key type, in this case, HOST for the hostname. The bit range will vary according to the algorithm. The following example creates a host key using a 128-bit key and the HMAC-MD5 encryption algorithm:

```
dnssec-keygen -a HMAC-MD5 -b 128 -n HOST turtle.mytrek.com
```

This creates a private key and a public key, located in the **.key** and **.private** files. In a TSIG scheme, both hosts would use the same private key for authentication. For example, to enable a DHCP server to update a DNS server, both would need the private (secret) key for a TSIG authentication. The HMAC-MD5 key is used as a shared private key, generating both the same private and public keys in the **.key** and **.private** files.

The Key Statement

You then specify a key in the **named** configuration file with the **key** statement. For the algorithm option, you list the HMAC-MD5 algorithm, and for the secret option, you list the private key. This key will be listed in both the **.private** and **.key** files. The preceding example would generate key and private files called **Kturtle.mytrek.com.+157.43080.key** and **Kturtle.mytrek.com.+157.43080.private**. The contents of the **.key** file consist of a resource record shown here:

```
turtle.mytrek.com. IN KEY 512 3 157 ONQAfbBLnvWU9H8hRqq/WA==
```

The contents of the private file show the same key along with the algorithm.

```
Private-key-format: v1.2
Algorithm: 157 (HMAC_MD5)
Key: ONQAfbBLnvWU9H8hRqq/WA==
```

Within the **named** configuration file, you then name the key using a **key** statement:

```
key myserver {
algorithm HMAC-MD5;
secret "ONQAfbBLnvWU9H8hRqq/WA==";
};
```

The key's name can then be used to reference the key in other named statements, such as **allow-update** statements.

```
allow-update myserver;
```

The DNS server or DHCP server with which you are setting up communication will also have to have the same key. See the earlier section "Dynamic Update: DHCP and Journal Files". For communication between two DNS servers, each would have to have a server statement specifying the shared key. In the following example, the **named.conf** file for the DNS server on 192.168.0.1 would have to have the following server statement to communicate with the DNS server on 10.0.0.1, using the shared myserver key. The **named.conf** file on the 10.0.0.1 DNS server would have to have a corresponding server statement for the 192.168.0.1 server.

```
server 10.0.0.1 {  keys (myserver;}; };
```

TLS statements

Should you want your DNS server to use TLS for communications, you can configure the connection for TLS in the **named.conf** file using the **tls** statement. Once configured you can reference TLS in the listen-on statements to receive requests on TLS. It can also be used for transfer requests between primary and secondary servers.

In the TLS statement you can configure various TLS options such as **cert-file** for the certificate, **ciphers** for the cipher to use, **protocols** for the versions of TLS allowed, and **key-file** for the TLS key. The **session_tickets** option allows the use of session tickets for easy resumption of connections, and **preferred -server** ciphers will prefer the use of the server ciphers instead of the client's. The **tls** statement has to be placed on the top level of the **named.conf** file. Keep in mind, that the TLS configuration is still under development. The example from the DNS manual follows:

```
tls local-tls {
    key-file "/path/to/key.pem";
    cert-file "/path/to/fullchain_cert.pem";
    dhparam-file "/path/to/dhparam.pem";
    ciphers
"HIGH:!kRSA:!aNULL:!eNULL:!RC4:!3DES:!MD5:!EXP:!PSK:!SRP:!DSS:!SHA1:!SHA256:!SHA3
84";
    prefer-server-ciphers yes;
    session-tickets no;
};
```

The **dhparam-file** option specifies the file holding the diffie-helmun parameters used for ciphers using the diffie-helmum key exchange (DHE). You can generate the file with and openssl command.

```
openssl dhparam -out dhparam.pem
```

By default the TLS statement implements opportunistic TLS, which provides no authentication. For strict TLS, which enables authentication, you would use the **remote-hostname** option to specify the host and the **ca-file** option for the certificate to use. Mutual TLS also provides authentication, but requires only a **ca-file** option that references a file holding client certificates. Mutual TLS does not require the use of TSIG keys for authentication.

Split DNS: Views

BIND 9 allows you to divide DNS space into internal and external views. This organization into separate views is referred to as split DNS. Such a configuration is helpful to manage a local network that is connected to a larger network, such as the Internet. Your internal view would include DNS information on hosts in the local network, whereas an external view would show only the part of the DNS space that is accessible to other networks. DNS views are often used when you have a local network that you want to protect from a larger network such as the Internet. In effect, you protect DNS information for hosts on a local network from a larger external network.

Internal and External Views

To implement a split DNS space, you need to set up different DNS servers for the internal and external views. The internal DNS servers will hold DNS information about local hosts. The external DNS server maintains connections to the Internet through a gateway, as well as manages DNS information about any local hosts that allow external access, such as FTP or websites. The gateways and Internet-accessible sites make up the external view of hosts on the network. The internal servers handle all queries to the local hosts or subdomains. Queries to external hosts, such as Internet sites are sent to the external servers, which then forward them on to the Internet. Queries sent to those local hosts that operate external servers such as Internet FTP and websites are sent to the external DNS servers for processing. Mail sent to local hosts from the Internet is handled first by the external servers, which then forward messages on to the internal servers. With a split DNS configuration, local hosts can access other local hosts, Internet sites, and local hosts maintaining Internet servers. Internet users can access only those hosts open to the Internet (served by external servers) such as those with Internet servers like FTP and HTTP. Internet users can, however, send mail messages to any of the local hosts, internal and external.

You can also use DNS views to manage connections for a private network that may use only one Internet address to connect its hosts to the Internet. In this case, the internal view holds the private addresses (192.168.), and the external view connects a gateway host with an Internet address to the Internet. This adds another level of security, providing a result similar to IP masquerading.

Configuring Views

DNS views are configured with the **allow** statements such as **allow-query** and **allow-transfer**. With these statements, you can specify the hosts that a zone can send and receive queries and transfers to and from. For example, the internal zone could accept queries from other local hosts, but not from local hosts with external access such as Internet servers. The local Internet servers, though, can accept queries from the local hosts. All Internet queries are forwarded to the gateway. In the external configuration, the local Internet servers can accept queries from anywhere. The gateways receive queries from both the local hosts and the local Internet servers.

In the following example, a network of three internal hosts and one external host is set up with a split view. There are two DNS servers: one for the internal network and one for external access, based on the external host. In reality, these make up one network but they are split into two views. The internal view is known as **mygolf.com**, and the external as **greatgolf.com**. In each configuration, the internal hosts are designated in ACL-labeled internals, and the external host is designated in ACL-labeled externals. Should you want to designate an entire IP address range as internal, you could simply use the network address, as in 192.168.0.0/24. In the options section, allow-query, allow-recursion, and allow-transfers restrict access within the network.

Split View Example

The following example shows only the configuration entries needed to implement an internal view (see next page). In the **mygolf.com** zone, queries and transfers are allowed only among internal hosts. The global allow-recursion option allows recursion among internals.

Internal DNS server

```
acl internals { 192.168.0.1; 192.168.0.2; 192.168.0.3; };
acl externals {10.0.0.1;};
options {
            forward only;
            forwarders {10.0.0.1;}; // forward to external servers
            allow-transfer { none; }; // allow-transfer to no one by default
            allow-query { internals; externals; };// restrict query access
            allow-recursion { internals; }; // restrict recursion to internals
            }
zone "mygolf.com" {
            type primary;
            file "mygolf";
            forwarders { };
            allow-query { internals; };
            allow-transfer { internals; }
            };
```

In the configuration for the external DNS server, the same ACLs are set up for internals and externals. In the options statement, recursion is now allowed for both externals and internals. In the **mygolf.com** zone, queries are allowed from anywhere, and recursion is allowed for externals and internals. Transfers are not allowed at all.

External DNS server

```
acl internals { 192.168.0.1; 192.168.0.2; 192.168.0.3; };
acl externals {10.0.0.1;};
options {
            allow-transfer { none; }; // allow-transfer to no one
            allow-query { internals; externals; };// restrict query access
            allow-recursion { internals; externals }; // restrict recursion
            };

zone "greatgolf.com" {
            type primary;
            file "greatgolf";
            allow-query { any; };
            allow-transfer { internals; externals; };
};
```

Response Policy Zones (DNS RPZ): DNS Firewall

Response Policy Zones allow you to control the response you give to different clients or queries. You can setup a policy for a specific zone that determines what responses to give for certain requests. Such zones are called Response Policy Zones (RPZ). An RPZ zone can intercept and block an attack, in effect, setting up a zone based DNS Firewall. The RPZ zone contains rules, much like a firewall rule with a trigger and an action. DNS firewall is often used to block domains, preventing clients from accessing known malicious sites. For more information see "Configuring BIND to use Response Policy Zones", **https://www.isc.org/docs/BIND_RPZ.pdf**.

Catalog Zones

Should a primary server have multiple secondary servers, it would normally have to list each one in its **named** configuration file. Managing multiple secondary servers can become complex, especially if they change often. Instead you can use a catalog zone to list and manage the secondary servers. The primary server needs only to reference the catalog zone, instead of each secondary server.

In a **named.conf** file, you would specify the name of the catalog zone in a **catalog-zones** statement placed in the options or view statements.

```
catalog-zones
    zone "mycatalog"
    default-primaries { 192.168,0.1;  }
    in-memory no
    zone-directory "mycatzones"
    min-update-interval 10;
};
```

The **default-primaries** option lists default primaries for the catalog zone's secondary zones. The **in-memory** option allows the member zones to be stored in memory. If **in-memory** is set to no, you can specify a directory where they can be stored with the **zone-directory** option. The **min-update-interval** option sets the minimum update interval for secondary servers.

You then set up a **catalog** zone file with an SOA record.

```
catalog.mytrek.com   IN SOA turtle.mytrek.com. hostprimary.turtle.mytrek.com. (
                              93071200 ; Serial (yymmddxx)
                                   900 ; Refresh
                                   600 ; Retry
                                 86400 ; Expire
                                    1) ; Minimum

    catalog.mytrek.com      IN NS turtle.mytrek.com.
    version.catalog.mytrek.com IN TXT "1"

    primaries.catalog.mytrek.com IN A  192.168.0.1

    0000000.zones.catalog.mytrek.com. IN TPTR mytrek.com.
```

Note: Dynamically Loadable Zones allows zone configurations to be transferred from external databases. DynDB allows data to be loaded directly from an external database. It is an alternative to DLZ, which requires translation.

ubuntu

16. Network Autoconfiguration with IPv6, DHCPv6, and DHCP

IPv6 Stateless Autoconfiguration

IPv6 Stateful Autoconfiguration: DHCPv6

DHCP for IPv4

Kea DHCP

Many networks now provide either IPv6 autoconfiguration or the DHCP (Dynamic Host Configuration Protocol) service, which automatically provides network configuration for all connected hosts. Autoconfiguration can be either stateless, as in the case of IPv6, or stateful, as with DHCP. Stateless IPv6 autoconfiguration requires no independent server or source to connect to a network. It is a direct plug-and-play operation, where the hardware network interfaces and routers can directly determine the correct addresses. DHCP is an older method that requires a separate server to manage and assign all addresses. Should this server ever fail, hosts cannot connect.

With the DHCP protocol, an administrator uses a pool of IP addresses from which the administrator can assign an IP address to a host as needed. The protocol can also be used to provide all necessary network connection information such as the gateway address for the network or the netmask. Instead of having to configure each host separately, network configuration can be handled by a central DHCP server. The length of time that an address can be used can be controlled by means of leases, making effective use of available addresses. If your network is configuring your systems with DHCP, you will not have to configure it.

For clarity, the examples in this chapter use the traditional network device name (like **eth0** and **eth1**) instead of the predictable device names (like **enp7s0**). Keep in mind, that, unless you rename your network devices (see Chapter 2), the actual devices on your system will use a predictable device name (like **enp7s0**).

IPv6 Stateless Autoconfiguration

In an IPv6 network, the IPv6 protocol includes information that can directly configure a host. With IPv4 you either had to configure each host manually or rely on a DHCP server to provide configuration information. With IPv6, configuration information is integrated into the Internet protocol directly. IPv6 address autoconfiguration is described in detail in RFC 2462.

IPv6 autoconfiguration capabilities are known as stateless, meaning that it can directly configure a host without recourse of an external server. Alternatively, DHCP, including DHCPv6, is stateful, where the host relies on an external DHCP server to provide configuration information. Stateless autoconfiguration has the advantage of hosts not having to rely on a DHCP server to maintain connections to a network. Networks can even become mobile, hooking into one subnet or another, automatically generating addresses as needed. Hosts are no longer tied to a particular DHCP server.

Generating the Local Address

To autoconfigure hosts on a local network, IPv6 makes use of each network device's hardware MAC address. This address is used to generate a temporary address, with which the host can be queried and configured.

The MAC address is used to create a link-local address, one with a link-local prefix, **FE80::0**, followed by an interface identifier. The link-local prefix is used for physically connected hosts such as those on a small local network.

A uniqueness test is then performed on the generated address. Using the Neighbor Discovery Protocol (NDP), other hosts on the network are checked to determine whether another host is already using the generated link-local address. If no other host is using the address, the address is assigned to that local network. At this point, the host has only a local address valid within the local physical network. Link-local addresses cannot be routed to a larger network.

Figure 16-1: Stateless IPv6 address autoconfiguration

Generating the Full Address: Router Advertisements

Once the link-local address has been determined, the router for the network is queried for additional configuration information. The information can be stateful, stateless, or both. For stateless configuration, information such as the network address is provided directly, whereas, for stateful configuration, the host is referred to a DHCPv6 server where it can obtain configuration information. The two can work together. Often the stateless method is used for addresses, and the stateful DHCPv6 server is used to provide other configuration information such as DNS server addresses.

In the case of stateless addresses, the router provides the larger network address, such as the network's Internet address. This address is then added to the local address, replacing the original link-local prefix, giving either a complete global Internet address or, in the case of private networks, unique-local addresses. Routers will routinely advertise this address information, though it can also be specifically requested. The NDP is used to query the information. Before the address is assigned officially, a duplicate address detection procedure checks to see if the address is already in use. The process depends on the router providing the appropriate addressing information in the form of router advertisements. If there is no router, or there are no router advertisements, then a stateful method like DHCPv6 or manual configuration must be used to provide the addresses.

IPv6 Router Renumbering

Figure 16-2: Router renumbering with IPv6 autoconfiguration

Figure 16-1 shows a network that is configured with stateless address autoconfiguration. Each host first determines its interface identifier using its own MAC hardware address to create a temporary link-local address for each host using the **FE80::0** prefix. This allows initial communication with the network's router. The router then uses its network prefix to create full Internet addresses, replacing the link-local prefix.

Router Renumbering

With IPv6, routers have the ability to renumber the addresses on their networks by changing the network prefix. Renumbering is carried out through the Router Renumbering (RR) Protocol. (See RFC 2894 for a description of router renumbering.) Renumbering is often used when a network changes ISP providers and requires that the net address for all hosts be changed (see Figure 16-2). It can also be used for mobile networks in which a network can be plugged into different larger networks, renumbering each time.

With renumbering, routers place a time limit on addresses, similar to the lease time in DHCP, by specifying an expiration limit for the network prefix when the address is generated. To ease the transition, interfaces still keep their old addresses as deprecated addresses, while the new addresses are first being used. The new addresses will be the preferred addresses used for any new connections, while deprecated addresses are used for older connections. In effect, a host can have two addresses, one deprecated and one preferred. This regeneration of addresses effectively renumbers the hosts.

Linux as an IPv6 Router: radvd

For a Linux system that operates as a router, you would use the **radvd** (Router ADVertisement Daemon) to advertise addresses, specifying a network prefix in the **/etc/radvd.conf** file (Ubuntu main repository). The **radvd** daemon will detect router network address requests from hosts, known as router solicitations, and provide them with a network address using a router advertisement. These router advertisements will also be broadcast to provide the network address to any hosts that do not send in requests. For **radvd** to work, you will have to turn on IPv6 forwarding. Use **sysctl** and set **net.ipv6.conf.all.forwarding** to 1. To start up the **radvd** daemon, you use the **radvd.service** systemd script. To check the router addresses **radvd** is sending, you can use **radvdump**.

```
sudo systemctl enable radvd
sudo systemctl start radvd
```

You will have to configure the **radvd** daemon yourself, specifying the network address to broadcast. Configuration is simple, as the full address will be automatically generated using the host's hardware address. A configuration consists of interface entries, which in turn list interface options, prefix definitions, and options, along with router definitions if needed. The configuration is placed in the **/etc/radvd.conf** file, which will look something like this:

```
interface eth0 {
    AdvSendAdvert on;
        prefix fc00:0:0:0::/64
        {
        AdvOnLink on;
        AdvAutonomous on;
        };
};
```

This assumes one interface is used for the local network, **eth0** in this example (you can find the interface name for your network with the **ifconfig** command. Wired connection begin with **en**. **eth** is an older naming convention). This interface configuration lists an interface option (AdvSendAdvert) and a prefix definition, along with two prefix options (AdvOnLink and AdvAutonomous). To specify prefix options for a specific prefix, add them within parentheses following the prefix definition. The prefix definition specifies your IPv6 network address. If a local area network has its own network address, you will need to provide its IPv6 network prefix address. For a private network, such as a home network, you can use the unique-local IPv6 prefix, which operates like the IPv4 private network addresses, 192.168.0. The preceding example uses a unique-local address that is used for private IPv6 networks, fc00:0:0:0::, which has a length of 64 bits.

The AdvSendAdvert interface option turns on network address advertising to the hosts. The AdvAutonomous network prefix option provides automatic address configuration, and AdvOnLink simply means that host requests can be received on the specified network interface.

A second network interface is then used to connect the Linux system to an ISP or larger network. If the ISP supports IPv6, this is a matter of sending a router solicitation to the ISP router. This automatically generates your Internet address, using the hardware address of the network interface that connects to the Internet and the ISP router's advertised network address. In Figure 16-2, shown earlier, the **eth0** network interface connects to the local network, whereas **eth1** connects to the Internet.

DHCP

DHCP provides configuration information to systems connected to a TCP/IP network, whether the Internet or an intranet. The hosts on the network operate as DHCP clients, obtaining their network configuration information from a DHCP server on their network. A host on the network runs a DHCP client daemon that automatically receives its network configuration information from its network's DHCP server. The information includes its IP address, along with the network's name server, gateway, and proxy addresses, including the netmask. Nothing has to be configured manually on the local system, except to specify the DHCP server it should get its network configuration from. This has the added advantage of centralizing control over network configuration for the different systems on the network. A network administrator can manage the network configurations for all the systems on the network from the DHCP server.

A DHCP server supports several methods for IP address allocation: automatic, dynamic, and manual. Automatic allocation assigns a permanent IP address for a host. Manual allocation assigns an IP address designated by the network administrator. With dynamic allocation, a DHCP server can allocate an IP address to a host on the network only when the host actually needs to use it. Dynamic allocation takes addresses from a pool of IP addresses that hosts can use when needed and releases them when they are finished.

The current version of DHCP supports the DHCP failover protocol, in which two DHCP servers support the same address pool. Should one fail, the other can continue to provide DHCP services for a network. Both servers are in sync and have the same copy of network support information for each host on the network. Primary and secondary servers in this scheme are designated with the primary and secondary statements.

A variety of DHCP servers and clients are available for different operating systems. The Ubuntu main repository provides DHCP version 4.4 software from the Internet Software Consortium (ISC) at **https://www.isc.org**. See **https://www.isc.org/dhcp/**. It integrates support for both IPv4 and IPv6 addressing. The software available includes a DHCP server (**isc-dhcp-server**), common DHCP files (**isc-dhcp-common**), a client (**isc-dhcp-client**), and a relay agent (**isc-dhcp-relay**). Ubuntu no longer supports DHCP version 3.

```
sudo apt install isc-dhcp-server
```

Configuring DHCP Client Hosts

Configuring hosts to use a DHCP server is a simple matter of setting options for the host's network interface device, such as an Ethernet card. On the Ubuntu desktop, selecting Automatic on the network tool's IPv tab selects DHCP.

Client support is carried out by the **dhclient** tool. When your network starts up, it uses **dhclient** to set up your DHCP connection. Though defaults are usually adequate, you can further configure the DHCP client using the **/etc/dhcp/dhclient.conf** file. Consult the **dhclient.conf** Man page for a detailed list of configuration options. Further configuration is provided in the **/etc/dhcp/dhclient-enter-hooks.d** and **/etc/dhcp/dhclient-exit-hooks.d** files for Avahi, Samba, the time server (Chrony), and debugging. Check the **dhclient-script** man page for more details. Lease information on the DCHP connection is kept in the **/var/lib/dhcp/dhclient.leases** file. You can also directly run **dhclient** to configure DHCP connections.

```
dhclient
```

Configuring the DHCP Server

The DHCP server package provided a single server, **dhcpd**, for both IPv4 addressing and for IPv6 addressing. Each form of addressing has a separate configuration file: for IPv4 it is **/etc/dhcp/dhcpd.conf**, and for IPv6 it is **/etc/dhcp/dhcpd6.conf**. Documentation for IPv6 configuration is integrated into the man pages for the DHCP server. See the man pages for **dhcpd.conf** for details on both IPv4 and the IPv6 addressing. The IPv6 sections are labeled DHCP6. The **dhcp-options** man page lists the DHCP/DHCP6 options. Any server runtime parameter can be set in the corresponding **/etc/default** files for the two methods of addressing: **/etc/default/dhcpd** and **/etc/default/dhcpd6**. Arguments are assigned to the DHCPDARGS variable.

For IPv4 addressing, **systemd** manages the DHCP server using the **isc-dhcp-server.service** file in the **/lib/systemd/system** directory. For IPv6 addressing it uses the **isc-dhcp-server6.service** file. The DHCP server is started after networking (After) and for the multi-user.target (WantedBy). It is started using the **/usr/sbin/dhcpd** command which reads configuration from **dhcpd.conf**. The **isc-dhcp-server6.service** file is the same except that the **dhcpd** command reads the **dhcpd6.conf** file and has the option **-6** for IPv6.

isc-dhcp-server.service

```
[Unit]
Description=ISC DHCP Ipv4 server
Documentation=man:dhcpd(8)
Wants=network-online.target
After=network-online.target
After=time-sync.target
ConditionPathExists=/etc/default/isc-dhcp-server
ConditionPathExists=/etc/ltsp/dhcpd.conf
ConditionPathExists=/etc/dhcp/dhcpd.conf

[Service]
EnvironmentFile=/etc/default/isc-dhcp-server
RuntimeDirectory=dhcp-server
#The leases file needs to be root:root even when dropping privileges
ExecStart=/bind/sh -ec '\
    CONFIG_FILE=/etc/dhcp/dhcpd.conf
    if [ -f /etc/ltsp/dhcpd.conf ]; then CONFIG_FILE=/etc/ltsp/dhcpd.conf; fi; \
    [ -e /var/ lib/dhcp/dhcpd.leases ] || touch /var/lib/hdcp/dhcpd.leases; \
    chown root:root /var/lib/dhcp  /var/lib/dhcp/dhcpd.leases*; \
    chmod 775 /var/lib/dhcp : chmod 664 /var/lib/dhcp/dhcpd.leases; \
    exec dhcpd -user dhcpd -group dhcpd -f -4 -pf /run/dhcp-server/dhcpd.pid -cf
$CONFIG_FILE $INTERFACESv4'

[Install]
WantedBy=multi-user.target
```

Use **systemctl** command with the **isc-dhcp-server** or **isc-dhcp-server6** command with the **start**, **restart**, and **stop** options. The following examples start the dhcp server with either IPv4 or IPv6 addressing. Use the **stop** option to shut it down and **restart** to restart them.

```
sudo systemctl start isc-dhcp-server
sudo systemctl start isc-dhcp-server6
```

Dynamically allocated IP addresses, known as leases, will be assigned for a given time. When a lease expires it can be extended, or a new one generated. Current leases are listed in the **dhcpd.leases** file located in the **/var/lib/dhcp** directory. A lease entry will specify the IP address and the start and end times of the lease along with the client's hostname.

/etc/dhcp/dhcpd.conf

The configuration file for the DHCP server is **/etc/dhcp/dhcpd.conf**. Here you specify parameters and declarations that define how different DHCP clients on your network are accessed by the DHCP server, along with options that define information passed to the clients by the DHCP server. These parameters, declarations, and options can be defined globally for certain sub-networks or for specific hosts. Global parameters, declarations, and options apply to all clients unless overridden by corresponding declarations and options in subnet or host declarations. Technically, all entries in a **dhcpd.conf** file are statements that can be either declarations or parameters.

All statements end with a semicolon. Options are specified in **options** parameter statements. Parameters differ from declarations in that they define if and how to perform tasks, such as how long a lease is allocated. Declarations describe network features such as the range of addresses to allocate or the networks that are accessible. See Table 16-1 for a listing of commonly used declarations and options.

Declarations provide information for the DHCP server or designate actions it is to perform. For example, the **range** declaration is used to specify the range of IP addresses to be dynamically allocated to hosts:

```
range 192.168.0.5 192.168.0.128;
```

With parameters, you can specify how the server is to treat clients. For example, the **default-lease-time** declaration sets the number of seconds a lease is assigned to a client. The **filename** declaration specifies the boot file to be used by the client. The **server-name** declaration informs the client of the host from which it is booting. The **fixed-address** declaration can be used to assign a static IP address to a client. See the Man page for **dhcpd.conf** for a complete listing.

Options provide information to clients that they may need to access network services, such as the domain name of the network, the domain name servers that clients use, or the broadcast address. See the Man page for **dhcp-options** for a complete listing. This information is provided by **option** parameters as shown here.

```
option broadcast-address 192.168.0.255;
option domain-name "mytrek.com";
option domain-name-servers 192.168.0.1, 192.168.0.4;
```

Your **dhcpd.conf** file will usually begin with declarations, parameters, and options that you define for the network serviced by the DHCP server. The following example provides router (gateway), netmask, domain name, and DNS server information to clients. Additional parameters define the default and maximum lease times for dynamically allocated IP addresses.

Entries	Description
Declarations	
`shared-network` *name*	Indicates if some subnets share the same physical network.
`subnet` *subnet-number netmask*	References an entire subnet of addresses.
`range` [*dynamic-bootp*] *low-address* [*high-address*] ;	Provides the highest and lowest dynamically allocated IP addresses.
`host` *hostname*	References a particular host.
`group`	Lets you label a group of parameters and declarations and then use the label to apply them to subnets and hosts.
`allow unknown-clients;` `deny unknown-clients;`	Does not dynamically assign addresses to unknown clients.
`allow bootp; deny bootp;`	Determines whether to respond to `bootp` queries.
`allow booting; deny booting;`	Determines whether to respond to client queries.
Parameters	
`default-lease-time` *time* ;	Assigns length in seconds to a lease.
`max-lease-time` *time* ;	Assigns maximum length of lease.
`hardware` *hardware-type hardware-address* ;	Specifies network hardware type (Ethernet or token ring) and address.
`filename` "*filename*" ;	Specifies name of the initial boot file.
`server-name` "*name*" ;	Specifies name of the server from which a client is booting.
`next-server` *server-name* ;	Specifies server that loads the initial boot file specified in the filename.
`fixed-address` *address* [, *address* ...] ;	Assigns a fixed address to a client.
`get-lease-hostnames` *flag* ;	Determines whether to look up and use IP addresses of clients.
`authoritative;` `not authoritative;`	Denies invalid address requests.
`server-identifier` *hostname* ;	Specifies the server.
Options	
`option subnet-mask` *ip-address* ;	Specifies client's subnet mask.
`option routers` *ip-address* [, *ip-address*...] ;	Specifies list of router IP addresses

	on client's subnet.
`option domain-name-servers` *ip-address* [, *ip-address...*] ;	Specifies list of domain name servers used by the client.
`option log-servers` *ip-address* [, *ip-address...*] ;	Specifies list of log servers used by the client.
`option host-name` *string*;	Specifies client's hostname.
`option domain-name` *string*;	Specifies client's domain name.
`option broadcast-address` *ip-address*;	Specifies client's broadcast address.
`option nis-domain` *string*;	Specifies client's Network Information Service domain.
`option nis-servers` *ip-address* [, *ip-address...*] ;	Specifies NIS servers the client can use.
`option smtp-server` *ip-address* [, *ip-address...*] ;	Lists SMTP servers used by the client.
`option pop-server` *ip-address* [, *ip-address...*] ;	Lists POP servers used by the client.
`option nntp-server` *ip-address* [, *ip-address...*] ;	Lists NNTP servers used by the client.
`option www-server` *ip-address* [, *ip-address...*] ;	Lists web servers used by the client.

Table 16-1: DHCP Declarations, Parameters, and Options

```
option routers 192.168.0.1;
option subnet-mask 255.255.255.0;
option domain-name "mytrek.com ";
option domain-name-servers 192.168.0.1;
default-lease-time 600;
max-lease-time 7200;
```

With the subnet, host, and group declarations, you can reference clients in a specific network, particular clients, or different groupings of clients across networks. Within these declarations, you can enter parameters, declarations, or options that will apply only to those clients. Scoped declarations, parameters, and options are enclosed in braces. For example, to define a declaration for a particular host, use the **host** declaration as shown here.

```
host rabbit {
        declarations, parameters, or options;
        }
```

You can collect different subnet, global, and host declaration into groups using the **group** declaration. In this case, the global declarations are applied only to those subnets and hosts declared within the group.

Dynamic IPv4 Addresses for DHCP

Your DHCP server can be configured to select IP addresses from a given range and assign them to different clients. Given a situation where you have many clients that may not always be connected to the network, you can effectively service them with a smaller pool of IP addresses. IP addresses are assigned only when they are needed. With the **range** declaration, you specify a range of addresses that can be dynamically allocated to clients. The declaration takes two arguments, the first and last addresses in the range.

```
range 192.168.1.5 192.168.1.128;
```

For example, if you are setting up your own small home network, you would use a network address beginning with 192.168. The range would specify possible IP addresses with that network. So, for a network with the address 192.168.0.0, you place a **range** declaration along with any other information you want to give to your client hosts. In the following example, a range of IP addresses extending from 192.168.0.1 to 192.168.0.128 can be allocated to the hosts on that network.

```
range 192.168.0.5 192.168.0.128;
```

You should also define your lease times, both a default and a maximum:

```
default-lease-time 600;
max-lease-time 7200;
```

For a small, simple home network, you just need to list the **range** declaration along with any global options. If your DHCP server is managing several sub-networks, you will have to use the **subnet** declarations.

In order to assign dynamic addresses to a network, the DHCP server will require that your network topology is mapped. This means it needs to know what network addresses belong to a given network. Even if you use only one network, you will need to specify the address space for it. You define a network with the **subnet** declaration. Within this **subnet** declaration, you can specify any parameters, declarations, or options to use for that network. The **subnet** declaration informs the DHCP server of the possible IP addresses encompassed by a given subnet. This is determined by the network IP address and the netmask for that network. The next example defines a local network with address spaces from 192.168.0.0 to 192.168.0.255. The **range** declaration allows addresses to be allocated from 192.168.0.5 to 192.168.0.128.

```
subnet 192.168.1.0 netmask 255.255.255.0 {
        range 192.168.0.5 192.168.0.128;
}
```

DHCP 4 does not require that you map connected network interfaces that are not being served by DHCP. These unmapped network interfaces are ignored.

The implementation of a very simple DHCP server for dynamic addresses is shown in the sample **dhcpd.conf** file that follows:

/etc/dhcp/dhcpd.conf

```
option subnet-mask 255.255.255.0;
option domain-name "mytrek.com ";
option domain-name-servers 192.168.0.1;

subnet 192.168.1.0 netmask 255.255.255.0 {
        range 192.168.0.5 192.168.0.128;
        default-lease-time 21600;
        max-lease-time 43200;
```

```
        option routers 192.168.0.1;
        }
```

DHCP Dynamic DNS Updates

For networks that also support a Domain Name Server, dynamic allocation of IP addresses currently needs to address one major constraint: DHCP needs to sync with a DNS server. A DNS server associates hostnames with particular IP addresses, whereas, in the case of dynamic allocation, the DHCP server randomly assigns its own IP addresses to different hosts. These may or may not be the same as the IP addresses that the DNS server expects to associate with a hostname. A solution to this problem is Dynamic DNS. With Dynamic DNS, the DHCP server is able to automatically update the DNS server with the IP addresses the DHCP server has assigned to different hosts. You can find detailed information about dynamic DNS in the **dhcpd.conf** Man page.

Note: Alternatively, if you want to statically synchronize your DHCP and DNS servers with fixed addresses, you configure DHCP to assign those fixed addresses to hosts. You can then have the DHCP server perform a DNS lookup to obtain the IP address it should assign, or you can manually assign the same IP address in the DHCP configuration file. Performing a DNS lookup has the advantage of specifying the IP address in one place, the DNS server.

The DHCP server has the ability to dynamically update BIND DNS server zone configuration files. You enable dynamic updates on a DNS server for a zone file by specifying the **allow-update** option for it in the **named.conf** file. It is strongly encouraged that you use TSIG signature keys to reference and authenticate the BIND and DHCP servers. Enabling the use of a TSIG key involves syncing configurations for both your DHCP and DNS servers. Both have to be configured to use the same key for the same domains. First, you need to create a shared secret TSIG signature key using **dnssec-keygen**. In the DNS server, you place TSIG key declarations and **allow-update** entries in the server's **named.conf** file, as shown in this example.

```
key mydhcpserver {
algorithm HMAC-MD5;
secret "ONQAfbBLnvWU9H8hRqq/WA==";
};


zone "mytrek.com" {
        type primary;
        file "mytrek.com";
        allow-update {key mydhcpserver;};
 };

zone "1.168.192.IN-ADDR.ARPA" {
        type primary;
        file "192.168.0";
        allow-update {key mydhcpserver;};
};
```

In the DHCP server, you place a corresponding TSIG key declaration and **allow-update** entries in the server's **dhcpd.conf** file, as shown in this example. The **key** declaration has the same syntax as the DNS server. DHCP **zone** statements are then used to specify the IP address of the domain and the TSIG key to use. The domain names and IP addresses need to match exactly in the configuration files for both the DNS and DHCP servers. Unlike in a **named** configuration file, there are no quotes around the domain name or IP addresses in the **dhcpd.conf** file. In the **dhcpd.conf** file, the domain names and IP addresses used in the **zone** statement also need to end with a period, as they do in the DNS zone files. The **key** statement lists the key to use. Though the DHCP server will try to determine the DNS servers to update, it is recommended that you explicitly identify them with a primary statement in a **zone** entry.

```
key mydhcpserver {
    algorithm HMAC-MD5;
    secret "ONQAfbBLnvWU9H8hRqq/WA==";
    };

zone mytrek.com. {                 #DNS domain zone to update
    primary 192.168.0.1;           #address of DNS server
    key mydhcpserver;              #TSIG signature key
 };

zone 1.168.192.IN-ADDR.ARPA. {    #domain PTR zone to update
    primary 192.168.0.1;           #address of DNS server
    key mydhcpserver;              # TSIG signature key
};
```

To generate a fully qualified hostname to use in a DNS update, the DHCP server will normally use its own domain name and the hostname provided by a DHCP client (see the **dhcpd.conf** Man page for exceptions). Should you want to assign a specific hostname to a host, you can use the **ddns-hostname** statement to specify it in the host's hardware section. The domain name is specified in the **domain-name** option:

```
option domain-name "mytrek.com"
```

The DNS update capability can be turned on or off for all domains with the **ddns-update-style** statement. It is off by default. Set it to **yes** to turn it on. To turn off DNS updates for particular domains, you can use the **ddns-updates** statement.

```
ddns-updates-style yes;
```

DHCP Subnetworks

If you are dividing your network space into several subnetworks, you can use a single DHCP server to manage them. In that case, you will have a **subnet** declaration for each subnetwork. If you are setting up your own small network, you use a network address beginning with 192.168. The range specifies possible IP addresses within that network so, for a network with the address 192.168.0.0, you create a **subnet** declaration with the netmask 255.255.255.0. Within this declaration, you place a **range** declaration along with any other information you want to give to your client hosts. In the following example, a range of IP addresses extending from 192.168.0.1 to 192.168.0.75 can be allocated to the hosts on that network.

```
subnet 192.168.0.0 netmask 255.255.255.0 {
 range 192.168.0.5 192.168.0.75;
 }
```

You may want to specify different policies for each subnetwork, such as different lease times. Any entries in a **subnet** declaration will override global settings. So if you already have a global lease time set, a lease setting in a **subnet** declaration will override it for that subnet. The next example sets different lease times for different subnets, as well as different address allocations. The lease times for the first subnet are taken from the global lease time settings, whereas the second subnet defines its own lease times.

```
default-lease-time 21600;
max-lease-time 43200;

subnet 192.168.1.0 netmask 255.255.255.0 {
      range 192.168.0.5 192.168.0.75;
      }
subnet 192.168.1.128 netmask 255.255.255.252 {
      range 192.168.0.129 192.168.0.215;
      default-lease-time 56000;
      max-lease-time 62000;
       }
```

If your subnetworks are part of the same physical network, you need to inform the server of this fact by declaring them as shared networks. You do this by placing subnet declarations within a **shared-network** declaration, specifying the shared network's name. The name can be any descriptive name, though you can use the domain name. Any options specified within the **shared-network** declaration and outside the subnet declarations will be global to those subnets. In the next example, the subnets are part of the same physical network and so are placed within a **shared-network** declaration.

```
shared-network mytrek.com
{
default-lease-time 21600;
max-lease-time 43200;
subnet 192.168.1.0 netmask 255.255.255.0 {
        range 192.168.0.5 192.168.0.75;
        }
subnet 192.168.1.128 netmask 255.255.255.252 {
        range 192.168.0.129 192.168.0.215;
        default-lease-time 56000;
        max-lease-time 62000;
        }
}
```

DHCP Fixed Addresses

Instead of using a pool of possible IP addresses for your hosts, you may want to give each one a specific address. Using the DHCP server still gives you control over which address will be assigned to a given host. However, to assign an address to a particular host, you need to know the hardware address for that host's network interface card (NIC). In effect, you need to inform the DHCP server that it has to associate a particular network connection device with a specified IP address. To do that, the DHCP server needs to know which network device you are referring to. You can identify a network device by its hardware address, known as its MAC address. To find out a client's hardware address, log in to the client and use the **ifconfig** command to find out information about your network devices. To list all network devices, use the **-a** option. If you know your network device name, you can use that. The next example will list all information about the Ethernet device, **enp7s0**:

```
ifconfig enps7s0
```

This will list information on all the client's network connection devices. The entry (usually the first) with the term **HWaddr** will display the MAC address. Once you have the MAC address, you can use it on the DHCP server to assign a specific IP address to that device.

In the **dhcpd.conf** file, you use a **host** declaration to set up a fixed address for a client. Within the **host** declaration, you place a **hardware** option in which you list the type of network connection device and its MAC address. Then use the **fixed-address** parameter to specify the IP address to be assigned to that device. In the following example, the client's network device with a MAC address of 08:00:2b:4c:29:32 is given the IP address 192.168.0.2.

```
host rabbit {
          option host-name "rabbit.mytrek.com"
          hardware ethernet 08:00:2b:4c:29:32;
          fixed-address 192.168.0.2;
          }
```

You can also have the DHCP server perform a DNS lookup to obtain the host's IP address. This has the advantage of letting you manage IP addresses in only one place, the DNS server. This requires that the DNS server is operating so that the DHCP server can determine the IP address. For example, a proxy server connection (which can provide direct web access) needs just an IP address, not a DNS hostname, to operate. If the DNS server were down, the preceding example would still assign an IP address to the host, whereas the following example would not.

```
host rabbit {
          option host-name "rabbit.mytrek.com"
          hardware ethernet 08:00:2b:4c:29:32;
          fixed-address rabbit.mytrek.com;
          }
```

You can also use the **host** declaration to define network information for a diskless workstation or terminal. In this case, you add a **filename** parameter specifying the boot file to use for that workstation or terminal. Here the terminal called **myterm** obtains boot information from the server **turtle.mytrek.com**.

```
host myterm {
          option host-name "myterm.mytrek.com"
          filename "/boot/vmlinuz";
          hardware ethernet 08:00:2b:4c:29:32;
          server-name "turtle.mytrek.com";
          }
```

A common candidate for a fixed address is the DNS server for a network. Usually, you want the DNS server located at the same IP address, so that it can be directly accessed. The DHCP server can then provide this IP address to its clients.

DHCP Client Classes

DCHP supports the use of classes of clients. Classes are defined and selected based on values derived from DHCP packets. You use the **class** statement to define a class. Once defined you can select a class. A class can be vendor or user determined. Vendors may include vendor identification information in a packet that can be detected and used by a DHCP server to configure or control access to different types of computers. A user based class can group computers by tasks, such as computers in an accounting department or those used on a special project. Such classes could be assigned a certain subset of addresses. Each client would use an option statement to specify what class they belong to. To select a class of clients you use the DCHP **match** command within a **class** statement, or additional DCHP conditional commands such as **if**.

The conditional command and its expressions are described in the **dhcp-eval** man page. The operators used for the **if** command expressions are designed to read and test certain data in a packet or to manipulate that data, such as a substring operation. The **option** function returns specified options contained in the packet. You can then use operators to test that value. The **dhcp-user-class** option is used to specify a user class. DHCP options are listed in the **dhcp-options** man page.

Kea DHCP Servers

Though not yet directly supported by Ubuntu, the new ISC Kea DHCP server is also available (Universe repository). There is a Kea IPv4, IPv6, and a dynamic DNS update server (DDNS). Install the **kea-dhcp4-server**, **kea-dhcp6-server**, and the **kea-dhcp-ddns-server** packages, as well as **kea-doc**. The **kea-admin** package provides a shell script to manage Kea datbases.

```
sudo apt install kea-dhcp4-server
```

Examples can be found in the **/usr/share/doc/kea/examples** directory. The man pages for the servers are **kea-dhcp4**, **kea-dhcp6**, and **kea-dhcp-ddns**. Check the Administrative Reference Manual at: **https://kea.readthedocs.io/**. The reference manual is also located on your system at **/usr/share/doc/kea/html** along with the man pages for Kea commands.

Kea is the replacement for DHCP, completely redesigned for the current large scale network environment. It features support for database backends such as MySQL and can be easily extended. Configuration is in the form a JSON (JavaScript Object Notation) files located in the **/etc/kea** directory. Each server has a separate configuration file such as **kea-dhcp4.conf** for the kea-dhcp4 server.

To convert an ISC DHCP configuration to a Kea DHCP configuration you can use the Kea Migration Assistant, isc-dhcp-keama. It is not yet available on the Ubuntu supported repositories. You can download the source code from github at **https://gitlab.isc.org/isc-projects/dhcp/-/tree/master/keama**.

ubuntu

17. Firewalls

Firewalls management tools

UFW and GUFW

FirewallD

nftables: rulesets, families, tables, chains, and rules

nftables expressions and statements

nftables connection tracking

nftables masquerading and mangle operations

nftables stateful objects, sets, maps, and verdict maps

IPtables

Most systems currently connected to the Internet are open to attempts by outside users to gain unauthorized access. Outside users can try to gain access directly by setting up an illegal connection, by intercepting valid communications from users remotely connected to the system, or by pretending to be valid users. Firewalls, encryption, and authentication procedures are ways of protecting against such attacks. A firewall prevents any direct unauthorized attempts at access, encryption protects transmissions from authorized remote users, and authentication verifies that a user requesting access has the right to do so. The current Linux kernel incorporates support for firewalls using the Netfilter (nftables) packet filtering package. To implement a firewall, you provide a series of rules to govern what kind of access you want to allow on your system. If that system is also a gateway for a private network, the system's firewall capability can effectively help protect the network from outside attacks.

Web Site	Security Application
https://www.netfilter.org	Netfilter project, nftables, and NAT
www.openssh.org	Secure Shell encryption
www.squid-cache.org	Squid Web Proxy server
web.mit.edu/Kerberos	Kerberos network authentication

Table 17-1: Network Security Applications

To provide protection for remote communications, transmission can be simply encrypted. For Linux systems, you can use the Secure Shell (SSH) suite of programs to encrypt any transmissions, preventing them from being read by anyone else. Kerberos authentication provides another level of security whereby individual services can be protected, allowing use of a service only to users who are cleared for access. Outside users may also try to gain unauthorized access through any Internet services you may be hosting, such as a website. In such a case, you can set up a proxy to protect your site from attack. For Linux systems, use Squid proxy software to set up a proxy to protect your Web server. Table 17-1 lists several network security applications commonly used on Linux.

For clarity, the examples in this chapter use the traditional network device name (like **eth0** and **eth1**) instead of the predictable device names (like **enp7s0**). Keep in mind, that, unless you rename your network devices (see Chapter 2), the actual devices on your system will use a predictable device name (like **enp7s0**).

nftables and IPtables

IPtables has been replaced by nftables. Whereas IPtables works like an interpreter, processing each individual rule one at a time, nftables operates more like a programming language, able to handle many rules at once on incoming packets. On Ubuntu 24.04, the **/usr/sbin/iptables** command is a link to the **/etc/alternatives/iptables** command, which, in turn, is a link to **/usr/sbin/xtables-nft**, which, in turn, is a link to the **/usr/sbin/xtables-nft-multi** command. The commands **xtables-nft-save** and **iptables-nft-restore** follow a similar path of links to the same **xtables-nft-multi** command. The **xtables-nft-multi** command read IPtables rules and convert them to nftables format using the **nft_compat** module. Though the ufw frontend manages IPtables rules, these rules are converted and used by nftables. FirewallD, on the other hand, operates as a frontend for nftables directly. Also, if you have to add rules directly to your firewall and you need to convert from IPtables to nftables, you can use the **iptables-translate** command. The **iptables-translate** command takes as its argument an IPtables rule and generates the nftables equivalent. It is also a link directly to the **/usr/sbin/xtables-nft-multi** command. You can find out more about nftables at **https://wiki.nftables.org/**.

You can still use the older IPtables firewall with the **iptables-legacy** commands (**iptables-legacy**, **iptables-legacy-save**, and **iptables-legacy-restore**). These are links to the **xtables-legacy-multi** command. By default the standard iptables commands follow a path of links to the nftables **iptables-nft-multi** command. These links are symbolic links that can be easily changed. The links to change are located in the **/etc/alternatives** directory, which holds the iptables commands (**iptables**, **iptables-save**, and **iptables-restore**), which are only links. If you want to use the older IPtables firewall instead of nftables, you would change these links to reference the **iptables-legacy** commands in the **/usr/sbin** directory. These, in turn, all reference the **iptables-legacy-multi** command. The ufw firewall would then use the older IPtables firewall instead of nftables. To return to using nftables, change the iptables command links in the **/etc/alternatives** directory to link back to using the iptables-nft commands, also in **/usr/sbin**.

The links to change for switching between IPtables and nftables are located in the **/etc/alternatives** directory. To use the older IPtables firewall, use the following link operation for the **iptables-legacy** commands in **/usr/sbin**. Be sure include the **-f** option to force the change on an existing link.

```
sudo ln -s -f /usr/sbin/iptables-legacy   /etc/alternatives/iptables
sudo ln -s -f /usr/sbin/iptables-legacy-save  /etc/alternatives/iptables-save
sudo ln -s -f /usr/sbin/iptables-legacy-restore  /etc/alternatives/iptables-restore
```

To return to using nftables, link the iptables commands in **/etc/alternatives** to the corresponding **iptables-nft** commands in **/usr/sbin**.

```
sudo ln -s -f /usr/sbin/iptables-nft   /etc/alternatives/iptables
sudo ln -s -f /usr/sbin/iptables-nft-save   /etc/alternatives/iptables-save
sudo ln -s -f /usr/sbin/iptables-nft-restore   /etc/alternatives/iptables-restore
```

Firewall management tools

You can choose from several different popular firewall management tools (see Table 17-2). Ubuntu provides a firewall configuration tool called the Uncomplicated Firewall (ufw). IPtables and ufw are on the Ubuntu main repository, and other firewall tools are in the Universe repository. You can also choose to use other popular management tools such as Fwbuilder. Gufw provides a frontend desktop interface, technically using IPtables as its backend. Search Synaptic Package Manager for firewall to see a complete listing. In addition, you can use the FirewallD dynamic firewall front end application, whose backend is nftables.

Firewall	Description
nftables	nftables: netfilter, NAT, and mangle. **https://netfilter.org** (Main repository), replaces IPtables
IPTables	IPtables older form of firewall rules, replaced by nftables
ufw	Uncomplicated Firewall, ufw. **https://wiki.ubuntu.com/UncomplicatedFirewall** (Ubuntu Main repository), also see Ubuntu Server Guide at **https://ubuntu.com/server/docs**. Still generates IPtable rules, which are automatically converted to nftables rules by the system.
Gufw	GNOME frontend interface for Uncomplicated Firewall, ufw. **https://help.ubuntu.com/community/Gufw**
Fwbuilder	Firewall configuration tool, allow for more complex configuration **https://sourceforge.net/projects/fwbuilder/** (Universe repository)
Shorewall	Shoreline firewall (Universe repository)
FirewallD	Dynamic Firewall daemon, frontend for nftables backend https://fedorahosted.org/firewalld/ (Universe repository)

Table 17-2: Ubuntu Firewall configuration tools

The Uncomplicated Firewall: ufw

The Uncomplicated Firewall, ufw, is the official firewall application for Ubuntu. It provides a simple firewall that can be managed with a few command-line operations. ufw still uses IPtables to define rules and run the firewall. The ufw application is just a frontend management interface for IPtables. Default IPtables rules are kept in before and after files, with added rules in user files. The IPtables rule files are held in the **/etc/ufw** directory. These IPtables rules are automatically converted to nftables rules. Firewall configuration for certain packages will be placed in the **/usr/share/ufw** directory. You can find out more about ufw at the Ubuntu Firewall site at **https://wiki.ubuntu.com/UncomplicatedFirewall** and at the Ubuntu firewall section in the Ubuntu Server Guide at **https://ubuntu.com/server/docs/security-firewall**. The Server Guide also shows information on how to implement IP Masquerading on ufw. You can manage the ufw firewall with either the **ufw** command or using the Gufw desktop tool. Runtime configuration is read from **/etc/default/ufw**. The ufw **systemd** unit files manage static IPtables rules. The ufw operation runs an **ufw-init** script to start and stop the firewall. As noted, the **/sbin/iptables** command is a link to the **/etc/alternatives/iptables** command, which, in turn, is a link to the **/usr/sbin/iptables-nft-multi**, which is one of the **iptables-nft** commands. The **iptables-nft** commands read IPtables rules and converts them to nftables format using the **nft_compat** module.

ufw.service

```
[Unit]
Description=Uncomplicated firewall
Documentation=man:ufw(8)
DefaultDependencies=no
Before=network.target
Wants=network-pre.target local-fs.target
After=local-fs.target

[Service]
Type=oneshot
RemainAfterExit=yes
ExecStart=/lib/ufw/ufw-init start quiet
ExecStop=/lib/ufw/ufw-init stop

[Install]
WantedBy=multi-user.target
```

ufw commands

IPtables firewall rules can be set up using **ufw** commands entered on the command line and in a Terminal window. Most users may only need to use **ufw** commands to allow or deny access by services like the Web server or Samba server. A **ufw** command requires administrative access and must be run with the **sudo** command. To check the current firewall status, listing those services allowed or blocked, use the **status** command.

```
sudo ufw status
```

If the firewall is not enabled, you will first have to enable it with the **enable** command.

```
sudo ufw enable
```

You can restart the firewall, reloading your rules, using the **systemctl** command with the **restart** option.

```
sudo systemctl restart ufw
```

You can then add rules using allow and deny commands and their options as listed in Table 17-3. To allow a service, use the allow command and the service name. This is the name for the service listed in the **/etc/services** file. For connection rate limiting, use the **limit** option in place of **allow**. The following command allows the ftp service.

```
sudo ufw allow ftp
```

If the service you want is not listed in **/etc/services**, and you know the port and protocol it uses, you can specify the port and protocol directly. For example, the Samba service uses port 445 and protocol tcp.

```
sudo ufw allow 445/tcp
```

The status operation will then show what services are allowed.

Commands	Description
enable | disable	Turn the firewall on or off
status	Display status along with services allowed or denied.
logging on | off	Turn logging on or off
default allow | deny	Set the default policy, **allow** is open, whereas **deny** is restrictive
allow *service*	Allow access by a service. Services are defined in **/etc/services** which specify the ports for that service.
allow *port-number/protocol*	Allow access on a particular port using specified protocol. The protocol is optional.
deny *service*	Deny access by a service
delete *rule*	Delete an installed rule, use **allow**, **deny**, or **limit** and include rule specifics.
proto *protocol*	Specify protocol in **allow**, **deny**, or **limit** rule
from *address*	Specify source address in **allow**, **deny**, or **limit** rule
to *address*	Specify destination address in **allow**, **deny**, or **limit** rule
port *port*	Specify port in **allow**, **deny**, or **limit** rule for **from** and **to** address operations

Table 17-3: UFW firewall operations

```
sudo ufw status
To                 Action        From
21:tcp             ALLOW         Anywhere
21:udp             ALLOW         Anywhere
139,445:tcp          ALLOW          Anywhere
```

To remove a rule, prefix it with the **delete** command.

```
sudo ufw delete allow 445/tcp
```

A range of ports can be specified using the colon. Samba also uses the 137 and 138 ports with the UDP protocol.

```
sudo ufw allow 137:138/udp
```

Provided ports use the same protocol, you can list several in the same rule separated by commas. The Samba service uses both ports 445 and 135 with the TCP protocol.

```
sudo ufw allow 135,445/tcp
```

More detailed rules can be specified using address, port, and protocol commands. These are similar to the actual IPtables commands. Packets to and from particular networks, hosts, and ports can be controlled. The following denies SSH access (port 22) from host 192.168.03.

```
sudo ufw deny proto tcp from 192.168.03 to any port 22
```

UFW also supports connection rate limiting. Use the **limit** option in place of **allow**. With **limit**, connections are limited to 6 per 30 seconds on the specified port. It is meant to protect against brute force attacks.

The rules you add are placed in the **/etc/ufw/user.rules** file as IPtables rules (corresponding IPv6 rules are placed in the **user6.rules** file). ufw is just a front-end for **iptables-restore** which will read this file and set up the firewall using **iptables** commands. **ufw** will also have **iptables-restore** read the **before.rules** and **after.rules** files in the **/etc/ufw** directory. These files are considered administrative files that include needed supporting rules for your IPtables firewall. Administrators can add their own IPtables rules to these files for system specific features like IP Masquerading.

Note: The Ubuntu Server Guide shows information on how to implement IP masquerading on ufw (**https://ubuntu.com/server/docs/security-firewall**).

The **before.rules** file will specify a table with the * symbol, as in ***filter** for the netfilter table (the corresponding IPv6 before rules are in the **before6.rules** file). For the NAT table, you would use ***nat**. At the end of each table segment, a COMMIT command is needed to instruct ufw to apply the rules. Rules use **-A** for allow and **-D** for deny, assuming the **iptables** command. The following would implement IP Forwarding when placed at the end of the **before.rules** file (see Ubuntu firewall server documentation on Firewalls). This particular rule works on the first Ethernet device (eth0 in this example) for a local network (192.168.0.0/24).

```
# nat Table rules
*nat
:POSTROUTING ACCEPT [0:0]
# Forward traffic from eth1 through eth0.
-A POSTROUTING -s 192.168.0.0/24 -o eth0 -j MASQUERADE
# don't delete the 'COMMIT' line or these nat table rules won't be processed
COMMIT
```

Default settings for ufw are placed in **/etc/default/ufw**. Here you will find the default INPUT, OUTPUT, and FORWARD policies specified by setting associated variables, like DEFAULT_INPUT_POLICY for INPUT and DEFAULT_OUTPUT_POLICY for OUTPUT. The DEFAULT_INPUT_POLICY variable is set to DROP, making DROP the default policy for the INPUT rule. The DEFAULT_OUTPUT_POLICY variable is set to ACCEPT, and the DEFAULT_FORWARD_POLICY variable is set to DROP. To allow IP Masquerading, DEFAULT_FORWARD_POLICY would have to be set to ACCEPT. These entries set default policies only. Any user rules you have set up would take precedence.

Managing the ufw firewall on the desktop with Gufw

Gufw provides an easy to use GNOME interface for managing your ufw firewall. A simple interface lets you add rules, both custom and standard. You can install Gufw from Ubuntu Software as Firewall Configuration (Snap repository) or from the Synaptic Package Manager (Universe repository, **gufw** package). On the Applications overview, search on firewall and choose Firewall Configuration. If Gufw does not start, you may also have to install the **python-gobject** package.

```
sudo apt-get install python-gobject
```

By default, the IPtables rules Gufw generates are converted automatically to nftables rules. In this sense, it operates as a front end for nftables. Should you want to change to using IPtables instead, you have to change the iptables command links in the **/etc/alternatives** directory to use the **iptables-legacy** commands as described in the previous section.

Gufw will initially open with the firewall disabled, with no ports configured. The application is locked initially. The Status button is set to off, and the shield image will be gray. To enable the firewall, click the left side of the Status button, setting the status to on. The shield image will be colored and the firewall rules will be listed. Figure 15-1 shows the firewall enabled and several rules listed. Rules for both IPv4 and IPv6 (**v6**) network protocols are listed.

Figure 17-1: Gufw

The Gufw dialog has a Firewall section and three tabs: Rules, Report, and Log. The Firewall section has a Status button for turning the firewall on or off. There is a Profile menu for Home, Office, and Public configurations. The Incoming and Outgoing drop down menus are for setting the default firewall rules. Available options are Deny, Reject, or Allow, and are applied to incoming and outgoing traffic, respectively. By default, incoming traffic is denied (Deny), and outgoing traffic is allowed (Allow). Rules you specified in the Rules tab will make exceptions, allowing only certain traffic in or out. Should you select the Allow option, the firewall accepts all incoming traffic. In this case you should set up rules to deny access to some traffic, otherwise, the firewall becomes ineffective, allowing access to all traffic. The Report tab lists active services and ports such as the Samba server on port 139. The Log tab list firewall notices. You can copy notices, as well as delete a log. The Home tab provides basic help on how to use Gufw.

To add a rule, click the Rules tab, and then click the plus button (+) on the lower left corner of the Rules tab to open the "Add a Firewall Rule" dialog, which has three tabs for managing rules: Preconfigured, Simple, and Advanced. The Preconfigured tab provides five menus: the first for the policy (Allow, Deny, Reject, and Limit), the second for the traffic direction (In or Out), the third for the category of the application, the fourth for a subcategory, and the fifth for the particular application or service for the rule. The list of possible applications is extensive. You can narrow the list down by using the Category and Subcategory menus. The main categories are Audio video, Games, Network, Office, and System. The Network category with the Services subcategory lists most network services like SSH, Samba, and FTP. You could also simply use the search box (Application Filter) to search for a service.

If there is a security issue with the rule, a warning is displayed. Should you need to modify the default rule for an application, you can click on the arrow button to the right of the search box to open the Advanced tab for that rule.

Click the Add button to add the rule. Once added, a port entry for the rule appears in the Rules section. In Figure 17-2 the Samba service has been selected and then added, showing up in the Rules section as "137,138/udp ALLOW IN Anywhere."

Figure 17-2: Gufw Preconfigured rules

Applications and services can also be blocked. To prevent access by the FTP service, you would first select Deny, then Service, and then the FTP entry.

Besides Allow and Deny, you can also choose a Limit option. The Limit option will enable connection rate limiting, restricting connections to no more than 6 every 30 seconds for a given port. This is meant to protect against brute force attacks.

Figure 17-3: Gufw Simple rules

Should there be no preconfigured entry, you can use the Simple tab to allow access to a port (see Figure 17-3). The first menu is for the rule (Allow, Deny, Reject, and Limit), and the second for the protocol (TCP, UDP, or both). In the Port text box, you enter the port number.

On the Advanced tab, you can enter more complex rules. You can set up allow or deny rules for tcp or udp protocols, and specify the incoming and outgoing host (ip) and port (see Figure 17-4).

Figure 17-4: Gufw Advanced rules

If you decide to remove a rule, select it in the Rules section and then click the minus button on the lower left corner (-). To remove several rules, click and press Shift-click or use Ctrl-click to select a collection of rules, and then click the minus button.

You can edit any rule by selecting it and clicking the edit button (gear image) to open an "Update a Firewall Rule" dialog (see Figure 17-5). For a default or simple rule, you can only change a few options, but you can turn on logging.

Figure 17-5: Gufw edit a rule

You can also create rules for detected active ports. Click the Report tab and then select a port and click on the plus button at the bottom of the tab. An "Add a Firewall Rule" dialog opens to the Advanced tab with the name of the service active on that port and the port number (see Figure 17-6). You can change any of the options. The port number is already entered.

Should you want to you can pause any activity on a port by selecting it and clicking the pause button at the bottom of the tab. The button will change to a play button. Select the port and click the play button to activate the port.

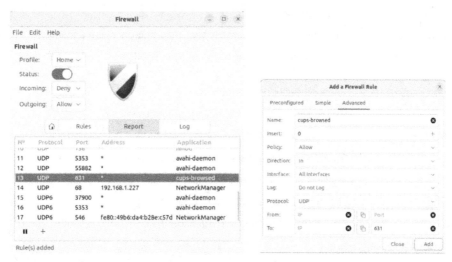

Figure 17-6: Gufw create a rule for an active port

Dynamic Firewall with FirewallD

FirewallD runs as a daemon implementing a dynamic firewall. Instead of loading rules offline from a file, you add them directly to the FirewallD daemon. FirewallD operates as a frontend for nftables, directly. FirewallD is not supported by Ubuntu but is available on the Ubuntu repository. It is the default firewall for Fedora and Suse Linux. For documentation see:

```
https://fedoraproject.org/wiki/FirewallD
```

FirewallD Zones

FirewallD sets up network zones to define the level of trust for different kinds of network connections (see Table 17-4). Each zone can have several connections, but a connection can belong only to one zone. FirewallD defines several zones, most of which you can change (mutable). The drop and block zones are immutable and designed to stop all incoming packets. The public, external, and dmz zones are designed for untrusted networks, exposing only part of your system. The work, home, and internal zones are used for trusted networks. The trusted zone (also immutable) allows all network connections.

Zone configurations are located in **/etc/firewalld/zones**. You can use **firewall-config** or **firewall-cmd** to manage your zones and add new ones. The default zone is set in the **/etc/firewalld/firewalld.conf** configuration files by the DefaultZone variable. Initially, it is set to public. The default and fallback zones are saved in **/lib/firewalld/zones**.

Zone files are saved as XML files which list the zone name and the services and ports allowed, along with any masquerade, ICMP, and port forwarding options.

Zone	Description
drop (immutable)	Deny all incoming connections, outgoing ones are accepted.
block (immutable)	Deny all incoming connections, with ICMP host prohibited messages issued.
trusted (immutable)	Allow all network connections
public	Public areas, do not trust other computers
external	For computers with masquerading enabled, protecting a local network
dmz	For computers publicly accessible with restricted access.
work	For trusted work areas
home	For trusted home network connections
internal	For internal network, restrict incoming connections

Table 17-4: FirewallD zones

Dynamic and Static Firewalls: FirewallD and the iptables command

Traditionally firewalls were static. You modified firewall rules and then restarted your firewall to load the rules. A dynamic firewall, such as FirewallD, can apply modified rules without restarting the firewall. Rules, however, have to be managed directly by the FirewallD daemon. You use the **firewall-config** and **firewall-cmd** tools to directly configure your firewall. FirewallD is front end for nftables, which performs the actual firewall operations. nftables is the default firewall for Ubuntu, superseding the older IPtables.

Though not supported by Ubuntu directly, you can use the FirewallD dynamic firewall daemon to set up a firewall. You can disable and enable FirewallD manually using the **systemctl** command.

```
sudo systemctl enable firewalld
sudo systemctl disable firewalld
```

On Ubuntu, FirewallD is managed by the **firewalld** service script. You can start and stop it using the **systemctl** command. You will have to start the FirewallD daemon in a terminal window with the following command.

```
sudo systemctl start firewalld
```

You can stop it with a stop command.

```
sudo systemctl stop firewalld
```

firewall-cmd

The **firewall-cmd** command works on a command line interface, using options to set features for different zones. Zone modification options such as **--add-service**, can be either runtime or permanent. Runtime changes expire after a restart or reload. To make the changes permanent you add the **--permanent** option, making changes for a persistent configuration, instead of a runtime one.

Use the **get** options to display information about the firewall. The **--get-zones** option lists your zones, the **--get-services** option list services supported by the current zone, and the **--get-icmptypes** lists the ICMP types.

```
firewall-cmd --get-zones
firewall-cmd --get-services
firewall-cmd --get-icmptypes
```

The **--get-default-zone** option lists the default zone, and **--set-default-zone** sets up a new default zone.

```
firewall-cmd --set-default-zone  home
```

To find out what features have been enabled for a zone, use the **--list-all** option with a **--zone=** option to specify the zone.

```
firewall-cmd home --zone=home  --list-all
```

Zone are assigned network interfaces. There are interface options to add, remove, or change an interface. Use the query option to check if an interface belongs to a zone.

```
firewall-cmd --zone=home  --query-interface=enp7s0
```

The service, port, masquerade, icmp, and forwarding options can be either runtime or persistent (permanent). The **--service** options can add and remove services to a zone.

```
firewall-cmd -add-service=vsftp
```

To make the change permanent (persistent mode), add the **--permanent** option.

```
firewall-cmd --permanent -add-service=vsftp
```

The **--query-service** option checks to see if a service is enabled for a zone.

```
firewall-cmd --zone=home -query-service=http
```

The **--port** options are used to add, remove, or query ports.

```
firewall-cmd --zone=home --add-port=22
```

Add the **--permanent** option to make it permanent.

```
firewall-cmd --permanent --zone=home --add-port=22
```

The **masquerade** options add, removes, and queries zones for masquerading.

```
firewall-cmd --zone=work --add-masquerade
```

The **icmp-block** options add, remove, and query ICMP types.

```
firewall-cmd --zone=work --add-icmp-block=echo-reply
```

Should your firewall have to use custom firewall rules, you can add, remove, and list them using the **--direct** option. These are rules written in the IPtables syntax. You have to specify the protocol, table, chain, and arguments. The following lists the rules you added to the netfilter table. The rules are not saved and have to be added again each time you restart or reload. You could have a script of **firewall-cmd** rules to do this.

```
firewall-cmd --direct --get-rules ipv4 netfilter
```

The following adds a simple netfilter rule.

```
Firewall-cmd --direct -add-rule ipv4 netfilter INPUT  Deny
```

Managing FirewallD on the desktop with firewall-config

On the desktop, you can use **firewalld-config** to configure Firewalld. You can also use the **firewalld-cmd** command from the command line. To set up your firewall, run **firewall-config**, (see Figure 17-7). The top button bar has a button to Reload your saved firewall.

Figure 17-7: firewall-config: Runtime Configuration

With **firewall-config,** you can configure either a Runtime or Permanent configuration. Select one from the Configuration menu. The Runtime configuration shows your current runtime set up, whereas a Permanent configuration does not take effect until you reload or restart. If you wish to edit your zones and services, you need to choose the Permanent Configuration (see Figure 17-8). This view displays a zone toolbar for editing zone at the bottom of the zone scroll box, and an Edit Services button on the Services tab for editing service protocols, ports, and destination addresses.

Additional tabs can be displayed from the View menu for configuring ICMP types, and for adding firewall rules directly (Direct Configuration).

From the Options menu, you can reload your saved firewall.

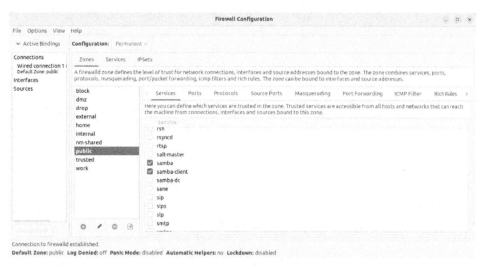

Figure 17-8: firewall-config: Permanent Configuration

A firewall configuration is set up for a given zone, such as a home, work, internal, external, or public zone. Zones provide an added level of protection by the firewall. They divide the network protected by the Firewall into separate segments, which can only communicate as permitted by the firewall. In effect, zones separate one part of your network from another. Each zone has its own configuration. Zones are listed in the Zone scroll box on the left side of the firewall-config window. Select the one you want to configure. The firewall-config window opens to the default zone, Public. You can choose the default zone from the System Default Zone dialog (see Figure 17-9), which you open from the Options menu as "Change Default Zone."

Figure 17-9: Default Zone

To the left of the Zones tab is the Active Bindings section, which list the network connections, interfaces, and sources on your system. For each active connection the zone bound to it is listed, such as the public zone bound to the wired connection. To change the zone bound to a connection you select the entry and click the Change Zone button at the bottom of the Active

Binding section. This open a Select zone dialog where you can choose a different zone to be bound to a connection. You can choose from any of the zones in the zones tab. You can also change a connection binding from the Options menu by choosing "Change Zones of Connections."

If you choose Permanent Configuration from the Current View Menu, a toolbar for zones is displayed below the Zone scroll box. The plus button lets you add a zone and the minus button removes a zone. The pencil button lets you edit a zone. The add and edit buttons open the Base Zone Settings dialog, where you enter or edit the zone name, version, description, and the target (see Figure 17-10). The default target is ACCEPT. Other options are REJECT and DROP. The Load Zone Defaults button (yellow arrow) loads default settings, removing any you have made.

Each zone, in turn, can have one or more network connections. From the Options menu choose "Change Zones of Connections" to select a network connection for the zone.

For a given zone you can configure services, ports, masquerading, port forwarding, and ICMP filter. A Linux system is often used to run servers for a network. If you are creating a strong firewall but still want to run a service such as a Web server, an FTP server, Samba desktop browsing, or SSH encrypted connections, you must specify them in the Services tab. Samba desktop browsing lets you access your Samba shares, like remote Windows file systems, from your Ubuntu desktop.

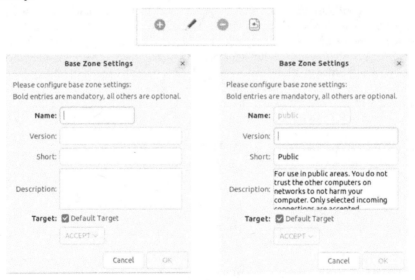

Figure 17-10: Base Zone Settings

For a selected service, you can specify service settings such as ports and protocols it uses, any modules, and specific network addresses. Default settings are already set up for you such as port 139 for Samba, using the TCP protocol. To modify the settings for a service, click the Services tab on the Firewall Configuration window to list your services (see Figure 17-11). Choose the service you want to edit from the Service scroll box at the left. For a given service you can then use the Ports, Protocols, Source Port, Modules, and Destination tabs to specify ports, protocols, modules, and addresses. On the Ports tab, click the Add button to open the Port and Protocol dialog where you can add a port or port range, and choose a protocol from the Protocol menu (see Figure 17-12). On the Destination tab, you can enter an IPv4 or IPv6 destination address for the service.

Figure 17-11: Service Settings

Figure 17-12: Service Protocols and Ports

On the Zones tab, the Ports tab lets you specify ports that you may want opened for certain services, like BitTorrent. Click the Add button to open a dialog where you can select the port number along with the protocol to control (tcp or udp), or enter a specific port number or range.

If your system is being used as a gateway to the Internet for your local network, you can implement masquerading to hide your local hosts from outside access from the Internet. This also requires IP forwarding which is automatically enabled when you choose masquerading. Local hosts will still be able to access the Internet, but they will masquerade as your gateway system. You would select for masquerading the interface that is connected to the Internet. Masquerading is available only for IPv4 networks, not IPv6 networks.

The Port Forwarding tab lets you set up port forwarding, channeling transmissions from one port to another, or to a different port on another system. Click the Add button to add a port, specifying its protocol and destination (see Figure 17-13).

Figure 17-13: Port Forwarding

Figure 17-14: ICMP Filters

The ICMP Filters tab allows you to block ICMP messages. By default, all ICMP messages are allowed. Blocking ICMP messages makes for a more secure system. Certain types of ICMP messages are often blocked as they can be used to infiltrate or overload a system, such as the ping and pong ICMP messages (see Figure 17-14).

If you have specific firewall rules to add, use the Direct Configuration tab (displayed from the View | Direct Configuration menu).

nftables

nftables is now the default firewall for Ubuntu, replacing IPtables. The **nftables** man page provides detailed documentation. It is installed by default (the **nftables** package). Examples of nftable rules (**.nft** files) can be found at:

```
/usr/share/doc/nftables/examples
```

There are examples for filter, nat, and mangle tables, for both IPv4 and IPv6 protocols, such as **ipv4-filter.nft** and **ipv6-nat.nft**.

A detailed explanation of **nftables** can be found at:

```
https://wiki.nftables.org/wiki-nftables/index.php/Main_Page
```

You use the **nft** command to manage nftables, adding, removing, and loading rules. nftables keeps firewall rules in either **.nft** files or in the **/etc/nftables.conf** file.

The older IPtables used a match and single action format, whereas nftables can have multiple expressions along with multiple statements. This allows for more complex rules much like statements in a programming language. Rules with multiple expressions are evaluated from left to right. If the first expression is a match, then the next expression is checked. If it matches, then the next one is checked, and so on. If all the expressions match, then the statements are executed. These may include actions to be taken on the packet, such as accepting or dropping it. nftables can also handle both IPv4 and IPv6 packets at the same time.

The nftables is managed by **systemd** using the **nftables.service** unit file, shown here. It is a simple file that is run before the network starts (Before) and is started by **sysinit.target** (WantedBy). It is run by the **/usr/sbin/nft** command which reads the **/etc/nftables.conf** file. When it is stopped, it will flush the ruleset, **nft flush ruleset**.

nftables.service

```
[Unit]
Description=nftables
Documentation=man:nft(8) http://wiki.nftables.org
Wants=network-pre.target
Before=network-pre.target shutdown.target
Conflicts=shutdown.target
DefaultDependencies=no

[Service]
Type=oneshot
RemainAfterExit=yes
StandardInput=null
ProtectSystem=full
ProtectHome=true
ExecStart=/usr/sbin/nft -f /etc/nftables.conf
ExecReload=/usr/sbin/nft -f /etc/nftables.conf
ExecStop=/usr/sbin/nft flush ruleset

[Install]
WantedBy=sysinit.target
```

You can start, stop, and restart, nftables with the **systemctl** command.

```
sudo systemctl start nftables
sudo systemctl stop nftables
sudo systemctl restart nftables
systemctl status nftables
```

Ubuntu does not enable the nftables firewall by default. You will have to enable it and then start it.

```
sudo systemctl enable nftables
sudo systemctl start nftables
```

You can convert from IPtables to nftables using several nftables tools. To convert a single IPtables rule, you can use the **iptables-translate** command. Notice that a **counter** statement is added to the nftables version. This is because IPtables automatically adds a **counter** statement to all its rules. Also, the table name is **filter** which is just a placeholder name for a table.

```
iptables-translate -A INPUT -j ACCEPT  -i lo
nft add rule ip filter INPUT iifname "lo" counter accept
```

To convert an entire file, use the **iptables-restore-translate** command with the name of your IPtables script. Redirect the output to an **.nft** file. You can then read the **.nft** file into nftables with the **nft -f** command.

```
iptables-restore-translate -f myiptables > mynftables.nft
nft -f mynftables.nft
```

If you are still using **iptables**, be sure to turn it off and disable it (use **systemctl**) before starting the **nftables** service.

Methods of entering nftable rulesets

For nftables, there are several different ways to enter the tables, chains, and rules that make up a firewall. The common method is to load rules from an **.nft** file with the **nft -f** command. This gives you greater flexibility. It is the method used in this section. Using this method you can enter the rules as single rules as you would an IPtables rule, or use a block method that organizes your rules much as you would a program.

You could enter the rules into the file, with a separate rule on each line.

```
add chain ip myfilter myinput { type filter hook input priority 0; }
```

With the block method you can arrange the entries as blocks, with rules placed in the block for their chain.

```
add chain ip myfilter myinput {
          type filter hook input priority 0;
          }
```

Should you want to run your nftables rules directly as an executable file, instead of entering the **nft -f** command from the shell, you would place the following command to invoke the **nft** shell. It must be the first entry in your file.

```
#!/usr/sbin/nft -f
```

There is also a default nftables file that is read automatically, **/etc/nftables.conf**. This file already has a basic set of rules. You can replace them with your own. As an executable file it has the invocation of the **nft** shell as its first line, **#!/usr/sbin/nft -f**. Be sure the leave it in when adding your rules.

Alternatively, you can enter your rules from the shell, much like IPtables rules were entered. This approach is not often used for nftables. Each rule would have to be preceded with the **sudo nft** command. nftables and the shell also use some of the same operators, such as the semicolon, which you would have to be careful to quote so that they are not evaluated by the shell.

```
sudo nft add chain ip myfilter myinput '{ type filter hook input priority 0; }'
```

Rulesets

One major difference from IPtables is that IPtables reads a shell script of iptables rules to configure a firewall, during which time the firewall is not operational. nftables, instead, reads its rules in such a way that the firewall is always operational. nftables performs an atomic operation. It uses an atomic object to hold the entire firewall configuration in memory. To read in new nftable rules, all the nft configuration files are read and a new atomic object is created in memory. Then the new atomic object replaces the current one. There is no time when the firewall is not operational.

You can save your ruleset by outputting the result of a **list** operation to a file, as in:

```
nft list table myfilter > myfilter-rules
```

Use the **ruleset** command to reference the ruleset for nftables. To reference the ruleset for just a particular family in the ruleset, specify the family. To list the ruleset just for a table, add the table name. For a chain in a table, add the chain name.

```
ruleset
ruleset ip
ruleset ip myfilter
ruleset ip myfilter myinput
```

Use **list** to display the rules for a ruleset.

```
nft list ruleset
nft list rulesetip myfilter
```

You can also use **ruleset** to flush the entire ruleset or just those for a family.

```
nft flush ruleset
nft flush ruleset ip
```

To restore a ruleset, you would want to first flush the current ruleset, removing those rules from your firewall before adding in the restoring ruleset.

First back up the ruleset as a precaution.

```
nft list ruleset > mybackup.nft
```

When you want to restore the ruleset, first flush the firewall.

```
nft flush ruleset
```

Then read in the **mybackup.nft** file.

```
nft  -f mybackup.nft
```

For a **.nft** script that holds the rules you load into the firewall, you could add the **flush** operation as the first line to ensure that the firewall is clear of any previous rules.

```
flush ruleset
```

.nft files

There are two file formats that **nft** can read, rule-based and block. Essentially, the rule-based file is one that contains a list of rules, just as the older IPtables files used a list of rules. The block format is meant to work much like a programming language. It organizes rules into blocks that can be more easily referenced.

You can place your rules in a text file with the extension **.nft** to be read by the **nft** command. In the file you can define variables, include other files, and place comments. **nft** reads in the **.nft** file as rules using the command **nft** and **-f** option. The **.nft** file can be any name.

```
nft -f myrules.nft
```

To include another file into the **nft** file, you use the **include** command and the name of the added file encased in single quotes.

```
include "myaddedrules.nft"
```

The file name can recognize matching characters. The following includes all files with the **.nft** extension.

```
include "*.nft"
```

You can also include all the files in a directory by using the directory name instead. Be sure to use the full path name of the directory. The following adds in all the files in the **/etc/myrulesdir** directory.

```
include "/etc/myrulesdir"
```

Comments are indicated with a # sign. Any line beginning with the # character is treated as a comment.

```
# These are my new rules
```

As noted, you can place your rules in bash shell scripts to be executed directly. The following command has to be placed as the first line in the nft script.

```
#!/usr/sbin/nft -f
```

The /etc/nftables.conf file

nftables will automatically load the rules in the the **/etc/nftables.conf** file. It has already set up a basic firewall with very simple table and chain definitions. The name of the ruleset table is **inet** and the type is **filter**, as shown here.

```
#!/usr/sbin/nft -f

flush ruleset

table inet filter {
      chain input {
            type filter hook input priority filter;
      }
      chain forward {
            type filter hook forward priority filter;
      }
      chain output {
            type filter hook output priority filter;
      }
}
```

You could simply replace this with an **include** statement for the **.nft** file you want to have automatically loaded. The **.nft** file has to be an administrative file (owned by the root user). A simple way to do this is to create an **/etc/nftables** directory (it can be any name). And then, as the administrative user (**sudo**) copy your **.nft** file to the that directory.

```
sudo mkdir /etc/nftables

sudo cp myfilter-rules.nft   /etc/nftables
```

Then you can include it in the **/etc/nftables.conf** file as shown here.

```
#!/usr/sbin/nft -f

flush ruleset
include "/etc/nftables/myfilter-rules.nft"
```

Should you want to automatically load a different file, change the **include** statement to that file name.

Families

nftables organizes addresses into families. Different tables can be set up for the different families of addresses (see Table 17-5). The address families are: **ip** for IPv4 addresses, **ip6** for IPv6 addresses, **inet** for both IPv4 and IPv6 addresses, **arp** for IPv4 ARP packets, **bridge** for Bridge addresses (those on a bridge device), and **netdev** for ingress and netgress packets. When adding a table, chain, or rule you should specify the address family. If no address family is specified, the default is used, **ip** for IPv4 addresses.

Family	Description
ip	IPv4 address family
ip6	IPv6 address family
inet	IPv4 and IPv6 address family
arp	IPv4 ARP addresses
bridge	Packets on a bridge device
netdeve	Packets on ingress and egress

Table 17-5: nftables address families

The address families have their packets accessed through hooks. The **ip**, **ip6**, and **inet** families support hooks for different points in packet processing. These are **prerouting**, **input**, **output**, **forward**, **postrouting**, and **ingres** (inet family only), (see Table 17-6). These hooks apply to packets for IPv4 and IPv6 addresses (**ip**, **ip6**, and **inet**).

Hook	Description
prerouting	Operations on packets when they are firs received
input	Packets received by the host
output	Packets sent out by the host
forward	Packets forwarded
postrouting	Packets leaving
ingress	Occurring before prerouting, it is for initial operations on packets when the first arrive.

Table 17-6: nftables ip, ip6, and inet address hooks

The **prerouting** hook is for IPv4 and IPv6 packets when they first arrive. Here is where operations such pre filtering tasks or route changes are performed. The **input** hook is for all packets arriving for the host. The **output** hook is for all packets being sent from the host. The **forward** hook is for those packets to be forwarded on to another host. The **postrouting** hook is for all packets as they leave, performing tasks such as changing routing if needed. The **ingress** hook applies only to packets for the **inet** address family (both IPv4 and IPv6) and can apply tasks when the packet first arrives, before even **prerouting**.

The ARP family supports only **input** and **output** hooks. The Bridge family supports the **ingress** and **egress** hooks, for when packets first arrive and when they leave.

Tables

nftables organizes rules into tables. Tables are the basic containers for chains. Within the chains you add and manage the rules. In nftables, a table is referenced with the keyword **table**. A table works with a specified family. So you can create tables for IPv4 packets (**ip4**), IPv6 packets (**ip6**), and for both (**inet**), as well as Arp packets and Bridge and netdev packets. See Table 17-7 for statements you can use on tables.

Command	Description
add table *family table-name*	Add a new table, specify the address family and a name. Also used to make table dormant or reactivated.
delete table *family table-name*	Delete a table
list table *family table-name*	List a table
flush table *family table-name*	Delete all chains and rules in a table
create table *family table-name*	Also creates a table, but check if it already exists.

Table 17-7: nftables table commands

To create a table use the **add table** statement with the table's family. The name of the table can be any name you want to give it. The following example creates a table for the **ip** family and is called **myfilter**.

```
nft add table ip myfilter
```

To remove a table use the **delete table** command, its family, and the table name.

```
nft delete table ip myfilter
```

To see what tables are in your firewall use the **list tables** command.

```
nft list tables
```

To see the chains and rules in a specific table use the **list table** command with the family and the table name.

```
nft list table ip myfilter
```

As with IPtables you can flush a table, removing all the rules. Use the **flush** command, the table's family, and the table name.

```
nft flush table ip myfilter
```

The flushing operation can also be applied in a more refined way to specific chains. Be sure to specify the chain.

```
nft flush table ip myfilter myinput
```

The **add table** command will not check if the table already exists, whereas the **create table** command will. It returns an error if the table already exists.

To disable a table you use the **dormant** flag. Use the **add table** command to add the **dormant** flag to the table.

```
add table ip mytable { flag dormant; }
```

To enable the table again use a simple **add table** command.

```
add table ip mytable
```

Note: The nftables documentation will use the name filter for the table in its examples. This can actually be any name. It does not have to be filter. Keep in mind that the term filter is the type used for adding a chain.

Chains

A table has chains which hold the table's rules. There are two kinds of chains, base and regular. The base chains are for addresses as they are processed. A regular chain is used as a jump target for organizing your rules. You manage your chains with the **chain** statements (see Table 17-8)

Command	Description
add chain *family table chain-name*	Add a new chain to the specified table.
delete chain *family table chain-name*	Delete a chain. Flush all rules from it first.
rename chain *family table chain-name new-name*	Rename a chain
list chain *family* table *table-name chain-name*	List the rules in the chain
flush chain *family table chain-name*	Delete all rules in a chain
create chain *family table chain-name*	Also creates a chain, but check if it already exists.

Table 17-8: nftables chain commands

To create a chain you use the **add chain** or **create chain** statement. The **create chain** statement checks to see the chain already exist and returns an error if it does. Otherwise the two statements operate the same. The name of the chain can be any name you want to give it. There are several chain parameters that can be set: **type, hook, device, priority, policy,** and **comments**. You have to specify the **type** for the chain and its **hook** or **device**, as well as the **priority** for processing the chain. You can also set a default policy, specify a device, and add comments. The following example creates a **myinput** chain in the **myfilter** table with the type **filter** that operates on the packets in the **input** hook. The chain has a **priority** of 0.

```
add chain ip myfilter myinput { type filter hook input priority 0; }
```

Chains that access packets, such as those that access packets in **input, output, forward, prerouting,** and **postrouting,** are known as base chains. These base chains must have a **type, hook,** and **priority** specified. The possible base chain types are **filter, route,** and **nat**. These are specified in the chain's **type** parameter. The **filter** type is the most common and is used to filter packets. The **route** chain re-routes packets, much like the mangle table did in iptables. The **nat** chains supports Network Address Translation (NAT).

You use the chain's **hook** parameter to determine where the chain operates in the packet stream. The type of hooks are **ingress, prerouting, input, forward, output,** and **postrouting**. The **ingress** type checks packets when the first arrive, before any other chain. **prerouting** then checks the arriving packets. **input** sees the incoming packets. **forward** can forward packets. **output** sees the outgoing packets. **postrouting** checks packets before they leave. Hooks are specified with the **hook** parameter.

```
hook prerouting
hook input
hook output
hook forward
hook postrouting
```

The **filter** type supports all families, and all hooks (see Table 17-9). The **nat** type supports only the **ip**, **ip6**, and **inet** families, as well as only the **prerouting**, **input**, **output**, and **postrouting** hooks (not the **forward** hook). The **route** type supports only the **ip** and **ip6** families and the **output** hook.

In addition, the ARP family only supports the **input** and **output** hooks with a chain type of **filter**. The **inet** family also supports the **ingress** hook with type **filter**. The **netdev** family only supports **ingress** and **egress**, both with type **filter**, as well a requiring that device be specified.

Type	Families	Hooks	Description
filter	all famlies	all hooks	commonly used chain type
nat	ip, ip6, inet	prerouting, input, output, postrouting	NAT (Native Address Translation) chains
route	ip, ip6	output	Re-route a packet

Table 17-9: nftables base chain types

nftables also supports regular chains. These are user defined chains and can have any name.

Use the **delete** statement to remove a chain and the **flush** statement to remove all rules in a chain. Be sure to specify the table and chain.

```
nft delete chain ip myfilter myinput

nft flush chain myfilter myinput
```

You can have multiple chains in a table. Each chain is given a priority, using its **priority** parameter. The chain with the highest priority (staring from 0) is evaluated first. If the evaluation does not result in a drop operation, the next chain is evaluated.

```
priority 0
priority -100
```

Instead of a number, you can use a priority name, called a standard name. These are priorities given to common network services, such as a Web or FTP server. The names are available to certain families with specific hooks (see Table 17-10). A name is simply another way to specify the number. In any chain, you can still use the value directly instead of a standard name. The bridge family is more restricted with only four standard names (see Table 17-11).

Name	Value	Family	Hooks
raw	-300	ip, ip6, inet	all hooks
mangle	-150	ip, ip6, inet	all hooks
dstnat	-100	ip, ip6, inet	prerouting
filter	0	ip, ip6, inet, arp, netdev	all hooks
security	50	ip, ip6, inet	all hooks
srcnat	100	ip, ip6, inet	postrouting

Table 17-10: nftables standard names for priorities

Name	Value	Hooks
dstnat	-300	prerouting
filter	-2000	all hooks
out	100	output
srcnat	300	postrouting

Table 17-11: nftables standard priority names for bridge familty

The default policy for a chain can be either **accept** or **drop**, which are indicated by the **policy** parameter and the keywords **accept** and **drop**.

```
policy accept
```

Moving to chains: jump and goto

Chains can contain rules. You can treat a chain much as you would a function in a programming language, in that you can jump from a rule to a chain to have the packets processed by the rules in that chain. You would then automatically return to the calling chain and continue with the next rule in line. You use the **jump** statement to jump to another chain for processing. Chain flow of control is usually arranged like a tree, connecting different chains through **jump** statements.

As an example, if you want to count all incoming tcp packets, instead of repeating a **counter** statements for each tcp rule, you could simply jump to a chain with a counter in it. In the next example the **my-tcp-counter** chain is created and a rule added to it with the **counter** statement.

```
add chain ip myfilter my-tcp-counter-chain
add rule ip myfilter my-tcp-counter-chain counter
```

Then a rule is added for the **myiput** chain that will jump to the **my-tcp-counter** chain to count all input packets for the tcp protocol.

```
add rule ip myfilter myinput ip protocol tcp jump my-tcp-counter-chain
```

Alternatively, you could use the **goto** statement to change to another chain. With the **goto** statement, you are not returned automatically to the next rule in the calling chain. You leave that chain and do not return.

Rules

For each chain you can add rules which perform actions on matched packets. A rule supports two kinds of components: expressions and statements. Usually a rule consists of two parts: a pattern matching section used to detect a packet, followed by statements used to perform actions on the packet. Expressions can be used in either section. Rules are managed with the rule statements such as **add rule** to add a rule and **delete rule** to remove one (see Table 17-12). The **add rule** statement adds rules to those already in the chain, and the **insert rule** statement adds a rule as the first rule.

Command	Description
add rule *family table chain rule*	Add a new rule to the specified chain. The rule is appended to the end of the list of current rules in chain.
insert rule *family table chain*	Insert a rule to the beginning of the rules in a chain
insert rule *family table chain* handle *handle-number rule*	Insert a rule to a chain
insert rule *family table chain* index *handle-number rule*	Rename a chain
delete rule *family table chain rule* handle *handle-number*	Delete a rules.
replace rule *family table chain rule* handle *handle-number statement*	Rename a chain

Table 17-12: nftables rule statements

Note: Be warned that nft uses shell script operators in its syntax. If you are adding a rule directly from the shell instead of a file, to ensure that the shell does not try to evaluate the operators, either enclose the entire rule within single quotes or prefix each operator with a backslash. Shell and nft operators include brackets, periods, semi-colons, and colons.

To add a rule, you use the **add rule** statement. Each rule must specify the table and chain it is being added to. The following would add a rule to the **myoutput** chain in the **myfilter** table, placing it at the end of the rules for the **myoutput** chain.

```
add rule myfilter output ip daddr 192.168.0.3 counter
```

The following example uses the **insert rule** statement to add the rule to the top of the rules in the **myoutput** chain.

```
insert rule myfilter myoutput ip daddr 192.168.0.1 counter
```

Each rule can be given a priority to determine the order in which they are evaluated. Rules with the same priority are evaluated randomly.

Should you want to add a rule to a specific place in the set of rules already in the chain, you will need to know its position. Rules are referenced by their **handle** or **index**. A **handle** is a unique value the kernel uses to reference a rule. Use the **-n** and **-a** options with the **list** command to find the handles for rules in the chains. The **-a** option shows the handles in your ruleset. The handle is listed at the end of each rule, preceded by **#handle**

```
nft -n -a list chain myfilter myoutput
```

The output for a rule would look like this.

```
ip daddr 10.0.0.5 counter packets 0 bytes 0 accept # handle 97
```

You can use the **insert rule** statement with a specified rule handle to insert the rule before the one with that handle. Enter the statement **handle** with the handle number of the rule you want to insert the new rule before.

```
nft insert rule myfilter myoutput handle 97 ip daddr 192.168.0.1 counter
```

The handle of the inserted rule would become the handle of the rule it was inserted before.

```
ip daddr 192.168.0.1 counter packets 0 bytes 0 accept # handle 97
```

The **index** is a user specified rank, whereas the **handle** is referenced by the kernel.

Use the **delete rule** statement to remove a rule from a chain, referencing the rule by its handle. As noted, a handle is a unique value the kernel uses to reference a rule. Use the **-a** option with the **list** command to find the handles for rules in a chain.

```
nft delete rule myfilter myoutput handle 5
```

You can also use a handle to replace a rule. Use the **replace rul**e statement with the table and chain name along with the replacement rule.

```
nft replace rule myfilter myoutput handle 5 counter
```

Expressions

Expressions can be either constants, common expressions such as comparison or mathematical operations, complex operations used in matching packets information, or operations deriving information from a packet. Expressions are used extensively for a wide range of possible network data types. See the **nft** man page for a detailed explanation of all the supported expression data types. See Table 17-13 for a list of some of the common basic data types.

Expressions are identified by their data types. To find out more information about a data type or expression, use the **describe** statement. The following describes the data type **daddr**, which is an **ip** expression.

```
sudo nft describe ip daddr
payload expression, datatype ipv4_addr (IPv4 address) (basetype integer), 32 bits
```

Data types are key to how expressions are handled. They determine the size, parsing, allowed symbols, and compatibility. Some data types are dynamic, such as strings, and others are constants. You can use the **describe** statement to find a constant data type's value. There are lower level types such as **integer** which are used for higher level types such as an addresses. Expressions can be combinations of sub expressions from which a data type is derived.

Data type	size	Name	Base type
integer	variable	Integer	
string	variable	String	
bitmask	variable	Bitmask	integer
ipv4_addr	32 bit	IPv4 Address<	integer
ipv6_addr	128 bit	IPv6 Address<	integer
icmp_type	8 bit	ICMP Type	integer
ct_state	4 byte	contrack state	bitmask
ct_status	4 byte	contrack status	bitmask
dccp_pkttype	4 bit	DCCP packet type	integer

Table 17-13: nftables common data types

Relational operators will work on numbers and strings, as well as addresses and ports (see Table 17-14).

Operator	Operator	Description
==	eq	equal
!=	ne	not equal
<	lt	less than, for shell escape use \<
>	>	greater than, for shell escape use \>
le	<=	less than or equal
ge	>=	greater than or equal

Table 17-14: nftables expression operators

For example, the integer data type is used for numbers. You can use relational operators on them to create a complex expressions. To test for ports higher than 1024 use the following expression.

```
tcp dport  >= 1024
```

Not including 1024, use a greater than, >, operator.

```
tcp dport > 1024
```

For ports not tcp 22, use !=.

```
dcp dport != 22
```

Primary Expressions

You can use primary expressions such as meta, ipv4, and ct (connection tracking) to access and match on information in a packet. These are primary expressions which represent a constant or a single piece of data.

There are several other primary expressions such as **socket** expressions for searching connected TCP/UPD sockets, **osf** expressions for passive operating system fingerprinting, **fib** expressions to search the forwarding information base, **rt** for routing information, **ipsec** for accessing IPSEC data in a packet, and **payload** expressions to access data in the packet's payload such as an address (see Table 17-18).

Keyword	data type	Description
pktype	pkt_type	packet type
length	integer (32 bit)	packet length in bytes
protocol	ether_type	packet protocol
nfproto	integer (32 bit)	netfilter packet protocol family
l4proto	integer (8bit(	layer 4 protocol

Table 17-15: nftables meta data protocols infomation

Keyword	data type	Description
iif	iface_index	input interface index
iifname	ifname	input interface name
iiftype	iface_type	input interface type
iifkind	ifkind	input interface kind
iifgroup	devgroup	input interface group
oif	iface_index	output interface index
oifname	ifname	output interface name
oiftype	iface_type	output interface type
oifkind	ifkind	output interface kind
oifgroup	devgroup	output interface group
ibrname	ifname	input bridge interface name
obrname	ifname	output bridge interface name
ibrvproto	ether_type	input bridge vlan protocol
sdif	integer	slave device interface index
sdifname	ifname	slave device interface name

Table 17-16: nftables meta expressions used for packet match by interface

Meta Expressions

You can match on and access the meta data in a packet using a **meta** expression, accessing information such as the package name or interface it traverses. Meta information includes data such as the length of the packet or its protocol (see Table 17-15). You can also match on interfaces, both incoming and outgoing, as well as bridges (see Table 17-16). You can match on the time by date, day of the week, or time of day (see Table 17-17). There are also meta security expressions you can use such as **cpu** for the CPU processing the packet, and **ipsec** to see if it is encrypted. You can even match on the User or Group IDs of the originating socket.

To use a meta expression, precede it with the **meta** keywork and a meta expressions.

```
meta iifname lo
meta priority 2
```

For example, you could use the **iifname** expression to reference the **lo** loopback device by name.

```
input meta iifname "lo" accept
```

You could use **skuid** to access the user id of a socket.

```
meta skuid 1002
```

Keyword	data type	Description
mark	mark	packet mark
priority	tc_handle	tc packet priority
rtclassid	realm	routing realm
ID		
skuid	uid	UID for originating socket
skgid	gid	GID for originating socket
Time		
time	time	timestamp of packet when received
day	day	day of week (as integer 1 to 6) or string as weekday such as Monday, Mon, or mon)
hour	hour	hour of day (format is HH:MM:SS)
Security		
cpu	integer	CPU processing packet
cgroup		socket control group
secmark		packet secmark
ipsec		true if ipsec encrypted

Table 17-17: nftables meta expressions for packet match by mark, priory, route, ID, time, and security

Expression	Description
meta	Meta expression
socket	Socket expression for open TCP/UDP sockets
osf	Passive OS fingerprinting
fib	Access forwarding information base
rt	Routing data such as mtu and next hop
ipsec	IPSEC information such as the source or destination address

Table 17-18: nftables primary expressions for packet information

Payload Expressions

Payload expressions reference the packet's payload, such as the address and protocol header information. The **ether** expression matches on the destination address (**daddr**), source address (**saddr**), and the **ether** type (**type**).

```
ether daddr
```

The **vlan** header expression obtains any Vlan information: **id** for the Vlan id, **del** for drop indicator, **pcp** for the prior code point, and **type** for the ether type.

There are also expressions for different protocols such as ARP, IPv4, IPv6, ICMP, TCP, UDP, and DCCP. Use the **ar** expression for ARP, **ip** for IPv4, **ip6** for IPv6, and **udp** for UDP (see Table 17-19).

You can also access information in extended headers for IPv6, IPv4, and TCP. Use the **exthdr** expression for IPv6. For TCP and IPv4 use the **tcp option** and **ip option** expressions.

Expression	Description
ether	Ethernet header expression
vlan	Vlan information
arp	ARP header information
ip	IPv4 header information
Ip6	IPv6 header information
icmp	ICMP header information such as type, checksum, id, and gateway
imcpv6	ICMPv6 header information such as packet-to-big and max-delay
tcp	TCP information such as the source and destination port
udp	UDP information such as the ports, length, and checksum
sctp	SCTP information
dccp	DCCP information, address and type
ah	Authenticaion information such as length, sequence number, and security parameter index
esp	Encrypted security payload information
comp	IPCOMP infromation
@*base,offset,length*	Raw payload expressing to access specified subsets of the payload's raw data. Has the same format as a substring operation.
exthdr	IPv6 extended headers information
tcp option ip option	TCP and IPv4 extended header information

Table 17-19: nftables payload expressions

Statements.

Statements perform the actions in a rule. There are two kinds of statements: terminal and non-terminal. A terminal statements ends a rule, unconditionally. No further evaluation of the rule is performed. There can be only one terminal statement in a rule. Non-terminal statements can also end a rule, but would do so conditionally. You could also have a non-terminal statement that does not end a rule. Within a rule you can have as many non-terminal statements as you want. Statements and their flags are listing in Table-20.

Commands	Description
accept	Accept a packet
drop	Drop a packet
reject	Reject a packet
counter	count the packets and bytes for an element
elements	Initialize set with values
Flags	
constant	Values of the elements cannot be changed
interval	Set can have intervals
timeout	Elements can have timeout command

Table 17-20: nftables statements

Verdict Statements: accept and drop

Verdict statements are terminal statements that set a policy for a packet or changes the flow of control of the firewall rules by moving to another rule or chain (see Table 17-21).

Statement	Description
accept	Accept a packet, other hooks or chains could evaluate it
drop	Drop a packet, no further evaluation by any other hooks or chains
reject	Drop a packet, no further evaluation by any other hooks or chains, returns an error message.
queue	Queue a packet to user space
continue	Continue to next rule. Also the default for all rules.
return	Return to the next rule in the chain the current chain was invoked from
jump *chain*	Jump to another chain, evaluating the rules in that chain.
goto *chain*	Go to another chain without a return to the calling chain

Table 17-21: nftables verdict statements

Use the **accept** and **drop** statements to accept and drop packets. The following rule accepts all packets.

```
myfilter myinput accept
```

The **reject** statement is the same as the drop statement, but will also return an error message. The **reject** statement can only be used in the **input**, **output**, and **forward** hooks, or for user defined chains based on them.

```
reject with icmp type host-unreachable
myfilter myinput ct state new reject
```

The following example will drop all incoming packets from the address 192.168.0.45.

```
add rule ip myfilter myinput ip saddr 192.168.0.45 drop
```

You can turn a rule into its inverse with an **!=** operator. For example, to accept all incoming packets except those from a specific address, place an **!=** operator after the **saddr** expression and before that address. The following example will accept all packets except those from the IP address 192.168.0.45.

```
add rule ip filter INPUT ip saddr != 192.168.0.45 accept
```

You can specify an individual address using its domain name or its IP number. For a range of addresses, you can use the IP number of their network and the network IP mask. The IP mask can be an IP number or the number of bits making up the mask. For example, all of the addresses in network 192.168.0 can be represented by 192.168.0.0/225.255.255.0 or by 192.168.0.0/24. To specify any address, you can use 0.0.0.0/0.0.0.0 or simply 0/0. By default, rules reference any address if no **saddr** or **daddr** specification exists. The following example accepts messages coming in that are from (source) any host in the 192.168.0.0 network and that are going (destination) anywhere at all.

```
add rule ip myfilter myinput ip saddr 192.168.0.0/24 accept
```

The nftables rules are usually applied to a specific network interface such as the Ethernet interface used to connect to the Internet. For a single system connected to the Internet, you will have two interfaces, one that is your Internet connection, and a loopback interface (**lo**) for internal connections between users on your system. The network interface for the Internet is referenced using the device name for the interface. For example, the first Ethernet card with the device name would be referenced by the device name **eth0**. A modem using PPP protocols with the device name **ppp0** would have the name **ppp0**. In nftable rules, you use the **iifname** option to indicate the input device, with the device name in double quotes. The **oifname** option indicates the output device. Rules can then be applied to packets arriving and leaving on network devices. In the following examples, the first rule references the Ethernet device **eth0**, and the second, the localhost.

```
add rule ip myfilter myinput iifname "eth0" saddr 192.168.0.45 drop
add rule ip myfilter myinput iifname "lo" accept
```

The **continue**, **return**, **jump**, and **goto** statement change the flow of control for the ruleset, moving to a specific rule or chain. The **continue** statement moves to the next statement immediately. All rules automatically move the next statement when they finish evaluating by default. The **return**, **jump**, and **goto** statements move to another chain and start evaluating the rules in that chain.

The **jump** statement returns to the chain from which it was called, continuing to evaluate the next rule in that chain. The calling chain continues from where it left off when it executed the jump. The **goto** statement, though, does not return to the calling chain. It continues on to the next chain. The **return** statement returns immediately to the chain the current chain was called from, say from a **jump** or **goto** statement.

Multiple statements

Unlike IPtables, you can perform more than one statement on a rule. You do not need separate rules. The following rules can be combined into one rule, with both statements listed (**log** and **drop**).

```
add rule ip myfilter input iifname "eth1" ip saddr != 192.168.0.0/24 log
add rule ip myfilter input iifname "eth1" ip saddr != 192.168.0.0/24 drop
```

The combined rule is shown here.

```
add rule ip myfilter input iifname "eth1" ip saddr != 192.168.0.0/24 log drop
```

Payload Statements

Payload statements change the values in a packets. It consists of a payload expression to match on the payload content, and then a **set** statement to assign a new value. In the following example, the **ether daddr** payload expression sets the destination address to 192.168.0.7. This is the mechanism used for packet mangling, where you can change the address in a packet.

```
ether daddr set 192.168.0.7
```

Log Statements

You can use the **log** statements to log information such as headers for all matched packets, saving them in the syslog logs. The **log** statements are non-terminating. You can add one along with other statements in a rule. The **log** statement has several options to better tailor the information saved. The **prefix** option lets you specify a log prefix string. With the **level** option you can choose the syslog logging level: **emerg**, **alert**, **crit**, **err**, **warn**, **notice**, **info**, **debug**, or **audit**. The **warn** level is the default. The **queue-threshold** option will let you specify the number of packets to first queue before logging them to syslog.

```
log level crit
log prefix "FTP connection"
log queue-threshold 35 level info
```

The **log** flags lets you specify certain information to be logged. You can specify several on the same rule. The **tcp sequence** flag logs TCP sequence numbers. The **skuid** option logs the user id of the process that generated the packet. The **ether** flag decodes the MAC address and protocol. The **tcp options** and **ip options** flags logs options from the TCP and IPv4/IPv6 headers respectively. The **all** flag implements all the flags.

```
log flags skuid flags ether
log flags all
```

You could also have logs sent to a logging group over the network, using the **ulogd2** logging daemon. It would replace syslog. Be sure to install and run the **ulogd2** package. The daemon is referenced on nftables as **nflog** (on IPtables it is **ulog**). If you have set up your ulog groups, you can reference them with the nftables **group** option. For this option you specify the ulog group to send the logs to. The **snaplen** option lets you choose the amount of the packet payload to send to the daemon.

```
log group 1 snaplen 40
```

Meta Statement

The meta statement lets you assign a meta expression using a **set** statement. The meta fields you can assign are **mark**, **priority**, **pkttype**, and **nftrace**. The **priority** field sets a packet's priority, with a **tc_handle** type for its value. The **mark** field is the packet's mark (**mark** type),

pkttype is the packet's type (**pkt_type** type), and **nftrace** is a flag that turns tracing on or off. It can be 0 or 1.

```
meta priority set 100
meta nftrace set 0
```

Interface and Socket Direction: dup, fwd, and tproxy

The **dup** statement lets you duplicate a packet and send the copy to a gateway or interface.

```
dup to 192.168.0.7
dup to "eth1"
dup to 192.168.0.7 device "eth1"
```

The **fwd** statement redirects a packet to another interface.

```
fwd to "eth1"
```

The **tproxy to** statement directs a packet to a local socket directly. No changes are made to the packet. It takes as its argument a port or socket address.

```
tproxy to 192.168.0.8
tproxy to :ssh
```

ICMP Packets

Firewalls often block certain Internet Control Message Protocol (ICMP) messages. ICMP redirect messages can take control of your routing tasks. You need to enable some ICMP messages, such as those needed for ping, traceroute, and destination-unreachable operations. In most cases, you always need to make sure destination-unreachable packets are allowed. Otherwise, domain name queries could hang. Some of the more common ICMP packet types are listed in Table 17-22.

Number	Name	Required By
0	echo-reply	ping
3	destination-unreachable	Any TCP/UDP traffic
5	redirect	Routing if not running routing daemon
8	echo-request	ping
11	time-exceeded	traceroute

Table 17-22: Common ICMP Packets

You can enable an ICMP type of packet with the **icmp type** specification, which takes as its argument a number or a name representing the message. The following examples enable the use of echo-reply, echo-request, and destination-unreachable messages, which have the numbers 0, 8, and 3.

```
add rule ip filter input iifname "eth0" ip daddr 10.0.0.1 icmp type echo-reply
accept

add rule ip filter input iifname "eth0" ip daddr 10.0.0.1 icmp type echo-request
accept

add rule ip filter input iifname "eth0" ip daddr 10.0.0.1 icmp type destination-
unreachable accept
```

Ping operations need to be further controlled to avoid the ping-of-death security threat. You can do this several ways. One way is to deny any ping fragments. Ping packets are normally small. You can block ping-of-death attacks by denying any ICMP packet that is a fragment. Use the **frag-off** option to indicate fragments.

```
add rule ip filter input ip frag-off & 0x1fff != ip protocol icmp drop
```

Another way is to limit the number of matches received for ping packets. You use the **limit** statement to control the number of matches on the ICMP ping operation. Use **limit rate** to specify the number of allowed matches. **1/second bursts** will allow one match per second.

```
add rule ip filter forward icmp type echo-request limit rate 1/second bursts
packets accept
```

Connection Tracking

Connection tracking maintains information about a connection such as its source, destination, and port. For example, it provides an effective means for determining which packets belong to an established or related connection.

Connection Tracking Expressions

Connection tracking expressions let you access a packet's connection tracking data. Some data require a direction key, others are direction neutral and require no key. Connection tracking expressions are specified with a **ct** expression, consisting of the **ct** keyword and a connection tracking key such as **state** for the connection state.

```
ct state
```

You can access connection tracking information such as the **direction**, **status**, **expiration** (set connection limits), source and destination addresses (**saddr** and **daddr**), the **protocol**, the count of current connections (**count**), and the **zone** (assign connections to a zone). Some have a connection tracking specific type such as **ct_state** for **state**, **ct_dir** for **direction**, and **ct_status** for **status**.

Connection Tracking Statement

The connection tracking statement, **ct**, is used to mark and label meta data for a connection. The meta data is set in the prerouting and output stages. There are several mark and label options you can use: **event**, **mark**, **label**, and **zone**. The **helper** option lets you assign a connection tracking helper to the meta data. You can use the **notrack** statement to disable connection tracking.

Connection Tracking States: ct state

To use connection tracking, you specify the state expression first with **ct state** for connection tracking state (see Table 17-23).

State	Description
new	A packet that creates a new connection
established	A packet that belongs to an existing connection
related	A packet that is related to, but not part of, an existing connection, such as an ICMP error or a packet establishing an FTP data connection
invalid	A packet that could not be identified for some reason
untracked	A packet that is excluded from conntrack

Table 17-23: Connection Tracking states

If you are designing a firewall that is meant to protect your local network from any attempts to penetrate it from an outside network, you may want to restrict packets coming in. Simply denying access by all packets is unfeasible, because users connected to outside servers on the Internet must receive information from them. You can, instead, deny access by a particular kind of packet used to initiate a connection. The idea is that an attacker must initiate a connection from the outside. The headers of these kinds of packets have their SYN bit set on and their FIN and ACK bits empty. The **state** option **new** matches on any such SYN packet. By specifying a **drop** policy for such packets, you deny access by any packet that is part of an attempt to make a connection with your system. Anyone trying to connect to your system from the outside is unable to do so. Users on your local system who have initiated connections with outside hosts, can still communicate with them. The following example will drop any packets trying to create a new connection on the **eth0** interface, though they will be accepted on any other interface.

```
add rule ip filter input iifname "eth0" ct state new drop
```

You can use the ! operator on the **eth0** device combined with an **accept** statement to compose a rule that will accept any new packets except those on the **eth0** device. If the **eth0** device is the only one that connects to the Internet, this still effectively blocks outside access. At the same time, input operation for other devices such as your localhost are free to make new connections. This kind of conditional **input** rule is used to allow access overall with exceptions. It usually assumes that a later rule, such as a chain policy, will drop remaining packets.

```
add rule ip filter input iifname != "eth0" ct state new accept
```

The next example will accept any packets that are part of an established connection (**established**) or related to such a connection (**related**) on the **eth0** interface.

```
add rule ip filter input ct state related,established accept
```

Specialized Connection Tracking: ct helper.

To track certain kinds of packets, nftables uses specialized connection tracking helpers. A helper is used for connections that could use a variety of different ports, such as FTP. The helper aids in locating those ports. Available helpers include, FTP, IRC, Amanda, TFTP, NetBIOS, PPTP,

SANE, SIP, H.323, and SNMP. It also provides user space helpers such as MDNS, RPC, NFSv3, DNSPv6, SSDP, SLP, and Oracle TNS. These all have corresponding kernel names in lower case such as **ftp** for FTP. Use the **helper** option with the type of connection for the **ct state** statement to indicate the connection tracking helper directly.

```
add rule ,myfilter myinput ct state helper "ftp"
```

You can create a named connection tracking helper with the **add ct helper** command. Specify the type and protocol. The type is the name of the helper you want to use placed in quotes, such as "ftp" for FTP.

```
add ct helper myfilter myftp { type "ftp" protocol tcp ; }
```

You can then use the helper in a rule invoking it with the **ct helper set** statement.

```
ct helper set "myftp"
```

You can delete a connection tracking helper with the **delete ct helper** statement using just its name.

```
delete ct helper myfilter myftp
```

To see a list of all your helpers use the following **list** statement.

```
nft list ct helpers
```

Connection Tracking Connlimit: ct count

Use the **ct count** statement to create an anonymous connlimit stateful object that sets a limit to the allowed connection tracking connections. This lets you limit the number of connections. Specify the allowed number of connection tracking connections. The following example allows only up to 50 connection tracking connections.

```
ct count 50
```

The following statement would limit the number of connection tracking connections on port 80.

```
dport 80 ct count 50 accept
```

Use the **over** options to check when the number of connections tracking connections exceeds the specified number.

```
ct count over 100
```

Connection Timeout Policy: ct timeouts

You can set up a connection tracking timeout object to implement a timeout policy that you can then apply to a rule. You would first create a named timeout object using the **ct timeout** statement and then specify the protocol (**protocol**) it applies to and its policy (**policy**) states along with the timeout values for each. The policy states can be close, close_wait, established, fin_wait, syn_recv, retrans, syn_sent, last_ack, unack, and time_wait.

```
ct timeout mytimeout { protocol tcp ; policy = {established: 120, close: 20 } }
```

To apply it to a rule use the **ct timeout set** statement

```
ct timeout set "mytimeout"
```

To delete it use the **delete ct timeout** statement with the table name and timeout name.

```
delete ct timeout myfilter mytimeout
```

Connection Tracking Expectations: ct expectation

You can set up a connection tracking expectation policy for a specific protocol and port using the **ct expectation** statement. Connection tracking expectation confirms the number of connections for a port within a given time limit. You have to specify the **protocol**, **port**, **timeout**, and **size**. You can also specify the level 3 protocol (**l3proto**) such as **ip** if you want. In the following example the protocol is tcp, the time allotment is 9 minutes and the number of connections is 16.

```
ct expectation myexpect { protocol tcp ; timeout  9m ; dport 3286 ; size 16 ; }
```

You can then use the **ct expectation set** statement to invoke your connection tracking expectation object.

```
ct expectation set "myexpect"
```

To delete it use the **delete ct expectation** statement with the table name and the expectation name.

```
delete ct expectation myfilter myexpect
```

Note: Synproxy is an alternative to connection tracking that uses cookies to perform the same tracking functions. Use the **synproxy** statement to implement it.

Network Address Translation on nftables (NAT)

Network address translation (NAT) is the process whereby a system will change the destination or source of packets as they pass through the system. A packet will traverse several linked systems on a network before it reaches its final destination. Normally, they will simply pass the packet on. However, if one of these systems performs a NAT operation on a packet, it can change the source or destination. A packet sent to a particular destination could have its destination address changed. To make this work, the system also needs to remember such changes so that the source and destination for any reply packets are altered back to the original addresses of the packet being replied to.

NAT is often used to provide access to systems that may be connected to the Internet through only one IP address. Such is the case with networking features such as IP masquerading, support for multiple servers, and transparent proxying. With IP masquerading, NAT operations will change the destination and source of a packet moving through a firewall/gateway linking the Internet to computers on a local network. The gateway has a single IP address that the other local computers can use through NAT operations. If you have multiple servers but only one IP address, you can use NAT operations to send packets to the alternate servers. You can also use NAT operations to have your IP address reference a particular server application such as a Web server (transparent proxy).

Adding NAT Rules

Packet selection rules for NAT operations are added to the NAT table. You first have to define a table with the **nft table** statement. You can call the table anything you want.

```
nft table mynat
```

To add a chain to the NAT table, you would have to specify its **type** as the **nat** parameter as shown here for the **prerouting** chain.

```
nft add chain mynat prerouting { type nat hook prerouting priority dstnat }
```

You can then add a rule to your NAT table.

```
nft add rule mynat prerouting
```

With the **list** command, you can list the rules you have added to your NAT table.

```
nft table mynat list
```

Adding the **-n** option will list IP addresses and ports in numeric form. This will speed up the listing, as nftables will not attempt to do a DNS lookup to determine the hostname for the IP address.

```
nft table mynat list -n
```

NAT statements

There are four NAT statements: **snat**, **dnat**, **masquerade**, and **redirect** (see Table 17-24). The **snat** statement is used for rules that alter source addresses, and the **dnat** statement, for those that alter destination addresses. The addresses can be of type **ipv4_addr** for IPv4 addresses, and **ipv6_addr** for IPv6 addresses.

Three chains in the NAT table are used by the kernel for NAT operations. These are **prerouting**, **postrouting** , and **output**. **prerouting** is used for destination NAT (**dnat**) rules. These are packets that are arriving. **postrouting** is used for source NAT (**snat**) rules. These are for packets leaving. They are destination NAT rules for locally generated packets.

Statement	Description
snat	Modify source address
dnat	Modify destination address
redirect	Redirect a packet.
masquerade	IP masquerading.

Table 17-24: nftables nat statements

As with packet filtering, you can specify source (**snat**) and destination (**dnat**) addresses, as well as the input and output devices. You would implement IP masquerading by adding a **masquerade** statement to the **prerouting** chain:

```
add rule ip mynat postrouting oifname "eth0" masquerade
```

To change the source address of a packet leaving your system, you would use the **prerouting** rule with the **snat** statement. For the **snat** statement, you use the **to** option to specify the source address,

```
add rule ip mynat postrouting iifname "eth0" snat to 192.168.0.4
```

To change the destination address of packets arriving on your system, you would use the **prerouting** rule with the **dnat** statement and the **to** option.

```
add rule ip mynat postrouting iifname "eth0" dnat to 192.168.0.3
```

Specifying a port lets you change destinations for packets arriving on a particular port. In effect, this lets you implement port forwarding. The port is specified by its port number. In the next example, every packet arriving on port 80 (the Web service port) is redirected to 10.0.0.3, which in this case would be a system running a Web server.

```
add rule ip mynat prerouting iifname "eth0" tcp dport 80 dnat to 10.0.0.3
```

NAT tables can be used to implement packet redirection, a process transparent to the user. Redirection is commonly used to implement a transparent proxy. The **redirect** statement is a form of the **dnat** statement that redirects to the local host. For example, with transparent proxies, packets received can be automatically redirected to a proxy server. Also, packets arriving on the Web service port, 80, can be redirected to the Squid Proxy service port, usually 3128. This involves a redirection of the packet, using the **redirect** statement on the **prerouting** chain. Use the **dport** option to specify its original destination port.

```
add rule ip nat prerouting iifname "eth1" tcp dport 80 redirect to :3128
```

Packet Mangling on nftables: the set statement

Packet mangling is used to actually modify packet information. Rules applied specifically to this packet mangling are often designed to control the mundane behavior of packets, like routing, connection size, and priority. Packet mangling rules that actually modify a packet, rather than simply redirecting or stopping it, are defined using the **set** statement to change a matched value on a packet. The chains for the rule to mangle packets would have **mangle** priority, the value -150. You could, if you wish, set up a separate table that you could use for your mangle rules. You can then think of this as your mangle table.

This example creates a table called **mymangle** to be use for mangle chains.

```
add table mymangle
```

A basic mangle operation can change the destination of incoming packets. A **prerouting** chain is then defined with the **mangle** priority.

```
add chain mymangle prerouting { type filter hook prerouting priority mangle }
```

A rule is then added to mangle packets using the **set** command to change its destination address.

```
add rule mymangle prerouting tcp daddr 19.168.0.200 tcp daddr set 19.168.0.4
```

An nftables Rule-based Script Example: IPv4

You now have enough information to create a simple nftables script that will provide basic protection for a single system connected to the Internet. The following script, **myfilter-rules.nft**, provides an nftables filtering process to protect a local network and a website from outside attacks. This example uses nftables rules and IPv4 addressing. **eth0** and **eth1**, are used here for clarity. Your system's actual device names will be different, following predictable naming formats (see Chapter 3). For simplicity, the script uses the same rule-based format as IPtables. It is simply a sequence of rules.

The script first creates the ip and nat tables, along with their chains. The ip table created is named **myfilter**. Chains for the input, output, and forward hooks are defined, named **myinput**, **myoutput**, and **myforward**. Their chain type is **filter**. The nat table, called **mynat**, is created with chains for **postrouting** and **prerouting**. Their type is **nat** and the they access the prerouting and postrouting hooks.

myfilter-rules.nft

```
# Firewall Gateway system IP address is 10.0.0.1 using Ethernet device eth0
# Private network address is 192.168.0.0 using Ethernet device eth1
# Web site address is 10.0.0.2

# Create an ip table called myfilter and a nat table called mynat
add table ip myfilter
add table mynat

# add the input, output, and forward chains for the myfilter ip table and set (policy)
add chain ip myfilter myinput { type filter hook input priority 0; policy drop; }
add chain ip myfilter myoutput { type filter hook output priority 0; policy accept; }
add chain ip myfilter myforward { type filter hook forward priority 0; policy accept; }

# add prerouting and postrouting chains for the mynat nat table and set (policy)
add chain mynat prerouting { type nat hook prerouting priority dstnat; }
add chain mynat postrouting { type nat hook postrouting priority srcnat; }


# Flush chain rules
flush chain ip myfilter myinput
flush chain ip myfilter myoutput
flush chain ip myfilter myforward
flush chain ip mynat prerouting
flush chain ip mynat postrouting

# IP spoofing, deny any packets on the internal network that have an external source address
add rule ip myfilter myinput iifname "eth1" ip saddr != 192.168.0.0/24 counter log
add rule ip myfilter myinput iifname "eth1" ip saddr != 192.168.0.0/24 drop
add rule ip myfilter myforward  iifname "eth1" ip saddr != 192.168.0.0/24 drop

# source addr4ess of the internal network
add rule ip myfilter myinput iifname != "eth1" ip saddr 192.168.0.0/24 drop
add rule ip myfilter myforward  iifname != "eth1" ip saddr 192.168.0.0/24 drop

# IP spoofing, deny any outside packets with localhost address
# (packets not on the lo interface (any on eth0 or eth1) that have source address localhost)
add rule ip myfilter myinput iifname != "lo" ip saddr 127.0.0.0/8 drop
add rule ip myfilter myforward  iifname != "lo" ip saddr 127.0.0.0/8 drop

# allow all incoming messages for users on your firewall system
add rule ip myfilter myinput iifname "lo" accept

# allow  communication to the Web server (address 10.0.0.2), port www
add rule ip myfilter myinput iifname "eth0" ip saddr 10.0.0.2 tcp dport 80 accept
# Allow  established connections from Web servers to internal network
add rule ip myfilter myinput iifname "eth0" ip saddr 10.0.0.2 ip daddr 192.168.0.0/24 ct
state related,established  tcp sport 80 accept

# Prevent new  connections from Web servers to internal network
add rule ip myfilter myoutput oifname "eth0" ip daddr 192.168.0.0/24 ct state new  tcp sport
80 drop
```

```
# allow established and related outside communication to your system
# and allow outside communication to the firewall, except for ICMP packets
add rule ip myfilter myinput iifname "eth0" ip protocol != icmp ct state related,established
accept

# prevent outside initiated connections
add rule ip myfilter myinput iifname "eth0" ct state new  drop
add rule ip myfilter myforward  iifname "eth0" ct state new  drop

# allow all local communication to and from the firewall on eth1  from the local network
add rule ip myfilter myinput iifname "eth1" ip saddr 192.168.0.0/24 accept

# Set up masquerading to allow internal machines access to outside network
add rule ip mynat postrouting oifname "eth0" masquerade

# Accept ICMP Ping and Destination unreachable messages
# Others will be rejected by myinput and output DROP policy
add rule ip myfilter myinput iifname "eth0" ip daddr 10.0.0.1 icmp type echo-
reply accept
add rule ip myfilter myinput iifname "eth0" ip daddr 10.0.0.1 icmp type echo-
request accept
add rule ip myfilter myinput iifname "eth0" ip daddr 10.0.0.1 icmp type
destination-unreachable accept
```

Figure 17-15: A network with a firewall

The script configures a simple firewall for a private network. In this configuration, all remote access initiated from the outside is blocked, but two-way communication is allowed for connections that users in the network make with outside systems. In this example, the firewall system functions as a gateway for a private network whose network address is 192.168.0.0 (see Figure 17-15). The Internet address is, for the sake of this example, 10.0.0.1. The system has two

Ethernet devices: one for the private network (**eth1**) and one for the Internet (**eth0**). The gateway firewall system also supports a Web server at address 10.0.0.2. Entries in this example that are too large to fit on one line are continued on a second line, with the newline quoted with a backslash. The basic rules as they apply to different parts of the network are illustrated in Figure 17-16.

The script has an **.nft** extension. It is loaded with the **nft -f** shell command.

```
nft -f myfilter-rules.nft
```

Note: The **counter** statement is used to keep an anonymous count of each time a rule is used, which IPtables did by default.

This is what the output of a **list** operation on this ruleset look like.

```
sudo nft -s list ruleset

table ip myfilter {
        chain myinput {
                type filter hook input priority filter; policy drop;
                iifname "eth1" ip saddr != 192.168.0.0/24 counter log
                iifname "eth1" ip saddr != 192.168.0.0/24 drop
                iifname != "eth1" ip saddr 192.168.0.0/24 drop
                iifname != "lo" ip saddr 127.0.0.0/8 drop
                iifname "lo" accept
                iifname "eth0" ip saddr 10.0.0.2 tcp dport 80 accept
                iifname "eth0" ip saddr 10.0.0.2 ip daddr 192.168.0.0/24 ct state
established,related tcp sport 80 accept
                iifname "eth0" ip protocol != icmp ct state established,related accept
                iifname "eth0" ct state new drop
                iifname "eth1" ip saddr 192.168.0.0/24 accept
                iifname "eth0" ip daddr 10.0.0.1 icmp type echo-reply accept
                iifname "eth0" ip daddr 10.0.0.1 icmp type echo-request accept
                iifname "eth0" ip daddr 10.0.0.1 icmp type destination-unreachable accept
        }

        chain myoutput {
                type filter hook output priority filter; policy accept;
                oifname "eth0" ip daddr 192.168.0.0/24 ct state new tcp sport 80 drop
        }

        chain myforward {
                type filter hook forward priority filter; policy accept;
                iifname "eth1" ip saddr != 192.168.0.0/24 drop
                iifname != "eth1" ip saddr 192.168.0.0/24 drop
                iifname != "lo" ip saddr 127.0.0.0/8 drop
                iifname "eth0" ct state new drop
        }
}
table ip mynat {
        chain prerouting {
                type nat hook prerouting priority dstnat; policy accept;
        }

        chain postrouting {
                type nat hook postrouting priority srcnat; policy accept;
                oifname "eth0" masquerade}
}
```

Drop Policy

First, a **drop** policy is set up for **input** and **forward** built-in hooks for the IPv4 family of addresses. This means that if a packet does not meet a criterion in any of the rules to let it pass, it will be dropped. Then both IP spoofing attacks and any attempts from the outside to initiate connections (SYN packets) are rejected.

Outside connection attempts are also logged. This is a very basic configuration that can easily be refined to your own needs by adding nftables rules.

```
add chain ip myfilter myinput { type filter hook input priority 0; policy drop; }
add chain ip myfilter myoutput { type filter hook output priority 0; policy accept; }
add chain ip myfilter myforward { type filter hook forward priority 0; policy accept; }
```

Figure 17-16: Firewall rules applied to a local network example

IP Spoofing

One way to protect the private network from the IP spoofing of any packets is to check for any outside addresses on the Ethernet device dedicated to the private network. In this example, any packet on device **eth1** (dedicated to the private network) whose source address is not that of the private network (**! -s 192.168.0.0**) is denied. Also, check to see if any packets coming from the outside are designating the private network as their source. In this example, any packets with the source address of the private network on any Ethernet device other than for the private network (**eth1**) are denied. The same strategy can be applied to the local host.

Then, you would set up rules to allow all packets sent and received within your system, the localhost (**lo**), to pass.

```
add rule ip filter input iifname "lo" accept
```

```
# IP spoofing, deny any packets on the internal network
# that has an external source address.

add rule ip myfilter myinput iifname "eth1" ip saddr != 192.168.0.0/24 log
add rule ip myfilter myinput iifname "eth1" ip saddr != 192.168.0.0/24 drop
add rule ip myfilter myforward iifname "eth1" ip saddr != 192.168.0.0/24 drop


# IP spoofing, deny any outside packets (any not on eth1)
# that have the source address of the internal network
add rule ip myfilter myinput iifname != "eth1" ip saddr 192.168.0.0/24 drop
add rule ip myfilter myforward iifname != "eth1" ip saddr 192.168.0.0/24 drop

# IP spoofing, deny any outside packets with localhost address
# (packets not on the lo interface (any on eth0 or eth1)
# that have the source address of localhost)

add rule ip myfilter myinput iifname != "lo" ip saddr 127.0.0.0/8 drop
add rule ip myfilter myforward iifname != "lo" ip saddr 127.0.0.0/8 drop
```

Server Access

For the Web server, you want to allow access by outside users but block access by anyone attempting to initiate a connection from the Web server into the private network. In the next example, all messages are accepted to the Web server, but the Web server cannot initiate contact with the private network. This prevents anyone from breaking into the local network through the Web server, which is open to outside access. Established connections are allowed, permitting the private network to use the Web server.

```
# allow  communication to the Web server (address 10.0.0.2), port www
add rule ip myfilter myinput iifname "eth0" ip saddr 10.0.0.2 tcp dport 80 accept

# Allow  established connections from Web servers to internal network
add rule ip myfilter myinput iifname "eth0" ip saddr 10.0.0.2 ip daddr
192.168.0.0/24 ct state related,established  tcp sport 80 accept

# Prevent new  connections from Web servers to internal network
add rule ip myfilter myoutput oifname "eth0" ip daddr 192.168.0.0/24 ct state new
tcp sport 80 drop
```

Firewall Outside Access

To allow access by the firewall to outside networks, you allow input by all packets except for ICMP packets. These are handled later. The firewall is specified by the firewall device, **eth0**. First, your firewall should allow established and related connections to proceed, as shown here. Then you would block outside access as described later.

```
# allow outside communication to the firewall,except for ICMP packets

add rule ip myfilter myinput iifname "eth0" ip protocol != icmp ct state
related,established accept
```

Blocking Outside Initiated Access

To prevent outsiders from initiating any access to your system, create a rule to block access by SYN packets from the outside using the connection tracking state (**ct state**) with the **new** option. Drop any new connections on the **eth0** connection (assumes only **eth0** is connected to the Internet or outside network).

```
# prevent outside initiated connections
add rule ip myfilter myinput iifname "eth0" ct state new  drop
add rule ip myfilter myforward iifname "eth0" ct state new  drop
```

Local Network Access

To allow interaction by the internal network with the firewall, you allow input by all packets on the internal Ethernet connection, **eth1**. The valid internal network addresses are designated as the input source.

```
add rule ip myfilter myinput iifname "eth1" ip saddr 192.168.0.0/24 accept
```

User-Defined Chains

For more complex rules, you may want to create your own chain to reduce repetition. A common method is to define a user chain for both **input** and **forward** hooks so that you do not have to repeat **drop** operations for each. Instead, you would have only one user chain that both **forward** and **input** hooks would feed into for **drop** operations. Keep in mind that both **forward** and input operations may have separate rules in addition to the ones they share. In the next example, a user-defined chain called **arriving** is created. The chain is defined with the **add chain** command option at the top of the script.

```
add chain ip filter arriving { type filter hook input priority 0; policy accept; }
```

A user chain has to be defined before it can be used as a target in other rules. So, you have to first define and add all the rules for that chain, and then use it as a target. The **arriving** chain is first defined and its rules added. Then, at the end of the file, it is used as a target for both the **myinput** and **myforward** chains.

```
#Create an arriving chain
add chain ip myfilter arriving { type filter hook input priority 0; policy accept; }
flush chain ip myfilter arriving

add rule ip myfilter arriving iifname "eth0" ip saddr 192.168.0.45 drop
add rule ip myfilter arriving iifname "lo" accept


# entries at end of script

add rule ip myfilter myinput jump arriving
add rule ip myfilter myforward jump arriving
```

For rules where chains may differ, you will still need to enter separate rules. In the **myfilter** script, the the **myforward** hook has an **accept** policy, allowing all forwarded packets to the local network to pass through the firewall. If the **myforward** chain had a **drop** policy, like the **myinput** chain, then you may need to define separate rules under which the **myforward** chain could accept packets. In this example, the **myforward** and **myinput** chains have different rules for accepting packets on the **eth1** device. The **myinput** rule is more restrictive. To enable the local network to receive forwarded packets through the firewall, you could enable forwarding on its device using a separate **forward** rule, as shown here.

```
add rule ip myfilter myforward iifname "eth1" accept
```

The **myinput** chain would accept packets only from the local network.

```
add rule ip myfilter myinput iifname "eth1" ip saddr 192.168.0.0/24 accept
```

Masquerading Local Networks

To implement masquerading, where systems on the private network can use the gateway's Internet address to connect to Internet hosts, you create a NAT table **postrouting** hook with a **masquerade** statement.

```
add rule mynat postrouting oifname "eth0" masquerade
```

Controlling ICMP Packets

In addition, to allow ping and destination-reachable ICMP packets, you enter input rules with the firewall as the destination. To enable ping operations, you use both echo-reply and echo-request ICMP types, and for destination unreachable, you use the destination-unreachable type.

```
add rule ip myfilter myinput iifname "eth0" ip daddr 10.0.0.1 icmp type echo-reply
accept
add rule ip myfilter myinput iifname "eth0" ip daddr 10.0.0.1 icmp type echo-
request accept
add rule ip myfilter myinput iifname "eth0" ip daddr 10.0.0.1 icmp type
destination-unreachable accept
```

Simple LAN Configuration

To create a script to support a simple LAN without any Internet services like Web servers, you would not include rules for supporting those services. You would still need **forward** and **postrouting** rules for connecting your local hosts to the Internet, as well as rules governing interaction between the hosts and the firewall. To modify the example script to support a simple LAN without the Web server, remove the three rules governing the Web server. Leave everything else the same.

LAN Configuration with Internet Services on the Firewall System

Often, the same system that runs a firewall is also used to run Internet servers, like Web and FTP servers. In this case, the firewall rules are applied to the ports used for those services. The example script dealt with a Web server running on a separate host system. If the Web server were, instead, running on the firewall system, you would apply the Web server firewall rules to the port that the Web server uses. Normally the port used for a Web server is 80. In the following example, the nftables rules for the Web server have been applied to port www, port 80, on the firewall system. The modification simply requires removing the old Web server host address references, 10.0.0.2.

```
# allow  communication to the Web server, port www (port 80)
add rule ip myfilter myinput iifname "eth0" tcp dport 80 accept

# Allow  established connections from Web servers to internal network
add rule ip myfilter myinput iifname "eth0" ip daddr 192.168.0.0/24 ct state
related,established  tcp sport 80 accept
# Prevent new  connections from Web servers to internal network
add rule ip myfilter myoutput oifname "eth0" ip daddr 192.168.0.0/24 ct state new
tcp sport 80 drop
```

Similar entries could be set up for an FTP server. Should you run several Internet services, you could use a user-defined rule to run the same rules on each service, rather than repeating three separate rules per service. Working from the example script, you would use two defined rules, one for input and one for output, controlling incoming and outgoing packets for the services.

```
add chain ip myfilter inputservice { type filter hook input priority 0; policy drop; }
add chain ip myfilter outputservice { type filter hook output priority 0; policy drop; }
flush chain ip myfilter inputservice
flush chain ip myfilter outputservice

# allow  communication to the service
add rule ip myfilter inputservice iifname "eth0" ip protocol tcp accept

# Allow  established connections from the service to internal network
add rule ip myfilter inputservice iifname "eth0" ip protocol tcp ip daddr
192.168.0.0/24 ct state related,established accept

add rule ip myfilter outputservice oifname "eth0" ip protocol tcp ip daddr
192.168.0.0/24 ct state new drop

.......................
# Run rules for the Web server, port www (port 80)
add rule ip myfilter myinput tcp dport 80 jump inputservice
add rule ip myfilter myinput tcp dport 80 jump outputservice

# Run rules for the FTP server, port ftp (port 21)
add rule ip myfilter myoutput tcp dport 21 jump inputservice
add rule ip myfilter myoutput tcp dport 21 jump outputservice
```

nftables Block format

You do not have to enter the rules as separate rules as you would IPtables. You can, instead, use the block format as shown in the listing of the ruleset. Each table has a block encased in braces listing its chains, and, within each chain, its rules. Enter them in as you would a programming language, with rules and type specifications on separate lines. Each chain has a block listing its type and its rules. This format can make for a much more readable and easily modified ruleset. The nftables examples in the **/usr/share/doc/examples** directory uses this format.

For example, the following NAT table chains and rules shown here as separate rules can be written as a block instead.

```
add table mynat
add chain mynat prerouting { type nat hook prerouting priority dstnat; }
```

```
add chain mynat postrouting { type nat hook postrouting priority srcnat; }
add rule ip mynat postrouting oifname "eth0" masquerade
```

This is the block version. The **mynat** table is defined with two chains, **prerouting** and **postrouting**. The **postrouting** chain has a **masquerade** rule.

```
table ip mynat {
      chain prerouting {
              type nat hook prerouting priority dstnat; policy accept;
      }

      chain postrouting {
              type nat hook postrouting priority srcnat; policy accept;
              oifname "eth0" masquerade}
 }
```

nftables Symbolic Variables

You can define symbolic variables in a **.nft** file using the **define** statement. The format of the **define** statement is the keyword **define** followed by the name of the variable, and = operator, followed by an expression to be assigned.

```
define net_dev2 = eth1
define int_net =192.168.0.0/24
```

You can then access the variable's value by preceding it with a **$** in a rule or chain.

```
add rule ip myfilter myinput iifname $net_dev2 ip saddr != $int_net counter log
```

For example, using a variable definition for the ethernet device, should the device have to be changed, you would only need to change its variable definition, instead of each rule the device is used in.

Using a block format, the scope of a variable is the block it is defined in, as well as any block within that block.

You can undefine a variable with the **undefine** statement, and reassign a value to it with the **redefine** statement.

```
# Firewall Gateway system IP address is 10.0.0.1 using Ethernet device eth0
# Private network address is 192.168.0.0 using Ethernet device eth1
# Web site address is 10.0.0.2

# Flush ruleset
flush ruleset

define net_dev1 = eth0
define net_dev2 = eth1
define int_net = 192.168.0.0/24
define local_net =  127.0.0.0/8
define ext_gateway = 10.0.0.1
define web_server = 10.0.0.2


add table ip myfilter
add table mynat
```

```
add chain ip myfilter myinput { type filter hook input priority 0; policy drop; }
add chain ip myfilter myoutput { type filter hook output priority 0; policy
accept; }
add chain ip myfilter myforward { type filter hook forward priority 0; policy
accept; }

add chain mynat prerouting { type nat hook prerouting priority dstnat; }
add chain mynat postrouting { type nat hook postrouting priority srcnat; }

add rule ip myfilter myinput iifname $net_dev2 ip saddr != $int_net counter log
add rule ip myfilter myinput iifname $net_dev2 ip saddr != $int_net drop
add rule ip myfilter myforward  iifname $net_dev2 ip saddr != $int_net drop

add rule ip myfilter myinput iifname != $net_dev2 ip saddr $int_net drop
add rule ip myfilter myforward  iifname != $net_dev2 ip saddr $int_net drop

add rule ip myfilter myinput iifname != "lo" ip saddr $local_net drop
add rule ip myfilter myforward  iifname != "lo" ip saddr $local_net drop

add rule ip myfilter myinput iifname "lo" accept

add rule ip myfilter myinput iifname $net_dev1 ip saddr 10.0.0.2 tcp dport 80
accept
add rule ip myfilter myinput iifname $net_dev1 ip saddr 10.0.0.2 ip daddr
$int_net ct state related,established  tcp sport 80 accept

add rule ip myfilter myoutput oifname $net_dev1 ip daddr $int_net ct state new
tcp sport 80 drop

add rule ip myfilter myinput iifname $net_dev1 ip protocol != icmp ct state
related,established  accept

add rule ip myfilter myinput iifname $net_dev1 ct state new  drop
add rule ip myfilter myforward  iifname $net_dev1 ct state new  drop

$net_dev2  from the local network
add rule ip myfilter myinput iifname $net_dev2 ip saddr $int_net accept

add rule ip mynat postrouting oifname $net_dev1 masquerade

add rule ip myfilter myinput iifname $net_dev1 ip daddr $ext_gateway icmp type
echo-reply accept
add rule ip myfilter myinput iifname $net_dev1 ip daddr $ext_gateway icmp type
echo-request accept
add rule ip myfilter myinput iifname $net_dev1 ip daddr $ext_gateway icmp type
destination-unreachable accept
```

The ruleset will automatically evaluate the variables.

```
table ip myfilter {
        chain myinput {
                type filter hook input priority filter; policy drop;
                iifname "eth1" ip saddr != 192.168.0.0/24 counter log
                iifname "eth1" ip saddr != 192.168.0.0/24 drop
                iifname != "eth1" ip saddr 192.168.0.0/24 drop
                iifname != "lo" ip saddr 127.0.0.0/8 drop
                iifname "lo" accept
                iifname "eth0" ip saddr 10.0.0.2 tcp dport 80 accept
                iifname "eth0" ip saddr 10.0.0.2 ip daddr 192.168.0.0/24 ct state
established,related tcp sport 80 accept
                iifname "eth0" ip protocol != icmp ct state established,related
accept
                iifname "eth0" ct state new drop
                iifname "eth1" ip saddr 192.168.0.0/24 accept
                iifname "eth0" ip daddr 10.0.0.1 icmp type echo-reply accept
                iifname "eth0" ip daddr 10.0.0.1 icmp type echo-request accept
                iifname "eth0" ip daddr 10.0.0.1 icmp type destination-unreachable
accept
        }

        chain myoutput {
                type filter hook output priority filter; policy accept;
                oifname "eth0" ip daddr 192.168.0.0/24 ct state new tcp sport 80
drop
        }

        chain myforward {
                type filter hook forward priority filter; policy accept;
                iifname "eth1" ip saddr != 192.168.0.0/24 drop
                iifname != "eth1" ip saddr 192.168.0.0/24 drop
                iifname != "lo" ip saddr 127.0.0.0/8 drop
                iifname "eth0" ct state new drop
        }
}
table ip mynat {
        chain prerouting {
                type nat hook prerouting priority dstnat; policy accept;
        }

        chain postrouting {
                type nat hook postrouting priority srcnat; policy accept;
                oifname "eth0" masquerade
        }
}
```

In the block format, you can scope variables, as shown here.

```
flush ruleset

define net_dev1 = eth0
define net_dev2 = eth1

table ip myfilter {
        define int_net = 192.168.0.0/24
        define local_net =  127.0.0.0/8
        define ext_gateway = 10.0.0.1
        define web_server = 10.0.0.2

        chain myinput {
                type filter hook input priority filter; policy drop;
                iifname $net_dev2 ip saddr != $int_net counter log drop
                iifname != $net_dev2 ip saddr $int_net drop
                iifname != "lo" ip saddr $local_net drop
                iifname "lo" accept
                iifname $net_dev1 ip saddr $web_server tcp dport 80 accept
                iifname $net_dev1 ip saddr $web_server ip daddr $int_net ct state
established,related tcp sport 80 accept
                iifname $net_dev1 ip protocol != icmp ct state established,related
accept
                iifname $net_dev1 ct state new drop
                iifname $net_dev2 ip saddr $int_net accept
                iifname $net_dev1 ip daddr $ext_gateway icmp type { echo-reply,
destination-unreachable, echo-request } accept
        }

        chain myoutput {
                type filter hook output priority filter; policy accept;
                oifname $net_dev1 ip daddr $int_net ct state new tcp sport 80 drop
        }

        chain myforward {
                type filter hook forward priority filter; policy accept;
                iifname $net_dev2 ip saddr != $int_net drop
                iifname != $net_dev2 ip saddr $int_net drop
                iifname != "lo" ip saddr $local_net drop
                iifname $net_dev1 ct state new drop
        }
}
table ip mynat {
        chain prerouting {
                type nat hook prerouting priority dstnat; policy accept;
        }

        chain postrouting {
                type nat hook postrouting priority srcnat; policy accept;
                oifname $net_dev1 masquerade
        }
}
```

IP Masquerading

On Linux systems, you can set up a network in which you can have one connection to the Internet that several systems on your network can use. This way, using only one IP address, several different systems can connect to the Internet. This method is called IP masquerading, where a system masquerades as another system, using that system's IP address. In such a network, one system is connected to the Internet with its own IP address, while the other systems are connected on a local area network (LAN) to this system. When a local system wants to access the network, it masquerades as the Internet-connected system, borrowing its IP address.

IP masquerading is implemented on Linux using the nftables firewall tool. In effect, you set up a firewall, which you then configure to do IP masquerading. Currently, IP masquerading supports all the common network services, such as Web browsing, FTP, and ping. Any services you want local systems to access must also be on the firewall system because request and response actually are handled by services on that system.

With IP masquerading, as implemented on Linux systems, the machine with the Internet address is also the firewall and gateway for the LAN of machines that use the firewall's Internet address to connect to the Internet. Firewalls that also implement IP masquerading are sometimes referred to as MASQ gates. With IP masquerading, the Internet-connected host (the firewall) listens for Internet requests from hosts on its LAN. When it receives one, it replaces the requesting local host's IP address with the Internet IP address of the firewall and then passes the request out to the Internet, as if the request were its own. Replies from the Internet are then sent to the firewall host. The replies the firewall receives are addressed to the firewall using its Internet address. The firewall then determines the local host to whose request the reply is responding. It then strips off its IP address and sends the response on to the local host across the LAN. The connection is transparent from the perspective of the local machines. They appear to be connected directly to the Internet.

Masquerading Local Networks

IP masquerading is often used to allow machines on a private network to access the Internet. These could be machines in a home network or a small LAN, such as for a small business. Such a network might have only one machine with Internet access, and as such, only the one Internet address. The local private network would have IP addresses chosen from the private network allocations (10., 172.16., or 192.168.). Ideally, the firewall has two Ethernet cards: one for an interface to the LAN (for example, **eth1**) and one for an interface to the Internet, such as **eth0**. The card for the Internet connection (**eth0**) would be assigned the Internet IP address. The Ethernet interface for the local network (**eth1**, in this example) is the firewall Ethernet interface. Your private LAN would have a network address like 192.168.0. Its Ethernet firewall interface (**eth1**) would be assigned the IP address 192.168.0.1. In effect, the firewall interface lets the firewall operate as the local network's gateway. The firewall is then configured to masquerade any packets coming from the private network. Your LAN needs to have its own domain name server, identifying the machines on your network, including your firewall. Each local machine needs to have the firewall specified as its gateway. Use separate interfaces for them, such as two Ethernet cards.

```
add table mynat
add chain mynat prerouting { type nat hook prerouting priority dstnat; }
add chain mynat postrouting {type nat hook postrouting priority srcnat; }
```

Masquerading NAT Rules

Use the masquerade statement to implement masquerading on nftables. The following example adds a rule to the **postrouting** chain with the **oifname** option specifying the output device and the **masquerade** statement.

```
nft add rule ip mynatpostrouting oifname "eth0" masquerade
```

IP Forwarding

The next step is to turn on IP forwarding, either manually or by setting the **net.ipv4.ip_forward** variable in the **/etc/sysctl.conf** file and running **sysctl** with the **-p** option. IP forwarding will be turned off by default. For IPv6, use **net.ipv6.conf.all.forwarding**. The **/etc/sysctl.conf** entries are shown here.

```
net.ipv4.ip_forward = 1
net.ipv6.conf.all.forwarding = 1
```

You then run **sysctl** with the **-p** option.

```
sysctl -p
```

You can directly change the respective forwarding files with an **echo** command as shown here.

```
echo 1 > /proc/sys/net/ipv4/ip_forward
```

For IPv6, you would use the forwarding file in the corresponding **/proc/sys/net/ipv6** directory, **conf/all/forwarding**.

```
echo 1 > /proc/sys/net/ipv6/conf/all/forwarding
```

Masquerading Selected Hosts

Instead of masquerading all local hosts as the single IP address of the firewall/gateway host, you could use the NAT table to rewrite addresses for a few selected hosts. Such an approach is often applied to setups where you want several local hosts to appear as Internet servers. Using the **dnat** and **snat** statements, you can direct packets to specific local hosts. You would use rules on the **prerouting** and **postrouting** chains to direct input and output packets.

For example, the Web server described in the previous example could have been configured as a local host to which a DNAT target could redirect any packets originally received for 10.0.0.2. Say the Web server was set up on 192.168.0.5. It could appear as having the address 10.0.0.2 on the Internet. Packets sent to 10.0.0.2 would be rewritten and directed to 192.168.0.5 by the NAT table. In the **mynat** table **prerouting** chain, the **tcp ip daddr** statement matches on all TCP IPv4 packets destined to 10.0.0.2. You would then use the **dnat to** statement (destination) to direct the packet to 192.168.0.5.

```
add rule ip mynat prerouting ip protocol tcp ip daddr 10.0.0.2 dnat to
192.168.0.5

add rule ip mynat postrouting ip protocol tcp ip saddr 192.168.0.5 snat to
10.0.0.2

add rule mynat postrouting oifname "eth0" snat to 192.168.0.5
add rule mynat prerouting oifname "eth0" dnat to 10.0.0.2
add rule mynat postrouting oifname "eth0" masquerade
```

Stateful Objects: counters, quotas, and limits

Stateful object provide stateful information derived from rules in a particular table. They can have any unique name you want to give them. Stateful objects can be counters, quotas, or limits. Counters keep counts as specified by the rules they are used in, such as a count of all the new connections in the input chain. Quotas specify a quota, and limits enforce a limit within a rule such as the number of connections an FTP port can support. Use the **add**, **delete**, **list**, and **reset** statements to manage your stateful objects. Use the **add** statement to add a new stateful object to a table. You can list the value of a stateful object with **list** statement. With **reset** you can reset the a stateful object to zero. To delete a stateful object, you need to know its handle. Use the **nft -a list counters** statement to first determine its handle. Then use the **delete** statement with the type of stateful object, the table, and the keyword **handle** and the handle to delete it.

```
add counter myfilter mycount
reset quota myfilter myquota
delete limit myfilter handle 6
```

To see a list of all the counters, quotas, or limits in a family, use the **list** statement along with the plural version of these stateful objects: **counters**, **quotas**, and **limits**.

```
list counters ip
list limits inet
list quotas ip6
```

Counters: anonymous and named

Counters will count packets, such as those from an input source. You can have anonymous or named packets. Anonymous packets are restricted to the rule they are used in, whereas a named counter can be used in any rule. You create a counter with the **counter** statement. For the counter statement you can specify the number of packets to count with the **packets** option, as well as the number of bytes to count (**bytes** option). Without options, a simple **counter** statement counts all the packets.

```
counter
counter packets 5
counter bytes 40
```

IPtables would anonymously count the number of times a rule was applied. A rule for all incoming packets would automatically count the number of incoming packets. nftables does not perform an automatic count. You have to explicitly specify it with the **counter** statement. Adding a **counter** statement to a rule will set up an automatic anonymous count for the rule.

```
protocol tcp counter
```

Named counters operate much like named sets. Named counters have to be declared first. Then they can be used throughout the firewall. To declare a counter use the **counter** statement and the name you want to give the counter. To use the counter in rule use the **name counter** statement.

The following **counter** statement declares a named counter called **count_logs** for the **myfilter** table.

```
add counter myfilter count_logs
```

A rule is then added that uses the **count_logs** counter to count logging on the eth1 device.

```
add rule ip myfilter input iifname "eth1" ip saddr != 192.168.0.0/24 log counter
name count_logs
```

Named counters can also be added to ports. The following declares a counter named **www_count**. It is then used in a rule to count access to port 80, the Web server port.

```
add counter myfilter www_count
```

```
add rule ip myfilter input iifname "eth0" ip saddr 10.0.0.2 tcp dport 80 counter
name www_count accept
```

Use the **list counters** command to list your named counters and their values.

```
list counters
```

You can also reference a named counter by its name.

```
list counter ip myfilter www_count
```

The following lists all the counters in the **myfilter** table.

```
list counters table ip myfilter
```

Use the **reset counters** command to reset all counters to zero.

```
reset counters
```

To reset just those in a table, reference the table.

```
reset counters table ip myfilter
```

You can use **reset counter** to reset specified named counters.

```
reset counter ip www_count
```

Quotas: anonymous and named

Like counters, quotas can be named or anonymous. For an anonymous quota use the **quota** statement with **over** or **until** options and a number for the quota in **bytes**, **kbytes**, or **mbytes**.

```
quota until 200 kbytes
```

For a named quota, use the **add quota** statement with the table and a name to create a quota. Use the **over** or **until** options to specify the quota in bytes, kbytes, or mbytes.

```
add quota myfilter myquota { over mybytes 10 |
```

To reference the named quota use the **quota name** statement along with the quota's name in quotes.

```
quota name myquota
```

For example

```
dport 80 quota name "myquota"
```

The **used** option lets you specify the initial value of a quota.

Use the **reset quota** statement to reset a particular quota, and the **reset quotas** statement to reset all quotas.

```
reset quota ip myquota
reset quotas ip table myfilter
```

To remove the named quota use the **delete quota** statement with the table and the quota name.

```
delete quota myfilter myquota
```

Use the **list quota** statement to list a particular named quota.

```
list quota ip myquota
```

With the **list quotas** statement you can list all the quotas in a table or ruleset.

```
list quotas ip table myfilter
```

Limits: anonymous and named

You can use the limit statement to set limits on matching or logging in a rule. For an anonymous limit, you use the **limit rate** statement and the packet number. You can limit by the number of packets or the number of bytes. For the bytes limit you also specify the kind of byte unit: **bytes**, **kbytes**, or **mbytes**. You can use the **over** option to match over the rate. You can also specify a time unit such as **second**, **minute**, **hour**, **day**.

```
limit rate 50
limit rate 100 mbytes
```

For a named limit, use the **limit** statement with the limit name to create a named limit. Use the **rate** option to specify the rate as **second**, **minute**, **hour**, **day**. You can use the **comment** option to add a comment.

```
limit myfilter mylimit { rate 200/minute ; }
```

To reference the named limit use the **limit name** statement along with the limit's name in quotes.

```
limit name "mylimit"
```

For example

```
dport 21 limit name "mylimit" accept
```

To remove the named limit use the **delete limit** statement with the table and the limit name.

```
delete limit myfilter mylimit
```

Use the **list limit** statement to list a named limit.

```
list quota ip myfilter mylimit
```

With the **list limits** statement you can list all the limits in a table or ruleset.

```
list limits ip table myfilter
```

Concatenations

You can combine elements using the period operator, letting you reference more than one address, port, protocol, or device in a list. You can string together multiple values of different kinds.

Concatenations operate as an AND operator. All the concatenated elements are activated. If addresses are concatenated, then all those addresses are referenced. Same for ports, or combinations of addresses and ports, as well as device interfaces and protocols. A set, on the other hand, operates, instead, as an OR operation. For a set of addresses, any one of the addresses can be referenced, instead of all of them.

The following references two addresses.

```
{192.168.0.1 . 192.168.0.3}
```

The following references two ports.

```
{80 . 21}
```

The following references both the input and output devices.

```
{oif . iif}
```

This reference both the tcp and udp protocols.

```
{tcp . udp}
```

You can use concatenations as elements in sets. This set references both two addresses and the tcp protocol, and one address with the udp protocol.

```
{192.168.0.1 . 192.168.0.5 . tcp , 192.168.0.3 . udp}
```

For named sets, be sure to specify the concatenation of allowable types.

```
add set ip myfilter myset2 { type ipv4_addr . ipv4_addr . inet_service ; }
```

You could then use concatenation in the set.

```
add element ip myfilter myset2 { 192.168.0.15 . 192.168.0.25 . 36 , 10.0.0.14 . 10.0.0.27 . 4055 }
```

You can use concatenations also as elements in maps. Be sure to specify concatenations in the element types.

```
add map ip myfilter mymap2 { type ipv4_addr . inet_service : inet_proto ; }
```

The following adds the concatenated address and port as an element to a map.

```
add element ip myfilter mymap2 { 192.168.0.11 . 22 : tcp , 192.168.0.16 . 35 : udp }
```

The **get element** statement requires that you enter values for the entire concatenation.

```
get element ip myfilter mymap2 { 192.168.0.15 . 22 }
```

Intervals (ranges)

Intervals designate a range of addresses or ports. In a rule you can depict an interval by placing two addresses separated by a dash. The following would show a range between 192.168.0.11 and 192.168.0.16.

```
192.168.0.11-192.168.0.16
```

The same could be done for ports.

```
21-24
```

The following example would accept only the range of addresses from 192.168.0.11 to 192.168.0.16 to be accepted on device eth1.

```
add rule ip myfilter myinput iifname "eth1" ip saddr 192.168.0.11-192.168.0.16
accept
```

This example uses port ranges.

```
tcp port 21-24 accept
```

You can also use ranges in anonymous sets.

```
{ 192.168.0.11-192.168.0.16 , 10.0.0.14-10.0.0.27 }
```

For named sets and maps, be sure to set the **interval** flag, which allows elements to have ranges.

```
add set ip myfilter myset3 { type ipv4_addr ; flags interval ; }
```

You could then use intervals in the set.

```
add element ip myfilter myset3 { 192.168.0.11-192.168.0.16 , 10.0.0.14-10.0.0.27
}
```

Be sure to also set the interval flag for named maps.

```
add map ip myfilter mymap3 { type ipv4_addr: inet_service ; flags interval ; }
```

The following adds a range of addresses as an element to a map.

```
add element ip myfilter mymap3 { 192.168.0.11-192.168.0.16 : 22 }
```

The **get element** statement will retrieve any address or port in an element's range.

```
get element ip myfilter mymap3 { 192.168.0.15 }
```

Sets

nftables sets operate much like an array. Sets hold elements. Using the elements in the set, nftables generates an identical rule with those values substituted inline. Instead of repeating a group of nearly identical rules, as you would with IPtables, you use just one rule with a set listing the values that are different.

Anonymous Sets

Sets can be anonymous or named. An anonymous set operates much liked an array of constants. It consists of a list of values which cannot be referenced, changed, or updated.

You define an anonymous set in a rule by encasing the elements within braces and separating the elements with commas. The following creates an anonymous set consisting of different ICMP packet types.

```
{ echo-reply, destination-unreachable, echo-request}
```

Using sets you can easily combine repetitive rules that vary with only one element. The three following rules can be combined into one using a set.

```
add rule ip myfilter input iifname "eth0" ip daddr 10.0.0.1 icmp type echo-reply
accept
add rule ip myfilter input iifname "eth0" ip daddr 10.0.0.1 icmp type echo-
request accept
add rule ip myfilter input iifname "eth0" ip daddr 10.0.0.1 icmp type
destination-unreachable accept
```

These rules can be written as one rule using a set for the icmp type.

```
add rule ip myfilter input iifname "eth0" ip daddr 10.0.0.1 icmp type { echo-
reply, destination-unreachable, echo-request} accept
```

Anonymous sets are often used for collections of ports, addresses, and subnets. You could write a rule for both FTP (port 21) and Web (port 80), using a set. The following is a simple rule to accept all packets for FTP and Web ports.

```
tcp port { 21, 80} accept
```

You could do something similar with subnets (addresses). The following accepts all packets from 192.168.0.0/24 and for 10.3.0.0/24.

```
ip saddr { 192.168.0.0/24, 10.3.0.0/24 }
```

You could also reference specific addresses.

```
ip daddr { 192.168.0.5, 192.168.0.32, 10.0.0.5 }
```

You can use multiple sets in the same rule.

```
 ip saddr { 192.168.0.0/24, 10.3.0.0/24 } tcp port { 21, 80 } accept
```

Named Sets

Named sets operate similar to arrays in programming languages. They can be referenced by their name and you can add, change, or delete elements from them. Should you need to repeat a set in another rule, you could name the set and then just refer to the name. You do not have to enter the set again, as you would have to do with an anonymous set.

A named set is defined by the user with a **type** specification for the type of data used for its elements along with flags to control them such as the **constant** flag for unchangeable values and the **interval** flag for allowing address or port ranges. Named sets only work for specific types of data as listed in Table 17-26.

To create a named set, you first define the name and the set's types with the **add set** command. Essentially a name definition. In a sense, you are defining a structure or array, giving a name to it and specifying the type of data it will hold. Then you use the **add element** command to add data elements to the named set. You could list the elements to add several elements at once. Tale 17-25 lists named sets statements.

Commands	Description
add set *family table set-name* { }	Create a named set
list set *family table set-name*	Display the elements in a named set
list sets *family*	List all the sets in a family
flush set *family table set-name*	Remove the elements in a named set, emptying the set
delete set *family table* handle *handle-number*	Delete a set
add element *family table set-name* { *element* }	Add an element to a set
delete element *family table set-name* { *element* }	Remove an element from a set

Table 17-25: nftables named set statements

When defining a named set, you also need to specify the type of values in the set. There are several value types, all specified by the keyword **type**. The type specification follows the set name and is enclosed in braces. The most common types used are **ether_addr**, **ipv4_addr**, **ipv6_addr**, and **inet_service** (the network service). The types are listed in Table 17-26.

Type	Description
ipv4_addr	IPv4 address
ipv6_addr	IPv6 address
ether_addr	Ethernet address
inet_proto	internet protocols: tcp, udp, udplite, exp, ah, icmp, icmpv6, comp dccp, sctp
inet_service	network service port number: udp, tcp, updlite, sctp, dccp
mark	Mark type: meta, socket, fib, ct

Table 17-26: nftables named set types

With nftables version 0.9.4 the **typeof** option can be used that can detect the type from an expression. Instead of using the **ipv4_addr** type, you can use **typeof ip saddr**.

```
add set myaddr { type ipv4_addr ; }
add set myaddr { typeof ip saddr ; }
```

Once you define a named set, you can reference it in a rule by prefixing the name with the **@** sign.

In the following example, the **add set** statement defines the **myaddreses** set, which holds IPv4 addresses. Be sure to end the type parameter with a semicolon. Each parameter in a set definition has to end with a semicolon.

```
add set ip myfilter myaddreses { type ipv4_addr ; }
```

The **add element** statements are then used to add elements to the set containing IPv4 addresses.

```
add element ip myfilter myaddresses { 192.168.0.45 , 10.0.0.9 }
add element ip myfilter myaddresses { 192.168.0.67 }
```

In a rule, the **myaddresses** set is referenced using the **@** operator. It accepts only packets with addresses destined for those in the **myaddresses** set.

```
add rule ip myfilter myinput ip daddr @myaddresses accept
```

You could combined the **add set** and **add element** rules into one by adding the **elements={}** parameter to the set definition. Be sure to separate the **type** and **elements** parameters with a semicolon.

```
add set ip myfilter myaddreses { type ipv4_addr ; elements={192.168.0.45 ,
10.0.0.9 , 192.168.0.67} ; }
```

You can list the contents of a named set with the **list set** command.

```
nft list set ip myfilter myaddreses
```

To check to see if a given value is presents as an element of a set, you can use the **get element** command.

```
get element ip myfilter myaddresses {192.168.0.67}
```

You can use the **list** command to list the elements in a set, and the **flush** command remove its elements, emptying the set (see table 17-27). Use the **delete** command to remove a set. To delete a set, you will need to know the set's handle. The following example lists all sets in the **ip** (IPv4) family, then all sets in the **myfilter** table, and all sets in the **myfilter myinput** chain

```
list sets ip
list sets table myfilter
list sets table myfilter myinput
```

You can add parameters to a set to control how the elements in it are used (see Table 17-33). The **size** command sets a maximum number of elements for the named set.

```
add set ip myfilter myaddreses { type ipv4_addr ; size 15 ; }
```

The **policy** parameter either optimizes for performance or memory.

```
add set ip myfilter myaddreses { type ipv4_addr ; policy performance; }
```

The **timeout** parameter can apply to the entire set, or to specific elements if the **timeout** flag is set. It specifies how long an element remains in a named set. You specify a number with a unit code indicating the time. The unit can be **d** for day, **h** for hour, **m** for month, and **s** for week. In the following example the entire set has a timeout of 2 hours.

```
add set ip myfilter myaddreses { type ipv4_addr ; timeout 2h ; }
```

Flags specify allowed operations for the elements. The flags available are **constant**, **interval**, and **timeout**. The **constant** flag will not allow the values in a named set to be changed. The **interval** flag allows a set to have a range of addresses, services, or ports as a value instead of a single value, and the **timeout** flag allows elements in a set to have their own timeouts.

Flags are listed with the **flags** parameter for the set (see Table 17-28).

```
add set ip myfilter myaddreses { type ipv4_addr ; flags interval, constant ; }
```

With the **interval** and **constant** flags set the elements can have ranges but they cannot be changed.

```
add element ip myfilter myaddresses { 192.168.0.45-192.168.0.68 , 10.0.0.9 }
```

The **timeout** flag allows each element to have its own timeout parameter. Enter the **timeout** as a parameter to the element's value.

```
add set ip myfilter myaddreses { type ipv4_addr ; flags timeout , interval ; }
```

In this example, some elements have different timeouts. The timeout for each element is added as a parameter to its value.

```
add element ip myfilter myaddresses { 192.168.0.45 timeout 2s , 10.0.0.9 timeout
5m }
```

If you are invoking a rule from the Bash shell with the **nft** command instead of a file, be sure to quote any shell operators such as the semicolon. In the named set definition, the type, parameters, and flags each end with a semi-colon. Because the semi-colon is also a shell command, for firewall rules, you have to prefix the semi-colon with a backslash, \;.

```
nft add set myfilter myset {type ipv4_addr \; flags constant \;
elements={192.168.0.5 , 10.0.0.55} \;}
```

Commands	Description
type	Set type of values for elements in the set. Type must me one of those listed in table 17-10
typeof	Derives type from an expression
timeout	time limit for value in a set. The length of the time out is specified by a number and unit code (d, h, m, s for week).
size	Maximum number of elements in a set (64 bit integer)
policy	Either performance (the default) or memory
elements	Initialize set with values
gc-interval	Set interval for values
auto-merge	For interval elements, merges adjacent or overlapping elements
flags	Specify capabilities and limitations of the set's elements (see Table 17-10).

Table 17-27: nftables named set element parameters

Flags	Description
constant	Values of the elements cannot be changed
interval	The set can have intervals
timeout	Elements can have timeout command.
dynamic	Values can be changed (default)

Table 17-28: nftables named set flags

It is possible to dynamically add to or update a set based on received packets, such as those meant for a black list or banned list. For that you use the **set update** and **set add** statements with a @ operation to reference the list.

First you define the set.

```
add set myflter mybadaddr { type ipv4_addr ; }
```

Then reference it with a **set add** or **set update** operation, using a @ operator.

```
add rule myfilter myinput set add ip saddr @mybadaddr
```

The difference between the **update** and **add** statements is that if you have a timeout for the set elements, with the **add** statement the timeout is not refreshed, whereas with the **update** statement it is refreshed.

Maps

A map works much like an array used in programming languages. Maps use the same structure as sets. Like an associative array in programming languages which assign values to character-based indexes, you can use a map to associate values to keys. You can then use the keys to retrieve the value or reference the entire set of associations in a rule. For example, you could associate addresses with ports, using the ports as the keys and the addresses as the values. Certain addresses would be associated with specific ports. Maps are an simple way to perform port redirection, specifying to what address packets from certain ports are to be directed. Like sets, maps can be either anonymous or named. An anonymous map can be defined and used directly in a rule, whereas named maps are first defined and can be referenced in different rules.

Anonymous Maps

An anonymous map is specified much like a set, except that its elements consist of a key and value pair. Each key and value are separated by a colon. Elements are separated by commas. The entire map, like a set, is encased in braces. You define a map with the **map** statement followed by the set of key and value elements. The following map has elements with the first element having the key 80 (the Web port) with a value of the address 192.168.0.1, and the second element having the key 21 (the FTP port) with the value of the address 192.168.0.3.

```
map {80 : 192.168.0.1 , 21 : 19.168.0.3}
```

The next example shows an anonymous map defined for the **mynat** table

```
add rule ip mynat prerouting dnat to tcp dport map {80 : 192.168.0.1 , 21 :
19.168.0.3}
```

Named Maps

Named maps operate much like named sets. You first have a rule to define the map, followed by a rule to assign its keys and values. You can then use the map in different rules by referencing its name. Use the **map** statements to manage a map: creating a map, deleting it, and listing its values (see Table 17-29).

Commands	Description
add map *family table map-name* { }	Create a named map
list map *family table map-name*	Display the elements in a named set
list maps *family*	List all the maps in a family
flush map *family table map-name*	Remove the elements in a named map, emptying the map
delete map *family table map-name*	Delete a map

Table 17-29: nftables named map commands

To implement a map you first define it with the **add map** statement and then add keys and their values to the map with the **add element** statement. To define a map use the **add map** statement to specify its name followed by the keyword **type** with the key type and the value type, separated by a colon. The allowed types for an element are listed in table 17-30.

```
add map mynat myports { type inet_service : ipv4_addr ; }
```

Type	Description
ipv4_addr	IPv4 address
ipv6_addr	IPv6 address
ether_addr	Ethernet address
inet_proto	internet protocols: tcp, udp, udplite, exp, ah, icmp, icmpv6, comp dccp, sctp
inet_service	network service port number: udp, tcp, updlite, sctp, dccp
mark	Mark type: meta, socket, fib, ct
counter	count (cannot use a counter for a key)
quota	quota (cannot use a quota for a key)

Table 17-30: nftables named map types for type command

You can add parameters to a map to control how the elements in it are used (see Table 17-31). The **size** sets a maximum number or elements for the named map. **policy** can be either performance or memory (the default). Flags specify allowed operations for the elements. Flags available are **constant** and **interval**. The **constant** flag will not allow the values in a named set to be changed. The **interval** flag allows a value to have ranges.

Commands	Description
type	Set type of values for elements in the map. Type must me one of those listed in table 17-10
typeof	Derives type from an expression
elements	Initialize map with keys and their values
size	Maximum number of elements in a set (64 bit integer)
policy	Map policy can be either performance or memory, performance is the default.
comment	Comment for the map
flags	Specify capabilities and limitations of the set's elements. There are two map flags: **constant** and **interval**. The **interval** flag allows a range of values to be stored in an element.

Table 17-31: nftables named map parameters

You use the element related map statements to manage the elements in the map (see Table 17-32). Use the map statement to add elements, remove them, and to display elements. To add elements to a map, use the **add element** statement, listing a set of keys and their values. Each element consists of a key and value separated by a colons. The elements are separated with commas.

```
add element mynat myports {80 : 192.168.0.1 , 21 : 19.168.0.3}
```

Commands	Description
add element *family table map-name* { *element-list* }	Add elements to a map
create element *family table map-name* { *element-list* }	Add elements to a map if they do not already exist in the map
delete element *family table map-name* { *element-keys* }	Remove elements from a map with the specified keys
get element *family table map-name* { *element-list* }	Check to see if elements are already in a map and then display them if they are.

Table 17-32: nftables named map element statements

You can then reference the map in any rule in the table using the **map** statement and the **@** prefix with the map name, as in **@myports**. Be sure to specify how the keys in the map are to be used, in this case **tcp dport**.

```
add rule ip mynat postrouting snat to tcp dport map @myports
```

The **create element** command only adds an element if it is not already in the map.

The element's value is an expression. It can be a simple expressions such as an address or port. It can also be a complex expression such as a concatenation. For example, to use both an address and port as a value, you could use a concatenation expression for the address and port. The concatenation operator is a period. Be sure to specify the type for the values in the expression in the map **type** definition.

```
add map mynat myports { type inet_service : ipv4_addr . inet_service \; }
add element mynat myports {80 : 192.168.0.1 . 5001 , 21 : 19.168.0.3 . 5002}
```

You can use the **delete element** statement to remove an element. Be sure to specify the element's key.

```
delete element mynat myports {21 : 19.168.0.3}
```

With the **get element** statement you can check to see if an element is part of a map, and then display it.

```
get element mynat myports {80 : 192.168.0.1}
```

There are also options you can apply just to elements (see Table 17-33). The **timeout** option specifies how long an element remains in a named map. You specify a number with a unit code indicating the time. The unit can be **d** for day, **h** for hour, **m** for month, and **s** for week. The **expires** option sets a time when the element expires. The **comment** option lets you enter a specific comment for the element.

Commands	Description
timeout	Time limit for value in a map. The length of the time out is specified by a number and unit code (d, h, m, s for week).
expires	The time when an element expires
comment	An element's comment

Table 17-33: nftables named map element options

Verdict Maps

A verdict map allows you to associate an action such as **accept** or **drop**, with a key. These actions are called verdict statements. A verdict map is a map that has only verdict statements for its values. A verdict statement performs a decision such as to drop or accept a packet, or to perform a jump to another chain. The allowed verdict statements are listed in table 17-26. Verdict maps work much like case statements in programming languages. If a certain address is detected, then its associated verdict statement is executed. You could have keys such as addresses or ports associated with a specific verdict statement.

Like maps, a verdict map can be either anonymous or named. An anonymous verdict map is created with a **vmap** statement and a set of key and verdict statements for the map.

```
add rule ip myfilter myinput ip protocol vmap {80 : jump www-chain , 21 : jump ftp-chain }
```

Named verdict maps are first defined with the **add map** command, using the **verdict** type for the value type.

```
add map myfilter mymap {type ipv4_addr : verdict ; }
```

You can then add elements with the **add element** statement, specifying verdict statements for the values.

```
add element myfilter mymap {192.168.0.1 : drop , 192.168.0.3 : accept }
```

You can then reference the verdict array in a rule with the **vmap** statement and its name and the **@** prefix, as in **@mymap**.

```
add rule myfilter input ip saddr vmap @mymap
```

An nftables Script Example with Sets

The following script shows the example using a set and a multiple statement. You would load it with the **nft -f** command.

myfilter-rules-2.nft

```
# Firewall Gateway system IP address is 10.0.0.1 using Ethernet device eth0
# Private network address is 192.168.0.0 using Ethernet device eth1
# Web site address is 10.0.0.2

# Flush the ruleset, removing all tables, chains, and rules
flush ruleset

# Create an ip table called myfilter and a nat table called mynat
add table ip myfilter
add table mynat

# add the input, output, and forward chains for the myfilter ip table and set
(policy)
add chain ip myfilter myinput { type filter hook input priority 0; policy drop; }
add chain ip myfilter myoutput { type filter hook output priority 0; policy
accept; }
add chain ip myfilter myforward { type filter hook forward priority 0; policy
accept; }

# add prerouting and postrouting chains for the mynat nat table and set (policy)
add chain mynat prerouting { type nat hook prerouting priority dstnat; }
add chain mynat postrouting { type nat hook postrouting priority srcnat; }

# IP spoofing, deny any packets on the internal network that have an external
source address
add rule ip myfilter myinput iifname "eth1" ip saddr != 192.168.0.0/24 counter
log drop
add rule ip myfilter myforward  iifname "eth1" ip saddr != 192.168.0.0/24 drop

# source addr4ess of the internal network
add rule ip myfilter myinput iifname != "eth1" ip saddr 192.168.0.0/24 drop
add rule ip myfilter myforward  iifname != "eth1" ip saddr 192.168.0.0/24 drop

# IP spoofing, deny any outside packets with localhost address
# (packets not on the lo interface (any on eth0 or eth1) that have source address
localhost)
add rule ip myfilter myinput iifname != "lo" ip saddr 127.0.0.0/8 drop
```

```
add rule ip myfilter myforward  iifname != "lo" ip saddr 127.0.0.0/8 drop

# allow all incoming messages for users on your firewall system
add rule ip myfilter myinput iifname "lo" accept

# allow  communication to the Web server (address 10.0.0.2), port www
add rule ip myfilter myinput iifname "eth0" ip saddr 10.0.0.2 tcp dport 80 accept
# Allow  established connections from Web servers to internal network
add rule ip myfilter myinput iifname "eth0" ip saddr 10.0.0.2 ip daddr
192.168.0.0/24 ct state related,established  tcp sport 80 accept

# Prevent new  connections from Web servers to internal network
add rule ip myfilter myoutput oifname "eth0" ip daddr 192.168.0.0/24 ct state new
tcp sport 80 drop

# allow established and related outside communication to your system
# and allow outside communication to the firewall, except for ICMP packets
add rule ip myfilter myinput iifname "eth0" ip protocol != icmp ct state
related,established  accept

# prevent outside initiated connections
add rule ip myfilter myinput iifname "eth0" ct state new  drop
add rule ip myfilter myforward  iifname "eth0" ct state new  drop

# allow all local communication to and from the firewall on eth1  from the local
network
add rule ip myfilter myinput iifname "eth1" ip saddr 192.168.0.0/24 accept

# Set up masquerading to allow internal machines access to outside network
add rule ip mynat postrouting oifname "eth0" masquerade

# Accept ICMP Ping and Destination unreachable messages
# Others will be rejected by myinput and output DROP policy
add rule ip myfilter myinput iifname "eth0" ip daddr 10.0.0.1 icmp type map {
echo-reply , echo-request , destination-unreachable } accept
```

The ruleset looks like this:

```
table ip myfilter {
        chain myinput {
                type filter hook input priority filter; policy drop;
                iifname "eth1" ip saddr != 192.168.0.0/24 counter log drop
                iifname != "eth1" ip saddr 192.168.0.0/24 drop
                iifname != "lo" ip saddr 127.0.0.0/8 drop
                iifname "lo" accept
                iifname "eth0" ip saddr 10.0.0.2 tcp dport 80 accept
                iifname "eth0" ip saddr 10.0.0.2 ip daddr 192.168.0.0/24 ct state
established,related tcp sport 80 accept
                iifname "eth0" ip protocol != icmp ct state established,related accept
                iifname "eth0" ct state new drop
                iifname "eth1" ip saddr 192.168.0.0/24 accept
                iifname "eth0" ip daddr 10.0.0.1 icmp type { echo-reply, destination-
unreachable, echo-request } accept
        }

        chain myoutput {
```

```
                type filter hook output priority filter; policy accept;
                oifname "eth0" ip daddr 192.168.0.0/24 ct state new tcp sport 80 drop
        }

        chain myforward {
                type filter hook forward priority filter; policy accept;
                iifname "eth1" ip saddr != 192.168.0.0/24 drop
                iifname != "eth1" ip saddr 192.168.0.0/24 drop
                iifname != "lo" ip saddr 127.0.0.0/8 drop
                iifname "eth0" ct state new drop
        }
}
table ip mynat {
        chain prerouting {
                type nat hook prerouting priority dstnat; policy accept;
        }

        chain postrouting {
                type nat hook postrouting priority srcnat; policy accept;
                oifname "eth0" masquerade
        }
}
```

You can also assign sets to variables.

```
define myicmps = { echo-reply, destination-unreachable, echo-request }

add rule ip myfilter myinput iifname $net_dev1 ip daddr 10.0.0.1 $myicmps accept
```

Iptables

The older IPtables information is provided here for those that still want to work with IPtables rules, especially for older complex firewalls. You can use IPtables rules on the Ubuntu **nftables** firewall. The rules are automatically converted to **nftables** rules and the run on the firewall.

The command used to execute packet filtering and NAT tasks in IPtables is **iptables**. Netfilter implements packet filtering and NAT tasks separately using different tables of rules. This approach streamlines the packet-filtering task, letting IPtables perform packet-filtering checks without the overhead of also having to do address translations. NAT operations are also freed from being mixed in with packet-filtering checks. You use the **iptables** command for packet filtering, NAT tasks, and packet mangling. Each operation has its own table of rules: filter for packet filtering, nat for NAT tasks, and mangle for packet mangling. For NAT you specify the NAT table with the **-t nat** option. For the mangle table, you use the **-t mangle** option. The packet filtering is the default. It can be specified with the **-t filter** option, but it is usually left out, assuming that if a table is not specified it is a filter operation. In addition, netfilter also handles certain exemptions to connection tracking operations in a **raw** table.

On Ubuntu, firewall applications, such as ufw, will set up their own iptables files containing **iptables** commands. When these are run, they will set up the tables and rules used to filter, translate, and mangle packets. The iptables files are located at **/etc/ufw**. If you want to set up rules manually and start them automatically you can use the iptables-persistent service (**iptables-persistent** package). The iptables-persistent service will run IPtables rules using rules you have set up in the **/etc/iptables/rules** files. Use the **iptables-persistent** script to run **iptables-restore** to load rules from the rules file.

```
sudo service iptables-persistent start
```

ip6tables

The **ip6tables** command provides support for IPv6 addressing. It is identical to IPtables, except that it allows the use of IPv6 addresses instead of IPv4 addresses. Both filter and mangle tables are supported in ip6tables, but not NAT tables. The filter tables support the same options and commands as supported in IPtables. The mangle tables will allow specialized packet changes like those for IPtables, using PREROUTING, INPUT, OUTPUT, FORWARD, and POSTROUTING rules. Some extensions have ipv6 labels for their names, such as ipv6-icmp, which correspond to the IPtables icmp extension. The ipv6headers extension is used to select IPv6 headers.

arptables

The arptables tool allows you to manage rules for the IPv4 Address Resolution Protocol (ARP). The ARP is used on IPv4 local networks to discover the hardware address (MAC address) associated with an IP address. Once the association is made, connections can be made to that address. In this way, a host on a local network can detect and connect to another host. arptables sets up IPtables rules for controlling access between these hosts. The filter, mangle, and nat tables are supported. Install the arptables package. arptables has its own commands for saving and loading ARP rules, **arptables-restore** and **arptables-save**. It is used for managing transmissions on local networks.

xtables

xtables is an underlying framework that combines the code for iptables, ip6tables, and arptables. Firewall modules hook into this framework. Modules that connect directly to this framework begin the **xt** prefix.

IPtables Netfilter

Netfilter is essentially a framework for packet management that can check packets for particular network protocols and notify parts of the kernel listening for them. Built on the Netfilter framework is the packet selection system implemented by IPtables. With IPtables, different tables of rules can be set up to select packets according to differing criteria. Netfilter currently supports three tables: filter, nat, and mangle. Packet filtering is implemented using a filter table that holds rules for dropping or accepting packets. Network address translation operations such as IP masquerading are implemented using the NAT table that holds IP masquerading rules. The mangle table is used for specialized packet changes. Changes can be made to packets before they are sent out when they are received, or as they are being forwarded. This structure is extensible in that new modules can define their own tables with their own rules. This also greatly improves efficiency. Instead of all packets checking one large table, they access only the table of rules they need.

IP table rules are managed using the **iptables** command. For this command, you have to specify the table you want to manage. The default is the filter table, which does not need to be specified. You can list the rules you have added at any time with the **-L** and **-n** options, as shown next. The **-n** option says to use only numeric output for both IP addresses and ports, avoiding a DNS lookup for hostnames. You could, however, just use the **-L** option to see the port labels and hostnames.

```
iptables -L -n
```

Chains

Rules are combined into different chains. The kernel uses chains to manage packets it receives and sends out. A chain is simply a checklist of rules. These rules specify what action to take for packets containing certain headers. The rules operate with an if-then-else structure. If a packet does not match the first rule, the next rule is then checked, and so on. If the packet does not match any rules, the kernel consults chain policy. Usually, at this point, the packet is rejected. If the packet does match a rule, it is passed to its target, which determines what to do with the packet. The standard targets are listed in Table 17-34. If a packet does not match any of the rules, it is passed to the chain's default target.

Target	Function
ACCEPT	Allow packet to pass through the firewall.
DROP	Deny access by the packet.
REJECT	Deny access and notify the sender.
QUEUE	Send packets to user space.
RETURN	Jump to the end of the chain and let the default target process it.

Table 17-34: IPtables Targets

Targets

A target could, in turn, be another chain of rules, or even a chain of user-defined rules. A packet could be passed through several chains before finally reaching a target. In the case of user-defined chains, the default target is always the next rule in the chains from which it was called. This sets up a procedure or function-call-like flow of control found in programming languages. When a rule has a user-defined chain as its target, when activated, that user-defined chain is executed. If no rules are matched, execution returns to the next rule in the originating chain.

Firewall and NAT Chains

The kernel uses three firewall chains: INPUT, OUTPUT, and FORWARD. When a packet is received through an interface, the INPUT chain is used to determine what to do with it. The kernel then uses its routing information to decide where to send it. If the kernel sends the packet to another host, the FORWARD chain is checked. Before the packet is actually sent, the OUTPUT chain is also checked. In addition, two NAT table chains, POSTROUTING and PREROUTING, are implemented to handle masquerading and packet address modifications. The built-in Netfilter chains are listed in Table 17-35.

Adding and Changing Rules

You add and modify chain rules using the iptables commands. An iptables command consists of the command **iptables**, followed by an argument denoting the command to execute. For example, **iptables -A** is the command to add a new rule, whereas **iptables -D** is the command to delete a rule. The iptables commands are listed in Table 17-36.

Chain	Description
INPUT	Rules for incoming packets
OUTPUT	Rules for outgoing packets
FORWARD	Rules for forwarded packets
PREROUTING	Rules for redirecting or modifying incoming packets, NAT table only
POSTROUTING	Rules for redirecting or modifying outgoing packets, NAT table only

Table 17-35: IPtables Netfilter Built-in Chains

The following command simply lists the chains along with their rules currently defined for your system. The output shows the default values created by iptables commands.

```
iptables -L -n
Chain input (policy ACCEPT):
Chain forward (policy ACCEPT):
Chain output (policy ACCEPT):
```

Option	Function
-A *chain*	Appends a rule to a chain.
-D *chain* [*rulenum*]	Deletes matching rules from a chain. Deletes rule *rulenum* (1 = first) from *chain*.
-I *chain* [*rulenum*]	Inserts in *chain* as *rulenum* (default 1 = first).
-R *chain rulenum*	Replaces rule *rulenum* (1 = first) in *chain*.
-L [*chain*]	Lists the rules in *chain* or all chains.
-E [*chain*]	Renames a chain.
-F [*chain*]	Deletes (flushes) all rules in *chain* or all chains.
-R *chain*	Replaces a rule; rules are numbered from 1.
-Z [*chain*]	Zero counters in *chain* or all chains.
-N *chain*	Creates a new user-defined chain.
-X *chain*	Deletes a user-defined chain.
-P *chain target*	Changes policy on *chain* to *target*.

Table 17-36: IPtables Commands

To add a new rule to a chain, you use **-A**. Use **-D** to remove it, and **-R** to replace it. Following the command, list the chain to which the rule applies, such as the INPUT, OUTPUT, or FORWARD chain, or a user-defined chain. Next, you list different options that specify the actions you want taken (most are the same as those used for IP Chains, with a few exceptions). The **-s** option specifies the source address attached to the packet, **-d** specifies the destination address, and the **-j** option specifies the target of the rule. The ACCEPT target will allow a packet to pass. The **-i** option indicates the input device and can be used only with the INPUT and FORWARD chains. The **-o** option indicates the output device and can be used only for OUTPUT and FORWARD chains. Table 17-37 lists several basic options.

IPtables Options

The IPtables package is designed to be extensible, and a number of options with selection criteria can be included with IPtables (see Table 17-37). For example, the TCP extension includes the **--syn** option that checks for SYN packets. The ICMP extension provides the **--icmp-type** option for specifying ICMP packets as those used in ping operations. The limit extension includes the **--limit** option, with which you can limit the maximum number of matching packets in a specified time period, such as a second.

Note: In IPtables commands, chain names have to be entered in uppercase, as with the chain names INPUT, OUTPUT, and FORWARD.

In the following example, the user adds a rule to the INPUT chain to accept all packets originating from the address 192.168.0.55. Any packets that are received (INPUT) whose source address (**-s**) matches 192.168.0.55 are accepted and passed through (-j ACCEPT):

```
iptables -A INPUT -s 192.168.0.55 -j ACCEPT
```

Option	Function
`-p [!]` *proto*	Specifies a protocol, such as TCP, UDP, ICMP, or ALL.
`-s [!]` *address*[`/mask`] `[!]` [*port*[`:port`]]	Source address to match. With the *port* argument, you can specify the port.
`--sport [!]` [*port*[`:port`]]	Source port specification. You can specify a range of ports using the colon, *port:port*.
`-d [!]` *address*[`/mask`] `[!]` [*port*[`:port`]]	Destination address to match. With the *port* argument, you can specify the port.
`--dport [!]`[*port*[`:port`]]	Destination port specification.
`--icmp-type [!]` *typename*	Specifies ICMP type.
`-i [!]` *name*[`+`]	Specifies an input network interface using its name. The + symbol functions as a wildcard. The + attached to the end of the name matches all interfaces with that prefix (`eth+` matches all Ethernet interfaces). Can be used only with the INPUT chain.
`-j` *target* [`port`]	Specifies the target for a rule (specify [`port`] for REDIRECT target).
`--to-source` < *ipaddr*>[`-<` *ipaddr*>] [`:` *port-port*]	Used with the SNAT target, rewrites packets with new source IP address.
`--to-destination` < *ipaddr*>[`-<` *ipaddr*>] [`:` *port- port*]	Used with the DNAT target, rewrites packets with new destination IP address.
`-n`	Numeric output of addresses and ports, used with `-L`.

`-o [!] name[+]`	Specifies an output network interface using its name. Can be used only with FORWARD and OUTPUT chains.
`-t table`	Specifies a table to use, as in `-t nat` for the NAT table.
`-v`	Verbose mode, shows rule details, used with `-L`.
`-x`	Expands numbers (displays exact values), used with `-L`.
`[!] -f`	Matches second through last fragments of a fragmented packet.
`[!] -V`	Prints package version.
`!`	Negates an option or address.
`-m`	Specifies a module to use, such as state.
`--state`	Specifies options for the state module such as NEW, INVALID, RELATED, and ESTABLISHED. Used to detect packet's state. NEW references SYN packets (new connections).
`--syn`	SYN packets, new connections.
`--tcp-flags`	TCP flags: SYN, ACK, FIN, RST, URG, PS, and ALL for all flags.
`--limit`	Option for the limit module (`-m limit`). Used to control the rate of matches, matching a given number of times per second.
`--limit-burst`	Option for the limit module (`-m limit`). Specifies maximum burst before the limit kicks in. Used to control denial-of-service attacks.

Table 17-37: IPtables Options

Accepting and Denying Packets: DROP and ACCEPT

There are two built-in targets: DROP and ACCEPT. Other targets can be either user-defined chains or extensions added on, such as REJECT. Two special targets are used to manage chains, RETURN and QUEUE. RETURN indicates the end of a chain and returns to the chain it started from. QUEUE is used to send packets to user space. The following example will drop all incoming packets from the **www.myjunk.com** site.

```
iptables -A INPUT -s www.myjunk.com -j DROP
```

You can turn a rule into its inverse with an **!** symbol. For example, to accept all incoming packets except those from a specific address, place an **!** symbol before the **-s** option and that address. The following example will accept all packets except those from the IP address 192.168.0.45.

```
iptables -A INPUT -j ACCEPT ! -s 192.168.0.45
```

You can specify an individual address using its domain name or its IP number. For a range of addresses, you can use the IP number of their network and the network IP mask. The IP mask can be an IP number or simply the number of bits making up the mask. For example, all of the addresses in network 192.168.0 can be represented by 192.168.0.0/225.255.255.0 or by 192.168.0.0/24. To specify any address, you can use 0.0.0.0/0.0.0.0 or simply 0/0. By default, rules reference any address if no **-s** or **-d** specification exists. The following example accepts messages coming in that are from (source) any host in the 192.168.0.0 network and that are going (destination) anywhere at all (the -d option is left out or could be written as -d 0/0).

```
iptables -A INPUT -s 192.168.0.0/24  -j ACCEPT
```

The IPtables rules are usually applied to a specific network interface such as the Ethernet interface used to connect to the Internet. For a single system connected to the Internet, you will have two interfaces, one that is your Internet connection, and a loopback interface (**lo**) for internal connections between users on your system. The network interface for the Internet is referenced using the device name for the interface. For example, the first Ethernet card with the device name would be referenced by the device name **eth0**. A modem using PPP protocols with the device name **ppp0** would have the name **ppp0**. In IPtables rules, you use the **-i** option to indicate the input device; it can be used only with the INPUT and FORWARD chains. The **-o** option indicates the output device and can be used only for OUTPUT and FORWARD chains. Rules can then be applied to packets arriving and leaving on network devices. In the following examples, the first rule references the Ethernet device **eth0**, and the second, the localhost.

```
iptables -A INPUT -j DROP -i eth0 -s 192.168.0.45
iptables -A INPUT -j ACCEPT  -i lo
```

User-Defined Chains

With IPtables, the FORWARD and INPUT chains are evaluated separately. One does not feed into the other. This means that if you want to completely block certain addresses from passing through your system, you will need to add both a FORWARD rule and an INPUT rule for them.

```
iptables -A INPUT -j DROP -i eth0 -s 192.168.0.45
iptables -A FORWARD -j DROP -i eth0 -s 192.168.0.45
```

A common method for reducing repeated INPUT and FORWARD rules is to create a user chain into which both the INPUT and FORWARD feed. You define a user chain with the **-N** option. The next example shows the basic format for this arrangement. A new chain is created called incoming (it can be any name you choose). The rules you would define for your FORWARD and INPUT chains are now defined for the incoming chain. The INPUT and FORWARD chains then use the incoming chain as a target, jumping directly to it and using its rules to process any packets they receive.

```
iptables -N incoming

iptables -A incoming -j DROP -i eth0 -s 192.168.0.45
iptables -A incoming -j ACCEPT  -i lo

iptables -A FORWARD -j incoming
iptables -A INPUT -j incoming
```

ICMP Packets

Firewalls often block certain Internet Control Message Protocol (ICMP) messages. ICMP redirect messages can take control of your routing tasks. You need to enable some ICMP messages, such as those needed for ping, traceroute, and destination-unreachable operations. In most cases, you always need to make sure destination-unreachable packets are allowed. Otherwise, domain name queries could hang. Some of the more common ICMP packet types are listed in Table 17-38. You can enable an ICMP type of packet with the **--icmp-type** option, which takes as its argument a number or a name representing the message. The following examples enable the use of echo-reply, echo-request, and destination-unreachable messages, which have the numbers 0, 8, and 3.

```
iptables -A INPUT -j ACCEPT -i eth0 -p icmp --icmp -type  echo-reply -d 10.0.0.1
iptables -A INPUT -j ACCEPT -i eth0 -p icmp --icmp-type  echo-request -d 10.0.0.1
iptables -A INPUT -j ACCEPT -i eth0 -p icmp --icmp-type destination-unreachable -d 10.0.0.1
```

Their rule listing will look like this:

```
ACCEPT     icmp --  0.0.0.0/0          10.0.0.1           icmp type 0
ACCEPT     icmp --  0.0.0.0/0          10.0.0.1           icmp type 8
ACCEPT     icmp --  0.0.0.0/0          10.0.0.1           icmp type 3
```

Number	Name	Required By
0	echo-reply	ping
3	destination-unreachable	Any TCP/UDP traffic
5	redirect	Routing if not running routing daemon
8	echo-request	ping
11	time-exceeded	traceroute

Table 17-38: IPtables Common ICMP Packets

Ping operations need to be further controlled to avoid the ping-of-death security threat. You can do this several ways. One way is to deny any ping fragments. Ping packets are normally small. You can block ping-of-death attacks by denying any ICMP packet that is a fragment. Use the **-f** option to indicate fragments.

```
iptables -A INPUT -p icmp -j DROP -f
```

Another way is to limit the number of matches received for ping packets. You use the limit module to control the number of matches on the ICMP ping operation. Use **-m** limit to use the limit module, and **--limit** to specify the number of allowed matches. **1/s** will allow one match per second.

```
iptables -A FORWARD -p icmp --icmp-type echo-request -m limit --limit 1/s -j ACCEPT
```

Controlling Port Access

If your system is hosting an Internet service, such as a Web or FTP server, you can use IPtables to control access to it. You can specify a particular service by using the source port (**--sport**) or destination port (**--dport**) options with the port that the service uses. IPtables lets you use names for ports such as **www** for the Web server port. The names of services and the ports they use are listed in the **/etc/services** file, which maps ports to particular services. For a domain name server, the port would be **domain**. You can also use the port number if you want, preceding the number with a colon. The following example accepts all messages to the Web server located at 192.168.0.43.

```
iptables -A INPUT -d 192.168.0.43 -p tcp --dport www -j ACCEPT
```

Common ports checked and their labels are shown here:

Service	Port Number	Port Label
Auth	113	auth
FTP	21	ftp
rpcbind	111	sunrpc
Telnet	23	telnet
Web server	80	www

You can also use port references to protect certain services and deny others. This approach is often used if you are designing a firewall that is much more open to the Internet, letting users make freer use of Internet connections. Certain services you know can be harmful, such as Telnet, can be denied selectively. For example, to deny any kind of Telnet operation on your firewall, you can drop all packets coming in on the Telnet port, 23. To protect NFS operations, you can deny access to the port used for the rpcbind, 111. You can use either the port number or the port name.

```
# deny outside access to rpcbind port on firewall.
iptables -A arriving  -j DROP -p tcp -i eth0  --dport 111
# deny outside access to telnet port on firewall.
iptables -A arriving  -j DROP -p tcp -i eth0  --dport telnet
```

The rule listing will look like this:

```
DROP      tcp  --  0.0.0.0/0    0.0.0.0/0    tcp dpt:111
DROP      tcp  --  0.0.0.0/0    0.0.0.0/0    tcp dpt:23
```

One port-related security problem is access to your X server ports that range from 6000 to 6009. On a relatively open firewall, these ports could be used to illegally access your system through your X server. A range of ports can be specified with a colon, as in 6000:6009. You can also use x11 for the first port, x11:6009. Sessions on the X server can be secured by using SSH, which normally accesses the X server on port 6010.

```
iptables -A arriving  -j DROP -p tcp -i eth0 --dport 6000:6009
```

Packet States: Connection Tracking

One of the more useful extensions is the state extension, which can easily detect tracking information for a packet. Connection tracking maintains information about a connection such as its source, destination, and port. It provides an effective means for determining which packets belong to an established or related connection. To use connection tracking, you specify the state module first with **-m** state. Then you can use the **--state** option. You can specify any of the following states:

State	Description
NEW	A packet that creates a new connection
ESTABLISHED	A packet that belongs to an existing connection
RELATED	A packet that is related to, but not part of, an existing connection, such as an ICMP error or a packet establishing an FTP data connection
INVALID	A packet that could not be identified for some reason
RELATED+REPLY	A packet that is related to an established connection, but not part of one directly

If you are designing a firewall that is meant to protect your local network from any attempts to penetrate it from an outside network, you may want to restrict packets coming in. Simply denying access by all packets is unfeasible, because users connected to outside servers on the Internet must receive information from them. You can, instead, deny access by a particular kind of packet used to initiate a connection. The idea is that an attacker must initiate a connection from the outside. The headers of these kinds of packets have their SYN bit set on and their FIN and ACK bits empty. The state module's NEW state matches on any such SYN packet. By specifying a DROP target for such packets, you deny access by any packet that is part of an attempt to make a connection with your system. Anyone trying to connect to your system from the outside is unable to do so. Users on your local system who have initiated connections with outside hosts can still communicate with them. The following example will drop any packets trying to create a new connection on the **eth0** interface, though they will be accepted on any other interface.

```
iptables -A INPUT -m state --state NEW -i eth0 -j DROP
```

You can use the ! operator on the **eth0** device combined with an ACCEPT target to compose a rule that will accept any new packets except those on the **eth0** device. If the **eth0** device is the only one that connects to the Internet, this still effectively blocks outside access. At the same time, input operation for other devices such as your localhost are free to make new connections. This kind of conditional INPUT rule is used to allow access overall with exceptions. It usually assumes that a later rule, such as a chain policy, will drop remaining packets.

```
iptables -A INPUT -m state --state NEW ! -i eth0 -j ACCEPT
```

The next example will accept any packets that are part of an established connection or related to such a connection on the **eth0** interface.

```
iptables -A INPUT -m state --state ESTABLISHED,RELATED -j ACCEPT
```

Specialized Connection Tracking: ftp, irc, Amanda, tftp.

To track certain kinds of packets, IPtables uses specialized connection tracking modules. These are optional modules that you need to have loaded manually. To track passive FTP connections, you would have to load the ip_conntrack_ftp module. To add NAT table support, you would also load the ip_nat_ftp module. For IRC connections, you use ip_conntrack_irc and ip_nat_irc. There are corresponding modules for Amanda (the backup server) and TFTP (Trivial FTP).

If you are writing your own iptables script, you would have to add **modprobe** commands to load the modules.

```
modprobe ip_conntrack ip_conntrack_ftp ip_nat_ftp
modprobe ip_conntrack_amanda ip_nat_amanda
```

Network Address Translation on IPtables (NAT)

Network address translation (NAT) is the process whereby a system will change the destination or source of packets as they pass through the system. A packet will traverse several linked systems on a network before it reaches its final destination. Normally, they will simply pass the packet on. However, if one of these systems performs a NAT operation on a packet, it can change the source or destination. A packet sent to a particular destination could have its destination address changed. To make this work, the system also needs to remember such changes so that the source and destination for any reply packets are altered back to the original addresses of the packet being replied to.

NAT is often used to provide access to systems that may be connected to the Internet through only one IP address. Such is the case with networking features such as IP masquerading, support for multiple servers, and transparent proxying. With IP masquerading, NAT operations will change the destination and source of a packet moving through a firewall/gateway linking the Internet to computers on a local network. The gateway has a single IP address that the other local computers can use through NAT operations. If you have multiple servers but only one IP address, you can use NAT operations to send packets to the alternate servers. You can also use NAT operations to have your IP address reference a particular server application such as a Web server (transparent proxy). NAT tables are not implemented for ip6tables.

Adding NAT Rules

Packet selection rules for NAT operations are added to the NAT table managed by the **iptables** command. To add a rule to the NAT table, you would have to specify the NAT table with the **-t nat** option as shown here.

```
iptables -t nat
```

With the **-L** option, you can list the rules you have added to the NAT table.

```
iptables -t nat -L -n
```

Adding the **-n** option will list IP addresses and ports in numeric form. This will speed up the listing, as iptables will not attempt to do a DNS lookup to determine the hostname for the IP address.

Nat Targets and Chains

In addition, there are two types of NAT operations: source NAT, specified as SNAT target, and destination NAT, specified as DNAT target. The SNAT target is used for rules that alter source addresses, and DNAT target, for those that alter destination addresses.

Three chains in the NAT table are used by the kernel for NAT operations. These are PREROUTING, POSTROUTING, and OUTPUT. PREROUTING is used for destination NAT (DNAT) rules. These are packets that are arriving. POSTROUTING is used for source NAT (SNAT) rules. These are for packets leaving. OUTPUT is used for destination NAT rules for locally generated packets.

The targets valid only for the NAT table are shown here:

SNAT	Modify source address, use `--to-source` option to specify new source address.
DNAT	Modify destination address, use `--to-destination` option to specify new destination address.
REDIRECT	Redirect a packet.
MASQUERADE	IP masquerading.
MIRROR	Reverse source and destination and send back to sender.
MARK	Modify the Mark field to control message routing.

As with packet filtering, you can specify source (**-s**) and destination (**-d**) addresses, as well as the input (**-i**) and output (**-o**) devices. The **-j** option will specify a target such as MASQUERADE. You would implement IP masquerading by adding a MASQUERADE rule to the POSTROUTING chain:

```
iptables -t nat -A POSTROUTING -o eth0 -j MASQUERADE
```

To change the source address of a packet leaving your system, you would use the POSTROUTING rule with the SNAT target. For the SNAT target, you use the **--to-source** option to specify the source address,

```
iptables -t nat -A POSTROUTING -o eth0 -j SNAT --to-source 192.168.0.4
```

To change the destination address of packets arriving on your system, you would use the PREROUTING rule with the DNAT target and the **--to-destination** option.

```
iptables -t nat -A PRETROUTING -i eth0 -j DNAT --to-destination 192.168.0.3
```

Specifying a port lets you change destinations for packets arriving on a particular port. In effect, this lets you implement port forwarding. In the next example, every packet arriving on port 80 (the Web service port) is redirected to 10.0.0.3, which in this case would be a system running a Web server.

```
iptables -t nat -A PRETROUTING -i eth0 -p tcp --dport 80 -j DNAT --to-destination 10.0.0.3
```

With the TOS and MARK targets, you can mangle the packet to control its routing or priority. A TOS target sets the type of service for a packet, which can set the priority using criteria such as normal-service, minimize-cost, or maximize-throughput, among others.

Nat Redirection: Transparent Proxies

NAT tables can be used to implement any kind of packet redirection, a process transparent to the user. Redirection is commonly used to implement a transparent proxy. Redirection of packets is carried out with the REDIRECT target. With transparent proxies, packets received can be automatically redirected to a proxy server. For example, packets arriving on the Web service port, 80, can be redirected to the Squid Proxy service port, usually 3128. This involves a command to redirect a packet, using the REDIRECT target on the PREROUTING chain.

```
# iptables -t nat -A PREROUTING -i eth1 -p tcp --dport 80 -j REDIRECT --to-port 3128
```

Packet Mangling on IPtables: the Mangle Table

The packet mangling table is used to actually modify packet information. Rules applied specifically to this table are often designed to control the mundane behavior of packets, like routing, connection size, and priority. Rules that actually modify a packet, rather than simply redirecting or stopping it, can be used only in the mangle table. For example, the TOS target can be used directly in the mangle table to change the Type of Service field to modifying a packet's priority. A TCPMSS target could be set to control the size of a connection. The ECN target lets you work around ECN black holes, and the DSCP target will let you change DSCP bits. Several extensions such as the ROUTE extension will change a packet, in this case, rewriting its destination, rather than just redirecting it.

The mangle table is indicated with the **-t** mangle option. Use the following command to see what chains are listed in your mangle table.

```
iptables -t mangle  -L
```

Several mangle table targets are shown here:

TOS	Modify the Type of Service field to manage the priority of the packet.
TCPMSS	Modify the allowed size of packets for a connection, enabling larger transmissions.
ECN	Remove ECN black hole information.
DSCP	Change DSCP bits.
ROUTE	Extension TARGET to modify destination information in the packet.

Note: The IPtables package is designed to be extensible, allowing customized targets to be added easily. This involves applying patches to the kernel and rebuilding it. See **https://www.netfilter.org** for more details, along with a listing of extended targets.

IPtables Scripts

Though you can enter IPtables rules from the shell command line, when you shut down your system, these commands will be lost. You will most likely need to place your IPtables rules in a script that can then be executed directly. This way you can edit and manage a complex set of rules, adding comments and maintaining their ordering.

To load the rules, use the **iptables-restore** script to read the IPtables commands from that file.

```
sudo iptables-restore < myfilter
```

The **iptables-save** command will save currently loaded firewall rules to a file of your choosing using the redirection operator, >. You could use this command to save a copy of rules set up by another firewall application like ufw, and then use that file as a basis for customizing firewall rules manually. You could then use **iptables-restore** to load your customized rules. The **iptables-save** command will save whatever rules are loaded currently, even those you may have entered directly using the **iptables** command.

```
sudo iptables-save > mycurrentfirewall
```

An IPtables Script Example: IPv4

You now have enough information to create a simple IPtables script that will provide basic protection for a single system connected to the Internet. The following script, **myfilter**, provides an IPtables filtering process to protect a local network and a website from outside attacks. This example uses IPtables and IPv4 addressing. For IPv6 addressing, you would use ip6tables, which has corresponding commands, except for the NAT rules, which would be implemented as mangle rules.

eth0 and **eth1**, are used here for clarity. Your system's actual device names will be different, following predictable naming formats (see Chapter 3).

myfilter

```
# Firewall Gateway system IP address is 10.0.0.1 using Ethernet device eth0
# Private network address is 192.168.0.0 using Ethernet device eth1
# Web site address is 10.0.0.2
# turn off IP forwarding
echo 0 > /proc/sys/net/ipv4/ip_forward
# Flush chain rules
iptables -F INPUT
iptables -F OUTPUT
iptables -F FORWARD
# set default (policy) rules
iptables -P INPUT DROP
iptables -P OUTPUT ACCEPT
iptables -P FORWARD ACCEPT


# IP spoofing, deny any packets on the internal network that have an external source address
iptables -A INPUT -j LOG  -i eth1 \! -s 192.168.0.0/24
iptables -A INPUT -j DROP  -i eth1 \! -s 192.168.0.0/24
iptables -A FORWARD -j DROP  -i eth1 \! -s 192.168.0.0/24
# IP spoofing, deny any outside packets (any not on eth1) that have the
# source address of the internal network
iptables -A INPUT -j DROP \! -i eth1 -s 192.168.0.0/24
iptables -A FORWARD -j DROP \! -i eth1 -s 192.168.0.0/24
# IP spoofing, deny any outside packets with localhost address
# (packets not on the lo interface (any on eth0 or eth1) that have source address localhost)
iptables -A INPUT -j DROP  -i \! lo  -s  127.0.0.0/255.0.0.0
iptables -A FORWARD -j DROP  -i \! lo  -s  127.0.0.0/255.0.0.0


# allow all incoming messages for users on your firewall system
iptables -A INPUT -j ACCEPT  -i lo


# allow  communication to the Web server (address 10.0.0.2), port www
iptables -A INPUT  -j ACCEPT -p tcp -i eth0  --dport www -s 10.0.0.2
# Allow  established connections from Web servers to internal network
iptables -A INPUT -m state --state ESTABLISHED,RELATED -i eth0 -p tcp  --sport www -s
10.0.0.2 -d 192.168.0.0/24  -j ACCEPT
# Prevent new  connections from Web servers to internal network
iptables -A OUTPUT -m state --state  NEW -o eth0 -p tcp --sport www -d 192.168.0.0/24 -j DROP


# allow established and related outside communication to your system
# allow outside communication to the firewall, except for ICMP packets
iptables -A INPUT -m state --state ESTABLISHED,RELATED -i eth0 -p \! icmp -j ACCEPT
# prevent outside initiated connections
iptables -A INPUT -m state --state NEW -i eth0 -j DROP
iptables -A FORWARD -m state --state NEW -i eth0 -j DROP
# allow all local communication to and from the firewall on eth1  from the local network
```

```
iptables -A INPUT -j ACCEPT -p all -i eth1 -s 192.168.0.0/24

# Set up masquerading to allow internal machines access to outside network
iptables -t nat -A POSTROUTING -o eth0 -j MASQUERADE

# Accept ICMP Ping and Destination unreachable messages
# Others will be rejected by INPUT and OUTPUT DROP policy
iptables -A INPUT -j ACCEPT  -p icmp -i eth0 --icmp-type  echo-reply -d 10.0.0.1
iptables -A INPUT -j ACCEPT  -p icmp -i eth0 --icmp-type  echo-request -d 10.0.0.1
iptables -A INPUT -j ACCEPT -p icmp -i eth0 --icmp-type  destination-unreachable -d 10.0.0.1
# Turn on IP Forwarding
echo 1 > /proc/sys/net/ipv4/ip_forward
```

Figure 17-17: A network with a firewall

The script configures a simple firewall for a private network. In this configuration, all remote access initiated from the outside is blocked, but two-way communication is allowed for connections that users in the network make with outside systems. In this example, the firewall system functions as a gateway for a private network whose network address is 192.168.0.0 (see Figure 17-17). The Internet address is, for the sake of this example, 10.0.0.1. The system has two Ethernet devices: one for the private network (**eth1**) and one for the Internet (**eth0**). The gateway firewall system also supports a Web server at address 10.0.0.2. Entries in this example that are too large to fit on one line are continued on a second line, with the newline quoted with a backslash. The basic rules as they apply to different parts of the network are illustrated in Figure 17-18.

Initially, in the script, you would clear your current IPtables with the flush option (**-F**), and then set the policies (default targets) for the non-user-defined rules. IP forwarding should also be turned off while the chain rules are being set.

```
echo 0 > /proc/sys/net/ipv4/ip_forward
```

Drop Policy

First, a DROP policy is set up for INPUT and FORWARD built-in IP chains. This means that if a packet does not meet a criterion in any of the rules to let it pass, it will be dropped. Then both IP spoofing attacks and any attempts from the outside to initiate connections (SYN packets) are rejected.

Outside connection attempts are also logged. This is a very basic configuration that can easily be refined to your own needs by adding IPtables rules.

```
iptables -P INPUT DROP
iptables -P OUTPUT ACCEPT
iptables -P FORWARD ACCEPT
```

Figure 17-18: Firewall rules applied to a local network example

IP Spoofing

One way to protect the private network from the IP spoofing of any packets is to check for any outside addresses on the Ethernet device dedicated to the private network. In this example, any packet on device **eth1** (dedicated to the private network) whose source address is not that of the private network (! -s 192.168.0.0) is denied. Also, check to see if any packets coming from the outside are designating the private network as their source. In this example, any packets with the source address of the private network on any Ethernet device other than for the private network (**eth1**) are denied. The same strategy can be applied to the local host.

```
# IP spoofing, deny any packets on the internal network
# that has an external source address.
iptables -A INPUT -j LOG  -i eth1 \! -s 192.168.0.0/24
iptables -A INPUT -j DROP  -i eth1 \! -s 192.168.0.0/24
iptables -A FORWARD -j DROP  -i eth1 \! -s 192.168.0.0/24
# IP spoofing, deny any outside packets (any not on eth1)
# that have the source address of the internal network
iptables -A INPUT -j DROP \! -i eth1 -s 192.168.0.0/24
iptables -A FORWARD -j DROP \! -i eth1 -s 192.168.0.0/24
# IP spoofing, deny any outside packets with localhost address
# (packets not on the lo interface (any on eth0 or eth1)
# that have the source address of localhost)
iptables -A INPUT -j DROP  -i \! lo  -s  127.0.0.0/255.0.0.0
iptables -A FORWARD -j DROP  -i \! lo  -s  127.0.0.0/255.0.0.0
```

Then, you would set up rules to allow all packets sent and received within your system (localhost) to pass.

```
iptables -A INPUT -j ACCEPT  -i lo
```

Server Access

For the Web server, you want to allow access by outside users but block access by anyone attempting to initiate a connection from the Web server into the private network. In the next example, all messages are accepted to the Web server, but the Web server cannot initiate contact with the private network. This prevents anyone from breaking into the local network through the Web server, which is open to outside access. Established connections are allowed, permitting the private network to use the Web server.

```
# allow  communication to the Web server (address 10.0.0.2), port www
iptables -A INPUT  -j ACCEPT -p tcp -i eth0  --dport www -s 10.0.0.2
# Allow  established connections from Web servers to internal network
iptables -A INPUT -m state --state ESTABLISHED,RELATED -i eth0 \
   -p tcp  --sport www -s 10.0.0.2 -d 192.168.0.0/24  -j ACCEPT
# Prevent new  connections from Web servers to internal network
iptables -A OUTPUT -m state --state  NEW -o eth0 -p tcp \
  --sport www -d 192.168.0.1.0/24  -j DROP
```

Firewall Outside Access

To allow access by the firewall to outside networks, you allow input by all packets except for ICMP packets. These are handled later. The firewall is specified by the firewall device, **eth0**. First, your firewall should allow established and related connections to proceed, as shown here. Then you would block outside access as described later.

```
# allow outside communication to the firewall,
# except for ICMP packets
iptables -A INPUT -m state --state ESTABLISHED,RELATED \
        -i eth0 -p \! icmp -j ACCEPT
```

Blocking Outside Initiated Access

To prevent outsiders from initiating any access to your system, create a rule to block access by SYN packets from the outside using the state option with NEW. Drop any new connections on the **eth0** connection (assumes only **eth0** is connected to the Internet or outside network).

```
# prevent outside initiated connections
iptables -A INPUT -m state --state NEW -i eth0 -j DROP
iptables -A FORWARD -m state --state NEW -i eth0 -j DROP
```

Local Network Access

To allow interaction by the internal network with the firewall, you allow input by all packets on the internal Ethernet connection, **eth1**. The valid internal network addresses are designated as the input source.

```
iptables -A INPUT -j ACCEPT -p all -i eth1 -s 192.168.0.0/24
```

Listing Rules

A listing of these **iptables** options shows the different rules for each option, as shown here.

```
$ iptables -L
Chain INPUT (policy DROP)
target     prot opt source          destination
LOG        all  -- !192.168.0.0/24  anywhere          LOG level warning
DROP       all  -- !192.168.0.0/24  anywhere
DROP       all  -- 192.168.0.0/24   anywhere
DROP       all  -- 127.0.0.0/8      anywhere
ACCEPT     all  -- anywhere         anywhere
ACCEPT     tcp  -- 10.0.0.2         anywhere          tcp dpt:http
ACCEPT     tcp  -- 10.0.0.2         192.168.0.0/24    state RELATED,ESTABLISHED tcp spt:http
ACCEPT     !icmp -- anywhere        anywhere          state RELATED,ESTABLISHED
DROP       all  -- anywhere         anywhere          state NEW
ACCEPT     all  -- 192.168.0.0/24   anywhere
ACCEPT     icmp -- anywhere         10.0.0.1          icmp echo-reply
ACCEPT     icmp -- anywhere         10.0.0.1          icmp echo-request
ACCEPT     icmp -- anywhere         10.0.0.1          icmp destination-unreachable
Chain FORWARD (policy ACCEPT)
target     prot opt source          destination
DROP       all  -- !192.168.0.0/24  anywhere
DROP       all  -- 192.168.0.0/24   anywhere
DROP       all  -- 127.0.0.0/8      anywhere
DROP       all  -- anywhere         anywhere          state NEW

Chain OUTPUT (policy ACCEPT)
target     prot opt source       destination
DROP       tcp  -- anywhere      192.168.0.0/24  state NEW tcp spt:http


$ iptables -t nat -L
Chain PREROUTING (policy ACCEPT)
target        prot opt source        destination
Chain POSTROUTING (policy ACCEPT)
target        prot opt source        destination
MASQUERADE all  -- anywhere       anywhere
Chain OUTPUT (policy ACCEPT)
target        prot opt source        destination
```

User-Defined Rules

For more complex rules, you may want to create your own chain to reduce repetition. A common method is to define a user chain for both INPUT and FORWARD chains so that you do not have to repeat DROP operations for each. Instead, you would have only one user chain that both FORWARD and INPUT chains would feed into for DROP operations. Keep in mind that both FORWARD and INPUT operations may have separate rules in addition to the ones they share. In the next example, a user-defined chain called arriving is created. The chain is defined with the **-N** option at the top of the script.

```
iptables -N arriving
```

A user chain has to be defined before it can be used as a target in other rules. So, you have to first define and add all the rules for that chain, and then use it as a target. The arriving chain is first defined and its rules added. Then, at the end of the file, it is used as a target for both the INPUT and FORWARD chains. The INPUT chain lists rules for accepting packets, whereas the FORWARD chain has an ACCEPT policy that will accept them by default.

```
iptables -N arriving
iptables -F arriving
# IP spoofing, deny any packets on the internal network
# that has an external source address.
iptables -A arriving -j LOG  -i eth1 \! -s 192.168.0.0/24
iptables -A arriving -j DROP  -i eth1 \! -s 192.168.0.0/24
iptables -A arriving -j DROP \! -i eth1 -s 192.168.0.0/24
............................
# entries at end of script
iptables -A INPUT -j arriving
iptables -A FORWARD -j arriving
```

A listing of the corresponding rules is shown here.

```
Chain INPUT (policy DROP)
target     prot opt source            destination
arriving   all  --  0.0.0.0/0          0.0.0.0/0
Chain FORWARD (policy ACCEPT)
target     prot opt source            destination
arriving   all  --  0.0.0.0/0          0.0.0.0/0
Chain arriving (2 references)
target     prot opt source            destination
LOG        all  -- !192.168.0.0/24    0.0.0.0/0       LOG flags 0 level 4
DROP       all  -- !192.168.0.0/24    0.0.0.0/0
DROP       all  --  192.168.0.0/24    0.0.0.0/0
```

For rules where chains may differ, you will still need to enter separate rules. In the **myfilter** script, the FORWARD chain has an ACCEPT policy, allowing all forwarded packets to the local network to pass through the firewall. If the FORWARD chain had a DROP policy, like the INPUT chain, then you may need to define separate rules under which the FORWARD chain could accept packets. In this example, the FORWARD and INPUT chains have different rules for accepting packets on the **eth1** device. The INPUT rule is more restrictive. To enable the local network to receive forwarded packets through the firewall, you could enable forwarding on its device using a separate FORWARD rule, as shown here.

```
iptables -A FORWARD -j ACCEPT -p all -i eth1
```

The INPUT chain would accept packets only from the local network.

```
iptables -A INPUT -j ACCEPT -p all -i eth1 -s 192.168.0.0/24
```

Masquerading Local Networks

To implement masquerading, where systems on the private network can use the gateway's Internet address to connect to Internet hosts, you create a NAT table (**-t nat**) POSTROUTING rule with a MASQUERADE target.

```
iptables -t nat -A POSTROUTING -o eth0 -j MASQUERADE
```

Controlling ICMP Packets

In addition, to allow ping and destination-reachable ICMP packets, you enter INPUT rules with the firewall as the destination. To enable ping operations, you use both echo-reply and echo-request ICMP types, and for destination unreachable, you use the destination-unreachable type.

```
iptables -A INPUT -j ACCEPT  -p icmp -i eth0 --icmp-type echo-reply -d 10.0.0.1
iptables -A INPUT -j ACCEPT  -p icmp -i eth0 --icmp-type echo-request -d 10.0.0.1
iptables -A INPUT -j ACCEPT -p icmp -i eth0 --icmp-type destination-unreachable -d 10.0.0.1
```

At the end, IP forwarding is turned on again.

```
echo 1 > /proc/sys/net/ipv4/ip_forward
```

Simple LAN Configuration

To create a script to support a simple LAN without any Internet services like Web servers, you would not include rules for supporting those services. You would still need FORWARD and POSTROUTING rules for connecting your local hosts to the Internet, as well as rules governing interaction between the hosts and the firewall. To modify the example script to support a simple LAN without the Web server, remove the three rules governing the Web server. Leave everything else the same.

LAN Configuration with Internet Services on the Firewall System

Often, the same system that runs a firewall is also used to run Internet servers, like Web and FTP servers. In this case, the firewall rules are applied to the ports used for those services. The example script dealt with a Web server running on a separate host system. If the Web server were, instead, running on the firewall system, you would apply the Web server firewall rules to the port that the Web server uses. Normally the port used for a Web server is 80. In the following example, the IPtables rules for the Web server have been applied to port www, port 80, on the firewall system. The modification simply requires removing the old Web server host address references, 10.0.0.2.

```
# allow  communication to the Web server, port www (port 80)
iptables -A INPUT  -j ACCEPT -p tcp -i eth0  --dport www
# Allow  established connections from Web servers to internal network
iptables -A INPUT -m state --state ESTABLISHED,RELATED -i eth0 \
   -p tcp  --sport www -d 192.168.0.0/24  -j ACCEPT
# Prevent new  connections from Web servers to internal network
iptables -A OUTPUT -m state --state  NEW -o eth0 -p tcp \
  --sport www -d 192.168.0.1.0/24 -j DROP
```

Similar entries could be set up for an FTP server. Should you run several Internet services, you could use a user-defined rule to run the same rules on each service, rather than repeating three separate rules per service. Working from the example script, you would use two defined rules, one for INPUT and one for OUTPUT, controlling incoming and outgoing packets for the services.

```
iptables -N inputservice
iptables -N outputservice
iptables -F inputservice
iptables -F outputservice

# allow  communication to the service
iptables -A inputservice  -j ACCEPT -p tcp -i eth0
# Allow  established connections from the service to internal network
iptables -A inputservice -m state --state ESTABLISHED,RELATED -i eth0 \
   -p tcp  -d 192.168.0.0/24  -j ACCEPT
# Prevent new  connections from service to internal network
iptables -A outputservice -m state --state  NEW -o eth0 -p tcp \
   -d 192.168.0.1.0/24 -j DROP

# Run rules for the Web server, port www (port 80)
iptables -A INPUT  --dport www -j inputservice
iptables -A INPUT  --dport www -j outputservice
# Run rules for the FTP server, port ftp (port 21)
iptables -A OUTPUT  --dport ftp -j inputservice
iptables -A OUTPUT  --dport ftp -j outputservice
```

IP Masquerading

On Linux systems, you can set up a network in which you can have one connection to the Internet that several systems on your network can use. This way, using only one IP address, several different systems can connect to the Internet. This method is called IP masquerading, where a system masquerades as another system, using that system's IP address. In such a network, one system is connected to the Internet with its own IP address, while the other systems are connected on a local area network (LAN) to this system. When a local system wants to access the network, it masquerades as the Internet-connected system, borrowing its IP address.

IP masquerading is implemented on Linux using the IPtables firewall tool. In effect, you set up a firewall, which you then configure to do IP masquerading. Currently, IP masquerading supports all the common network services. as does IPtables firewall, such as Web browsing, Telnet, and ping. Other services, such as IRC and FTP, require the use of certain modules. Any services you want local systems to access must also be on the firewall system because request and response actually are handled by services on that system.

With IP masquerading, as implemented on Linux systems, the machine with the Internet address is also the firewall and gateway for the LAN of machines that use the firewall's Internet address to connect to the Internet. Firewalls that also implement IP masquerading are sometimes referred to as MASQ gates. With IP masquerading, the Internet-connected system (the firewall) listens for Internet requests from hosts on its LAN. When it receives one, it replaces the requesting local host's IP address with the Internet IP address of the firewall and then passes the request out to the Internet, as if the request were its own. Replies from the Internet are then sent to the firewall system. The replies the firewall receives are addressed to the firewall using its Internet address. The firewall then determines the local system to whose request the reply is responding. It then strips off its IP address and sends the response on to the local host across the LAN. The connection is transparent from the perspective of the local machines. They appear to be connected directly to the Internet.

Masquerading Local Networks

IP masquerading is often used to allow machines on a private network to access the Internet. These could be machines in a home network or a small LAN, such as for a small business. Such a network might have only one machine with Internet access, and as such, only the one Internet address. The local private network would have IP addresses chosen from the private network allocations (10., 172.16., or 192.168.). Ideally, the firewall has two Ethernet cards: one for an interface to the LAN (for example, **eth1**) and one for an interface to the Internet, such as **eth0**. The card for the Internet connection (**eth0**) would be assigned the Internet IP address. The Ethernet interface for the local network (**eth1**, in this example) is the firewall Ethernet interface. Your private LAN would have a network address like 192.168.0. Its Ethernet firewall interface (**eth1**) would be assigned the IP address 192.168.0.1. In effect, the firewall interface lets the firewall operate as the local network's gateway. The firewall is then configured to masquerade any packets coming from the private network. Your LAN needs to have its own domain name server, identifying the machines on your network, including your firewall. Each local machine needs to have the firewall specified as its gateway. Use separate interfaces for them, such as two Ethernet cards.

Masquerading NAT Rules

In Netfilter, IP masquerading is a NAT operation and is not integrated with packet filtering as in IP Chains. IP masquerading commands are placed on the NAT table and treated separately from the packet-filtering commands. Use IPtables to place a masquerade rule on the NAT table. First, reference the NAT table with the **-t nat** option. Then add a rule to the POSTROUTING chain with the **-o** option specifying the output device and the **-j** option with the MASQUERADE command.

```
iptables -t nat -A POSTROUTING -o eth0 -j MASQUERADE
```

IP Forwarding

The next step is to turn on IP forwarding, either manually or by setting the **net.ipv4.ip_forward** variable in the **/etc/sysctl.conf** file and running **sysctl** with the **-p** option. IP forwarding will be turned off by default. For IPv6, use **net.ipv6.conf.all.forwarding**. The **/etc/sysctl.conf** entries are shown here.

```
net.ipv4.ip_forward = 1
net.ipv6.conf.all.forwarding = 1
```

You then run **sysctl** with the **-p** option.

```
sysctl -p
```

You can directly change the respective forwarding files with an **echo** command as shown here.

```
echo 1 > /proc/sys/net/ipv4/ip_forward
```

For IPv6, you would use the forwarding file in the corresponding **/proc/sys/net/ipv6** directory, **conf/all/forwarding**.

```
echo 1 > /proc/sys/net/ipv6/conf/all/forwarding
```

Masquerading Selected Hosts

Instead of masquerading all local hosts as the single IP address of the firewall/gateway host, you could use the NAT table to rewrite addresses for a few selected hosts. Such an approach is often applied to setups where you want several local hosts to appear as Internet servers. Using the DNAT and SNAT targets, you can direct packets to specific local hosts. You would use rules on the PREROUTING and POSTROUTING chains to direct input and output packets.

For example, the Web server described in the previous example could have been configured as a local host to which a DNAT target could redirect any packets originally received for 10.0.0.2. Say the Web server was set up on 192.168.0.5. It could appear as having the address 10.0.0.2 on the Internet. Packets sent to 10.0.0.2 would be rewritten and directed to 192.168.0.5 by the NAT table. You would use the PREROUTING chain with the **-d** option to handle incoming packets and POSTROUTING with the **-s** option for outgoing packets.

```
iptables -t nat -A PREROUTING -d 10.0.0.2 -p tcp 80 -j DNAT --to-destination
192.168.0.5
iptables -t nat -A POSTROUTING -s 192.168.0.5 -p tcp  -j DNAT --to-source
10.0.0.2
```

Tip: Masquerading is not combined with the FORWARD chain. If you specify a DROP policy for the FORWARD chain, you will also have to specifically enable FORWARD operation for the network that is being masqueraded. You will need both a POSTROUTING rule and a FORWARD rule.

ubuntu

18. Administering TCP/IP Networks

TCP/IP Protocol Suite

IPv4 and IPv6

TCP/IP Network Addresses

IPv6 Addressing

IPv6 and IPv4 Coexistence Methods

TCP/IP Configuration Files

Domain Name Service (DNS)

Network Interfaces and Routes: ifconfig and route

Monitoring Your Network

Wireshark

Network Tools

Linux systems are configured to connect with networks that use the TCP/IP protocols. These are the same protocols used by the Internet and many local area networks (LANs). TCP/IP is a robust set of protocols designed to provide communications among systems with different operating systems and hardware. The TCP/IP protocols were developed in the 1970s as a special project of the Defense Advanced Research Projects Agency (DARPA) to enhance communications between universities and research centers. These protocols were originally developed on UNIX systems, with much of the research carried out at the University of California, Berkeley.

Linux, as a version of UNIX, benefits from much of this original focus on UNIX. Currently, the TCP/IP protocol development is managed by the Internet Engineering Task Force (IETF), which, in turn, is supervised by the Internet Society (ISOC). The ISOC oversees several groups responsible for different areas of Internet development, such as the Internet Assigned Numbers Authority (IANA), which is responsible for Internet addressing (see Table 18-1). Over the years, TCP/IP protocol standards and documentation have been issued in the form of Request for Comments (RFC) documents. Check the most recent RFCs for current developments at the IETF website at **https://www.ietf.org/**.

TCP/IP Protocol Suite

The TCP/IP protocol suite consists of several different protocols, each designed for a specific task in a TCP/IP network. The three basic protocols are the Transmission Control Protocol (TCP), which handles receiving and sending out communications, the Internet Protocol (IP), which handles the actual transmissions, and the User Datagram Protocol (UDP), which also handles receiving and sending packets. The Internet Protocol (IP), which is the base protocol that all others use, handles the actual transmissions, handling the packets of data with sender and receiver information in each. The TCP protocol is designed to work with cohesive messages or data. This protocol checks received packets and sorts them into their designated order, forming the original message. For data sent out, the TCP protocol breaks the data into separate packets, designating their order. The UDP protocol, meant to work on a lower level, also breaks down data into packets but does not check their order. The TCP/IP protocol is designed to provide stable and reliable connections that ensure that all data is received and reorganized into its original order. UDP, on the other hand, is designed simply to send as much data as possible, with no guarantee that packets will all be received or placed in the proper order. UDP is often used for transmitting large amounts of data of the type that can survive the loss of a few packets, for example, temporary images, video, and banners displayed on the Internet.

Other protocols provide various network and user services. The Domain Name Service (DNS) provides address resolution, the File Transfer Protocol (FTP) provides file transmission, and the Network File System (NFS) provides access to remote file systems. Table 18-2 lists the protocols in the TCP/IP suite. These protocols make use of either TCP or UDP to send and receive packets, which in turn uses the IP protocol for transmitting the packets.

In a TCP/IP network, messages are broken into small components, called datagrams, which are then transmitted through various interlocking routes and delivered to their destination computers. Once received, the datagrams are reassembled into the original message. Datagrams themselves can be broken down into smaller packets. The packet is the physical message unit actually transmitted among networks. Sending messages as small components has proven to be far more reliable and faster than sending them as one large transmission. With small components, if one is lost or damaged, only that component must be re-sent, whereas if any part of a large transmission is corrupted or lost, the entire message has to be re-sent.

Group	Title	Description
ISOC	Internet Society	Professional membership organization of Internet experts that oversees boards and task forces dealing with network policy issues **www.isoc.org**
IESG	The Internet Engineering Steering Group	Responsible for technical management of IETF activities and the Internet standards process **www.ietf.org/iesg.html**
IANA	Internet Assigned Numbers Authority	Responsible for Internet Protocol (IP) addresses **www.iana.org**
IAB	Internet Architecture Board	Defines the overall architecture of the Internet, providing guidance and broad direction to the IETF **www.iab.org**
IETF	Internet Engineering Task Force	Protocol engineering and development arm of the Internet **www.ietf.org**

Table 18-1: TCP/IP Protocol Development Groups

The configuration of a TCP/IP network on your Linux system is implemented using a set of network configuration files (see Table 18-6). Many of these files can be managed using network tools on your desktop like NetworkManager. NetworkManager also has a command line interface command called **nmcli** that you can use to configure your network. You can also use more specialized programs, such as **netstat**, **ifconfig**, Wireshark, and **route**. Some configuration files are easy to modify yourself using a text editor. The **ifconfig** utility enables you to configure your network interfaces, adding new ones and modifying others. The **ifconfig** and **route** utilities are lower-level programs that require more specific knowledge of your network to use effectively. Most **ifconfig** and **route** operations can be implemented using **nmcli**. The **netstat** utility provides you with information about the status of your network connections. Wireshark is a network protocol analyzer that lets you capture packets as they are transmitted across your network, selecting those you want to check.

An alternative to NetworkManager is the systemd based network manager called **systemd-networkd**. It is currently used for basic operations. It is a small, fast, and simple alternative to the larger NetworkManager. **systemd-networkd** is the default network manager for Ubuntu server, whereas NetworkManager is still used for the Ubuntu desktop.

Zero Configuration Networking: Avahi and Link Local Addressing

Zero Configuration Networking (Zeroconf) allows the setup of non-routable private networks without the need of a DHCP server or static IP addresses. A Zeroconf configuration lets users automatically connect to a network and access all network resources, such as printers, without having to perform any configuration. On Linux, Zeroconf networking is implemented by Avahi (**http://avahi.org**), which includes multicast DNS (mDNS) and DNS service discovery (DNS-SD) support that automatically detects services on a network. IP addresses are determined using either

IPv6 or IPv4 Link Local (IPv4LL) addressing. IPv4 Link Local addresses are assigned from the 168.254.0.0 network pool. Derived from Apple's Bonjour Zeroconf implementation, it is a free and open source version currently used by desktop tools. Ubuntu implements full Zeroconf network support with the Avahi daemon that implements multicast DNS discover, and **avahi-autoipd** that provides dynamic configuration of local IPv4 addresses. Both are installed as part of the desktop configuration.

Avahi support tools like **avahi-browse** and **avahi-publish** are located in the **avahi-utils** package. Specialized tools like SSH and Shell tools are located in the **avahi-ui-tools** package. The KDE Zeroconf solution is also provided using Avahi (**kde-zeroconf**).

IPv4 and IPv6

Traditionally, a TCP/IP address is organized into four segments, consisting of numbers separated by periods. This is called the IP address. The IP address actually represents a 32-bit integer whose binary values identify the network and host. This form of IP addressing adheres to Internet Protocol, version 4, also known as IPv4. IPv4, the kind of IP addressing described here, is still in use.

Version 6 of the IP protocol, called IPv6, replaces the older IPv4 version. IPv6 expands the number of possible IP addresses by using 128 bits. It is fully compatible with systems still using IPv4. IPv6 addresses are represented differently, using a set of eight 16-bit segments, each separated from the next by a colon. Each segment is represented by a hexadecimal number. A sample address would be:

```
FC00:0:0:0:800:BA98:7654:3210
```

Advantages of IPv6 include the following:

IPv6 features simplified headers that allow for faster processing.

IPv6 provides support for encryption and authentication along with virtual private networks (VPN), using the integrated IPsec protocol.

One of its most significant advantages lies in extending the address space to cover 2 to the power of 128 possible hosts (billions of billions). This extends far beyond the 4.2 billion supported by IPv4.

IPv6 supports stateless autoconfiguration of addresses for hosts, bypassing the need for DHCP to configure such addresses. Addresses can be generated directly using the MAC (Media Access Control) hardware address of an interface.

IPv6 supports Quality of Service (QoS) operations, providing sufficient response times for services like multimedia and telecom tasks.

Multicast capabilities are built into the protocol, providing direct support for multimedia tasks. Multicast addressing also provides that same function as IPv4 broadcast addressing.

More robust transmissions can be ensured with anycast addressing, where packets can be directed to an anycast group of systems, only one of which needs to receive them.

IPv6 provides better access for mobile nodes, like PDAs, notebooks, and cell phones.

Transport	Description
TCP	Transmission Control Protocol; places systems in direct communication
UDP	User Datagram Protocol
IP	Internet Protocol; transmits data
ICMP	Internet Control Message Protocol; status messages for IP
Routing	**Description**
RIP	Routing Information Protocol; determines routing
OSPF	Open Shortest Path First; determines routing
Network Addresses	**Description**
ARP	Address Resolution Protocol; determines unique IP address of systems
DNS	Domain Name Service; translates hostnames into IP addresses
RARP	Reverse Address Resolution Protocol; determines addresses of systems
User Service	**Description**
FTP	File Transfer Protocol; transmits files from one system to another using TCP
TFTP	Trivial File Transfer Protocol; transfers files using UDP
Telnet	Remote login to another system on the network
SMTP	Simple Mail Transfer Protocol; transfers e-mail between systems
RPC	Remote Procedure Call; allows remote systems to communicate
Gateway	**Description**
EGP	Exterior Gateway Protocol; provides routing for external networks
GGP	Gateway-to-Gateway Protocol; provides routing between gateways
IGP	Interior Gateway Protocol; provides routing for internal networks
Network Service	**Description**
NFS	Network File System; allows mounting of file systems on remote machines
NIS	Network Information Service; maintains user accounts across a network
BOOTP	Boot Protocol; starts system using boot information on server for network
SNMP	Simple Network Management Protocol; provides status messages on TCP/IP configuration
DHCP	Dynamic Host Configuration Protocol; automatically provides network configuration information to host systems

Table 18-2: TCP/IP Protocol Suite

TCP/IP Network Addresses

The traditional IPv4 TCP/IP address is organized into four segments, consisting of numbers separated by periods. Part of an IP address is used for the network address, and the other part is used to identify a particular interface on a host in that network. Keep in mind that IP addresses are assigned to interfaces, such as Ethernet cards or modems, and not to the host computer. Usually, a computer has only one interface and is accessed using only that interface's IP address. In that way, an IP address can be thought of as identifying a particular host system on a network, so the IP address is usually referred to as the host address.

Often, a host system could have several interfaces, each with its own IP address. This is the case for computers that operate as gateways and firewalls from a local network to the Internet. One interface usually connects to a local network and another to the Internet using two Ethernet cards. Each interface (such as an Ethernet card) has its own IP address. Other Ethernet cards have their own IP addresses. If you use a modem to connect to an ISP, you would set up a Point-to-Point Protocol (PPP) interface that would also have its own IP address (usually dynamically assigned by the ISP).

IPv4 Network Addresses

The IP address is divided into two parts: one part identifies the network, and the other part identifies a particular host. The network address identifies the network of which a particular interface on a host is a part. Two methods exist for implementing the network and host parts of an IP address: the original class-based IP addressing and the current Classless Interdomain Routing (CIDR) addressing. Class-based IP addressing designates officially predetermined parts of the address for the network and host addresses, whereas CIDR addressing allows the parts to be determined dynamically using a netmask.

Class-Based IP Addressing

Originally, IP addresses were organized according to classes. On the Internet, IPv4 networks are organized into three classes depending on their size, classes A, B, and C. A class A network uses only the first segment for the network address and the remaining three for the host, allowing a great many computers to be connected to the same network. Most IP addresses reference smaller, class C, networks. For a class C network, the first three segments are used to identify the network, and only the last segment identifies the host. Altogether, this forms a unique address with which to identify any network interface on computers in a TCP/IP network. For example, in the IP address 192.168.1.72, the network part is 192.168.1 and the interface/host part is 72. The interface/host is a part of a network whose own address is 192.168.1.0.

In a class C network, the first three numbers identify the network part of the IP address. This part is divided into three network numbers, each identifying a subnet. Networks on the Internet are organized into subnets, beginning with the largest and narrowing to small subnetworks. The last number is used to identify a particular computer, referred to as a host. You can think of the Internet as a series of networks with subnetworks. These subnetworks have their own subnetworks. The right-most number identifies the host computer, and the number preceding it identifies the subnetwork of which the computer is a part. The number to the left of that identifies the network the subnetwork is part of, and so on. The Internet address 192.168.187.4 references the fourth computer connected to the network identified by the number 187. Network 187 is a subnet to a larger network identified as 168. This larger network is itself a subnet of the network identified as 192.

192.168.187.4	IPv4 address
192.168.187	Network identification
4	Host identification

Netmask

Systems derive the network address from the host address using the netmask. You can think of an IP address as a series of 32 binary bits, some of which are used for the network and the remainder for the host. The netmask has the network set of bits set to 1s, with the host bits set to 0s (see Figure 18-1). In a standard class-based IP address, all the numbers in the network part of your host address are set to 255, and the host part is set to 0. This has the effect of setting all the binary bits making up the network address to 1s. This, then, is your netmask. So, the netmask for the host address 192.168.1.72 is 255.255.255.0. The network part, 192.168.1, has been set to 255.255.255, and the host part, 72, has been set to 0. Systems can then use your netmask to derive your network address from your host address. They can determine what part of your host address makes up your network address and what those numbers are.

For those familiar with computer programming, a bitwise AND operation on the netmask and the host address results in zeroing the host part, leaving you with the network part of the host address. You can think of the address as being implemented as a four-byte integer, with each byte corresponding to a segment of the address. In a class C address, the three network segments correspond to the first three bytes, and the host segment corresponds to the fourth byte. A netmask is designed to mask out the host part of the address, leaving the network segments alone. In the netmask for a standard class C network, the first three bytes are all 1s and the last byte consists of 0s. The 0s in the last byte mask out the host part of the address and the 1s in the first three bytes leave the network part of the address alone. Figure 18-1 shows the bitwise operation of the netmask on the address 192.168.1.4. This is a class C address to the mask, which consists of twenty-four 1s making up the first three bytes and eight 0s making up the last byte. When it is applied to the address 192.168.1.4, the network address remains (192.168.1) and the host address is masked out (4), giving you 192.168.1.0 as the network address.

The netmask as used in Classless Interdomain Routing (CIDR) is much more flexible. Instead of having the size of the network address and its mask determined by the network class, it is determined by a number attached to the end of the IP address. This number simply specifies the size of the network address, how many bits in the address it takes up. For example, in an IP address whose network part takes up the first three bytes (segments), the number of bits used for that network part is 24, eight bits to a byte (segment). Instead of using a netmask to determine the network address, the number for the network size is attached to the end of the address with a slash, as shown here.

```
192.168.1.72/24
```

CIDR gives you the advantage of specifying networks that are any size bits, instead of only three possible segments. You could have a network whose addresses take up 14 bits, 22 bits, or even 25 bits. The host address can use whatever bits are left over. An IP address with 21 bits for the network can cover host addresses using the remaining 11 bits, 0 to 2,047.

Classless Interdomain Routing (CIDR)

The class-based organization of IP addresses is being replaced by the CIDR format. CIDR was designed for midsized networks, those between a class C, and classes with numbers of hosts greater than 256 and smaller than 65,534. A class C network–based IP address uses only one segment, an 8-bit integer, with a maximum value of 256. A class B network based IP address uses two segments, which make up a 16-bit integer, whose maximum value is 65,534. You can think of an address as a 32-bit integer taking up four bytes, where each byte is 8 bits. Each segment conforms to one of the four bytes. A class C network uses three segments, or 24 bits, to make up its network address. A class B network, in turn, uses two segments, or 16 bits, for its address. With this scheme, allowable host and network addresses are changed an entire byte at a time, segment to segment. With CIDR addressing, you can define host and network addresses by bits, instead of whole segments. For example, you can use CIDR addressing to expand the host segment from 8 bits to 9, rather than having to jump it to a class B 16 bits (two segments).

Class-based Addressing

IP Address   192.168.1.4

	Network			Host
binary	11000000	10101000	00000001	00000100
numeric	192	168	1	4

Netmask   255.255.255.0

binary	11111111	11111111	11111111	00000000
numeric	255	255	255	000

Network Address   192.168.1.0

binary	11000000	10101000	00000001	00000000
numeric	192	168	1	0

Netmask Operation

IP Address	11000000	10101000	00000001	00000100
Netmask	11111111	11111111	11111111	00000000
Net Address	11000000	10101000	00000001	00000000

Figure 18-1: Class-based netmask operations

CIDR addressing notation achieves this by incorporating netmask information in the IP address (the netmask is applied to an IP address to determine the network part of the address). In the CIDR notation, the number of bits making up the network address is placed after the IP address, following a slash. For example, the CIDR form of the class C 192.168.187.4 IP address is:

```
192.168.187.4/24
```

Figure 18-2 shows an example of a CIDR address and its network mask. The IP address is 192.168.1.6 with a network mask of 22 bits, 192.168.1.6/22. The network address takes up the first 22 bits of the IP address, and the remaining 10 bits are used for the host address. The host address is taking up the equivalent of a class-based IP address's fourth segment (8 bits) and 2 bits from the third segment.

Table 18-3 lists the different IPv4 CIDR network masks available along with the maximum number of hosts. Both the short forms and the full forms of the netmasks are listed.

CIDR Addressing

IP Address   192.168.4.6/22

		Network		Host
binary	11000000	10101000	000001 00	00000110
numeric	192	168	4	6

Netmask 255.255.252.0   22 bits

binary	11111111	11111111	111111 00	00000000
numeric	255	255	252	000

Figure 18-2: CIDR addressing

IPv4 CIDR Addressing

The network address for any standard class C IPv4 IP address takes up the first three segments, 24 bits. If you want to create a network with a maximum of 512 hosts, you can give them IP addresses where the network address is 23 bits and the host address takes up 9 bits (0–511). The IP address notation remains the same, using the four 8-bit segments. This means a given segment's number could be used for both a network address and a host address. Segments are no longer wholly part of either the host address or the network address. Assigning a 23-bit network address and a 9-bit host address means that the number in the third segment is part of the network address and the host address, the first 7 bits for the network and the last bit for the host. In this following example, the third number, 145, is used as the end of the network address and as the beginning of the host address.

```
192.168.145.67/23
```

This situation complicates CIDR addressing, and in some cases, the only way to represent the address is to specify two or more network addresses. Check RFC 1520 at **https://www.ietf.org/** for more details.

CIDR also allows a network administrator to take what is officially the host part of an IP address, and break it up into subnetworks with fewer hosts. This is referred to as subnetting. A given network will have its official IP network address recognized on the Internet or by a larger network. The network administrator for that network could, in turn, create several smaller networks within it using CIDR network masking. A classic example is to take a standard class C network with 254 hosts and break it up into two smaller networks, each with 64 hosts. You do this by using a CIDR netmask to take a bit from the host part of the IP address and use it for the subnetworks. Numbers within the range of the original 254 addresses whose first bit would be set to 1 would represent one subnet, and the others, whose first bit would be set to 0, would constitute the remaining network. In the network whose network address is 192.168.187.0, where the last segment is used for the hostnames, that last host segment could be further split into two subnets, each with its own hosts. For two subnets, you would use the first bit in the last 8-bit segment for the network. The remaining 7 bits could then be used for host addresses, giving you a range of 127 hosts per network. The subnet whose bit is set to 0 would have a range of 1 to 127, with a CIDR netmask of 25. The 8-bit segment for the first host would be 00000001. So, the host with the address of 1 in that network would have this IP address.

```
192.168.187.1/25
```

For the subnet where the first bit is 1, the first host would have an address of 129, with the CIDR netmask of 25, as shown here. The 8-bit sequence for the first host would be 10000001.

```
192.168.187.129/25
```

Note: A simple way to calculate the number of hosts a network can address is to take the number of bits in its host segment as a power of 2, and then subtract 2, that is, 2 to the number of host bits, minus 2. For example, an 8-bit host segment would be 2 to the power of 8, which equals 256. Subtract 2 (1 for the broadcast address, 255, and 1 for the zero value, 000) to leave you with 254 possible hosts.

Each subnet would have a set of 126 addresses, the first from 1 to 126, and the second from 129 to 254. 127 is the broadcast address for the first subnet, and 128 is the network address for the second subnet. The possible subnets and their masks that you could use are shown here.

Subnetwork	CIDR Address	Binary Mask
First subnet network address	.0/25	00000000
Second subnet network address	.128/25	10000000
First subnet broadcast address	.127/25	01111111
Second subnet broadcast address	.255/25	11111111
First address in first subnet	.1/25	00000001
First address in second subnet	.129/25	10000001
Last address in first subnet	.126/25	01111110
Last address in second subnet	.254/25	11111110

IPv6 CIDR Addressing

IPv6 CIDR addressing works much the same as with the IPv4 method. The number of bits used for the network information is indicated by the number following the address. A host (interface) address could take up much more than the 64 bits that it usually does in an IPv6 address, making the network prefix (address) section smaller than 64 bits. How many bits that the network prefix uses is indicated by the following number. In the next example, the network prefix (address) uses only the first 48 bits of the IPv6 address, and the host address uses the remaining 80 bits.

```
FC00:0000:0000:0000:FEDC:BA98:7654:3210/48
```

You can also use a two-colon notation (::) for the compressed version.

```
FC00::FEDC:BA98:7654:3210/48
```

Though you can use CIDR to subnet addresses, IPv6 also supports a subnet field that can be used for subnets.

Obtaining an IP Address

IP addresses are officially allocated by IANA, which manages all aspects of Internet addressing (**https://www.iana.org/**). IANA oversees Internet Registries, which, in turn, maintain Internet addresses on regional and local levels. The Internet Registry for the Americas is the American Registry for Internet Numbers (ARIN), whose website is at **https://www.arin.net**. These addresses are provided to users by Internet service providers (ISPs). You can obtain your own Internet address from an ISP, or if you are on a network already connected to the Internet, your network administrator can assign you one. If you are using an ISP, the ISP may temporarily assign one from a pool it has on hand with each use.

Short Form	Full Form	Maximum Number of Hosts
/8	/255.0.0.0	16,777,215 (A class)
/16	/255.255.0.0	65,535 (B class)
/17	/255.255.128.0	32,767
/18	/255.255.192.0	16,383
/19	/255.255.224.0	8,191
/20	/255.255.240.0	4,095
/21	/255.255.248.0	2,047
/22	/255.255.252.0	1,023
/23	/255.255.254.0	511
/24	/255.255.255.0	255 (C class)
/25	/255.255.255.128	127
/26	/255.255.255.192	63
/27	/255.255.255.224	31
/28	/255.255.255.240	15
/29	/255.255.255.248	7
/30	/255.255.255.252	3

Table 18-3: CIDR IPv4 Network Masks

IPv4 Reserved Addresses

Certain numbers are reserved. The numbers 127, 0, and 255 cannot be part of an official IP address. The number 127 is used to designate the network address for the loopback interface on your system. The loopback interface enables users on your system to communicate with each other, within the system, without having to route through a network connection. Its network address would be 127.0.0.0, and its IP address is 127.0.0.1. For class-based IP addressing, the number 255 is a special broadcast identifier you can use to broadcast messages to all sites on a network. Using 255 for any part of the IP address references all nodes connected at that level. For example, 192.168.255.255 broadcasts a message to all computers on network 192.168, all its subnetworks, and their hosts. The address 192.168.187.255 broadcasts to every computer on the local network. If you use 0 for the network part of the address, the host number references a computer within your local network. For example, 0.0.0.6 references the sixth computer in your local network. If you want to broadcast to all computers on your local network, you can use the number 0.0.0.255. For CIDR IP addressing, the broadcast address may appear much like a normal IP address. As indicated in the preceding section, CIDR addressing allows the use of any number of bits to make up the IP address for either the network or the host part. For a broadcast address, the host part must have all its bits set to 1 (see Figure 18-3).

A special set of numbers is reserved for use on non-Internet Local Area Networks (LANs) (see RFC 1918). These are numbers that begin with the special network number 192.168 (for class C networks), as used in these examples. If you are setting up a LAN, such as a small business or a home network, you are free to use these numbers for your local machines. You can set up an intranet using network cards, such as Ethernet cards and Ethernet hubs, and then configure your machines with IP addresses starting from 192.168.0.1. The host segment can go up to 256. If you have three machines on your home network, you could give them the addresses 192.168.0.1, 192.168.0.2, and 192.168.0.3. You can implement Internet services, such as FTP, Web, and mail services, on your local machines and use any of the Internet tools to make use of those services. They all use the same TCP/IP protocols used on the Internet. For example, with FTP tools, you can transfer files among the machines on your network. With mail tools, you can send messages from one machine to another, and with a Web browser, you can access local websites that may be installed on a machine running its own Web servers. If you want to have one of your machines connected to the Internet or some other network, you can set it up to be a gateway machine. By convention, the gateway machine is usually given the address 192.168.0.1. With IP masquerading, you can have any of the non-Internet machines use a gateway to connect to the Internet.

IPv4 Private Network Addresses	Network Classes
10.0.0.0	Class A network
172.16.0.0–172.31.255.255	Class B network
192.168.0.0	Class C network
127.0.0.0	Loopback network (for system self-communication)

Table 18-4: Non-Internet IPv4 Local Network IP Addresses

Numbers are also reserved for class A and class B non-Internet local networks. Table 18-4 lists these addresses. The possible addresses available span from 0 to 255 in the host segment of the address. For example, class B network addresses range from 172.16.0.0 to 172.31.255.255, providing you a total of 32,356 possible hosts. The class C network ranges from 192.168.0.0 to 192.168.255.255, providing you 256 possible subnetworks, each with 256 possible hosts. The network address 127.0.0.0 is reserved for a system's loopback interface, which allows it to communicate with itself, enabling users on the same system to send messages to each other.

Broadcast Addresses

The broadcast address allows a system to send the same message to all systems on your network at once. With IPv4 class-based IP addressing, you can easily determine the broadcast address using your host address: the broadcast address has the host part of your address set to 255. The network part remains untouched. So the broadcast address for the host address 192.168.1.72 is

192.168.1.255 (you combine the network part of the address with 255 in the host part). For CIDR IP addressing, you need to know the number of bits in the netmask. The remaining bits are set to 1 (see Figure 18-3). For example, an IP address of 192.168.4.6/22 has a broadcast address of 192.168.7.255/22. In this case, the first 22 bits are the network address and the last 10 bits are the host part set to the broadcast value (all 1s).

Class-based Broadcast Addressing

Broadcast Address 192.168.1.255

| binary | 11000000 | 10101000 | 00000001 | 11111111 |
| numeric | 192 | 168 | 1 | 255 |

CIDR Broadcast Addressing

Broadcast Address 192.168.7.255/22

		Network		Host
binary	11000000	10101000	000001	11 11111111
numeric	192	168	7	255

Figure 18-3: Class-based and CIDR broadcast addressing

You can think of a class C broadcast address as a CIDR address using 24 bits (the first three segments) for the network address, and the last 8 bits (the fourth segment) as the broadcast address. The value 255 expressed in binary terms is simply 8 bits that are all 1s. 255 is the same as 11111111.

IP Address	Broadcast Address	IP Broadcast Number	Binary Equivalent
192.168.1.72	192.168.1.255	255	11111111
192.168.4.6/22	192.168.7.255/22	7.255 (last 2 bits in 7)	1111111111

Gateway Addresses

Some networks have a computer designated as the gateway to other networks. All connections to and from a network to other networks pass through this gateway computer. Most local networks use gateways to establish a connection to the Internet. If you are on this type of network, you must provide the gateway address. If your network does not have a connection to the Internet or a larger network, you may not need a gateway address. The gateway address is the address of the host system providing the gateway service to the network. On many networks, this host is given a host ID of 1, so the gateway address for a network with the address 192.168.0 would be 192.168.0.1, but this is only a convention. To be sure of your gateway address, ask your network administrator.

Name Server Addresses

Many networks, including the Internet, have computers that provide a Domain Name Service (DNS) that translates the domain names of networks and hosts into IP addresses. These are known as the network's domain name servers. DNS makes your computer identifiable on a network, using your domain name, rather than your IP address. You can also use the domain names of other systems to reference them, so you do not have to know their IP addresses. You must know the IP addresses of any domain name servers for your network, however. You can obtain the addresses from your system administrator (often more than one address exists). Even if you are using an ISP, you must know the address of the domain name servers your ISP operates for the Internet.

IPv6 Addressing

IPv6 addressing introduces major changes to the format and method of addressing systems under the Internet Protocol (see RFC 3513 at **https://www.ietf.org/rfc/** or **www.faqs.org** for more details). There are several different kinds of addressing with different fields for the network segment. The host segment has been expanded to a 64-bit address, allowing direct addressing for a far larger number of systems. Each address begins with a type field specifying the kind of address, which will then determine how its network segment is organized. These changes are designed, not only to expand the address space but to also provide greater control over transmissions at the address level.

Note: Ubuntu is distributed with IPv6 support already enabled in the kernel. Kernel support for IPv6 is provided by the IPv6 kernel module.

IPv6 Address Format

An IPv6 address consists of 128 bits, up from the 32 bits used in IPv4 addresses. The first 64 bits are used for network addressing, of which the first few bits are reserved for indicating the address type. The last 64 bits are used for the interface address, known as the interface identifier field. The amount of bits used for subnetting can be adjusted with a CIDR mask, much like that in IPv4 CIDR addressing (see the preceding section).

An IPv6 address is written as eight segments representing 16 bits each (128 bits total). To represent 16-bit binary numbers more easily, hexadecimal numbers are used. Hexadecimal numbers use 16 unique numbers, instead of the 8 used in octal numbering. These are 0–9, continuing with the characters A–F.

In the next example, the first four segments represent the network part of the IPv6 address, and the following four segments represent the interface (host) address.

```
FC00:0000:0000:0000:0008:0800:200C:417A
```

You can cut any preceding zeros, but not trailing zeros, in any given segment. Segments with all zeros can be reduced to a single zero.

```
FC00:0:0:0:8:800:200C:417A
```

The loopback address used for localhost addressing can be written with seven preceding zeros and a 1.

```
0:0:0:0:0:0:0:1
```

Many addresses will have sequences of zeros. IPv6 supports a shorthand symbol for representing a sequence of several zeros in adjacent fields. This consists of a double colon (::). There can be only one use of the :: symbol per address.

```
FC00::8:800:200C:417A
```

The loopback address 0000000000000001 can be reduced to just the following.

```
::1
```

To ease the transition from IPv4 addressing to IPv6, a form of addressing incorporating IPv4 addresses is also supported. In this case, the IPv4 address (32 bits) can be used to represent the last two segments of an IPv6 address and can be written using IPv4 notation.

```
FC00::192.168.0.3
```

IPv6 Interface Identifiers

The identifier part of the IPv6 address takes up the second 64 bits, consisting of four segments containing four hexadecimal numbers. The interface ID is a 64-bit (four-segment) Extended Unique Identifier (EUI-64) generated from a network device's Media Access Control (MAC) address.

IPv6 Address types

There are three basic kinds of IPv6 addresses: unicast, multicast, and anycast.

A *unicast* address is used for a packet that is sent to a single destination.

An *anycast* address is used for a packet that can be sent to more than one destination.

A *multicast* address is used to broadcast a packet to a range of destinations.

IPv6 Addresses Format Prefixes and Reserved Addresses	Description
3	Unicast global addresses
FE8	Unicast link-local addresses, used for physically connected hosts on a network, used for DHCP equivalents.
FC00	Unicast unique-local addresses, comparable to IPv4 private addresses.
0000000000000001	Unicast loopback address (for system self-communication, localhost)
0000000000000000	Unspecified address
FF	Multicast addresses

Table 18-5: IPv6 Format Prefixes and Reserved Addresses

In IPv6, addressing is controlled by the format prefix that operates as a kind of address type. The format prefix is the first field of the IP address. The three major kinds of unicast network addresses are global, link-local, and unique-local. Global, unique-local, and link-local are indicated by their own format prefix (see Table 18-5).

Global addresses begin with the address type 3, unique-local with FE00, and link-local with FE8. Global addresses can be sent across the Internet.

Link-local addresses are used for physically connected systems on a local network. It is often used for DHCP addresses.

Unique-local can be used for any hosts on a local network. Unique-local addresses operate like IPv4 private addresses. They are used only for local access and cannot be used to transmit over the Internet.

In addition, IPv6 has two special reserved addresses. The address 0000000000000001 is reserved for the loopback address used for a system's localhost address, and the address 0000000000000000 is the unspecified address.

IPv6 Unicast Global Addresses

IPv6 global addresses currently use four fields: the format prefix, a global routing prefix, the subnet identifier, and the interface identifier. The format prefix for a unicast global address is 3 (3 bits). The global routing prefix references the network address (45 bits), and the subnet ID references a subnet within the site (16 bits).

IPv6 Unicast Local Use Addresses: Link-Local and Unique-Local Addresses

For local use, IPv6 provides both link-local and unique-local addresses. Link-local addressing is used for interfaces (hosts) that are physically connected to a network. This is usually a small local network. A link-local address uses only three fields, the format prefix **FE8** (10 bits), an empty field (54 bits), and the interface identifier (host address) (64 bits). In effect, the network section is empty.

IPv6 unique-local addresses have three fields: the format prefix (10 bits), the subnet identifier (54 bits), and the interface identifier (64 bits). Except for any local subnetting, there is no network address. The unique local address has a format prefix of **FC00**. The unique-local addresses (also known as unique local addresses) fulfill the same function as private addresses in IPv4 (192.168.0).

IPv6 Multicast Addresses

Multicast addresses have a format prefix of FF (8 bits) with flag and scope fields to indicate whether the multicast group is permanent or temporary and whether it is local or global in scope. A group identifier (112 bits) references the multicast group. For the scope, 2 is link-local, 5 is unique-local, and E is global. In addition to their interface identifiers, hosts will also have a group ID that can be used as a broadcast address. You use this address to broadcast to the hosts. The following example will broadcast only to those hosts on the local network (5) with the group ID 101.

```
FF05:0:0:0:0:0:0:101
```

To broadcast to all the hosts in a link-local scope, you would use the broadcast address.

```
FF02:0:0:0:0:0:0:1
```

For a unique-local scope, a local network, you would use.

```
FF05:0:0:0:0:0:0:2
```

IPv6 and IPv4 Coexistence Methods

In the transition from IPv4 to IPv6, many networks will find the need to support both. Some will be connected to networks that use the contrary protocol, and others will connect through other network connections that use that protocol. There are several official IETF methods for providing IPv6 and IPv4 cooperation, which fall into three main categories:

Dual-stack   Allows IPv4 and IPv6 to coexist on the same networks.

Translation   Enables IPv6 devices to communicate with IPv4 devices.

Tunneling   Allows transmission from one IPv6 network to another through IPv4 networks as well as allowing IPv6 hosts to operate on or through IPv4 networks.

In the dual-stack methods, both IPv6 and IPv4 addresses are supported on the network. Applications and DNS servers can use either to transmit data.

Translation uses NAT tables to translate IPv6 addresses to corresponding IPv4 address and vice versa, as needed. IPv4 applications can then freely interact with IPv6 applications. IPv6-to-IPv6 transmissions are passed directly through, enabling full IPv6 functionality.

Tunneling is used when one IPv6 network needs to transmit to another through an IPv4 network that cannot handle IPv6 addresses. With tunneling, the IPv6 packet is encapsulated within an IPv4 packet, where the IPv4 network then uses the outer IPv4 addressing to pass on the packet. Several methods are used for tunneling, as shown here, as well as direct manual manipulation:

6-over-4   Used within a network to use IPv4 multicasting to implement a virtual LAN to support IPv6 hosts, without an IPv6 router (RFC 2529)

6-to-4   Used to allow IPv6 networks to connect to and through a larger IPv4 network (the Internet), using the IPv4 network address as an IPv6 network prefix (RFC 3056)

Tunnel brokers   Web-based services that create tunnels (RFC 3053)

TCP/IP Configuration Files

A set of configuration files in the **/etc** directory, shown in Table 18-6, are used to set up and manage your TCP/IP network. These configuration files specify such network information as host and domain names, IP addresses, and interface options. The IP addresses and domain names of other Internet hosts you want to access are entered in these files. If you configured your network during installation, you can already find that information in these files.

Identifying Hostnames: /etc/hosts

Without the unique IP address the TCP/IP network uses to identify computers, a particular computer cannot be located. Because IP addresses are difficult to use or remember, domain names are used instead. For each IP address, a domain name exists. When you use a domain name to reference a computer on the network, your system translates it into its associated IP address, which can then be used by your network to locate that computer.

Originally, every computer on the network was responsible for maintaining a list of the hostnames and their IP addresses. This list is still kept in the **/etc/hosts** file. When you use a domain name, your system looks up its IP address in the **hosts** file. The system administrator is responsible for maintaining this list. Because of the size of the Internet and the development of larger networks, the responsibility for associating domain names and IP addresses has been taken over by domain name servers. The **hosts** file is still used to hold the domain names and IP addresses of frequently accessed hosts. Your system normally checks your **hosts** file for the IP address of a domain name before taking the added step of accessing a domain name server.

Address	Description
Host address	IP address of your system; it has a network part to identify the network you are on and a host part to identify your own system
Network address	IP address of your network
Broadcast address	IP address for sending messages to all hosts on your network at once
Gateway address	IP address of your gateway system, if you have one (usually the network part of your host IP address with the host part set to 1)
Domain name server addresses	IP addresses of domain name servers your network use
Netmask	Used to determine the network and host parts of your IP address
File	**Description**
/etc/hosts	Associates hostnames with IP addresses, lists domain names for remote hosts with their IP addresses
/etc/network/interfaces	Network interfaces
/etc/network	Network connection startup scripts for services
/etc/host.conf	Lists resolver options
/etc/nsswitch.conf	Name Switch Service configuration (see Chapter 11)
/etc/resolv.conf	Lists domain name server names, IP addresses (nameserver), and domain names where remote hosts may be located (search)
/etc/protocols	Lists protocols available on your system
/etc/services	Lists available network services, such as FTP and Telnet, and the ports they use

Table 18-6: TCP/IP Configuration Addresses and Files

The format of a domain name entry in the **hosts** file is the IP address followed by the domain name, separated by a space. You can then add aliases for the hostname. After the entry, on the same line, you can enter a comment. A comment is always preceded by a # symbol. You can already find an entry in your **hosts** file for localhost with the IP address 127.0.0.1; **localhost** is a special identification used by your computer to enable users on your system to communicate locally with each other. The domain name for the local host is **localhost**. The IP address 127.0.0.1 is a special reserved address used by every computer for this purpose. It identifies what is technically referred to as a loopback device. The corresponding IPV6 localhost address is **::1**, which also has the domain name **localhost6** and the name **localhost6**. For compatibility, it is also given the names **localhost** as well as **ip6-localhost** and **ip6-loopback**. You should never remove the **localhost** and **ip6-localhost** or **ip6-loopback** entries. A sample **/etc/hosts** file is shown here.

/etc/hosts

```
192.168.0.1          turtle.mytrek.com
192.168.0.2          rabbit.mytrek.com
192.168.34.56        pango1.mytrain.com
127.0.0.1            localhost
::1                  turtle.mytrek.com localhost6
127.0.1.1            turtle.mytrek.com

# The following lines are desirable for IPv6 capable hosts
::1      localhost ip6-localhost ip6-loopback
fe00::0 ip6-localnet
ff00::0 ip6-mcastprefix
ff02::1 ip6-allnodes
ff02::2 ip6-allrouters
ff02::3 ip6-allhosts
```

/etc/resolv.conf

The **/etc/resolv.conf** file holds the IP addresses for your DNS servers along with domains to search. A DNS entry will begin with the term nameserver followed by the name server's IP address. A search entry will list network domain addresses. Check this file to see if your network DNS servers have been correctly listed. An example is shown here.

/etc/resolv.conf

```
nameserver  192.168.0.1
search  mytrek.com   mytrain.com
```

For DHCP connections, the **resolv.conf** file is a link to the **/run/resolvconf/resolv.conf** file, which holds the DNS server and search domains provided by the DHCP server.

/etc/netplan

The **/etc/netplan** directory holds network service and interface information for configuring your network device. The actual configuration file is generated when the system starts up and placed in the **/var/run** directory. There is no static configuration file in the **/etc** directory. Instead a simple netplan configuration file in the **/etc/netplan** directory is used to generate the network configuration file. The **/etc/netplan** files are written using YAML (YAML Ain't Markup Language) and have the extension **.yaml**. This method provides a level of abstraction that make configuration of different available network services much more flexible. The default network service is **networkd**, which is used for the Ubuntu server. But you could specify other services such as NetworkManager.

For the Ubuntu server, the run time file generated by netplan for network configuration will be located in **/var/run/systemd/network** and will have a name that includes "netplan" and the network device name, such as **10-netplan-enp7s0.network**.

Several examples of Netplan configuration files can be found at **/usr/share/doc/netplan/examples**. These include files such as those for static, vlan, bridge, bonding, wireless, and network-manager configurations.

/etc/network

The **/etc/network** directory holds the older network interface information used by **ifup** and **ifdown** to start up and shut down your networking. It, along with **ifup** and **ifdown,** have been replaced by **/etc/netplan** which used systemd directly. Some service such as BIND DNS, may still use the ifup and ifdown scripts. Within the directory are subdirectories for the **ifup** and **ifdown** operations, like **if-up.d** and **if-down.d**, which hold configuration scripts for certain network-related services, such as multicast DNS discover with Avahi, network time update, or remote file system mounting with NFS. The subdirectories included are **if-down.d, if-post-down.d, if-pre-up.d**, and **if-up.d**.

/etc/network/interfaces (ifupdown)

Ubuntu no longer uses the **ifupdown** software to manage network connections. Instead it uses Netplan. Should you still want to use **ifupdown**, you can install it. Should **ifpudown** be installed, the network interfaces will be defined in **/etc/network/interfaces** file, which usually holds only the configuration for the internal loopback interface. A standard Ubuntu version defines the loopback interface, the local network interface for your computer. The **auto** command will automatically activate the network interface when you boot up.

```
auto lo
iface lo inet loopback
```

The **/etc/network/interfaces** file holds manual network configuration settings, such as those you set with Network Manager. Automatic configurations are also managed by NetworkManager. NetworkManager will run any **if-up** and **if-down** scripts in the **/etc/network** subdirectories.

Should you need to configure your connection manually, you could enter configuration entries directly by editing the **/etc/network/interfaces** file. The **iface** command defines the interface. Its arguments are the interface name, the protocol it uses (**inet** for IPv4 and **inet6** for IPv6), and the connection type: **static**, **dhcp**, **ppp** (dial-up), or **bootp**. Each protocol and connection type can support different options. Check the interface's man page for details.

The following example sets up a static IP address for the first Ethernet device, **enp7s0**, using the IPv4 protocol. The address entry specifies the IP address, along with netmask and gateway for the IP addresses for those servers.

```
auto enp7s0
iface enp7s0 inet static
address 192.168.0.5
netmask 255.255.255.0
gateway 192.168.0.1
```

Should you be using a DHCP server to set up your address information, you would specify **dhcp**.

```
auto enp7s0
iface enp7s0 inet dhcp
```

/etc/services

The **/etc/services** file lists network services available on your system, such as FTP and Telnet, and associates each with a particular port. Here, you can find out what port your Web server is checking or what port is used for your FTP server. You can give a service an alias, which you specify after the port number. You can then reference the service using the alias.

/etc/protocols

The **/etc/protocols** file lists the TCP/IP protocols currently supported by your system. Each entry shows the protocol number, its keyword identifier, and a brief description. See **http://www.iana.org/assignments/protocol-numbers** for a complete listing.

/etc/hostname and hostnamectl

The **/etc/hostname** file contains your hostname. You can use the **hostnamectl** command to display your current hostname and all information pertaining to it such as the machine ID, the kernel used, the architecture, chassis (type of computer), and the operating system (you can add the **status** option if you want). Three different kinds of hostnames are supported: static, pretty, and transient. You can set each with the **hostnamectl**'s **set-hostname** command with the corresponding type. The static hostname is used to identify your computer on the network (usually a fully qualified hostname). You can use the **--static** option to set it. The pretty hostname is a descriptive hostname made available to users on the computer. This can be set by **set-hostname** with the **-- pretty** option. The transient hostname is one allocated by a network service such as DHCP, and can be managed with the **--transient** option. Without options, the **set-hostname** command will apply the name to all the hostname types.

```
hostnamectl set-hostname --pretty "my computer"
```

The **set-chassis** command sets the computer type, which can be desktop, laptop, server, tablet, handset, and vm (virtual system). Without a type specified it reverts to the default for the system. The **set-icon-name** sets the name used by the graphical applications for the host.

/etc/host.conf

Name servers are queried by resolvers. These are programs specially designed to obtain addresses from name servers. To use domain names on your system, a resolver must be set up. Your local resolver is configured with your **/etc/host.conf** and **/etc/resolv.conf** files.

Your **host.conf** file lists resolver options (shown in Table 18-7). Each option can have several fields, separated by spaces or tabs. You can use a # at the beginning of a line to enter a comment. The options tell the resolver what services to use. The order of the list is important. The resolver begins with the first option listed and moves on to the next in turn. You can find the **host.conf** file in your **/etc** directory, along with other configuration files.

Your **host.conf** file will be set up already with a standard configuration for accessing most DNS services. The default **host.conf** file is shown here. The **order** option instructs your resolver first to look up names in your local **/etc/hosts** file, and then, if that fails, to query domain name servers. The system does not have multiple addresses.

/etc/host.conf

```
# The "order" line is only used by old versions of the C library.
order hosts,bind
# multiple addresses
multi on
```

Option	Description
order	Specifies sequence of name resolution methods: **hosts** Checks for name in the local **/etc/host** file **bind** Queries a DNS name server for an address **nis** Uses Network Information Service protocol to obtain an address
alert	Checks addresses of remote sites attempting to access your system; you turn it on or off with the **on** and **off** options
nospoof	Confirms addresses of remote sites attempting to access your system
trim	Checks your local host's file; removes the domain name and checks only for the hostname; enables you to use only a hostname in your host file for an IP address
multi	Checks your local hosts file; allows a host to have several IP addresses; you turn it on or off with the **on** and **off** options

Table 18-7: Resolver Options, host.conf

Network Interfaces and Routes: ifconfig and route

Your connection to a network is made by your system through a particular hardware interface, such as an Ethernet card or a modem. Data passing through this interface is then routed to your network. The **ifconfig** command configures your network interfaces, and the **route** command sets up network connections accordingly. If you configure an interface with a network configuration tool like Network Manager, you needn't use **ifconfig** or **route**. You can also configure interfaces directly using **ifconfig** and **route**. Every time you start your system, the network interfaces and their routes must be established. This is done automatically for you by NetworkManager. Alternatively, you can run your own direct configuration with **ifconfig** and **route** commands.

Note: As an alternative to **ifconfig** and **route**, you can use **ip**. This is a tool provided by the **iproute** package. The syntax is much the same. Route commands use the **route** option, **ip route**. The **ifconfig** operations on addresses would use the **addr** option, **ip addr**.

Simple Network Startup: systemd-networkd.service

A simple network startup process is provided by the **systemd-networkd.service** file. This file will activate your network interface cards (NICs). You can manually shut down and start your network interface using this script and the **restart**, **start**, or **stop** options, as well as NetworkManager. You can run the script with the **ifconfig** command. The following commands shut down and then start up your network interface.

```
sudo systemctl stop systemd-networkd
sudo systemctl start systemd-networkd
```

      If you are changing network configuration, you will have to restart your network interface for the changes to take effect:

```
sudo systemctl restart systemd-networkd
```

      To test if your interface is working, use the **status** option

```
systemctl status systemd-networkd
```

ifconfig

      The **ifconfig** command takes as its arguments the name of an interface and an IP address, as well as options. You can install it with the **net-tools** package. The **ifconfig** command then assigns the IP address to the interface. Your system now knows that such an interface exists and that it references a particular IP address. In addition, you can specify whether the IP address is a host address or a network address. You can use a domain name for the IP address, provided the domain name is listed along with its IP address in the **/etc/hosts** file. The syntax for the **ifconfig** command is as follows:

```
ifconfig interface -host_net_flag address options
```

      The host_net_flag can be either **-host** or **-net** to indicate a host or network IP address. The **-host** flag is the default. The **ifconfig** command can have several options, which set different features of the interface, such as the maximum number of bytes it can transfer (**mtu**) or the broadcast address. The **up** and **down** options activate and deactivate the interface. In the next example, the **ifconfig** command configures an Ethernet interface.

```
ifconfig enp7s0 192.168.0.1
```

      For a simple configuration such as this, **ifconfig** automatically generates a standard broadcast address and netmask. The standard broadcast address is the network address with the number 255 for the host address. For a class C network, the standard netmask is 255.255.255.0, whereas, for a class A network, the standard netmask is 255.0.0.0. If you are connected to a network with a particular netmask and broadcast address, however, you must specify them when you use **ifconfig**. The option for specifying the broadcast address is **broadcast**. For the network mask, it is **netmask**. Table 18-8 lists several **ifconfig** options. In the next example, **ifconfig** includes the netmask and broadcast address.

```
ifconfig enp7s0 192.168.0.1 broadcast 192.168.0.255 netmask 255.255.255.0
```

      Once you configure your interface, you can use **ifconfig** with the **up** option to activate it and with the **down** option to deactivate it. If you specify an IP address in an **ifconfig** operation, as in the preceding example, the **up** option is implied.

```
ifconfig enp7s0 up
```

      Point-to-point interfaces such as Parallel IP (PLIP), Serial Line IP (SLIP), and Point-to-Point Protocol (PPP) require you to include the **pointopoint** option. A PLIP interface name is identified with the name **plip** with an attached number. For example, **plip0** is the first PLIP interface. SLIP interfaces use **slip0**. PPP interfaces start with **ppp0**. Point-to-point interfaces are those that usually operate between only two hosts, such as two computers connected over a modem. When you specify the **pointopoint** option, you need to include the IP address of the host. In the next example, a PLIP interface is configured that connects the computer at IP address 192.168.1.72

with one at 192.166.254.14. If domain addresses were listed for these systems in **/etc/hosts**, those domain names could be used in place of the IP addresses.

```
ifconfig plip0 192.168.1.72 pointopoint 192.166.254.14
```

Option	Description
Interface	Name of the network interface,(wired ethernet interfaces begin with **en**, wireless with **wl**)
`up`	Activates an interface; implied if IP address is specified
`down`	Deactivates an interface
`allmulti`	Turns on or off the promiscuous mode; preceding hyphen (–) turns it off; this allows network monitoring
`mtu` *n*	Maximum number of bytes that can be sent on this interface per transmission
`dstaddr` *address*	Destination IP address on a point-to-point connection
`netmask` *address*	IP network mask; preceding hyphen (–) turns it off
`broadcast` *address*	Broadcast address; preceding hyphen (–) turns it off
`point-to-point` *address*	Point-to-point mode for interface; if address is included, it is assigned to remote system
`hw`	Sets hardware address of interface
Address	IP address assigned to interface

Table 18-8: The ifconfig Options

If you need to, you can also use **ifconfig** to configure your loopback device. The name of the loopback device is **lo**, and its IP address is the special address 127.0.0.1. The following example shows the configuration.

```
ifconfig lo 127.0.0.1
```

The **ifconfig** command is useful for checking on the status of an interface. If you enter the **ifconfig** command along with the name of the interface, information about that interface is displayed.

```
ifconfig enp7s0
```

To see if your loopback interface is configured, you can use **ifconfig** with the loopback interface name, **lo**.

Routing

A packet that is part of a transmission takes a certain route to reach its destination. On a large network, packets are transmitted from one computer to another until the destination computer is reached. The route determines where the process starts and to what computer your system needs to send the packet for it to reach its destination. On small networks, routing may be static, that is, the route from one system to another is fixed. One system knows how to reach another, moving through fixed paths. On larger networks and on the Internet, routing is dynamic. Your system knows the first computer to send its packet off to, and then that computer takes the packet from there, passing it on to another computer, which then determines where to pass it on. For dynamic routing, your system needs to know little. Static routing, however, can become complex because you have to keep track of all the network connections.

Your routes are listed in your routing table in the **/proc/net/route** file. To display the routing table, enter **route** with no arguments (the **netstat -r** command will also display the routing table).

```
$ route
Kernel routing table
Destination Gateway       Genmask       Flags Metric Ref Use  Iface
192.168.0.0    *          255.255.255.0 U     0      0   0    enp7s0
192.168.0.0    *          255.255.255.0 U     0      0   0    wlp6s0
link-local     *          255.255.0.0   U     1000   0   0    enp7s0
default     192.168.0.1   0.0.0.0       UG    0      0   0    enp7s0
```

Each entry in the routing table has several fields, providing information such as the route destination and the type of interface used. The different fields are listed in Table 18-9.

Field	Description
Destination	Destination IP address of the route
Gateway	IP address or hostname of the gateway the route uses; * indicates no gateway is used
Genmask	The netmask for the route
Flags	Type of route: U = up, H = host, G = gateway, D = dynamic, M = modified
Metric	Metric cost of route
Ref	Number of routes that depend on this one
Window	TCP window for AX.25 networks
Use	Number of times used
Iface	Type of interface this route uses

Table 18-9: Routing Table Entries

With the **add** argument, you can add routes either for networks with the **-net** option or with the **-host** option for IP interfaces (hosts). The **-host** option is the default. In addition, you can then specify several parameters for information, such as the netmask (**netmask**), the gateway (**gw**), the interface device (**dev**), and the default route (**default**). If you have more than one IP interface on your system, such as several Ethernet cards, you must specify the name of the interface using the **dev** parameter. If your network has a gateway host, you use the **gw** parameter to specify it. If your system is connected to a network, at least one entry should be in your routing table that specifies the default route. This is the route taken by a message packet when no other route entry leads to its destination. The following example is the routing of an Ethernet interface.

```
route add 192.168.1.2 dev enp7s0
```

If your system has only the single Ethernet device as your IP interface, you could leave out the **dev** parameter.

```
route add 192.168.1.2
```

You can delete any route you establish by invoking **ifconfig** with the **del** argument and the IP address of that route, as in this example.

```
route del 192.168.1.2
```

For a gateway, you first add a route to the gateway interface and then add a route specifying that it is a gateway. The address of the gateway interface in this example is 192.168.1.1.

```
route add 192.168.1.1
route add default gw 192.168.1.1
```

If you are using the gateway to access a subnet, add the network address for that network (in this example, 192.168.23.0).

```
route add -net 192.168.23.0 gw dev eth1
```

To add another IP address to a different network interface on your system, use the **ifconfig** and **route** commands with the new IP address. The following command configures a second Ethernet card (**eth1**) with the IP address 192.168.1.3.

```
ifconfig eth1 192.168.1.3
route add 192.168.1.3 dev enp7s0
```

You can also use **nmcli** to manage routes if you are running NetworkManager. Use the plus sign with **ipv4.routes** property to add a route, **+ipv4.routes**.

```
nmcli con modify enp7s0 ipv4.routes 192.168.1.3
```

Monitoring Your Network: ping, netstat, tcpdump, Ettercap, Wireshark, and Nagios

Several applications are available on Linux to let you monitor your network activity. Graphical applications like EtherApe, Ettercap, and Wireshark provide detailed displays and logs to let you analyze and detect network usage patterns. Other tools like **ping**, **netstat**, and **traceroute** offer specific services. Table 18-10 lists various network information tools.

The EtherApe, Ettercap, and Wireshark tools can be accessed on a desktop. Tools like **ping**, **traceroute**, and **netstat** can be accessed from Network Tools, or they can be run individually on a command line. EtherApe provides a simple graphical display for your protocol activity. The Preferences dialog lets you set features like the protocol to check and the kind of traffic to report.

GNOME Network Tools: gnome-nettool

The GNOME Nettool utility (**gnome-nettool**) provides a desktop interface for network information tools, like the ping and traceroute operations as well as Finger, Whois, and Lookup for querying users and hosts on the network (see Figure 18-4). The first tab, Devices, describes your connected network devices, including configuration and transmission information about each device, such as the hardware address and bytes transmitted. Both IPv4 and IPv6 host IP addresses are listed.

```
sudo apt install gnome-nettool
```

Network Information Tools	Description
ping	Detects whether a system is connected to the network.
finger	Obtains information about users on the network.
who	Checks what users are currently online.
whois	Obtains domain information.
host	Obtains network address information about a remote host.
traceroute	Tracks the sequence of computer networks and hosts your message passes through.
wireshark	Protocol analyzer to examine network traffic.
gnome-nettool	GNOME interface for various network tools including ping, finger, and traceroute.
mtr	My traceroute combines both ping and traceroute operations.
EtherApe	Analyze protocol activity
Ettercap	Sniffer program for man-in-middle attacks
netstat	Real time network status monitor
tcpdump	Capture and save network packets
Nagios	Nagios network monitoring, **nagio4** packages, **/etc/nagios4** configuration directory, **http://localhost/nagios4** browser access

Table 18-10: Network Tools

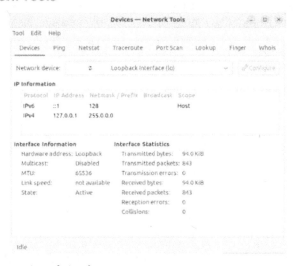

Figure 18-4: Gnome network tool

You can use the ping, finger, lookup, whois, and traceroute operations to find out status information about systems and users on your network. The ping operation is used to check if a remote system is up and running. You use finger to find out information about other users on your network, seeing if they are logged in or if they have received mail. The traceroute tool can be used to track the sequence of computer networks and systems your message passed through on its way to you. Whois will provide domain name information about a particular domain, and Lookup will provide both domain name and IP addresses. Netstat shows your network routing (addresses used) and active service (open ports and the protocols they use). Port Scan lists the ports and services they use on a given connection (address).

Network Information: ping, finger, traceroute, and host

You can use the **ping**, **finger**, **traceroute**, and **host** commands to find out status information about systems and users on your network. The **ping** command is used to check if a remote system is up and running. You use **finger** to find out information about other users on your network, seeing if they are logged in or if they have received mail. **host** displays address information about a system on your network, giving you a system's IP and domain name addresses. **traceroute** can be used to track the sequence of computer networks and systems your message passed through on its way to you.

ping

The **ping** command detects whether a system is up and running. **ping** takes as its argument the name of the system you want to check. If the system you want to check is down, **ping** issues a timeout message indicating a connection could not be made. **ping** sends a request to the host for a reply. The host then sends a reply back, and it is displayed on your screen. **ping** continually sends such a request until you stop it with a break command, by pressing **Ctrl-c**. You see one reply after another scroll by on your screen until you stop the program. If **ping** cannot access a host, it issues a message saying the host is unreachable. If **ping** fails, it can indicate that your network connection is not working, such as a hardware failure, a basic configuration problem, or a bad physical connection. Networks may block these protocols as a security measure, also preventing **ping** from working. A **ping** failure may simply indicate a security precaution on the part of the queried network.

To use **ping**, enter the **ping** command and the name of the host. The next example checks to see if **www.ubuntu.com** is up and connected to the network:

```
$ ping www.ubuntu.com
PING www.ubuntu.com(elvira.canonical.com (2001:67c:1562::1f)) 56 data bytes
64 bytes from elvira.canonical.com (2001:67c:1562::1f): icmp_seq=1 ttl=47 time=75.9 ms
64 bytes from elvira.canonical.com (2001:67c:1562::1f): icmp_seq=2 ttl=47 time=75.9 ms
64 bytes from elvira.canonical.com (2001:67c:1562::1f): icmp_seq=3 ttl=47 time=75.5 ms
64 bytes from elvira.canonical.com (2001:67c:1562::1f): icmp_seq=4 ttl=47 time=75.6 ms
^C
--- www.ubuntu.com ping statistics ---
4 packets transmitted, 4 received, 0% packet loss, time 3003ms
rtt min/avg/max/mdev = 75.479/75.732/75.910/0.178 ms
```

You can also use **ping** with an IP address instead of a domain name. With an IP address, **ping** can try to detect the remote system directly without having to go through a domain name server to translate the domain name to an IP address. This can be helpful for situations where your network's domain name server may be temporarily down and you want to check if a particular remote host on your network is connected. **ping** will work with either IPv4 or IPv6 addresses.

```
ping 2001:67c:1562::1f
PING 2001:67c:1562::1f(2001:67c:1562::1f) 56 data bytes
64 bytes from 2001:67c:1562::1f: icmp_seq=1 ttl=47 time=75.6 ms
64 bytes from 2001:67c:1562::1f: icmp_seq=2 ttl=47 time=75.4 ms
64 bytes from 2001:67c:1562::1f: icmp_seq=3 ttl=47 time=75.3 ms
64 bytes from 2001:67c:1562::1f: icmp_seq=4 ttl=47 time=75.4 ms
^C
--- 2001:67c:1562::1f ping statistics ---
4 packets transmitted, 4 received, 0% packet loss, time 3002ms
rtt min/avg/max/mdev = 75.304/75.417/75.593/0.108 ms
```

finger and who

You can use the **finger** command to obtain information about other users on your network and the **who** command to see what users are currently online on your system. The **who** and **w** commands lists all users currently connected, along with when, how long, and where they logged in. The **w** command provides more detailed information. It has several options for specifying the level of detail. The **who** command is meant to operate on a local system or network. The **finger** command can operate on large networks, including the Internet, though most systems block it for security reasons.

host

With the **host** command, you can find network address information about a remote system connected to your network. The information usually consists of a system's IP address, domain name address, domain name nicknames, and mail server. This information is obtained from your network's domain name server. For the Internet, this includes all systems you can connect to over the Internet.

The **host** command is an effective way to determine a remote site's IP address or URL. If you have only the IP address of a site, you can use **host** to find out its domain name. For network administration, an IP address can be helpful for making your own domain name entries in your **/etc/host** file. That way, you do not have to rely on a remote domain name server (DNS) for locating a site.

```
$ host gnome.org
gnome.org has address 8.43.85.23
gnome.org mail is handled by 10 smtp.gnome.org.

$ host 209.132.180.168
23.85.43.8.in-addr.arpa domain name pointer proxy01.gnome.org.
```

traceroute

Internet connections are made through various routes, traveling through a series of interconnected gateway hosts. The path from one system to another could take different routes, some of which may be faster than others. For a slow connection, you can use **traceroute** to check the route through which you are connected to a host, monitoring the speed and the number of intervening gateway connections a route takes. The **traceroute** command takes as its argument the hostname or IP addresses for the system whose route you want to check. Options are available for specifying parameters like the type of service (**-t**) or the source host (**-s**). The **traceroute** command will return a list of hosts the route traverses, along with the times for three probes sent to each gateway. Times greater than five seconds are displayed with a asterisk, *. Install with the **traceroute** package.

```
traceroute rabbit.mytrek.com
```

Note: You can also use the My Traceroute tool (**mtr** package) to perform both ping and traces. **mtr** provides a cursor-based screen you can run on the command line.

Ettercap

Ettercap is a sniffer program designed to detect Man in the Middle attacks. In this kind of attack, packets are detected and modified in transit to let an unauthorized user access a network. You can use either its graphical interface or its command line interface. Ettercap can perform Unified sniffing on all connections, or Bridged sniffing on a connection between network interfaces. Ettercap uses plugins for specific tasks, like dos_attack to detect Denial of Service attacks and dns_spoof for DNS spoofing detection. Check the plugins Help tab, or enter **ettercap -P list** for a complete listing. Ettercap can be run in several modes, including a text mode, a command line cursor mode, a script mode using commands in a file, and even as a daemon logging results automatically. Install either the **ettercap-text-only** or, if you are using a desktop, **ettercap-graphical** package.

Wireshark

Wireshark is a network protocol analyzer that lets you capture packets transmitted across your network, selecting and examining those from protocols you want to check. You can examine packets from particular transmissions, displaying the data in readable formats. You can run Wireshark on a desktop such as GNOME or KDE. The Wireshark interface displays three panes: a listing of current packets, the protocol tree for the currently selected packet, and a display of the selected packets contents. The first pane categorizes entries by time, source, destination, and protocol, with button headers for each. To sort a set of entries by a particular category, you click its header. For example, to group entries by protocol, click the Protocol button. For destinations, click the Destination button.

Capture Options

To configure Wireshark, you select the Options entry from the Capture menu (Capture | Options). This opens an options window where you can select the network interface to watch. Here you can also select options, such as the file in which to hold your captured information and a size limit for the capture, along with a filter to screen packets. With the promiscuous mode selected, you can see all network traffic passing through that device, whereas with it off, you will see only those packets destined for that device. You can then click the start button to start Wireshark. To stop and start Wireshark, you select the Stop and Start entries on the Capture menu.

Capture Files lets you select a file to save your capture in. If no file is selected, then data is simply displayed in the Wireshark window. If you want to keep a continuous running snapshot of your network traffic, you can use ring buffers. These are a series of files that are used to save captured data. When they fill up, the capture begins saving again to the first file, and so on. Check "Use multiple files" to enable this option.

Limit lets you set a limit for the capture packet size.

Capture Filter lets you choose the type of protocol you want to check.

Display Options control whether packets are displayed in real time on the Wireshark window.

"Enable network name resolution" enables the display of host and domain names instead of IP addresses, if possible.

Wireshark Filters

A filter lets you select packets that match specified criteria, such as packets from a particular host. Criteria are specified using expressions supported by the Packet Capture Library and implemented by **tcpdump**. Wireshark filters use expressions similar to those used by the **tcpdump** command. Check the **tcpdump** Man page for detailed descriptions.

You can set up either a Search filter in the Find tab (Edit menu) to search for certain packets, or set up a Capture Filter in the Options tab (Capture menu) to select which packets to record. The filter window is the same for both. On the filter window, you can select the protocol you want to search or capture. The Filter name and string will appear in the Properties segment. You can also enter your own string, setting up a new filter of your own. The string must be a filter expression.

To create a new filter, enter the name you want to give it in the Filter Name box. Then in the Filter String box, enter the filter expression, like **icmp**. Then click New. Your new filter will appear in the list. To change a filter, select it and change its expression in the Filter String box, then click Change.

A filter expression consists of an ID, such as the name or number of host, and a qualifier. Qualifiers come in three types: type, direction, and protocol. The type can reference the host, network, or port. The type qualifiers are **host**, **net**, and **port**. Direction selects either source or destination packets, or both. The source qualifier is **src**, and the destination qualifier is **dst**. With no destination qualifier, both directions are selected. Protocol lets you specify packets for a certain protocol. Protocols are represented using their lowercase names, such as **icmp** for ICMP. For example, the expression to list all packets coming in from a particular host would be **src host** hostname, where hostname is the source host. The following example will display all packets from the 192.168.0.3 host.

```
src host 192.168.0.3
```

Using just **host** will check for all packets going out as well as coming in for that host. The **port** qualifier will check for packets passing through a particular port. To check for a particular protocol, you use the protocol name. For example, to check for all ICMP packets you would use the expression:

```
icmp
```

There are also several special qualifiers that let you further control your selection. The **gateway** qualifier lets you detect packets passing through a gateway. The **tcpdump** and **multi-cast** qualifiers detect packets broadcast to a network. The **greater** and **less** qualifiers can be applied to numbers such as ports or IP addresses.

You can combine expressions into a single complex Boolean expression using **and**, **or**, or **not**. This lets you create a more refined filter. For example, to capture only the ICMP packets coming in from host 192.168.0.2, you can use:

```
src host 192.168.0.3 and icmp
```

tcpdump

Like Wireshark, **tcpdump** will capture network packets, saving them in a file where you can examine them. **tcpdump** operates entirely from the command line. Using various options, you can refine your capture, specifying the kinds of packets you want. **tcpdump** uses a set of options to specify actions you want to take, which include limiting the size of the capture, deciding which file to save it to, and choosing any filter you want to apply to it. Check the **tcpdump** Man page for a complete listing of options. Be sure to run it with the **sudo** command.

The **-i** option lets you specify an interface to listen to.

With the **-c** option, you can limit the number of packets to capture.

Packets will be output to the standard output by default. To save them to a file, you can use the **-w** option.

You can later read a packet file using the **-r** option and apply a filter expression to it.

The **tcpdump** command takes as its argument a filter expression that you can use to refine your capture. Wireshark uses the same filter expressions as **tcpdump** (see the filters discussion in Wireshark).

netstat

The netstat program provides real-time information on the status of your network connections, as well as network statistics and the routing table. The **netstat** command has several options you can use to display different sorts of information about your network. Install with the **net-tools** package.

The **netstat** command with no options lists the network connections on your system. First, active TCP connections are listed, and then the active domain sockets are listed. The domain sockets contain processes used to set up communications among your system and other systems. You can use **netstat** with the **-r** option to display the routing table, and **netstat** with the **-i** option displays the uses of the different network interfaces.

```
$ netstat
Active Internet connections
Proto Recv-Q Send-Q Local Address Foreign Address (State) User
tcp 0 0 turtle.mytrek.com:01 pango1.mytrain.com.:ftp ESTABLISHED dylan
Active UNIX domain sockets
Proto RefCnt Flags Type State Path
unix 1 [ ACC ] SOCK_STREAM LISTENING /dev/printer
unix 2 [ ] SOCK_STREAM CONNECTED /dev/log
unix 1 [ ACC ] SOCK_STREAM LISTENING /dev/nwapi
unix 2 [ ] SOCK_STREAM CONNECTED /dev/log
unix 2 [ ] SOCK_STREAM CONNECTED
unix 1 [ ACC ] SOCK_STREAM LISTENING /dev/log
```

Nagios4

Ubuntu also supports Nagios4, the enterprise level network monitoring software. You can install Nagios4 with the **nagios4** package. All dependent Nagios packages will be selected and installed, including **nagios4-doc** for documentation and **nagios-plugins** for servers like DNS and MySQL. To install you can use **apt**, **apt-get**, **aptitude**, or the Synaptic Package Manager.

```
sudo apt install nagios4
```

Make sure that the Nagios4 server is running. If not, enter the following at the command line or in a terminal window to start it.

```
sudo systemctl start nagios4
```

When you install Nagios4, you will be prompted to select the server type and the host. You no longer have to enter a password as access, as configured, is open to all.

You then open your browser and access your Nagios interface with the following URL.

```
http://localhost/nagios4
```

The Nagios Web interface is then displayed as shown in Figure 18-5.

Figure 18-5: Nagios 4 network monitoring Web interface

Using the links listed on the left sidebar you can then display different monitoring information like the service status for hosts on your network (see Figure 18-6). It is possible to run Nagios from the command line using the **lynx** Web browser.

Figure 18-6: Nagios 4 network monitoring Service Status

Configuration files for Nagios4 are located at **/etc/nagios4**, and the configuration files for different plugins are located at **/etc/nagios-plugins/config**. The main configuration file is **nagios.cfg**, an editable text file with detailed comments for each directive. The **apache2.conf** file sets up aliases mapping Nagios to the Nagios4 directories and files. An AuthUserFile directive specifies that the Nagios Web page user and password file is **/etc/nagios4/htdigest.users**. If you want to use user and password authentication, configure the **/etc/nagios4/apache2.conf** file to require them.

You can create or change a nagios user and password with the following command entered in a terminal window. You will be prompted to enter a new password twice.

```
sudo htpasswd -c /etc/nagios4/htdigest.users  nagiosadmin
```

The Nagios application and plugins are supported directly by Ubuntu as part of the main repository. Nagios also provides a remote plugin server that allows Nagios plugins to run on remote hosts. The Nagios Remote Plugin Executor server (NRPE) is part of the Universe repository. Install both the **nagios-nrpe-server** and the **nagios-nrpe-plugin** packages.

```
sudo apt install nagios-nrpe-server nagios-nrpe-plugin
```

The NRPE server script is **nagios-nrpe-server**.

```
sudo systemctl start nagios-nrpe-server
```

The configuration files for the NRPE server are located at **/etc/nagios**.

Telegraf, Prometheus, and Grafana

With Telegraf you can generate data on the performance of a system in your network. The data generated on each system can then be collected by Prometheus and sent to specified output sources. You can then use Grafana to display this data in a graph format. Prometheus would be installed on a system used to monitor the other systems running Telegraf.

Telegraf

Telegraf would be installed and run on the different computers on your network. Telegraf is an entirely plugin driven monitoring tool capable of monitoring a variety of systems. Telegraf is a Snap package you can install with the **snap** command. It is a classic package that access files outside the Snap sandbox, which requires the **--classic** option to install.

```
sudo snap install --classic telegraf
```

The configuration file for Telegraf on Ubuntu is **/etc/telegraf/telegraf.conf** with additional configuration files in the **/etc/telegraf/telegraf.d** directory. The documentation for Telegraf configuration is:

```
https://docs.influxdata.com/telegraf/v1.24/
```

The **telegraf.conf** file list the plugins available for your system. Those active are uncommented. To activate one remove its comments. Telegraf configuration is written in TOML (Tom's Obviously Minimal Language, **https://github.com/toml-lang/toml#toml**), a simple YAML language designed specifically for configuration files. The configuration file is composed of blocks of directives. The first block lists global settings, **[global_tags]**, the second lists agent settings, **[agent]**. The rest of the configuration files contains blocks for output, processor, aggregator, and input plugins. The list of plugins in the configuration file is extensive. Most are commented out. The Aggregator plugins gather metrics over a certain time periods.

The output plugins list the metrics, usually to a specified location. The output plugins include those for Google cloud, Azure, syslog servers, as well as various Amazon services. Most of the output plugins are commented out. Several of the processor output plugins are active. There is an extensive list of input plugins.

The input plugins generate metrics. The input plugins for the CPU and disk are active, as well as for the Telegraf agent and global_tags blocks. Input plugins include those for the Apache, Bind, MySQL, Postfix, LAPD, Nginx, and Chrony servers, and IPtables.

Prometheus

Prometheus is an open source monitoring service that generates time series statistics of jobs on your systems, such as processor use. Monitoring is carried out by the Prometheus server, which collects data provided by Telegraf on the different systems on a network.

Specialized exporter packages can provide metrics on certain services such as MySql, node/system (processor), HAProxy, SNMP, and Statd. In addition there are numerous unofficial exporters for services such as Apache, MongoDB, PostgreSQL, and Squid. Some services do not need exporters as they already provide metrics in Prometheus formats, such as BIND, JSON, OpenStack, SSH, and Xen. Prometheus also features a pushgateway for obtaining metrics on short-lived jobs that it would normally miss.

You can find out more about Prometheus at:

```
https://prometheus.io/
```

Documentation is located at:

```
https://prometheus.io/docs/introduction/overview/
```

On Ubuntu, the **prometheus** and **prometheus-alertmanager** packages are available on both on the Snap repository and the universe repository (APT). Ubuntu Software may only list the Snap repository version. The APT version installs both the Prometheus server and the node exporter, whereas they are installed separately for the Snap repository. If installed from Snap, use the **snap services** command to see if the Prometheus server is running.

```
snap services prometheus
```

For the Snap version, configuration is located at **/var/snap/prometheus/current/** in the **prometheus.yaml** file. The APT version would be located at **/etc/prometheus**. Prometheus uses the YAML language to configure the server. At the end of the configuration file, you can add custom scrape operations for your data in the **scrape_configs** section of the **prometheus.yml** file. Check the Prometheus documentation for details.

You can use the Prometheus expression browser to see if Prometheus is working properly (see Figure 18-7). Open your browser and access port 9090.

```
http://localhost:9090
```

In the expression query box enter an expression, usually beginning with a term such as "process" or "prometheus." Upon entering the initial part of the term a drop down menu is displayed with full queries you can choose from. Once selected, click the execute command to display the metric.

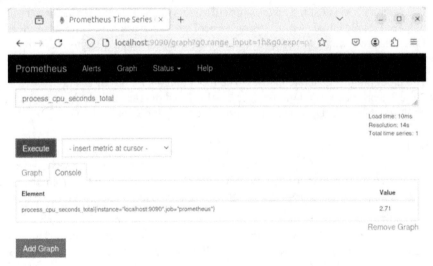

Figure 18-7: Prometheus expression browser

Alerts are managed by the Prometheus Alert Manager. You can configure the Prometheus configuration to read an alerts files with the alerts you want.

Grafana

Grafana is an open source visualization application for metrics. With it you can display graphs of your data. Once you have installed and started Prometheus, you can then use Grafana to display and analyze the metrics it provides.

You can find out more about Grafana at:

```
https://grafana.com/
```

For documentation and tutorials check the following site under the Learn tab.

```
https://grafana.com/docs/
```

You can install Grafana from the Snap repository using the **snap** command or Ubuntu Software. Configuration is located in a **defaults.ini** file, which you would not access. You could set up your own for custom configuration at **/var/snap/grafana/current/conf** in an **.ini** file.

To run Grafana, start your browser and access port 3000 (see Figure 18-8). To select the Prometheus data source click on the configuration icon on the left side and select "Data Source" to display data source configuration options. To display a list of possible data sources, click on the "Add data source" button. For Prometheus, move the mouse to the Prometheus entry and then click the Select button. A configuration panel opens where you can specify the data source options such as the URL to use, where to make it the default, and authentication options. Buttons at the bottom allow you to save and test the changes, as well as delete the data source. You could set up several Prometheus data sources, each with a different configuration.

```
http://localhost:3000
```

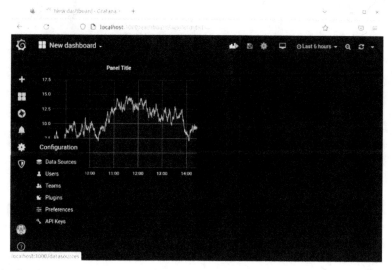

Figure 18-8: Grafana

Grafana uses a dashboard to display metrics from a data source. Click on the plus button (+) to create a new dashboard. The panel configuration is displayed showing the panel (see Figure 18-9). Buttons to the lower left let you enter and add queries, change the visualization, set the panel tiles and description, and set alerts. Buttons at the top right let you share, save, configure, and refresh the panel, as well as set the time frame.

Figure 18-9: Grafana Dashboard

Part 5: Shells

Shells
Files and Directories
Shell Variables and Scripts
Shell Configuration

ubuntu

19. Shells

The Command Line

History

Filename Expansion: *, ?, [ ]

Standard Input/Output and Redirection

The shell is a command interpreter that provides a line-oriented interactive and non-interactive interface between the user and the operating system. You enter commands on a command line. They are interpreted by the shell and then sent as instructions to the operating system (the command line interface is accessible from GNOME and KDE desktops through a Terminal window). You can also place commands in a script file to be consecutively executed, much like a program. This interpretive capability of the shell provides for many sophisticated features. For example, the shell has a set of file expansion characters that can generate filenames. The shell can redirect input and output, as well as run operations in the background, freeing you to perform other tasks.

Shell	Web Site
www.gnu.org/software/bash	BASH website with online-manual, FAQ, and current releases
www.gnu.org/software/bash/manual/bash.html	BASH online manual
www.zsh.org	Z shell website with referrals to FAQs and current downloads.
www.tcsh.org	TCSH website with detailed support including manual, tips, FAQ, and recent releases
www.kornshell.com	Korn shell site with manual, FAQ, and references

Table 19-1: Linux Shells

Several different types of shells have been developed for Linux: the Bourne Again shell (BASH), the Korn shell, the TCSH shell, and the Z shell. All shells are available for your use, although the BASH shell is the default. You only need one type of shell to do your work. Ubuntu Linux includes all the major shells, although it installs and uses the BASH shell as the default. If you use the command line shell, you will be using the BASH shell unless you specify another. This chapter discusses the BASH shell, which shares many of the same features as other shells.

You can find out more about shells at their respective websites as listed in Table 19-1. Also, a detailed online manual is available for each installed shell. Use the **man** command and the shell's keyword to access them, **bash** for the BASH shell, **ksh** for the Korn shell, **zsh** for the Z shell, and **tsch** for the TSCH shell. For example, the following command will access the BASH shell online manual.

```
man bash
```

Note: You can find out more about the BASH shell at https://www.gnu.org/software/bash/. A detailed online manual is available on your Linux system using the **man** command with the **bash** keyword.

The Command Line

The Linux command line interface consists of a single line into which you enter commands with any of their options and arguments. From the desktop, you can access the command line interface by opening a terminal window. Should you start Linux with the command line interface, as is the case with the server version of Ubuntu, you will be presented with a BASH shell command line when you log in.

By default, the BASH shell has a dollar sign ($) prompt, but Linux has several other types of shells, each with its own prompt (like **%** for the C shell). The root user will have a different prompt, the **#**. A shell prompt, such as the one shown here, marks the beginning of the command line.

```
$
```

You can enter a command along with options and arguments at the prompt. For example, with an **-l** option, the **ls** command will display a line of information about each file, listing such data as its size and the date and time it was last modified. In the next example, the user enters the **ls** command followed by a **-l** option. The dash before the **-l** option is required. Linux uses it to distinguish an option from an argument.

```
$ ls -l
```

If you wanted only the information displayed for a particular file, you could add that file's name as the argument, following the **-l** option:

```
$ ls -l mydata
-rw-r--r-- 1 chris weather 207 Feb 20 11:55 mydata
```

Tip: Some commands can be complex and take some time to execute. When you mistakenly execute the wrong command, you can interrupt and stop such commands with the interrupt key, CTRL-c.

You can enter a command on several lines by typing a backslash just before you press ENTER. The backslash "escapes" the ENTER key, effectively continuing the same command line to the next line. In the next example, the **cp** command is entered on three lines. The first two lines end in a backslash, effectively making all three lines one command line.

```
$ cp -i \
mydata \
/home/george/myproject/newdata
```

You can also enter several commands on the same line by separating them with a semicolon (;). In effect, the semicolon operates as an execute operation. Commands will be executed in the sequence in which they are entered. The following command executes an **ls** command followed by a **date** command.

```
$ ls ; date
```

You can also conditionally run several commands on the same line with the **&&** operator. A command is executed only if the previous command is true. This feature is useful for running several dependent scripts on the same line. In the next example, the **ls** command is run only if the **date** command is successfully executed.

```
$ date && ls
```

TIP: Commands can also be run as arguments on a command line, using their results for other commands. To run a command within a command line, you encase the command in back quotes.

Movement Commands	Operation
CTRL-F, RIGHT-ARROW	Move forward a character
CTRL-B, LEFT-ARROW	Move backward a character
CTRL-A or HOME	Move to beginning of line
CTRL-E or END	Move to end of line
ALT-F	Move forward a word
ALT-B	Move backward a word
CTRL-L	Clear screen and place line at top
Editing Commands	**Operation**
CTRL-D or DEL	Delete character cursor is on
CTRL-H or BACKSPACE	Delete character before the cursor
CTRL-K	Cut remainder of line from cursor position
CTRL-U	Cut from cursor position to beginning of line
CTRL-W	Cut the previous word
CTRL-C	Cut entire line
ALT-D	Cut the remainder of a word
ALT-DEL	Cut from the cursor to the beginning of a word
CTRL-Y	Paste previous cut text
ALT-Y	Paste from set of previously cut text
CTRL-Y	Paste previous cut text
CTRL-V	Insert quoted text, used for inserting control or meta (Alt) keys as text, such as CTRL-B for backspace or CTRL-T for tabs
ALT-T	Transpose current and previous word
ALT-L	Lowercase current word
ALT-U	Uppercase current word
ALT-C	Capitalize current word
CTRL-SHIFT-_	Undo previous change

Table 19-2: Command Line Editing Operations

Command Line Editing

The BASH shell, which is your default shell, has special command line editing capabilities (see Table 19-2). You can modify commands you have entered before executing them, moving anywhere on the command line and inserting or deleting characters. This is especially helpful for complex commands.

You can press CTRL-f or the RIGHT ARROW key to move forward a character, or the CTRL-b or LEFT ARROW key to move back a character. CTRL-d or DEL deletes the character the cursor is on, and CTRL-h or BACKSPACE deletes the character preceding the cursor. To add text, you use the arrow keys to move the cursor to where you want to insert text and type the new characters.

You can even cut words with the CTRL-w or ALT-d key, and then press the CTRL-**y** key to paste them back in at a different position, effectively moving the words. As a rule, the CTRL version of the command operates on characters, and the ALT version works on words, such as CTRL-t to transpose characters and ALT-t to transpose words. At any time, you can press ENTER to execute the command. For example, if you make a spelling mistake when entering a command, rather than re-entering the entire command, you can use the editing operations to correct the mistake. The actual associations of keys and their tasks, along with global settings, are specified in the **/etc/inputrc** file.

The editing capabilities of the BASH shell command line are provided by Readline. Readline supports numerous editing operations. You can even bind a key to a selected editing operation. Readline uses the **/etc/inputrc** file to configure key bindings. This file is read automatically by your **/etc/profile** shell configuration file when you log in. Users can customize their editing commands by creating an **.inputrc** file in their home directory (this is a dot file). It may be best to first copy the **/etc/inputrc** file as your **.inputrc** file and then edit it. **/etc/profile** will first check for a local **.inputrc** file before accessing the **/etc/inputrc** file. You can find out more about Readline from the Readline manual on the GNU Manuals page at **https://www.gnu.org/manual/manual.html**.

Command and Filename Completion

The BASH command line has a built-in feature that performs command line and filename completion. Automatic completions can be effected by pressing the TAB key. If you enter an incomplete pattern as a command or filename argument, you can press the TAB key to activate the command and filename completion feature, which completes the pattern. A directory will have a forward slash (/) attached to its name. If more than one command or file has the same prefix, the shell simply beeps and waits for you to press the TAB key again. It then displays a list of possible command completions and waits for you to add enough characters to select a unique command or filename. For situations where you know multiple possibilities are likely, you can just press the ESC key instead of two TABs. In the next example, the user issues a **cat** command with an incomplete filename. When the user presses the TAB key, the system searches for a match and, when it finds one, fills in the filename. The user can then press ENTER to execute the command.

```
$ cat pre <tab>
$ cat preface
```

The automatic completions also work with the names of variables, users, and hosts. In this case, the partial text needs to be preceded by a special character, indicating the type of name. A listing of possible automatic completions follows.

Filenames begin with any text or /.

Shell variable text begins with a $ sign.

Username text begins with a ~ sign.

Hostname text begins with a @.

Commands, aliases, and text in files begin with normal text.

Variables begin with a **$** sign, so any text beginning with a dollar sign is treated as a variable to be completed. Variables are selected from previously defined variables, like system shell variables. Usernames begin with a tilde **(~)**. Hostnames begin with a **@** sign, with possible names taken from the **/etc/hosts** file. For example, to complete the variable HOME given just $HOM, press a TAB key.

```
$ echo $HOM <tab>
$ echo $HOME
```

If you entered just an **H**, then you could press TAB twice to see all possible variables beginning with H. The command line is redisplayed, letting you complete the name.

```
$ echo $H <tab> <tab>
$HISTCMD $HISTFILE $HOME $HOSTTYPE HISTFILE  $HISTSIZE $HISTNAME
$ echo $H
```

You can also specifically select the kind of text to complete, using corresponding command keys. In this case, it does not matter what kind of sign a name begins with.

Command (CTRL-R for listing possible completions)	Description
TAB	Automatic completion
TAB TAB or ESC	List possible completions
ALT-/, CTRL-R-/	Filename completion, normal text for automatic
ALT-$, CTRL-R-$	Shell variable completion, $ for automatic
ALT-~, CTRL-R-~	Username completion, ~ for automatic
ALT-@, CTRL-R-@	Hostname completion, @ for automatic
ALT-!, CTRL-R-!	Command name completion, normal text for automatic

Table 19-3: Command Line Text Completion Commands

For example, the pressing ALT-~ will treat the current text as a username. Pressing ALT-@ will treat it as a hostname, and ALT-$, as a variable. Pressing Alt-! will treat it as a command. To display a list of possible completions, press the CTRL-x key with the appropriate completion key, as in CTRL-x-$ to list possible variable completions. See Table 19-3 for a complete listing.

History

The BASH shell keeps a history list, of your previously entered commands. You can display each command, in turn, on your command line by pressing the UP ARROW key. Press the

DOWN ARROW key to move down the list. You can modify and execute any of these previous commands when you display them on the command line.

Tip: The ability to redisplay a command is helpful when you've already executed a command you had entered incorrectly. In this case, you would be presented with an error message and a new, empty command line. By pressing the UP ARROW key, you can redisplay the previous command, make corrections to it, and then execute it again.

History Events

In the BASH shell, the history utility keeps a record of the most recent commands you have executed. The commands are numbered starting at 1, and a limit exists to the number of commands remembered. The default is 500. The history utility is a kind of short-term memory, keeping track of the most recent commands you have executed. To see the set of your most recent commands, type **history** on the command line and press enter. A list of your most recent commands is then displayed, preceded by a number.

```
$ history
1 cp mydata today
2 vi mydata
3 mv mydata reports
4 cd reports
5 ls
```

Each of these commands is technically referred to as an event. An event describes an action that has been taken, a command that has been executed. The events are numbered according to their sequence of execution. The most recent event has the highest number. Each of these events can be identified by its number or beginning characters in the command.

The history utility lets you reference a former event, placing it on your command line so you can execute it. The easiest way to do this is to use the UP ARROW and DOWN ARROW keys to place history events on the command line, one at a time. You do not have to display the list first with **history**. Pressing the UP ARROW key once places the last history event on the command line. Pressing it again places the next history event on the command line. Pressing the DOWN ARROW key places the previous event on the command line.

You can use certain control and meta keys to perform other history operations like searching the history list. A meta key is the ALT key, and the ESC key on keyboards that have no ALT key. Pressing ALT-< will move you to the beginning of the history list. ALT-n will search it. CTRL-s and CTRL-r will perform incremental searches, displaying matching commands as you type in a search string. Table 19-4 lists the different commands for referencing the history list.

Tip: If more than one history event matches what you have entered, you will hear a beep, and you can then enter more characters to help uniquely identify the event.

You can also reference and execute history events using the ! history command. The ! is followed by a reference that identifies the command. The reference can be either the number of the event or a beginning set of characters in the event. In the next example, the third command in the history list is referenced first by number and then by the beginning characters.

```
$ !3
mv mydata reports
$ !mv my
mv mydata reports
```

History Commands	Description
CTRL-N or DOWN ARROW	Moves down to the next event in the history list
CTRL-P or UP ARROW	Moves up to the previous event in the history list
ALT-<	Moves to the beginning of the history event list
ALT->	Moves to the end of the history event list
ALT-N	Forward Search, next matching item
ALT-P	Backward Search, previous matching item
CTRL-S	Forward Search History, forward incremental search
CTRL-R	Reverse Search History, reverse incremental search
fc *event-reference*	Edits an event with the standard editor and then executes it **Options** **-l** List recent history events; same as **history** command **-e** *editor event-reference* Invokes a specified editor to edit a specific event
History Event References	
! *event num*	References an event with an event number
! !	References the previous command
! *characters*	References an event with beginning characters
!? *pattern*?	References an event with a pattern in the event
! –*event num*	References an event with an offset from the first event
! *num*–*num*	References a range of events

Table 19-4: History Commands and History Event References

You can also reference an event using an offset from the end of the list. A negative number will offset from the end of the list to that event, thereby referencing it. In the next example, the fourth command, **cd mydata**, is referenced using a negative offset, and then executed. Remember that you are offsetting from the end of the list, in this example event 5, up toward the beginning of the list, event 1. An offset of 4 beginning from event 5 places you at event 2.

```
$ !-4
vi mydata
```

To reference the last event, you use a following **!**, as in **!!**. In the next example, the command **!!** executes the last command the user executed, in this case, **ls**.

```
$ !!
ls
mydata today reports
```

Filename Expansion: *, ?, [ ]

Filenames are the most common arguments used in a command. Often you will know only part of the filename, or you will want to reference several filenames that have the same extension or begin with the same characters. The shell provides a set of special characters that search out, match, and generate a list of filenames. These are the asterisk, the question mark, and brackets (*, ?, []). Given a partial filename, the shell uses these matching operators to search for files and expand to a list of filenames found. The shell replaces the partial filename argument with the expanded list of matched filenames. This list of filenames can then become the arguments for commands such as **ls**, which can operate on many files. Table 19-5 lists the shell's file expansion characters.

Matching Multiple Characters

The asterisk (*) references files beginning or ending with a specific set of characters. You place the asterisk before or after a set of characters that form a pattern to be searched for in filenames.

If the asterisk is placed before the pattern, filenames that end in that pattern are searched for. If the asterisk is placed after the pattern, filenames that begin with that pattern are searched for. Any matching filename is copied into a list of filenames generated by this operation.

In the next example, all filenames beginning with the pattern "doc" are searched for and a list generated. Then all filenames ending with the pattern "day" are searched for and a list is generated. The last example shows how the * can be used in any combination of characters.

```
$ ls
doc1 doc2 document docs mydoc monday tuesday
$ ls doc*
doc1 doc2 document docs
$ ls *day
monday tuesday
$ ls m*d*
monday
$
```

Filenames often include an extension specified with a period and followed by a string denoting the file type, such as **.c** for C files, **.cpp** for C++ files, or **.jpg** for JPEG image files. The extension has no special status and is only part of the characters making up the filename. Using the asterisk makes it easy to select files with a given extension. In the next example, the asterisk is used to list only those files with a **.c** extension. The asterisk placed before the **.c** constitutes the argument for **ls**.

```
$ ls *.c
calc.c main.c
```

You can use * with the **rm** command to erase several files at once. The asterisk first selects a list of files with a given extension, or beginning or ending with a given set of characters, and then it presents this list of files to the **rm** command to be erased. In the next example, the **rm** command erases all files beginning with the pattern "doc".

```
$ rm doc*
```

Common Shell Symbols	Execution
ENTER	Execute a command line.
;	Separate commands on the same command line.
`command`	Execute a command.
$ (command)	Execute a command.
[ ]	Match on a class of possible characters in filenames.
\	Quote the following character. Used to quote special characters.
		Pipe the standard output of one command as input for another command.
&	Execute a command in the background.
!	History command.
File Expansion Symbols	**Execution**
*	Match on any set of characters in filenames.
?	Match on any single character in filenames.
[ ]	Match on a class of characters in filenames.
Redirection Symbols	**Execution**
>	Redirect the standard output to a file or device, creating the file if it does not exist and overwriting the file if it does exist.
>!	The exclamation point forces the overwriting of a file if it already exists.
<	Redirect the standard input from a file or device to a program.
>>	Redirect the standard output to a file or device, appending the output to the end of the file.
Standard Error Redirection Symbols	**Execution**
2>	Redirect the standard error to a file or device.
2>>	Redirect and append the standard error to a file or device.
2>&1	Redirect the standard error to the standard output.

Table 19-5: Shell Symbols

Tip: Use the * file expansion character carefully and sparingly with the rm command. The combination can be dangerous. A misplaced * in an rm command without the -i option could easily erase all the files in your current directory. The -i option will first prompt the user to confirm whether the file should be deleted.

Matching Single Characters

The question mark (**?**) matches only a single incomplete character in filenames. Suppose you want to match the files **doc1** and **docA**, but not the file **document**. Whereas the asterisk will match filenames of any length, the question mark limits the match to one extra character. The next example matches files that begin with the word "doc" followed by a single differing letter.

```
$ ls
doc1 docA document
$ ls doc?
doc1 docA
```

Matching a Range of Characters

Whereas the ***** and **?** file expansion characters specify incomplete portions of a filename, the brackets (**[]**) enable you to specify a set of valid characters to search for. Any character placed within the brackets will be matched in the filename. In the next example, files are listed that begin with "doc", but only end in **1** or **A**. Filenames ending in **2** or **B**, or any other character are not listed.

```
$ ls
doc1 doc2 doc3 docA docB docD document
$ ls doc[1A]
doc1 docA
```

You can also specify a set of characters as a range, rather than listing them one by one. A dash placed between the upper and lower bounds of a range of characters selects all characters within that range. The range is usually determined by the character set in use. In an ASCII character set, the range "a-g" will select all lowercase alphabetic characters from **a** through **g**, inclusive. In the next example, files beginning with the pattern "doc" and ending in characters **1** through **3** are selected. Then, those ending in characters **B** through **E** are matched.

```
$ ls doc[1-3]
doc1 doc2 doc3
$ ls doc[B-E]
docB docD
```

You can combine the brackets with other file expansion characters to form flexible matching operators. Suppose you want to list only filenames ending in either a **.c** or **.o** extension, but no other extension. You can use a combination of the asterisk and brackets: *** [co]**. The asterisk matches all filenames, and the brackets match only filenames with extension **.c** or **.o**.

```
$ ls *.[co]
main.c  main.o  calc.c
```

Matching Shell Symbols

At times, a file expansion character is actually part of a filename. In these cases, you need to quote the character by preceding it with a backslash (****) to reference the file. In the next example, the user needs to reference a file that ends with the **?** character, called **answers?**. The **?** is, however, a file expansion character and would match any filename beginning with "answers" that has one or more characters. In this case, the user quotes the **?** with a preceding backslash to reference the filename.

```
$ ls answers\?
answers?
```

Placing the filename in double quotes will also quote the character.

```
$ ls "answers?"
answers?
```

This is also true for filenames or directories that have white space characters like the space character. In this case, you could either use the backslash to quote the space character in the file or directory name, or place the entire name in double quotes.

```
$ ls My\ Documents
My Documents
$ ls "My Documents"
My Documents
```

Generating Patterns

Though not a file expansion operation, {} is often useful for generating names that you can use to create or modify files and directories. The braces operation only generates a list of names. It does not match on existing filenames. Patterns are placed within the braces and separated with commas. Any pattern placed within the braces will be used to generate a version of the pattern, using either the preceding or following pattern, or both. The following example generates a list of names beginning with "doc", but ending only in the patterns "ument", "final", and "draft".

```
$ echo doc{ument,final,draft}
document docfinal docdraft
```

Since the names generated do not have to exist, you could use the {} operation in a command to create directories, as shown here.

```
$ mkdir {fall,winter,spring}report
$ ls
fallreport springreport winterreport
```

Standard Input/Output and Redirection

The data in input and output operations are organized like a file. Data input at the keyboard is placed in a data stream arranged as a continuous set of bytes. Data output from a command or program is also placed in a data stream and arranged as a continuous set of bytes. This input data stream is referred to as the standard input, while the output data stream is called the standard output. A separate output data stream reserved solely for error messages is called the standard error.

Because the standard input and standard output have the same organization as that of a file, they can easily interact with files. Linux has a redirection capability that lets you easily move data in and out of files. You can redirect the standard output so that, instead of displaying the output on a screen, you can save it in a file. You can also redirect the standard input away from the keyboard to a file so that input is read from a file instead of from your keyboard.

When a Linux command is executed that produces output, this output is placed in the standard output data stream. The default destination for the standard output data stream is a device, usually the screen. Devices, such as the keyboard and screen, are treated as files. They receive and send out streams of bytes with the same organization as that of a byte-stream file. The screen is a device that displays a continuous stream of bytes. By default, the standard output will send its data to the screen device, which will then display the data.

For example, the **ls** command generates a list of all filenames and outputs this list to the standard output. Next, this stream of bytes in the standard output is directed to the screen device. The list of filenames is then printed on the screen. The **cat** command also sends output to the standard output. The contents of a file are copied to the standard output, whose default destination is the screen. The contents of the file are then displayed on the screen.

Redirecting the Standard Output: > and >>

Suppose that instead of displaying a list of files on the screen, you would like to save this list in a file. In other words, you would like to direct the standard output to a file rather than the screen. To do this, you place the output redirection operator, the greater-than sign (>), followed by the name of a file on the command line after the Linux command. Table 19-6 lists the different ways you can use the redirection operators. In the next example, the output of the **ls** command is redirected from the screen device to a file:

```
$ ls -l *.c > programlist
```

The redirection operation creates the new destination file. If the file already exists, it will be overwritten with the data in the standard output. You can set the **noclobber** feature to prevent overwriting an existing file with the redirection operation. In this case, the redirection operation on an existing file will fail. You can overcome the **noclobber** feature by placing an exclamation point after the redirection operator. You can place the **noclobber** command in a shell configuration file to make it an automatic default operation. The next example sets the **noclobber** feature for the BASH shell and then forces the overwriting of the **oldarticle** file if it already exists:

```
$ set -o noclobber
$ cat myarticle >! oldarticle
```

Although the redirection operator and the filename are placed after the command, the redirection operation is not executed after the command. It is executed before the command. The redirection operation creates the file and sets up the redirection before it receives any data from the standard output. If the file already exists, it will be destroyed and replaced by a file of the same name. In effect, the command generating the output is executed only after the redirected file has been created.

In the next example, the output of the **ls** command is redirected from the screen device to a file. First, the **ls** command lists files, and in the next command, **ls** redirects its file list to the **listf** file. Then the **cat** command displays the list of files saved in **listf**. Notice the list of files in **listf** includes the **listf** filename. The list of filenames generated by the **ls** command includes the name of the file created by the redirection operation, in this case, **listf**. The **listf** file is first created by the redirection operation, and then the **ls** command lists it along with other files. This file list output by **ls** is then redirected to the **listf** file, instead of being printed on the screen.

```
$ ls
mydata intro preface
$ ls > listf
$ cat listf
mydata intro listf preface
```

Command	Execution
ENTER	Execute a command line
;	Separate commands on the same command line
command\ opts args	Enter backslash before carriage return to continue entering a command on the next line
`command`	Execute a command
Special Characters for Filename Expansion	**Execution**
*	Match on any set of characters
?	Match on any single characters
[]	Match on a class of possible characters
\	Quote the following character. Used to quote special characters
Redirection	**Execution**
command > filename	Redirect the standard output to a file or device, creating the file if it does not exist and overwriting the file if it does exist
command < filename	Redirect the standard input from a file or device to a program.
command >> filename	Redirect the standard output to a file or device, appending the output to the end of the file
command 2> filename	Redirect the standard error to a file or device
command 2>> filename	Redirect and append the standard error to a file or device
command 2>&1	Redirect the standard error to the standard output in the Bourne shell
command >& filename	Redirect the standard error to a file or device in the C shell
Pipes	**Execution**
command	command	Pipe the standard output of one command as input for another command

Table 19-6: The Shell Operations

Tip: Errors occur when you try to use the same filename for both an input file for the command and the redirected destination file. In this case, because the redirection operation is executed first, the input file, because it exists, is destroyed and replaced by a file of the same name. When the command is executed, it finds an input file that is empty.

You can also append the standard output to an existing file using the >> redirection operator. Instead of overwriting the file, the data in the standard output is added at the end of the file. In the next example, the **myarticle** and **oldarticle** files are appended to the **allarticles** file. The **allarticles** file will then contain the contents of both **myarticle** and **oldarticle**.

```
$ cat myarticle >> allarticles
$ cat oldarticle >> allarticles
```

The Standard Input

Many Linux commands can receive data from the standard input. The standard input itself receives data from a device or a file. The default device for the standard input is the keyboard. Characters typed on the keyboard are placed in the standard input, which is then directed to the Linux command. Just as with the standard output, you can also redirect the standard input, receiving input from a file rather than the keyboard. The operator for redirecting the standard input is the less-than sign (<). In the next example, the standard input is redirected to receive input from the **myarticle** file, rather than the keyboard device (use CTRL-d to end the typed input). The contents of **myarticle** are read into the standard input by the redirection operation. Then the **cat** command reads the standard input and displays the contents of **myarticle**.

```
$ cat < myarticle
hello Christopher
How are you today
$
```

You can combine the redirection operations for both standard input and standard output. In the next example, the **cat** command has no filename arguments. Without filename arguments, the **cat** command receives input from the standard input and sends output to the standard output. The standard input has been redirected to receive its data from a file, while the standard output has been redirected to place its data in a file.

```
$ cat < myarticle > newarticle
```

Redirecting the Standard Error: >&, 2>, |&

When you execute commands, it is possible for an error to occur. You may give the wrong number of arguments or some kind of system error could take place. When an error occurs, the system will issue an error message. Usually, such error messages are displayed on the screen along with the standard output. Error messages are placed in another standard byte stream called the standard error. In the next example, the **cat** command is given as its argument the name of a file that does not exist, **myintro**. In this case, the **cat** command will simply issue an error. Redirection operators are listed in Table 19-6.

```
$ cat myintro
cat : myintro not found
```

Because error messages are in a separate data stream from the standard output, this means that if you have redirected the standard output to a file, error messages will still appear on the screen for you to see. Though the standard output may be redirected to a file, the standard error is still directed to the screen. In the next example, the standard output of the **cat** command is redirected to the file **mydata**. The standard error, containing the error messages, is still directed toward the screen

```
$ cat myintro > mydata
cat : myintro not found
```

Like the standard output, you can also redirect the standard error. This is helpful if you need to save a record of the error messages. Like the standard output, the standard error's default destination is the display. Using special redirection operators, you can redirect the standard error to any file or device that you choose. If you redirect the standard error, the error messages will not be displayed on the screen. You can examine them later by viewing the contents of the file in which you saved them.

All the standard byte streams can be referenced in redirection operations with numbers. The numbers 0, 1, and 2 reference the standard input, standard output, and standard error respectively. By default an output redirection, >, operates on the standard output, 1. You can modify the output redirection to operate on the standard error by preceding the output redirection operator with the number 2, **2>**. In the next example, the **cat** command again will generate an error. The error message is redirected to the standard byte stream represented by number 2, the standard error.

```
$ cat nodata 2> myerrors
$ cat myerrors
cat : nodata not found
```

You can also append the standard error to a file by using the number 2 and the redirection append operator, >>. In the next example, the user appends the standard error to the **myerrors** file, which then functions as a log of errors.

```
$ cat nodata 2>> myerrors
$ cat compls 2>> myerrors
$ cat myerrors
cat : nodata not found
cat : compls not found
$
```

To redirect both the standard output as well as the standard error, you would need a separate redirection operation and file for each. In the next example, the standard output is redirected to the file **mydata**, and the standard error is redirected to **myerrors**. If the file **nodata** were to exist, then **mydata** would hold a copy of its contents.

```
$ cat nodata 1> mydata 2> myerrors
cat myerrors
cat : nodata not found
```

If, however, you want to save a record of your errors in the same file as that used for the redirected standard output, you need to redirect the standard error into the standard output. You can reference a standard byte stream by preceding its number with an ampersand. **&1** references the standard output. You can use such a reference in a redirection operation to make a standard byte stream a destination file. The redirection operation **2>&1** redirects the standard error into the standard output. In effect, the standard output becomes the destination file for the standard error. Conversely, the redirection operation **1>&2** would redirect the standard input into the standard error.

Pipes: |

You may encounter situations in which you need to send data from one command to another. In other words, you may want to send the standard output of a command to another command, rather than to a destination file. Suppose you want to send a list of your filenames to the printer to be printed. You need two commands to do this: the **ls** command to generate a list of filenames and the **lpr** command to send the list to the printer. In effect, you need to take the output of the **ls** command and use it as input for the **lpr** command. You can think of the data as flowing from one command to another. To form such a connection in Linux, you use what is called a pipe. The pipe operator (|, the vertical bar character) placed between two commands forms a connection between them. The standard output of one command becomes the standard input for the other. The pipe operation receives output from the command placed before the pipe and sends this data as input to the command placed after the pipe. As shown in the next example, you can connect the **ls** command and the **lpr** command with a pipe. The list of filenames output by the **ls** command is piped into the **lpr** command.

```
$ ls | lpr
```

You can combine the **pipe** operation with other shell features, such as file expansion characters, to perform specialized operations. The next example prints only files with a **.c** extension. The **ls** command is used with the asterisk and ".c" to generate a list of filenames with the **.c** extension. Then this list is piped to the **lpr** command.

```
$ ls *.c | lpr
```

In the preceding example, a list of filenames was used as input, but what is important to note is that pipes operate on the standard output of a command, whatever that might be. The contents of whole files, or even several files, can be piped from one command to another. In the next example, the **cat** command reads and outputs the contents of the **mydata** file, which are then piped to the **lpr** command:

```
$ cat mydata | lpr
```

Linux has many commands that generate modified output. For example, the **sort** command takes the contents of a file and generates a version with each line sorted in alphabetic order. The **sort** command works best with files that are lists of items. Commands such as **sort** that output a modified version of its input are referred to as filters. Filters are often used with pipes. In the next example, a sorted version of **mylist** is generated and piped into the **more** command for display on the screen. The original file, **mylist**, has not been changed and is not sorted. Only the output of **sort** in the standard output is sorted.

```
$ sort mylist | more
```

The standard input piped into a command can be more carefully controlled with the standard input argument (-). When you use the dash as an argument for a command, it represents the standard input.

ubuntu

20. Working with files and directories

Linux Files

The File Structure

Listing, Displaying, and Printing Files: ls, cat, more, less, and lpr

Managing Directories: mkdir, rmdir, ls, cd, pwd

File and Directory Operations: find, cp, mv, rm, ln

Archiving and Compressing Files

In Linux, all files are organized into directories that, in turn, are hierarchically connected to each other in one overall file structure. A file is referenced not according to just its name, but also according to its place in this file structure. You can create as many new directories as you want, adding more directories to the file structure. The Linux file commands can perform sophisticated operations, such as moving or copying whole directories along with their subdirectories. You can use file operations such as **find**, **cp**, **mv**, and **ln** to locate files and copy, move, or link them from one directory to another. Desktop file managers provide a desktop interface to perform the same operations using icons, windows, and menus. This chapter will focus on the commands you use in the shell command line to manage files, such as **cp** and **mv**. Whether you use the command line or a desktop file manager, the underlying file structure is the same.

Archives are used to back up files or to combine them into a package, which can then be transferred as one file over the Internet or posted on an FTP site for easy downloading. The standard archive utility used on Linux and UNIX systems is **tar**. You have several compression programs to choose from, including GNU zip (**gzip**), Zip, **bzip**, and **compress**.

Linux Files

You can name a file using any letters, underscores, and numbers. You can also include periods and commas. Except in certain special cases, you should never begin a filename with a period. Other characters, such as slashes, question marks, or asterisks, are reserved for use as special characters by the system and should not be part of a filename. Filenames can be as long as 256 characters. Filenames can also include spaces, though to reference such filenames from the command line, be sure to encase them in quotes.

You can include an extension as part of a filename. A period is used to distinguish the filename proper from the extension. Extensions can be useful for categorizing your files. For example, C source code files always have a **.c** extension. Files that contain compiled object code have an **.o** extension. You can make up your own file extensions. The following examples are all valid Linux filenames. Keep in mind that to reference the name with spaces on the command line, you would have to encase it in quotes, for example the name "New book review".

```
preface
chapter2
9700info
New_Revisions
calc.c
intro.bk1
New book review
```

Special initialization files are also used to hold shell configuration commands. These are the hidden, or dot, files, which begin with a period. Dot files used by commands and applications have predetermined names, such as the **.mozilla** directory used to hold your Mozilla Web browser data and configuration files. When you use **ls** to display your filenames, the dot files will not be displayed. To include the dot files, you use **ls** with the **-a** option.

The **ls -l** command displays detailed information about a file. First, the permissions are displayed, followed by the number of links, the owner of the file, the name of the group to which the user belongs, the file size in bytes, the date and time the file was last modified, and the name of the file. Permissions indicate who can access the file: the user, members of a group, or all other users. The group name indicates the group permitted to access the file object. The file type for

mydata is that of an ordinary file. Only one link exists, indicating the file has no other names and no other links. The owner's name is **chris**, the same as the login name, and the group name is **weather**. Other users probably also belong to the **weather** group. The size of the file is 207 bytes, and it was last modified on February 20 at 11:55 A.M. The name of the file is **mydata**.

If you want to display this detailed information for all the files in a directory, use the **ls -l** command without an argument.

```
$ ls -l
-rw-r--r-- 1 chris weather 207 Feb 20 11:55 mydata
-rw-rw-r-- 1 chris weather 568 Feb 14 10:30 today
-rw-rw-r-- 1 chris weather 308 Feb 17 12:40 monday
```

All files in Linux have one physical format, a byte stream, which is simply a sequence of bytes. This allows Linux to apply the file concept to every data component in the system. Directories are classified as files, as are devices. Treating everything as a file allows Linux to organize and exchange data more easily. The data in a file can be sent directly to a device such as a screen because a device interfaces with the system using the same byte-stream file format used by regular files.

This same file format is used to implement other operating system components. The interface to a device, such as the screen or keyboard, is designated as a file. Other components, such as directories, are themselves byte-stream files, but they have a special internal organization. A directory file contains information about a directory, organized in a directory format. Because these different components are treated as files, they can be said to constitute different file types. A character device is one file type. A directory is another file type. The number of these file types may vary according to your specific implementation of Linux. Five common types of files exist: ordinary files, directory files, first-in-first-out (FIFO) pipes, character device files, and block device files.

Although all ordinary files have a byte-stream format, they may be used in different ways. The most significant difference is between binary and text files. Compiled programs are examples of binary files. Text files can be further classified according to their different uses. You can have files that contain C programming source code or shell commands or even a file that is empty. The file could be an executable program or a directory file. The Linux **file** command helps you determine what a file is used for. It examines the first few lines of a file and tries to determine a classification for it. The **file** command looks for special keywords or special numbers in those first few lines, but it is not always accurate. In the next example, the **file** command examines the contents of two files and determines a classification for them.

```
$ file monday reports
monday: text
reports: directory
```

If you need to examine the entire file byte by byte, you can do so with the **od** (octal dump) command, which performs a dump of a file. By default, it prints every byte in its octal representation. You can also specify a character, decimal, or hexadecimal representation. The **od** command is helpful when you need to detect any special character in your file or if you want to display a binary file.

The File Structure

Linux organizes files into a hierarchically connected set of directories. Each directory may contain either files or other directories. In this respect, directories perform two important functions. A directory holds files, much like files held in a file drawer, and a directory connects to other directories, much as a branch in a tree is connected to other branches. Because of the similarities to a tree, such a structure is referred to as a tree structure.

The Linux file structure branches into several directories beginning with a root directory, /. Within the root directory, several system directories contain files and programs that are features of the Linux system. The root directory also contains a directory called **/home** that contains the home directories of all the users in the system. Each user's home directory, in turn, contains the directories users have created for their own use. Each of these can also contain directories. Such nested directories branch out from the user's home directory.

Note: The user's home directory can be any directory, though it is usually the directory that bears the user's login name. This directory is located in the directory named **/home** on your Linux system. For example, a user named **dylan** will have a home directory called **dylan** located in the system's **/home** directory. The user's home directory is a subdirectory of the directory called **/home** on your system.

Home Directories

When you log in to the system, you are placed within your home directory. The name given to this directory by the system is the same as your login name. Any files you create when you first log in are organized within your home directory. Within your home directory, you can create more directories. You can then change to these directories and store files in them. The same is true for other users on the system. Each user has a home directory, identified by the appropriate login name. Users, in turn, can create their own directories.

You can access a directory either through its name or by making it your working directory. Each directory is given a name when it is created. You can use this name in file operations to access files in that directory. You can also make the directory your working directory. If you do not use any directory names in a file operation, the working directory will be accessed. The working directory is the one from which you are currently working. When you log in, the working directory is your home directory, which usually has the same name as your login name. You can change the working directory by using the **cd** command to move to another directory.

Pathnames

The name you give to a directory or file when you create it is not its full name. The full name of a directory is its pathname. The hierarchically nested relationship among directories forms paths and these paths can be used to identify and reference any directory or file uniquely or absolutely. Each directory in the file structure can be said to have its own unique path. The actual name by which the system identifies a directory always begins with the root directory and consists of all directories nested below that directory.

In Linux, you write a pathname by listing each directory in the path separated from the last by a forward slash. A slash preceding the first directory in the path represents the root. The pathname for the **chris** directory is **/home/chris**. If the **chris** directory has a subdirectory called **reports**, then the full the pathname for the **reports** directory would be **/home/chris/reports**.

Pathnames also apply to files. When you create a file within a directory, you give the file a name. The actual name by which the system identifies the file is the filename combined with the path of directories from the root to the file's directory. As an example, the pathname for **monday** is **/home/chris/reports/monday** (the root directory is represented by the first slash). The path for the **monday** file consists of the root, **home**, **chris**, and **reports** directories and the filename **monday**.

Directory	Function
I	Begins the file system structure, called the *root*.
/home	Contains users' home directories.
/bin	Holds all the standard commands and utility programs.
/usr	Holds those files and commands used by the system; this directory breaks down into several subdirectories.
/usr/bin	Holds user-oriented commands and utility programs.
/usr/sbin	Holds system administration commands.
/usr/lib	Holds libraries for programming languages.
/usr/share/doc	Holds Linux documentation.
/usr/share/man	Holds the online Man files.
/var/spool	Holds spooled files, such as those generated for printing jobs and network transfers.
/sbin	Holds system administration commands for booting the system.
/var	Holds files that vary, such as mailbox files.
/dev	Holds file interfaces for devices such as the terminals and printers (dynamically generated by udev, do not edit).
/etc	Holds system configuration files and any other system files.

Table 20-1: Standard System Directories in Linux

Pathnames may be absolute or relative. An absolute pathname is the complete pathname of a file or directory beginning with the root directory. A relative pathname begins from your working directory. It is the path of a file relative to your working directory. The working directory is the one you are currently operating in. Using the previous example, if **chris** is your working directory, the relative pathname for the file **monday** is **reports/monday**. The absolute pathname for **monday** is **/home/chris/reports/monday**.

The absolute pathname from the root to your home directory can be especially complex and, at times, even subject to change by the system administrator. To make it easier to reference, you can use the tilde (~) character, which represents the absolute pathname of your home directory. You must specify the rest of the path from your home directory. In the next example, the user references the **monday** file in the **reports** directory. The tilde represents the path to the user's home directory, **/home/chris**, and then the rest of the path to the **monday** file is specified.

```
$ cat ~/reports/monday
```

System Directories

The root directory that begins the Linux file structure contains several system directories that contain files and programs used to run and maintain the system. Many also contain other subdirectories with programs for executing specific features of Linux. For example, the directory **/usr/bin** contains the various Linux commands that users execute, such as **ls**. The directory **/bin** holds system level commands. Table 20-1 lists the basic system directories.

Listing, Displaying, and Printing Files: ls, cat, more, less, and lpr

You may need to perform certain basic output operations on your files, such as displaying them on your screen or printing them. The BASH shell provides a set of commands that perform basic file-management operations, such as listing, displaying, and printing files, as well as copying, renaming, and erasing files. These commands are usually made up of abbreviated versions of words. For example, the **ls** command is a shortened form of "list" and lists the files in your directory. The **lpr** command is an abbreviated form of "line print" and will print a file. The **cat**, **less**, and **more** commands display the contents of a file on the screen. The **ls** command has many possible options for displaying filenames according to specific features. Table 20-2 lists these commands with their different options.

Command or Option	Execution
`ls`	This command lists file and directory names.
`cat` *filenames*	This filter can be used to display a file. It can take filenames for its arguments. It outputs the contents of those files directly to the standard output, which, by default, is directed to the screen.
`more` *filenames*	This utility displays a file screen by screen. Press the SPACEBAR to continue to the next screen and **q** to quit.
`less` *filenames*	This utility also displays a file screen by screen. Press the SPACEBAR to continue to the next screen and **q** to quit.
`lpr` *filenames*	Sends a file to the line printer to be printed; a list of files may be used as arguments. Use the **-P** option to specify a printer.
`lpq`	Lists the print queue for printing jobs.
`lprm`	Removes a printing job from the print queue.

Table 20-2: Listing, Displaying, and Printing Files

Displaying Files: cat, less, and more

The **cat** and **more** commands display the contents of a file on the screen. The name **cat** stands for concatenate.

```
$ cat mydata
computers
```

The **cat** command outputs the entire text of a file to the screen at once. This presents a problem for a large file because its text quickly speeds past on the screen. The **more** and **less** commands are designed to overcome this limitation by displaying one screen of text at a time. You can then move forward or backward in the text as you wish. You invoke the **more** or **less** command by entering the command name followed by the name of the file you want to view (**less** is a more powerful and configurable display utility).

```
$ less mydata
```

When **more** or **less** invoke a file, the first screen of text is displayed. To continue to the next screen, you press the **f** key or the SPACEBAR. To move back in the text, you press the **b** key. You can quit at any time by pressing the **q** key.

Printing Files: lpr, lpq, and lprm

With the printer commands such as **lpr** and **lprm**, you can perform printing operations such as printing files or canceling print jobs (see Table 20-2). When you need to print files, use the **lpr** command to send files to the printer connected to your system. In the next example, the user prints the **mydata** file.

```
$ lpr mydata
```

If you want to print several files at once, you can specify more than one file on the command line after the **lpr** command. In the next example, the user prints out both the **mydata** and **preface** files.

```
$ lpr mydata preface
```

Printing jobs are placed in a queue and printed one at a time in the background. You can continue with other work as your files print. You can see the position of a particular printing job at any given time with the **lpq** command, which gives the owner of the printing job (the login name of the user who sent the job), the print job ID, the size in bytes, and the temporary file in which it is currently held.

If you need to cancel an unwanted printing job, you can do so with the **lprm** command, which takes as its argument either the ID number of the printing job, or the owner's name. It then removes the print job from the print queue. For this task, **lpq** is helpful, for it provides you with the ID number and owner of the printing job you need to use with **lprm**.

Managing Directories: mkdir, rmdir, ls, cd, pwd

You can create and remove your own directories, as well as change your working directory, with the **mkdir**, **rmdir**, and **cd** commands. Each of these commands can take as its argument the pathname for a directory. The **pwd** command displays the absolute pathname of your working directory. In addition to these commands, the special characters represented by a single dot, a double dot, and a tilde can be used to reference the working directory, the parent of the working directory, and the home directory, respectively. Taken together, these commands enable you to manage your directories. You can create nested directories, move from one directory to another, and use pathnames to reference any of your directories. Those commands commonly used to manage directories are listed in Table 20-3.

Command	Execution
`mkdir` *directory*	Creates a directory.
`rmdir` *directory*	Erases a directory.
`ls -F`	Lists directory name with a preceding slash.
`ls -R`	Lists working directory as well as all subdirectories.
`cd` *directory name*	Changes to the specified directory, making it the working directory. **cd** without a directory name changes back to the home directory: **$ cd reports**
`pwd`	Displays the pathname of the working directory.
directory name / *filename*	A slash is used in pathnames to separate each directory name. In the case of pathnames for files, a slash separates the preceding directory names from the filename.
`. .`	References the parent directory. You can use it as an argument or as part of a pathname. **$ cd ..** **$ mv ../larisa oldarticles**
`.`	References the working directory. You can use it as an argument or as part of a pathname. **$ ls .**
`~/` *pathname*	The tilde is a special character that represents the pathname for the home directory. It is useful when you need to use an absolute pathname for a file or directory: **$ cp monday ~/today**

Table 20-3: Directory Commands

Creating and Deleting Directories

You create and remove directories with the **mkdir** and **rmdir** commands. In either case, you can also use pathnames for the directories. In the next example, the user creates the directory **reports**. Then the user creates the directory **articles** using a pathname.

```
$ mkdir reports
$ mkdir /home/chris/articles
```

You can remove a directory with the **rmdir** command followed by the directory name. In the next example, the user removes the directory **reports** with the **rmdir** command.

```
$ rmdir reports
```

To remove a directory and all its subdirectories, you use the **rm** command with the **-r** option. This is a very powerful command and could easily be used to erase all your files. You will be prompted for each file. To simply remove all files and subdirectories without prompts, add the **-f** option. The following example deletes the **reports** directory and all its subdirectories.

```
rm -rf reports
```

Displaying Directory Contents

To distinguish between file and directory names, you use the **ls** command with the **-F** option. A slash is then placed after each directory name in the list.

```
$ ls
weather reports articles
$ ls -F
weather reports/ articles/
```

The **ls** command also takes as an argument any directory name or directory pathname. This enables you to list the files in any directory without first having to change to that directory. In the next example, the **ls** command takes as its argument the name of a directory, **reports**. Then the **ls** command is executed again, only, this time, the absolute pathname of **reports** is used.

```
$ ls reports
monday tuesday
$ ls /home/chris/reports
monday tuesday
$
```

Moving Through Directories

The **cd** command takes as its argument the name of the directory to which you want to move. The name of the directory can be the name of a subdirectory in your working directory or the full pathname of any directory on the system. If you want to change back to your home directory, you need to enter only the **cd** command by itself, without a filename argument.

```
$ cd reports
$ pwd
/home/chris/reports
```

Referencing the Parent Directory

A directory always has a parent (except, of course, for the root). For example, in the preceding listing, the parent for **reports** is the **chris** directory. When a directory is created, two entries are made: one represented with a dot (.), and the other with double dots (..). The dot represents the pathnames of the directory, and the double dots represent the pathname of its parent directory. Double dots, used as an argument in a command, reference a parent directory. The single dot references the directory itself.

You can use the single dot to reference your working directory, instead of using its pathname. For example, to copy a file to the working directory retaining the same name, the dot can be used in place of the working directory's pathname. In this sense, the dot is another name for the working directory. In the next example, the user copies the **weather** file from the **chris** directory to the **reports** directory. The **reports** directory is the working directory and can be represented with the single dot.

```
$ cd reports
$ cp /home/chris/weather .
```

The **..** symbol is used to reference files in the parent directory. In the next example, the **cat** command displays the **weather** file in the parent directory. The pathname for the file is the **..** symbol (for the parent directory) followed by a slash and the filename.

```
$ cat ../weather
raining and warm
```

Tip: You can use the cd command with the . . symbol to step back through successive parent directories of the directory tree from a lower directory.

File and Directory Operations: find, cp, mv, rm, ln

As you create files, you may want to back them up, change their names, erase some of them, or even give them added names. Linux provides several file commands that you can use to search for files, copy files, rename files, or remove files (see Table 20-5). If you have a large number of files, you can also search them to locate a specific one. The commands are usually shortened forms of full words, consisting of only two characters. The **cp** command stands for "copy" and copies a file, **mv** stands for "move" and renames or moves a file, **rm** stands for "remove" and erases a file, and **ln** stands for "link" and adds another name for a file, often used as a shortcut to the original. The **find** command performs searches of your filenames to find a file.

Searching Directories: find

You may need to search files stored in many different directories to locate a specific file, or files, of a certain type. The **find** command enables you to perform such a search from the command line. The **find** command takes as its arguments directory names followed by several possible options that specify the type of search and the criteria for the search. It then searches within the directories listed and their subdirectories for files that meet these criteria. The **find** command can search for a file by name, type, owner, and even the time of the last update.

```
$ find directory-list -option criteria
```

The **-name** option has as its criteria a pattern and instructs **find** to search for the filename that matches that pattern. To search for a file by name, you use the **find** command with the directory name followed by the **-name** option and the name of the file.

```
$ find directory-list -name filename
```

The **find** command also has options that perform actions, such as outputting the results of a search. If you want **find** to display the filenames it has located, you include the **-print** option on the command line along with any other options. The **-print** option is an action that instructs **find** to write to the standard output the names of all the files it locates (you can also use the **-ls** option instead to list files in the long format). In the next example, the user searches for all the files in the **reports** directory with the name **monday**. Once located, the file, with its relative pathname, is printed.

```
$ find reports -name monday -print
reports/monday
```

The **find** command prints out the filenames using the directory name specified in the directory list. If you specify an absolute pathname, the absolute path of the found directories will be output. If you specify a relative pathname, only the relative pathname is output. In the preceding example, the user specified a relative pathname, **reports**, in the directory list. Located filenames were output beginning with this relative pathname. In the next example, the user specifies an absolute pathname in the directory list. Located filenames are then output using this absolute pathname.

```
$ find /home/chris  -name monday -print
/home/chris/reports/monday
```

Tip: Should you need to find the location of a specific program or configuration file, you could use `find` to search for the file from the root directory. Log in as the root user and use */* as the directory. This command searched for the location of the `more` command and files on the entire file system: `find / -name more -print`.

Searching the Working Directory

If you want to search your working directory, you can use the dot in the directory pathname to represent your working directory. The double dots would represent the parent directory. The next example searches all files and subdirectories in the working directory, using the dot to represent the working directory. If your working directory is your home directory, this is a convenient way to search through all your own directories. Notice that the located filenames that are output begin with a dot.

```
$ find . -name  weather -print
./weather
```

You can use shell wildcard characters as part of the pattern criteria for searching files. The special character must be quoted to avoid evaluation by the shell. In the next example, all files (indicated by the asterisk, *****) with the **.c** extension in the **programs** directory are searched for and then displayed in the long format using the **-ls** action.

```
$ find programs -name '*.c' -ls
```

Locating Directories

You can also use the **find** command to locate other directories. In Linux, a directory is officially classified as a special type of file. Although all files have a byte-stream format, some files, such as directories, are used in special ways. In this sense, a file can be said to have a file type. The **find** command has an option called **-type** that searches for a file of a given type. The **-type** option takes a one-character modifier that represents the file type. The modifier that represents a directory is a **d**. In the next example, both the directory name and the directory file type are used to search for the directory called **travel**.

```
$ find /home/chris -name travel -type d -print
/home/chris/articles/travel
$
```

File types are not so much different types of files, as they are the file format applied to other components of the operating system, such as devices. In this sense, a device is treated as a type of file, and you can use **find** to search for devices and directories, as well as ordinary files. Table 20-4 lists the different types available for the **find** command's **-type** option.

Command or Option	Execution
`find`	Searches directories for files according to search criteria. This command has several options that specify the type of criteria and actions to be taken.
`-name` *pattern*	Searches for files with the *pattern* in the name.
`-lname` *pattern*	Searches for symbolic link files.
`-group` *name*	Searches for files belonging to the group *name*.
`-gid` *name*	Searches for files belonging to a group according to group ID.
`-user` *name*	Searches for files belonging to a user.
`-uid` *name*	Searches for files belonging to a user according to user ID.
`-size` *numc*	Searches for files with the size *num* in blocks. If **c** is added after *num*, the size in bytes (characters) is searched for.
`-mtime` *num*	Searches for files last modified *num* days ago.
`-newer` *pattern*	Searches for files modified after the one matched by *pattern*.
`-context` *scontext*	Searches for files according to security context (SE Linux).
`-print`	Outputs the result of the search to the standard output. The result is usually a list of filenames, including their full pathnames.
`-type` *filetype*	Searches for files with the specified file type. File type can be **b** for block device, **c** for character device, **d** for directory, **f** for file, or **l** for symbolic link.
`-perm` *permission*	Searches for files with certain permissions set. Use octal or symbolic format for permissions.
`-ls`	Provides a detailed listing of each file, with owner, permission, size, and date information.
`-exec` *command*	Executes command when files found.

Table 20-4: The find Command

You can also use the find operation to search for files by ownership or security criteria, like those belonging to a specific user or those with a certain security context. The **-user** option lets to locate all files belonging to a certain user. The following example lists all files that the user **chris** has created or owns on the entire system. To list those just in a user's home directory, you would use **/home** for the starting search directory. This would find all those in a user's home directory as well as any owned by that user in other user directories.

```
$ find / -user chris -print
```

Copying Files

To make a copy of a file, you give **cp** command two filenames as its arguments (see Table 20-5). The first filename is the name of the file to be copied, the one that already exists. This is often referred to as the source file. The second filename is the name you want for the copy. This will be a new file containing a copy of all the data in the source file. This second argument is referred to as the destination file. The syntax for the **cp** command follows.

```
$ cp source-file destination-file
```

In the next example, the user copies a file called **proposal** to a new file called **oldprop**.

```
$ cp proposal oldprop
```

Command	Execution
cp *filename filename*	Copies a file. **cp** takes two arguments: the original file and the name of the new copy. You can use pathnames for the files to copy across directories.
cp -r *dirname dirname*	Copies a subdirectory from one directory to another. The copied directory includes all its own subdirectories.
mv *filename filename*	Moves (renames) a file. The **mv** command takes two arguments: the first is the file to be moved. The second argument can be the new filename or the pathname of a directory. If it is the name of a directory, then the file is literally moved to that directory, changing the file's pathname.
mv *dirname dirname*	Moves directories. In this case, the first and last arguments are directories.
ln *filename filename*	Creates added names for files referred to as links. A link can be created in one directory that references a file in another directory.
rm *filenames*	Removes (erases) a file. Can take any number of filenames as its arguments. Literally, removes links to a file. If a file has more than one link, you need to remove all of them to erase a file.

Table 20-5: File Operations

You could unintentionally destroy another file with the **cp** command. The **cp** command generates a copy by first creating a file and then copying data into it. If another file has the same name as the destination file, that file is destroyed and a new file with that name is created. By default, Ubuntu configures your system to check for an existing copy by the same name (**cp** is aliased with the **-i** option). To copy a file from your working directory to another directory, you need to use that directory name as the second argument in the **cp** command. In the next example, the **proposal** file is overwritten by the **newprop** file. The **proposal** file already exists.

```
$ cp newprop proposal
```

You can use any of the wildcard characters to generate a list of filenames to use with **cp** or **mv**. For example, suppose you need to copy all your C source code files to a given directory. Instead of listing each one individually on the command line, you could use an * character with the **.c** extension to match on and generate a list of C source code files (all files with a **.c** extension). In the next example, the user copies all source code files in the current directory to the **sourcebks** directory.

```
$ cp *.c sourcebks
```

If you want to copy all the files in a given directory to another directory, you could use * to match on and generate a list of all those files in a **cp** command. In the next example, the user copies all the files in the **props** directory to the **oldprop** directory. Notice the use of a **props** pathname preceding the * special characters. In this context, **props** is a pathname that will be appended before each file in the list that * generates.

```
$ cp props/* oldprop
```

You can, of course, use any of the other special characters, such as **.**, **?**, or **[]**. In the next example, the user copies both source code and object code files (**.c** and **.o**) to the **projbk** directory.

```
$ cp *.[oc] projbk
```

When you copy a file, you can give the copy a name that is different from the original. To do so, place the new filename after the directory name, separated by a slash.

```
$ cp filename directory-name/new-filename
```

Moving Files

You can use the **mv** command to either rename a file or to move a file from one directory to another. When using **mv** to rename a file, you simply use the new filename as the second argument. The first argument is the current name of the file you are renaming. If you want to rename a file when you move it, you can specify the new name of the file after the directory name. In the next example, the **proposal** file is renamed with the name **version1**.

```
$ mv proposal version1
```

As with **cp**, it is easy for **mv** to erase a file accidentally. When renaming a file, you might accidentally choose a filename already used by another file. In this case, that other file will be erased. The **mv** command also has an **-i** option that checks first to see if a file by that name already exists.

You can also use any of the special characters to generate a list of filenames to use with **mv**. In the next example, the user moves all source code files in the current directory to the **newproj** directory.

```
$ mv *.c newproj
```

If you want to move all the files in a given directory to another directory, you can use * to match on and generate a list of all those files. In the next example, the user moves all the files in the **reports** directory to the **repbks** directory.

```
$ mv reports/* repbks
```

Copying and Moving Directories

You can also copy or move whole directories at once. Both **cp** and **mv** can take as their first argument a directory name, enabling you to copy or move subdirectories from one directory into another (see Table 20-5). The first argument is the name of the directory to be moved or copied, and the second argument is the name of the directory within which it is to be placed. The same pathname structure used for files applies to moving or copying directories.

You can just as easily copy subdirectories from one directory to another. To copy a directory, the **cp** command requires you to use the **-r** option, which stands for "recursive." It directs the **cp** command to copy a directory, as well as any subdirectories it may contain. The entire directory subtree, from that directory on, will be copied. In the next example, the **travel** directory is copied to the **oldarticles** directory. Now two **travel** subdirectories exist, one in **articles** and one in **oldarticles**.

```
$ cp -r articles/travel oldarticles
$ ls -F articles
/travel
$ ls -F oldarticles
/travel
```

Erasing Files and Directories: the rm Command

As you use Linux, you will find the number of files you use increases rapidly. Generating files in Linux is easy. You can remove them with the **rm** command. The **rm** command can take any number of arguments, enabling you to list several filenames and erase them all at the same time. In the next example, the file **oldprop** is erased.

```
$ rm oldprop
```

Be careful when using the **rm** command. It is irrevocable. Once a file is removed, it cannot be restored. There is no undo. With the **-i** option, you are prompted separately for each file and asked whether you really want to remove it. If you enter **y**, the file will be removed. If you enter anything else, the file is not removed. In the next example, the **rm** command is instructed to erase the files **proposal** and **oldprop**. The **rm** command then asks for confirmation for each file. The user decides to remove **oldprop,** but not **proposal**.

```
$ rm -i proposal oldprop
Remove proposal? n
Remove oldprop? y
$
```

Links: the ln Command

You can give a file more than one name using the **ln** command. You might do this because you want to reference a file using different filenames to access it from different directories. The added names are often referred to as links. Linux supports two different types of links, hard and symbolic. Hard links are literally another name for the same file, whereas symbolic links function like shortcuts referencing another file. Symbolic links are much more flexible and can work over many different file systems, while hard links are limited to your local file system. Hard links introduce security concerns, as they allow direct access from a link that may have public access to an original file that you may want protected. Links are usually implemented as symbolic links.

Symbolic Links

To set up a symbolic link, you use the **ln** command with the **-s** option and two arguments: the name of the original file and the new, added filename. The **ls** operation lists both filenames, but only one physical file will exist.

```
$ ln -s original-file-name added-file-name
```

In the next example, the **today** file is given the additional name **weather**. It is just another name for the **today** file.

```
$ ls
today
$ ln -s today weather
$ ls
today weather
```

You can give the same file several names by using the **ln** command on the same file many times. In the next example, the file **today** is assigned the names **weather** and **weekend**.

```
$ ln -s today weather
$ ln -s today weekend
$ ls
today weather weekend
```

If you list the full information about a symbolic link and its file, you will find the information displayed is different. In the next example, the user lists the full information for both **lunch** and **/home/george/veglist** using the **ls** command with the **-l** option. The first character in the line specifies the file type. Symbolic links have their own file type, represented by an **l**. The file type for **lunch** is **l**, indicating it is a symbolic link, not an ordinary file. The number after the term "group" is the size of the file. Notice the sizes differ. The size of the **lunch** file is only 4 bytes. This is because **lunch** is only a symbolic link (a file that holds the pathname of another file) and a pathname takes up only a few bytes. It is not a direct hard link to the **veglist** file.

```
$ ls -l lunch /home/george/veglist
lrw-rw-r-- 1 chris group 4 Feb 14 10:30 lunch
-rw-rw-r-- 1 george group 793 Feb 14 10:30 veglist
```

To erase a file, you need to remove only its original name (and any hard links to it). If any symbolic links are left over, they will be unable to access the file. In this case, a symbolic link would hold the pathname of a file that no longer exists.

Hard Links

You can give the same file several names by using the **ln** command on the same file many times. To set up a hard link, you use the **ln** command with no **-s** option and two arguments: the name of the original file and the new, added filename. The **ls** operation lists both filenames, but only one physical file will exist.

```
$ ln original-file-name added-file-name
```

In the next example, the **monday** file is given the additional name **storm**. It is just another name for the **monday** file.

```
$ ls
today
$ ln monday storm
$ ls
monday storm
```

To erase a file that has hard links, you need to remove all its hard links. The name of a file is actually considered a link to that file, hence the command **rm** that removes the link to the file. If you have several links to the file and remove only one of them, the others stay in place and you can reference the file through them. The same is true even if you remove the original link, the original name of the file. Any added links will work just as well. In the next example, the **today** file is removed with the **rm** command. However, a link to that same file exists, called **weather**. The file can then be referenced under the name **weather**.

```
$ ln today weather
$ rm today
$ cat weather
The storm broke today
and the sun came out.
$
```

Archiving and Compressing Files

Archives are used to back up files or to combine them into a package, which can then be transferred as one file over the Internet or posted on an FTP site for easy downloading. The standard archive utility used on Linux and Unix systems is **tar**, for which several desktop front ends exist. You have several compression programs to choose from, including GNU zip (**gzip**), Zip, **bzip**, and **compress**. Table 20-6 lists the commonly used archive and compressions applications.

Applications	Description
tar	Archive creation and extraction www.gnu.org/software/tar/manual/tar.html
FileRoller (Archive Manager)	GNOME front end for tar and gzip/bzip2
gzip	File, directory, and archive compression www.gnu.org/software/gzip/manual/
bzip2	File, directory, and archive compression www.gnu.org/software/gzip/manual/
zip	File, directory, and archive compression

Table 20-6: Archive and Compression Applications

Archiving and Compressing Files with File Roller

GNOME provides the File Roller tool (labeled Archive Manager) that operates as a desktop front end to archive and compress files, letting you perform Zip, gzip, tar, and bzip2 operation using a desktop interface. You can examine the contents of archives, extract the files you want, and create new compressed archives. When you create an archive, you determine its compression method by specifying its filename extension, such as **.gz** for gzip or **.bz2** for bzip2. You can select the different extensions from the File Type menu or enter the extension yourself. To both archive and compress files, you can choose a combined extension like **.tar.bz2**, which both archives with **tar** and compresses with **bzip2**. Click Add to add files to your archive. To extract files from an archive, open the archive to display the list of archive files. You can then click Extract to extract particular files or the entire archive.

File Roller can also be used to examine the contents of an archive file. From the file manager, right-click the archive and select Open With Archive Manager. The list of files and directories in that archive will be displayed. For subdirectories, double-click their entries. This method also works for DEB software files, letting you browse all the files that make up a software package.

Archive Files and Devices: tar

The **tar** utility creates archives for files and directories. With **tar**, you can archive specific files, update them in the archive, and add new files as you want to that archive. You can even archive entire directories with all their files and subdirectories, all of which can be restored from the archive. The **tar** utility was originally designed to create archives on tapes. The term "tar" stands for tape archive. You can create archives on any device, such as a floppy disk, or you can create an archive file to hold the archive. The **tar** utility is ideal for making backups of your files or combining several files into a single file for transmission across a network. File Roller is a GNOME desktop application for **tar**. For more information on **tar**, check the man page or the online man page at **https://www.gnu.org/software/tar/manual/tar.html**.

Note: As an alternative to tar, you can use pax, which is designed to work with different kinds of Unix archive formats such as cpio, bcpio, and tar. You can extract, list, and create archives. The pax utility is helpful if you are handling archives created on Unix systems that are using different archive formats.

Displaying Archive Contents on Desktops

The file manager for the GNOME desktop has the capability to display the contents of a **tar** archive file automatically. The contents are displayed as though they were files in a directory. You can list the files as icons or with details, sorting them by name, type, or other fields. You can even display the contents of files. Clicking a text file opens it with a text editor, and an image is displayed with an image viewer. If the file manager cannot determine what program to use to display the file, it prompts you to select an application. The file manager can also perform operations on archives residing on remote file systems, such as tar archives on FTP sites. You can obtain a listing of their contents and even read their readme files. The file manager can also extract an archive.

Creating Archives

On Linux, **tar** is often used to create archives on devices or files. You can direct **tar** to archive files to a specific device or a file by using the **f** option with the name of the device or file. The syntax for the **tar** command using the **f** option is shown in the next example. The device or filename is often referred to as the archive name. When creating a file for a **tar** archive, the filename is usually given the extension **.tar**. This is a convention only and is not required. You can list as many filenames as you want. If a directory name is specified, all its subdirectories are included in the archive.

```
$ tar optionsf archive-name.tar directory-and-file-names
```

To create an archive, use the **c** option. Combined with the **f** option, **c** creates an archive on a file or device. You enter this option before and right next to the **f** option. Notice no dash precedes a **tar** option. Table 20-7 lists the different options you can use with **tar**. In the next example, the directory **mydir** and all its subdirectories are saved in the file **myarch.tar**. In this example, the **mydir** directory holds two files, **mymeeting** and **party**, as well as a directory called **reports** that has three files: **weather**, **monday**, and **friday**.

Commands	Execution
`tar` *options files*	Backs up files to tape, device, or archive file.
`tar` *options*f *archive_name filelist*	Backs up files to a specific file or device specified as *archive_name. filelist*; can be filenames or directories.
Options	
`c`	Creates a new archive.
`t`	Lists the names of files in an archive.
`r`	Appends files to an archive.
`U`	Updates an archive with new and changed files; adds only those files modified since they were archived or files not already present in the archive.
`--delete`	Removes a file from the archive.
`w`	Waits for a confirmation from the user before archiving each file; enables you to update an archive selectively.
`x`	Extracts files from an archive.
`m`	When extracting a file from an archive, no new timestamp is assigned.
`M`	Creates a multiple-volume archive that may be stored on several floppy disks.
`f` *archive-name*	Saves the tape archive to the file archive name, instead of to the default tape device. When given an archive name, the `f` option saves the tar archive in a file of that name.
`f` *device-name*	Saves a tar archive to a device such as a floppy disk or tape. **/dev/fd0** is the device name for your floppy disk; the default device is held in **/etc/default/tar-file**.
`v`	Displays each filename as it is archived.
`z`	Compresses or decompresses archived files using gzip.
`j`	Compresses or decompresses archived files using bzip2.

Table 20-7: File Archives: tar

```
$ tar cvf myarch.tar mydir
mydir/
mydir/reports/
mydir/reports/weather
mydir/reports/monday
mydir/reports/friday
mydir/mymeeting
mydir/party
```

Extracting Archives

The user can later extract the directories from the tape using the **x** option. The **xf** option extracts files from an archive file or device. The **tar** extraction operation generates all subdirectories. In the next example, the **xf** option directs **tar** to extract all the files and subdirectories from the **tar** file **myarch.tar**.

```
$ tar xvf myarch.tar
mydir/
mydir/reports/
mydir/reports/weather
mydir/reports/monday
mydir/reports/friday
mydir/mymeeting
mydir/party
```

You use the **r** option to add files to an already-created archive. The **r** option appends the files to the archive. In the next example, the user appends the files in the **letters** directory to the **myarch.tar** archive. Here, the directory **mydocs** and its files are added to the **myarch.tar** archive.

```
$ tar rvf myarch.tar mydocs
mydocs/
mydocs/doc1
```

Updating Archives

If you change any of the files in the directories you previously archived, you can use the **u** option to instruct **tar** to update the archive with any modified files. The **tar** command compares the time of the last update for each archived file with those in the user's directory and copies into the archive any files that have been changed since they were last archived. Any newly created files in these directories are also added to the archive. In the next example, the user updates the **myarch.tar** file with any recently modified or newly created files in the **mydir** directory. In this case, the **gifts** file was added to the **mydir** directory.

```
tar uvf myarch.tar mydir
mydir/
mydir/gifts
```

If you need to see what files are stored in an archive, you can use the **tar** command with the **t** option. The next example lists all the files stored in the **myarch.tar** archive.

```
tar tvf myarch.tar
drwxr-xr-x root/root 0 2000-10-24 21:38:18 mydir/
drwxr-xr-x root/root 0 2000-10-24 21:38:51 mydir/reports/
-rw-r--r-- root/root 22 2000-10-24 21:38:40 mydir/reports/weather
-rw-r--r-- root/root 22 2000-10-24 21:38:45 mydir/reports/monday
-rw-r--r-- root/root 22 2000-10-24 21:38:51 mydir/reports/friday
-rw-r--r-- root/root 22 2000-10-24 21:38:18 mydir/mymeeting
-rw-r--r-- root/root 22 2000-10-24 21:36:42 mydir/party
drwxr-xr-x root/root 0 2000-10-24 21:48:45 mydocs/
-rw-r--r-- root/root 22 2000-10-24 21:48:45 mydocs/doc1
drwxr-xr-x root/root 0 2000-10-24 21:54:03 mydir/
-rw-r--r-- root/root 22 2000-10-24 21:54:03 mydir/gifts
```

Note: To backup files using several CD/DVD-ROMs, you would first create a split archive, one consisting of several files, using the -M option, the multi-volume option. The tape size for an ISO DVD would be specified with the tape-length option, --tape-length=2294900.

Compressing Archives

The **tar** operation does not perform compression on archived files. If you want to compress the archived files, you can instruct **tar** to invoke the **gzip** utility to compress them. With the lowercase **z** option, **tar** first uses **gzip** to compress files before archiving them. The same **z** option invokes **gzip** to decompress them when extracting files.

```
$ tar czf myarch.tar.gz mydir
```

To use **bzip** instead of **gzip** to compress files before archiving them, you use the **j** option. The same **j** option invokes **bzip** to decompress them when extracting files.

```
$ tar cjf myarch.tar.bz2 mydir
```

Remember, a difference exists between compressing individual files in an archive and compressing the entire archive as a whole. Often, an archive is created for transferring several files at once as one tar file. To shorten transmission time, the archive should be as small as possible. You can use the compression utility **gzip** on the archive tar file to compress it, reducing its size, and then send the compressed version. The person receiving it can decompress it, restoring the **tar** file. Using **gzip** on a **tar** file results in a file with the extension **.tar.gz**. The extension **.gz** is added to a compressed **gzip** file. The next example creates a compressed version of **myarch.tar** using the same name with the extension **.gz**.

```
$ gzip myarch.tar
$ ls
$ myarch.tar.gz
```

Instead of retyping the **tar** command for different files, you can place the command in a script and pass the files to it. Be sure to make the script executable. In the following example, a simple **myarchprog** script is created that will archive filenames listed as its arguments.

myarchprog

```
tar   cvf   myarch.tar   $*
```

A run of the **myarchprog** script with multiple arguments is shown here.

```
$ myarchprog mydata preface
mydata
preface
```

Archiving to Tape

If you have a default device specified, such as a tape, and you want to create an archive on it, you can simply use tar without the **f** option and a device or filename. This can be helpful for making backups of your files. The name of the default device is held in a file called **/etc/default/tar**. The syntax for the **tar** command using the default tape device is shown in the following example. If a directory name is specified, all its subdirectories are included in the archive.

```
$ tar option directory-and-file-names
```

In the next example, the directory **mydir** and all its subdirectories are saved on a tape in the default tape device.

```
$ tar c mydir
```

In this example, the **mydir** directory and all its files and subdirectories are extracted from the default tape device and placed in the user's working directory.

```
$ tar x mydir
```

Note: There are other archive programs you can use such as **cpio**, **pax**, and **shar**. However, **tar** is the one most commonly used for archiving application software.

File Compression: gzip, bzip2, and zip

Several reasons exist for reducing the size of a file. The two most common are to save space or, if you are transferring the file across a network, to save transmission time. You can effectively reduce a file size by creating a compressed copy of it. Anytime you need the file again, you decompress it. Compression is used in combination with archiving to enable you to compress whole directories and their files at once. Decompression generates a copy of the archive file, which can then be extracted, generating a copy of those files and directories. File Roller provides a desktop interface for these tasks.

Compression with gzip

Several compression utilities are available for use on Linux and Unix systems. Most software for Linux systems uses the GNU **gzip** and **gunzip** utilities. The **gzip** command compresses files, and **gunzip** decompresses them. For more information on gzip, check the man page or the online man page at **https://www.gnu.org/software/gzip/manual/**.

To compress a file, enter the command **gzip** and the filename. This replaces the file with a compressed version of it with the extension **.gz**.

```
$ gzip mydata
$ ls
mydata.gz
```

To decompress a gzip file, use either **gzip** with the **-d** option or the command **gunzip**. These commands decompress a compressed file with the **.gz** extension and replace it with a decompressed version with the same root name but without the **.gz** extension. When you use **gunzip**, you do not have to use the **.gz** extension. **gunzip** and **gzip -d** assume it. Table 20-8 lists the different **gzip** options.

```
$ gunzip mydata.gz
$ ls
mydata
```

Option	Execution
-c	Sends compressed version of file to standard output; each file listed is separately compressed. `gzip -c mydata preface > myfiles.gz`

-d	Decompresses a compressed file; or you can use gunzip.
	`gzip -d myfiles.gz`
	`gunzip myfiles.gz`

-h	Displays help listing.
-l *file-list*	Displays compressed and uncompressed size of each file listed. `gzip -l myfiles.gz.`
-r *directory-name*	Recursively searches for specified directories and compresses all the files in them; the search begins from the current working directory. When used with `gunzip`, compressed files of a specified directory are uncompressed.
-v *file-list*	For each compressed or decompressed file, displays its name and the percentage of its reduction in size.
-num	Determines the speed and size of the compression; the range is from –1 to –9. A lower number gives greater speed but less compression, resulting in a larger file that compresses and decompresses quickly. Thus –1 gives the quickest compression but with the largest size; –9 results in a very small file that takes longer to compress and decompress. The default is –6.

Table 20-8: The gzip Options

You can also compress archived **tar** files. This results in files with the extensions **.tar.gz**. Compressed archived files are often used for transmitting extremely large files across networks.

```
$ gzip myarch.tar
$ ls
myarch.tar.gz
```

You can compress **tar** file members individually using the **tar z** option that invokes **gzip**. With the **z** option, **tar** invokes **gzip** to compress a file before placing it in an archive. Archives with members compressed with the **z** option, however, cannot be updated, nor is it possible to add to them. All members must be compressed, and all must be added at the same time.

The compress and uncompress Commands

You can also use the **compress** and **uncompress** commands to create compressed files. They generate a file that has a **.Z** extension and use a different compression format from **gzip**. The **compress** and **uncompress** commands are not that widely used, but you may run across **.Z** files occasionally. You can use the **uncompress** command to decompress a **.Z** file. The **gzip** utility is the standard GNU compression utility and should be used instead of **compress**.

Compressing with bzip2

Another popular compression utility is **bzip2**. It compresses files using the Burrows-Wheeler block-sorting text compression algorithm and Huffman coding. The command line options are similar to **gzip** by design, but they are not exactly the same (see the **bzip2** Man page for a complete listing). For more information on bzip2 check its man page or the online documentation at **https://www.sourceware.org/bzip2/docs.html**.

You compress files using the **bzip2** command and decompress with **bunzip2**. The **bzip2** command creates files with the extension **.bz2**. You can use **bzcat** to output compressed data to the standard output. The **bzip2** command compresses files in blocks and enables you to specify their size (larger blocks give you greater compression). As when using **gzip**, you can use **bzip2** to compress **tar** archive files. The following example compresses the **mydata** file into a bzip compressed file with the extension **.bz2**.

```
$ bzip2 mydata
$ ls
mydata.bz2
```

To decompress, use the **bunzip2** command on a bzip file.

```
$ bunzip2 mydata.bz2
```

Using Zip

Zip is a compression and archive utility modeled on the older PKZIP. Zip is a cross-platform utility used on Windows, Mac, MS-DOS, OS/2, Unix, and Linux systems. You compress a file using the **zip** command. This creates a Zip file with the **.zip** extension. If no files are listed, Zip outputs the compressed data to the standard output. You can also use the - argument to have Zip read from the standard input. To compress a directory, you include the **-r** option. The first example archives and compresses a file.

```
$ zip mydata
$ ls
mydata.zip
```

The next example archives and compresses the **reports** directory.

```
$ zip -r reports
```

A full set of archive operations is supported. With the **-f** option, you can update a particular file in the Zip archive with a newer version. The **-u** option replaces or adds files, and the **-d** option deletes files from the Zip archive. Options also exist for encrypting files and including hidden files.

To decompress and extract the Zip file, you use the **unzip** command.

```
$ unzip mydata.zip
```

21. Shell Variables and Scripts

Shell Variables

Environment Variables

Control Structures

A shell script combines Linux commands in such a way as to perform a specific task. The different kinds of shells provide many programming tools that you can use to create shell scripts. You can define variables and assign values to them. You can also define variables in a script file, and have a user interactively enter values for them when the script is executed. The shell provides loop and conditional control structures that repeat Linux commands or make decisions on which commands you want to execute. You can also construct expressions that perform arithmetic or comparison operations. All these shell programming tools operate in ways similar to those found in other programming languages.

The BASH, TCSH, and Z shells are types of shells. You can have many instances of a particular kind of shell. A shell is an interpretive environment within which you execute commands. You can have many environments running at the same time, of either the same or different types of shells. You could have several shells running at the same time that are of the BASH shell type.

This chapter will cover the basics of creating a shell script using the BASH shell, the default shell for most Linux systems. You will learn how to create your own scripts, define shell variables, and develop user interfaces, as well as learn the more difficult task of combining control structures to create complex programs. Tables throughout the chapter list shell commands and operators, while numerous examples show how they are implemented.

Usually, the instructions making up a shell program are entered into a script file that can then be executed. You can even distribute your program among several script files, which will contain instructions on how to execute others. You can think of variables, expressions, and control structures as tools you can use to bring together several Linux commands into one operation. In this sense, a shell program is a new and complex Linux command that you have created.

The BASH shell has a flexible and powerful set of programming commands that allows you to build complex scripts. It supports variables that can be either local to the given shell or exported to other shells. You can pass arguments from one script to another. The BASH shell has a complete set of control structures, including loops and if structures, as well as case structures. All shell commands interact with redirection and piping operations that allow them to accept input from the standard input or send it to the standard output.

Shell Variables

Within each shell, you can enter and execute commands. You can further enhance the capabilities of a shell using shell variables. A shell variable lets you hold data that you can reference over and over again as you execute different commands within a shell. For example, you can define a shell variable to hold the name of a complex filename. Then, instead of retyping the filename in different commands, you can reference it with the shell variable.

You define variables within a shell, and such variables are known as shell variables. Some utilities have their own shells with their own shell variables. You can also create your own shell using shell scripts. You have a user shell that becomes active as soon as you log in. This is often referred to as the login shell. Special system-level parameter variables are defined within this login shell. Shell variables can also be used to define a shell's environment.

Note: Shell variables exist as long as your shell is active, that is, until you exit the shell. For example, logging out will exit the login shell. When you log in again, any variables you may need in your login shell must be defined again.

Definition and Evaluation of Variables: =, $, set, unset

You define a variable in a shell when you first use the variable's name. A variable's name may be any set of alphabetic characters, including the underscore. The name may also include a number, but the number cannot be the first character in the name. A name may not have any other type of character, such as an exclamation point, an ampersand, or even a space. Such symbols are reserved by the shell for its own use. Also, a variable name may not include more than one word. The shell uses spaces on the command line to distinguish different components of a command such as options, arguments, and the command name.

You assign a value to a variable with the assignment operator (=). You type the variable name, the assignment operator, and then the value assigned. Do not place any spaces around the assignment operator. The assignment operation **poet = Virgil**, for example, will fail. (The C shell has a slightly different type of assignment operation.) You can assign any set of characters to a variable. In the next example, the variable poet is assigned the string Virgil.

```
$ poet=Virgil
```

Once you have assigned a value to a variable, you can use the variable name to reference the value. Often you use the values of variables as arguments for a command. You can reference the value of a variable using the variable name preceded by the $ operator. The dollar sign is a special operator that uses the variable name to reference a variable's value, in effect evaluating the variable. Evaluation retrieves a variable's value, usually a set of characters. This set of characters then replaces the variable name on the command line. Wherever a $ is placed before the variable name, the variable name is replaced with the value of the variable. In the next example, the shell variable **poet** is evaluated and its contents, Virgil, is used as the argument for an **echo** command. The **echo** command simply echoes or prints a set of characters to the screen.

```
$ echo $poet
Virgil
```

You must be careful to distinguish between the evaluation of a variable and its name alone. If you leave out the $ operator before the variable name, all you have is the variable name itself. In the next example, the $ operator is absent from the variable name. In this case, the **echo** command has as its argument the word **poet**, and so prints out **poet**.

```
$ echo poet
poet
```

The contents of a variable are often used as command arguments. A common command argument is a directory pathname. It can be time consuming to retype a directory path that is being used over and over again. If you assign the directory pathname to a variable, you can simply use the evaluated variable in its place. The directory path you assign to the variable is retrieved when the variable is evaluated with the $ operator. The next example assigns a directory pathname to a variable, and then uses the evaluated variable in a copy command. The evaluation of **ldir**, which is **$ldir**, results in the pathname **/home/chris/letters**. The copy command evaluates to **cp myletter /home/chris/letters**.

```
$ ldir=/home/chris/letters
$ cp myletter $ldir
```

You can obtain a list of all the defined variables with the **set** command. If you decide you do not want a certain variable, you can remove it with the **unset** command. The **unset** command undefines a variable.

Variable Values: Strings

The values that you assign to variables may consist of any set of characters. These characters may be a character string that you explicitly type in or the result obtained from executing a Linux command. In most cases, you will need to quote your values using either single quotes, double quotes, backslashes, or back quotes. Single quotes, double quotes, and backslashes allow you to quote strings in different ways. Back quotes have the special function of executing a Linux command and using its results as arguments on the command line.

Quoting Strings: Double Quotes, Single Quotes, and Backslashes

Variable values can be made up of any characters. Problems occur when you want to include characters that are also used by the shell as operators. Your shell has certain metacharacters that it uses in evaluating the command line, such as the space, asterisk, and period. A space is used to parse arguments on the command line. The asterisk, question mark, and brackets are metacharacters used to generate lists of filenames. The period represents the current directory. The dollar sign, **$**, is used to evaluate variables, and the greater-than and less-than characters , > <, are redirection operators. The ampersand, **&**, is used to execute background commands and the bar pipes output. If you want to use any of these characters as part of the value of a variable, you first need to quote them. Quoting a metacharacter on a command line makes it just another character. It is not evaluated by the shell.

You can use double quotes, single quotes, and backslashes to quote such metacharacters. Double and single quotes allow you to quote several metacharacters at a time. Any metacharacters within double or single quotes are quoted. A backslash quotes the single character that follows it.

If you want to assign more than one word to a variable, you need to quote the spaces separating the words. You can do so by enclosing all the words within double quotes. You can think of this as creating a character string to be assigned to the variable. Any other metacharacters enclosed within the double quotes are also quoted.

In the following first example, the double quotes enclose words separated by spaces. Because the spaces are enclosed within double quotes, they are treated as characters, not as separators used to parse command line arguments. In the second example, double quotes enclose a period, treating it as just a character. In the third example, an asterisk is enclosed within the double quotes. The asterisk is considered just another character in the string and is not evaluated.

```
$ notice="The meeting will be tomorrow"
$ echo $notice
The meeting will be tomorrow

$ message="The project is on time."
$ echo $message
The project is on time.

$ notice="You can get a list of files with ls *.c"
$ echo $notice
You can get a list of files with ls *.c
```

Double quotes do not quote the dollar sign, the operator that evaluates variables. A **$** operator next to a variable name enclosed within double quotes will still be evaluated, replacing the variable name with its value. The value of the variable will then become part of the string, not the variable name. There may be times when you want a variable within quotes to be evaluated. In the next example, the double quotes are used so that the winner's name will be included in the notice.

```
$ winner=dylan
$ notice="The person who won is $winner"
$ echo $notice
The person who won is dylan
```

On the other hand, there may be times when you do not want a variable within quotes to be evaluated. In that case, you have to use the single quotes. Single quotes suppress any variable evaluation and treat the dollar sign as just another character. In the next example, single quotes prevent the evaluation of the **winner** variable.

```
$ winner=dylan
$ result='The name is in the $winner variable'
$ echo $result
The name is in the $winner variable
```

If the double quotes were used instead, an unintended variable evaluation would take place. In the next example, the characters **"$winner"** are interpreted as a variable evaluation.

```
$ winner=dylan
$ result="The name is in the $winner variable"
$ echo $result
The name is in the dylan variable
```

You can always quote any metacharacter, including the **$** operator, by preceding it with a backslash. The use of the backslash is to quote ENTER keys (newlines). The backslash is useful when you want to both evaluate variables within a string and include **$** characters. In the next example, the backslash is placed before the **$** in order to treat it as a dollar sign character: \$. At the same time, the variable **$winner** is evaluated because the double quotes that are used do not quote the **$** operator.

```
$ winner=dylan
$ result="$winner won \$100.00"
$ echo $result
dylan won $100.00
```

Quoting Commands: Single Quotes

There are times when you may want to use single quotes around a Linux command. Single quotes allow you to assign the written command to a variable. If you do so, you can then use that variable name as another name for the Linux command. Entering in the variable name, preceded by the **$** operator on the command line, will execute the command. In the next example, a shell variable is assigned the characters that make up a Linux command to list files, **'ls -F'**. Notice the single quotes around the command. When the shell variable is evaluated on the command line, the Linux command it contains will become a command line argument, and it will be executed by the shell. In effect, you are creating another name for a command, like an alias.

```
$ lsf='ls -F'
$ $lsf
mydata /reports /letters
$
```

Values from Linux Commands: Back quotes

Although you can create variable values by typing in characters or character strings, you can also obtain values from other Linux commands. To assign the result of Linux command to a variable, you first need to execute the command. If you place a Linux command within back quotes (`` ` ``) on the command line, that command is first executed and its result becomes an argument on the command line. In the case of assignments, the result of a command can be assigned to a variable by placing the command within back quotes first to execute it. The back quotes can be thought of as an expression consisting of a command to be executed whose result is then assigned to the variable. The characters making up the command itself are not assigned. In the next example, the command **ls *.c** is executed and its result is then assigned to the variable **listc**. **ls *.c**, which generates a list of all files with a **.c** extension. This list of files is then assigned to the **listc** variable.

```
$ listc=`ls `*.c`
$ echo $listc
main.c prog.c lib.c
```

Keep in mind the difference between single quotes and back quotes. Single quotes treat a Linux command as a set of characters. Back quotes force execution of the Linux command. There may be times when you accidentally enter single quotes when you mean to use back quotes. In the following first example, the assignment for the **lscc** variable has single quotes, not back quotes, placed around the **ls *.c** command. In this case, **ls *.c** are just characters to be assigned to the variable **lscc**. In the second example, back quotes are placed around the **ls *.c** command, forcing evaluation of the command. A list of filenames ending in **.c** is generated and assigned as the value of **lscc**.

```
$ lscc='ls *.c'
$ echo $lscc
ls *.c
```

```
$ lscc=`ls *.c`
$ echo $lscc
main.c  prog.c
```

Shell Scripts: User-Defined Commands

You can place shell commands within a file and then have the shell read and execute the commands in the file. In this sense, the file functions as a shell program, executing shell commands as if they were statements in a program. A file that contains shell commands is called a shell script.

You enter shell commands into a script file using a standard text editor such as the Vi editor. The **sh** or **.** command used with the script's filename will read the script file and execute the commands. In the next example, the text file called **lsc** contains an **ls** command that displays only files with the extension **.c**.

lsc

```
ls *.c
```

A run of the **lsc** script is shown here.

```
$ sh lsc
main.c calc.c
$ . lsc
main.c calc.c
```

Executing Scripts

You can dispense with the **sh** and **.** commands by setting the executable permission of a script file. When the script file is first created by your text editor, it is given only read and write permission. The **chmod** command with the **+x** option will give the script file executable permission. Once it is executable, entering the name of the script file at the shell prompt and pressing ENTER will execute the script file and the shell commands in it. In effect, the script's filename becomes a new shell command. In this way, you can use shell scripts to design and create your own Linux commands. You need to set the permission only once.

In the next example, the **lsc** file's executable permission for the owner is set to on. Then the **lsc** shell script is directly executed like any Linux command.

```
$ chmod u+x lsc
$ lsc
main.c calc.c
```

You may have to specify that the script you are using is in your current working directory. You do this by prefixing the script name with a period and slash combination, as in **./lsc**. The period is a special character representing the name of your current working directory. The slash is a directory pathname separator. The following example shows how to execute the **lsc** script.

```
$ ./lsc
main.c calc.c
```

Script Arguments

Just as any Linux command can take arguments, so also can a shell script. Arguments on the command line are referenced sequentially starting with 1. An argument is referenced using the **$** operator and the number of its position. The first argument is referenced with **$1**, the second, with **$2**, and so on. In the next example, the **lsext** script prints out files with a specified extension. The first argument is the extension. The script is then executed with the argument **c**. Be sure that the script has executable permission.

lsext

```
ls *.$1
```

A run of the `lsext` script with an argument is shown here.

```
$ lsext c
main.c calc.c
```

In the next example, the commands to print out a file with line numbers have been placed in an executable file called **lpnum**, which takes a filename as its argument. The **cat** command with the **-n** option first outputs the contents of the file with line numbers. Then this output is piped into the **lpr** command, which prints it. The command to print out the line numbers is executed in the background.

lpnum

```
cat -n $1 | lpr &
```

A run of the **lpnum** script with an argument is shown here.

```
$ lpnum mydata
```

You may need to reference more than one argument at a time. The number of arguments used may vary. In **lpnum**, you may want to print out three files at one time and five files at some other time. The **$** operator with the asterisk, **$***, references all the arguments on the command line. Using **$*** enables you to create scripts that take a varying number of arguments. In the next example, **lpnum** is rewritten using **$*** so that it can take a different number of arguments each time you use it.

lpnum

```
cat -n $* | lpr &
```

A run of the **lpnum** script with multiple arguments is shown here.

```
$ lpnum mydata preface
```

Environment Variables

When you log in to your account, your Linux system generates your user shell. Within this shell, you can issue commands and declare variables. You can also create and execute shell scripts. However, when you execute a shell script, the system generates a subshell. You then have two shells, the one you logged in to and the one generated for the script. Within the script shell, you can execute another shell script, which will then have its own shell. When a script has finished execution, its shell terminates and you enter back to the shell from which it was executed. In this sense, you can have many shells, each nested within the other.

Variables that you define within a shell are local to it. If you define a variable in a shell script, then, when the script is run, the variable is defined with that script's shell and is local to it. No other shell can reference it. In a sense, the variable is hidden within its shell.

To illustrate this situation, the next example will use two scripts, one of which is called from within the other. When the first script executes, it generates its own shell. From within this shell, another script is executed which, in turn, generates its own shell. In the next example, the user first executes the **dispfirst** script, which displays a first name. When the **dispfirst** script executes, it generates its own shell and then, within that shell, it defines the **firstname** variable. After it displays the contents of **firstname**, the script executes another script: **displast**. When **displast** executes, it generates its own shell. It defines the **lastname** variable within its shell and then displays the contents of **lastname**. It then tries to reference **firstname** and display its contents. It cannot do so because **firstname** is local to **dispfirst's** shell and cannot be referenced outside it. An error message is displayed indicating that for the **displast** shell, **firstname** is an undefined variable.

dispfirst

```
firstname="Charles"
echo "First name is $firstname"

displast
```

displast

```
lastname="Dickens"

echo "Last name is $lastname"
echo "$firstname $lastname"
```

The run of the **dispfirst** script is shown here.

```
$ dispfirst
First name is Charles
Last name is Dickens
 Dickens
sh: firstname: not found
```

If you want the same value of a variable, used both in a script's shell and a subshell, you can simply define the variable twice, once in each script, and assign it the same value. In the previous example, there is a **myfile** variable defined in **dispfile** and in **printfile**. The user executes the **dispfile** script, which first displays the list file with line numbers. When the **dispfile** script executes, it generates its own shell and then, within that shell, it defines the **myfile** variable. After it displays the contents of the file, the script then executes another script **printfile**. When **printfile** executes, it generates its own shell. It defines its own **myfile** variable within its shell and then sends a file to the printer.

What if you want to define a variable in one shell and have its value referenced in any subshell? For example, what if you want to define the **myfile** variable in the **dispfile** script and have its value, "List", referenced from within the **printfile** script, rather than explicitly defining another variable in **printfile**? Since variables are local to the shell they are defined in, there is no way you can do this with ordinary variables. However, there is a type of variable called an environment variable that allows its value to be referenced by any subshells. Environment variables constitute an environment for the shell and any subshell it generates, no matter how deeply nested.

dispfile

```
myfile="List"

echo "Displaying $myfile"
pr -t -n $myfile
```

printfile

```
printfile

myfile="List"

echo "Printing $myfile"
lp $myfile &
```

The run of the **dispfile** script is shown here.

```
$ dispfile
Displaying List
1 screen
2 modem
3 paper
Printing List
```

You can define environment variables in the three major types of shells: Bourne, Korn, and C. The strategy used to implement environmental variables in the Bourne and Korn shells is very different from that of the C shell. In the Bourne and Korn shells, environmental variables are exported. This means that a copy of an environmental variable is made in each subshell. In a sense, if the **myfile** variable is exported, a copy is automatically defined in each subshell for you. In the C shell, on the other hand, an environmental variable is defined only once and can be directly referenced by any subshell.

Shell Environment Variables

In the Bourne, BASH, and Korn shells, an environment variable can be thought of as a regular variable with added capabilities. To make an environment variable, you apply the **export** command to a variable you have already defined. The **export** command instructs the system to define a copy of that variable for each new shell generated. Each new shell will have its own copy of the environment variable. This process is called exporting variables.

In the next example, the variable **myfile** is defined in the **dispfile** script. It is then turned into an environment variable using the **export** command. The **myfile** variable will consequently be exported to any subshells, such as that generated when **printfile** is executed.

dispfile

```
myfile="List"
export myfile

echo "Displaying $myfile"
pr -t -n $myfile

printfile
```

printfile

```
echo "Printing $myfile"
lp $myfile &
```

The run of the **dispfile** script is shown here.

```
$ dispfile
Displaying List
1 screen
2 modem
3 paper
Printing List
```

When **printfile** is executed it will be given its own copy of **myfile** and can reference that copy within its own shell. You no longer need to explicitly define another **myfile** variable in **printfile**.

It is a mistake to think of exported environment variables as global variables. A new shell can never reference a variable outside of itself. Instead, a copy of the variable with its value is generated for the new shell. You can think of exported variables as exporting their values to a shell, not themselves. For those familiar with programming structures, exported variables can be thought of as a form of call-by-value.

Control Structures

You can control the execution of Linux commands in a shell script with control structures. Control structures allow you to repeat commands and to select certain commands over others. A control structure consists of two major components: a test and commands. If the test is successful, then the commands are executed. In this way, you can use control structures to make decisions as to whether commands should be executed.

Two different kinds of control structures are used: loops, which repeat commands, and conditions, which execute commands when certain conditions are met. The BASH shell has three loop control structures, **while**, **for**, and **for-in**, and two condition structures, **if** and **case**. The control structures have as their test the execution of a Linux command. All Linux commands return an exit status after they have finished executing. If a command is successful, its exit status will be 0. If the command fails for any reason, its exit status will be a positive value referencing the type of failure that occurred. The control structures check to see whether the exit status of a Linux command is 0 or some other value. For the control structures, such as the **if** and **while**, if the exit status is a 0 value, the command was successful and the structure continues.

Test Operations

With the **test** command, you can compare integers and strings, and even perform logical operations. The command consists of the keyword **test**, followed by the values being compared, separated by an option that specifies what kind of comparison is taking place. The option can be thought of as the operator, but it is written, like other options, with a minus sign and letter codes. For example, **-eq** is the option that represents the equality comparison. Two string operations, however, actually use an operator instead of an option. When you compare two strings for equality, you use the equal sign (=). For inequality you use **!=**. Table 21-1 lists some of the commonly used options and operators used by **test**. The syntax for the test command is shown here.

```
test value -option value
test string = string
```

Integer Comparisons	Function
-gt	Greater-than
-lt	Less-than
-ge	Greater-than-or-equal-to
-le	Less-than-or-equal-to
-eq	Equal
-ne	Not-equal
String Comparisons	
-z	Tests for empty string
=	Equal strings
!=	Not-equal strings
Logical Operations	
-a	Logical AND
-o	Logical OR
!	Logical NOT
File Tests	
-f	File exists and is a regular file
-s	File is not empty
-r	File is readable
-w	File can be written to, modified
-x	File is executable
-d	Filename is a directory name

Table 21-1: BASH Shell Test Operators

The next example compares two integer values to determine whether they are equal. In this case, the equality option, **-eq**, should be used. The exit status of the **test** command is examined to determine the result of the test operation. The shell special variable **$?** holds the exit status of the most recently executed Linux command.

```
$ num=5
$ test $num -eq 10
$ echo $?
1
```

Instead of using the keyword **test** for the test command, you can use enclosing brackets. The command test **$greeting = "hi"** can be written as

```
$ [ $greeting = "hi" ]
```

Similarly, the command test **$num -eq 10** can be written as

```
$ [ $num -eq 10 ]
```

The brackets themselves must be surrounded by white space: a space, tab, or new line. Without the spaces, the code is invalid.

Conditional Control Structures

The BASH shell has a set of conditional control structures that allow you to choose what Linux commands to execute. Many of these are similar to conditional control structures found in programming languages, but there are some differences. The **if** condition tests the success of a Linux command, not an expression. The end of an **if-then** command must be indicated with the keyword **fi**, and the end of a case command is indicated with the keyword **esac**. The condition control structures are listed in Table 21-2.

The **if** structure places a condition on commands. That condition is the exit status of a specific Linux command. If a command is successful, returning an exit status of 0, then the commands within the **if** structure are executed. If the exit status is anything other than 0, the command has failed and the commands within the **if** structure are not executed. The **if** command begins with the keyword **if** and is followed by a Linux command whose exit condition will be evaluated. The keyword **fi** ends the command.

The **elsels** script in the next example executes the **ls** command to list files with two different possible options, either by size or with all file information. If the user enters an s, files are listed by size; otherwise, all file information is listed.

elsels

```
echo Enter s to list file sizes,
echo          otherwise all file information is listed.
echo -n "Please enter option: "
read choice
if [  "$choice" = s  ]
    then
         ls -s
    else
           ls -l
fi
echo Good-bye
```

Condition Control Structures: if, else, elif, case	Function
if *command* **then** *command* **fi**	**if** executes an action if its test command is true.

if *command* **then**
  command
else
  command
fi
	if-else executes an action if the exit status of its test command is true; if false, the **else** action is executed.

if *command* **then**	**elif** allows you to nest **if** structures, enabling selection

command **elif** *command* **then** *command* **else** *command* **fi**	among several alternatives; at the first true **if** structure, its commands are executed and control leaves the entire **elif** structure.
case *string* **in** *pattern*) *command;;* **esac**	**case** matches the string value to any of several patterns; if a pattern is matched, its associated commands are executed.
command **&&** *command*	The logical AND condition returns a true 0 value if both commands return a true 0 value; if one returns a nonzero value, then the AND condition is false and also returns a nonzero value.
command **||** *command*	The logical OR condition returns a true 0 value if one or the other command returns a true 0 value; if both commands return a nonzero value, then the OR condition is false and also returns a nonzero value.
! *command*	The logical NOT condition inverts the return value of the command.
Loop Control Structures: while, until, for, for-in, select	
while *command* **do** *command* **done**	**while** executes an action as long as its test command is true.
until *command* **do** *command* **done**	**until** executes an action as long as its test command is false.
for *variable* **in** *list-values* **do** *command* **done**	**for-in** is designed for use with lists of values; the variable operand is consecutively assigned the values in the list.
for *variable* **do** *command* **done**	**for** is designed for reference script arguments; the variable operand is consecutively assigned each argument value.
select *string* **in** *item-list* **do** *command* **done**	**select** creates a menu based on the items in the *item-list*; then it executes the command; the command is usually a **case**.

Table 21-2: BASH Shell Control Structures

A run of the program follows.

```
$ elsels
Enter s to list file sizes,
otherwise all file information is listed.
Please enter option: s
total 2
    1 monday     2 today
```

Loop Control Structures

The while loop repeats commands. A while loop begins with the keyword **while** and is followed by a Linux command. The keyword **do** follows on the next line. The end of the loop is specified by the keyword **done**. The Linux command used in **while** structures is often a test command indicated by enclosing brackets.

The **for-in** loop is designed to reference a list of values sequentially. It takes two operands: a variable and a list of values. The values in the list are assigned one by one to the variable in the **for-in** loop. Each time through the loop, the next value in the list is assigned to the variable. When the end of the list is reached, the loop stops. Like the **while** loop, the body of a **for-in** loop begins with the keyword **do** and ends with the keyword **done**. In the next example, the **cbackup** script makes a backup of each file and places it in a directory called **sourcebak**. Notice the use of the * special character to generate a list of all filenames with a **.c** extension.

cbackup

```
for backfile in *.c
do
    cp $backfile sourcebak/$backfile
 echo $backfile
done
```

A run of the program follows.

```
$ cbackup
io.c
lib.c
main.c
$
```

The **for** loop without a specified list of values takes as its list of values the command line arguments. The arguments specified on the command line when the shell file is invoked become a list of values referenced by the **for** command. The variable used in the **for** loop is set automatically to each argument value in sequence. The first time through the loop, the variable is set to the value of the first argument. The second time, it is set to the value of the second argument.

22. Shell Configuration

Shell Configuration Files

Configuration Directories and Files

Aliases

Controlling Shell Operations

Environment Variables and Subshells: export

Configuring Your Shell with Shell Parameters

Four different major shells are commonly used on Linux systems: the Bourne Again shell (BASH), the AT&T Korn shell, the TCSH shell, and the Z shell. The BASH shell is an advanced version of the Bourne shell, which includes most of the advanced features developed for the Korn shell and the C shell. TCSH is an enhanced version of the C shell, originally developed for BSD versions of UNIX. The Z shell is an enhanced version of the AT&T UNIX Korn shell. Although their UNIX counterparts differ greatly, the Linux shells share many of the same features. In Linux, the BASH shell incorporates all the advanced features of the Korn shell and C shell, as well as the TCSH shell. All four shells are available for your use.

Command	Description
bash	BASH shell, **/bin/bash**
bsh	BASH shell, **/bin/bsh** (link to **/bin/bash**)
sh	BASH shell, **/bin/sh** (link to **/bin/bash**)
tcsh	TCSH shell, **/usr/tcsh**
csh	TCSH shell , **/bin/csh** (link to **/bin/tcsh**)
ksh	Korn shell, **/bin/ksh** (also added link **/usr/bin/ksh**)
zsh	Z shell, **/bin/zsh**

Table 22-1: Shell Invocation Command Names

The BASH shell is the default shell for most Linux distributions. If you are logging in to a command line interface, you will be placed in the default shell automatically and given a shell prompt at which to enter your commands. The shell prompt for the BASH shell is a dollar sign ($). In the desktop interface, such as GNOME or KDE, you can open a terminal window that will display a command line interface with the prompt for the default shell (BASH). Though you log in to your default shell or display it automatically in a terminal window, you can change to another shell by entering its name. Entering **tcsh** invokes the TCSH shell, **bash** the BASH shell, **ksh** the Korn shell, and **zsh** the Z shell. You can leave a shell by pressing CTRL-D or using the **exit** command. You only need one type of shell to do your work. Table 22-1 shows the different commands you can use to invoke different shells. Some shells have added links you can use to invoke the same shell, like **sh** and **bsh**, which link to and invoke the **bash** command for the BASH shell.

This chapter describes common features of the BASH shell, such as aliases, as well as how to configure the shell to your own needs using shell variables and initialization files. The other shells share many of the same features and use similar variables and configuration files.

Though the basic shell features and configurations are shown here, you should consult the respective online manuals and FAQs for each shell for more detailed examples and explanations.

Shell Initialization and Configuration Files

Each type of shell has its own set of initialization and configuration files. The TCSH shell uses **.login**, **.tcshrc**, and **.logout** files in place of **.profile**, **.bashrc**, and **.bash_logout**. The Z shell has several initialization files: **.zshenv**, **.zlogin**, **.zprofile**, **.zschrc**, and **.zlogout**. See Table 22-2 for a listing. Check the Man pages for each shell to see how they are usually configured. When you install a shell, default versions of these files are automatically placed in user home directories. Except for the TCSH shell, all shells use much the same syntax for variable definitions and assigning values (TCSH uses a slightly different syntax, described in its Man pages).

Filename	Function
BASH Shell	
.profile	Login initialization file
.bashrc	BASH shell configuration file
.bash_logout	Logout name
.bash_history	History file
/etc/profile	System login initialization file
/etc/bash.bashrc	System BASH shell configuration file
/etc/profile.d	Directory for specialized BASH shell configuration files
/etc/bash_completion	Completion options for applications
TCSH Shell	
.login	Login initialization file
.tcshrc	TCSH shell configuration file
.logout	Logout file
Z Shell	
.zshenv	Shell login file (first read)
.zprofile	Login initialization file
.zlogin	Shell login file
.zshrc	Z shell configuration file
.zlogout	Logout file
Korn Shell	
.profile	Login initialization file
.kshrc	KORN shell configuration file

Table 22-2: Shell Configuration Files

Configuration Directories and Files

Applications often install configuration files in a user's home directory that contain specific configuration information, which tailors the application to the needs of that particular user. This may take the form of a single configuration file that begins with a period, or a directory that contains several configuration files. The directory name will also begin with a period. For example, Mozilla installs a directory called **.mozilla** in the user's home directory that contains configuration files. On the other hand, many mail applications use a single file called **.mailrc** to hold alias and feature settings set up by the user, though others like Evolution also have their own, **.evolution**. Most single configuration files end in the letters **rc**. **FTP** uses a file called **.netrc**. Most newsreaders use a file called **.newsrc**. Entries in configuration files are usually set by the application, though you can usually make entries directly by editing the file. Applications have their own set of special variables to which you can define and assign values. You can list the configuration files in your home directory with the **ls -a** command.

Aliases

You can use the **alias** command to create another name for a command. The **alias** command operates like a macro that expands to the command it represents. The alias does not literally replace the name of the command. It just gives another name to that command. An **alias** command begins with the keyword **alias** and the new name for the command, followed by an equal sign and the command the alias will reference.

Note: No spaces should be placed around the equal sign used in the **alias** command.

In the next example, **list** becomes another name for the **ls** command.

```
$ alias list=ls
$ ls
mydata today
$ list
mydata today
$
```

If you want an alias to be automatically defined, you have to enter the alias operation in a shell configuration file. On Ubuntu, aliases are defined in either the user's **.bashrc** file or in a **.bash_aliases** file. To use a .bash_aliases file, you have to first uncomment the commands in the **.bashrc** file that will read the **.bash_aliases** file. Just edit the **.bashrc** file and remove the preceding # so it appears like the following.

```
if [ -f ~/.bash_aliases ]; then
    . ~/.bash_aliases
fi
```

You can also place aliases in the **.bashrc** file directly. Some are already defined, though commented out. You can edit the **.bashrc** file and remove the # comment symbols from those lines to activate the aliases.

```
# some more ls aliases
alias ll='ls -l'
alias la='ls -A'
alias l='ls -CF'
```

Aliasing Commands and Options

You can also use an alias to substitute for a command and its option, but you need to enclose both the command and the option within single quotes. Any command you alias that contains spaces must be enclosed in single quotes as well. In the next example, the alias **lss** references the **ls** command with its -s option, and the alias **lsa** references the **ls** command with the -F option. The **ls** command with the -s option lists files and their sizes in blocks, and **ls** with the **-F** option places a slash after directory names. Notice how single quotes enclose the command and its option.

```
$ alias lss='ls -s'
$ lss
mydata 14   today  6    reports  1
$ alias lsa='ls -F'
$ lsa
mydata today reports/
$
```

Aliases are helpful for simplifying complex operations. In the next example, **listlong** becomes another name for the **ls** command with the -**l** option (the long format that lists all file information), as well as the -**h** option for using a human-readable format for file sizes. Be sure to encase the command and its arguments within single quotes so that they are taken as one argument and not parsed by the shell.

```
$ alias listlong='ls -lh'
$ listlong
-rw-r--r--   1 root   root   51K Sep  18  2008 mydata
-rw-r--r--   1 root   root   16K Sep  27  2008 today
```

Aliasing Commands and Arguments

You may often use an alias to include a command name with an argument. If you execute a command that has an argument with a complex combination of special characters on a regular basis, you may want to alias it. For example, suppose you often list just your source code and object code files, those files ending in either a **.c** or **.o**. You would need to use as an argument for **ls** a combination of special characters such as ***.[co]**. Instead, you can alias **ls** with the **.[co]** argument, giving it a simple name. In the next example, the user creates an alias called **lsc** for the command **ls.[co]**.

```
$ alias lsc='ls *.[co]'
$ lsc
main.c main.o lib.c lib.o
```

Aliasing Commands

You can also use the name of a command as an alias. This can be helpful in cases where you should use a command only with a specific option. In the case of the **rm**, **cp**, and **mv** commands, the -**i** option should always be used to ensure an existing file is not overwritten. Instead of always being careful to use the -**i** option each time you use one of these commands, you can alias the command name to include the option. In the next example, the **rm**, **cp**, and **mv** commands have been aliased to include the -**i** option.

```
$ alias rm='rm -i'
$ alias mv='mv -i'
$ alias cp='cp -i'
```

The **alias** command by itself provides a list of all aliases that have been defined, showing the commands they represent. You can remove an alias by using the **unalias** command. In the next example, the user lists the current aliases and then removes the **lsa** alias.

```
$ alias
lsa=ls -F
list=ls
rm=rm -i
$ unalias lsa
```

Controlling Shell Operations

The BASH shell has several features that enable you to control the way different shell operations work. For example, setting the **noclobber** feature prevents redirection from overwriting files. You can turn these features on and off like a toggle, using the **set** command. The **set** command takes two arguments: an option specifying on or off and the name of the feature. To set a feature on, you use the **-o** option, and to set it off, you use the **+o** option. Here is the basic form.

```
$ set -o feature          turn the feature on
$ set +o feature          turn the feature off
```

Features	Description
`$ set -+o feature`	BASH shell features are turned on and off with the `set` command; `-o` sets a feature on and `+o` turns it off. `$ set -o noclobber` *set noclobber on* `$ set +o noclobber` *set noclobber off*
`ignoreeof`	Disables CTRL-D logout
`noclobber`	Does not overwrite files through redirection
`noglob`	Disables special characters used for filename expansion: *, ?, ~, and []

Table 22-3: BASH Shell Special Features

Three of the most common features are **ignoreeof**, **noclobber**, and **noglob**. Table 22-3 lists these different features, as well as the **set** command. Setting **ignoreeof** enables a feature that prevents you from logging out of the user shell with CTRL-d. CTRL-d is not only used to log out of the user shell, but also to end user input entered directly into the standard input. CTRL-d is used often for the Mail program or for utilities such as **cat**. You can easily enter an extra CTRL-d in such circumstances and accidentally log yourself out. The **ignoreeof** feature prevents such accidental logouts. In the next example, the **ignoreeof** feature is turned on using the **set** command with the **-o** option. The user can then log out only by entering the **logout** command.

```
$ set -o ignoreeof
$ CTRL-D
Use exit to logout
$
```

Environment Variables and Subshells: export

When you log in to your account, Linux generates your user shell. Within this shell, you can issue commands and declare variables. You can also create and execute shell scripts. When you execute a shell script, however, the system generates a subshell. You then have two shells: the one you logged in to and the one generated for the script. Within the script shell, you can execute another shell script, which then has its own shell. When a script has finished execution, its shell terminates and you return to the shell from which it was executed. In this sense, you can have many shells, each nested within the other. Variables you define within a shell are local to it. If you define a variable in a shell script, then, when the script is run, the variable is defined with that script's shell and is local to it. No other shell can reference that variable. In a sense, the variable is hidden within its shell.

Shell Variables	Description
BASH	Holds full pathname of BASH command
BASH_VERSION	Displays the current BASH version number
GROUPS	Groups that the user belongs to
HISTCMD	Number of the current command in the history list
HOME	Pathname for user's home directory
HOSTNAME	The hostname
HOSTTYPE	Displays the type of machine the host runs on
OLDPWD	Previous working directory
OSTYPE	Operating system in use
PATH	List of pathnames for directories searched for executable commands
PPID	Process ID for shell's parent shell
PWD	User's working directory
RANDOM	Generates random number when referenced
SHLVL	Current shell level, number of shells invoked
UID	User ID of the current user

Table 22-4: Shell Variables, Set by the Shell

You can define environment variables in all types of shells, including the BASH shell, the Z shell, and the TCSH shell. The strategy used to implement environment variables in the BASH shell, however, is different from that of the TCSH shell. In the BASH shell, environment variables are exported. That is to say, a copy of an environment variable is made in each subshell. For example, if the EDITOR variable is exported, a copy is automatically defined in each subshell for you. In the TCSH shell, on the other hand, an environment variable is defined only once and can be directly referenced by any subshell.

In the BASH shell, an environment variable can be thought of as a regular variable with added capabilities. To make an environment variable, you apply the **export** command to a variable you have already defined. The **export** command instructs the system to define a copy of that variable for each new shell generated. Each new shell will have its own copy of the environment variable. This process is called exporting variables. To think of exported environment variables as global variables is a mistake. A new shell can never reference a variable outside of itself. Instead, a copy of the variable with its value is generated for the new shell.

Configuring Your Shell with Shell Parameters

When you log in, Linux will set certain parameters for your login shell. These parameters can take the form of variables or features. Linux reserves a predefined set of variables for shell and system use. These are assigned system values, in effect, setting parameters. Linux sets up parameter shell variables you can use to configure your user shell. Many of these parameter shell variables are defined by the system when you log in. Some parameter shell variables are set by the shell automatically, and others are set by initialization scripts, described later. Certain shell variables are set directly by the shell, and others are simply used by it. Many of these other variables are application specific, used for such tasks as mail, history, or editing. Functionally, it may be better to think of these as system-level variables, as they are used to configure your entire system, setting values such as the location of executable commands on your system, or the number of history commands allowable. See Table 22-4 for a list of those shell variables set by the shell for shell-specific tasks. Table 22-5 lists those used by the shell for supporting other applications.

A reserved set of keywords is used for the names of these system variables. You should not use these keywords as the names of any of your own variable names. The system shell variables are all specified in uppercase letters, making them easy to identify. Shell feature variables are in lowercase letters. For example, the keyword HOME is used by the system to define the HOME variable. HOME is a special environment variable that holds the pathname of the user's home directory. On the other hand, the keyword noclobber is used to set the noclobber feature on or off.

Shell Parameter Variables

Many of the shell parameter variables automatically defined and assigned initial values by the system when you log in can be changed if you wish. However, some parameter variables exist whose values should not be changed. For example, the HOME variable holds the pathname for your home directory. Commands such as **cd** reference the pathname in the HOME shell variable to locate your home directory. Some of the more common of these parameter variables are described in this section.

Other parameter variables are defined by the system and given an initial value that you are free to change. To do this, you redefine them and assign a new value. For example, the PATH variable is defined by the system and given an initial value. It contains the pathnames of directories where commands are located. Whenever you execute a command, the shell searches for it in these directories. You can add a new directory to be searched by redefining the PATH variable yourself so that it will include the new directory's pathname.

Still, other parameter variables exist that the system does not define. These are usually optional features, such as the EXINIT variable that enables you to set options for the Vi editor. Each time you log in, you must define and assign a value to such variables. Some of the more common parameter variables are SHELL, PATH, PS1, PS2, and MAIL. The SHELL variable holds the pathname of the program for the type of shell you log in to. The PATH variable lists the different directories to be searched for a Linux command. The PS1 and PS2 variables hold the prompt symbols. The MAIL variable holds the pathname of your mailbox file. You can modify the values for any of these to customize your shell.

Note: You can obtain a listing of the currently defined shell variables using the **env** command. The **env** command operates like the **set** command, but it lists only parameter variables.

Using Initialization Files

You can automatically define parameter variables using special shell scripts called initialization files. An initialization file is a specially named shell script executed whenever you enter a certain shell. You can edit the initialization file and place in it definitions and assignments for parameter variables. When you enter the shell, the initialization file will execute these definitions and assignments, effectively initializing parameter variables with your own values. For example, the BASH shell's **.profile** file is an initialization file executed every time you log in. It contains definitions and assignments of parameter variables. However, the **.profile** file is basically only a shell script, which you can edit with any text editor changing, if you wish, the values assigned to parameter variables.

In the BASH shell, all the parameter variables are designed to be environment variables. When you define or redefine a parameter variable, you also need to export it to make it an environment variable. This means any change you make to a parameter variable must be accompanied by an **export** command. You will see that at the end of the login initialization file, **.profile**, there is usually an **export** command for all the parameter variables defined in it.

Your Home Directory: HOME

The HOME variable contains the pathname of your home directory. Your home directory is determined by the parameter administrator when your account is created. The pathname for your home directory is automatically read into your HOME variable when you log in. In the next example, the **echo** command displays the contents of the HOME variable.

```
$ echo $HOME
/home/chris
```

The HOME variable is often used when you need to specify the absolute pathname of your home directory. In the next example, the absolute pathname of **reports** is specified using HOME for the home directory's path.

```
$ ls $HOME/reports
```

Command Locations: PATH

The PATH variable contains a series of directory paths separated by colons. Each time a command is executed, the paths listed in the PATH variable are searched, one by one, for that command. For example, the **cp** command resides on the system in the directory **/bin**. This directory path is one of the directories listed in the PATH variable. Each time you execute the **cp** command, this path is searched and the **cp** command located. The system defines and assigns PATH an initial set of pathnames. In Linux, the initial pathnames are **/bin** and **/usr/bin**.

Shell Variables	Description
BASH_VERSION	Displays the current BASH version number
CDPATH	Search path for the cd command
EXINIT	Initialization commands for Ex/Vi editor
FCEDIT	Editor used by the history fc command.
GROUPS	Groups that the user belongs to
HISTFILE	The pathname of the history file
HISTSIZE	Number of commands allowed for history
HISTFILESIZE	Size of the history file in lines
HOME	Pathname for user's home directory
IFS	Interfield delimiter symbol
IGNOREEOF	If not set, EOF character will close the shell. Can be set to the number of EOF characters to ignore before accepting one to close the shell (default is 10)
INPUTRC	Set the **inputrc** configuration file for Readline (command line). Default is current directory, **.inputrc**. Most Linux distributions set this to **/etc/inputrc**
KDEDIR	The pathname location for the KDE desktop
LOGNAME	Login name
MAIL	Name of specific mail file checked by Mail utility for received messages, if MAILPATH is not set
MAILCHECK	Interval for checking for received mail
MAILPATH	List of mail files to be checked by Mail for received messages
HOSTTYPE	Linux platforms, such as i686, x86_64, or ppc
PROMPT_COMMAND	Command to be executed before each prompt.
HISTFILE	The pathname of the history file
PS1	Primary shell prompt
PS2	Secondary shell prompt
SHELL	Pathname of program for type of shell you are using
TERM	Terminal type
TMOUT	Time that the shell remains active awaiting input
USER	Username
UID	Real user ID (numeric)

Table 22-5: System Environment Variables Used by the Shell

The shell can execute any executable file, including programs and scripts you have created. For this reason, the PATH variable can also reference your working directory. If you want to execute one of your own scripts or programs in your working directory, the shell can locate it.

No spaces are allowed between the pathnames in the string. A colon with no pathname specified references your working directory. Usually, a single colon is placed at the end of the pathnames as an empty entry specifying your working directory. For example, the pathname **//bin:/usr/bin:** references three directories: **/bin**, **/usr/bin**, and your current working directory.

```
$ echo $PATH
/bin:/usr/sbin:
```

You can add any new directory path you want to the PATH variable. This can be useful if you have created several of your own Linux commands using shell scripts. You can place these new shell script commands in a directory you create, and then add that directory to the PATH list. Then, no matter what directory you are in, you can execute one of your shell scripts. The PATH variable will contain the directory for that script so that directory will be searched each time you issue a command.

You add a directory to the PATH variable with a variable assignment. You can execute this assignment directly in your shell. In the next example, the user **chris** adds a new directory, called **bin,** to the PATH. Although you could carefully type in the complete pathnames listed in PATH for the assignment, you can also use an evaluation of PATH, **$PATH**, in its place. In this example, an evaluation of HOME is also used to designate the user's home directory in the new directory's pathname. Notice the last colon, which specifies the working directory.

```
$ PATH=$PATH:$HOME/mybin:
$ export PATH
$ echo $PATH
/bin:/usr/bin::/home/chris/mybin
```

If you add a directory to PATH yourself while you are logged in, the directory will be added only for the duration of your login session. When you log back in, the login initialization file, **.profile**, will again initialize your PATH with its original set of directories. The **.profile** file is described in detail later in this chapter. To add a new directory to your PATH permanently, you need to edit your **.profile** file and find the assignment for the PATH variable. Then, you can insert the directory, preceded by a colon, into the set of pathnames assigned to PATH.

Specifying the BASH Environment: BASH_ENV

The BASH_ENV variable holds the name of the BASH shell initialization file to be executed whenever a BASH shell is generated. For example, when a BASH shell script is executed, the BASH_ENV variable is checked, and the name of the script that it holds is executed before the shell script. The BASH_ENV variable usually holds **$HOME/.bashrc**. This is the **.bashrc** file in the user's home directory. You can specify a different file if you wish, using that instead of the **.bashrc** file for BASH shell scripts.

Configuring the Shell Prompt

The PS1 and PS2 variables contain the primary and secondary prompt symbols, respectively. The primary prompt symbol for the BASH shell is a dollar sign ($). You can change the prompt symbol by assigning a new set of characters to the PS1 variable. In the next example, the shell prompt is changed to the -> symbol.

```
$ PS1='->'
-> export PS1
->
```

The following table lists the codes for configuring your prompt.

Prompt Codes	Description
\!	Current history number
\$	Use $ as prompt for all users except the root user, which has the # as its prompt
\d	Current date
\#	History command number for just the current shell
\h	Hostname
\s	Shell type currently active
\t	Time of day in hours, minutes, and seconds.
\u	Username
\v	Shell version
\w	Full pathname of the current working directory
\W	Name of the current working directory
\\	Displays a backslash character
\n	Inserts a newline
\[\]	Allows entry of terminal specific display characters for features like color or bold font
\nnn	Character specified in octal format

You can change the prompt to be any set of characters, including a string, as shown in the next example.

```
$ PS1="Please enter a command: "
Please enter a command: export PS1
Please enter a command: ls
mydata /reports
Please enter a command:
```

The PS2 variable holds the secondary prompt symbol, which is used for commands that take several lines to complete. The default secondary prompt is >. The added command lines begin with the secondary prompt instead of the primary prompt. You can change the secondary prompt just as easily as the primary prompt, as shown here.

```
$ PS2="@"
```

Like the TCSH shell, the BASH shell provides you with a predefined set of codes you can use to configure your prompt. With them, you can make the time, your username, or your directory pathname a part of your prompt. You can even have your prompt display the history event number of the current command you are about to enter. Each code is preceded by a \ symbol: \w represents the current working directory, \t the time, and \u your username; \! will display the next history event number. In the next example, the user adds the current working directory to the prompt.

```
$ PS1="\w $"
/home/dylan $
```

The codes must be included within a quoted string. If no quotes exist, the code characters are not evaluated and are themselves used as the prompt. PS1=\w sets the prompt to the characters \w, not the working directory. The next example incorporates both the time and the history event number with a new prompt.

```
$ PS1="\t \! ->"
```

The default BASH prompt is \s-\v\$ to display the type of shell, the shell version, and the $ symbol as the prompt. Some distributions have changed this to a more complex command consisting of the username, the hostname, and the name of the current working directory. A sample configuration is shown here. A simple equivalent is shown here with @ sign in the hostname and a $ for the final prompt symbol. The home directory is represented with a tilde (~).

```
$ PS1="\u@\h:\w$"
richard@turtle.com:~$
```

Ubuntu also includes some complex prompt definitions in the **.bashrc** file to support color prompts and detect any remote user logins.

Specifying Your News Server

Several shell parameter variables are used to set values used by network applications, such as web browsers or newsreaders. NNTPSERVER is used to set the value of a remote news server accessible on your network. If you are using an ISP, the ISP usually provides a Usenet news server you can access with your newsreader applications. However, you first have to provide your newsreaders with the Internet address of the news server. This is the role of the NNTPSERVER variable. News servers on the Internet usually use the NNTP protocol. NNTPSERVER should hold the address of such a news server. For many news servers, the news server address is a domain name that begins with **nntp**. The following example assigns the news server address **nntp.myservice.com** to the NNTPSERVER shell variable. Newsreader applications automatically obtain the news server address from NNTPSERVER. Usually, this assignment is placed in the shell initialization file, **.profile**, so that it is automatically set each time a user logs in.

```
NNTPSERVER=news.myservice.com
export NNTPSERVER
```

Configuring Your Login Shell: .profile

The **.profile** file is the BASH shell's login initialization file. It is a script file that is automatically executed whenever a user logs in. The file contains shell commands that define system environment variables used to manage your shell. They may be either redefinitions of system-defined variables, or definitions of user-defined variables. For example, when you log in, your user shell needs to know what directories hold Linux commands. It will reference the **PATH** variable to find the pathnames for these directories. However, first, the **PATH** variable must be assigned those pathnames. In the **.profile** file, an assignment operation does just this. Because it is in the **.profile** file, the assignment is executed automatically when the user logs in.

.profile

```
# ~/.profile: executed by the command interpreter for login shells.
# This file is not read by bash(1), if ~/.bash_profile or ~/.bash_login
# exists.
# see /usr/share/doc/bash/examples/startup-files for examples.
# the files are located in the bash-doc package.

# the default umask is set in /etc/profile
# for ssh logins, install and configure the libpam-umask package.
#umask 022

# if running bash
if [ -n "$BASH_VERSION" ]; then
    # include .bashrc if it exists
    if [ -f "$HOME/.bashrc" ]; then
     . "$HOME/.bashrc"
    fi
fi

# set PATH so it includes user's private bin if it exists
if [ -d "$HOME/bin" ] ; then
    PATH="$HOME/bin:$PATH"
fi

# set PATH so it includes user's private bin if it exists
if [ -d "$HOME/local/bin" ] ; then
    PATH="$HOME/local/bin:$PATH"
fi
```

Exporting Variables

Any new parameter variables you may add to the **.profile** file will also need to be exported, using the export command. This makes them accessible to any subshells you may enter. You can export several variables in one export command by listing them as arguments. The **.profile** file contains no variable definitions, though you can add ones of your own. In this case, the **.profile** file would have an export command with a list of all the variables defined in the file. If a variable is missing from this list, you may be unable to access it. The **.bashrc** file contains a definition of the **HISTCONTROL** variable, which is then exported. You can also combine the assignment and export command into one operation as shown here for NNTPSERVER.

```
export NNTPSERVER=news.myservice.com
```

Variable Assignments

A copy of the standard **.profile** file, provided for you when your account is created, is listed in the next example. Notice how PATH is assigned. PATH is a parameter variable the system has already defined. PATH holds the pathnames of directories searched for any command you enter. The assignment PATH="$PATH:$HOME/bin" has the effect of redefining PATH to include your **bin** directory within your home directory so that your **bin** directory will also be searched for any commands, including ones you create yourself, such as scripts or programs.

Should you want to have your current working directory searched also, you can use any text editor to add another PATH line in your **.profile** file PATH="$PATH:". You would insert a colon : after PATH. In fact, you can change this entry to add as many directories as you want to search. Making commands automatically executable in your current working directory could be a security risk, allowing files in any directory to be executed, instead of in certain specified directories. An example of how to modify your **.profile** file is shown in the following section.

```
PATH="$PATH:"
```

Editing Your BASH Profile Script

Your **.profile** initialization file is a text file that can be edited by a text editor, like any other text file. You can easily add new directories to your PATH by editing **.profile** and using editing commands to insert a new directory pathname in the list of directory pathnames assigned to the PATH variable. You can even add new variable definitions. If you do so, be sure to include the new variable's name in the **export** command's argument list. For example, if your **.profile** file does not have any definition of the EXINIT variable, you can edit the file and add a new line that assigns a value to EXINIT. The definition EXINIT='set nu ai' will configure the Vi editor with line numbering and indentation. You then need to add EXINIT to the export command's argument list. When the **.profile** file executes again, the EXINIT variable will be set to the command **set nu ai**. When the Vi editor is invoked, the command in the EXINIT variable will be executed, setting the line number and auto-indent options automatically.

In the following example, the user's **.profile** has been modified to include definitions of EXINIT and redefinitions of PATH, PS1, and HISTSIZE. The PATH variable has the ending colon added to it that specifies the current working directory, enabling you to execute commands that may be located in either the home directory or the working directory. The redefinition of HISTSIZE reduces the number of history events saved, from 1,000 defined in the system's **.profile** file, to 30. The redefinition of the PS1 parameter variable changes the prompt to just show the pathname of the current working directory. Any changes you make to parameter variables within your **.profile** file override those made earlier by the system's **/etc/profile** file. All these parameter variables are then exported with the export command.

.profile

```
# ~/.profile: executed by the command interpreter for login shells.
# This file is not read by bash(1), if ~/.bash_profile or ~/.bash_login
# exists.
# see /usr/share/doc/bash/examples/startup-files for examples.
# the files are located in the bash-doc package.

# the default umask is set in /etc/profile
# for ssh logins, install and configure the libpam-umask package.
#umask 022

# if running bash
if [ -n "$BASH_VERSION" ]; then
    # include .bashrc if it exists
    if [ -f "$HOME/.bashrc" ]; then
    . "$HOME/.bashrc"
    fi
fi
```

```
# set PATH so it includes user's private bin if it exists
if [ -d "$HOME/bin" ] ; then
    PATH="$HOME/bin:$PATH"
fi

# set PATH so it includes user's private bin if it exists
if [ -d "$HOME/.local/bin" ] ; then
    PATH="$HOME/.local/bin:$PATH"
fi

HISTSIZE=30
NNTPSERVER=news.myserver.com
EXINIT='set nu ai'
PS1="\w \$"
export PATH HISTSIZE EXINIT PS1 NNTPSERVER
```

Manually Re-executing the .profile script

Although the **.profile** script is executed each time you log in, it is not automatically re-executed after you make changes to it. The **.profile** script is an initialization file that is executed only whenever you log in. If you want to take advantage of any changes you make to it without having to log out and log in again, you can re-execute the **.profile** script with the dot (.) command. The **.profile** script is a shell script and, like any shell script can be executed with the . command.

```
$ . .profile
```

Alternatively, you can use the source command to execute the **.profile** initialization file or any initialization file such as **.login** used in the TCSH shell or **.bashrc**.

```
$ source .profile
```

System Shell Profile Script

Your Linux system also has its own profile file that it executes whenever any user logs in. This system initialization file is simply called **profile** and is found in the **/etc** directory, **/etc/profile**. This file contains parameter variable definitions the system needs to provide for each user. On Ubuntu, the **/etc/profile** script checks the **/etc/profile.d** directory for any shell configuration scripts to run, and then runs the **/etc/bash.baschrc** script, which performs most of the configuration tasks.

The number of configuration settings needed for different applications would make the **/etc/profile** file much too large to manage. Instead, application task-specific aliases and variables are placed in separate configuration files located in the **/etc/profile.d** directory. There are corresponding scripts for both the BASH and C shells. The BASH shell scripts are run from **/etc/profile** with the following commands. A **for** loop sequentially accesses each script and executes it with the dot (.) operator.

```
for i in /etc/profile.d/*.sh; do
  if [ -r $i ]; then
    . $i
  fi
done
```

For a basic install, you will have only the **gvfs-bash-completion.sh** script. As you install other shells and application there may be more. The **/etc/profile.d** scripts are named for the kinds of tasks and applications they configure. Files run by the BASH shell end in the extension **.sh**, and those run by the C shell have the extension **.csh**. The **/etc/profile** script will also check first if the **PS1** variable is defined before running any **/etc/profile.d** scripts.

A copy of the system's **profile** file follows

/etc/profile

```
# /etc/profile: system-wide .profile file for the Bourne shell (sh(1))
# and Bourne compatible shells (bash(1), ksh(1), ash(1), ...).

if [ "$PS1" ]; then
  if [ "$BASH" ] && [ "$BASH" != "/bin/sh" ]; then
    # The file bash.bashrc already sets the default PS1.
    # PS1='\u@\h:\w\$ '
    if [ -f /etc/bash.bashrc ]; then
        . /etc/bash.bashrc
    fi
  else
    if [ "`id -u`" -eq 0 ]; then
      PS1='# '
    else
      PS1='$ '
    fi
  fi
fi

if [ -d /etc/profile.d ]; then
  for i in /etc/profile.d/*.sh; do
    if [ -r $i ]; then
      . $i
    fi
  done
  unset i
fi
```

Configuring the BASH Shell: .bashrc

The **.bashrc** script is a configuration file executed each time you enter the BASH shell or generate any subshells. If the BASH shell is your login shell, **.bashrc** is executed along with your **.profile** script when you log in. If you enter the BASH shell from another shell, the **.bashrc** script is automatically executed, and the variable and alias definitions it contains will be defined. If you enter a different type of shell, the configuration file for that shell will be executed instead. For example, if you were to enter the TCSH shell with the **tcsh** command, the **.tcshrc** configuration file would be executed instead of **.bashrc**.

The User .bashrc BASH Script

The **.bashrc** shell configuration file is actually executed each time you generate a BASH shell, such as when you run a shell script. In other words, each time a subshell is created, the **.bashrc** file is executed. This has the effect of exporting any local variables or aliases you have defined in the **.bashrc** shell initialization file. The **.bashrc** file usually contains the definition of aliases and any feature variables used to turn on shell features. Aliases and feature variables are locally defined within the shell. But the **.bashrc** file defines them in every shell. For this reason, the **.bashrc** file usually holds aliases and options you want defined for each shell. As an example of how you can add your own aliases and options, aliases for the **rm**, **cp**, and **mv** commands and the shell **noclobber** and **ignoreeof** options have been added to the example shown here. For the root user **.bashrc**, the **rm**, **cp**, and **mv** aliases have already been included in the root's **.bashrc** file.

The **.bashrc** file will check for aliases in a **.bash_aliases** file and run **/etc/bash_completion** for command completion directives.

The **.bashrc** file will set several features including history, prompt, alias, and command completion settings. The **HISTCONTROL** directive is defined to ignore duplicate commands and lines beginning with a space (**ignoreboth**). The history file is appended to, and the history size and history file sizes are set to 1000 and 2000.

```
# don't put duplicate lines or lines starting with space in the history
# See bash(1) for more options
HISTCONTROL=ignoreboth

# append to the history file, don't overwrite it
shopt -s histappend

# for setting history length see HISTSIZE and HISTFILESIZE in bash(1
HISTSIZE=1000
HISTFILESIZE=2000
```

Several commands then define terminal display features and command operations, including the shell prompt, beginning with **PS1=**.

The code for reading the user's **.bash_aliases** script is included. Possible aliases are also provided, some of which are commented. You can remove the comment symbols, #, to activate them. Aliases that provide color support for the **ls**, **grep**, **fgrep**, and **egrep** commands are listed. An alert alias is also provided which notifies you of long running commands.

```
# enable color support of ls and also add handy aliases
if [ -x /usr/bin/dircolors ]; then
    test -r ~/.dircolors && eval "$(dircolors -b ~/.dircolors)" || eval
"$(dircolors -b)"
    alias ls='ls --color=auto'
    #alias dir='dir --color=auto'
    #alias vdir='vdir --color=auto'

    alias grep='grep --color=auto'
    alias fgrep='fgrep --color=auto'
    alias egrep='egrep --color=auto'
fi
```

```
# some more ls aliases
#alias ll='ls -alF'
#alias la='ls -A'
#alias l='ls -CF'

# Add an "alert" alias for long running commands. Use like so:
# sleep 10; alert
alias alert='notify-send --urgency=low -i "$([ $? = 0 && echo terminal || echo
error)" "$(history | tial -n1 | sed -e '\''s/^\s*[0-
9]\+\s*//;s/[;&|]\s*alert$//'\'')"'

# Alias definitions.
# You may want to put all your additions into a separate file like
# ~/.bash_aliases, instead of adding them here directly.
# See /usr/share/doc/bash-doc/examples in the bash-doc package.

#if [ -f ~/.bash_aliases ]; then
#    . ~/.bash_aliases
#fi
```

The **bash_completion** file is then read to set up command completion options.

```
# enable programmable completion features (you don't need to enable
# this, if it's already enabled in /etc/bash.bashrc and /etc/profile
# sources /etc/bash.bashrc).

if ! shopt -oq posix; then
  if [ -f /usr/share/bash-conpletion/bash_completion ]; then
    . /usr/share/bash-completion/bash_completion

  elif [ -f /etc/bash_completion ]; then
    . /etc/bash_completion
  fi
fi
```

You can add any commands or definitions of your own to your **.bashrc** file. If you have made changes to **.bashrc** and you want them to take effect during your current login session, you need to re-execute the file with either the . or the **source** command.

```
$ . .bashrc
```

The System /etc/bash.bashrc BASH Script

Ubuntu also has a system **bashrc** file executed for all users, called **bash.bashrc**. Currently the **/etc/bash.bashrc** file sets the default shell prompt, updates the window size, identifies the root directory, and checks whether a user is authorized to use a command. The **bash.bashrc** file is shown here.

```
# System-wide .bashrc file for interactive bash(1) shells.

# To enable the settings / commands in this file for login shells as well,
# this file has to be sourced in /etc/profile.

# If not running interactively, don't do anything
[ -z "$PS1" ] && return

# check the window size after each command and, if necessary,
# update the values of LINES and COLUMNS.
shopt -s checkwinsize

# set variable identifying the chroot you work in (used in the prompt below)
if [ -z "$debian_chroot" ] && [ -r /etc/debian_chroot ]; then
    debian_chroot=$(cat /etc/debian_chroot)
fi
# set a fancy prompt (non-color, overwrite the one in /etc/profile)
# but only if not SUDOing and have SUDO-PS1 set; then assume smart user.
if ! [ -n "${SUDO_USER}" -a -n "${SUDO_PS1}" ]; then
    PS1='${debian_chroot:+($debian_chroot)}\u@\h:\w\$ '
fi


# sudo hint
if [ ! -e $HOME/.sudo_as_admin_successful ] && [ ! -e "$HOME/.hushlogin" ]; then
    case " $(groups) " in *\ admin\ *|*\ sudo\ *)
    if [ -x /usr/bin/sudo ]; then
      cat <<-EOF
      To run a command as administrator (user "root"), use "sudo <command>".
      See "man sudo_root" for details.

      EOF
    fi
    esac
fi

# if the command-not-found package is installed, use it
if [ -x /usr/lib/command-not-found -o -x /usr/share/command-not-found/command-
not-found ]; then
        function command_not_found_handle {
                # check because c-n-f could've been removed in the meantime
                if [ -x /usr/lib/command-not-found ]; then
                  /usr/bin/python /usr/lib/command-not-found -- "$1"
                   return $?
                elif [ -x /usr/share/command-not-found/command-not-found ]; then
                  /usr/bin/python /usr/share/command-not-found/command-not-found
-- "$1"
                   return $?
                else
                  printf "%s: command not found\n" "$1" >&2
                  return 127
                fi
        }
fi
```

Though commented out, the file also includes statements to set the title of a terminal window to the user, hostname, and directory, as well as to enable bash completion.

The BASH Shell Logout File: .bash_logout

The **.bash_logout** file is also a configuration file, but it is executed when the user logs out. It is designed to perform any operations you want to occur whenever you log out. Instead of variable definitions, the **.bash_logout** file usually contains shell commands that form a kind of shutdown procedure, actions you always want taken before you log out. One common logout command is to clear the screen and then issue a farewell message.

As with **.profile**, you can add your own shell commands to **.bash_logout**. In fact, the **.bash_logout** file is not automatically set up for you when your account is first created. You need to create it yourself, using a text editor. You could then add a farewell message or other operations. The default **.bash_logout** file includes instructions to invoke the **clear_console** command to clear the screen.

.bash_logout

```
# ~/.bash_logout: executed by bash(1) when login shell exits.
# when leaving the console clear the screen to increase privacy

    if [ "$SHLVL" = 1 ]; then
            [ -x /usr/bin/clear_console ] && /usr/bin/clear_console -q
    fi
```

Table Listing

Figure Listing

Index

www.ingramcontent.com/pod-product-compliance
Lightning Source LLC
LaVergne TN
LVHW062258060326
832902LV00013B/1939